T0179131

BEST PRACTICES SERIES

High-Performance Web Databases

Design, Development, and Deployment

THE AUERBACH
BEST PRACTICES SERIES

Broadband Networking,
James Trulove, Editor,
ISBN: 0-8493-9821-5

Business Continuity Planning,
Ken Doughty, Editor,
ISBN: 0-8493-0907-7

Designing a Total Data Solution: Technology, Implementation, and Deployment,
Roxanne E. Burkey and
Charles V. Breakfield, Editors,
ISBN: 0-8493-0893-3

High Performance Web Databases: Design, Development, and Deployment,
Sanjiv Purba, Editor,
ISBN: 0-8493-0882-8

Electronic Messaging,
Nancy Cox, Editor,
ISBN: 0-8493-9825-8

Enterprise Systems Integration,
John Wyzalek, Editor,
ISBN: 0-8493-9837-1

Financial Services Information Systems, Jessica Keyes, Editor,
ISBN: 0-8493-9834-7

Healthcare Information Systems, Phillip L. Davidson, Editor,
ISBN: 0-8493-9963-7

Internet Management,
Jessica Keyes, Editor,
ISBN: 0-8493-9987-4

Multi-Operating System Networking: Living with UNIX, NetWare, and NT, Raj Rajagopal,
Editor, ISBN: 0-8493-9831-2

Network Design, Gilbert Held,
Editor, ISBN: 0-8493-0859-3

Network Manager's Handbook,
John Lusa, Editor,
ISBN: 0-8493-9841-X

Project Management,
Paul C. Tinnirello, Editor,
ISBN: 0-8493-9998-X

Server Management,
Gilbert Held, Editor,
ISBN: 0-8493-9823-1

Web-to-Host Connectivity,
Lisa Lindgren and Anura Guruge,
Editors, ISBN: 0-8493-0835-6

Winning the Outsourcing Game: Making the Best Deals and Making Them Work,
Janet Butler, Editor,
ISBN: 0-8493-0875-5

BEST PRACTICES SERIES

High-Performance Web Databases

Design, Development, and Deployment

Editor

SANJIV PURBA

CRC Press
Taylor & Francis Group
Boca Raton London New York

CRC Press is an imprint of the
Taylor & Francis Group, an **informa** business

AN AUERBACH BOOK

First published 2001 by Auerbach Publications

Published 2019 by CRC Press
Taylor & Francis Group
6000 Broken Sound Parkway NW, Suite 300
Boca Raton, FL 33487-2742

©2001 by Taylor & Francis Group, LLC
CRC Press is an imprint of Taylor & Francis Group, an Informa business

First issued in paperback 2019

No claim to original U.S. Government works

ISBN-13: 978-0-367-45545-3 (pbk)
ISBN-13: 978-0-8493-0882-6 (hbk)

**Visit the Taylor & Francis Web site at
http://www.taylorandfrancis.com**

**and the CRC Press Web site at
http://www.crcpress.com**

Library of Congress Cataloging-in-Publication Data

High-performance Web databases: design, development, and deployment / edited by Sanjiv Purba.
      p. cm. — (Best practices series)
    Includes bibliographical references and index.
    ISBN 0-8493-0882-8 (alk. paper)
    1. Web databases. 2. Database design. I. Purba, Sanjiv. II. Best practices series
    (Boca Raton, Fla.)

QA76.9.W43 D47 2000
005.75′8—dc21
                                               00-044173
                                             CIP

Library of Congress Card Number 00-044173

Contributors

BRUCE ANDERSON, *Independent Consultant, Toronto, Ontario, Canada*

CHARLES BANYAY, *Manager, Deloitte & Touche Consulting Group, Toronto, Ontario, Canada*

RICHARD E. BIEHL, *Senior Consultant, Data-Oriented Quality Solutions, Pequannock, New Jersey*

DEBORAH L. BROOKS, *Data Specialist, MCI Telecommunications Corp., Arlington, Virginia*

DAVE BRUEGGEN, *Systems Analyst, Insurance and Pension Computer Systems, Union Central Life Insurance Co., Cincinnati, Ohio*

STEVEN CHEUNG, *Manager, Management Consulting West Practice, Ernst & Young, Seattle, Washington*

SOONG H. CHUNG, *Korea Electronics Technology, Seoul, Korea*

TREVOR CLARKE, *Management Consultant, Deloitte Consulting, Toronto, Ontario, Canada*

FRANK CULLEN, *Principal, Blackstone and Cullen, Atlanta, Georgia*

SEAN D. DOYLE, *Marketing Coordinator, Secure Systems Business Unit, Oracle Corp., Redwood Shores, California*

JEFFERY FELDMAN, *Manager, Deloitte & Touche Consulting Group, Toronto, Ontario, Canada*

CANDACE C. FLEMING, *Manager, Technology Planning and Information Management, Schering-Plough Corp., Kenilworth, New Jersey*

ELIZABETH N. FONG, *Computer Systems Laboratory, National Institute of Standards and Technology, Gaithersburg, Maryland*

PHILIP FRIEDLANDER, CPA, CDP, CISA, CIA, DBA, *Instructor, Information Technology Delivery Group, Ernst & Young*

IDO GILEADI, *Manager, Deloitte & Touche Consulting Group, Toronto, Ontario, Canada*

KATHRYN A. HARVILL, *Computer Systems Laboratory, National Institute of Standards and Technology, Gaithersburg, Maryland*

DAVID C. HAY, *President, Essential Strategies, Inc., Houston, Texas*

GILBERT HELD, *Director, 4-Degree Consulting, Macon, Georgia*

JONATHAN HELD, *U.S. Navy, Monterey, California*

WILLIAM H. INMON, *Senior Principal, American Management Systems, Fairfax, Virginia*

Contributors

ASHVIN IYENGAR, *Consultant, Object Technologies, Deloitte & Touche Consulting Group, Toronto, Ontario, Canada*

WOLFGANG KELLER, *Senior Manager, Software Design & Management, Ltd., Munich, Germany*

BONN-OH KIM, *Assistant Professor of Information Systems, Department of Management, University of Nebraska–Lincoln*

WILLIAM KROUSLIS, CDRP, CSP, CFPS, *Assistant Vice President, Chubb Services Corp., Warren, New Jersey*

MICHAEL P. KUSHNER, *Senior Software Engineer, Walklett Burns, Ltd., Great Valley, Pennsylvania*

JAMES A., LARSON, *Senior Software Engineer, Intel Architecture Lab, Hillsboro, Oregon*

CAROL L. LARSON, *Freelance Desktop Publisher, Hillsboro, Oregon*

SOOUN LEE, *Associate Professor, School of Business, Department of Decision Science and MIS, Miami University, Oxford, Ohio*

JONG-SUNG LEE, *Database Administrator, Department of Computer Information Systems, College of Business, Middle Tennessee State University, Murfreesboro, Tennessee*

CHANG-YANG LIN, *Associate Professor of Information Systems, Department of Finance and Business Systems, College of Business, Eastern Kentucky University, Richmond, Kentucky*

JENNIFER LITTLE, *Manager, Data Administration Programs, AmerInd, Inc., Alexandria, Virginia*

PHILLIP Q. MAIER, *Member, Secure Network Initiative, Lockheed Martin Corporation, Sunnyvale, California*

LYNDA L. MCGHIE, *Director, Information Security, Lockheed Martin Corporation, Bethesda, Maryland*

STEWART S. MILLER, *President and Owner, Executive Information Services, Carlsbad, California*

NATHAN J. MULLER, *Independent Consultant, Huntsville, Alabama*

MOHAMED NOUR, *Ph.D. candidate, School of Business, Kent State University, Kent, Ohio*

JONATHAN B. NOVAK, *Novak, Integrated Systems Solutions Corp., Atlanta, Georgia*

SRINIVAS PADMANABHARAO, *Consultant, Deloitte & Touche Consulting, Toronto, Ontario, Canada*

WILLIAM PEARSON, *Senior System Consultant and DB2 Database Administrator, Toronto, Ontario, Canada*

WILLIAM E. PERRY, CPA, CISA, CQA, *Executive Director, Quality Assurance Institute, Orlando, Florida*

SRIRAM PIDAPARTI, *Cargill Financial Services Corporation, Minnetonka, Minnesota*

SANJIV PURBA, *Senior Manager, Deloitte & Touche Consulting Group, Toronto, Ontario, Canada*

TERINIA REID, *Canadian Networking Manager, Deloitte & Touche Consulting, Toronto, Ontario, Canada*

LOIS RICHARDS, *Data Warehousing Project Manager, Dynamic Information Systems Corp., Boulder, Colorado*

RONALD G. ROSS, *Editor/Publisher, Database Newsletter, Database Research Group, Inc., Boston, Massachusetts*

ALICE SANDIFER, *Senior Database Analyst, Bristol-Myers Products, Somerville, New Jersey*

CHARLES L. SHEPPARD, *Computer Systems Laboratory, National Institute of Standards and Technology, Gaithersburg, Maryland*

MICHAEL SIMONYI, *Independent Consultant, Etobicoke, Ontario, Canada*

Il-YEOL SONG, *Assistant Professor, College of Information Studies, Drexel University, Philadelphia, Pennsylvania*

BHAVANI THURAISINGHAM, *Principal Engineer, Advanced Information Systems Center, MITRE Corp., Bedford, Massachusetts*

BARBARA VON HALLE, *Principal, Spectrum Technology Group, Inc., North Branch, New Jersey*

DAVID C. WALLACE, *Professor, Applied Computer Science Department, Illinois State University, Normal, Illinois*

KYU-YOUNG WHANG, *Associate Professor, Computer Science, Korea Advanced Institute of Science and Technology, Daejon, South Korea*

BO KAI WONG, *Department of Management, Williamson School of Business Administration, Youngstown State University, Youngstown, Ohio*

JAMES WOODS, *Independent Consultant, Lewisville, Texas*

MICHAEL ZIMMER, *Senior Data Administrator, Ministry of Health, Victoria, British Columbia, Canada*

Contents

SECTION 1   DATABASE PLANNING AND GETTING STARTED.   1

1   **Database Development Methodology and Organization** .   5
Sanjiv Purba

2   **Establishing Enterprise Data Standards**.   15
Sanjiv Purba

3   **Enterprise Data Management**.   25
Jonathan B. Novak

SECTION II   INFORMATION GATHERING AND ANALYSIS.   47

4   **Data, Processes, and Events:**
Keys to Comprehensive Analysis.   51
Philip Friedlander

5   **A Framework for Classifying Data**.   69
William H. Inmon

6   **One Concept Equals One Data Element:**
A Rule for Developing Data Elements.   79
Jennifer Little

7   **Leveraging Content**   93
Charles Banyay

SECTION III   MANAGING BUSINESS RULES.   107

8   **Business Rules: Capturing the Most Elusive**
Information Asset.   111
Alice Sandifer and Barbara von Halle

9   **Business Rules: A Case Study**.   129
Alice Sandifer and Barbara von Halle

ix

Contents

10   Modeling Business Rules 145
Ronald G. Ross

SECTION IV   PERFORMANCE MODELING METHODS 157

11   Enterprise Data Modeling Practices 161
Wolfgang Keller

**12   Evaluation of Four Languages for Specifying
Conceptual Database Designs** 171
James A. Larson and Carol L. Larson

**13   A Comparison of Three Systems Modeling
Methodologies** 195
Michael P. Kushner, Il-Yeol Song and Kyu-Young Whang

14   Building a Data Model 213
Candace C. Fleming and Barbara von Halle

15   Business Information Data Modeling 229
Deborah L. Brooks

16   Making Data Models Readable 241
David C. Hay

**17   Integrating Process and Data Models in
a Horizontal Organization** 261
David C. Wallace

18   Avoiding Pitfalls in Data Modeling 277
Steven Cheung

19   The Politics of Entity Identifiers 305
Deborah L. Brooks

**20   Practical Guidelines for Supertype and
Subtype Modeling** 319
Richard E. Biehl

SECTION V   PERFORMANCE DESIGN AND DEVELOPMENT 333

21   Physical Database Design 337
James A. Larson and Carol L. Larson

**22   Design, Implementation, and Management of
Distributed Databases — An Overview** 353
Elizabeth N. Fong, Charles L. Sheppard, and Kathryn A. Harvill

**23 Detailed Design and Application of
Distributed Database Management Systems** 365
Elizabeth N. Fong, Charles L. Sheppard, and Kathryn A. Harvill

24 Relational Database Design Using Semantic Objects 375
Jong-Sung Lee and Bo Kai Wong

25 Component Design for Relational Databases 385
Ashvin Iyengar

26 Designing Relational Databases 399
Candace C. Fleming and Barbara von Halle

SECTION VI DATABASE INTEGRITY AND QUALITY 411

27 What Is Wrong with My Data? 415
Jeffery Feldman

28 Referential Integrity for Database Design 427
Bonn-Oh Kim

29 Data Quality: An Architectural Solution 435
Sriram Pidaparti

30 Ensuring the Integrity of the Database 447
William E. Perry

**SECTION VII DISTRIBUTED DATABASES, PORTABILITY, AND
INTEROPERABILITY** 465

**31 Data Communications Requirements of
Distributed Database Systems** 469
Dave Brueggen and Sooun Lee

**32 Managing Multiple Databases Across
Heterogeneous Hardware and Software Systems** 479
James Woods

33 Providing Access to External Databases 489
Gilbert Held

**SECTION VIII DATABASE INTEGRATION WITH THE INTERNET
AND THE WEB** 495

**34 Developing Client/Server RDBMS Applications
Using Java Servlets and JDBC** 499
Jonathan Held

Contents

35   **Building Database-enabled Web Applications
      with IDC** 525
      Ido Gileadi

36   **Integrating EDMSs and DBMSs** 539
      Charles Banyay

37   **Database Management and the Internet:
      Developments and Challenges** 549
      Bhavani Thuraisingham

SECTION IX   DATA MIGRATION, CONVERSION, AND
             LEGACY APPLICATIONS 555

38   **Relational Database Conversion:
      Issues and Approaches** 559
      Chang-Yang Lin

39   **Data: Ever Changing and Eternally the Same** 569
      Bruce Anderson

40   **A Practical Example of Data Conversion** 579
      Charles Banyay

41   **Data Conversion: Doing It Right the First Time** 589
      Michael Zimmer

42   **Migrating Data to an Integrated Database** 605
      James A. Larson and Carol L. Larson

43   **Bridging Legacy Data with XML** 613
      Frank Cullen

SECTION X   PERFORMANCE TUNING 619

44   **Improving User Experience Through Improved
      Web Design and Database Performance** 623
      Srinivas Padmanabharao

45   **Web-based Testing and Capacity Planning** 631
      Trevor Clarke

46   **The Advancing Art of Indexing** 639
      Lois Richards

47   **Parallel Databases** 653
      Stewart S. Miller

48   **Leveraging Checkpoint Processing** 661
      William Pearson

49   **The Denormalization Decision in
      Relational Database Systems Design** 671
      Bonn-Oh Kim

SECTION XI   DATA ADMINISTRATION AND OPERATIONS 679

50   **Assessing a Data Administrative Program** 683
      Jennifer Little

51   **Managing Database Backup and Recovery** 693
      Michael Simonyi

52   **Database Compression Technologies** 705
      Nathan J. Muller

53   **How to Handle Data Loss and Backup** 717
      William Krouslis

SECTION XII   DATABASE SECURITY 723

54   **Security Management for the World Wide Web** 727
      Lynda L. McGhie and Phillip Q. Maier

55   **Establishing Security Controls in
      a Distributed Database** 753
      Sooun Lee, Mohamed Nour, and Soong H. Chung

56   **Understanding Relational Databases and
      Assessing Their Security** 763
      Sean D. Doyle

57   **Virus Protection in a Web Environment** 777
      Terinia Reid

ABOUT THE CONSULTING EDITOR 785

INDEX 787

Introduction

IN THE PAST FEW DECADES, DATABASE SOLUTIONS AND DATA MANAGEMENT OPERATIONS HAVE SUPPORTED AN EVER-EXPANDING RANGE OF SOLUTIONS AND TECHNOLOGY ARCHITECTURES. There is no abatement to this trend. Many end-to-end Information Technology (IT) solutions in the current environment include access to the World Wide Web and integration with one or more Web sites. This broadened scope adds another layer of complexity to database solutions, while retaining the traditional issues and challenges facing database management.

There are still more factors affecting the complexity of data management in the current IT environment. From a business perspective, corporate mergers, reorganization, and increased competition complicate the contents and ownership of information and data across the organization. From a technology perspective, Web-enabled applications can be built on top of a broad mix of technology architectures, including components, objects, layers, and tiers. Some applications are designed from the ground up; others are Web-enabled after they are constructed. There is also a broad range of development tools and products that need to be integrated to provide a full database solution to an organization.

Another level of complexity involves the ever-increasing level of user expectations. With most Web-based solutions, the power of choice has clearly shifted to the user or consumer. Users expect and demand respect for their time and flawless application execution. Competing Web sites are only a mouse-click, gesture, glance, touch, or word away. This makes it imperative to design a Web site for optimal end-to-end performance and usability from the ground up. The alternative is to lose customers.

PURPOSE OF THIS BOOK

This book provides best practices in building data-based applications that support Web-based, Internet-oriented applications. This is examined in the context of an end-to-end approach that includes traditional data management considerations, as well as support for the Internet-based architectures.

The chapters in this book are written by experienced and acknowledged experts in the Information Technology (IT) industry. Each author offers significant experiences, knowledge, and unique perspectives in data management, Web-based applications, Internet applications, performance tuning, or database operations.

This book flows from business to technology considerations, and from logical to physical designs. It begins by establishing a business framework and then proceeds to implement a well-tuned technology solution. The sections in this book are designed to support the specific needs or interests of readers who may be at any point within a project development or operations lifecycle.

SCOPE OF THIS BOOK

The scope of this book includes a full breadth of data management categories, including strategy, methodologies, standards, information-gathering methods, techniques, business rule management, performance modeling, performance design, performance development, data integrity, distributed databases, database integration with the Internet and the Web, data conversion, performance tuning, data administration, and data security.

INTENDED AUDIENCE

The intended audience for this book includes senior management, line management, project managers, business analysts, systems analysts, consultants, methodologists, developers, testers, Web masters, data analysts, data administrators, database administrators, and technical writers.

GETTING THE MOST FROM THIS BOOK

Many authors have contributed their experiences, knowledge, and ideas to the chapters in this book. These contributors are strong players in their respective niches in the industry. Taken as a whole, this best practices book sweeps across many data management categories and technologies. It is divided into twelve sections, each focusing on a particularly useful aspect of data management. These sections are described here.

Section I, "Database Planning and Getting Started," focuses on database development/management methodologies, the role of planning, establishing standards, and the database as an enterprise resource. This section is the place to get started in establishing a Web-enabled database environment from first principles.

Section II, "Information Gathering and Analysis," focuses on building and sharing content in a variety of formats, including over the Web. Techniques for gathering information and performing preliminary analysis to allow its classification and verification are also examined in this section.

Section III, "Managing Business Rules," examines approaches for turning information into business rules, as well as basic management of this important resource. In n-tier architecture, business rules encapsulate the core body of knowledge and proprietary practices of an organization.

Section IV, "Performance Modeling Methods," compares and contrasts data modeling techniques and modeling formats. Both the logical and physical data modeling formats are examined in this section. This section also examines approaches for allocating business rules to data models.

Section V, "Performance Design and Development," shows how to convert a physical data model into a database design. This section also examines component design and semantic objects. This section shows how to improve n-tier/Web application performance through iterative design, refinement, and testing approaches.

Section VI, "Database Integrity and Quality," examines approaches for ensuring data integrity at the atomic or referential level. This discussion includes an examination of architectural issues and quality-oriented procedures. Techniques to improve database integrity and to correct it are also examined.

Section VII, "Distributed Databases, Portability, and Interoperability," focuses on distributed databases, data communication, database portability, and database interoperability. This section shows how database distribution is a key consideration in Web-enabled applications.

Section VIII, "Database Integration with the Internet and the Web," focuses on integrating databases to the Internet and the World Wide Web. This section also examines development tools in the Web context.

Section IX, "Data Migration, Conversion, and Legacy Applications," examines approaches for migrating applications to another environment, along with data conversion operations. This section also examines methods to bridge Web-based applications to legacy data through XML, in order to avoid a data conversion process in some cases.

Section X, "Performance Tuning," examines approaches for tuning applications and databases. This section also examines Web-specific performance tuning methods, Web-based testing, and capacity planning.

Section XI, "Data Administration and Operations," focuses on database administration, backup, recovery, and data compression in a 7×24 Web-enabled production environment. This section also examines approaches for establishing an ongoing operations schedule.

Section XII, "Database Security," examines considerations for adopting effective security mechanisms in the Internet and Web environments. Controls and procedures are examined in this context. This section also provides considerations on how to protect a technology environment from computer viruses.

SANJIV PURBA, SENIOR MANAGER
Deloitte Consulting, Toronto, Ontario, Canada
April 2000

Section I
Database Planning and Getting Started

EFFECTIVE DATA-BASED SOLUTIONS IN AN ORGANIZATION MUST BE BUILT AROUND A SOLID STRATEGIC AND ORGANIZED FRAMEWORK. This must start with an organization's executive team. From here, the solutions must sweep across the organization, touching all relevant departments, processes, procedures, and user interfaces (e.g., reports, Web pages). An organized planning phase offers an organization the opportunity to define data sources, data presentation, ownership, timelines, and conflict resolution mechanisms pertaining to corporate data. The data ownership list should also include resources who are knowledgeable about the information in the organization.

This section contains chapters that define how effective data solutions can be formalized and implemented across an organization. The cornerstone of this involves the selection and implementation of data development methodologies. Data development methodologies offer a powerful tool set to define the activities and the deliverables produced in data-related projects. In some cases, data development methodologies are a component of a larger, full-cycle development methodology. Because data is a corporatewide resource, it is also necessary to define standards for its capture and communication across the enterprise. This section contains three chapters that present approaches for satisfying both of these initiatives, as well as offering an approach for establishing an enterprise data management framework.

Chapter 1, "Database Development Methodology and Organization," provides a framework for building databases from the logical to physical level at the enterprise level — with support for evolving technology architectures. The methodology is built around a generic system development lifecycle with a strong data-oriented approach. This chapter also discusses the roles and responsibilities required to support a database development methodology.

Chapter 2, "Establishing Enterprise Data Standards," provides practical examples and categories for building a set of enterprise data standards. The contents of this chapter are assembled from actual project experiences to describe techniques that work, and as importantly, do not work, when trying to build and implement enterprise data standards. Suggestions for avoiding the common pitfalls experienced by organizations during this initiative are also provided in this chapter.

Chapter 3, "Enterprise Data Management," describes an enterprise data management approach for identifying and establishing missions, objectives, strategies, and plans to align information management and business intelligence with enterprise objectives and requirements.

Chapter 1
Database Development Methodology and Organization

Sanjiv Purba

DATABASE DEVELOPMENT IS ONE OF THE FUNDAMENTAL OBJECTIVES of the data management function and certainly one of the end products of the process. In recent years, several trends have impacted the way that databases are built and the role they play in the overall organization. Some of these trends include data warehousing, object-oriented technology, E-commerce, and the emergence of very large databases (VLDBs). Other changes to the landscape include the popularity of complex data types (e.g., BLOBs, video), universal databases, and object databases. Despite these changes, the basis of many online transaction processing applications (OLTP) that run the business is still the relational database and the flat files. This fact is not going to change dramatically over the next few years. If anything, the relational database has proven its value as an enterprise enabler and, like the IBM mainframe, is here to stay for the foreseeable future.

This chapter defines a database development methodology and approach that has proven successful on a variety of projects, such as $100,000 to $15,000,000 budgets, mainframe, client/server, three-tier with OO, and package implementations. This approach promotes viewing methodologies as flexible frameworks that are customized for every specific instance. It allows data-oriented teams to use their personal insight and experience alongside the best practices embedded in the methodology. This chapter also defines organizational roles for a data-oriented environment.

0-8493-0882-8/00/$0.00+$.50
© 2001 by CRC Press LLC

BENEFITS

The complexity that is inherent in constructing relational database solutions can be reduced by using proven database development methodologies on projects. Methodologies are an excellent example of best practices and project lessons. Use of methodologies, therefore, reduces risk on development projects. Methodologies define activities and deliverables that are constructed in projects that were successful. Following these successful lessons can reduce project development time while increasing product quality. Furthermore, the use of methodologies simplifies the process of tracking project progress because there are clear benchmarks that can be reviewed by the project manager. Methodologies that offer templates/deliverables also allow a quickstart to the development process.

SELECTING A DATABASE DEVELOPMENT METHODOLOGY

Development methodologies with well-defined database development phases are commonly available in the marketplace. Some are freely available with modeling or project management tools, although others are found on the World Wide Web. Many of the larger consulting firms have developed proprietary methodologies based on their corporate project experiences and proven best practices. These can be purchased separately or they can be bundled with consulting/mentoring services retained from the firm. The following list identifies some of the features that should be included in any database development methodology that is being considered for deployment in an organization.

- *Linkage to a full lifecycle development methodology:* A full lifecycle methodology supports more than database development. The database development methodology chosen should either be a component of a larger full lifecycle methodology, or link seamlessly with one. Failure to do this could result in mismatched techniques or the development of deliverables that are not used.
- *Techniques:* Many popular development methodologies support a combination of techniques to streamline development of deliverables. The traditional waterfall approach involves producing deliverables in a sequential fashion. Deliverable B is not started until Deliverable A is completed and signed off. This approach, however, historically has proven to be slow on many projects of all sizes. As a result of this experience, a rapid application development (RAD) approach has gained popularity in the past 10 years. RAD produces deliverables in a much smaller timeframe than the older waterfall approach. Iteration and prototyping are cornerstones of most RAD approaches, as are teams that combine technical resources and users during the analysis and design phases of the project lifecycle. RAD has proven to be successful on smaller projects, but has been problematic on the larger ones due

to the complexity of the business requirements. A relatively new approach combines the best elements of both the waterfall and RAD approaches and has proven valuable on larger development projects.

- *Support:* A development methodology (or a database development methodology) is a product, whether an organization has paid for it or not. As such, it is important for the methodology to be supported by the vendor into the future. An unsupported methodology becomes obsolete in sort order. Some questions to ask the vendor include: "How much research is being conducted to improve the methodology?" "Is there a hotline for technical support?" and "When is the next release of the methodology being released?"

- *Price:* The price of the methodology should be considered in whole and in part and assessed against the value that is received. Consider the one-time cost, training costs, upgrade costs, yearly licence fees, costs per user, customization costs, hardware/software support costs, and costs for future releases.

- *Vendor:* Consider the stability and market share of the vendor providing the methodology. The vendor's references also should be checked to ascertain their support for clients. Vendors that are more stable and have more market share are more likely to improve their methodology with new techniques in the future.

- *Proven Success:* One of the surest ways of selecting a suitable methodology is to check the references of similar organizations that have used it successfully on development projects.

- *Electronic Availability:* The methodology should be available electronically through Lotus Notes, the Internet, or CD-ROM. It also should be available on paper. This makes the methodology widely available to those using it across the organization.

- *Templates/Deliverables:* Reusable templates and deliverables are a good source of best practices that provide the means for quick starting development projects. Many methodologies are demonstrated with these, but the templates/deliverables are not provided to customers. In such cases, it is valuable to try to negotiate the inclusion of templates/deliverables as part of the transaction. If the templates/deliverables still are not offered by the vendor, but the rest of the methodology is acceptable, a pilot project should be used to create reusable templates and deliverables for future projects to use. Although this may slow the pilot project down in the short term, subsequent projects will run more efficiently. It is also desirable to select a methodology architecture that allows additional templates and deliverables to be added to the database on an ongoing basis.

- *Linkages to newer architectures:* The methodology also should support linkages with modules that support data warehousing, object technology, E-commerce, and Web architectures. Flexibility in expanding the methodology directly or through deliverable linkages is desirable.

- *Ease of Learning and Use:* Methodologies that are easy to learn and use are more likely to be used on projects. Some methodologies are packaged with training courses from the vendor or other third parties.

It is not unusual to add to this list of features or to assign more weight to a handful of them because of their importance to a specific organization. Experience has shown that complicating the selection process does not necessarily improve the quality of the final selection. In fact, this can lead to wasted time and intense team debates or arguments that end in worthless stalemates. It is preferrable to build a short list of candidate methodologies by disqualifying candidates that are weak on one or two key features (e.g., not available electronically or purchase price is greater than $100,000). The short list then can be compared to maybe five or six of the features that are of key importance to the organization. It is useful to conduct a limited number of pilot projects that test the value of a methodology before making a final selection. It is also not unusual to pilot two different methodologies in a conference room pilot (CRP) to make a final determination. This process can take between six weeks and six months.

HIGH-LEVEL DATABASE DEVELOPMENT METHODOLOGY

This section defines a high-level methodology for database development. This methodology provides a good start for small- to medium-sized projects; however, a formal third-party methodology should be considered for projects that require more than six months of development effort. The activities discussed in this section are mapped to the standard project development framework, which consists of the following main phases: requirements, architecture, design, development, testing, implementation, and post-implementation. These phases can be conducted in parallel or sequentially depending on the exact nature of the methodology, and are restricted to database specific activities.

The subprocesses that are described in this section fit into a larger full lifecycle methodology that would address such activities as corporate sponsorship for the project, project plan definition, organization building, team building, user interface development, application design, technology selection, acceptance testing, and deployment. It is assumed that these activities are completed outside the database development methodology phases.

- *Define Business Requirements:* Business requirements are captured for any system development effort. The requirements also should be used to build the logical data model. They will feed such things as the number of entities, attribute names, and types of data stored in each attribute. These often are categorized by subject area.
- *Borrow or Create the Data Model:* With a solid understanding of the business requirements, it is a good idea to search the market for a data

model that can be purchased from a third party. This subsequently can be customized for the organization.

- *Build Logical Data Model:* The logical data model is built iteratively. The first view usually is done at a high level, beginning with a subject area or conceptual data model. Subsequent levels contain more detail. The process of normalization also is applied at this stage. There are many good books on normalization, so normal forms will not be covered. Foreign key fields and potential indexes also can be considered here. It is not necessary to build the logical data model for performance at this time, and physical considerations are left until a later process.

- *Verify the Data Model:* The logical data model is validated iteratively with users, the fields of the user interface, and process models. It is not unusual to make changes to the data model during this verification process. New requirements, which need to be fitted into the data model, also may be identified.

- *Build Data Architecture:* The data architecture is defined in the context of the physical data environment. Considerations, such as the database server, distribution, components, and partitioning, are considered in this step.

- *Build the Physical Data Model:* The logical data model is converted to a physical data model based on the specific database that is used. The physical data model will vary with the choice of database products and tools. The physical data model also contains such objects as indexes, foreign keys, triggers, views, and user-defined datatypes. The physical data model is optimized for performance and usually is denormalized for this reason. Denormalization can result in redundancy, but can improve system performance. Building the physical data model is not a one-stop process. Do not expect to build a final version of the physical data model on the first attempt.

- *Refine the Data Model:* The physical data model is refined continuously as more information becomes available, and the results of stress testing and benchmarking become available to the database development team. The logical data model also should be maintained as the physical data model is refined.

- *Complete Transaction Analysis:* Transaction analysis is used to review system transactions so that the physical data model can be refined for optimum system performance. Transaction analysis results are only meaningful after the business requirements and systems design are fairly solid. Transaction analysis produces statistics showing the access frequency for the tables in the database, time estimates, and data volumes.

- *Populate the Data:* After the database structure is established and the database is created, it is necessary to populate the database. This can be done through data scripts, applications, or data conversions. This can be an extensive set of activities that requires substantial data mapping, testing, and parallel activities. It is expected that the details of this are included in the full lifecycle methodology.

- *Complete Testing:* Testing a database usually is done in the context of applications and is covered in the full lifecycle methodology. Some specific types of testing, such as stress testing, benchmarking, and regression testing, can be used to refine the performance of the physical data model. These require high volumes of data, testing tools, and distribution tools.

DELIVERABLES

Some of the important deliverables that are created from inception to the creation of a physical database are discussed in this section. It is useful to build a reference database that contains samples of each of these deliverables so that project teams know in advance what they are attempting to build.

- *Requirements Document:* This is the statement of the business requirements for the application being developed. This deliverable can contain narrative and any number of models or prototypes to capture and represent the business requirements.
- *Conceptual Model/Subject Areas:* This is a high-level view of the business subject areas that are within the scope of the data model (e.g., accounting, administration, billing, engineering).
- *Logical Data Model:* This contains entities, attributes, and business rules within the subject areas. The model also shows relationships between the entities. Key fields and foreign keys also can be identified in this model.
- *Transaction Analysis:* This is a list of transactions supported by the system, the entities (and possibly the fields) that are accessed by the transactions, and the frequency with which they are accessed. A create, read, update, and delete (CRUD) matrix is a useful input for helping with this analysis.
- *Physical Data Model:* This is a denormalized version of the logical data model that is optimized for performance under a specific technical environment and refined through the transaction analysis results. The physical data model usually is refined throughout a development cycle and is not finished until implementation. The physical data model contains physical objects such as tables, fields, indexes, foreign keys, primary keys, views, user-defined data types, and rules.
- *Object Model:* An object model supports the logical data model. This often serves as an intermediate layer between an object-based user interface and a relational back-end database.
- *Validation Model:* This is a cross-reference of models, such as process models, to the logical data model to prove its validity. It often includes

a mapping between the logical data model with a user interface and reports to identify gaps.

- *Conversion Strategy:* This is a statement of the strategy used to convert data into a new application. The level of detail can vary signficantly. This could be anything from high-level principles to detailed conversion scripts.

TOOLS

Modeling tools are critical for the database development process. There are a number of tools with various add-ons that can be used in this process. Modeling tools should offer support for both data models and process models. It also is becoming more useful for modeling tools to support object models or to link to other tools that do. Tools that support reverse-reengineering from physical databases to generate logical data model or scripts are useful for organizations that require extensive changes to data structures (possibly following a corporate merger).

There are many other tools that are useful in the database development process. Some of these include CASE tools, conversion tools, testing tools, and database server tools.

ORGANIZATION

When staffing a project that involves a data initiative, it is necessary to fill specific roles. The roles defined in this section are generally specific to the data initiative. These roles often are complemented by other roles in full implementation projects. Projects that have high object-oriented content skew the organization towards object-modeling skillsets.

- *Project Sponsor:* Projects should not be initiated or conducted without a senior project sponsor who is positioned to remove obstacles and ensure that the project team has the full support they require to be successful.
- *Project Manager:* The project manager is in charge of the entire project, including the data initiative.
- *Business User:* This person provides the business rules for the application, which are used to derive the entities and attributes necessary to save the data.
- *Business Analyst:* The business analyst provides a critical link between the business user and the data architect by understanding the business requirements and translating them into technical words.
- *Data Architect:* This person has the responsibility of defining the data architecture. This could be distributed, central, standalone, or integrated with a sophisticated overall architecture.
- *Data Analyst:* The data analyst works with the business analyst to build a consistent view of each element of the data. This person

11

understands the linkage between the business and the individual items of data.

- *Data Modeler:* This person works with the data architect to build a logical relational data model and also may get involved in transforming the logical data model into a physical data model.
- *Object Modeler:* The object modeler becomes involved in projects to build an object model, including messages and methods. This person also may be responsible for mapping the object model to the corporate data model.
- *Database Administrator:* This person implements the physical database, maintains and optimizes the physical environment, restricts access to the database by controlling privilege levels for users, offers advice to the development team for converting the logical data model to the physical data model, and holds the overall responsibility for running the database environment on a data-to-day basis.
- *Network Administrator:* The network administrator maintains the physical network, has the responsibility for maintaining the integrity of the physical environment that supports the data environment, and operates at the operating system level and the hardware level. For example, this person would add more physical disk to support larger databases.
- *Developer:* This person uses the database(s) for application development.

PITFALLS

Misuse or misinterpretation of how methodologies should be executed can result in signficantly negative impacts to project timelines. It is not unusual for organizations to use methodologies as process charts or recipes without streamlining any of the activities. This can result in a considerable amount of wasted time as deliverables or activities are produced without an understanding of how they are leading toward a solution. Methodologies should be adjusted for specific projects. Activities or deliverables that are not necessary should be dropped from the project plan.

Methodologies that are too complicated or difficult to learn and used frequently are avoided by project teams. There are some methodologies that may contain information for thousands of project contingencies. However, they require thousands of megabytes of storage or dozens of manuals to store. During tight project timeframes, such methodologies are sidelined quickly.

It is important to update methodologies over time. New project experiences and best practices should be included in the methodology at specific intervals.

CONCLUSION

Database development methodologies are a subset of full lifecycle methodologies. Project teams can access a third-party database development methodology or follow the high-level framework described in this chapter for database development. Database development methodologies also should support parallel development, iteration, high-user involvement, and be accompanied by a database of reusable templates or sample deliverables.

References

Deloitte & Touche Consulting Group Framework for Computing Solutions.

Maguire, S., *Writing Solid Code*. Microsoft Press, Redmond, WA, 1993.

Purba, S., *Developing Client/Server Systems Using Sybase SQL Server System 11*. John Wiley & Sons, New York, 1995.

Smith, P. N., *Client/Server Computing. 2nd. ed.,* Sams Publishing, Indianapolis, IN, 1994.

Willian, P., *Effective Methods for Software Testing*. John Wiley & Sons, New York, 1995.

Chapter 2
Establishing Enterprise Data Standards

Sanjiv Purba

STANDARDS EXIST IN SOME FORM OR OTHER IN MOST ORGANIZATIONS AND TEND TO BE WIDE REACHING IN ESTABLISHING HOW WORK IS PERFORMED AND DELIVERED WITHIN THE ENVIRONMENT. In the strictest sense, standards should thoroughly describe procedures and outcomes for all the events in an organization. The benefit of this is consistent communication within an organization and reliable deliverables. Implementing standards is a tricky business that can lead to an entirely different set of problems that can also jeopardize the health of the organization. Ideally, it would be best to simply borrow standards that have already been used successfully on similar projects and adapt them with minimal effort. Unfortunately, this is not possible in many real world cases, so another approach is required. As shown in Exhibit 1, simplicity is the key to successfully implementing enterprise data standards in most organizations.

Enterprise data standards are part of the larger, broader "enterprise development standards" category, which includes such topics as development approach, walkthrough procedures, and coding conventions. This paper focuses on establishing enterprise data standards. There are other types of standards in organizations (e.g., development standards), but these are outside the scope of this article. This distinction can sometimes be subjective; for example, consider the case of form naming standards. Is this a data standard or a development standard? For grouping purposes, I prefer to categorize it as a naming convention under data standards. However, some would prefer to stay pure and categorize it under the more general naming conventions in the development standards.

OBJECTIVES AND BENEFITS OF ENTERPRISE DATA STANDARDS

Data exists within organizations in a variety of formats, some of which include: documents, databases, flat files, paper documents, binary objects,

Standards are only useful if they are used;
Standards will only be used if they are understood;
Standards will only be understood if they are simple;
Standards will only be understood if the organization has bought into them;
The organization will buy into standards if they are simple, easily understood, and there is a stake in using them.

Exhibit 2-1. Guiding principles.

voice, and video. Data is everywhere, and its value is in a constant state of flux, either being modified, deleted, changed, or manipulated in some way. All of this activity is supported by many human resources, both inside and outside the organization. Enterprise data standards support the objectives of bringing consistency and integrity across the organization based on the categories shown in Exhibit 2-2. This list is not exhaustive, but the categories that are identified are common across many organizations in a variety of industries and provide a good start for beginning this process.

The significant objectives and benefits of each of the categories defined in Exhibit 2 are described in this section, as they pertain to many organizations.

ARCHITECTURE AND PHYSICAL ENVIRONMENT CATEGORY

Objectives

This includes building a consistent technical data architecture including centralized databases, distributed database servers, and mobile databases. This also includes the physical storage of the data and associated data objects (e.g., indexes) and defines the methods for accessing the data

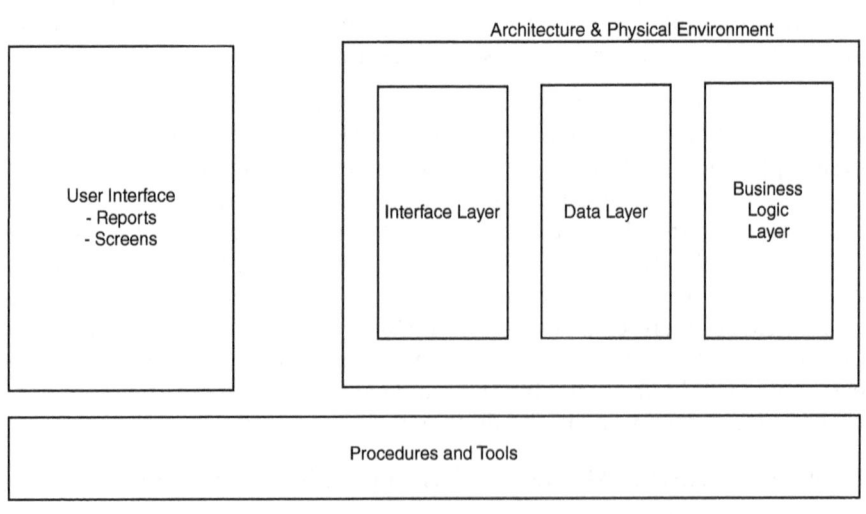

Exhibit 2-2. Categories of enterprise data standards.

in an n-tier environment from thin or fat clients using embedded SQL or remote procedure calls (RPCs). System management, change management, and version control tools are implemented to meet this objective based on procedures defined in the "Procedures Category."

Benefits

Provides a standard physical environment that is easier to support and enhance. Maintenance and support costs are also reduced. A standard architecture and physical environment also simplify application portability and interoperability.

PROCEDURES CATEGORY

Objectives

This includes all the procedures required to support data for operational or development groups. This can include system management, change management, and version control procedures. Included in this group are project naming standards (using tools like Microsoft Source-Save), module check in/check out procedures, support for multiple versions, and delta merging procedures.

Benefits

A significant benefit supported by this category includes the use of proven, consistent procedures for maintaining the integrity of the data environment. It is also becomes easier to measure compliance with the standards processes.

N-TIER/LAYERS CATEGORY

Objectives

This category contains anywhere from one to n-tiers, with three being the most common. The growing popularity of components will continue to increase the number of tiers. The predominant case includes three tiers, namely, user interface tier (or layer), data tier, and the business logic tier. The user interface tier is discussed in the next category. The n-tier category includes naming standards in terms of variable names, field names, data object names (e.g., tables, indexes, databases, user-defined datatypes, triggers, stored procedures), forms class libraries, and objects.

Benefits

There are significant benefits derived from standardizing in this category. Application modules are easier to read, build, and maintain. There is increased reuse of code and improved application portability and interoperability. This results in faster development and more accurate debugging.

There is a reduced learning curve. The end result is improved product quality.

USER INTERFACE CATEGORY

Objectives

This category includes all types of user interfaces, including application screens and reports (both online and printed). The objectives in this category are to specifiy placement of data on screens or printed forms. Categories such as screen navigation are outside the scope of this topic.

Benefits

Standards in this category result in consistent look and feel for user screens and printed reports. Users know where to search for specific types of information. An example of this is an error line on a screen or the page number on a report.

CATEGORIES OF ENTERPRISE DATA STANDARDS

Enterprise data standards are required to support both operational and development groups within an organization. Operational groups include those who perform the company's business on a day-to-day basis. These groups require access to information, the ability to manipulate information, procedures, and forms of various kinds. Development groups are more project-focused, in that they are restricted by some sort of timelines and deliverables. These groups require many of the data standards required by the operational groups, but their demands go further. Since development groups get right into the architecture and plumbing of applications, they are dependent on how data is stored, accessed, and manipulated at the code level.

The exhibits that are included in this section provide subcategories for each category defined previously. Each of the subcategories should be considered in your organization and allocated standards. Exhibit 3 shows the subcategories for the Architecture and Physical Environment category.

Exhibit 4 shows the subcategories that are included in the Procedures category. Most of these are focused on protecting data (in databases or files) during the development cycle.

Exhibit 5 shows the subcategories for the n-tier/Layers category. These are divided between the different tiers in the architecture model. This example covers the business logic tier and the data tier. The user interface layer is covered in Exhibit 6.

Exhibit 6 shows the subcategories for the User interface category. There are two primary subcategories, namely user screens and reports.

Exhibit 2-3.   Architecture and physical environment category.

Subcategory	Comments
Data Partitioning	Position nonvolatile data near the client platforms that access it.
Physical Architecture	Data architecture for development, testing, and production.
Data Access	Call stored procedures from client platforms to update database table data.
	Use views to select information from database tables.
	Return minimum number of data rows to the client.
Locking	Assume optimistic locking approach instead of the pessimistic.

PROCESS FOR DEFINING ENTERPRISE DATA STANDARDS

There are many approaches for defining enterprise data standards. Project experience has shown that the best approach for meeting the objectives identified earlier in this article is the early adoption of a simplified set of enterprise data standards that are easily understood and used across the organization. This is best achieved by starting with a set of proven standards from previous projects or from external vendors. For example, companies such as Microsoft, Forte, and Sybase all have publications that define standards to one degree or another. These can be readily found by searching the Websites of the vendors or phoning their marketing or technical departments. Exhibit 7 shows a high level view of a process that should be completed in your organization to define Enterprise Data Standards. This process has been defined through experiences on many small to large projects, and based on observations about what worked well and what did not work so well on the projects.

As shown in Exhibit 7, the "Borrow Approach" is the simplest to define or implement, which involves borrowing data standards from vendors, other successful projects, or organizations such as the American National Standards Institute (ANSI) or International Standards Organization (ISO) that define industry standards. A more complete list of organizations that define standards is provided at the end of this article. Such standards can

Exhibit 2-4.   Procedures category.

Subcategory	Comments
Change Management Standards	All database objects should be created with SQL Scripts. The scripts should be saved in tools such as Microsoft SourceSave.
System Management Standards	New client platforms will be configured using Microsoft SMS with local data tables for static data values.
Version Control Standards	Check in/Check out, delta management.

Exhibit 2-5.   n-tier/layers category.

Subcategory	Comments
General Naming Conventions	All variables names must be in lowercase
	Variables names should be mneumonic and reflect the contents of the variable
	Variable names should not exceed 40 characters in length
	Variable names should start with an alphabetic letter (a–z)
	The remainder of the name can be any combination of letters or digits or the symbol (_). The underscore (_) is used to separate parts of a name
	Variable names cannot contain include embedded spaces
Table Names	Maximum length is 20 characters
	Use the singular form (e.g., customer instead of customers)
	Do not use abbreviations
	Do not use restricted words
Column Names	Preface column name with first two letters of the table name
Index Names	Always contain part of the first 5 letters of the table name
	Number them sequentially starting with '_1'
Rules	Preface rule names with the table name
Views	Do not include more than 4 tables in a view
Stored Procedures	Always comment your Transact-SQL code
	Use the 'SET NOCOUNT ON' option to minimize data traffic
	Avoid the use of NULLS
	Log errors using master error file
	Stored procedure names should not exceed 30 characters in length
Triggers	Delete triggers prefaced with "dl". Insert triggers are prefaced with "in"; update triggers are prefaced with "up"
	Rollback any transactions that result in data integrity errors or which violate referential integrity
Datatypes	All tables must have a timestamp field
	Use ANSI-92 compatible datatypes only
	Minimize the storage required by variables by using the smallest datatype available (e.g., tinyint instead of int)
	Improve performance by using numerics instead of strings
	Avoid variable length strings
	Build ioins on columns that share compatible datatypes
	Avoid using NULLS

be used on a small number of sample projects and finetuned into a consistent set of data standards for a wider audience. A review team consisting of a Senior Sponsor (e.g., VP or CIO) and a combination of business analysts, systems analysts, and developers can then finetune the data standards and expand them for the enterprise before deploying them.

Exhibit 2-6.   User interface category.

Subcategory	Comments
Screens:	Include field sizes, field types, field objects
Help Screens	
Menu Screens	
Drop Down Menus	
Information Screens	
Transaction Screens	
Reports:	Include page headings, page footers, date, page
Project Plans	number, column headings, total columns
Status Reports	
Issue Logs	
Client Requests	Minimize number of SQL requests per transasction

Exhibit 7 also shows another approach that involves "creating" the data standards because there are no satisfactory ones to be borrowed from another source. The key for making this approach a success is to begin with a framework that is similar to the exhibits shown previously. You will probably want to modify the subcategories in the tables, or even to merge or expand the number of tables that are shown. A champion in the organization, perhaps a business analyst, should then review other projects and define a standard for each subcategory (e.g., all variable names must be

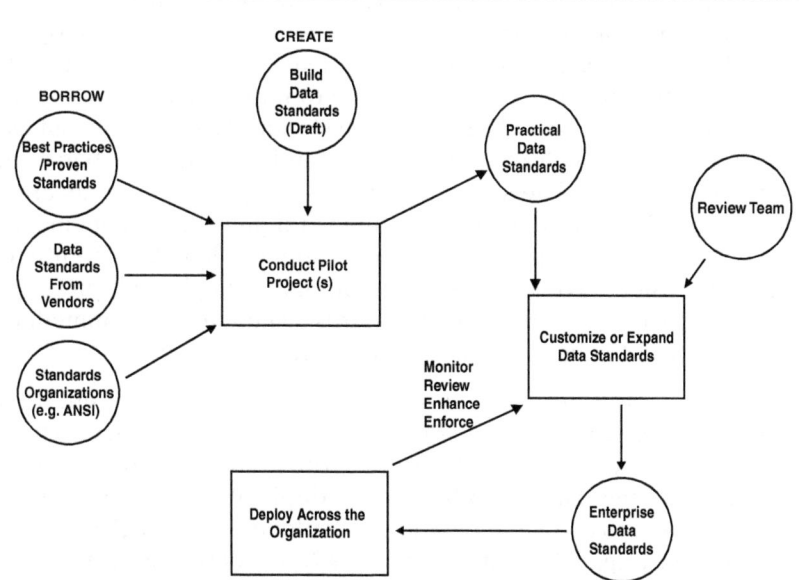

Exhibit 2-7. Process for defining enterprise data standards.

prefaced with their datatype, all databases will have project names). It is unlikely that this first pass will be complete. The primary challenge is to establish a standards baseline and to begin using them. As in the "borrow" approach, one or more pilot projects are used to validate and enhance the data standards. In the "create" approach, it is likely that several projects will be required to define a satisfactory set of data standards.

There is a third approach that involves combining the "borrow" and "create" approaches. In this instance, standards organizations such as ANSI or ISO can be used to provide a first cut at the data standards. These are then customized as discused in the "create" approach.

Exhibit 7 shows that after the enterprise data standards have been prepared and signed off by the corporate sponsor, the next task is wide deployment. The manner in which this is done is critical for the successful adoption of the enterprise data standards. The first step here is to ensure that the data standards are readily available electronically or on paper. The next step is to communicate the importance, location, and procedures for using the data standards by both the operations and development groups. This message must be communicated to the organization by a senior sponsor, such as a CIO or VP, in order to maximize corporate buy in.

COMMON PITFALLS AND TRAPS

There are several common pitfalls and traps that can befall an organization trying to establish enterprise data standards. One of the obvious problems springs from the "enterprise" term itself. Many organizations view the use of this term to mean "broad consensus required" or "slow adoption." This can lead to several problems, not the least of which is that the standards require too much attention and time to implement, or are too cumbersome to learn, use, or understand. Such standards are usually put aside during tight project timeframes. Too many standards can be as bad as having too few standards. The surest way of ensuring that standards are not used is to spend a lot of time defining them and publishing them in a hundred plus page manual. It is preferable to spend a few days conducting research, and then having a small team publish a single digit page document defining the suggested data standards which are then immediately passed to project teams to test and refine in actual projects.

Another common problem involves the inaccessibility of enterprise standards. To be effective, the standards must be readily accessible to project teams at any time. Furthermore, the standards should also be readily usable. They must also be easy to duplicate. A useful method of achieving these is to use a combination of deployment strategies. A central data repository (e.g., a Web site or a Lotus Notes database) can hold the enterprise standards. Project teams throughout the organization should have direct and remote access to the repositories. Reusable templates and deliverables (e.g., screen images) can also be included in the repositories to provide project teams with the ability to get started on their projects quickly. Paper-based, or CD/ROM-based, delivery of the standards and templates should accompany the electronic delivery modes.

MEASURING COMPLIANCE AND ENFORCING STANDARDS

During the pressure of development projects or unexpected operational emergencies, it is not uncommon for all standards, including data standards, to be suspended until the immediate problem is resolved. In some instances, this is acceptable in the short term. However, compliance is important in the long term, and several mechanisms should be used to measure and enforce this, as follows:

- Deliverable walk-throughs. Regular sessions should be scheduled to walkthrough and sign off on project deliverables to ensure that they comply with the published enterprise data standards. DBAs should be involved in this process.
- Audit. Infrequent audits of projects across the enterprise should be used to ensure ongoing compliance with the published standards. Resources on the audit teams can vary over time. A good size for the audit team is about three resources. It is a good idea to rotate resources on and off the teams over a period of time.
- Enforcement. Examples of noncompliance should be documented and the appropriate project manager(s) should be mandated to ensure that the standards are adhered to within a specific timeframe (e.g., one month).
- Quality plan. Every project plan should be accompanied by a quality plan that includes the activities that will be followed by the project teams to ensure compliance with the standards.

TEN TIPS FOR GETTING STARTED

Many projects have shown that the following tips greatly simplify the process of establishing enterprise-wide data standards:

1. Keep them simple.
2. Borrow, if possible, avoid creating.
3. Use samples from actual projects.
4. Make the standards readily accessible electronically.
5. Do not hesitate to modify enterprise data standards if a good argument is presented.
6. Use standards as reasonable guidelines.
7. Build early successes as showpieces.
8. Build data standard compliance right into the project plan or quality plan.
9. Never create standards in a vacuum.
10. Enforce the use of the data standards.

CONCLUSION

Enterprise data standards should be used by organizations that are building and maintaining nontrivial application systems. The key for establishing enterprise data standards is to keep them as simple as possible and to ensure that they are actually used on projects. It is recommended that standards be borrowed from third parties or vendors. Where this is not possible, it is recommended that a framework, such as the one included in this article, be used to build a first cut of the enterprise standards. These should then be validated in a few pilot projects before rolling them out to the enterprise.

LIST OF ORGANIZATIONS DEFINING STANDARDS

ISO	International Organization for Standardization (Global support)
OSF DCE	Open Software Foundation's (OSF) Distributed Computing Environment (middleware and enterprise standards)
POSIX	applications operating with OS. Deals with system calls, libraries, tools, interfaces, and testing
X/Open	European vendors and manufacturers
COSE	IBM, HP Santa Cruz Operation, Sun Microsystems, UNIX — application/OS implementations
CORBA	Object Management Group's Common Object Request Broker Architecture
IEEE	U.S. Standards body; works to get buy-in from ANSI
SQL Access Group	Call-Level Interface (CLI) and Remote Database Access (RDA)
ISOC	Internet Society. Internet standards and internetworking techniques

Chapter 3
Enterprise Data Management

Jonathan B. Novak

THE INFORMATION ENVIRONMENT TODAY IS CHARACTERIZED BY APPLICATION systems that develop and deliver data to specific groups. The data delivery is often achieved in a redundant and costly way because organizational and application barriers limit information transfer. More serious to the objectives of the enterprise is the limited access and often erroneous or, at best, inconsistent views of what the data represents.

To provide high-quality, consistent data, the enterprise must treat it as a corporate resource rather than the traditional application-specific domain. Application-specific databases were typically created to be independent from other applications, although often with similar elements. This situation is prominent because of the approach that addresses data requirements within the scope of a given application or process, with no concern or attention to requirements outside that scope for the same, similar, or related data.

To eliminate this tendency and to manage cross-process requirements, data must be addressed at the enterprise level. Resulting improvements in quality make it possible to manage by fact, because all functions and applications use a single logical image of data from the enterprise master copy of information rather than variations generated specifically by and for individual systems.

The core concept of this chapter is to support an architecture, methodology, and set of services to deliver timely, consistent, and quality data elements from a single logical source to all applications, end users, and clients. It is complementary but not limited to developing data information warehouse architectures. The objectives of Enterprise Data Management (EDM) include providing an enterprisewide data image developed from optimum data sources that populate an enterprise data information warehouse and are delivered to authorized end users and knowledge workers.

EDM PRINCIPLES

The appropriate corporate data environment requires the following EDM principles to be established

- *Data is a corporate asset.* Within this conceptual framework, data is treated as a corporate resource to be managed as an enterprise critical asset.
- *Data is organized by the business.* Data is organized into categories — subject data areas — and has specific functions and individuals that are accountable for its quality, value, and enterprise satisfaction.
- *Data is separated from the application.* Data development is separated from the traditional method of aligning with an application. Data is developed independently of applications that focus on its presentation or process for the end user.
- *Data is shared.* Data is shared and reused by all lines of business facilitated by an enterprise-managed data warehouse, architecture, and methodology.
- *Data has a single definition and source.* All information of interest or critical to the enterprise has a single data definition and source and can evolve as driven by business to meet specific requirements.
- *Data evolves.* The components of the enterprise warehouse and associated architecture should be developed in an evolutionary manner as needed to deliver information processes in support of business requirements.

ENTERPRISE DATA SCOPE

To determine and organize the enterprise data to be supported by the EDM, the key resources, entities, and functions required by the business must first be identified. This step lays the foundation of the relationships between the data areas and critical processes. Accordingly, the corporation can be assured that it is managing the right data for the right reasons rather than merely better identifying application-driven data requirements.

Subject data areas are enterprise resources and external tangible and intangible entities that are of interest or value to the business from a corporate perspective. Data area groupings are composed of related information and subgroupings identified with the enterprise (e.g., sales, financial, and product).

Functions are groupings of activities that support the mission of the enterprise. An organization is a grouping of corporate resources that are assigned to perform one or more functions of the enterprise and are not synonymous (e.g., marketing, finance, manufacturing, and human resources). Organizational structures are dynamic, whereas functions generally remain static.

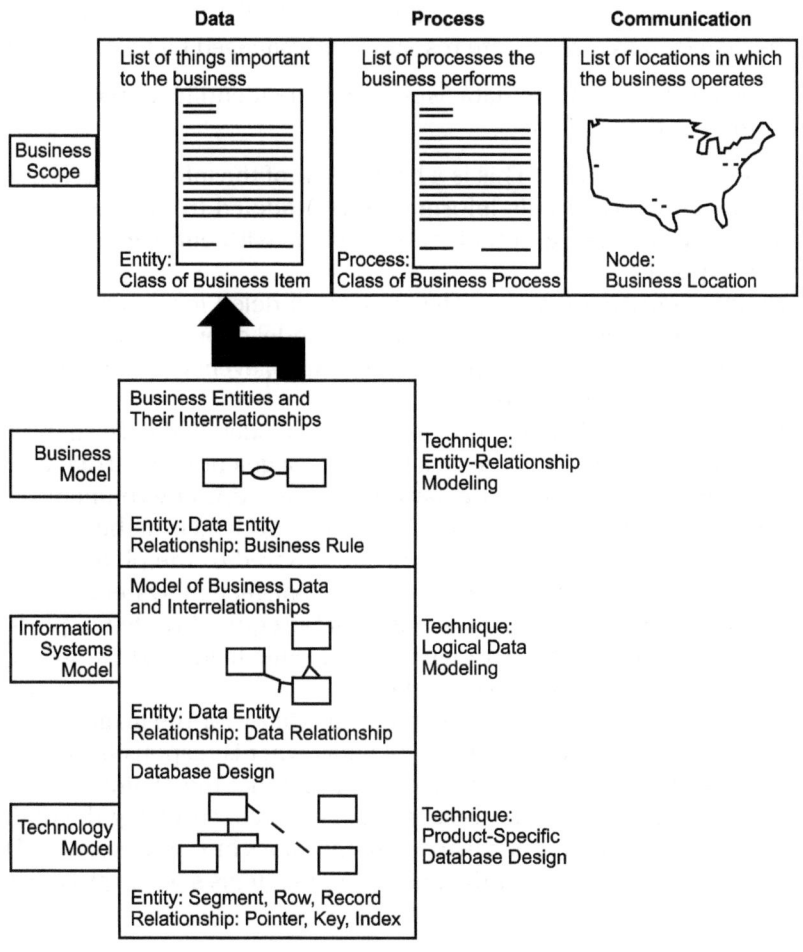

Exhibit 3-1. Zachman data architecture framework.

Much attention has been given to the requirements and processes of identifying and developing data relationships. Publications by IBM regarding information systems planning and the information warehouse; by John Zachman regarding the data architecture framework; by William Inmon regarding the data warehouse and structures; and by James Martin regarding information engineering all establish approaches to identify and establish critical aspects of managing information (see Exhibit 1).

It is the intention of this chapter to emphasize the need for the top layer of data areas to be identified by the business. Subsequent and parallel efforts can take place as supported by the corporation to understand and take advantage of information systems development approaches. Regardless of the time and resources applied to later efforts, the fist step is critical if data is to be managed as a corporate resource and managed by the enterprise.

The major layers for the data aspect and the identification of business owners of that data include

- *Enterprise data scope.* This is a broad view of the information required by the enterprise. This information is modeled from a subject data area or view level, and their relationships with enterprise functions are mapped.
- *Business data information.* This is data modeled for a particular segment or function of the enterprise — a model of business entities that represent facts about people, places, things, events, and concepts for a specific business segment.
- *Business system design information.* This is a detailed data analysis to support a business system or a business segment of a particular area without regard to the particular target computing environment.
- *Technology design information.* This is data derived from business system design information identified and tailored to the physical target computing environment and database management system.
- *Database design information.* This is data required to define physical data structures for the storage of data elements in a data store based on the technology design information.
- *Data ownership.* This is business accountability for the management of data as a vital corporate asset. The data owner is responsible for creating the logical model for the data, ensuring that the business views of the creating and using processes are supported, certifying the optimal source, and educating end users as to the data's business meaning. Data owners are supported by the information systems service providers.

EDM COMPONENTS

To manage the many and complex aspects of providing a total solution to data management and data warehousing, the following EDM components are identified:

- *Enterprise warehouse.* This provides a logical data store to contain enterprise managed data.
- *Enterprise data warehouse.* This provides a physical data store to contain the master data elements.
- *Client data warehouse.* This provides a downstream physical data store to contain distributed data.
- *Business information directory.* This provides a managed repository to contain metadata.
- *Optimum source.* This identifies the primary source to propagate quality operational data.

- *Extract.* This provides data enhancement and copy management for the data warehouse.
- *Distribution.* This provides seamless consistent data delivery to applications and end users.
- *Access.* This provides transparent user-initiated access, regardless of platforms.
- *Control.* This provides and maintains the rules that govern enterprise data.
- *Manager.* This individual provides the functions that monitor and direct EDM processes.
- *EDM execution.* This step provides the tools and utilities that execute EDM processes.

ENTERPRISE WAREHOUSE — THE DATA

In a logical sense, the enterprise warehouse component is a single master repository of enterprise data and metadata that produces the physical data structures required to store the subsequent informational data of the corporation. Physical implementation may warrant multiple data elements and fields; however, each replication is a clone of the logical master copy.

A single image of a data element is contained in a logical data store, which is the conceptual enterprise warehouse. The corporation has only one logical data element and its associated metadata for any given item. Actual physical data elements of the data are unlikely to be stored in one unique database. The physical layer of the enterprise warehouse are managed within the enterprise data warehouse or downstream client data warehouses (see Exhibit 2).

The enterprise data warehouse is the primary repository for the physical master data element. It is the first occurrence of physically depositing the master copy of an element or field in an enterprise managed data store.

The client data warehouse contains the subsets of these data elements stored in downstream physical locations to accommodate proximity and platforms. The elements contained therein are identical to the master logical image and are extracted from the enterprise data warehouse. In some instances, individual departmental-specific data elements not needed by other areas are stored in client data warehouses, and supersets are rolled into the enterprise data warehouse as required by the enterprise.

The enterprise warehouse is a logical view of data from a corporate perspective. It is not oriented toward the needs of the individual application, in the physical sense, but is modeled at a higher level to provide the consistent foundation for the data and relationships that different user constituents and applications have in common. It can eliminate the replication of

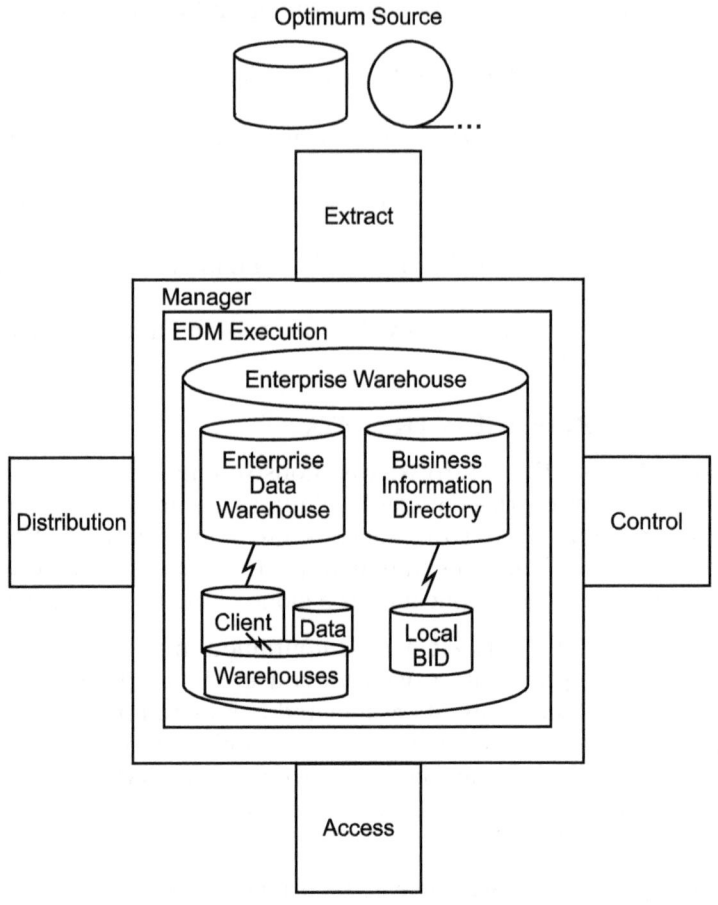

Exhibit 3-2. Enterprise data warehouse.

like data parts and the subsequent errors caused by the inconsistencies inherent in different definitions, schedules, and use.

For business and performance reasons, it may be appropriate to produce redundant physical copies of data elements and databases or files. These replications are managed within EDM to ensure consistency and quality of all enterprise data. Data is thus developed only once and duplicated only where justified, necessary, and controlled.

Duplicate physical enterprise data transported to databases located on other platforms (e.g., minicomputers, LANs, and personal workstations) are also client data warehouses of the enterprise data warehouse. Client data warehouses can be downstream of other client data warehouses in a distributed hierarchy. All client data warehouse copies are controlled and provide the single logical data image throughout the corporation to ensure consistency, integrity, and quality for the physical data and metadata. All copies have been justified for replication.

Data not managed by the enterprise is logically stored separately, and by definition these elements are used by only one application. Management of any application-specific data is the responsibility of the application even if physically it may be stored as an extension within a client data warehouse. If any element is later needed by another application, that element, again by definition, becomes of interest to the enterprise. Accordingly, those identified data elements must then be managed by the EDM process.

Metadata is managed in a like manner within the enterprise warehouse with the primary physical identifier stored in the master business information directory. Downstream copies of the metadata are managed by the enterprise and, like their data counterpart, are mirror images of their master copy. The downstream metadata may be stored as needed in a locally based business information directory.

DATA STATES

The following are enterprise warehouse data element states (see Exhibit 3):

- *Mirror image data.* This is data that has been identified and selected from the optimum source, unchanged in content, and stored in the enterprise warehouse.
- *Consolidated data.* This is data that has been identified from more than one source, consolidated into a single data attribute, and stored in the enterprise warehouse.
- *Derived data.* This is data that has been identified from one or more sources and formulated into a single attribute (e.g., a summation) and stored in the enterprise warehouse.
- *Historical data.* This is data that has been identified as point-in-time data (e.g., month-end, quarterly, or year-end accumulative) and stored in the enterprise warehouse. The key differentiator of historical data is the maintenance of additional data elements from current data elements to service historical trends and analysis information.
- *Developed data.* This is data for which content is not available from outside the enterprise warehouse, but developed and originated (i.e., value is added) and stored in the enterprise warehouse. In this case, the enterprise data warehouse data element becomes the optimum source.
- *Metadata.* This is data about the data that is stored in the enterprise warehouse. It is not the actual content of an element or field, but the information defining the attributes and descriptions, including business meaning, of the physical data.

31

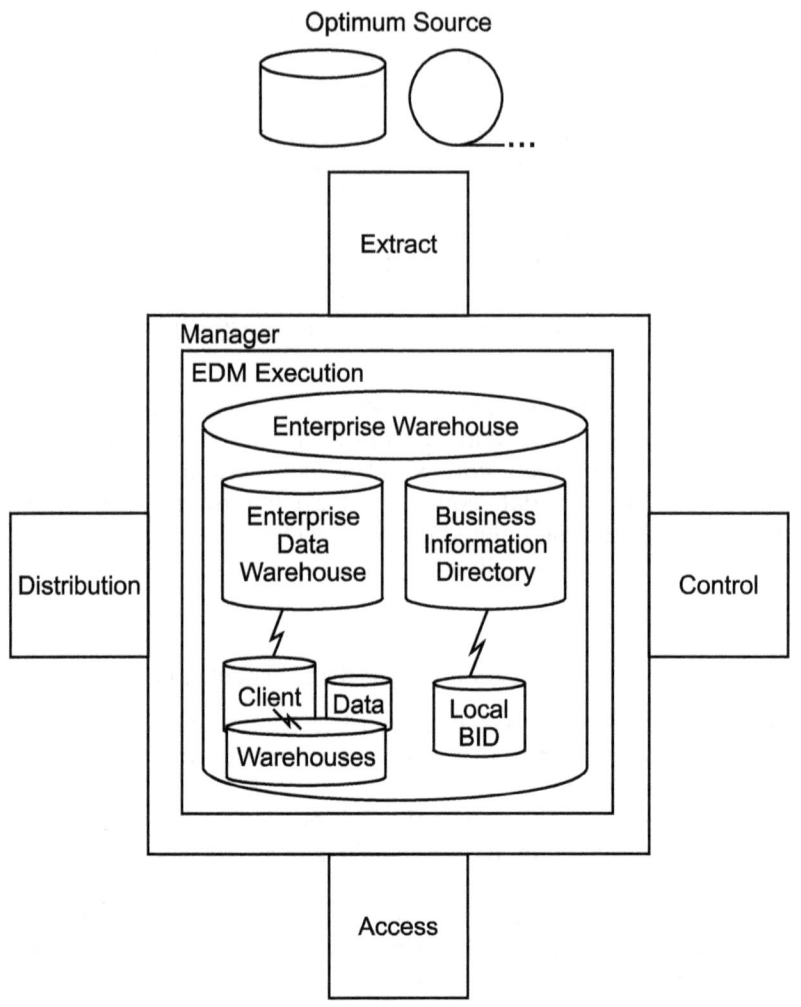

Exhibit 3-3. Enterprise warehouse element states.

BUSINESS INFORMATION DIRECTORY — THE METADATA

The associated metadata for each element is contained in the business information directory. The business information directory component provides the user with a single source or catalog of information about the data in the enterprise warehouse. The purpose of the directory is to provide a diversified set of users with the required information about the data that is available to them and how it is related to other information. This relationship further provides a link between the business and information systems development and its terms.

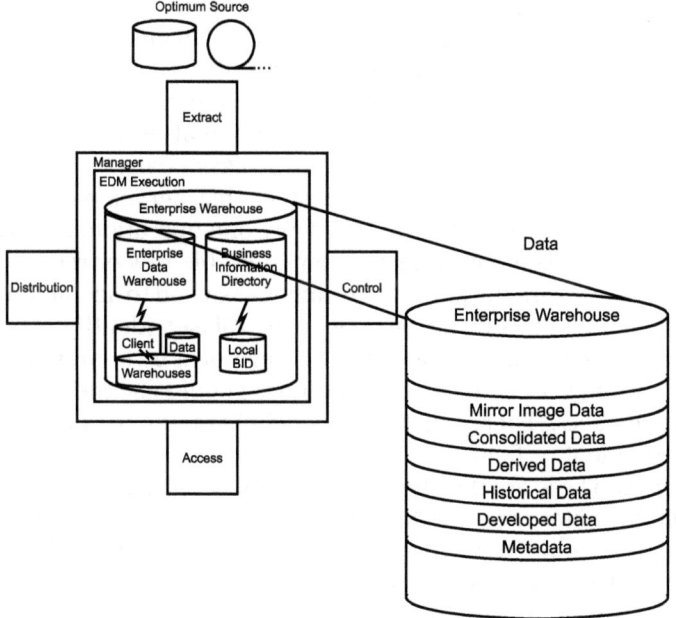

Exhibit 3-4. Business information directory metadata.

The business information directory contains the necessary information for its users to navigate in business terms to what information or data is available to them. That information includes definitions, owners, locations, current status, and what method is used to access it. The information in the directory is accessible at different levels (or views) depending on the user's orientation. For example, an IS developer may wish to access data at the table or database level, whereas a knowledge worker or data owner may wish to access information at the function, process, or application level.

The business information directory identifies data from the business perspective through data models, catalogs, directories, and dictionaries. The processes to build and maintain the directory objects must ensure consistent data definitions, names and attributes from such original sources as the enterprise data model, data dictionaries, DBMS catalogs and tables, and data owners.

METADATA CONTENTS

The following are some examples of the business information directory metadata contents (see Exhibit 4):

- *Name.* This is the business name of a data element or field. Only one of-ficial name exists for any element. The identical business name is to be used by all applications and processes that have the need and are authorized to have access to any given data element.

- *Definition.* This is the definition and description of a data element or field. Only one definition is linked to an element, although there may be layers of descriptors as needed by different users of any given element, including information systems professionals.
- *Source.* This is the operational system that serves as the optimum source for a data element or field. Only one operational source exists for any given element (at least at any possible row or record level).
- *Aliases.* These are the alternative names assigned to accommodate current investment in traditional systems. Aliases identify other names that a data element or field may also be known by in previously developed systems. New development efforts should use the official name.
- *Characteristics.* These are the physical characteristics and attributes of an element or field.
- *Locations.* These are the physical locations in which an element is stored within the enterprise warehouse, including client data warehouses. The physical location from where the data is obtained is also identified.
- *Models.* These are the enterprise, business, systems, and process model information and relationships.
- *Applications or processes.* These are the key applications and processes that are identified with an element.

OPTIMUM SOURCE — THE OPERATIONAL INPUT

The optimum source component addresses the identification, input, and management of data from key operational systems and databases. Data in the enterprise warehouse is grouped into logical subject data areas from a business point of view. Primary functions and applications are similarly grouped as major sourcing (i.e., creating) and reading of those data groups.

The optimum source is identified in support of projects being developed that use common shared data. Support is provided by information system organizations to develop an enterprise data model. Business owners are identified for each of the subject data areas and for the automated processes (e.g., operational systems applications) that support the business functions.

These efforts provide information to start the population of the repository or warehouses with the enterprise data required. It is the identification of the most appropriate operational systems and applications that are implemented or under development. This information is used to establish the process management and control information that is used to populate the enterprise warehouse and the business information directory.

As business changes are made, they are driven through the optimum source processes to determine data changes and expansions required,

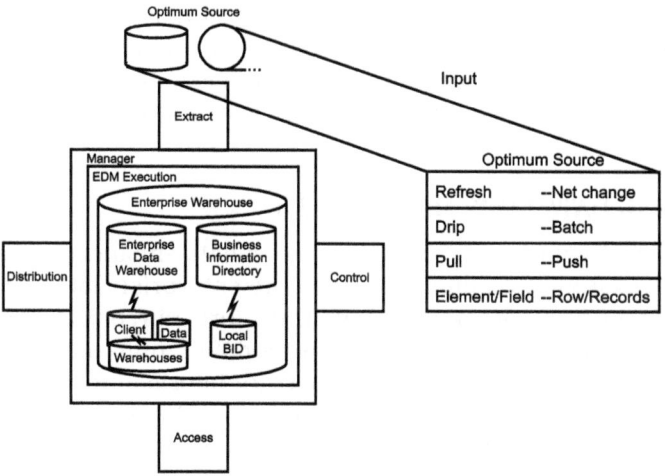

Exhibit 3-5. Optimum sourcing processes.

assess effects, and direct the appropriate changes in the enterprise ware-house. The business data owners are responsible for this process, for resolving any conflicts that result from data definitions and requirements, and for ensuring that the implementation of EDM meets their business needs.

The optimum source data and its operational process must be managed because by the nature of the extracting copy management processes, the operational data can affect propagation of the enterprise warehouse. It is this process that feeds the enterprise warehouse in an assortment of ways. These transport activities can occur at any point within the lifecycle of delivering data from the optimum source to any location managed within the enterprise data concept.

The following processes, shown in Exhibit 5, are not limited to optimum sourcing and can recur any time the data is extracted or distributed within the EDM process:

- *Refresh versus net change.* The refresh process entails all the data within a database or file being replaced on a periodic basis; with net change only those elements that had changes are affected (i.e., how much).
- *Drip versus batch.* In the drip process, data movement occurs continuously on a recurring basis as warranted by modifications, in batch mode, data is bulk-processed at end of completed operational processing (i.e., when).
- *Pull versus push.* Data can be pulled from operational sources as initiated by EDM, or data elements or fields can be pushed down from the operational systems when changes are noted (i.e., who initiates).

35

- *Element field versus rows and records.* Either only those data elements or fields required by EDM are provided by the operational systems, or completed rows or records are shipped transmitted to enterprise data sites with responsibility for segment selection remaining with those sites (i.e., what).

EXTRACT — DATA COPY MANAGEMENT

The extract component of EDM provides data enhancement and copy management from optimum sources to the enterprise data warehouses. System-initiated processes gather and transport source data, provide preparatory function to meet enterprisewide data requirements and structure, enhance as specified by data owners for informational specifications and decision support analysis, ensure update continuity, and store the finished element or field in the enterprise data warehouse.

A significant aspect of this component is to provide data extraction, transformation, enhancement, and storage into the master data store only once for all users. Because all applications and end users subsequently receive their data from a managed corporate data resource repository as defined by the enterprise, the traditional practice of each application developing and preparing its own data is eliminated.

The key functions provided by the extract component, shown in Exhibit 6, include:

- *Copy management.* This function transports data from optimal operational sources.
- *Data preparation.* This function transforms the data to meet enterprise-managed requirements.
- *Data enhancement.* This function develops data from an operational perspective to an informational and decision support perspective (e.g., point-in-time or summation).
- *Update.* This function ensures synchronization and consistency of data modifications that are authorized and initiated downstream from the warehouses.

DISTRIBUTION — DATA DELIVERY

The distribution component of EDM addresses system-initiated, process-driven delivery of data from the enterprise data warehouse to the subset client data warehouses, applications, and systems. Distribution provides transport processes to ensure consistent, seamless, and transparent data availability by applications regardless of location and movement.

Data delivery activity comprises all aspects of keeping the data accessible regardless of the location. It permits the movement of data and

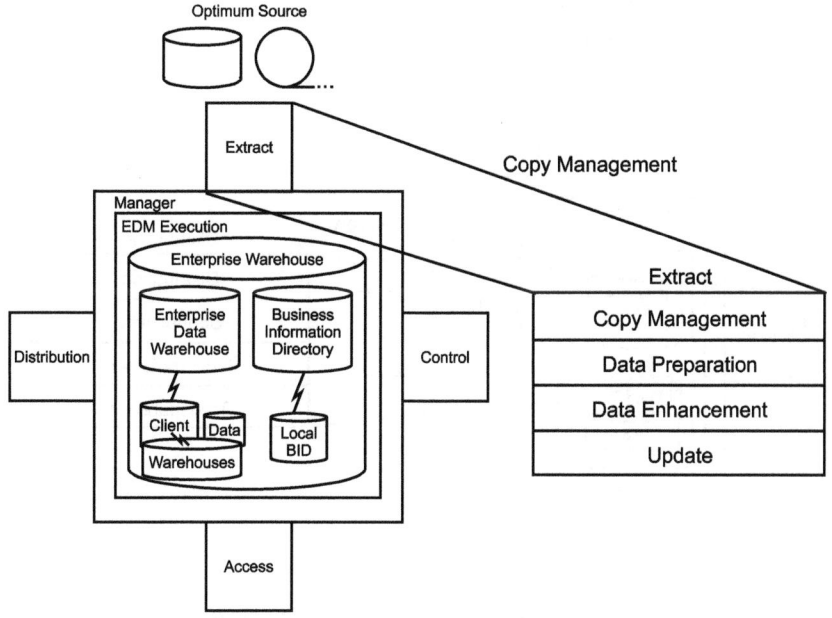

Exhibit 3-6. Extract component functions.

databases separated from the applications and users so that database configuration, performance, product, and technical advances are transparent to the development of the enterprise's information presentation and transaction systems.

Distribution establishes the bridges and hooks by which the applications address obtaining data from the data warehouse. This approach eliminates the need for each application to develop its own access procedures and, more important, permits managed control and synchronization of all enterprise data to ensure delivery of a single logical data image. In addition, all movement, modifications, and updates to a data element by an authorized application are reflected in a timely manner to all users of that element regardless of function, application, platform, or location.

As shown in Exhibit 7, the key functions provided by the distribution component include:

- *Distribution.* This refers to all managed client data warehouses, including intermediary nodes, client/servers, Wide Area Networks, LANs, and personal workstations.
- *Connectivity.* This refers to elements and rows because data is created separately from the application. Links and connectors are provided to applications for data availability.

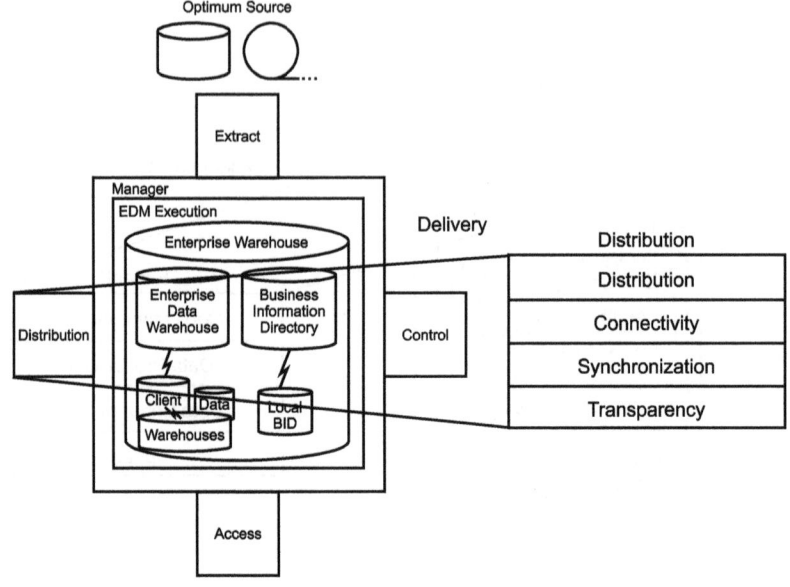

Exhibit 3-7. Distribution component functions.

- *Synchronization.* This applies to all copies of data elements to ensure timely and consistent data images, regardless of which managed data repository is accessed.
- *Transparency.* This refers to client data warehouse location or subsequent movement.

ACCESS — USER ACQUISITION

The access component of EDM provides seamless connectivity and access to warehouse client data by applications and ad hoc programs regardless of platform. It enables knowledge workers to initiate acquisition of data from a familiar interface and transparently locate and connect to the data requested by that end user. Although the extract and distribution components of EDM address the automated system initiated delivery of data from sources to warehouses and subsequent applications, the access component addresses end-user-initiated data retrieval from the user's terminal or personal workstation to structured and unstructured enterprisewide data.

The function is to establish an upstream accessibility from the final user system or tool to the enterprise warehouse over multiple operating systems, hardware, and interfaces without the end user's needing to know or care where or on what type of system the data resides. By information contained in the business information directory, the access component

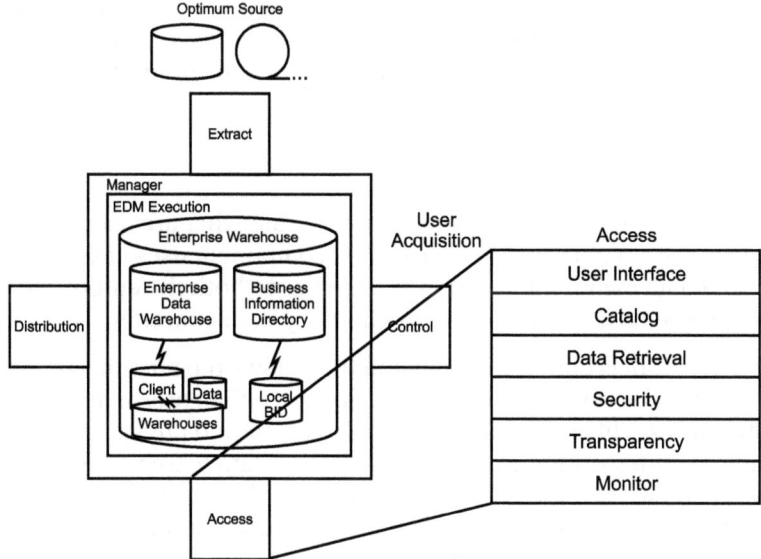

Exhibit 3-8. Access component functions.

locates specific data elements and provides the user with either its image or the actual data itself as previously established. Because critical navigational information is available for all data within the enterprise warehouse, the system is able to obtain any and all elements requested by the end user without prior data requirements being defined.

As shown in Exhibit 8, the key functions provided by the access component include

- *User interface.* This provides user-initiated data request interface either directly or by an application that interacts with the end user.
- *Catalog.* This presents the contents of the business information directory to the user.
- *Data retrieval.* This retrieves data from any source known to the business information directory.
- *Security.* This ensures security through user identification and authentication.
- *Transparency.* This provides consistent navigation regardless of data location or platform.
- *Monitoring.* This monitors user access to data.

CONTROL — THE RULES

The control component of EDM contains the rules to manage the data store and access to that data. The control component contains the rules to propagate data among the warehouses and to ensure that the data is accessible only to those who are authorized to view, modify, or obtain that data. Four major subcomponents are defined within control: data control, process control, user control, and standards.

Data Control

The data control component contains the rules that are used to manage the data in the enterprise warehouse. This component uses enterprise data model and data owner information and applies to both the enterprise warehouse and the business information directory data contents.

The data models contain information that allows the mapping of the data selected from the optimal operational sources to the enterprise warehouse data structures. This mapping is to both the logical and physical views of the data and includes optimum source, enterprise data warehouse, and client data warehouse locations. Through the use of these models and the processes that build the enterprise warehouse, data redundancy can be controlled and the integrity of the data maintained.

Process Control

The process control component contains the rules that are used to manage the data processes that propagate and deliver the data in the enterprise warehouse. This component incorporates data process models and application owner information and applies to both the enterprise warehouse and the business information directory.

The process models are used to identify the flow of data from the operational systems into the enterprise warehouse. They can identify the processes that are required to perform a task, the sequence in which the tasks are executed, the status of tasks, the scheduling information to be used, and execution initiation for the tasks.

Additional information that is available from the process models pertains to the priority of processing in the event multiple sources of information are available, to the indications of the data's current state, and to the identification of information that can be shared, or reused, by other processes.

User Control

User control is composed of security and registration functions and any associated profiles. Additional security is required to control access at the specific data element level. This control is usually managed at the application level today and is typically controlled by a job, data set, or terminal log-on classification with authorization codes for access.

A registration function is the primarily administrative task of identifying people, data sets, or jobs to the system. This function includes the initial entry into the system; the revalidation process to control current status; and the deletion of the access when it is no longer valid.

Profiles to identify a wide variety of user information are developed for proper routing of information and capturing user customization information. These profiles are user controlled and are used by applications and tools to pick up defaults or other variable information at the time of execution. These profiles exist at the system, application, and user level.

Standards

Standards to manage and introduce consistency for data naming, definitions, attributes, and contents must be developed. Establishing a standardized common base for enterprise data ensures that the user can consistently access data elements and extract information regardless of the application or location of the data. The data owner of each category controls the description and contents of data from the business perspective.

Technical standards must be developed consistent with industry direction and tool capabilities to manage data. A variety of tools are used to maintain the data linked to their respective models. These tools are primarily industry standards in information engineering (e.g., AD/Cycle and Computer-Aided Software Engineering products). These tools must be defined and installed on development workbenches and within the business organizations where necessary.

Control Types

The control component can be broken down into six subsets or groups of control information (listed in Exhibit 9) that are used to manage the data and related components and ensure compliance with EDM direction and architecture:

- *Security.* This information identifies authorization levels to access data.
- *Standards.* This information establishes conformity.
- *Policies and Rules.* This information establishes governing factors.
- *Procedures.* This information identifies enforcement steps to ensure compliance.
- *Guidelines.* This information identifies recommendations.
- *Processes.* This information identifies process control parameters.

MANAGER — PROCESSES

The manager component addresses authorizing and monitoring the processes necessary to manage and implement the enterprise data concept.

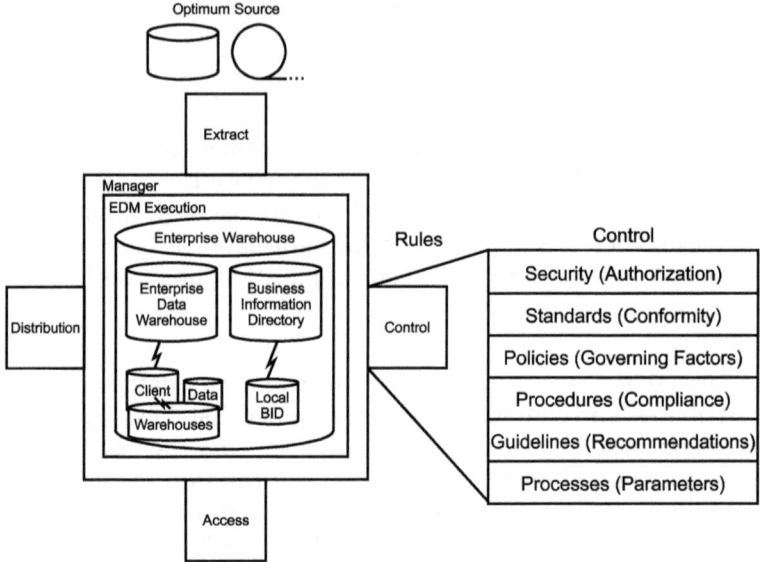

Exhibit 3-9. Control information types.

The manager services the requirements EDM and ensures appropriate actions are executed and exceptions are noted.

The manager uses the rules contained in the control component to determine when and how the processes are to be initiated to identify, source, maintain, access, or distribute the data contained in the data warehouses. As required, movement of data to subsequent databases is supervised by the manager and delivered by the distribution component. Actual system processing is accomplished by the execution component as directed by the manager.

Enterprise warehouse manager activity comprises all aspects of keeping the data up to date, available, and usable. It includes the validation and enhancement of operational data, the processing of complete file replacements as well as net change files, and the processing of end-user-generated information. This activity applies to individual files and across files where multiple data stores are available. In addition, the removal of obsolete data and reorganization of the databases are addressed.

The manager ensures both data and referential integrity in the repository through the application of controls, management of process execution, and monitoring of data delivery to keep all enterprise data elements accessible regardless of the location. Providing overall availability of the data to the end user includes preparing for unexpected outages. Procedures for backup and recovery as well as for the business interruption (i.e., disaster) planning are addressed.

42

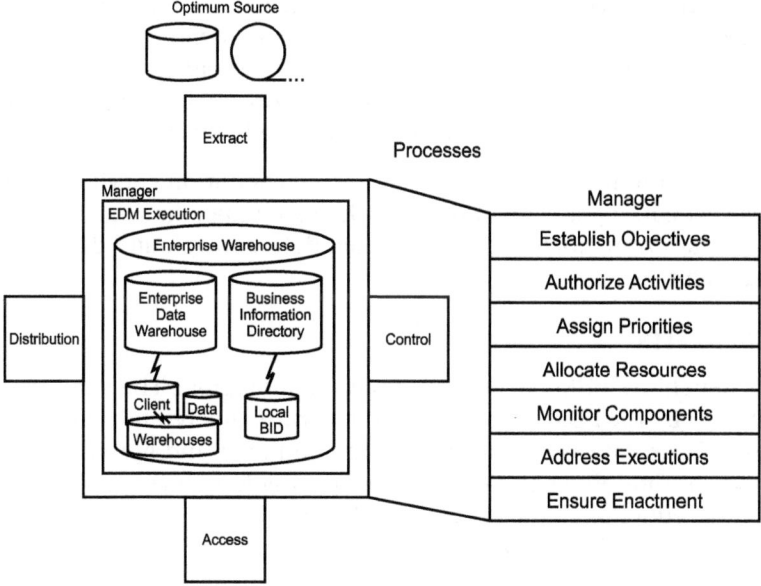

Exhibit 3-10. Manager processes.

Modifications to EDM are driven by the needs of the business as organizations and business processes change and are reflected within the EDM architecture. The information systems department assesses these changes, identifies the effects, determines the implementation approach, and communicates the changes and plans to those affected by modifications.

The key functions are to manage data coming into the enterprise warehouse and its development and storage and to provide access and delivery of data to the client (see Exhibit 10). To ensure the provision of necessary data services, the management component must: establish objectives, authorize activities, assign priorities, allocate resources, monitor components, address exceptions, and ensure enactment.

EXECUTION — PRODUCTS

The execution component comprises the actual products, tools, utilities, hooks, and processes that are executed to provide services for EDM. It addresses the actual performing of all the processes necessary to manage the enterprise data and related EDM components.

These utilities and interfaces must have consistently updated and available data elements to provide a single logical image to all applications and users. The central processing of data requirements eliminates the redundant development and processing that would be necessary if all applications and users produced and managed their own data activities, as in a traditional environment.

These supporting products and utilities must be developed and designed to evolve with the current priorities and technical solutions available. Data and data services can be modified and enhanced in a modular manner such that, as new technologies and products emerge, segments can be swapped in and out as warranted by the business.

Products and tools provide the following execution services for EDM: process execution, data identification, data sourcing, data extraction, data storage, data transport, data acquisition, data control, and data services management.

EDM BENEFITS

The benefits of EDM are both tangible and intangible. The quality of data distributed by the EDM is consistently accurate, timely, and synchronized. Access to this data is transparent to the end user and applications. The iterative methodology and data reuse approach fosters quicker deliverables by a reduction in the development cycle through the recurring use of the single logical data resources and processes.

Among the intangible benefits of EDM is that it provides a common source of information to be used by the corporation in processing its operations and making business decisions. The synergism attained by having all functions access and retain information in a common data store improves decision-making processes and allows the system to be more responsive to the needs of the business.

EDM reduces:

- *Code and data redundancy.* This is managed at the data level, eliminating application re-creation of like elements and fields.
- *The effect of input data.* This is controlled from operational data sources with single update for all data stores and subsequent use functions.
- *Processing requirements.* This is needed only once because not all applications and users repeat data development and extract processes.

Conversely, EDM provides:

- *Consistency of data names and definitions.* It ensures that a common element is available for all applications and end users.
- *Enhanced data integrity and currency.* This ensures consistency in accessing a single data element or field.
- *More timely data delivery.* This ensures the downloading of this common element is provided as part of EDM to the application or end user.
- *Improved quality of information available to the business.* This ensures consistency in meaning, updates, delivery, and contents of data.
- *Improved quality and performance in accessing business.* This ensures consistency in access, catalog, and extract of data to end users.

CONCLUSION

The information most organizations need to control, manage, and run their business already exists. The data is now effectively being used in day-to-day operations. Many corporations recognize that they must look beyond today's systems to use data assets in new ways to:

- Improve productivity of knowledge workers.
- Recognize patterns, spot trends, and improve competitive analysis.
- Integrate diverse activities of the enterprise.
- Understand customer and corporate needs.
- Provide better service.

To accomplish these results first requires managing the data as an enterprise-corporate resource. This EDM involves more than the collection and storing of data parts in a master warehouse. In addition to meeting the business requirements of specific departments and applications, it must also include the numerous components to manage a complete systems integration solution for the needs of the company as a whole entity — both operational and informational.

To help visualize a foundation for achieving an integrated, enterprise-driven information resource, corporate IS departments should develop an infrastructure that can evolve with the current business priorities and technical solutions available. To ensure effective evolution requires a disciplined and strategic architecture.

Section II
Information Gathering and Analysis

RAW DATA BECOMES INFORMATION WHEN IT HAS SPECIFIC INTERPRETATIONS WITHIN A BUSINESS CONTEXT. In terms of business solutions, collected information must be meaningful, thorough, and correct. Information-gathering activities are used to collect corporate data so that it can be used in solutions to solve business problems. Analysis activities are used to classify and validate the information that is gathered. These two sets of activities are generally done interatively until the activities are complete.

Information gathering and analysis activities can be consistently applied across technology architectures. The fact that the ultimate platform is Web based is generally not a differentiating factor at this stage. Information gathering involves using the results from the planning activities, specifically, the data owners, to collect, classify, and validate data across the organization. Some preliminary analysis is also performed to improve the value of the classification and the correctness of the data. However, how the collected information is formatted, modeled, stored, and accessed is examined in more detail in other sections of this book.

This section of the book contains four chapters. Chapter 4, "Data, Processes, and Events: Keys to Comprehensive Analysis," provides an approach for relating data, processes, and events to build an analytical framework used to build logical and ultimately physical data structures.

Chapter 5, "A Framework for Classifying Data," describes classic methods for classifying raw data into subsets. Because this approach spans the complexity of an organization, working with subsets simplifies the overall approach for managing complex data.

Chapter 6, "One Concept Equals One Data Element: A Rule for Developing Data Elements," provides guiding recommendations for defining data elements. The chapter also examines hazards of development data elements, standardization procedures, and when it is appropriate to violate rules.

Chapter 7, "Leveraging Content," examines approaches for collecting and classifying content across an organization. The results of physical activities are highly dependent on the type of technical architecture that supports a solution.

Chapter 4
Data, Processes, and Events: Keys to Comprehensive Analysis

Philip Friedlander

EVENT-DRIVEN ANALYSIS CAN ADD AN EXTRA DEGREE OF RIGOR TO BOTH DATA AND FUNCTIONAL MODELING AS WELL AS TO THE PROCESS OF SYSTEMS ANALYSIS. Event-driven analysis expands both the requirements gathering and requirements validation processes and introduces additional levels of depth and rigor to data, process, and event modeling techniques. This chapter introduces modeling tools that combine process, data, and event techniques.

ENTITY-LIFE HISTORIES AND DATA MODELING

Entity-life history (ELH) diagrams show all the events in the life of an entity; that is, all the states in which the entity can exist during its life. Each major data entity in the data model should have an ELH diagram that shows the major stages of its existence. However, more information than the stages of an entity's life are needed for a thorough understanding of the entity.

Most entities have certain required states (e.g., creation or instantiation, updating, and deletion). Exhibit 1 shows an ELH diagram for an entity called INSTRUCTOR. It has the required create, update, and delete stages. These stages are called the entity support stages, because these stages are required to support the entity's existence.

Exhibit 1 also shows an additional life stage, ASSIGN INSTRUCTOR TO CLASS. If this life stage does not support the entity, what is its purpose? The partial entity-relationship diagram (ERD) in Exhibit 2 shows that INSTRUCTOR teaches COURSE. The life stage of ASSIGN INSTRUCTOR TO

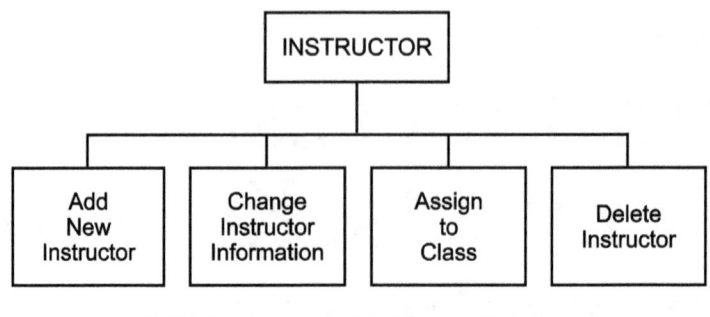

Exhibit 4-1. Entity-life history diagram.

COURSE supports the relationship that INSTRUCTOR has with COURSE. This type of entity-life stage is called a relationship support stage.

Therefore, each stage in an ELH must either support the entity or a relationship that the entity has with another entity. By understanding the differences between entity-support and relationship-support stages, a systems analyst can better understand the nature of relationships in data models. For example, a stage is an entity-support stage only if its event does not involve another entity; if another entity is involved, the stage is a relationship-support stage.

ELH AND PROCESS MODELING

Each stage of life of an entity is represented by one or more functions in a process model. A function may not equal a single process in the process model. The correspondence of functions to processes in the process model depends on the degree of abstraction with which the process model was developed. The degree to which there is one-to-one correspondence, however, is not critical during early analysis.

An important practice in analyzing life stages is that in addition to identifying the specific functionality required, analysts must also identify the events required to change the entity's state. A number of different analytical tools are available for the analysis of events. The most popular is the State-Transition Diagram. Although they effectively model events and states, State-Transition Diagram have little connection to data flow and entity relationship diagrams.

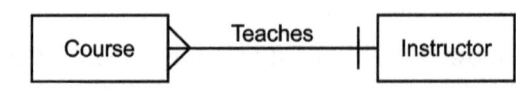

Exhibit 4-2. Sample of a partial entity-relationship diagram.

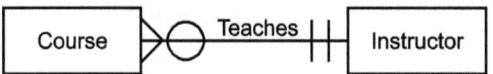

Exhibit 4-3. Existence criteria in an entity-relationship diagram.

EXISTENCE CRITERIA AND COUPLING

When examining a relationship between two entities, analysts must consider the relationship's cardinality and whether the relationship is required or optional for each entity. Exhibit 3 depicts existence criteria. The O symbol indicates that the relationship is optional, and the I symbol indicates that the relationship is required. Because all relationships are bidirectional, the analyst must show the existence criteria for each direction (i.e., entity). Exhibit 3 models the fact that a course must have an instructor. The two bars in the diagram indicate that a maximum of one instructor can teach a course. The O next to the COURSE entity indicates that an instructor does not have to teach any course.

In addition to existence criteria, the coupling of a relationship must also be examined. Coupling measures how much an action (i.e., change in stage) in one entity affects actions in a related entity. When assessing the coupling and existence criteria of a relationship, analysts must also determine whether the relationship is full or sparse. A relationship is considered full if the new occurrence of an entity immediately establishes a relationship with at least one occurrence of another entity. A full relationship is a form of moderate coupling, but this view of a relationship does not completely depict the nature of relationships.

In tightly coupled relationships, actions in one entity cause actions in another. There are nine possible combinations of a tightly coupled relationship. These nine possibilities are the product of combining create, update, and delete states in two entities (see Exhibit 4). The nine types of tightly coupled relationships are examined in the next section.

Types of Tightly Coupled Relationships

The following sections illustrate cases where action in one entity causes an action in another.

Create-Create. Exhibit 5 models an order-entity and billing system. A relationship exists between ORDER and LINE ITEMS. The ERD in Exhibit 5 shows that the relationship is required on both sides; that is, an order must have at least one line item and a line item must be associated with an order.

The relationship between these two entities has another dimension. The creation of an ORDER immediately establishes a relationship with a LINE

Casual Entity \ Affected Entity	Create	Update	Delete
Create	Create Create	Create Update	Create Delete
Update	Update Create	Update Update	Update Delete
Delete	Delete Create	Delete Update	Delete Delete

Exhibit 4-4. The nine combinations of tight coupling.

ITEM. Not only is this a full relationship but, more specific, the creation of an occurrence of one entity causes the creation of an occurrence of another entity. The creation of an ORDER does not just establish a relationship with an existing occurrence of LINE ITEM, it creates a new occurrence of LINE ITEM. In this tightly coupled relationship, the create state in one entity causes a create state in another entity.

Create-Update. Exhibit 5 shows that CUSTOMER has many INVOICES. The CUSTOMER entity has a data element called Date of Last Invoice. Thus, a new occurrence (i.e., creation) of INVOICE causes Date of Last Invoice to be updated.

Create-Delete. In the order-entry system, a customer who fails to pay after a certain period is placed in a bad customer file, which is used by the collections department. Such a customer is no longer allowed to conduct business with the supplier. The ERD in Exhibit 5 illustrates that the creation of an occurrence of a BAD CUSTOMER entity causes an instance of the CUSTOMER entity to be deleted.

Update-Create. The order-entry system must handle price changes, which can be volatile. The PRODUCT entity has a data element that stores the latest price, and for each price change a new instance of the PRICE CHANGE JOURNAL entity records the date, time, person changing, and old and new prices. In other words, an update in the PRODUCT entity causes the creation of a new occurrence of PRODUCT CHANGE JOURNAL.

Update-Update. The system must store the price and availability of all products from every vendor. The PRODUCT entity must always reflect the

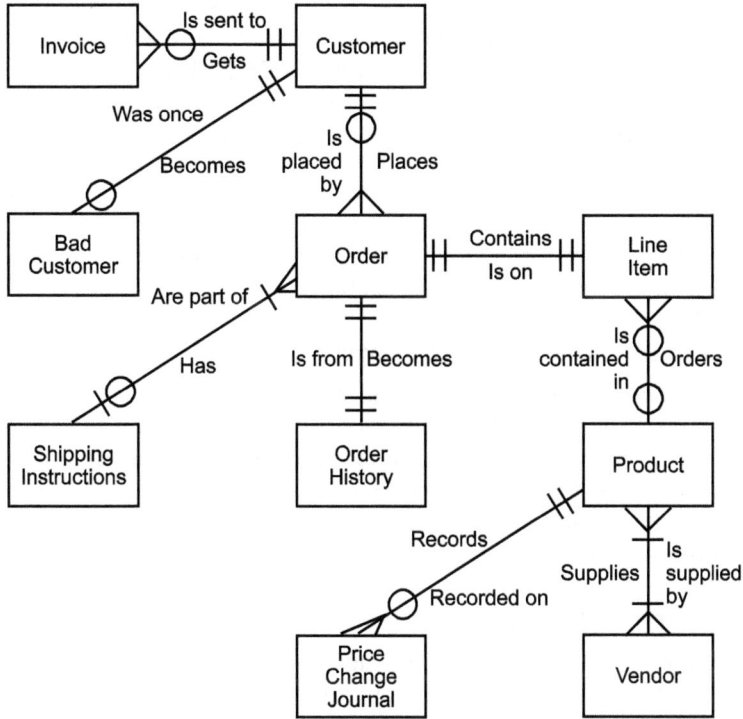

Exhibit 4-5. Entity-relationship diagram of an order entry system.

best price of a product and its vendor. When the availability of a product is updated in the VENDOR entity, the summary of product availability is also updated in the PRODUCT entity.

Update-Delete. The system must record special handling and shipping instructions for a small percentage of orders. Often, special shipping instructions are canceled by the customer after the order has been taken. In such a case, an update to one entity causes the deletion of an occurrence of another. When special shipping instruction information is removed from the ORDER entity, the relationship with the SHIPPING INSTRUCTIONS entity changes, and that instance of the SHIPPING INSTRUCTIONS entity involved in the old relationship is deleted. An update to ORDER causes a deletion of SHIPPING INSTRUCTIONS.

Delete-Create. The ERD in Exhibit 5 shows that when an order is closed, information about the order is recorded in the ORDER HISTORY entity. Thus, the deletion of an instance of ORDER creates a new occurrence of ORDER HISTORY. Obviously, the rules concerning the timing of the delete-create event can vary by application.

Delete-Update. The system also tracks customers who have outstanding invoices. When an invoice is paid in full, the occurrence of that invoice is deleted from the INVOICE entity, and the CUSTOMER entity is updated to reflect the invoice-number date, and amount of the last invoice paid in full. Deletion in INVOICE causes an update to CUSTOMER.

Delete-Delete. There are cases, of course, when the deletion of an occurrence of an entity causes the deletion of one or more occurrences of another entity. For example, if an instance of ORDER is deleted, all related LINE ITEM instances must also be deleted.

The Basis of the Event-Driven Approach

The nine types of slightly coupled relationships are the basis of the event-driven approach. This approach makes use of the ELH diagram. Unfortunately, the ELH diagram as it has been defined does not provide the richness and vigor required of an effective analysis tool. Although it can show changes, it cannot show what causes the change and how the change affects other entities.

The Four Types of Events

An event triggers a change in life stage of one or more entities. Based on this definition, there are only four categories of events.

1. Outside Influence. Exhibit 6 shows a simple ELH diagram for the ORDER entity of the example order entry system. The ORDER entity's first stage of life is the creation or addition of a new occurrence of the entity. This first stage is triggered by an outside influence. A new occurrence of ORDER would not have been created without the outside influence of the customer placing an order; this is modeled by Is Placed By relationship in the ERD in Exhibit 5. Outside influence is the most easily identified type of event.

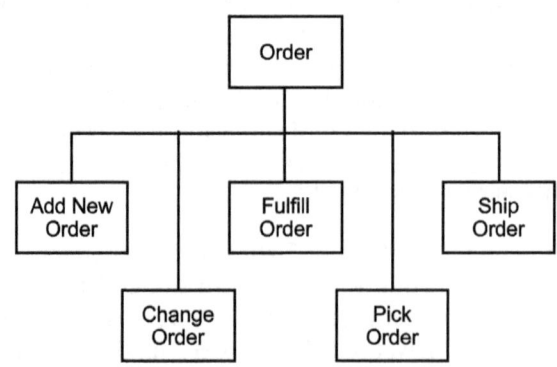

Exhibit 4-6. Entity-life history of the ORDER entity.

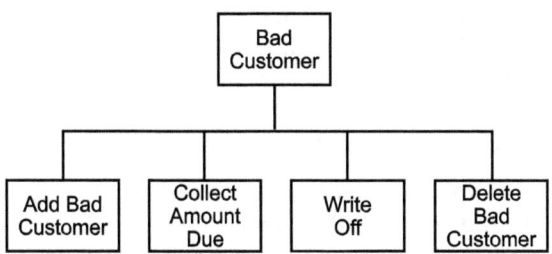

Exhibit 4-7. Entity-life history diagram of the BAD CUSTOMER entity.

2. Time. Time is another common trigger of state changes. Often, there are daily, weekly, monthly, and end-of-year processing triggers. Such temporal triggers are obvious. Some time-based events are less obvious. For example, in Exhibit 5 there is a relationship between CUSTOMER and BAD CUSTOMER. This relationship is also illustrated in the ELH diagram for BAD CUSTOMER (see Exhibit 7). The creation of a new BAD CUSTOMER instance is triggered by time. A customer who does not pay a bill in a certain amount of time is classified a bad customer — a time-triggered event.

3. Stage Change in Another Entity. Often, a stage change in one entity is a direct result of a stage change in another entity. The nine examples of tight coupling illustrate the ways in which this can happen.

4. Stage Change in the Same Entity. In many cases, one change of stage in an entity can automatically trigger another in the same entity. In Exhibit 6, the creation of a new instance of ORDER can trigger the stage Fulfill Order. The fulfilling of the order can trigger the picking of the inventory for the order. The picking stage cannot be triggered by only fulfilling an order but also by time or an outside influence (i.e., someone writing the picking tickets). Often, an event occurs because of a combination of triggers.

TOWARD A MORE POWERFUL TOOL SET

The nine types of tight coupling and four types of events are used to formulate a new approach to requirements gathering and analysis. Analysis can be divided into two major steps: requirements gathering and requirements validation. There has been much progress in the past few years in the validation of requirements. Requirements validation includes such steps as refinement and normalization of the data model, horizontal and vertical balancing of the process model, and rigorous synchronization of both models.

The requirements gathering phase, however, has experienced less progress. Certainly, Joint Application Design and Joint Requirements Definition techniques have improved efficiency. These behavioral approaches, however, have two drawbacks. The first is that they depend on the skills of the facilitator; skills that are difficult to develop. The second drawback is that they are not highly structured and, moreover, cannot be readily replicated. The next objective, therefore, is to provide a framework for a more structured approach to requirements gathering, which can be repeated.

This framework specifies how to analyze the relationships between entities and each stage in the ELH. The first step in this technique requires that the major data entities be identified. Each pair of entities is analyzed for the nine potential combinations of tight coupling to derive the first-cut data relationships.

APPLYING THE APPROACH

The example used to illustrate this event-based approach is the order-entry system modeled in Exhibit 5. The four major entities — CUSTOMER, ORDER, LINE ITEM, and PRODUCT — have already been identified. Each pair of entities is examined for the nine combinations of tight coupling (see Exhibit 4).

The first entity pair is ORDER and LINE ITEM. One of the two is selected to be the causal entity and the other to be the affected entity. At this stage it does not matter which entity assumes which role because this exercise is repeated for the same pair in the other direction. This duality reflects the accepted concept that all data relationships are bidirectional. It is important to note that, the ORDER entity represents the header portion of an order and each occurrence of LINE ITEM reflects each line of an order.

The analyst compares each pair of entities to all nine types of tight coupling (see Exhibit 4) and examines each pair for relevance in the context of causal and affected entities. For example, starting with the upper left box, the analyst asks the client such a question as: Is there any case where the creation of an order (the causal entity) causes the creation of a line item (the affected entity)? The answer to this question is yes. When the system creates an order, the order must have at least one line item. The analyst checks the box to indicate the identification of an event.

These identified events are the building blocks of the requirements gathering process. At first, it is not necessary to explore these events in detail. The fact that these events require further exploration and decomposition must be recorded.

Is there any case where the creation of an ORDER would cause the system to update a LINE ITEM? Probably not, because at the time an ORDER is created there would not have been an existing line item to which the order relates. Is there any case where the creation of an ORDER is cause to delete a LINE ITEM? Again, probably not.

LINE ITEM Entity

		Create	Update	Delete
ORDER Entity	Create	1 New Order		
	Update		2 Change Customer Type	
	Delete			3 Delete or Cancel Order

Exhibit 4-8. Matrix for identifying events in a pair of entities.

Next considered is the update row of the causal entity. Is there any case where the update of the ORDER would cause the system to create a LINE ITEM? Once again, probably not. Is there any case where the update of ORDER would cause the system to update a line item? This would be a possibility if the ORDER contained an indication of customer type or order type that perhaps affects the pricing of each line item. If this is the case, it would once again be recorded as an event requiring further analysis. Is there any case where the update of an ORDER would cause the system to delete a LINE ITEM? Once again, probably not.

Proceeding to the final row (i.e., delete events), the practitioner asks the same set of questions. Is there any case where the deletion of an ORDER would cause the system to create a LINE ITEM? Probably not. Is there any case where the deletion of an ORDER would cause the system to update a LINE ITEM? Once again, probably not. Is there any case where the deletion of an ORDER would cause the system to delete an LINE ITEM? Definitely yes. When the system deletes an order it should delete all the line items attached to it. Once again, the practitioner records this as another event requiring further decomposition.

At least two and possibly three major events requiring further exploration have been identified. Exhibit 8 shows how an analyst would illustrate this in the matrix. Because all relationships are bidirectional, the practitioner must look at causes and effects in both directions.

Looking from the Other Direction

Now the practitioner must go through the same procedure using the LINE ITEM as the causal entity and ORDER as the affected entity. There would be no case where the creation of a LINE ITEM causes the system to create an ORDER because the opposite is true; the creation of the ORDER causes the system to create a LINE ITEM. The creation of a LINE ITEM would, however, cause the system to update an ORDER; if the system adds a new line item to the order, it must reflect that in the order by updating the total cost, quantity, and number of line items.

The update of a LINE ITEM may also require the system to update the order to reflect changes in quantity or cost. The same thing would be true for the deletion of a line item. Deleting a line item would cause the system to reduce the total order cost, quantity, and number of line items.

THE DOCUMENTATION OF EVENTS

Once all the events associated with every entity pair have been identified, they must be documented. What information must analysts know about an event? They must know which entities are affected by the event. These entities were identified when the events were identified. Analysts must also know the event's trigger. Four basic types of event triggers have been identified:

1. Time
2. Input
3. Stage change in another entity
4. Stage change in the same entity

The latter two types are not really end-source event types because they are always ultimately triggered by one of the first two.

For example, the creation of a new ORDER causes the creation of at least one new LINE ITEM. In other words, this event is triggered by a stage change in the causal entity. However, this stage change in the causal entity is caused by the input of a new order. It is useful to review what has been discovered. There is an event that is caused by the input of a new order. This input-type of event in ORDER causes the creation stage of ORDER. In addition, it triggers the creation stage of LINE ITEM.

The business event or input that causes this event should be recorded as part of the event documentation. For example, the analyst should describe the various ways in which a customer can place an order, the type of order, and other such information. The analyst can also record the activities the system performs to process an order as well as the required interactions with the users.

This information about events has implications for the process model. Each stage in the ELH becomes one or more processes in the process model. Because an event can be triggered by input, the analyst has to account for the input in the process model as an input user-view (i.e., a data flow from an external entity to a process).

Exhibit 4-9.   Sample event documentation.

Description:	Ship order
Primary entity:	Order
Trigger:	Order has been picked and end of the day
Action Required:	Mark order as shipped
Other Events Triggered:	Quantity added to shipped quantity
	History is added
	Update year-to-date amounts
	Order is deleted

ITEMS TO BE RECORDED ABOUT AN EVENT

Exhibit 9 shows a sample of event documentation. This shows the documentation of an event called Ship Order. In Exhibit 9, the event's triggers have been listed; an order is shipped if it has already been picked and it is the end of the day. This is an example of a compound trigger: time (i.e., end of day) and another event (i.e., the picking of the order).

The event documentation also identifies the primary entity (i.e., ORDER) and what happens to it as a result of this event (i.e., order is marked as shipped). The documentation also indicates the other events that are triggered by this event. Each of these triggered events has its own specific event documentation. This documentation can be used as process specifications for the process model.

EVENT NETWORKS

It is difficult to review each event document, its triggers, and resulting events and subsequently judge its correctness. It is difficult to visualize the trigger-to-trigger relationships of events. This difficulty can be overcome with aid of a graphic tool. This tool is an adaptation of the traditional Project Evaluation Review Technique/Critical Path Management (PERT/CPM) chart. Exhibit 10 shows how event objects are placed into a PERT/CPM-like network to show relationships and dependencies.

Exhibit 10 also shows that additional triggers can be added to the event network to visually illustrate the trigger dependencies of certain events. For example, the Ship Order event in the network depends on two events-the picking of the order and the time trigger of End-of-Day. In the chart, parallelograms indicate an input trigger and squares indicate a time trigger.

An additional degree of structure can be added to the network by arranging the event network by primary entities (see Exhibit 11). Exhibit 11 is so arranged that it traces the ELH of each entity. Exhibit 12 shows how the ELH for the ORDER entity can be derived from the structured event network.

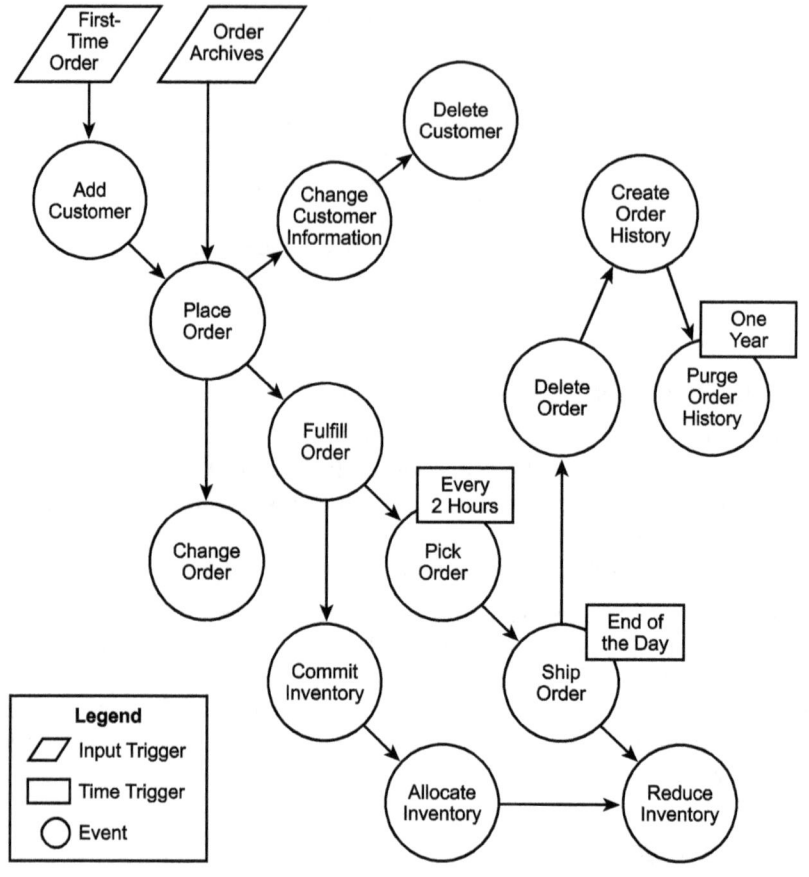

Exhibit 4-10. Event network for the order-entity system.

WEAKNESSES IN THE EXISTING TOOLS AND TECHNIQUES

The event network shown in Exhibit 11 has many similarities to a State-Transition Diagram that has been decomposed by entity. However, traditional state-transition diagram (STD) cannot relate events to data entities or processes. The event network takes into account the relationship between events and data. The entity-relationship model can effectively illustrate data and its relationships to other data. However, it cannot show events or transformations.

The data flow diagram (DFD) and other process models show both the movement and transformation of data. The Data Flow Diagram cannot explicitly show relationship among data entities and data dependencies. The ELH diagrams shows the life stages of the data entities and indirectly shows the transformations that take place. The ELH shows neither the triggers of events nor data dependencies.

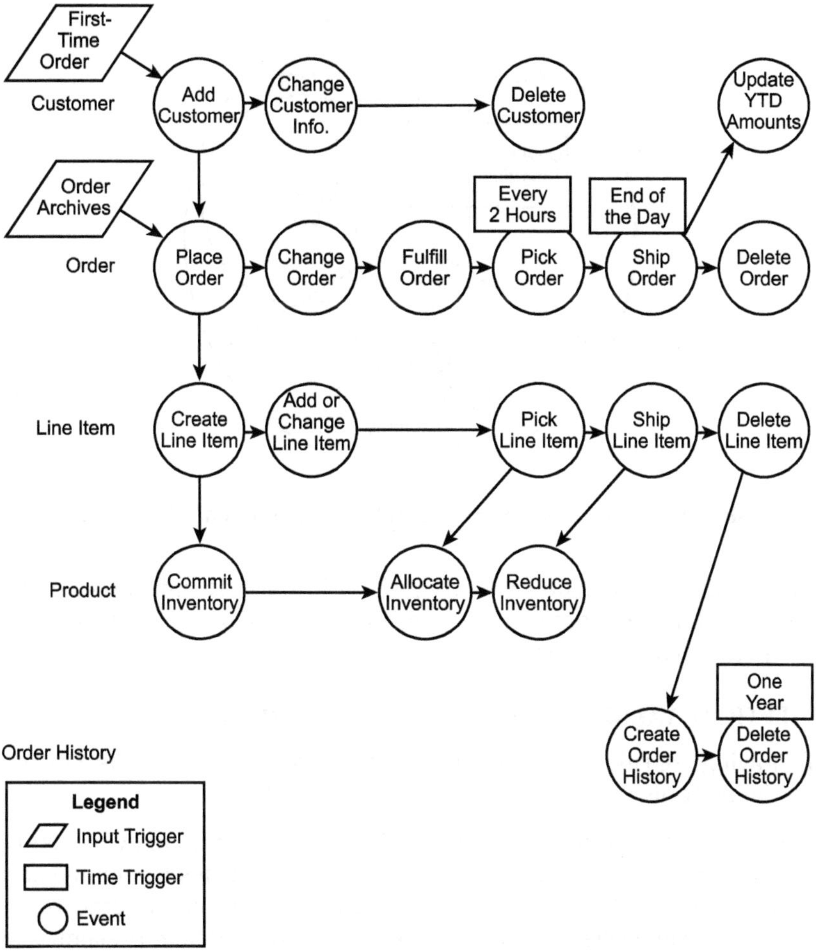

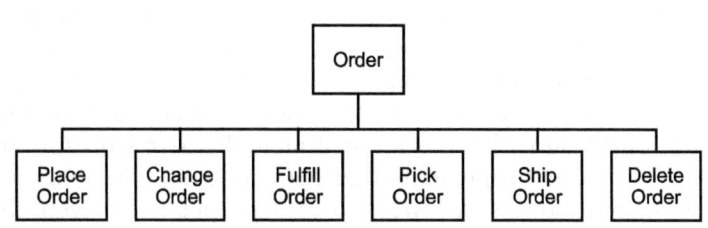

Exhibit 4-11. Structured event network for the order-entry system.

Exhibit 4-12. Entity-life history for the ORDER entity.

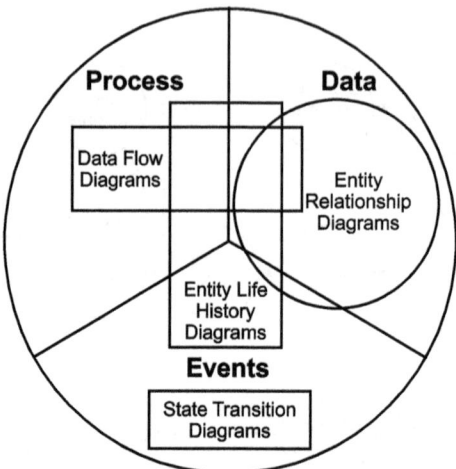

Exhibit 4-13. Areas of effectiveness for common analysis diagrams.

Exhibit 13 illustrates how effectively DFD, ERDs, ELH and state-transition diagram (STD) model data, processes, and events. Obviously, the effectiveness of each type of diagram must be extended.

ANALYTICAL VALIDATION OF ANALYSIS DIAGRAMS

Following are rules for cross-checking and validating the different types of modeling tools discussed in previous sections:

- Each event should be identified as a stage in the ELH of every data entity it affects. An event causes one or more entities to change stage. For each event documented, the entity or entities affected by that event are identified. Therefore, each event should be represented as a stage in the ELH of each entity it affects.
- Each stage in the ELH represents a function on the corresponding DFD. A stage in the life of an entity maps to a function in the process model. A function may or may not map one-to-one to a process on the process model at this stage. However, a function can be considered a fundamental unit of processing or task that must be performed.
- Each of those derived functions in a DFD should have the appropriate data stores attached to it. A corollary to the second rule, this rule is related to the principle known as horizontal process balancing or data conservation. Once the processes in the process model that represent a stage of the entity have been identified, the data stores in the Data Flow Diagram that represents that data entity should be attached to the identified processes. If the model refers back to the event that represents that stage in the ELH, other entities may be associated with

that event. The data stores that represent those entities should also be attached to the process.

- Each ELH stage triggered by input should have an input-user view associated with the corresponding processes. For each stage triggered by input, an analyst should review that stage's corresponding processes in the DFD. One or more of the processes should be associated with an input-user view, which is a data flow going from a process to an external entity. If the stage is triggered by input, its process should indicate that it is receiving input from the appropriate external entity.

- Each stage change triggered by a stage change in another entity should be represented in the ERD as a relationship between the two entities. A stage change caused by another stage change is a type of tight coupling, which is a unique kind of relationship. Thus, one entity cannot affect another entity unless the two are related.

- In the ELH diagram, each entity must have at least one create stage and at least one delete stage. An occurrence of any entity must first be created if it is to be used in a meaningful way. For most practical business purposes, information is not kept indefinitely. Even information that is archived is usually deleted at one point. Thus, all ELH diagrams, except those for historical or archival data entities, should end in a delete stage.

EXPANDING THE COVERAGE OF THE DIAGRAMS

The ELH Diagram. The ELH diagrams — the one in Exhibit 12 for example — are effective at showing the events affecting a single entity. However, it does not show graphically the triggers for a given event. It can be enhanced (see Exhibit 14) by using the trigger symbols used in event network diagrams.

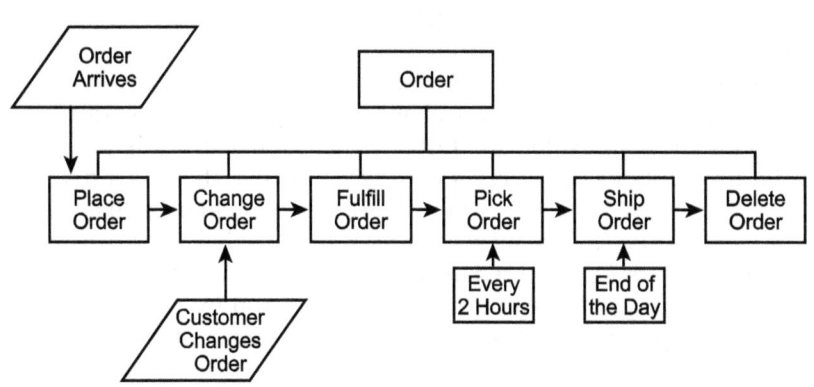

Exhibit 4-14. Entity-life history diagram enhanced with trigger symbols.

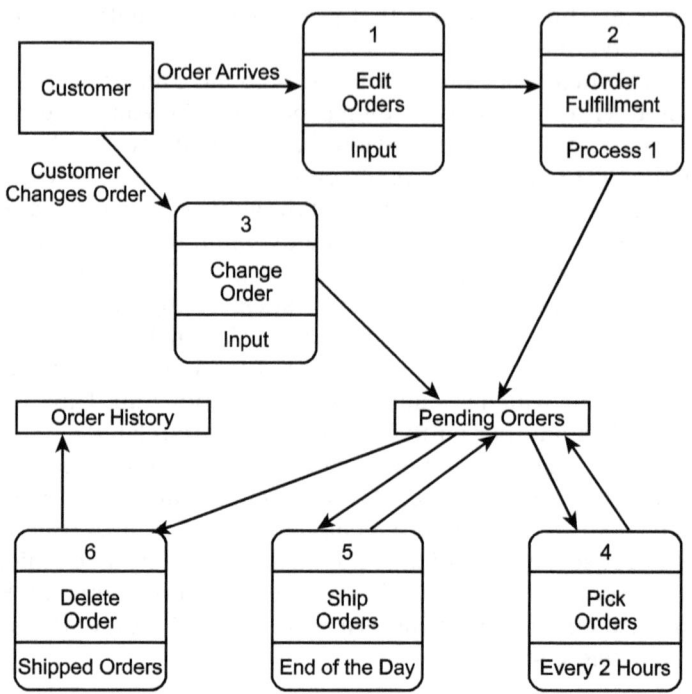

Exhibit 4-15. Data flow diagram enhanced with event symbols.

The Structured Event Network. This type of diagram (see Exhibit 11) effectively shows events and relates them to major data entities. However, it does not show the relationships among data entities other than through the perspective of events.

The DFD. The coverage of the Data Flow Diagram can easily be expanded by simply adding the event to the process legend, as shown in Exhibit 15. Various kinds of events can be illustrated in this manner. For example, the process-to-process data flow shown between processes 1and 2 in Exhibit 15 illustrates a stage change triggered by a change in state in the same entity. In other words, as the ELH in Exhibit 14 illustrates, as soon as an order is edited, it goes immediately to the fulfillment stage. Because there is a data store between processes 2 and 4 in Exhibit 15, the diagram implies that a waiting time or delay exists. The legend in process 4 confirms that it is triggered every two hours; process 2 is triggered by input that starts with process 1. Process 6 illustrates a stage change in one entity triggered by a stage change in another entity; process 6 deletes the order and creates order history.

The EERD

Although the techniques discussed in the previous section enhance the capabilities of the analysis tools discussed in this chapter, an event-driven

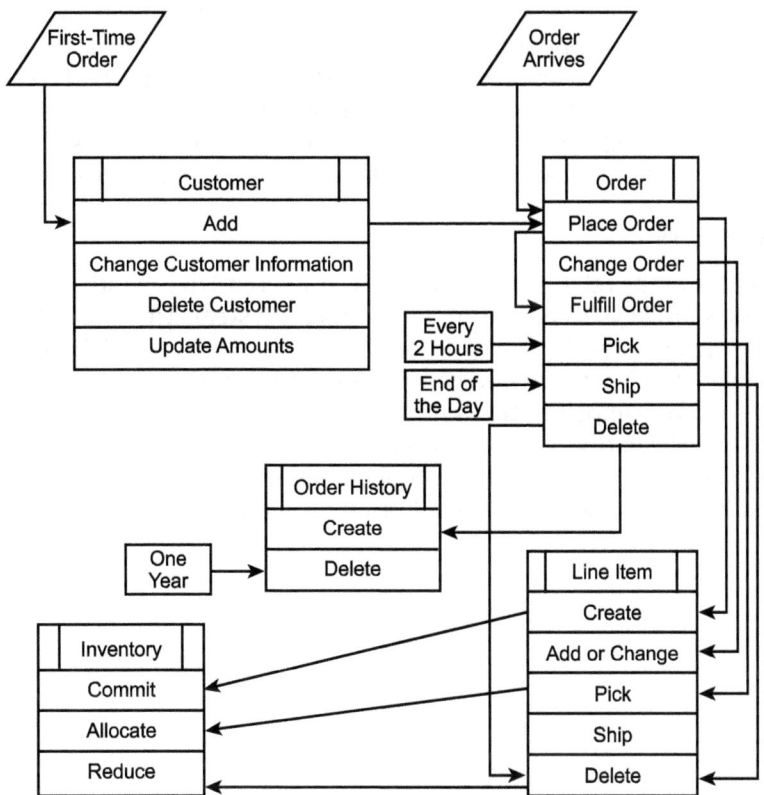

Exhibit 4-16. Entity-event-relationship diagram for the order-entry system.

diagram that significantly bonds events to data and stage changes in entities is still needed. The structured event network shows the relationship of events but is an unsatisfactory link to other diagrams.

Object-oriented analysis (OOA) has many useful diagrams. Object-Oriented Analysis notations can be used to show the relationships of events to data and other events in the EERD, which resembles an ERD. The boxes in the EERD still represent data entities, and the lines represent relationships. However, each data entity shows the stages it can enter.

Each entity can be thought of as a machine and each stage box as a button. Exhibit 16 is a partial EERD of the order entry system. It shows how one entity's event can push another entity's button. The direction of the arrows is important because it shows cause and effect. In addition, the standard symbols to show triggers from input (i.e., a parallelogram) and time (i.e., a box) have been added.

The diagram shows that the Pick event in ORDER triggers the Pickevent in LINE ITEM. In turn, the Pick event in LINE ITEM causes the Allocate event in INVENTORY. A backwards trace from causal events reveals the original causal event (e.g., input or time). For example, to find the event that causes the inventory level to be reduced (i.e., the Reduce event in INVENTORY), a backward trace reveals that it is triggered by the Ship event in LINE ITEM. This is in turn triggered by the Ship event in ORDER. This event is ultimately triggered by time (i.e., the End-of-the-Day event) as is indicated in the EERD.

CONCLUSION

Analysis of the relationships between entities and the events that trigger processes are keys to better understanding a system. There are also keys to developing more effective tools for analysis based on events. This chapter has illustrated how analysts can document the types of coupling in an entity's relationships to other entities as well as the types of events experienced by the entity. More important, this chapter has demonstrated the use of EERD. This tool can be used to relate events, data, and processes and adds rigor to the modeling of both data and functions.

Chapter 5
A Framework for Classifying Data

William H. Inmon

A USEFUL VEHICLE FOR THE EXAMINATION OF THE PROPERTIES AND CHAR-
ACTERISTICS OF THE DIFFERENT DATA TYPES IS THE DATA MODEL. A data
model is the classical vehicle by which organizations begin to make sense of
their data. The worth of a data model in the systems development process
is seldom questioned in today's sophisticated world of data management
and development.

A data model has the following characteristics:

- *It provides a paradigm for systematization.* The paradigm typically organizes data in subject areas, entities, and tables of data, all of which
  satisfy an organization's collective processing requirements.
- *It is a means of identifying commonality of data across applications.*
  Typically, subject areas such as customer, policy, account, and product apply across multiple applications.
- *It is a blueprint for the organization of details at all levels.* An orderly
  and rigorous transformation occurs in the structure of data from the
  subject area, the high level, to the low-level data model.
- *It is central to the relationship between primitive and derived data.*
  Knowing how to identify derived data, relate it back to its primitive
  source, and then eliminate it from the data model is crucial to the
  ability to build and implement a data model in a finite time period.

THE INTERNAL AND EXTERNAL DATA MODELS

In most cases the result of the data modeling exercise is a model of the
customer (or external) interaction with the organization. Banks, insurance
companies, retailers, and public utilities usually focus their data model on
the organization as it interacts with its external environment. Such a data
model is called an external data model because it is developed to facilitate
understanding of the external forces acting on (and interacting with) the
organization.

0-8493-0882-8/00/$0.00+$.50
© 2001 by CRC Press LLC

Another type of data model is an internal one; its focus is on the data reflecting the organization's internal components, dynamics, and relationships. The difference in focus between the internal and external data models is also evident in their content. Typical major subject areas found in the internal model are: mission, goal, strategy, objective, and problem. Typical major subject areas found in the external model are: product, customer, transaction, and account.

These areas are indicative of the great difference between the two types of models. From the external perspective, the customer is related to such concepts as products, accounts, and shipments. Although customers may be aware that the organization has underlying goals and objectives, as long as its products are of high quality and competitively priced, they do not need to know about the organization's internal issues and demographics. Similarly, for the manager focusing on the organization's internal relationships, such external factors as product, customer, and account(though still important) are a secondary consideration.

THE ADMINISTRATIVE AND DIRECTIONAL DATA MODELS

Another classification for data and data models is according to the organization's administrative and directional aspects. The focus of the administrative manager is on making short-term, frequently minor adjustments to the organization. The administrative decision maker typically is concerned with protecting existing market share and with attempts to minimize costs and maximize revenues. With an eye to the organization's continuity and stability, the administrative decision maker necessarily has a short-term horizon.

The counterpart of the administrative manager is the directional decision maker. This is the manager who handles longer-term issues (e.g., new markets, new uses of technology, and new investments). The directional decision maker makes decisions less frequently, but makes the ones that have broad consequences for the organization and that change the direction in which the organization is heading.

It is noteworthy that the decisions made by the administrative manager are often at odds with those made by the directional decision maker. This springs from a basic dichotomy between the administrative and operational management functions. Major subject areas that are typically relevant to the administrative manager include: employees, the organization chart, rate adjustment, the production quota, and late shipments. Subjects typically relevant to the directional manager include: competition, new technology, the economic forecast, and market share. A matrix (see Exhibit 1) can be constructed to distinguish between the internal and external perspectives of data and the administrative or directional perspectives.

Exhibit 5-1.   Representative data in the four quadrants.

	Internal	External
Administrative	• Organization Chart	• Customer
	• Employee Particulars	• Account
	• Compensation	• Transaction
	• Office Location	• Product
Directional	• Strategy	• Marketplace
	• Policy	• Technology
	• Mission	• Competition
	• Goals	• Economic Forecast

The focus in the internal administrative quadrant is an introspective look at the organization. Typical data found in this quadrant includes the organization chart, employee particulars, compensation, and office location. In the internal directional quadrant, the interest centers on such issues as the organization's strategy, policy, mission, and goals. The focus of the organization's external administrative quadrants is on the customers, accounts, transactions, and product. This quadrant is the most familiar to modelers because most data and most systems fit here. The focus of the external directional quadrant is the marketplace, technology, competition, and the economic forecast; these are broad subjects of interest to the organization as a whole.

An interesting feature of the matrix showing internal, external, administrative, and directional data is the tendency toward mutual exclusivity of data within the quadrant. Most data seems to fit naturally into one quadrant, and no others. This concept is discussed further in the next section.

Mutual Exclusivity

The tendency toward mutual exclusivity of data within the matrix is reflected in the data models that represent the data in each quadrant. In general, the data found in data models for each quadrant applies only to that quadrant-rarely does an organization's data model successfully include data from more than one quadrant. The most successful modeling efforts seem to be those that do not mix data from the different quadrants.

There is good reason for not mixing data from different quadrants in the data model. The goal of most modeling efforts is some form of systematization. From systematization there results payback to the organization, either through the leveraging of technology, or through the economies of consolidation that can be achieved through integration of common data and processing. Without some payback, however it is measured and realized, systematization makes no sense. A method of measuring payback is described in the next section.

**Exhibit 5-2.   Payback and systematization
ratings for the four quadrants.**

	Internal	External
Administrative	• Payback 2	• Payback 2
	• Systematization 9	• Systematization 9
Directional	• Payback 6	• Payback 10
	• Systematization 1	• Systematization 1

Rating the Quadrants

Each quadrant can be assigned a payback and systematization rating. On a scale of 1 to 10, a payback rating of 10 means that, historically, major payback is (or has been) possible from systematization in the quadrant. A payback rating of 1 indicates that very little payback has ever been achieved. A systematization rating of 10 indicates that the data represented in the quadrant has been methodically systematized in the past. A systematization rating of 1indicates the data has resisted attempts at systematization. Exhibit 2 shows the matrix with the payback and systematization ratings for each of the quadrants. An explanation of the ratings that have been assigned follows.

The Internal Administrative Quadrant. In this quadrant the payback of administrative internal systems is low. Typical systems would be those for employee payroll and employee education. Although an organization may run efficiently as far as its internal administrative systems are concerned, this efficiency does little toward winning new market share, lowering costs, and raising revenues. Because this quadrant does not directly affect profitability, there is only a small payback for systematization. Systematization in this quadrant is rated highly, however, because the data is fairly easy to systematize.

The Internal Directional Quadrant. This quadrant contains such data as mission, goal, and objective. There is a fairly high payback to the systematization of such data, but the track record of systematization here is very low. It is neither easy nor even appropriate in many cases to attempt to systematize strategy and objectives. The data in this quadrant is so ambiguous and amorphous as to be almost impervious to systematization.

The External Administrative Quadrant. This quadrant contains the classical data (e.g., that relating to customer, account, product, and transaction). No other quadrant has benefited from data automation to the extent that this quadrant has, and for good reason. The data in this quadrant has a fairly high payback for systematization and is fairly easily systematized, making it the most popular for automation.

Exhibit 5-3.   Combined payback and systematization ratings of each quadrant.

	Internal	External
Administrative	11	18
Directional	7	11

The External Directional Quadrant. This quadrant contains such data as new technology, competition, and economic conditions. Under any rules, there is a very high payback to the systematization of this data but there are also many problems. Some of these are:

- the irregularity of the availability of the data
- the extreme diversity of media over which information is transmitted
- the lack of uniformity of the data itself

In short, the data in this quadrant, as important as it is, resists systematization at every turn.

Adding the Ratings

Another, somewhat arbitrary, way to assess the affinity of the quadrants for automation is simply to add together the payback and the systematization ratings, as illustrated in Exhibit 3. The exhibit shows that the administrative external quadrant is easily the most favored target for automation, whereas the directional internal quadrant is the least amenable. An argument can be made that adding payback and systematization ratings further obscures an already obscure rating. But the rebuttal is that, whatever the payback, if systematization is very difficult, then the likelihood of automation is just as poor as if the systematization prospects were very high and the prospects for payback were poor.

The key for a customer is usually fairly clear, while the key for an objective is not. The attributes for a product are fairly clear, while the attributes for a goal are ambiguous. The specifics of, for instance, an insurance policy are clear and well defined, whereas the specifics for an organization's policy regarding overtime or employee absences are less clear. These reasons lead to the conclusion that internal data is difficult to automate and external data is not. If the purpose of a data model is to enhance or enable automation, it is questionable whether modeling the internal directional environment is even appropriate. Data from such areas as mission, strategy, and objective does not lend itself to automation in the same way that customer, product, and account data does. There may be real benefits to modeling the organization's internal workings, but these may not be easily realized by automation. Modeling the internal directional data of the organization can be useful in identifying and streamlining the organization's business practices. Some results of modeling this quadrant might be:

- identification of conflicting goals
- recognition of a strategy misalignment
- recognition that no objectives are identified
- discovery of misalignments in an organizational chart

The benefits of modeling in this quadrant are less tangible than those of modeling in other quadrants. Data models in this quadrant have the reputation of being blue-sky exercises that contribute little to the automation effort. As such, it is questionable whether they should be built in the first place.

Generic Data Models

Another interesting aspect of the internal directional quadrant is the potential for developing a generic internal directional (or even administrative) model. The models of most organizations are affected by their industry sector as a whole, at least insofar as the external model is concerned. But the internal model remains fairly constant regardless of the type of organization, the industry, and even the size of the organization. In other words, if there is any prospect at all for a generic data model, the model will most likely be of internal directional and administrative data. As with any data model, the more detailed it is, the less generic it is. At the high level, the model is likely to be highly generic, and at lower levels, successively less so.

An interesting phenomenon of modeling in the internal administrative and the internal directional quadrants is that the relationship between objects tends to be much more ambiguous than it is in other quadrants. In some cases, a relationship will apply so broadly as to be meaningless. An example of a broad relationship is that between strategy and mission. Such a relationship undoubtedly exists, but it is difficult to quantify and describe. In other cases, a relationship between data at the internal quadrants may be so specific and narrow as to be equally meaningless. The relationship of office location to compensation is valid, but it is of interest to so few people that its worth is questionable. The whole dimension of relationships in the internal quadrants, particularly the internal directional quadrant, needs to be thoroughly analyzed and established before the modeling process for this quadrant begins. Using standard techniques here for representation of relationships may prove to be more misleading than useful.

Overlapping Data

The mutual exclusivity of data from one quadrant to the next is not absolute; there is some overlap of data, particularly at the higher modeling levels. For example, for many environments the major subject (i.e., customer) fits into the external administrative and the external directional quadrants. However, what is meant by the term customer is not necessarily constant; and the more detailed the data attributes applied to it, the less commonality of data exists across quadrants.

For example, in the external administrative quadrant, the interest in customer focuses on current customers and on servicing their immediate needs to keep them. But in the external directional quadrant, the focus is more on potential customers and on demographics that are useful in helping the organization to attract new customers. In the external directional quadrant, there may be an interest in the existing customer base, but only insofar as the existing customer is also a potential candidate for new services or products.

The essential difference in the interest and focus of the data model or data administration in each of the quadrants shows up in at least two ways: the number of attributes in each quadrant, and the stability of the model in each quadrant. In the external administrative quadrant, data in a data model typically has many attributes. For example, the major subjects and their subtypes in account would have such attributes as:

- date opened
- domicile
- current balance
- type
- fund assignment
- statement date
- statement cycle
- social security number

The major subjects and their subtypes of loan have such attributes as

- interest rate
- collateral
- late payment penalty
- balloon payment
- renegotiation date

The major subjects and their subtypes of savings have such attributes as

- interest rate
- christmas club
- minimum balance
- minimum deposit
- withdrawal date

The data attributes found in the external administrative quadrant are relatively stable and numerous. But this is not so with regard to major categories in the external directional quadrant-customer, competition, and

75

new technology. The major subjects and their subtypes of customer have such attributes as:

- address
- age
- salary
- occupation
- number of dependents

The major subjects and their subtypes of competition have such attributes as

- market share
- product line
- length of time in business

The major subjects and their subtypes of new technology have such attributes as

- description
- developer
- potential uses

Not only are the attributes fewer and less stable, but the major subject areas in this quadrant are constantly changing. The gathering, use, and content of data in this quadrant are very different from those of data in other quadrants.

Other Dissimilarities

The dissimilarities of data from one quadrant to the next are not limited to the differences between the external administrative and the external directional quadrants. They extend to the representation of data from the external administrative and the internal directional quadrants. The data in the external administrative quadrant represents such tangible objects as shipments, products, parts, and customers. In addition, there are less eligible entities that have a legal and logical form, if not a physically tangible form. These include bank accounts, insurance claims, and financial transactions. In short, the external directional quadrant contains data that measures tangible objects.

In contrast to this, the objects represented in the internal directional quadrant tend to be intangible. Such data as objectives, goals, and motivations are found in this quadrant. The amorphous nature of these objects is reflected in the difficulty of trying to assign significant keys, attributes, and relationships to the data model representing them.

The very different nature of data in the various quadrants can also be seen from the perspective of the audience served by them. Some overlap exists between the audiences served, but to a great extent senior management is interested in the external directional quadrant, middle management in the internal administrative quadrant, and clerical personnel in the external administrative quadrant. In addition, the audience served by each quadrant can be categorized by job function. The marketing function is interested in the external directional quadrant; the sales function is interested in the external administrative quadrant; and the personnel administration function in the internal administrative quadrant.

CONCLUSION

The task of data modeling is confused enormously if all data is treated as if it were equal. To model data meaningfully, it should be broken into four general categories: internal administrative data, external administrative data, internal directional data, and external directional data. Each of these quadrants of data contains essentially different data with different characteristics. Models of data within any quadrant can be meaningfully created. But when data from one quadrant is mixed with that from another, the modeling process is best served by the creation of indirect relationships from one model to the next, rather than by mixing data models from different quadrants into a single integrated model.

Chapter 6
One Concept Equals One Data Element: A Rule for Developing Data Elements

Jennifer Little

DATA REPRESENTS SEPARATE FACTS ABOUT OBJECTS. A data element is the smallest unit used to collect and document these facts. Data elements specify the rules to which data must conform, thereby establishing the structure of the data. For example, the data element in Exhibit 1 establishes the structure in which people's last names are stored in a particular information system.

Because data elements provide structure for the data, poorly designed data elements lead to poor quality data. The most fundamental data element design principle is that a data element should encompass only one concept. Following the one-concept-equals-one-data-element rule when developing data elements can help ensure quality data elements. The rule can also help revise data elements during reengineering efforts to identify and improve problem data structures.

A data element has several parts (e.g., data element name, length, definition, format, and valid values), which are called data element attributes. When new data elements are developed, each attribute should be created to abide by the one-concept-equals-one-data-element rule. Also, when existing data elements are revised, the attributes can be examined to ensure that they conform to the rule. It is particularly critical to apply the one-concept-equals-one-data-element rule to two data element attributes — name and valid values. This chapter examines these two data element attributes and suggests ways to ensure compliance with the rule.

0-8493-0882-8/00/$0.00+$.50

Exhibit 6-1.   Sample Data element structure.

Data Element Name:	PERSON LAST NAME
Data Element Definition:	The full unabbreviated last name of a person
Data Element Length:	65
Data Element Format:	Alphabetic
Data Element Edit Rules:	Only alphabetic characters are allowed. Spaces and special characters are not allowed.

PURPOSE OF THE RULE

A concept is a single directly conceived or intuited object of thought. Therefore, following the one-concept-equals-one-data-element rule ensures that data elements represent the smallest unit of meaningful intelligence. When a data element complies with the one-concept-equals-one-data-element rule, it is correct to call it a data element. Violations of the rule, however, should not be called data elements; they are referred to as melded data chunks throughout the remainder of this chapter. All organizations have melded data chunks; Exhibit 2 represents a melded data chunk.

THE BENEFITS OF FLEXIBILITY

Data can be viewed as building blocks of information. Data that is collected using data elements is more flexible than data collected using melded data chunks. For example, a manager may want to know whether the training that a specific division received had any effect on its productivity. The division attended seven weeks of training during a one-year period, and the training was conducted in variable length segments with different people attending different segments at different times. The manager retrieves the productivity data from the personnel system that was created in the late 1960s to replace the manual monthly personnel productivity reports.

The productivity information is stored in the manner depicted in Exhibit 3, because the employees' pay rate for each month is based on their average monthly output. The manager would have difficulty determining what effect the training had. At the most, he or she may be able to see whether total productivity increased after one year. On the other hand, if the data elements in Exhibit 4 had been used in each personnel record, the manager would be able to make several comparisons of productivity and training to determine the effect of each training segment.

The issues of normalization notwithstanding and conceding the need to have equally flexible data elements to collect the training data, the second set provides more flexibility than the first. When all data elements conform to the one-concept-equals-one-data-element rule, the flexibility benefits not just the manager who wants to look at the relationship between the training

Exhibit 6-2.   Melded data chunk.

Name: NEW AND IMPROVED INSURANCE ELIGIBILITY

Description: Indicates a person's eligibility for the new and improved insurance coverage.

Valid Values:

Position 1

0 = Full-time Employee started at the company before 1949.

1 = Full-time Employee started at the company between 1950 and 1954

2 = Full-time Employee started at the company between 1955 and 1959

3 = Full-time Employee started at the company between 1960 and 1964

4 = Full-time Employee started at the company between 1965 and 1969

5 = Full-time Employee started at the company between 1970 and 1974

6 = Full-time Employee started at the company between 1975 and 1979

7 = Full-time Employee started at the company between 1980 and 1984

8 = Full-time Employee started at the company between 1985 and 1989

9 = Full-time Employee started at the company between 1990 and 1992

A = Full-time Employee started at the company between 1930 and 1970 and left for a period of longer than six months.

B = Full-time Employee started at the company between 1970 and the present, and tested positive for a communicable disease or refused the test.

C = Part-time Employee who is a relative of the owners of the company.

Positions 2-4

ABC = Employee currently has elected the ABC coverage plan for self only.

LNM = Employee currently has elected the LNM coverage plan for self only.

WIN = Employee currently has elected the WIN coverage plan for self only.

KJW = Employee currently has elected the KJW coverage plan for self only.

PRD = Employee currently has elected the PRD coverage plan for self only.

ABX = Employee currently has elected the ABC coverage plan for family.

LNX = Employee currently has elected the LNM coverage plan for family.

WIX = Employee currently has elected the WIN coverage plan for family.

KJX = Employee currently has elected the KJW coverage plan for family or had converted to KJW coverage (for self and/or family) after maintaining ABC coverage for self and family or WIN coverage for self or for self and family for at least 12 consecutive months anytime during the last ten years.

PRX = Employee currently has elected the PRD coverage plan for self OR family type coverage.

Positions 5-7

DEN = Denied optional coverage

MED = Failed physical

DIS = Disqualifying pre-existing condition

PRE = Pregnant

Exhibit 6-3.   Monthly productivity information.

Name	Definition
MONTHLY AVERAGE OUTPUT	The average number of widgets produced per month. Twelve occurrences are allowed.
AVERAGE OUTPUT MONTH	The month for which the average number of widgets is recorded for the employee.

Exhibit 6-4.   Revised productivity report.

Name	Definition
WIDGETS PRODUCED COUNT	The number of widgets produced by an employee per day. There is an unlimited number of occurrences allowed of this data element.
WIDGETS PRODUCED DATE	The sate (YYYYMMDD) on which the widgets were produced by an employee.

the division received and its productivity; it also benefits other managers in the organization with different information requirements. In other words, more questions can be answered with the data.

AN ANALOGY

An anecdote about building a house offers helpful analogies regarding the lack of flexibility caused by not following the one-concept-equals-one-data-element rule. After determining requirements for the house, it is decided that prefabricated house components will meet the needs in the easiest, cheapest, and fastest way. Prefabricated parts are melded components; and like melded data chunks, they contain more than one concept (i.e., component).

The house is built, and construction was cheap, fast, and easy. Two years later, however, it is decided to add an office with a separate entrance and a security system. Because the house was built with prefabricated parts, it is more complicated to make the addition. The prefabricated parts are melded components; consequently, an entire side of the house must be removed and rebuilt to accommodate the addition. Unfortunately, using the prefabricated components to begin with was faster, cheaper, and easier until changes needed to be made. The melded components' lack of flexibility caused the increased cost.

The Bottom Line

How can things (e.g., buildings or information) that have maximum flexibility for the future be created within today's budget? Large building

Exhibit 6-5.   Data element name structure.

Prime Word	Modifier	Class Word
PERSON	BIRTH	DATE

components that have specific, narrowly defined purposes (e.g., prefabricated parts) cannot be made into as many end-products as the individual substances of which they are composed. For example, prefabricated components cannot be taken apart and have unaffected nails, screws, pipes, glue, lumber, and plaster. Each of these ingredients has been altered by the process of constructing the prefabricated part, and they cannot return to their original state. Similarly, melded data chunks that are created for specific narrow purposes cannot be used to create as many end-products as data elements can. In addition, the benefits of flexible data elements that comply with the one-concept-equals-one-data-element rule apply not only when using them but when maintaining them. It is easier to make modifications to data elements than it is to change melded data chunks.

THE DATA ELEMENT NAMING PROCESS

Data Element Names

Most data element naming standards agree on a basic data element name structure: one prime word (which represents the thing about which the data is being collected), one class word (which provides the category of information and some indication of the format and structure), and one or more modifiers (i.e., adjectives that modify the prime word or class word) to make the data element name unique and meaningful. Exhibit 5 contains an example of this structure.

Existing naming standards, however, fail to produce data elements that comply with the one-concept-equals-one-data-element rule for at least two reasons: they do not provide guidelines for choosing appropriate modifiers, and they imply that developing data element names is the correct first step.

Modifiers

One of the deficiencies in data element standardization procedures is that they focus on naming data elements while other important data element development aspects are underrepresented. Some data element naming standard designers claim that using entity names from a data model as prime words ensures that the data element includes only one concept. Using entity names from a data model for the prime words is insufficient to ensure that a data element complies with the one-concept-equals-one-data-element rule. A naming convention of this type unnecessarily relies on the accuracy and completeness of the data model. Data element development

Exhibit 6-6.   Personnel department's melded data chunks.

EMPLOYEE FULL-TIME START DATE
EMPLOYEE PART-TIME START DATE
EMPLOYEE COOP STUDENT FIRST DAY
EMPLOYEE EXECUTIVE INITIAL STATUS DATE
EMPLOYEE DATE REINSTATED
EMPLOYEE MALE START DATE
EMPLOYEE FEMALE START DATE
EMPLOYEE HANDICAPPED START DATE
EMPLOYEE VETERAN START DATE
EMPLOYEE POSITION BEGIN DATE

rules should have the capability to be applied effectively outside any specific data modeling effort. They should also support data modeling efforts by providing a quality check of the content of the data model. In other words, if the data elements developed during modeling do not comply with the data element standards or if some of the standard data elements developed do not fit with the model, a closer look at the model would be prudent.

Data element naming standards must provide guidelines in selecting modifiers to ensure that the data element complies with the one-concept-equals-one-data-element rule. The following example illustrates how uncontrolled use of modifiers violates the rule and results in melded data chunks instead of data elements.

The melded data chunks in Exhibit 6 were created to meet the needs of an organization's personnel department. They may have been created over a period of 10 years as the personnel information system was modified to keep pace with the business requirements, or they may have been created all at one time to satisfy different divisions within the personnel department. Melded data chunks and redundant data elements are created inadvertently by carelessly inserting modifiers in data element names. If the previous examples were restricted to one prime word, one modifier, and one class word, the result — EMPLOYEE START DATE — makes it clear that the concept is the date the employee started working for the organization. The more modifiers a melded data chunk name has, the stronger the warning should sound that several concepts are included.

Some of those additional concepts are easier to spot than others, but they can be uncovered during data element cleanup efforts by restricting data element names to one modifier. Then, as large groups of related melded data chunks are being analyzed and refined into data elements, modifiers can be kept to a minimum. Typically during this process it becomes obvious how the quality of the data elements is related to the quality of the data model and logical database design. As many data elements are eliminated and some new data elements are created, new database designs can be contemplated.

Here, the key benefit obtained from ensuring that data elements comply to the one-concept-equals-one-data-element rule is reducing redundancy. Redundant data elements not only require more computer storage space, they frequently lead to lower data quality when different sources are updated at different times, allowing the data to become inconsistent.

The First Step

The problems caused by naming data elements before defining them also must be addressed. People become attached to labels assigned to objects and are reluctant to change those labels. Functional users, programmers, database administrators, and even data administrators usually rely on the data element name as the unique identifier of the data element (whether it is a full name or an abbreviated name). Therefore, the process of naming data elements should not be taken lightly. A suggested sequence of data element standardization involves the following steps:

- *Developing the data element definition.* This involves working with the proposed data element custodian, steward, sponsor, or responsible agent, ensuring that the data element definition includes only one concept.
- *Developing the valid values.* This involves ensuring that they include only one concept and are completely consistent with the definition. Then the length, format, and edit criteria must be established.
- *Developing the name from the definition.* This involves selecting words from the definition. All the words in the name should come from the definition, but not all the words in the definition should be included in the name. The urge to name the data element first should be resisted and the definition from the name should be created. The processes are not the same.
- *Developing the remaining required attributes.* These attributes differ, depending on the organization.

Dependence on Names

An inverse relationship exists between the number of data element attributes documented for a data element and the degree to which users must depend on the data element name for meaning. As depicted in Exhibit 7, as more attributes are documented for a data element, the user needs to depend on the name less and less to provide a complete understanding of the data element. The significance of this relationship is that organizations that are documenting (or intend to document) several attributes for their data elements need not rely on a rigidly structured naming standard.

Exhibit 6-7.   Multiple data element attributes.

Homogeneous Valid Values?	NO
PERSON HAIR COLOR:	1 = BROWN
	2 = BLACK
	3 = BLONDE
	4 = RED
	5 = GREY
	6 = BALD

On the other hand, organizations or projects that are documenting only the names of their data elements can benefit more from a stringent naming convention. For example, administrators working on high-level data modeling projects may find it unnecessary to document more than the name of the data elements in their models. Because the data element name is all that the readers of those models have on which to base their comprehension of the data elements, it is crucial that every word used in the names be chosen according to a well-thought-out naming standard and defined in the repository along with the model. Class words are usually limited to a small set of precisely defined terms, and prime words coming from a data model can rely on the definition of the entities. Modifiers also should be defined to avoid misunderstandings between business areas that use these common business terms differently.

Because dependence on the name for the data element's meaning decreases as more data element attributes are documented, data element naming is less crucial for projects in which data elements are fully defined. Data administrators should keep this in mind when developing data element standardization programs. They must ask, Who is the target community? Is it new systems development teams, data modeling teams, or systems reengineering teams? Data element standardization rules that are appropriate for one organization often do not apply to others.

DATA ELEMENT ATTRIBUTES

Valid Values

Homogeneous and mutually exclusive valid values will not, by themselves, ensure a quality data element. Many other features of data element design must be considered. Starting with these two goals, however, makes other common data element design problems easier to identify and avoid. The main goal in developing quality data elements is to make data elements as self-evident and useful as possible.

Usefulness is maximized through flexibility. If a data element can be used by only one small group of users in one small system because its definition and valid values are restrictive, it is not as useful as one that serves many needs in the organization. An example of an extremely useful data element is a Social Security number. Any information system that stores personal data can use this data element as the key to its personnel records with confidence that innumerable other systems are using the same data element.

Making data elements self-evident is one of the data administrator's main responsibilities. By constructing their data repository schema, data administrators establish the attributes to be documented for each data element. These attributes must be comprehensive enough to ensure that the data elements can be understood completely and consistently. Sometimes, data elements that are poorly named and not defined create no problems for the long-time users of the system because they already have a complete understanding. When systems are redeployed in a distributed environment or are reengineered and enhanced, however, both the previous users and the new users are likely to assign their own meaning to the new and revised data elements that are poorly named and defined. This may lead to incorrect reports to management, poor decisions, misunderstandings, or delayed business functions. Data administrators assist in the creation of data elements by developing the set of attributes that provides the structure to facilitate comprehensive definitions.

Homogeneity. Homogeneous valid values represent a set of like items. The valid values are the representations, or instances, of the concept that the data element embodies. Blue, green, and brown are all instances of eye color. The way in which the valid values are like each other is the concept. For example, it is helpful to ask what do blue, green, and brown have in common? Because they all represent colors of people's eyes, the concept is person eye color.

The presence of valid values that are not homogeneous indicates that more than one concept is being included. The example in Exhibit 8 contains valid values that are not homogeneous. These valid values represent more than one concept. The following phrases can be analyzed to determine the concepts they represent:

- the amount of hair a person has
- the color of the hair that a person has
- whether or not a person has hair

The phrases do not take into account whether the person wears a wig or whether the hair is more than one color (e.g., salt-and-pepper, has a white shock, or is dyed). If the amount of hair is concluded to be one of the concepts, the valid values for that concept must be determined.

Before continuing too far down this path, it would be wise to step back and look at the original concept. A data element may exist in personnel

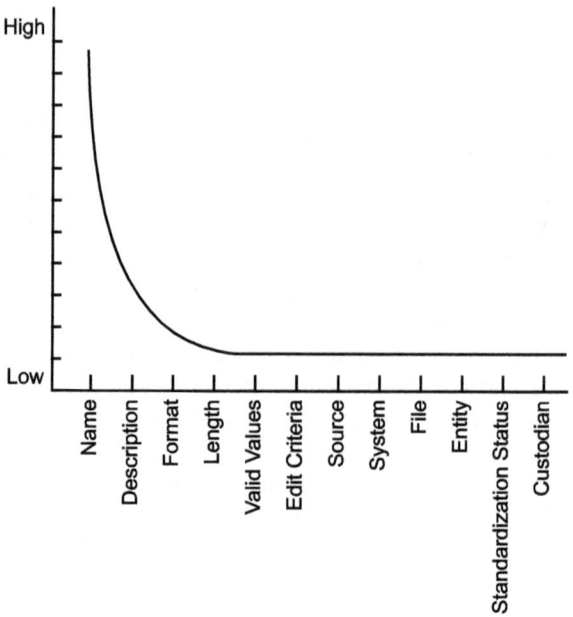

Exhibit 6-8. Nonhomogeneous valid values.

information systems because it is needed by the personnel business area to identify people. They may use it as one piece of data to visually observe someone's outward appearance to verify a person's identity. This instance is very different from a medical research laboratory that documents hair color by identifying and documenting the person's genetic structure responsible for hair color. It is important not to lose sight of the reason for collecting the data. Some data analysts have been accused of going off the deep end when it comes to developing data elements. A balance must be found between rigorous adherence to the one-concept-equals-one-data-element rule and the need for useful data elements.

Mutual Exclusivity. The other reason that abstracting to a higher level to combine concepts is risky is that the valid values themselves usually represent a combination of concepts. This results in valid values that are not mutually exclusive. The loss of flexibility in deriving meaningful information from values that are not mutually exclusive is the cost that must be paid.

A set of valid values are mutually exclusive when only one value applies to each instance. For example, the valid values in Exhibit 9 are not mutually exclusive because the term single can apply to someone who is widowed or divorced or who has never married. Also, someone could be divorced and remarried and both D and M would apply. Many data elements have valid

Exhibit 6-9.   Nonmutually exclusive valid values.

Data Element Name:	EMPLOYEE MARITAL STATUS CODE
Data Element Definition:	An employee's status with regard to any US state's law concerning marriage
Valid Values:	M = Married
	S = Single
	D = Divorced
	W = Widowed
	L = Legally separated
	I = Interlocutory
	A = Annulled

values like these, and the matter is usually dealt with by instructing the people who collect the data (e.g., customers, employees, or data entry clerks) to pick the choice that best fits. Relying on the data entry clerks or the people filling out the forms to pick the best choice indicates that someone knew that the choices were not mutually exclusive and that the quality of the data would probably suffer as a result.

Valid values that are not mutually exclusive often are developed for data elements that encompass more than one concept. In addition, data elements that include more than one concept are often developed to document the effect of implementing several related business rules on an instance of a business entity. The previous example implements the following implicit business rules:

- Only marriages that a U.S. state recognizes as valid are recognized as valid by the organization.
- Marriages can be legally created and dissolved only by one of the U.S. states.
- A person can be married to only one other person at a time.
- Once a valid marriage has been dissolved by the state, the persons can be legally married again.

Many laws define under what circumstances marriages can be dissolved by annulment or divorce. One data element, EMPLOYEE MARITAL STATUS CODE, attempts to document the relationship between an employee and all these business rules. The fact that this data element violates the one-concept-equals-one-data-element rule is evidenced by its valid values. It combines the following concepts: whether or not a person is currently married, whether or not a person was previously married, and what event caused the most recent previous marriage to end if the person has not remarried.

Exhibit 6-10.   Nonmeaningful indicators.

Person Blue Eye Color Indicator
Person Green Eye Color Indicator
Person Gray Eye Color Indicator
Person Brown Eye Color Indicator
Person Hazel Eye Color Indicator

Exhibit 6-11.   Higher-level indicators.

Person Smoking Indicator
Person Drinking Indicator
Person Exercise Indicator
Person Family History Indicator
Person High Blood Pressure Indicator
Person High Dietary Fat Intake Indicator

To remedy this situation, data elements that comply with the one-concept-equals-one-data-element rule can be developed for the concepts presented. A person's job may require the person to determine and analyze trends in marital relationships from a legal perspective; the data collected using the previous data element would be inadequate. Such persons would benefit from modeling their data requirements and constructing more precise data elements that would conform to the one-concept-equals-one-data-element rule.

Indicators

Homogeneity and mutual exclusivity among valid values help ensure that the data element addresses only one concept. However, there are other pitfalls to watch out for in developing valid values. Data elements with yes or no values are easy to create. They can be easily named and their valid values are mutually exclusive. But they often mask more meaningful data that may be more useful, and it is easy to end up with several yes or no data elements when a more comprehensive concept is more appropriate. The example in Exhibit 10 demonstrates this. The higher-level concept in the example in Exhibit 11 may be less obvious. These data elements could be assigned to the entity PERSON. A way to develop one meaningful data element to replace these, however, would be to reassign them as the valid values for a data element, Person Health Risk Code. This data element could be assigned to an entity called PERSON HEALTH RISK, which would be an associative entity between PERSON and HEALTH RISK. This associative entity could have data elements to document such additional concepts as date of onset, duration, and severity.

CONCLUSION

Strict adherence to the one-concept-equals-one-data-element rule is not always recommended. Situations do occur in which it is neither practical nor cost-effective to collect and store that level of detail because it will never be needed. These situations, however, are difficult to foresee. In addition, the data element designer is often not in a position to predict future users' data requirements. Therefore, the rule is an excellent foundation on which to build. If all data elements were initially developed to comply with this rule, changes to the data elements could be made selectively afterwards to the few that need not comply. This would then be done with full knowledge of the costs incurred by doing so. The cost is measured by the loss of flexibility and the subsequent risk that this lack of flexibility can cause when unforeseen requirements emerge.

Although data element development standards must be independent of data modeling efforts, they should support and be easily embraced by data modeling efforts (i.e., the data element standardization rules should be capable of being used with different modeling techniques). Also, even when organizations are not involved in full-scale modeling efforts, rudimentary data modeling during data element development often helps answer important questions. Data element development is often easier when done as part of a well-planned data modeling effort. The value of standardizing data elements in legacy systems, however, should not be ignored. Slow-moving cleanup efforts often provide steady improvements in data quality while new systems or databases are still in development.

Data element standardization, like data administration itself, will not yield significant benefits as a separate and disconnected activity. Developing flexible, long-lasting data elements must be an integral goal of all systems development activities, whether they are development or maintenance activities. The enforcement of the data element standardization policy also must be an integral component of the system development process. Monitoring data element development can provide necessary training to the developers in an informal setting and serve as an enforcement mechanism. The tools used by the developers place limits on the configuration and attributes allowed for data elements that frequently do not coincide with the requirements of the data element standardization policy of the organization. Therefore, the data administrator trying to monitor the data element development requires a powerful tool that can overcome these discrepancies.

Supporting Tools

Repositories to store complex relationships between nonstandard and standard data elements are needed to support the process of migrating from legacy data elements to standard data elements. Data element cleanup efforts can be accomplished without repositories that can do this, but they will take longer, cost more, and be more error prone. Few data repositories exist that can store these complex relationships; most must be modified in some way.

Unfortunately, the tasks needed to prepare for a data element analysis and cleanup efforts are often perceived as a delay in the actual work. The tasks of designing an appropriate repository structure, which requires knowledge of what problems are likely to be encountered and prediction of what aspects of those problems need to be documented, are additional pressures. The end result is often that very little forethought goes into designing the repository structure to support data element analysis and cleanup.

Data administrators should not standardize data elements for the sake of reporting growing numbers of standard data elements. The proponents, agents, users, custodians, and functional sponsors should understand the value of quality data elements and demand quality data elements. As is often the case with other information resource management concepts, data administrators take it on themselves to educate their proponents, agents, users, custodians, and functional sponsors. After these people see the light, the data administrator should not hide away with the data analysts pounding and pummeling melded data chunks into quality data elements. The information customers must remain involved in the analysis and creation of their data elements.

Well-designed data elements can provide many benefits to an organization. Information customers can confidently share data and discuss changes to the systems they use with the developers with confidence that they are speaking about the same things. Developers can forgo the inconvenience of inventing data element names or guessing about the meaning of names concocted by some other developer. However, standard data elements are not easy to develop. Using sloppy standardization policies may be worse than not having any standards because the developers and information customers may conclude that standardization has not helped them at all if they spent substantial resources complying with a poorly conceived standardization program. Large data element standardization programs in existence for several years have had varying degrees of success. Any organization just embarking on establishing a data element standardization program would be wise to thoroughly scrutinize those programs to identify what works, what does not, and why.

Chapter 7
Web Content Management

Charles Banyay

INFORMATION TECHNOLOGY (IT) HAS BEEN APPLIED TO THE SOLUTION OF BUSINESS PROBLEMS FOR THE PAST HALF CENTURY. Although studies have shown that most information in an enterprise is contained in unstructured data (i.e., content, documents, and tacit knowledge in the heads of the employees), traditional IT has done little to apply automation to any of these areas. During the second half of the twentieth century, the overwhelming proportion of IT attention, initiatives, and dollars has focused on the management and processing of structured data.

With the advent of doing business over the Internet, or e-Business, and the associated collaboration over wide geographic expanses and extensive publishing to the Web, the automation of content and documents and those processes that depend on them may be a critical requirement for most organizations. Those businesses that have not addressed content and document management issues may find their transition to the digital economy significantly slower and more challenging than originally imagined.

STRUCTURED DATA

Structured data is data that can be easily stored in a computer repository such as a relational database. Most of this data is comprised of numbers or simple text. Structured data is usually fixed in length or at least has an upper limit. It is easily encoded using some simple transformation to and from the binary code and is usually stored in a coded format.

The encoding format depends on the operating system and the chip set of the particular computer being used. The encoding is usually a base operation of either the operating system or the computer hardware, and in most instances is transparent to the application systems developers. It is totally transparent to the user. Some common examples of code formats are ASCII and EBCDIC. Because each character of structured data is encoded by the computer, it can be interpreted by the computer. Structured data, therefore, is sometimes referred to as content addressable data.

UNSTRUCTURED DATA (CONTENT AND DOCUMENTS)

There exists, however, another type of data that is far less structured. Unstructured data is neither encoded by the operating system nor the hardware. The encoding occurs at the higher level of application system software. The code is usually complex and is often proprietary to the specific application software used. For example, Microsoft Word and Corel WordPerfect are both popular word processing packages but they store their data in very different formats.

One consequence of this is that unstructured data is not directly understandable by most computers at the hardware or operating system software level. A developer cannot simply depend on access methods or services provided by the operating system to read unstructured data in a directly interpretable way. A further level of software — application software — is required. Another consequence of the application system level encoding is that there are sometimes as many formats as applications.

In addition to text such as that in most popular word processors, numbers and text in spreadsheets, presentation slides, images, video, or voice recordings are all examples of unstructured data. Most of this data is stored in some complex format that is proprietary to the application used to create it. Usually, one requires the application or a subset of it so that the data can be presented in some medium such as a computer display, or in print on paper, to enable interpretation by human beings.

Most documents are comprised of unstructured data. More precisely, documents are made up of multiple components. The components can be text, a picture, a drawing, or any of the other entities mentioned above. Each of these components is generally referred to as content. It is the content that is unstructured to begin with. Content is usually stored with limited presentation-level formatting. It saves space and processing time, and facilitates reuse.

Content components by themselves usually represent a single idea or concept. For example, content could be a single slide within a presentation, a single quote, or a picture. The primary objective of componentization is to facilitate easy content reuse. When content is stored together with other components as within a document, it is much more difficult to find and takes more effort to extract for reuse. There are no absolute rules defining what is content and what is a document. There are, however, some general rules-of-thumb. Documents are usually collections of multiple pieces of content. Some type of presentation formatting is applied to the aggregated content to provide an appropriate look-and-feel congruent with the intended message embedded within the document. The collective whole, aggregated content, formatted for presentation, is generally referred to as a document.

CONTENT VERSUS DOCUMENT MANAGEMENT

The tools and approaches for managing content are somewhat different from those used for documents. Document management is one of those tool sets for managing unstructured data that have been around for some time. Document management is generally considered arcane and is associated with library functions and records management. For this reason and for some of the reasons discussed later, document management has been difficult to get into the main stream of business IT. The base functional components generally associated with document management systems are:

- a conceptually centralized repository
- secured access
- search capability
- versioning capability
- check-in/check-out capability for editing

Some of the more sophisticated document management tool sets may offer additional functionality such as workflow for review, approve, and publish type document lifecycles, and integration to some of the desktop authoring tools. Some very high-end products may even offer integration with structured data management systems such as ERP applications.

Content management requires more sophisticated tools than document management. A content management system manages components of documents, so it requires all of the functionality of a document management system with some additions. The additions fall into three broad categories of functionality. The first is the ability to aggregate the components into documents and managing them in this aggregated form without keeping multiple copies. Some in the industry refer to this capability as virtual or compound document management. A compound document must be managed as any other document from the perspective of versioning and workflow. In addition, a compound document must be actively linked bi-directionally to each of its constituent content component parts. Compound document management can become very complex.

The second category of functionality is integration with the authoring tools used to create content. With the possible exception of some Web authoring tools, most tools in current use today were designed to create entire documents and not just content components. These authoring tools generally apply considerable presentation formatting to the unstructured data within the content. Most of this formatting must be stripped from the data before it is stored. The ability to create entire documents sometimes creates the requirement for disaggregation services; that is, the ability to componentize a document and store it as a collection of its constituent component content. This entire category of functionality should diminish in importance as the tools for creating content, especially those that will store the content in XML format, become more sophisticated.

The third category of functionality is publishing. This could cover publishing to any medium, including paper, personal devices, or the Web. Simple content is rarely published by itself. Usually, a document is published. Therefore, one of the first steps in publishing involves assembling the constituent components of the document. Assembly is different from the management of the aggregated components because management involves managing a set of pointers, whereas publishing involves assembling copies of the content into a unified whole. The next step after assembly is applying presentation formatting. This is done through the use of a template. The publishing system must be able to understand the unstructured data within each type of content component to some degree, to be able to apply the formatting and to be able to reproduce the formatted content in a meaningful way. As discussed previously, understanding the unstructured data can be complicated.

Publishing to the Web could almost be a category unto itself. In addition to the functionality for general publishing, publishing to the Web can require special hardware and software for Internet scalability. Special software may be required for the synchronization of multiple Web servers if more than one Web server is involved. Depending on the objective of providing the content over the Web, there may also be various application servers involved. For example, there may be commerce servers for buying and selling, or personalization servers to enable individuals to have a unique personal experience on a particular Web site. These application servers will require some integration with their indexing schemas.

As demonstrated, both content and documents are comprised of unstructured data. Unstructured data usually requires special tools, algorithms, and methodologies to effectively manage it. Standard IT tools such as relational databases by themselves are not effective.

All database management systems need to understand the content of the data in order to generate the indices that are used to store and retrieve the data. Because the computer cannot understand the content of unstructured data at the operating system level, it cannot generate the indices. Other tools, in addition to those provided in the standard IT toolkit, are required. One of the most common tools is the use of metadata or data describing the data (content). Metadata, however, needs to be generated by some intelligence that has at least a partial understanding of the meaning of the content. Metadata is stored externally as structured data in a relational database management system. The computer then uses this structured data and pointers to the content in the form of access paths provided by the operating system file access method, to manage information stored in the unstructured portion.

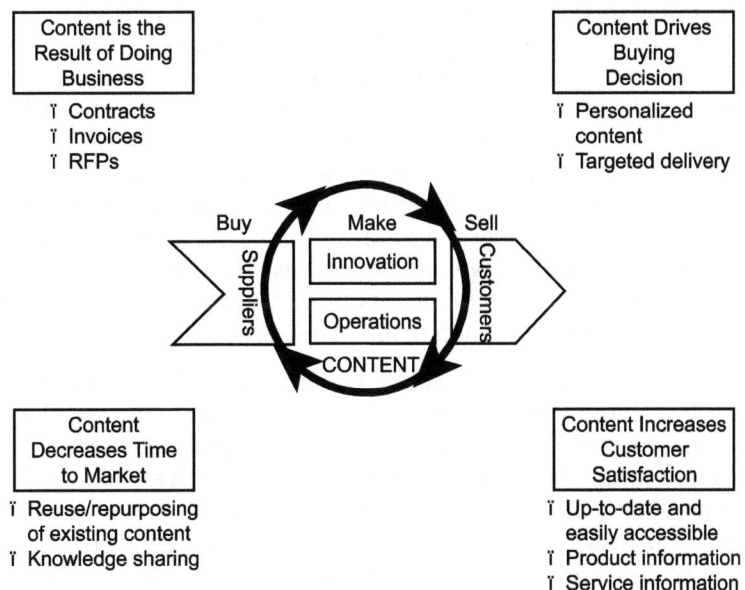

Exhibit 7-1. Things that affect content.

WHY HAS IT NOT DONE MORE TO AUTOMATE CONTENT AND DOCUMENTS?

Proprietary formats, the variety of formats, and their complexity are not the only challenges one faces when working with unstructured data or content. Until recently — and even to some extent continuing to this very day — special equipment was or is required to capture, store, present, and manipulate information stored as unstructured data. In addition, the endeavors that did try to bring automation to the world of unstructured data or content found that in most instances, the mastering of the technical issues was the easy part. The painful redesign of processes and changing the way in which people did their every-day work was far more of a challenge. Documents are pervasive in most businesses. Studies have shown that knowledge workers spend most of their time working with content and documents. Anything that affects content and documents generally has a major impact on knowledge workers, as shown in Exhibit 7-1.

To deal with complex data structures requires special training and, at times, significant effort. The process redesign requires special talents and skill sets usually not found in most IT organizations. The special software and hardware requirements can be costly. Taken collectively, this all strengthens the perception that IT endeavors around the management of documents and content are expensive and difficult to cost-justify in all but the largest of enterprises.

One result of this perception is that most IT organizations do not find the managing of documents and content an attractive area in which to build their competencies. Most IT organizations find much more success in focusing their efforts only on managing information stored as structured data. Most IT methodologies and tools, such as structured analysis and design, and data modeling, were specifically created to handle only structured data. The applicability and utility of these structured methodologies and tools in the content world are questionable. As a result, IT skills and methodologies that were developed to address the complexities of managing information stored as documents or content are often perceived as arcane and not within the realm of mainstream IT.

The collective end result is that currently, most IT professionals with standard IT backgrounds and skills often do not possess the additional skill sets to work effectively with unstructured data. In particular, they lack the in-depth understanding required to be able to effectively explain in business terms, the complexities around unstructured data to both colleagues and non-IT business professionals. More importantly, they lack the ability to recognize opportunities and to create effective business cases for addressing such IT endeavors.

HOW DID THE LACK OF AUTOMATION IN CONTENT AND DOCUMENT MANAGEMENT CONTRIBUTE TO TODAY'S BUSINESS DILEMMA?

Without IT support and the benefits of automation, most business people dealing with documents and content have been left to their own devices. They attempted many different non-IT solutions to minimize the inefficiencies that were left as a result of a nineteenth century approach to unstructured data in the office. Some examples of the attempts at a solution were:

- optimizing antiquated local filing systems
- retaining large numbers of administrative staff
- engraining the old processes in the culture and the organization structure in the name of efficiency
- expending considerable explicit and implicit effort into training people in the use of these antiquated filing systems
- retaining otherwise unproductive individuals who were the old-time gurus of these processes and filing systems
- optimizing paper processing, storage, and distribution
- implementing departmental imaging applications
- utilizing ever-increasing volumes of office space to enable the local presence of teams that needed to collaborate and access local files
- more creating huge LAN server farms with complex directory structures and folder hierarchies where people could store and sometimes find their unstructured information

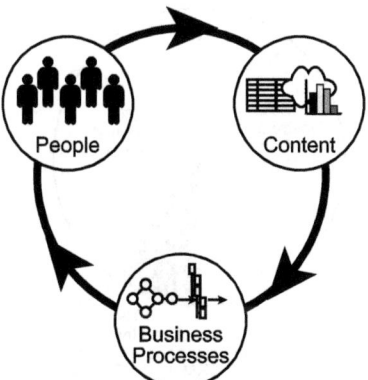

Exhibit 7-2. Departmental solution.

These attempts at a solution sometimes worked (an example is shown in Exhibit 7-2). The primary reason that they actually worked is that the problems were internally focused and so were the solutions. Most of the attempts at a solution were characterized by intimate familiarity with the internal processes and the physical knowledge repositories, and close geographic proximity to enable access to and sharing of knowledge content.

INTERNAL FOCUS EXACERBATES THE LACK OF AUTOMATION

In parallel with the focus on structured data by business leaders and their respective IT organizations was an absolute focus on internal process improvements — internal processes, as opposed to external processes such as those between an enterprise, its partners, suppliers, and customers. Nothing exemplifies this internal focus more than the tremendous success enjoyed by most ERP (enterprise resource planning) applications during the past decade. ERP applications are almost exclusively focused on internal productivity and effectiveness. It is not surprising that the overriding justification of most IT-related efforts during the past half century has been cost reduction.

This propensity to focus IT efforts internally allowed, and at times encouraged, a single dimensional approach to information or knowledge management focused on only the structured parts of data. The internal focus allowed IT to turn a blind eye to the unstructured world. IT could do what it knew best: how to manage structured data. The single dimensional approach fed on itself as there was perceived success. Had there been a compelling requirement to address external processes as well, there could possibly have been an earlier recognition that geographical proximity and intimate familiarity with internal norms and processes are not sound bases upon which to build business solutions.

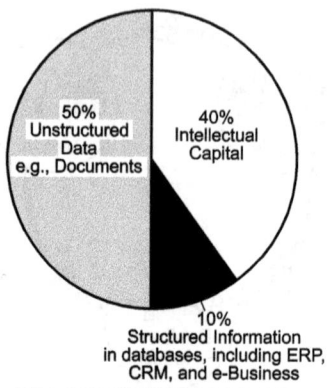

Exhibit 7-3. Where data lies.

The single dimensional approach to IT has prevailed for over half a century, despite disturbing statistics such as the one compiled by the *Harvard Business Review,* which seemed to indicate that office productivity had increased by only 1 percent since the application of modern information technology to business problems. Another statistic with similar disturbing implications was from a recent study done by PricewaterhouseCoopers, indicating that most information in an enterprise, upward of 80 to 90 percent, is stored as unstructured data. The study also confirmed that the large majority of this data was not automated (see Exhibit 7-3).

One of the unforeseen consequences of the internal business focus has been the formation of large conglomerates. These conglomerates have formed through numerous upstream and downstream integration along the value chain. One of the perceived advantages seen in these integrations has been the synergies or efficiency gained through internalizing and possibly sharing common business processes, especially administrative processes and those dealing with documents and content.

The lack of automated document and content management, however, has produced the opposite effects. Those entities within an enterprise dealing with documents and content have become dependent on intimate familiarity with the document-based processes and the physical knowledge repositories, and close geographic proximity. This has made it difficult for large conglomerates to outsource many of the internal business processes. Within the conglomerates, it has become exceedingly difficult to determine where value is added and where it is not. Many business processes have become inefficient because the internalization has protected them from external market forces, which could mandate efficiencies on them.

E-BUSINESS AND DISAGGREGATION

With the advent of transacting business over the Internet — a.k.a. B2B e-Business — the internal focus of many enterprises is quickly shifting. The ability to communicate and collaborate over the Internet, irrespective of geographic proximity, has been recognized by many early adopters of technology. They are using this aggressively for competitive advantage. This is forcing most organizations to shift their attention externally. They must address the external processes involving suppliers, partners, and possibly the customers.

The Internet is enabling many organizations to disaggregate along the value chain. The walls are coming down. Those internal components of large conglomerates that are primarily dealing with structured data and have the necessary IT tools to support their particular function are able to divorce the inefficient conglomerates and create a value proposition of their own. It is possible that during the next few years one could see the disaggregation of most high value-added functional units from the large conglomerates, leaving them with only the low value-added components. Another possible scenario is that all of the low value-added components or business processes will be outsourced to external business process providers.

There is an abundance of newly created organizations, offering a plethora of new services — in particular, business process outsourcing services. An example of this is the e-Procurement enterprise recently announced by Chase Manhattan and Deloitte Consulting. Most early adopting organizations of the disaggregated enterprise model are ones that deal primarily with structured data. They are supported by the required IT systems and infrastructure. These organizations will be subject to external market forces and therefore, in all probability, will offer far more efficient and effective service than an internal business process provider. The disaggregated component entities will be able to team with other providers of the most effective and efficient business processes, thereby collectively creating higher value for customers.

These early adopters should not be confused with some of the more careless players in this new market. There are other newly created entities taking up positions on the value chain. These entities may also deal primarily with structured data; however, they have not made the requisite investment in the necessary IT applications and infrastructure. These are some of the pure play .coms that have never earned a cent of profit, and will either learn or be obliterated by the natural market forces.

The more responsible component organizations mentioned above — the quick movers — are the entities that deal primarily with structured data and are already supported by the necessary IT systems and infrastructure. Because of the speed with which these entities have been able to move into

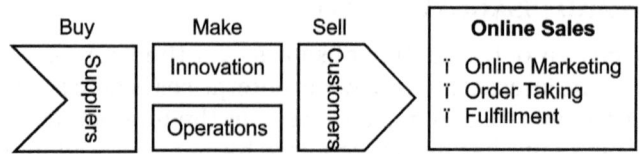

Exhibit 7-4. e-Commerce.

the new digital economic environment, they have created the expectation that this disaggregation will occur throughout the large conglomerates at the same speed. This may not be the case.

E-BUSINESS AND E-COMMERCE

If one rolls back the clock just one or two years, one might remember that these early adopters of the Internet or the digital economy were referred to as players within the realm of e-Commerce. The label here is quite important. Labeling them as e-Commerce players as opposed to e-Business players is quite appropriate. Most of these new organizations were involved in one way or another with selling and marketing (see Exhibit 7-4). Selling and marketing over the Internet is most appropriately referred to as e-Commerce. Central to this type of activity are secured financial transactions, and the backend integration to enterprise resource planning (ERP) applications for accounting and fulfillment. There may also be some limited customer relationship management (CRM) activity at the front end. The important point from the perspective of this discussion is that most e-Commerce activities, such as order transactions, billing, accounting, and interfaces to ERP and CRM applications, primarily involve structured data.

E-Business is far more than just e-Commerce (see Exhibit 7-5). This is not to underestimate or belittle the transformation from the old brick-and-mortar selling and marketing to that of e-Commerce. There are tremendous challenges

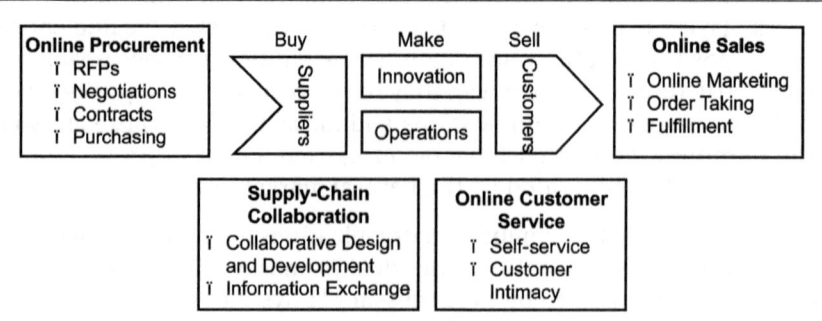

Exhibit 7-5. e-Business.

involved in just this single transformation. Transforming from a brick-and-mortar enterprise to e-Business, however, involves much more. E-Business incorporates e-Commerce. In addition, it also refers to activities involving online customer service, support, and possibly front-end collaboration. It involves innovation, design, and other supply-chain collaboration. Finally, it may involve online procurement.

Most of these activities involve business processes that are dependent on documents and content. By all estimates, these represent the majority of the business processes within an enterprise. This is corroborated by the fact that between 80 and 90 percent of information within an enterprise is in unstructured data. For many of these functional units, B2B interactions generally involve protracted negotiations or collaboration using content. These interactions can involve partners, suppliers, and possibly customers. This occurs throughout the value chain, generally involving the sharing and re-purposing of information, and knowledge (i.e., content).

CONTENT AND BUSINESS-TO-BUSINESS E-BUSINESS

Most organizations have had to develop an external focus. Competitive forces are mandating that the walls have to come down. However, for those entities owning processes within enterprises that depend on unstructured data, this may not be an easy process. There may be significant challenges. It has been found that in order to capture many of the benefits offered by e-Business, they cannot be encumbered by business solutions designed with the assumption of:

- intimate familiarity with the processes
- intimate familiarity with the physical knowledge repositories
- geographic proximity to enable collaboration, access to, and the sharing of knowledge content

Processes that were designed to operate with content management on a manual basis are proving to be grossly ineffective and in most cases just do not work in the B2B environment.

B2B interaction cannot suppose geographic proximity nor intimate familiarity with either the internal processes or the internal knowledge repositories. This mandates a focus on managing content in a way that IT has managed structured data during the past half century. The incentive for IT is that in the coming years, investment in content management could yield far greater returns than investments in standard IT. One reason may be simply due to the law of diminishing returns. Most of the structured data within organizations is computerized to a large degree, while the cherries in the content management orchard are yet to be picked.

To reduce risk and enhance efficiency and effectiveness, it is imperative that the content powering B2B interactions is trusted and is available through simple searches: (1) trusted because external entities cannot be expected to have intimate familiarity with the internal realities of other organizations against which they can compare content for validity; and (2) available through simple searches because they are not intimately familiar with the internal knowledge repositories in order to find content they require. Content must be managed. This managed environment at a minimum must ensure that:

- It can be scaled to an enterprise wide infrastructure (i.e., beyond just a few silos).
- Content goes through the necessary review and approval life cycle before it is available for consumption (i.e., published).
- There is an audit trail of each review and approval process.
- Content has integrity; that is, each instance of a particular content is the same in every physical repository.
- Content is versioned.
- Only published content is available for general consumption.
- Content is easily found through various metadata models such as attribute indexing, full text indexing, cabinet folder hierarchy indexing, and organizational ownership indexing.
- Only those with the appropriate authorization have access.
- Secured access is available at multiple levels for each content element, from no access at all through to full edit and deletion rights.
- Content can be aggregated and assembled without creating multiple copies.
- Aggregated content can be published in multiple formats.

Within this B2B environment, there must also exist the capability to collaborate. This requires spaces where shared content is readily available either through organizational ownership or cabinet folder hierarchy, metadata models, and where threaded discussions can occur. These collaboration spaces in essence are the electronic equivalent of bringing individuals who need to collaborate, be they departments or project teams, into the same physical location. Within this virtual physical location, they have the shared content that they require and have the ability to facilitate discussions and share ideas.

SUMMARY

In summary, since the inception of the industrial revolution, most businesses have been almost exclusively focused internally. For a number of reasons during the past half century, IT has done very little to address the business problems and issues around the management of unstructured data. Not the least of the reasons is that unstructured data is complex and the solutions of the problems around its management are not limited to just technical solutions. Most IT professionals with standard IT backgrounds and skills often do not possess the additional skill sets to work effectively with unstructured data. In particular, they lack the in-depth understanding required to be able to effectively explain in business terms, the complexities around unstructured data to both colleagues and non-IT business professionals. More importantly, they lack the ability to recognize opportunities and to create effective business cases for addressing such IT endeavors.

The internal focus of business leaders has allowed IT to limit its endeavors primarily to the automation of structured data. This has left business people dependent on unstructured data or content to their own devices. Without content automation, most of the attempts at a solution were characterized by intimate familiarity with the internal processes and the physical knowledge repositories, and close geographic proximity to enable access to and the sharing of knowledge content.

In the new digital economy, processes that were designed to operate with content management on a manual basis are proving to be grossly ineffective and in most cases just do not work. B2B interaction cannot suppose geographic proximity nor intimate familiarity with either the internal processes or the internal knowledge repositories. To reduce risk and to enhance efficiency and effectiveness, it is imperative that the content powering B2B interactions is trusted and available through simple searches. Content management can make a major difference. Trusted content provided through automation can truly power e-Business. Content managed through manual means can be the Achilles heel of many organizations looking to make the rapid transition into the digital economy.

Section III
Managing Business Rules

BUSINESS RULES HAVE BECOME THE MOST IMPORTANT TIER IN N-TIER AND WEB-BASED APPLICATIONS AND REPRESENT ONE OF THE STRONGEST ASSETS OF AN ORGANIZATION. Proper identification and encapsulation of business rules support the open, portable, and interoperable requirements of an n-tier-based architecture. The technical components of a system can arguably be commoditized and reused from organization to organization with relatively minor modifications. However, business rules represent the thoughts, ideas, and experience of a specific organization. In a rapidly evolving technical business environment, they offer a consistent competitive advantage that is not offered by the technology foundation. Business rules must be managed throughout a project and system lifecycle. They must be identified, captured, validated, owned, shared, and maintained consistently across an organization. This section builds a framework for achieving these objectives. The following chapters are included in this section.

Chapter 8, "Business Rules: Capturing the Most Elusive Information Asset," explains the importance of capturing business rules, in a natural language, early in a project lifecycle. A development lifecycle consisting of 15 steps is presented and offered as the basis for a business rule methodology. This spans clarification, identification, management, and promotion of business rules. This chapter also examines technology that can be used to capture business rules in a data model format and also to establish a central business rule repository.

Chapter 9, "Business Rules: A Case Study," provides a sample case study for collecting, analyzing, validating, and distributing business rules. The business rules are then classified into data modeling constructs consisting of entities and relationships. This chapter also offers recommendations for solutions that will support the defined business rules.

Chapter 10, "Modeling Business Rules," takes a shortcut to a generic project lifecycle by demonstrating how business rules can be modeled directly from existing data and object models using extensions. This is based on a graphical technique that models rules in a declarative form.

Chapter 8

Business Rules: Capturing the Most Elusive Information Asset

Alice Sandifer and Barbara von Halle

BUSINESS RULES ARE PERHAPS THE MOST IMPORTANT DELIVERABLE EN ROUTE TO A SHARED DATA ENVIRONMENT. Business rules reflect, in natural language, the true business meaning behind business information. They are the foundation for data sharing and the eventual integration of data and process modeling. However, they remain the most elusive and sometimes controversial information asset. This chapter discusses a formalized approach to capturing, validating, managing, and automating business rules.

A famous saying states that a picture is worth a thousand words. This is probably true, but does everyone internalize the picture using the exact same thousand words? Are there, in fact, as many different interpretations of the picture as there are viewers of the picture? Is each interpretation of the picture biased by the viewer's personal knowledge, experience, and desires?

Data specialists cannot be satisfied with an unjustified, biased perspective of business information. Their goal is to capture the true, pure business meaning behind the business information. In fact, data specialists must aim to represent business information accurately and minimize misinterpretations. Therefore, the most valuable deliverable from data management to the enterprise may not be the enterprise or information system data model or even the resulting databases, but the words behind the picture. These words are the business rules that reflect business practices and validate the data model. Unfortunately, good business rules are often the most elusive information asset. A business rule is a statement written in natural language describing terminology, definitions, rules, and policies about information that is used in conducting the enterprise's business.

THE VALUE ADDED BY BUSINESS RULES

An enterprise has much to gain by recognizing business rules as a formal deliverable of creating data models and databases. Those enterprises that have recognized the importance of business rules have developed formal procedures for capturing and validating them. Using a formal approach to documenting business rules allows data specialists to concentrate on user descriptions. Once the business community begins believing data specialists are listening diligently — and not distractively modeling — the pure business meaning behind the business information surfaces. Instead of conversations with business people revolving around the proper selection of entities, attributes, and relationships, they focus on sentences, precise use of terminology, and examples to clarify the meaning of business information.

Perhaps the greatest value business rules bring to an enterprise, however, is that they represent business knowledge in a format understandable by all business participants. When business rules are circulated to the business community for review, they serve as a valuable communication tool. Their natural language structure makes their validation and acceptance by the business community easier than if the information were being communicated with specialized terminology or notations. It follows, then, that business rules are the very foundation of data sharing. It is through the common understanding of business terminology, names, and definitions that business information becomes shareable. After business rules are accepted by the business community, business people may rely on them while composing ad hoc queries and interpreting query results.

The ultimate value of a repository of natural language business rules, however, has yet to be realized. Such a repository could be used to educate new employees as well as to assess commonality in business policy and culture when considering acquisitions and mergers. In progressive enterprises, a repository of business rules could form the basis for internal analysis, assist in the discovery of suboptimal business rules, and imply the necessity for reengineering major business functions.

HISTORICAL PERSPECTIVE OF BUSINESS RULES

Historically, data specialists have had to make assumptions about business rules because their importance was not truly recognized by enterprises. Without formal business rule procedures, the rules were generally embedded in information systems specifications and program documentation. More likely, most business rules were never recorded, and therefore remained in the minds of the business people, business analysts, and perhaps programmers who developed information systems. The greatest risk for an enterprise that does not formally capture business rules is that it is unable to differentiate rules that represent policy from those that are merely personal preferences.

Data modeling methodologies, data analysis guidelines, and automated tools have made it easier to understand the importance of capturing certain kinds of business rules. Data specialists have learned that the quality of a data model is directly related to exactly how much meaning has been captured about the business information and how readily available that meaning is to the business community. The information systems industry is still struggling with exactly how to capture all relevant business rules.

BUSINESS RULES DEVELOPMENT LIFECYCLE

Each business rule begins its life as a user utterance, typically a long, ambiguous, and perhaps unclear sentence. It must then be analyzed, decomposed, and refined until it becomes a concise, clear, atomic business rule that can be understood by all. In this atoned state, although simple and clear, the rule is parochial because it represents the knowledge or opinion of one or a few people. For use in a shared data environment, the parochial business rule should be expanded in scope until it reflects the truth as known by a major participants who have an interest in that business rule.

For example, to an order entry administrator, a customer is a person who currently has an open order with the enterprise. To a sales representative within the same enterprise, a customer is any person to whom the salesperson has spoken about the enterprise and its products, whether or not this person has ever placed an order for any product. In the same enterprise, a credit manager may perceive a customer as any person who has placed an order totaling more than $500 because such orders require a customer credit check. These definitions must either be combined into one general definition of customer that is all-encompassing, or they must be distilled into separate names and definitions when these differences are significant to the enterprise. The result is a true, shared business rule or set of rules.

After the business rule has been validated by the business community, and if the rule is within the scope of an information systems development project, it is next translated into appropriate data modeling constructs. This process, by its very nature, uncovers additional business rules.

This evolution of business rules suggests that they have a development lifecycle that can be divided into five major phases. The first phase is business rule acquisition, which is the process of obtaining facts from a business rule source. The second phase is business rule analysis, whereby an analyst converts user statements (verbal or written) into discrete, clear, and atomic business rules. Phase three is business rule validation, in which the business rules are circulated and subsequently modified to reflect commonality in understanding across organizational boundaries. The fourth phase is business rule storage, which includes the storage, update, and retrieval of business rules in a repository. The final phase of the lifecycle is

Exhibit 8-1. **Steps to a business rule methodology from Spectrum Technology Group, Inc.**

1. Determine scope of the enterprise
2. Develop project plan
3. Identify business rule sources
4. Determine acquisition approaches
5. Identify business rule tools and interfaces
6. Identify business rule standards and procedures
7. Conduct business rule acquisition sessions
8. Reword original sentence structures and content
9. Evolve a glossary of business terms
10. Translate original sentence into atomic units of thought
11. Organize business rules by business subject
12. Obtain source consent on preliminary set of business rules
13. Distribute business rules for business concurrence
14. Resolve conflicts
15. Classify business rules into data modeling types

business rule modeling, which is the translation of rules into technology-independent data model and process model constructs. Each of the five phases are comprised of more detailed steps. A sample set of detailed steps from Spectrum Technology Group, Inc.'s rule-driven data modeling course is presented in Exhibit 1.

BUSINESS RULE CLASSIFICATION

Business rules can be classified by many different methods. Most classifications, however, may be grouped into three basic categories: entity rules, relationship miles, and attribute rules. Business rules pertaining to entities include entity definition rules (e.g., a long rule and a short rule), entity identification rules (e.g., one for the primary identifier and others for alternate identifiers), entity cardinality rules (e.g., depicting minimum, maximum, and average expected number of occurrences), entity example rules, and entity miscellaneous rules (e.g., to cover anything else). Business rules pertaining to relationships consist of relationship definition rules, relationship cardinality rules (depicting minimum, maximum, and average ratio between entities), relationship justification rules (explaining exactly why the cardinality is as it is), relationship optionality rules, relationship referential integrity rules, relationship example miles, and relationship miscellaneous rules. Business rules pertaining to attributes include attribute definition rules (short and long), attribute domain rules, attribute trigger rules, attribute miscellaneous rules, and attribute example rules.

An additional category is business-specific business rules. These are rules that do not directly relate to an entity, attribute, or relationship, yet make a difference in understanding the enterprise and its business information. Unfortunately, data analysts neglect to gather business-specific work. In fact, most data specialists begin documenting business rules only when analyzing data modeling constructs because they are accustomed to viewing business information as a conglomeration of entities, attributes, and relationships.

Probably any combination of the above classifications are helpful for an enterprise. It is desirable for each enterprise to choose some method of business rule classification. The classifications provide more flexible ad hoe reporting of business rules from a repository.

WRITING A QUALITY BUSINESS RULE

Writing a quality business rule is usually achieved only after reiterative analysis and extensive questioning of the business community representatives. The following guidelines should be followed when constructing business rules.

Atomic

First, each business rule must represent one and only one fact. Typically, a sentence contains several facts joined together with a connector word (e.g., "and" or "or"). Business sentences that express more than one thought should be decomposed into separate facts. Data specialists must be careful to retain all business meaning when decomposing such business rules.

Sometimes, an initial business rule may actually be a combination of several types of business rules. For instance, a business rule may combine a sample instance of an entity in addition to providing a definition for the entity. To keep each business rule atoned, a separate business rule for the samples and the entity definition should be created. For example, the rule "A service is a task performed by a caregiver to aid a client (e.g., care of children or washing dishes)" is better expressed in two rules: "A service is a task performed by a caregiver to aid a client" and "An example of a service is taking care of children or washing dishes."

Complete

A business rule must also represent a complete fact. Each rule must specify everything that is necessary for the content of the rule to be understood by the average reader. For example, the initial business rule, "An application seeks to arrange employment for a caregiver for a client" is more complete when stated as "An application is a formal written request that prompts the agency to arrange for employment of a caregiver with a client." A guideline when constructing entity and attribute definition rules is that the object being defined (e.g., the entity or the attribute) should be stated followed by a nonaction verb (e.g., "is") and a meaningful descriptive noun. It is important to make clear distinctions (e.g., "agreements" versus "requests," "legal" versus "not legally binding," and "written" versus "verbal" characteristics). The person reading a business rule should not be confused — the rule should not be characterized by any ambiguity.

Similarly, each relationship definition business rule should be expressed in terms of a meaningful action verb or set of verbs along with minimum and maximum cardinalities. Generic verbs (e.g., "has," "exists," and "is") fail to fully describe a relationship. Instead, more specific action verbs should be used to describe the relationship (e.g., "generates," "groups," and "manufactures") because they convey more relevant information. To make a relationship definition rule complete, the relationship should be defined in both directions.

Explaining the purpose of a business rule is sometimes important in constructing a complete business rule. For example, a business rule describing a purpose could be "Although current skills are specified on an application, the agency maintains a complete list of a caregiver's skills for historical purposes." This rule explains the reason for associating skills with the caregiver entity rather than with the application entity. In many cases, including the purpose in the business rule may make the difference between an acceptable business rule and a quality one. Purpose gives the reader a frame of reference that allows for greater understanding of the business.

Consistency

Each business rule must be consistent with all other business rules in the enterprise and the repository of rules. Contradictory business rules create confusion for the end user querying the database as well as for developers and the programmer trying to use them as a guide for program logic. Because consistent business rules lay the foundation for a shared data environment, any inconsistencies must be flagged, investigated, and resolved. Unfortunately, such consistency checks are typically done manually.

Independent

Probably the most difficult task of constructing a quality business rule is to ensure it is unbiased in attitude towards any one information system or business area. Because a shared business rule must be valid for the entire enterprise, any business rules that pertain to a specific business group should be identified in the rule itself. Even so, these rules may be of interest to other parts of the enterprise.

Business

Every effort should be made to express each business rule in meaningful business terms. Although business rules should be in the language of the business, they must avoid slang and nonindustry-accepted phrases. A particular dictionary should be adopted as an enterprise standard for defining and using terms. Deviations from dictionary definitions should only be allowed for terms that have specific meaning to the enterprise or the industry of the enterprise. Creating an enterprise glossary to clarify commonly used phrases or terms ensures consistent use of terminology and assists in construction of business-oriented business rules.

Above all, business rules should never be expressed using information systems terminology, program specifications, program logic, or SQL. For example, referential integrity terms (e.g., "cascade" and "restrict") should be avoided. The data specialist should always remember that the primary audience for business rules is business people, not database analysts.

Clarity

Business rules must be written in clear, concise statements using proper grammar. Abstract or, ambiguous phrases make the meaning of the business rule confusing to the reader. Several guidelines may be followed to construct a clear business rule. First, all verbs in the business rule should be stated in the single active tense. The business rule, "A client has signed an employment contract" is more clearly stated as "A client signs employment contracts." Second, all components of each business rule should be stated positively, avoiding negative phrases. For example, "A client does not always sign an employment contract" is better stated as "A client may sign an employment contract." Reversing a negative phrase is not as easy as it seems and is not always possible. Because reversing a negative phrase may convey incorrect business meaning, this practice should be done with caution.

Another language construct that causes confusion for the reader is the connector "or." This word adds complications and creates a question in the reader's mind about whether to include or exclude an object. For example, "A caregiver may choose to live in his or her own home or the client's home" is better stated as "A caregiver may choose to live in his or her own home, instead of living in the client's home."

Similarly, the use of conditional words (e.g., "if" and "whether") may add unnecessary confusion. In these cases, phrases may be reversed and the conditional word substituted with a "when." For example, the business rule, "if the caregiver leaves, the agency will provide a substitute," is better stated as "The agency will provide a substitute when the caregiver leaves." Clarity may be enhanced by removing words (e.g., "all" or "some") from a business rule. For example, the business rule "Caregivers sign some employment contracts" is better stated as "A caregiver signs multiple employment contracts."

MANAGING BUSINESS RULES

Like any other information asset, business rules must be managed properly to ensure they are accurate, reliable, accessible, and secure. The individual responsible for meeting these objectives is the business rule administrator. This individual is most likely a data specialist from the data administration staff.

Business Rule Administration

The business rule administrator's primary responsibility is to ensure the quality and integrity of all business rules submitted to data administration. After business rules are collected, the administrator reviews each with discipline and rigor to ensure it is atomic, complete, consistent, unbiased, clear, and expressed in common business terms. Sharp analytical skills, in addition to a strong data modeling background, help the business rule administrator detect any inconsistencies between the business miles and the enterprise data model. Contradictions between different business area's viewpoints require the business rule administrator to be diplomatic and unbiased.

It is the responsibility of the business rule administrator to distribute rules to the appropriate areas for validation. The business rule administrator must choose appropriate functional area representatives to analyze rules, provide corrections, or indicate future changes based on anticipated business changes. This helps eliminate partially correct business rules.

The business rule administrator is also responsible for ensuring that the rules are accurate across all functional areas and for all participants in the shared data environment. As business rules evolve, so do the roles and responsibilities of the business rule administrator. In the future, the business rule administrator may evolve into a repository manager.

Business Rule Ownership

As a shared data environment is implemented, it becomes increasingly important to assign a guardian to each business rule. The term guardian implies responsibility for maintaining rules that reflect most current business practices. Some guidelines may be used in assigning business rule guardians. The guardian for entity definition rules and example rules should be the same as the guardian for the entity they describe. Similarly, referential integrity and trigger business rules should be assigned to the relationship that they describe. Identifying appropriate guardians for relationships, however, may not be so straightforward. When relationships associate two entities that have the same guardian, the guardian of the relationship definition is likely to be the same as the entity guardian. When relationships connect entities whose guardians are different, it may be difficult to determine the proper rule guardian. Likewise, if an entity has more than one guardian because different attributes have different guardians, the choice of a relationship guardian becomes debatable.

It is extremely important to recognize that the business rule administrator is not the true guardian of any business rules. Of course, in reality, the business rule administrator may need to assume a guardianship role when business guardians are not available or are not interested. Because the business rule administrator's responsibility is to ensure that business rules are submitted and approved by the appropriate business people, the administrator is generally responsible for resolving conflicting or inconsistent business rules in a politically acceptable and expedient manner. One workable mechanism is the creation of a committee of high-level business managers who meet periodically to resolve such issues.

Business Rule Maintenance

Generally, business rule maintenance is initiated by the business rule guardian and performed by the business rule administrator. The business rule guardian, knowing current business practices, is in the best position to judge when an update to a business rule is appropriate. As data and business rules apply to a shared data environment, it is likely that the business guardian function for a rule will evolve to become the responsibility of a team of business people, all of whom are stakeholders in the business rule. When changes in business practice or policy trigger necessary changes to the business rules, the administrator must again circulate rules to all appropriate business functional areas and then control the maintenance to each rule.

Business Rules and Vendor Packages

When an application package is chosen to support an information system, business rules should still be captured and stored. In fact, business rules should be captured by the enterprise before the decision to purchase a vendor package is made. Once a vendor package has been chosen, the enterprise should also document how the package influences the business areas. When constructing these rules, extra caution should be taken to avoid references to specific vendor package terms and concepts.

SELLING BUSINESS RULES

Selling the concept and usefulness of business rules to the business community and the data processing staff is a slow process that must be cultivated carefully and deliberately. The best selling style is through friendly persuasion. Generally, the data administration manager leads this effort and data administration staff members reinforce it. Data administration should emphasize the value added to the organization when business rules are incorporated into the development of information systems. Emphasis should be placed on the value added to the organization when business rules are captured before data modeling and physical database implementation. The persuasion should also identify resources wasted when rules are not included in the development of information systems.

Several steps may help ensure the successful sale of business rules to any organization. These include educating business and information systems people about business rules. They also include incorporation of business rules into the systems development life cycle and use of business rules in data model presentations. The selling of business miles is also facilitated by business rule storage and automation procedures and publicity.

Business Rule Education

Education is the most important critical success factor for incorporating the concept and use of business rules into an organization. The concept of formally capturing, storing, and managing business rules is for most organizations an extremely new phenomenon. Most individuals are not aware of the basic principles behind the formulation of business miles. Business rule education should emphasize the formal development and documentation of business miles and stress the benefits. Because few business rule courses are offered, the data administration function usually inherits the responsibility of developing and delivering this education.

Business Rules in the SDLC

After introducing the concepts of business rules into an organization's vocabulary, the next challenge is encouraging their consistent use. To make business rules an integral component of an organization's data-oriented philosophy, they should be embedded in its systems development life cycle (SDLC).

The typical SDLC consists of major phases (e.g., planning, scoping and feasibility, analysis, design, construction, production, and maintenance). Gathering business rules becomes most intense during SDLC analysis. As soon as potential entities or data groups are identified for a target information system during analysis, business rules that have already been collected (perhaps on behalf of other information systems projects) should be examined for relevance. Therefore, each analysis or design phase begins with the benefits of business knowledge that has already been captured. In addition, new or updated business rules should be required as deliverables in critical points in the development process. First-version business rules for entity definitions, relationship definitions, and any important miscellaneous rules should be included, along with the preliminary data model diagram at the end of a feasibility study, requirements analysis, and preliminary design. More complete business rules for entity definitions, relationship definitions, as well as referential integrity rules and business-specific rules should be required on completion of detailed design. Business rules should be well understood before the management-level or detailed data model is considered complete. Data administration should effectively enforce the submission of business rules either from business people or from the information systems staff to the business rule administrator before the creation of physical database structures. Including business rules as a separate deliverable in the SDLC at this time gives data administration greater leverage to ensure the rules are formally captured and agreed on before application implementation.

The business rule administrator should round out the rules at critical points in the SDLC, ensuring business rules match the data model. When reviewing a management-level data model, common business rule definitions should exist for each entity and relationship. In reviewing a detailed data model, entity identifier rules for each entity, referential integrity rules for every relationship, and a rule for each supertype data structure should exist.

Presentation of Data Models

Data administration can reinforce the importance of formally documenting business rules by presenting them to the audience along with the data model at a data model review. This is an excellent opportunity to uncover discrepancies in business rules because the audience will likely be cross-functional. Reviewing each business rule in a joint database review meeting streamlines data model validation. Because business rules are the supporting documentation for a data model, it is practical for data administration to present them to the business community when reviewing the data model. Often business people do not understand a complex entity-relationship diagram. They find following relationships between multiple associations entities difficult, but they can understand natural language. Unfortunately, most automated tools do not support a presentation format that integrates business rules with an entity-relationship diagram. Typically, data administration members need to present the entity-relationship diagram along with an accompanying report of business rules. One exception is ERWIN (from Logic Works), which can produce an entity-relationship diagram that encompasses at least entity definitions.

BUSINESS RULE STORAGE AND AUTOMATION

Data administration may have greater success selling the use of business rules when an automated mechanism for capturing them exists. Three basic alternatives exist for automated business rule storage: word-processor, computer-assisted software engineering (CASE) tool, and centralized repository. A fourth alternative is a combination of some or all of these basic alternatives.

Word Processors

The least complex alternative for automating business rules storage is to use word processors. Although word processors are easy to use for business people and information systems professionals, they lack ad hoc reporting capability. In addition, word processors are inadequate for providing update control and coordinating different versions of rules. This alternative for business rule storage requires manual management procedures and probably a centralized updater of all business rules.

CASE Tools

Another alternative for automating business rule storage is to use CASE tools. Although CASE tools provide more sophisticated support for handling business rules, they lack the ability to capture business specific rules. The only business rules that are easily documented in CASE tools are those that relate specifically to one entity, one relationship, or one attribute. These modeling constructs, rather than the business itself, become the focal point for capturing business rules.

One option for capturing business-specific business rules in a CASE tool is to bury them in free-format text. This alternative is not very flexible because free-format text is not conducive to ad hoc reporting. Another option is to store business-specific business rules in word processors. A third option is to use other facilities of a CASE tool. For example, some organizations have used Excelerator management objects for capturing business-specific business rules. A fourth option is to enhance the capability of a CASE tool to include business rule documentation facilities. Some organizations using Excelerator have customized the basic CASE tool to include business rule screens and reporting facilities.

Unfortunately, business rules housed in CASE products are not easily accessible to the business community. Business people are unlikely to use the CASE tool themselves for business rule reporting. Therefore, immediate access and even ownership and maintenance of these rules is more closely aligned with information systems professionals than with the business community. Another disadvantage of using CASE tools as the mechanism for capturing business rules is that unless the CASE tool has a mainframe or network version, business rules are available only to one workstation.

Nevertheless, some practical advantages to housing some business miles in a CASE tool do exist. Capturing entity, attribute, and relationship rules in a CASE tool provides the framework for automatic generation of data definition language (DDL). For this reason, at the very least, data administration should encourage the use of a CASE tool for data modeling by all information systems staff.

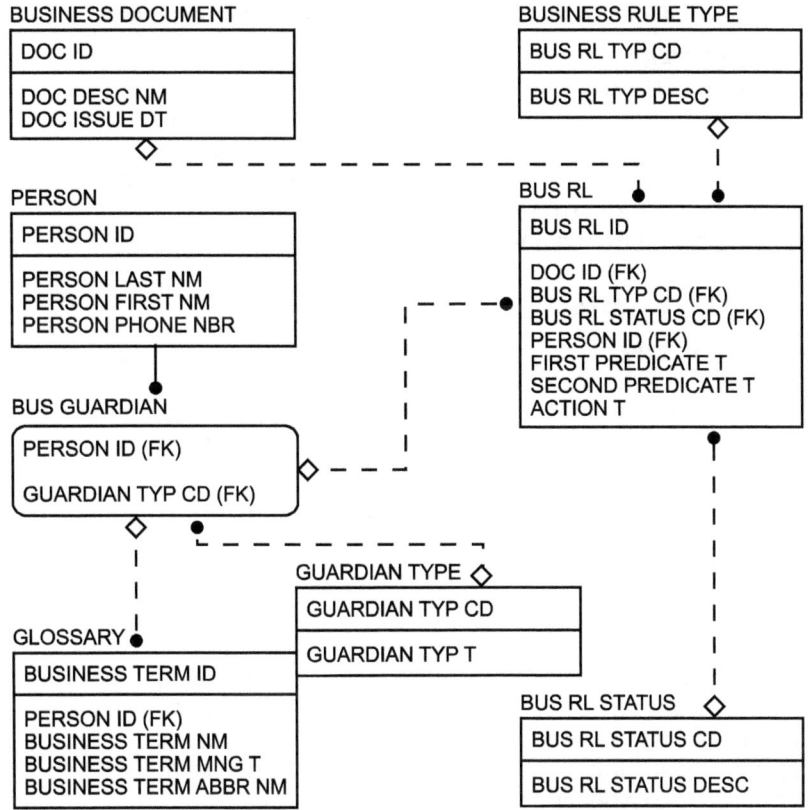

BUSINESS DOCUMENT

DOC ID
DOC DESC NM DOC ISSUE DT

BUSINESS RULE TYPE

BUS RL TYP CD
BUS RL TYP DESC

PERSON

PERSON ID
PERSON LAST NM PERSON FIRST NM PERSON PHONE NBR

BUS RL

BUS RL ID
DOC ID (FK) BUS RL TYP CD (FK) BUS RL STATUS CD (FK) PERSON ID (FK) FIRST PREDICATE T SECOND PREDICATE T ACTION T

BUS GUARDIAN

PERSON ID (FK)
GUARDIAN TYP CD (FK)

GUARDIAN TYPE

GUARDIAN TYP CD
GUARDIAN TYP T

GLOSSARY

BUSINESS TERM ID
PERSON ID (FK) BUSINESS TERM NM BUSINESS TERM MNG T BUSINESS TERM ABBR NM

BUS RL STATUS

BUS RL STATUS CD
BUS RL STATUS DESC

Exhibit 8-2. Data model for a business rule database.

Business Rule Repository

Another alternative for storing business rules is to create a centralized, user-friendly repository. This can be done with a relational database. Queries against this database may group business rules according to business source, entity, use (e.g., information system or business area), and effective date. Exhibit 2 depicts a data model for a business rule database. Exhibit 3 contains the corresponding DDL to create these relational tables. Although these tables represent only the storage of the business rules themselves, they may be expanded or joined with catalog, dictionary, or repository tables to correlate each business rule to its data model constructs.

In rare instances, organizations have developed front-end applications to business rule tables. Providing easy data entry for business rules significantly increases the probability that business people will be willing to capture and maintain them.

Exhibit 8-3.   Data definition language for a business rule database.

BUSINESS DOCUMENT
```
CREATE TABLE BUS_DOC
     (DOC_ID                   INTEGER        NOT NULL,
     DOC_DESC_NM               CHARACTER(30)  NOT NULL,
     DOC_ISSUE_DT              DATE           NOT NULL WITH DEFAULT,
     PRIMARY KEY(DOC_ID));
CREATE UNIQUE INDEX XPKBUS_DOC
     ON BUS_DOC
         (DOC_ID ASC);
```

BUSINESS RULE TYPE
```
CREATE TABLE BUS_RL_TYP
     (BUS_RL_TYP_CD            SMALLINT       NOT NULL,
     BUS_RL_TYP_DESC           CHARACTER(18)  NOT NULL,
     PRIMARY KEY(BUS_RL_TYP_CD));
CREATE UNIQUE INDEX XPKBUS_RL_TYP
     ON BUS_RL_TYP
         (BUS_RL_TYP_CD ASC);
```

PERSON
```
CREATE TABLE PERSON
     (PERSON_ID                INTEGER        NOT NULL,
     PERSON_LAST_NM            CHAR(18)       NOT NULL,
     PERSON_FIRST_NM           CHAR(18)       NOT NULL,
     PERSON_PHONE_NBR          CHAR(18)       NOT NULL,
     PRIMARY KEY(PERSON_ID));
CREATE UNIQUE INDEX XPKPERSON
     ON PERSON
         (PERSON_ID ASC);
```

BUSINESS RULE STATUS
```
CREATE TABLE BUS_RT STATUS
     (BUS_RL_STATUS_CD         SMALLINT       NOT NULL,
     BUS_RL_STATUS_DESC        CHAR(18)       NOT NULL,
     PRIMARY KEY (BUS_RL STATUS_CD));
CREATE UNIQUE INDEX XPKBUS_RL STATUS
     ON BUS_RL_STATUS
         (BUS_RL_STATUS_CD ASC);
```

BUSINESS GUARDIAN TYPE
```
CREATE TABLE GUARDIAN_TYP
     (GUARDIAN_TYP_CD          SMALLINT       NOT NULL,
     GUARDIAN_TYP_T            CHAR(L 8)      NOT NULL,
     PRIMARY KEY(GUARDIAN_TYP_CD));
CREATE UNIQUE INDEX XPKGUARDIAN_TYP
     ON GUARDIAN_TYP
         (GUARDIAN_TYP_CD);
```

Exhibit 8-3.   Data definition language for a business rule database. (*continued*)

BUSINESS GUARDIAN

```
CREATE TABLE BUS_GUARDIAN
    (PERSON_ID              INTEGER        NOT NULL,
    GUARDIAN_TYP_CD         SMALLINT       NOT NULL,
    PRIMARY KEY(PERSON_ID),
    FOREIGN KEY R/24(PERSON_ID)
        REFERENCES PERSON
        ON DELETE RESTRICT,
    FOREIGN KEY R/B(GUARDIAN_TYP_CD)
        REFERENCES GUARDIAN_TYP
        ON DELETE SET RESTRICT);
CREATE UNIQUE INDEX XPKBUS_GUARDIAN
    ON BUS_GUARDIAN
        (PERSON_ID ASC);
```

BUSINESS RULE

```
CREATE TABLE BUS_RL
    (BUS_RL_ID              INTEGER        NOT NULL,
    BUS_RL_TYP_CD           SMALLINT       NOT NULL,
    BUS_RL_STATUS_CD        SMALLINT       NOT NULL,
    PERSON_ID               INTEGER,
    DOC_ID                  INTEGER,
    FIRST_PREDICATE_T       VARCHAR(50)    NOT NULL,
    SECOND_PREDICATE_T      VARCHAR(50)    NOT NULL,
    ACTION_TX               CHAR(250)      NOT NULL,
    PRIMARY KEY(BUS_RL_ID),
    FOREIGN KEY R/4(BUS_RL_TYP_CD)
        REFERENCES BUS_RL_TYP
        ON DELETE RESTRICT,
    FOREIGN KEY R/6(BUS_RL_STATUS_CD)
        REFERENCES BUS_RL_STATUS
        ON DELETE RESTRICT,
    FOREIGN KEY R/7(PERSON_ID)
        REFERENCES BUS_GUARDIAN
        ON DELETE RESTRICT,
    FOREIGN KEY R/12(DOC_ID)
        REFERENCES BUS_DOC
        ON DELETE RESTRICT);
CREATE UNIQUE INDEX XPKBUS_RL
    ON BUS_RL
        (BUS_RL_ID);
```

GLOSSARY

```
CREATE TABLE GLOSSARY
    (BUS_TERM_ID            CHAR(18)       NOT NULL,
    PERSON_ID               INTEGER        NOT NULL,
```

125

Exhibit 8-3.   Data definition language for a business rule database. (*continued*)

```
        BUS_TERM_NM              CHAR(18)           NOT NULL,
        BUS_TERM_MNG_T           CHAR(18)           NOT NULL,
        BUS_TERM_ABBR_NM         CHAR(L 8)          NOT NULL,
        PRIMARY KEY (BUS_TERM_ID));
CREATE UNIQUE INDEX XPKGLOSSARY
    ON GLOSSARY
        (BUS_TERM_ID);
```

Business Rule Repository and CASE Tool

Most organizations that are serious about automating business rule storage do so by implementing a combination of CASE tool and repository storage. Both options are based on the philosophy that all business rules should first be housed in a centralized repository and subsequently moved to a CASE tool for data modeling and DDL activities.

The first implementation alternative calls for all business rules to be entered into a user-friendly front-end application that is connected to a centralized repository of business rules. The application's front-end intelligence would prompt the user to construct atomic, complete, independent, and clear business rules by referring to standard dictionary terms, an enterprise glossary, and existing business rules. Once each initial business rule was formatted concisely, the front-end application would specify the initial rule in the database as new and automatically distribute it to the appropriate business people for review. After business rule validation by the business community, data modelers could carefully review the rules and classify them according to appropriate data modeling constructs.

Once classified, the business rules could be downloaded into a specific CASE tool to automatically create data model diagrams based upon the business rule's classification. The CASE tool would have to be careful to integrate the information systems data models with the evolving enterprise data model. As the resulting data models were critiqued and refined, additional business rules could be uploaded to the repository for concurrence. Although this alternative is ideal, it is not currently implemented in any organization as far as the authors are aware.

A second alternative is to initially place all business rules into a centralized repository of business rules — a relational business rule database. After downloading business rules from the business rule database into the CASE tool, data specialists could manually convert appropriate business rules into data model constructs. A disadvantage of using this alternative is that redundant copies of business rules without synchronized update procedures would exist. The advantages are that all business rules would be housed in the repository and only those business miles needed for data modeling and DDL generation would be downloaded into the CASE tool.

Business Rule Publicity

Whenever opportunity arises, data administration should publicize the concept of business rules to the information systems staff and the business community in the form of written articles. These articles should be non-technical and emphasize the benefits for specific job functions. It is most useful to make available canned business rule queries that vary by entity or use (e.g., information system or business area).

Another method of publicizing business rules is to provide a copy of relevant business rules to individuals when they request the authority to perform their own ad hoc reporting. Such sharing of business rules encourages consistent reporting and use of the business information accessed through user queries.

When enhancements to an information system are required, developers should consult the business rule administrator for the most current business rules. They may find that working with business rules established before implementation makes it easier to judge alternative enhancement solutions. Less time is wasted creating functionally inadequate code and reinventing business rules.

SUMMARY

After the concept of formalizing the capture of business rules is sold and management realizes their benefits, the next step is for the enterprise to accept them as a corporate asset. The business knowledge that the rules document should be elevated to a status equal to that of other enterprise assets. Business rules must be obtained, managed, stored, and secured like any piece of equipment or inventory item.

Why then, is it so difficult to obtain organizational commitment? Why are business rules truly the most elusive information asset? The first reason is a cultural one. The development of commonly accepted business rules requires organizational commitment, a willingness to accept change, and an ability for business people and information systems professionals to make compromises for the good of the entire enterprise. The second reason is that business rules represent the initial integration of data and process — a phenomenon that the information systems industry is still struggling with.

Because business information and data processing requirements first appear together in conversations between information systems professionals and business people, it seems that uncovering business rules may be the first step in understanding this relationship. As the information systems industry progresses towards a better understanding of process and data modeling, business rules are likely to play an active role in blending the two together in an effective and business-oriented manner.

The contents of this chapter do not necessarily represent the views of Bristol-Myers Products. The authors would like to acknowledge valuable insight and experience provided by Judith Reeder on this subject.

Chapter 9
Business Rules: A Case Study

Alice Sandifer and Barbara von Halle

BUSINESS RULES ARE THE VERY FOUNDATION OF DATA SHARING. Effective collection of business rules requires validation across the enterprise before they are truly an information asset. This requires careful project planning, interviewing skills, analytical abilities, and diplomacy. This chapter highlights the most challenging aspects of dealing with business rules: the identification of scope and resolution of conflict.

The case study centers on a professional business rule administrator who works for a consulting enterprise that is very data-oriented in its development of information systems. The first assignment is to collect business rules pertaining to a local nanny agency. After business rules are collected, analyzed, validated, and distributed, the consulting company recommends a set of information systems to support the nanny agency's thriving business.

The business rules written for this case study are only for illustrative purposes. Although the authors have attempted to create a realistic view of a nanny agency's business, the business rule text used to describe the nanny agency is not factually correct in all instances. The business rules presented in this case study are not intended to imply legal advice or to propose how to conduct such a business.

DETERMINING THE SCOPE OF BUSINESS RULES

The first step the business rule administrator must follow is to determine the scope of the enterprise. Therefore, the administrator must determine the appropriate scope over which business rules are to be collected and subsequently validated.

The first step in determining scope is to analyze a management-level enterprise function model for the nanny agency and determine exactly which business functions are the target for initial information systems development. In this way, business rule collection can focus on a discrete business area or set of business areas. It is here that the business rule

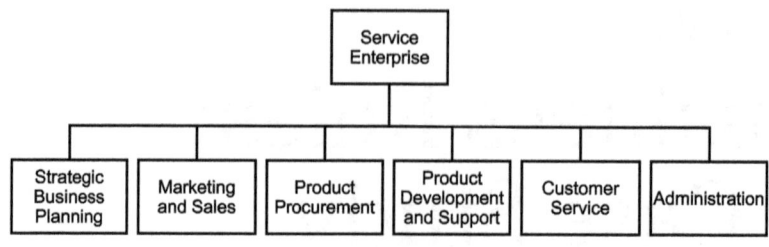

Exhibit 9-1. Management level enterprise function model for a service enterprise.

administrator faces two immediate challenges. The first challenge: no enterprise function model exists and no time or resources to create one is available.

Faced with this common dilemma, the business rule administrator creates a preliminary enterprise function model based on other models for service-oriented enterprises. In other words, the business rule administrator assumes that the nanny agency performs, even if in informal and incomplete ways, the following functions: strategic business planning, marketing and sales, procurement of product (i.e., nannies), customer service, product development and support (i.e., nanny networking and career development), and miscellaneous administrative services (e.g., making airline reservations). Exhibit 1 depicts this preliminary enterprise function model.

The second challenge is that neither the consulting company nor the nanny agency has yet determined which business functions are most in need of automation. Therefore, the scope of the business rules must include all functions of the nanny agency.

DEVELOPING A PROJECT PLAN

The second step in the business rule procedures is to develop a project plan. The business rule administrator outlines a plan that includes time for three to five business rule acquisition sessions, each lasting one to two hours. In addition, the business rule administrator allocates four to eight hours before each session for preparation and four to eight hours after each session to organize and analyze session results. The plan includes one week to distribute business rules to gain concurrence and updates. Another week is allocated to resolution of conflicts. Anticipating a relatively uncomplicated data model, the business rule administrator allows one week to develop a detailed data model.

Timeframes for other business rule projects for other enterprises might be significantly longer.

IDENTIFYING BUSINESS RULE SOURCES

The third step is to identify business rule sources. The business rule administrator begins with Mary Jones, the owner of the agency, but notes that it may be advantageous to meet with one to two customers.

DETERMINING ACQUISITION APPROACHES

The fourth step is the determination of business rule acquisition approaches. For this, the business rule administrator decides to conduct one-on-one face-to-face interviews, when possible, with phone and fax follow-up as needed.

IDENTIFYING BUSINESS RULE TOOLS, INTERFACES, STANDARDS, AND PROCEDURES

The fifth step is the identification of tools for documenting business rules. For the nanny agency, the business rules are entered into the agency's word processor. The sixth step is to determine standards for writing business rules.

CONDUCTING BUSINESS RULE ACQUISITION SESSIONS

The business rule administrator begins step seven with the first business rule acquisition session with Mary. When scheduling the meeting with Mary, the administrator asked her to forward sample documents she uses to conduct business (e.g., nanny employment applications, customer applications, fill-in-the-blank reference forms, and contracts).

After an introduction, the administrator begins by asking about the primary purpose of the agency. "We match high-quality, dependable nannies with good, supportive families in need of child care services," Mary answers. The business rule administrator immediately notices some imprecise terms (e.g., high-quality, dependable, good, and supportive). The business rule administrator focuses the conversation on the business nouns in the sentence nanny, family, and childcare services.

What is a nanny? "A nanny is usually a young female who provides care for children for payment." This sounds like the beginning of a business rule, but it contains imprecision.

Does a nanny have to be female? "No, although female nannies are more common than males." The business rule administrator notes that a nanny is a person, not necessarily a female. In addition, the term young requires further clarification. What is the minimum age you will accept for a nanny? "Eighteen." And, at what age must they no longer be a nanny? "No upper age limit is set."

Is the care always for children? "Yes, maybe. . ." Experience leads the business rule administrator to sense opportunity for future vision. Would you ever expand beyond the care of children? "That is an excellent question, perhaps a realistic possibility. Many people call and ask us to provide similar care for the elderly." The business rule administrator makes a note that the nanny agency may not limit itself to child-care services. Perhaps we should use the term dependent care rather than childcare? "That would be fine." Would you ever provide other kinds of care, such as for the handicapped? "No, that kind of business is really beyond our capabilities-probably for the foreseeable future."

What did you mean by the term childcare services? Should we probably rephrase that as dependent-care services? "It is actually a wide range of possibilities, such as bathing children, cooking for them, feeding them, dressing them, and so on." The business rule administrator writes down a first business rule: A CAREGIVER IS A PERSON WHOSE LIVELIHOOD IS TO PROVIDE DEPENDENT CARE AND LIGHT HOUSEKEEPING SERVICES FOR A FAMILY IN THE FAMILY'S HOME.

Your customers are families? "Yes." How do you define a family? "A group of people who live in a house together and need child care or housekeeping services." So, you really mean those families that are in need of your services. You do not mean all possible families? "Correct." Must the people in a family be related to each other by marriage or by blood? "No." Must they live in a house — what about other housing arrangements? "They can live in an apartment or condo." Or trailer? "Yes." The business rule administrator notes another business rule: A FAMILY IS A GROUP OF PEOPLE WHO SHARE A COMMON DWELLING AND WHO DESIRE EITHER DEPENDENT CARE OR LIGHT HOUSEKEEPING SUPPORT OR BOTH.

So, your goal, then, is to match a caregiver to a family? Can a family employ multiple caregivers? "No, well, I suppose eventually a family may desire a caregiver for the children as well as a caregiver for aging grandparents." Can a caregiver service more than one family? "No, a caregiver services only the family that has contracted for the services." Do you always find a suitable caregiver for a family? "No, sometimes the needs of the family cannot be met." Is it correct to say A FAMILY EMPLOYS ZERO, ONE, OR MANY CAREGIVERS? A CAREGIVER PROVIDES SERVICES FOR ONE AND ONLY ONE FAMILY? "Yes."

How do you formalize the employment relationship? Is there a contract? "Yes, here is a sample." So an employment contract is an agreement signed by a family and a caregiver? "Yes." What is specified in the contract? "The contract outlines the specific dependent care or housekeeping duties the caregiver will do, the salary the family is to pay the caregiver, and so on." Can this be a verbal agreement? "No, the agency insists that it must be written to eliminate misconceptions by both parties." The business rule administrator writes another business rule: A CONTRACT IS A WRITTEN EMPLOYMENT AGREEMENT SIGNED BY A FAMILY AND A CAREGIVER WHICH IS DESIGNED TO ELIMINATE JOB MISCONCEPTIONS. A CONTRACT SPECIFIES DEPENDENT CARE, HOUSEKEEPING SERVICES, CAREGIVER SALARY SCHEDULE, AND CAREGIVER BENEFITS.

Tell me a bit more about the caregiver and where they live. "A caregiver does not have to live in the same dwelling as the family." If the caregiver does not live with the family, where does the caregiver live? "Caregivers live in their own dwellings or someone else's." Who determines where the caregiver lives? "It is the choice of the caregiver." The latest business rule becomes: A CAREGIVER MAY LIVE IN THE FAMILY'S HOME OR ELSEWHERE.

What other services does your agency provide after the employment contract is signed and the caregiver begins work? "We may provide a substitute at no extra charge if the caregiver leaves abruptly." What constitutes abruptly? "When the caregiver leaves before the end date of the contract and without good cause." The business rule administrator seeks clarification. What constitutes without good cause? "Good cause would be serious personal or family illness. It might also include a disagreement on ethics between a family and a caregiver. Homesickness, however, is not good cause."

Are there conditions that the family must fulfill in order for the agency to provide a substitute free of charge? "Absolutely, the family must pay the agency fee in full on time." What do you mean by on time? "One week before the caregiver's first day on the job." The business rule administrator makes a note: THE AGENCY WILL PROVIDE A SUBSTITUTE CAREGIVER AT NO EXTRA CHARGE TO THE FAMILY IF THE ORIGINAL CAREGIVER LEAVES WITHOUT GOOD CAUSE. THIS GUARANTEE WILL ONLY APPLY IF THE FAMILY HAS PAID THE FULL AGENCY FEE AT LEAST ONE WEEK PRIOR TO CAREGIVER'S FIRST DAY ON THE JOB.

Can we talk a bit about the employment application? "Sure, here is the one that I use." Who completes the application? "Both the caregiver and the family. I also have two other applications: one for a caregiver who is seeking employment and one for a family seeking a caregiver." Does a caregiver application require different information than a family one? "Yes, a caregiver application requires specification of previous job experience." Must all of these applications always be written? "Yes." The business rule administrator notes: AN EMPLOYMENT APPLICATION IS A WRITTEN REQUEST FOR EMPLOYMENT FROM A CAREGIVER WHICH SPECIFIES NAME, ADDRESS, EXPERIENCE, SALARY REQUIREMENTS, REFERENCES, AND RELIGION.

Must a caregiver specify religious affiliation, as noted here? "No, but the caregiver may do so if desired." Can a caregiver have many re4ons? "We keep track of only one." May a religion be affiliated with many caregivers? "Yes." Why is a caregiver's religious affiliation important? "We use it to assist in setting up social networks for the nannies-many request to have a contact at a local religious group." The business rule is: A CAREGIVER IS AFFILIATED WITH ZERO OR ONE RELIGION. A RELIGION IS AFFILIATED WITH ZERO, ONE, OR MANY CAREGIVERS.

Do you keep these employment applications forever? "No, after one year, an employment application is removed from the file." "Who removes them from the file? "The agency, usually myself or temporary support person." Is the employment application removed and also the family application removed? "Only the family application is removed after one year." Why is it removed? "Because no contract was signed between the family and a caregiver." Is the family's record discarded also? "Yes." The administrator's next rule is: AFTER ONE YEAR, THE AGENCY REMOVES A FAMILY'S APPLICATION FOR FAMILIES WHO HAVE NOT CONTRACTED WITH A CAREGIVER.

Let's move on to the family application. What is it? "An application requesting services that require specific skills." Again, this is a written request? "Yes." Do both applications request services? "No, only the family application." The next two rules become: A FAMILY APPLICATION REQUESTS ONE OR MANY SERVICES. A SERVICE IS REQUESTED BY ZERO, ONE, OR MANY FAMILY APPLICATIONS AND A SERVICE REQUIRES ZERO, ONE, OR MANY SKILLS. A SKILL IS REQUIRED BY ZERO, ONE, OR MANY SERVICES.

Mary has no more time available. The initial business rule acquisition session comes to a cordial close. Although the business rule steps include specific steps for reworking original sentences and decomposing business rules into atomic facts, the business rule administrator accomplished these tasks during the business rule acquisition session. The 13 initial business rules are depicted in Exhibit 2.

EVOLVING A GLOSSARY OF BUSINESS TERMS

In step nine of the business rule procedure, the business rule administrator evaluates the need for an enterprise glossary for the agency. The following terms are listed as needing a definition as they apply specifically to the nanny agency. livelihood, dependent care, light housekeeping, dwelling, agency, good cause, and fee.

ORGANIZING BUSINESS RULES BY SUBJECT

Step 11 suggests that the business rules be organized by data subject. Doing so enables better comprehension and cross-referencing of related rides by the reader. Therefore, the business rule administrator suggests four major subjects and relates the rules as follows:

Exhibit 9-2.   Preliminary 13 business rules for the nanny agency.

1. A caregiver is a person whose livelihood is to provide dependent care and light housekeeping services for a family in the family's home.
2. A family is a group of people who share a common dwelling and who desire either dependent care, light housekeeping support, or both.
3. A family employs zero, one, or many caregivers. A caregiver provides services for zero or one family.
4. A contract is a written agreement signed by a family and a caregiver which is designed to eliminate job misconceptions.
5. A contract specifies dependent care, housekeeping services, caregiver salary, caregiver payment schedule, and caregiver benefits.
6. A caregiver may live with the family or may live elsewhere.
7. The agency provides a substitute caregiver at no extra charge to the family if the original caregiver leaves without advance notice and without good cause.
8. The substitute caregiver is guaranteed only if the family pays the full agency fee at least one week prior to the caregiver's first day on the job.
9. An employment application is a written request from a caregiver which specifies caregiver name, address, experience, salary requirements, references, and religion.
10. A caregiver is affiliated with zero or one religion. A religion is affiliated with zero, one, or many caregivers.
11. The agency removes a family application after one year if the family has not contracted with a caregiver in that time.
12. A family application requests one or many services. A service is requested by zero, one, or many family applications,
13. A service requires zero, one, or many skills. A skill is required by zero, one, or many services.

- Caregiver — Rules 1, 3, 6, 7, 9, and 12
- Family — Rules 2, 3, 6, 7, 8, and 11
- Contract — Rules 4, 5, 9, and 12
- Services — Rules 12 and 13

Some business rules (e.g., rule 3) are associated with more than one data subject.

During this exercise, the business suspects that the term family should be expanded in Scope and renamed Customer. A note is made to bring this to Mary's attention.

OBTAINING CONSENT FROM BUSINESS RULE SOURCE

For step 12, the business rule administrator faxes Mary a copy of the 13 business rules and asks for updates, comments, and approval on the work. The project plan is updated to include a potential business rule acquisition session with a caregiver to gather additional rules and to expand the scope of these initial rules.

DISTRIBUTING BUSINESS RULES FOR BUSINESS CONCURRENCE

Step 13 requires that business rules be distributed to all business parties that are stakeholders in the rules. The business rule administrator recognizes that the 13 business rules represent one point of view: that of the nanny agency owner.

In searching for appropriate reviewers and for additional sources of business miles, the business rule administrator makes use of the preliminary enterprise function model. From here, with Mary's assistance, the administrator identifies other people who perform some of these functions and who are stakeholders in the rules.

With Mary's help, the business rule administrator identifies customers and nannies to contact. The business rule administrator also knows that Mary is likely to provide the names of satisfied customers and nannies, so even this view is not totally without bias. Subsequently, the business rule administrator discovers another player in the business. Mary has part-time help from her neighbor when business is busy. As an aside, it is often very insightful to correct business rules about an enterprise from sources outside the enterprise.

RESOLVING CONFLICTS

Step 14 resolves conflicts. The business rule administrator quickly discovers one area of discrepancy over the definition of a caregiver. The nanny states that a caregiver need not ever provide housekeeping services and so the rule should be reworked as A CAREGIVER IS A PERSON WHOSE LIVELIHOOD IS TO PROVIDE DEPENDENT CARE OR LIGHT HOUSEKEEPING SERVICES FOR A FAMILY IN THE FAMILY'S HOME.

When Mary is presented with the proposed update to the business rules, she insists that all of her caregivers will provide some housekeeping — what is open to negotiation is the term light housekeeping. After all, she places only high-quality, dependable nannies who are very amenable to provide housekeeping services to the family.

The neighbor concurs with the nanny, stating that she herself has placed nannies who she is certain will not perform any housekeeping duties. Again, the business rule administrator faces a dilemma and must reevaluate the scope of business rules. Are the business rules to reflect those of ownership, support staff, customers, and products (e.g., nannies)? Are they to reflect the business as it currently actually operates, as it should operate, or as it will operate?

The business rule administrator discusses these matters with Mary. Because Mary is the CEO of the enterprise, she is the ultimate business authority and business custodian of the data. This is not so easily decided in a large enterprise. The business rules have already provided value to Mary; they uncovered serious misconceptions about quality of service. Mary can now publish these rules to better educate both her staff and nanny applicants.

When the business rule administrator reviews the remainder of the rules with the nanny, the nanny adds that a contract is for one year of service. The nanny states that subsequent negotiations for future years is between the caregiver and the family and does not involve the agency at all. Mary concurs with this.

The nanny would like to clarify the term "without due cause." The nanny wants to include the following as just causes: unfair treatment of the caregiver by the family (e.g., decreasing the availability of a car, restricting use of the phone, permission for daytime and overnight visitors). Mary has to think about these business rules before giving her approval.

CLASSIFYING BUSINESS RULES INTO DATA MODELING CONSTRUCTS

The business rule administrator — or perhaps a data modeler — is now ready to classify each of the 13 business rules into data modeling constructs, using an entity-relationship data modeling approach.

The business rule administrator classifies rules 1,2,4, and 9 as potential entity definition business rules. Therefore, the detailed data model initially contains entities for. CAREGIVER, FAMILY, CONTRACT, AND EMPLOYMENT APPLICATION. In addition, the business rule administrator determines that EMPLOYMENT APPLICATION is a subtype of CONTRACT. The business rule administrator decides to pursue the need for additional entities (e.g., SERVICE, SKILL, DEPENDENT CARE SERVICE, HOUSEKEEPING SERVICE, HOME OR DWELLING, ADDRESS, CAREGIVER BENEFIT, and RELIGION). If any of these are to be an entity, a business rule must define it.

In the second step of detailed data modeling, the business rule administrator determines relationships between entities. In this case, rules 3, 10, 12, and 13 are classified as relationship definition business rules that also include cardinality and optionality information. The business rule administrator decides that a many-to-many relationship may be needed among caregivers to indicate a specific social networking provided by the agency. If so, a new business rule is needed to define this relationship.

Business rules 6, 7, and 8 are business-specific business rules because they do not define a particular entity, relationship, or attribute. Rather, they add more clarity to those that are already defined and modeled. Business rule 11 is actually an archive business rule, indicating appropriate purge or archive requirements for entity occurrences.

The business rule administrator cannot address data modeling step LDM3 because no business rules exist to uncover primary entity identifiers

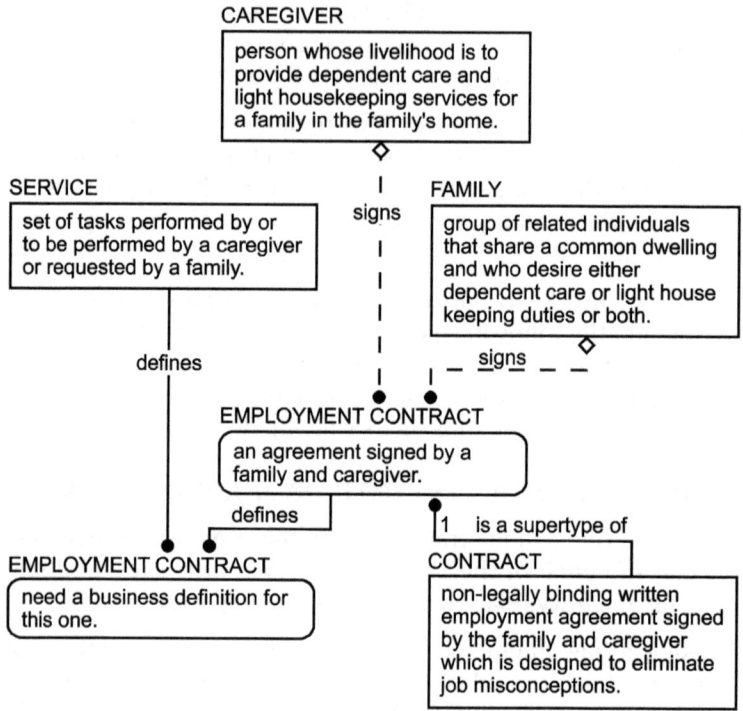

CAREGIVER
person whose livelihood is to provide dependent care and light housekeeping services for a family in the family's home.

SERVICE
set of tasks performed by or to be performed by a caregiver or requested by a family.

signs

FAMILY
group of related individuals that share a common dwelling and who desire either dependent care or light house keeping duties or both.

defines

signs

EMPLOYMENT CONTRACT
an agreement signed by a family and caregiver.

defines

1 is a supertype of

EMPLOYMENT CONTRACT
need a business definition for this one.

CONTRACT
non-legally binding written employment agreement signed by the family and caregiver which is designed to eliminate job misconceptions.

Exhibit 9-3. Erwin entity-relationship model showing entity definition rules.

(LDM3). Similarly, without primary identifier rules, step LDM4, propagation of foreign keys, cannot be completed. LDM5, identification of key insert and delete rules, also requires additional business rules.

Step LDM6, add non-key attributes, requires more investigation, although business rule 5 hints at some attributes for the CONTRACT entity. Each of these attributes needs its own attribute definition and domain business rule. Additional attributes also need to be discovered for this and other entities.

The business rule administrator begins to feel confident that classification of these business rules into data modeling constructs validates the business rules themselves. Business rule-driven data modeling is an excellent approach to developing entity-relationship models.

Additional business rule acquisition sessions are needed to solicit more business rules. A preliminary entity-relationship diagram, however, can be presented to Mary, the nanny, the customer, and the neighbor. Exhibit 3 depicts a sample entity-relationship diagram produced using ERwin from Logic Works, Inc. In this rendition of the diagram, the entity boxes display the business rule that defines the entity, although this model does not specifically depict the 13 business rules.

Exhibit 4 lists a more comprehensive set of business rules that may have been collected about the nanny agency's business. Exhibit 5 shows an entity-relationship diagram that depicts these rules.

SUMMARY

This case study, although simple, highlights some important aspects of business rule collection, analysis, validation, and modeling. First, the qualities of a business rule administrator include the ability to develop and refine a project plan, skills for good listening and analysis, as well as diplomacy and objectivity in dealing with business people and issues.

One of the most difficult parts of business rule capture is the identification of a definable and appropriate scope. Business rule scope comes in three varieties:

1. The scope over which to collect business rules (e.g., whom do you talk to?)
2. The scope over which to validate business rules (e.g., who has the overriding power to finalize the wording of a business rule?)
3. The purpose for which business rules are collected (e.g., to document current practices, to identify opportunity for improvement, or to embark on significant business reengineering)

In this case study, the scope of business rule collection was wider than that of validation (i.e., business rules were collected from the owner, nanny, helper, and customer, but the final validator was the owner). In most cases, the scope of business rule collection is usually narrower than that of business rule validation (i.e., initial business rules may be collected from one business function, but distributed for validation across many business functions).

Determination of scope is not only the decision of who to talk to, who to involve in resolution of conflicts, but also methods for resolving conflict in a politically palatable manner. Even in large enterprises, the ultimate business custodian may be the CEO or shareholders. Yet, it is desirable to resolve most conflicts at lower levels. Even after conflict is resolved, the task of enforcing these rules and making them available to nannies, helpers, and customers lies ahead.

The translation of business rules into data modeling constructs is perhaps the least controversial of the steps, although it is fraught with its own challenges. The authors are concerned that most enterprises devote much effort in the data modeling stage, but do not place sufficient emphasis on the more difficult, controversial aspects. It is proper identification of scope, business custodianship, and tactics for palatable resolution that can truly determine the shareability and stability of the data environment.

The contents of this chapter do not necessarily represent the views of Bristol-Myers Products.

Exhibit 9-4.   Comprehensive business rules for nanny agency.

BUSINESS RULES
Entity Definitions

1. A CAREGIVER is a person who has completed a CAREGIVER APPLICATION because they desire to pursue a career of providing SERVICEs in a CLIENT's home.
2. A CLIENT is one or more individuals who have completed a CLIENT APPLICATION because they desire assistance with SERVICEs in their home.
8. An EMPLOYMENT CONTRACT is a written agreement signed by the CLIENT and CAREGIVER which defines the specific terms and expectations of a work assignment in a CLIENT's home.
12. An APPLICATION is a formal written request that the agency act to arrange employment for a CAREGIVER or SERVICEs for a CLIENT.
14. A CLIENT APPLICATION is a type of APPLICATION completed by the CLIENT that requests the agency to arrange for specific SERVICEs for them in exchange for a fee.
16. A CAREGIVER APPLICATION is a type of APPLICATION completed by the CAREGIVER that requests the agency to arrange employment for them based upon JOB EXPERIENCE.
22. A RELIGION is an organized system of beliefs and rituals focusing on one or more supernatural beings.
23. A COUNTRY is a geographical area of land that is distinguishable by features of topography, biology, and culture.
24. CAREGIVER SALARY SCHEDULE is a timetable defined in an EMPLOYMENT CONTRACT that identifies the time intervals a CAREGIVER should expect to receive compensation along with the amount of compensation to be paid by the CLIENT at each interval.
25. CAREGIVER JOB EXPERIENCE is a listing of all employment positions previously or currently held by a CAREGIVER that are specified in a CAREGIVER APPLICATION.
27. An APPLICATION REFERENCE is an individual specified in an APPLICATION who would recommend a CAREGIVER as an employee or a CLIENT as an employer.
29. A DEPENDENT is an individual who requires the emotional, physical, or financial support of a CLIENT to maintain their existence in life.
31. A SERVICE is a task performed by a CAREGIVER to aid a CLIENT.
32. A DEPENDENT CARE SERVICE is a type of SERVICE that provides maintenance support activities or life enrichment activities to the DEPENDENTs of a CLIENT.
34. A HOUSEKEEPING SERVICE is a type of SERVICE that provides domestic services to the CLIENT.
37. A CAREGIVER SKILL is an association of what SKILLs are possessed by a particular CAREGIVER.
38. A SERVICE SKILL is an association of what SKILLs are required by a particular SERVICE.
39. A SKILL is an expertise required to perform a particular SERVICE.
40. EMPLOYMENT CONTRACT SERVICE is an association of what SERVICEs are defined in a particular EMPLOYMENT CONTRACT.
62. A CLIENT APPLICATION SERVICE is an association of what SERVICEs are requested on a particular CLIENT APPLICATION.

Exhibit 9-4.   Comprehensive business rules for nanny agency. (*continued*)

Relationships

3. A CLIENT signs zero, one, or many EMPLOYMENT CONTRACTS. An EMPLOYMENT CONTRACT is signed by one and only one CLIENT.

5. A CAREGIVER signs zero, one, or many EMPLOYMENT CONTRACTS. An EMPLOYMENT CONTRACT is signed by one and only one CAREGIVER.

19. A SERVICE requires zero, one, or many SERVICE SKILLS. A SERVICE SKILL is required by one and only one SERVICE.

20. A SKILL is required by zero, one, or many SERVICE SKILLS. A SERVICE SKILL requires one and only one SKILL.

21. A CAFIEGIVER is affiliated with zero or one RELIGION. A RELIGION is affiliated with zero, one, or many CAREGIVERS.

41. An APPLICATION specifies one or many APPLICATION REFERENCES. An APPLICATION REFERENCE is specified in one and only one APPLICATION.

42. An APPLICATION is a supertype for zero or one CLIENT APPLICATION. A CLIENT APPLICATION is a subset of one and only one APPLICATION.

43. An APPLICATION is a supertype for zero or one CAREGIVER APPLICATION. A CAREGIVER APPLICATION is a subset of one and only one APPLICATION.

44. A CLIENT APPLICATION requests one or many CLIENT APPLICATION SERVICES. A CLIENT APPLICATION SERVICE is requested by one and only one CLIENT APPLICATION.

45. A SERVICE is requested by zero, one, or many CLIENT APPLICATION SERVICES. A CLIENT APPLICATION SERVICE requests one and only one SERVICE.

46. A SERVICE is a supertype for zero or one HOUSEKEEPING SERVICE. A HOUSEKEEPING SERVICE is a subset of one and only one SERVICE.

47. A SERVICE is a supertype for zero or one DEPENDENT CARE SERVICE. A DEPENDENT CARE SERVICE is a subset of one and only one SERVICE.

48. A CAFIEGIVER APPLICATION is completed by one and only one CAREGIVER. A CAREGIVER completes one or many CAREGIVER APPLICATIONS.

49. A CAREGIVER APPLICATION lists one or many CAREGIVER JOB EXPERIENCES. A CAREGIVER JOB EXPERIENCE is listed on one and only one CAREGIVER APPLICATION.

50. A CAREGIVER is a citizen of one and only one COUNTRY. A COUNTRY is the legal residence of zero, one, or many CAREGIVERS.

51. A CAREGIVER possesses zero, one, or many CAREGIVER SKILLS. A CAREGIVER SKILL is possessed by one and only one CAREGIVER.

52. A SKILL is possessed by zero, one, or many CAREGIVER SKILLS. A CAREGIVER SKILL possesses one and only one SKILL.

53. An EMPLOYMENT CONTRACT defines one or many CAREGIVER SALARY SCHEDULES. A CAREGIVER SALARY SCHEDULE is defined for one and only one EMPLOYMENT CONTRACT.

54. An EMPLOYMENT CONTRACT defines one or many EMPLOYMENT CONTRACT SERVICES. An EMPLOYMENT CONTRACT SERVICE is defined in one and only one EMPLOYMENT CONTRACT.

55. A SERVICE is defined in zero, one, or many EMPLOYMENT CONTRACT SERVICES. An EMPLOYMENT CONTRACT SERVICE defines one and only one SERVICE.

58. A CLIENT supports zero, one, or many DEPENDENTS. A DEPENDENT is supported by one and only one CLIENT.

Exhibit 9-4.   Comprehensive business rules for nanny agency. (*continued*)

60. A CLIENT completes one or many CLIENT APPLICATIONS. A CLIENT APPLICATION is completed by one and only one CLIENT.
63. A CAREGIVER APPLICATION lists one or many CAREGIVER JOB EXPERIENCES. A CAREGIVER JOB EXPERIENCE is listed on one and only one CAFIEGIVER APPLICATION.

Business-Specific Rules

4. The agency may fail to arrange for a CAREGIVEFI to provide the SERVICES required in a CLIENT APPLICATION because the agency may not have CAREGIVER APPLICATIONS for CAREGIVERS who possess the appropriate SKILLS requested by the CLIENT.
7. The agency may fail to arrange for CAREGIVER to provide SERVICES for a CLIENT because the CAREGIVER may possess CAREGIVER SKILLS which are not required by any SERVICE requested in any CLIENT APPLICATION.
9. An EMPLOYMENT CONTRACT describes all SERVICES to be provided to the CLIENT by the CAREGIVER as well as specifies the SALARY SCHEDULE to be paid to the CAREGIVER by the CLIENT.
10. A CAREGIVER may choose to live in their own dwelling, instead of living with the CLIENT in their home.
11. The agency provides a substitute CAREGIVER to the CLIENT when the original CAREGIVER leaves within four months of their employment start date. This guarantee will only apply it the CLIENT has paid the agency fee in full one week prior to CAREGIVER arrival in the home.
13. An APPLICATION specifies name, address, salary requirement, and APPLICATION REFERENCEs.
15. A CLIENT APPLICATION specifies the specific SERVICES required by a CLIENT.
17. A CAREGIVER APPLICATION specifies a CAREGIVER's JOB EXPERIENCE.
26. The agency keeps records of all CAREGIVER JOB EXPERIENCES specified in a particular CAREGIVER APPLICATION for historical purposes.
28. The agency requires three APPLICATION REFERENCES be specified on each APPLICATION and approved before the agency considers matching CLIENT SERVICES with CAREGIVER SKILLS. This requirement ensures that only quality CAREGIVERs are placed in employment positions with quality CLIENTS.
36. Only SERVICES which have been reviewed and approved by the agency may be stated in an EMPLOYMENT CONTRACT.
56. The agency is not responsible for any actions performed by the CAREGIVER while they are performing SERVICES for a CLIENT.
57. Although current SKILLS are specified on a CAREGIVER APPLICATION by a CAREGIVER, the agency maintains a complete list of CAREGIVER SKILLS for historical purposes.
59. A CAREGIVER may complete many CAREGIVER APPLICATIONS because a CAREGIVER'S SKILLS or skill expertise level may change as the person acquires new job experiences.
61. A CLIENT may complete many CLIENT APPLICATIONS because their CLIENT SKILL requirements may change as DEPENDENTS no longer need assistance.

Exhibit 9-4.   Comprehensive business rules for nanny agency. (*continued*)

Referential Integrity Rules

6. The agency purges all records of the CAREGIVER and any information regarding their APPLICATION when a CAREGIVER does not sign an EMPLOYMENT CONTRACT within five years of application date.
18. The agency purges all records of the CLIENT and any information regarding their APPLICATION when a CLIENT does not sign an EMPLOYMENT CONTRACT within two years of application date.

Example Rules

30. Examples of DEPENDENTs are a small child, a handicapped person, or an aging parent.
33. Examples of DEPENDENT CARE SERVICEs are preparing dependent meals, giving dependents a bath, reading books to dependents, or supervising dependents' free time.
35. Examples of HOUSEKEEPING SERVICEs are washing dishes, keeping DEPENDENT rooms clean, running household errands, or ironing clothes.

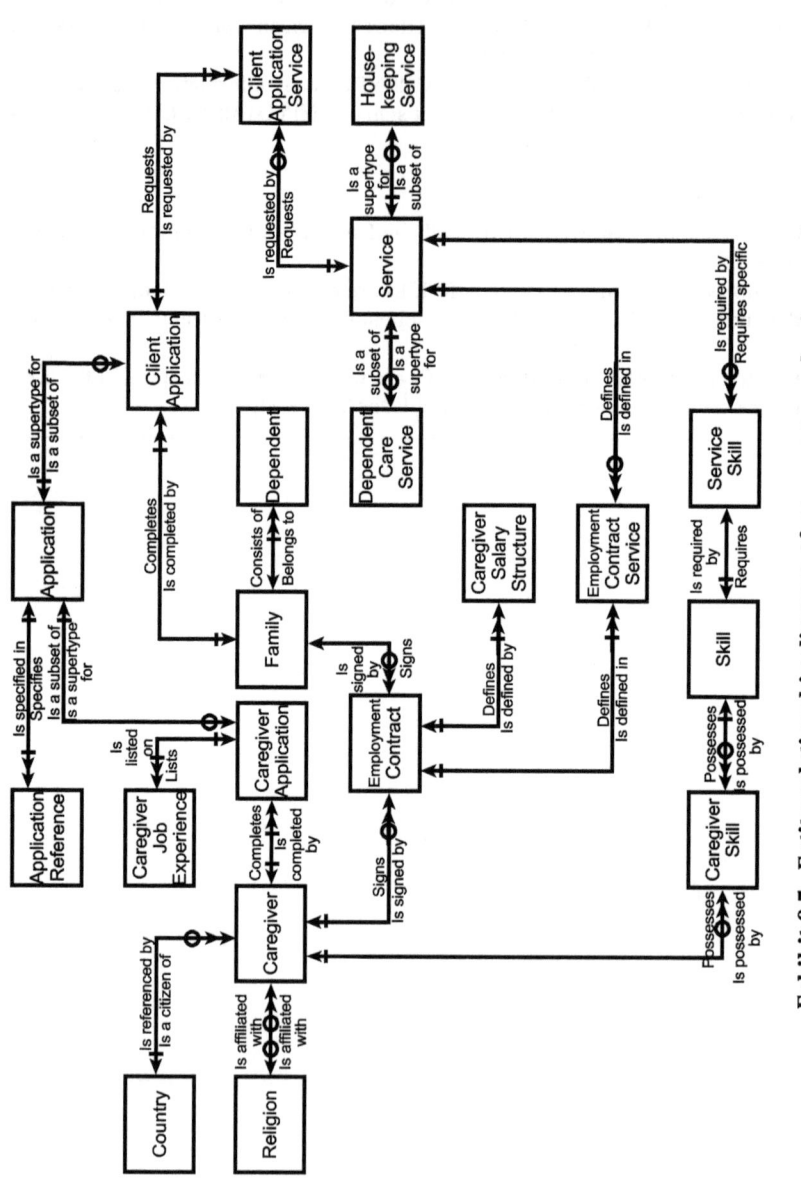

Exhibit 9-5. Entity-relationship diagram of nanny agency business rules.

Chapter 10
Modeling Business Rules

Ronald G. Ross

BUSINESS RULES TRADITIONALLY HAVE BEEN IMPLEMENTED IN PROCEDURAL LOGIC BURIED DEEP IN APPLICATION PROGRAMS — IN A FORM THAT IS VIRTUALLY UNRECOGNIZABLE, AND FAR REMOVED FROM ORIGINAL BUSINESS INTENT. Such strategies not only produce highly inconsistent enforcement of the business rules, but make rapid change in them virtually impossible. Sadly, this has been true even for information engineering, and other data-driven approaches. Process-oriented approaches have proven much worse.

A rule may be defined as a constraint, or a test, exercised for the purpose of maintaining the integrity (i.e., correctness) of persistent data. Every rule defined for a database should have a specific type, which should be selected from a standard set. The purpose of a rule generally is to control the updating of persistent data — in other words, the results that the execution of actions are permitted to leave behind.

Such control reflects desired patters for business behavior. A rule therefore embodies a formal, implementable expression of some user requirement, or business rule, usually stated in textual form using a natural language (e.g., English). Business rules indicate a discrete, operational practice or policy in running the business, without reference to any particular implementation strategy or specific technology. Users, of course, generally should not be concerned with how business rules actually are enforced.

The textual statement of business rules is extremely important. Every rule should be accompanied by an English-language expression of the rule's business intent. Unfortunately, textual statements often are ambiguous, and cannot be translated directly into an actual implementation (i.e., into running code). The task of the designer therefore is to translate textual business rules into formal, precise (and implementable) rules.

Some business rules translate directly to corresponding rules. Most, however, are more involved, and may require multiple rules to express fully. Often such rules can be interconnected in building-block fashion, enabling the database designer to work from standard rule components. This simplifies the task of translation significantly.

EXTENDING DATA (AND OBJECT) MODELS

A successful approach to modeling business rules requires careful attention to several crucial objectives, as follows:

- Rules depend on specification of underlying data types; these data types must be defined comprehensively and uniquely.
- To achieve maximum consistency and adaptability, rules themselves should be specified in discrete and nonredundant fashion.
- Users generally are not concerned with how business rules are implemented; therefore nonprocedural specification of rules is preferred.
- Communication of business intent usually is served best by pictures.

The framework that satisfies all these objectives most fully is provided by data models. Object models also may satisfy these objectives. This is discussed briefly in the following sections. Ross Method therefore uses data models as a given in specifying rules.

This preference is grounded in fundamental beliefs about the nature of production-level business operations. The computing problem this environment represents is the extreme opposite of single-user systems (even highly complex ones). The defining characteristic of the operational level of a business is extensive, multipurpose concurrency. It includes significant ad hoc access to persistent data by query language. The processing requirements of different concurrent users often are significantly different — and not infrequently, at odds with one another.

In environments of this type, ensuring consistency on the process side (by embedding support for business rules in all the processes) ultimately is futile. The only feasible solution is viewing specification of rules as an extension of the database problem, and using data models (or possibly object models) as the specification vehicle to achieve it.

Ross Method does not address data (or object) modeling per se. Rather, it assumes a robust, state-of-the-art technique already is familiar. Such technique must include complete, unencumbered support for type hierarchies. Any data modeling technique that satisfies these criteria may be used. The rule-modeling approach of Ross Method therefore is intended as a self-contained set of extensions to general modeling practices.

This includes many object-oriented (OO) approaches, assuming the following: the given approach permits properties of objects to be viewed publicly. (Certain OO approaches might be described as featuring hard-core encapsulation. These permit no access to the properties of an object except through messages to its operations. How declarative rules might be specified under these approaches is unclear.)

RULE TYPES

The power of the rule-based design approach prescribed by Ross Method arises in part from selection of standard, high-level rule types. These indicate the types of test a rule may perform. Recognized rule types can be organized into families sharing common purpose and mechanics, as follows:

- *Instance verifiers.* Rule types that test for possession of instances, present, or past.
- *Type verifiers.* Rule types that test for co-existence of instances of different types.
- *Sequence verifiers.* Rule types that test for patterns of aging (sequence of states).
- *Position selectors.* Rule types that test for rank or position by value or age.
- *Functional evaluators.* Rule types that test for patterns of values.
- *Comparative evaluators.* Rule types that compare values.
- *Calculators.* Rule types that compute values.
- *Update controllers.* Rule types that provide direct control over updating.
- *Timing controllers.* Rule types that test how long instances have existed.

The basic rule types in these families are atomic (i.e., they cannot be derived from combinations of other rule types). The rule families and their individual rule types therefore represent a fundamental classification scheme for business rules.

Rule types can be viewed as an alphabet for a business-rule language (or more precisely, for a sublanguage for integrity). Words are formed from this alphabet by selecting the rule type appropriate for a rule, then combining these rules in building-block fashion. The syntax presented in the remainder of this article indicates how this is accomplished.

Rule types also can be viewed as equivalent to the atomic elements in the Periodic Table used in chemistry. To form various chemical compounds (of which millions exist), the atomic elements (of which slightly more than a hundred exist) are combined (bonded) in appropriate fashion. The properties of a compound depend on which elements have been combined, and in what fashion. The same also is true for rule types, which similarly exist in atomic types. These can be combined in building-block fashion to form compound business rules.

INTEGRITY CONSTRAINTS VERSUS CONDITIONS

Rules are of two, and only two, varieties — those that possess built-in enforcement power, and those that do not. A rule with built-in enforcement power is called an integrity constraint; a rule without such power is called a condition.

Integrity
Constraint

Condition

11. Enforce a rule, or merely test it?

Exhibit 10-1. Integrity constraint versus condition.

More precisely, a rule can be viewed as a logical expression yielding either true or false (or null, if it is switched off).

- An integrity constraint is a rule that always must yield true (or null). It has enforcement power because it never is permitted to yield false. Business rules for which integrity constraints are appropriate generally indicate the sense of must.
- A condition is a rule that may yield either true or false (or null). Because it is permitted to yield false, it lacks direct enforcement power. Its usefulness arises in providing a test for the enforcement (or testing) of one or more other rules. Specifically, these other rules are enforced (or tested) only while the condition yields true. (Conditions therefore provide one important means for connecting rules in building-block fashion.) Business rules for which conditions are appropriate generally indicate the sense of if.

Integrity constraints and conditions must be distinguished in modeling business rules. Each is given a distinct graphic symbol, as illustrated in Exhibit 1. These symbols may be rotated to any position in 360.

Each of the two graphic symbols is directional in an important sense — each symbol has a back, a front, and two sides. The back and front are essential in modeling every individual rule; the sides provide points for connecting different rules in building-block fashion. Recognizing this directionality is a key element of the rule syntax.

MODELING RULES

Selection of rule type is crucial for rules. All rules must have a rule type. Generally, these rule types are selected from a standard set such as the set offered by Ross Method. Other rule types are possible, however, including derivatives. These are discussed later.

With practice, selection of rule types for most business rules becomes relatively straightforward. Each rule type has a particular sense, which always is applied in its interpretation. Exhibits 2 and 3 provide simple examples. It is important to note that all rule types can be used either for integrity constraints or for conditions.

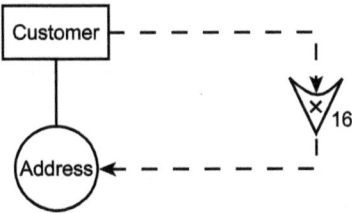

16. A customer must have an address.

Exhibit 10-2. A simple integrity constraint.

In Exhibit 2, the rule type has been indicated as MANDATORY (abbreviated X) within the integrity constraint symbol for rule #16. This selection of rule type was based on the sense of the business rule, which suggested possession of a property (must have).

Exhibit 2 also illustrates that every rule must have special connections (the dashed lines) with the data types it affects.

- The dashed line coming into the back of the integrity constraint symbol connects from the rule's constrained object (i.e., customer). Instances of customer therefore provide reference points for interpretation of this rule (i.e., an instance may exist only if the rule is satisfied). Every rule is considered to be a property of its constrained object.
- The dashed line coming out the front of the integrity constraint symbol connects to the rule's constraining object (i.e., address). Instances of this type are referenced to determine whether the rule is satisfied.

Very simple business rules (e.g., the example in Exhibit 2) often can be abbreviated. Typical business rules, however, are much more complicated, and require full specification.

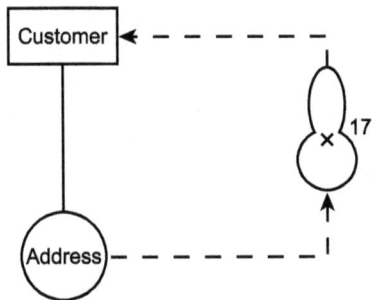

17. If a customer has an address, then . . .

Exhibit 10-3. A simple condition.

Exhibit 3 presents a modification of the previous examples. The rule type again has been specified as MANDATORY (abbreviated X),but now within a condition symbol, as appropriate for rule #17. As before, this selection of rule type was based on the sense of the business rule, which suggests (a test for) possession of a property (has). Specification of the condition itself now is complete. Without specification of what rule is to fire while the condition itself now is complete. Without specification of what rule is to fire while the condition yields true (the "then..." portion of the business rule), however, rule #17 remains without effect. This is illustrated later.

Enablers and Timers

Most rule types, when used as integrity constraints, have enforcement power, but are not capable of updates on their own. There are two notable exceptions, which are crucial in modeling more complex business rules. These two exceptions, enablers and timers, are discussed briefly in the following paragraphs.

An enabler is an integrity constraint of rule type ENABLED (abbreviated EA), or ENABLED-WITH-REVERSAL (abbreviated REA), with a lower or fixed enumeration type (which may be implicit). An enabler actually creates (i.e., enables, or switches on) instances of the constraining object when an instance of the constrained object exists.

- If the constraining object is a valued object, the enabler creates actual instances in the database. (This represents a simple form of inference.)
- If the constraining object is another rule, the enabler switches on (i.e., enables) this other rule. (Otherwise the rule remains disabled, in other words, off.)
- If the constraining object is an action, the enabler makes execution possible. (Otherwise, the action may not be executed.)

In Exhibit 4, rule #20.1 is indicated as an integrity constraint of type ENABLED-WITH-REVERSAL (with an implicit lower enumeration type). This indicates its being an enabler, capable of update actions on its own. Specifically, if an instance of its constrained object (address) exists, rule #20.1 enables instances of action #20.2, its constraining object. (This action has not been specified fully in the rule diagram.) Consequently, the action may be executed. The enabler disables (switches off) instances of action #20.2 for an instance of address when deleted. This renders them incapable of execution.

A timer is an integrity constraint of rule type TIMED (abbreviated TI) with an upper or fixed enumeration type. A timer actually deletes (i.e., disables, or switches off) instances of the constraining object for an instance of the constrained object after a specified amount of time:

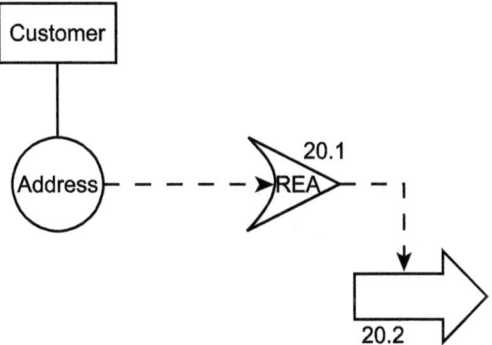

20. Enable execution of action #20.2
for a customer that has an address.

Exhibit 10-4. An enabler.

- If the constraining object is a valued object, the timer deletes actual instances on the database.
- If the constraining object is another rule, the timer switches off (i.e., disables) this other rule. (Otherwise the rule is enables, in other words, on.)
- If the constraining object is an action, the enabler makes execution impossible. (Otherwise, the action is ready to execute.)

In Exhibit 5, rule #21.1 is indicated as an integrity constraint of type TIMED with a fixed enumeration type. This indicates its being a timer, capable of update actions on its own. Specifically, for an instance of the rule's constrained object, address, once exactly five days have accumulated in which instances of action #21.2 are enabled (i.e., capable of being executed), the enabler will disable them automatically. (The action has not been specified fully in the rule diagram.) Once disabled, the instances of the action no longer may be executed.

Yield Rules

As mentioned, rules may be interconnected in building-block fashion to model more complex business rules. The first manner in which this may be accomplished is by indicating one rule as the constrained object of another rule. This makes the latter rule, called a yield rule, dependent on the yield of the former rule. Usually, this former rule is a condition, and therefore may yield either true or false. An example can illustrate this concept.

In Exhibit 6, rule #22.1, a condition of type MANDATORY, is indicated as the constrained object of rule #22.2,an integrity constraint. This indicates that rule #22.2 (not specified in full) is a yield rule, and therefore is dependent on the truth value of rule #22.1. If this condition yields true, rule #22.2 must be

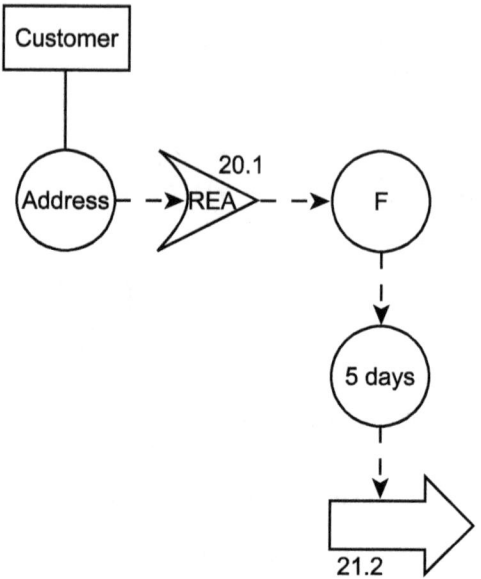

21. Disable execution of
action #21.2 after 5 days.

Exhibit 10-5. A timer.

enforced; if the condition yields false (or null), rule #22.2 is not enforced (i.e., must yield null). Rule #22.2 may be an enabler for some other rule (not shown), which now also will be dependent (indirectly) on the yield of condition #22.1.

Inclusion Rules

The second manner in which rules may be interconnected in building-block fashion to model more complex business rules is for one rule to be

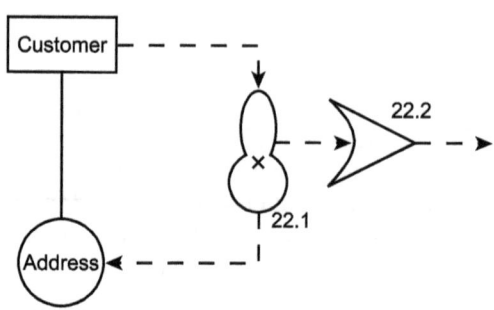

22. If a customer has an address,
then enforce rule #22.2.

Exhibit 10-6. A yield rule.

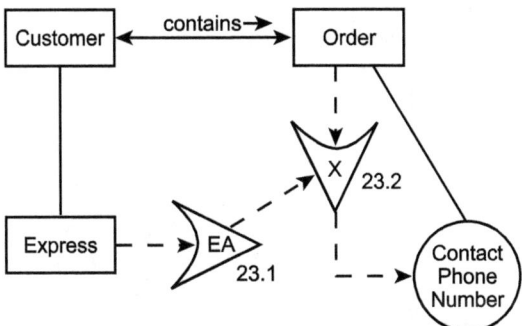

23. Orders contained on an express shipment
must have a contact phone number.

Exhibit 10-7. An inclusion rule.

indicated as the constraining object of another rule. This other rule, called an inclusion rule, often (but not always) is an enabler or timer. (Very sophisticated rules may be modeled using rule types other than enablers or timers as inclusion rules.)

All inclusion rules always effect the interpretation of scope for the constraining rule (i.e., for which instances, and in what manner, the rule will be applied). If the inclusion rule is an enabler or timer, it also may reduce the scope of the constraining rule by enabling only certain instances, or disabling other. An example illustrates this.

In Exhibit 7, rule #23.1, an enabler, indicates another rule (#23.2) as its constraining object. This indicates the enabler as being an inclusion rule. Typically, rule #23.2, an integrity constraint type MANDATORY, would be enforced for every instance of its constrained object, Order. The inclusion rule, however, changes this usual interpretation. Specifically, the enabler switches on (i.e., enables) rule #23.2 for only those orders contained on express shipments. Those orders on shipments not indicated as express, or contained on no shipment whatsoever, are not subject to rule #23.2 (i.e., rule #23.2 remains disabled for such orders). The inclusion rule acts to reduce the scope of rule #23.2 (i.e., to reduce the enforcement of rule #23.2 to only selected instances of Order).

Yield Value

Every rule performs some test for instances of the constrained object and constraining object(s), as indicated by its rule type. This test always requires these instances to be reflected, evaluated, tallied or computed in some manner unique to that rule type. For each instance of the rule's constrained object, this always produces a single-valued result at any point in time.

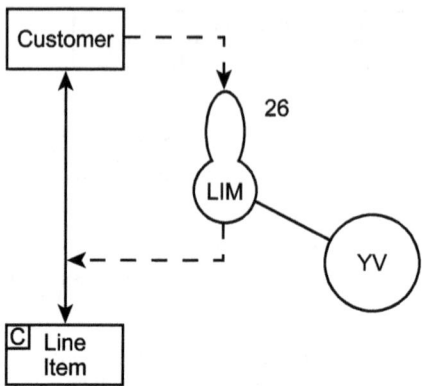

26. The number of line
items on an order is . . .

Exhibit 10-8. Yield value.

Usually, this result, called the yield value (abbreviated yv), is transparent. It is used internally by the rule to apply some test, or to enforce some constraint (i.e., to achieve the appropriate truth value for the rule). The yield value of every rule type is discrete and unique, and always is separate from truth value.

Sometimes, business rules require testing the yield value of a rule directly. Often, but not always, this occurs for condition-type rules, rather than for integrity constraints.

To satisfy this need, the yield value of a rule may be externalized. When externalized in this fashion, the yield value appears as an attribute type for the rule itself. As such it may appear as the constrained object or the constraining object for other rules. This is another way in which rules may be combined in building-block fashion to satisfy more complex business rules. The following example illustrates.

In Exhibit 8, rule #26, a condition of type LIMITED, indicates its yield value externalized as an attribute type. The yield value of a LIMITED-type rule counts the current number of instances of the rule's constraining object for each instance of its constrained object. Therefore, the yield value of condition#26 provides a current count of the number of line items for each instance of order. This yield value may be tested by other rules.

Derivatives

A derivative is any rule type that may also be expressed by specification of other rules. Such a rule type therefore is not a basic or atomic rule type — that is, one that cannot be derived from expression of other rules.

Sometimes the specification of the other rules for a derivative can become quite complex, involving many rules of basic types (or other derivatives) interconnected in building-block fashion. (Such specification is called the derivative's template.) If the derivative were not pre-defined, this template would have to be specified (correctly) for every business rule to which it applies.

Derivatives are similar to all other rule types in the following ways:

- They must follow rigorous specification conventions, which must be delineated beforehand. These conventions must be consistent with the general prescriptions for expressing rules described earlier.
- They must produce a yield value specific to their type. This yield value may be externalized for use by other rules. (The yield value for a derivative, of course, can be produced from the other rules that comprise its template. In this sense, the yield value of a derivative also is not basic like that of atomic rule types.)

In summary, derivative represents a convenient short-hand (i.e., a single utility rule type) for some test that appears frequently in business rules, or that is highly complex, or both. Derivatives represent an important means by which the set of standard atomic rule types may be extended.

CONCLUSION

Traditional business rule strategies have been inconsistent at best — making change almost impossible. Turning this trend around requires a new attitude toward building information systems. To that end, this chapter described a method for modeling business rules directly, using extensions to existing data and object models.

Section IV
Performance Modeling Methods

DATA MODELING ACTIVITIES GENERALLY FOLLOW THE INFORMATION COL-
LECTION AND ANALYSIS PHASE. A data model consists of many components, including entities, relationships, and attributes. Business rules are
also generally related to a data model.

There are many approaches or techniques for modeling data and as
many unique types of data models. Data models generally have several
forms associated with them as well. The two common ones are logical and
physical. Logical data models are independent of implementation details
and technology solutions. Their purpose is to represent data and relationships in the abstract sense. Physical data models are implementations of
the logical data model under a specific technology solution. A technology
infrastructure supporting a solution can be altered by generating a new
physical implementation of the same logical data model. Choices made at
the physical modeling stage can affect the performance, integrity, and
value of the ultimate production solution.

It is common practice to begin with a definition of a logical data model
and then to transform it into a physical database with refinements for
application performance improvements. This section consists of the following chapters that describe the different steps and issues in building
useful data models.

Chapter 11, "Enterprise Data Modeling Practices," provides an approach
for enterprisewide data modeling activties with particular emphasis on
how to avoid pitfalls that organizations typically encounter. Standards that
can be adopted by organizations are also presented in this chapter.

Chapter 12, "Evaluation of Four Languages for Specifying Conceptual
Database Designs," describes four conceptual database design languages
(CDDLs) from several different perspectives. These include the following
CDDL approaches: (1) English or other natural languages; (2) entity-rela-
tionship diagrams; (3) SQL; and (4) relational diagrams.

Chapter 13, "A Comparison of Three Systems Modeling Methodologies,"
describes the entity-relationship diagram, information model, and object
modeling techniques as three techniques for representing diverse corporate data.

Chapter 14, "Building a Data Model," provides an overview of a methodology for logical data modeling based on a data-driven approach. The objective of this approach is to facilitate optimal data design that encompasses
the principles of data correctness, consistency, sharing, and flexibility. The
data model is presented as the first step to effective database design.

Chapter 15, "Business Information Data Modeling," describes how to build
data models based on different types of business information. This chapter
examines derived business information, time-dependent business informa-

tion, historical information, and externally controlled business information. It also provides an approach for modeling difficult business information.

Chapter 16, "Making Data Models Readable," describes why some practitioners have had difficulties with data models, and then provides guidelines for building more usable data models. This includes how data models should be constructed, named, and communicated within an organization. Several modeling approaches are considered, including a basic E-R diagram, Chen's relationships, Oracle method cardinality and optionality, James Martin cardinality and optionality, and the Shlaer and Mellor cardinality and optionality.

Chapter 17, "Integrating Process and Data Models in a Horizontal Organization" describes approaches for integrating process models and data models into a unified solution. This chapter defines the characteristics of a horizational organization and describes a process- and data-focused approach for achieving strategic objectives.

Chapter 18, "Avoiding Pitfalls in Data Modeling," examines approaches for avoiding commonly encountered pitfalls in building data models at the enterprise level.

Chapter 19, "The Politics of Entity Identifiers," describes how to leverage entity identifiers to improve logical and physical database design. This is based on establishing data element properties and defining data element sets. This chapter also examines some commonly encountered entity identifier problems.

Chapter 20, "Practical Guidelines for Supertype and Subtype Modeling," describes a goal-oriented approach to supertype and subtype modeling. It also describes expectations from other parts of the organization, including IT management, data administration, and architecture, for building these models.

Chapter 11
Enterprise Data Modeling Practices
Wolfgang Keller

ENTERPRISE DATA MODELING HAS RECENTLY BEEN IN THE CROSSFIRE OF ATTACKS ASSERTING THAT IT IS COMPLETELY USELESS. Most critics say that such an inflexible, top-down, and centralist approach is not equipped to deal with problems like changing environments, pressure from global markets, and decentralization. A central data model is said to be a contradiction to a decentralized organization. Critics say that the rapid change will make the data model outdated before the data analysts can bring it to the market.

If analyzed, most of the arguments against data modeling have their roots in existing problems and frequent errors in practice. But this does not mean that enterprise data modeling in general is faulty or useless. Many of the arguments can be attributed to improper use of data modeling equipment.

Data modeling was invented to avoid the problems associated with isolated, nonintegrated systems. This chapter is designed to help users avoid some typical errors by focusing on correct data modeling practices.

ARGUMENTS AGAINST ENTERPRISEWIDE DATA MODELS

The following is a list of common arguments against data modeling. Many financial institutions and other organizations are reconsidering their data modeling practices in light of the bad press it has been receiving. A financial application is used as an example throughout this article because information processing is one of the core activities of the banking business.

Critics of data modeling assert that it:

- Is not able to keep pace with new developments. Information processing systems of financial institutions must be adapted to change rapidly because of the globalization of markets and new requirements for customer service.

- Cannot provide a bank with information systems that adapt with the speed of innovation. New financial instruments require fast adaptation of IS capabilities.
- Acts as a brake and not a booster for rapid systems development.
- Promotes structures that should not be changed. Change is the norm in systems development. This adds to the characterization of data modeling as a brake.
- Creates additional complexity in the process of software development. Applications development is impaired by the use of top-down data modeling practices.
- Can lead to the violation of normalization rules, with the consequent need to adapt the integrated systems.
- Has to incorporate all possible future options of a system, which slows operation down to a standstill. The level of abstraction tends to increase indefinitely until no one is able to understand the results of the process.
- Is useless, if purchased off the shelf as prefabricated data models.

STARTING POINTS FOR BETTER DATA MODELING

The following four requirements should be the starting points for data modeling. These goals are essential to a reasonable process of software development. Despite the criticism, these basic requirements are often acknowledged as essentials of any software development process:

- Integrated systems are a prerequisite for the survival of a financial institution, to manage complexity and to master interdependencies. Data modeling was invented to integrate systems and important terminology. The goals of this effort are reuse and data integration.
- The separate systems of an enterprise must use consistent terms to provide a consistent processing of data across the boundaries of several systems.
- Integration of old and new systems is necessary for routine systems development. As system integration is the norm in systems development, bottom-up strategies and reengineering of old systems must be supported. Good data modeling practice will provide support for this process.
- Fundamental structures or invariants of a business are the basis for all systems development.

Is Enterprise Data Modeling Really That Bad?

The rebuttals to the arguments will show that most of the problems with data modeling can be fixed by a data modeling process that is oriented toward goals.

Data Modeling Does Not Accommodate Rapid Change. Rebuttal: No attempt should be made to model transitory facts in a data model. Hardwired organization schemes are not subject to data modeling. The core of business activities and business rules is subject, however, to data modeling. A bank account will stay the same for years. Such an object is not subject to rapid change. Data modeling should concentrate on such core entities.

Data Modeling Is Inefficient for Financial Instruments. Rebuttal: There are data models for financial instruments that use factorization to describe them. A new instrument is a combination of known elements — a pattern of thinking that is well known from linear or polynomial functions or from industrial part list problems. No developer will try to model each new function or product; instead, it is sufficient to find the set of parameters that fully describe the function. This decomposition is often called a "high level of abstraction." Some argue that it is too high to understand. This depends on the granularity of the basic elements used to describe a product or instrument.

Data Modeling Slows Down Projects. Rebuttal: Data modeling can accelerate projects by acting as a service function. Data Administration groups can report on entities that already exist and about how other groups solved problems in a reference model. A Data administration group that does reviews only after project completion is indeed a slowdown. A Data administration group that helps projects by reporting on current problem-solving efforts is a very important step toward reuse and reusable objects.

Data Modeling Promotes Inflexible Structures. Rebuttal: The basic structure of a bank account is an entity that does not change.

Applications Development Is Slowed by Top-Down Methods. Rebuttal: There is no law that says developers have to work from the top down when practicing data modeling. There should be a framework, called a top-level data model, (e.g., level A or B of an enterprise data model). But no developer will seriously try to go all the way down to level C before starting his or her first project. Instead, most developers recommend a process that creates a top-down frame of about 50 entities on a B level. This frame is then filled from the bottom up by projects with their project data models.

Normal Forms Are Violated. Rebuttal: There is also no law saying there must be a fifth normal form. Models, such as reference models, are often highly normalized. This should not lead to the conclusion that denormalization at the logical level is forbidden in every case. In a level C logical data model, there is no need to stick with the highest normal form available on the market at the time of creation.

Data Modeling Is Inflexible for Future Change. Rebuttal: The problem of having to model all future options in a certain problem can be discussed using the example of financial instruments. The same approach is valid for the abstraction level of several reference data models — it has to fit the needs of many corporations. To adapt a reference model to individual needs, it should not be made more abstract, but it should be simplified to adapt it to the needs of the organization that uses it.

Reference Data Models Are Useless. Rebuttal: Reference data models, also called application platforms, are often mistaken for off-the-shelf, prefabricated data models intended for use in every financial institution. However, they are very useful, and can be tailored to specific organizations.

Alternatives to Data Modeling. The question most of the critics leave unanswered is, what happens if data modeling is not performed? The first alternative is to build island solutions, as in the pioneering days of data processing. These islands are connected via interfaces. The lack of common terminology leads to problems and considerable effort. The negative experiences with these solutions resulted in a data modeling approach to fix those problems.

Another approach is to take business processes as the fixed point of analysis. Processes can be analyzed, and in most cases, elementary processes will be found that will be grouped in entities. This approach is a purely dogmatic, bottom-up, object-oriented approach.

A practical approach is somewhere between bottom-up and top-down. A healthy mixture of a top-down approach, manifested in level A and B enterprise object models and bottom-up methods represented by project-driven level C logical models, should be much better than any pure, dogmatic approach.

ORGANIZATIONAL ASPECTS-DEFINING GOALS

A formal definition of goals and objectives for data modeling may seem bureaucratic. But a short statement defining the goals of data modeling in a company can be helpful for new employees in the Data Administration department or for the more experienced employees as a reminder of their goals.

When looking at an organization's data modeling procedures, quality and technical issues pertaining to the integration of data modeling should be checked in the software development organization. The following list of questions is derived from the criticisms and rebuttals of data modeling and should help organizations identify weak spots in their data modeling practice:

- Is there a written definition of the objectives for the Data Administration group?
- Are the goals consistent with goals stated in this chapter?
- What are the project goals of systems development projects in aspects of data modeling?
- Is there a top-level data model that is publicized and available?

Data Administration as a Service Provider

A Data administration group can be of enormous use to project teams, or it can be an enormous source of frustration. If a Data administration group comes up with some sound solutions or possible designs before a project starts with specification of details, it can be of great assistance. The Data administration department is a service and not a control function. Management may want to ask:

- Is the Data administration a service provider or only a review institution?
- Do they have a written statement that they are a service provider?
- What do the project managers think about the service provided by Data administration?
- What is the ratio between services and control functions in the Data administration department?

Integration of Data Modeling Activities into the Process of Specification

Data modeling should be an integral part of the specification process right from the beginning. This practice will promote reuse and avoid revisiting old arguments. To ensure that data modeling is properly integrated, managers should ask themselves:

- When do the project teams usually meet the Data Administration group — at the start of a project or at the end in the review?
- Are there separated project data models?
- Are there people who do data modeling on a C level for their own sake without a project needing it?
- Is there a mechanism that allows projects to borrow parts of the data model for rework and new developments?
- How do projects integrate their results into the global master enterprise data model? Is there any assistance or tool for integration?
- Who supervises the process of integration?

Separated Levels of a Data Model

Reference models separate clearly between different levels of abstraction in a data model. This is required because different levels are different blueprints for different groups of people (A, B levels for business administration, C for data systems professionals). The Data administration group should ask:

- Do we have level A and B data models that are more than just a pure copy of a reference model?
- What do the users think about data modeling?
- Is there a repository that strictly separates levels of the data model?
- Will users working on projects see at once which level they are currently looking at when dealing with the dictionary?

Quality of Data Model Contents

The quality of the contents of a data model is often intangible. Typical errors can be seen in existing data models — for example, an account number is the number of an account. Definitions such as this often occur when old pools of data have been reengineered in a sloppy manner. Data administration groups should make sure that data models are of high quality, and if not, examine the reasons why. Sometimes projects lack the budget to do a proper job, or employees may lack the motivation.

Rate of Change

A low rate of change, combined with efficient software development and systems integration, is an indicator for high-quality data modeling. If data modeling describes the core of the business rather than listing simple organizational facts, the indicator will show a decrease in change.

Managers of Data administration should ask themselves:

- Does the Data administration monitor the change rate? If so, is it an automatic function?
- Is the change rate seen as a problem? If so, why? What are the reasons for frequent change?
- Is the Data administration department clogged with change requests?

Is the Data Model Up to Date?

A data model should reflect the current state of the business for which it is designed. The terminology must reflect the corporate facts and the meaning of certain terms. The Data administration department should ensure that the data model is fully up to date and carefully monitor the time it takes to process a change request — the shorter the better.

Quality of Upper Model Levels

The upper level (i.e., A and B levels) of a data model should be understood and approved by the users, because they are the people who run the business and generate the profits that pay for Data administration. Data administration should make every effort to find out what users think about modeling efforts. It is also wise for Data administration to find out how project teams perceive the quality of the data model.

Data Types as Entities

Data administration should know whether:

- There are data types that are being modeled as entities (e.g., records that have no natural key, but a key that consists of all attributes).
- There are enumeration types coded as attributes that occur in several entities.

DATA ADMINISTRATION: QUALITY ASSURANCE AND SELF-CONTROL

Quality cannot be reached simply by defining formal objectives for Quality Assurance. In some cases explicit goals for quality assurance will help lead activities down the right path. This is also true for data modeling activities. In the absence of other goals, some Data Administration departments adhere to normal forms and similar theoretical approaches as indicators of quality — but this is not the essential goal. It is better to use business-driven objectives such as integration, reuse, and modeling of the core business.

Quality Objectives

There should be a documented statement of the Data administration department's quality goals. The goals will be either business driven or theory driven — the order of goals will imply which.

Reuse

Reuse is an explicit goal of many IS organizations and should be measured. The reuse quota is an indicator for the quality of data modeling activities.

Typical reuse quotas from projects are about 50 percent. Some are less and some are more, depending on the project and previous activities. Projects retrieve information about known entities from a variety of sources. For example, information can be retrieved from a host-based repository only (an adequate method) or from discussions with the Data administration group during the design process (a better method) as well as from a repository.

Data Integration at the Physical Level

Physical data integration across several applications is an indicator for good data modeling practice. Another good sign is the presence of logical objects that are implemented over and over again.

Reference models are not off-the-shelf production data models. They have to be fitted to fulfill the individual needs of the organization using them. They should best be separated physically or logically from the production data model.

The Data administration group may want to analyze its data integration attempts by posing the following questions:

- Is there a physical border between logical, physical, and reference data models?
- Is there a clear logical border? Is it possible to see at first glance whether an entity is in production or an entity from a reference model?
- Is the reference model subject to a version concept?

- Is the production model subject to a version concept? If so, is this separated from the versions of the reference model?
- How is the reference model acquired — paper, or files for a Computer-Aided Software Engineering tool?

Level of Abstraction

Reference models often have a level of abstraction that is too high for the needs of a single company. The other case, a production model with a higher level of abstraction, should occur only as a rare exception. In most cases, it is useless to raise the production data model to an even higher level of abstraction than a reference model. If there are examples of production models having a higher level of abstraction than reference models in an organization, the reasoning for this should be investigated thoroughly.

Transforming the Logical to a Physical Data Model

A one-to-one implementation of a logical data model can be successful, but in many cases it leads to slow implementations. The transformation process from logical to physical data models requires a great deal of knowledge and experience. It is not economical, and also not very probable, that every analyst has the know-how required for this delicate task. Before attempting this task, Data administration should find out the following:

- Do projects teams document their decisions? Can those decisions be retrieved by Data administration or other projects?
- Are there reviews of the physical data model? If so, who does them?
- Is there a set of design rules somewhere in the company? If not, is there capable help for documenting them?

Dialogs and Data Modeling

The acceptance of data modeling — especially of physical data modeling — will rise when data models and check routines are directly coupled. Automation is crucial for the development of large, consistent systems. Before automation is undertaken, the Data administration group should ask:

- Is there an automatic link between the data model or another repository, screen elements, and their captions?
- Is there an automatic reference between screen elements, check routines, and data type definitions?
- Are screen element tables in specifications generated automatically?

Database Access Layers

Database access layers for logical views on a physical model should be generated automatically from relation descriptions. Many companies use either no access layers at all or code frames for access layers. The generation of access layers is not possible without a rigid data modeling practice. The effort saved by not performing access layer programming is a very tangible effect of data modeling. It should be determined whether the software development department uses access layers, and if so, whether they are generated or at least standardized.

Data Types

Most COBOL or PL/I shops do not have a concept of data types. This leads to enumeration types being redundantly described in textual attribute descriptions, structures being described as entities, and other design flaws. It is helpful if an organization has a data type concept that is supported by code-generation facilities and a repository that allows a data type concept.

Data Dictionary Product Properties

It is important for data dictionary software to support requirements concerning the separation of model layers, version concepts, and data types. It is a good sign if the software developers and project teams like the look and feel of the data dictionary. A data dictionary should:

- Support data types such as enumeration types, records, range types, and a code generation facility.
- Be adaptable to changes in its metamodel. Improvement of the software development process can be slowed or made impossible by an inflexible dictionary.
- Have a version concept.
- Support integration of project data models. This is best done using check tools that support the Data administration group.
- Support separation of levels, documentation of transformations between levels, and separated production and reference models.

CONCLUSION

A broad range of criticism has been brought against data modeling. This article focused on the criticism to derive several lists of critical questions concerning organizational, technical, and quality success factors for a good data modeling practice. These questions were used to check the data modeling practice of a large financial institution. Exploring the issues covered and considering the questions posed should help Data Administration groups avoid some of the problems common to data modeling.

Chapter 12

Evaluation of Four Languages for Specifying Conceptual Database Designs

James Larson and Carol Larson

DATABASE ADMINISTRATORS (DBAS) NEED TO KNOW HOW TO DESCRIBE REAL-WORLD OBJECTS AND THEIR RELATIONSHIPS IN A FORM THAT IS BOTH PRACTICAL AND MEANINGFUL TO THE DATABASE USER AND STILL BE EFFICIENTLY USABLE BY THE DATABASE MANAGEMENT SYSTEM. Defining a conceptual schema is important because it describes the objects in a database at an abstract level, which hides many of the low-level storage details. This chapter describes four conceptual database design languages from several perspectives and in sufficient detail so that a DBA, who must know the strengths and weaknesses of each design language, can use them to construct a conceptual schema that meets the needs of the database user.

DESIGN LANGUAGES AND CONCEPTUAL SCHEMAS

The conceptual schema describes data stored in a database to reflect a collection of real-world objects and relationships. It defines the names of objects in a database and the relationships in which the objects may participate. The conceptual schema also defines the constraints on the values of objects. These constraints are called business rules. Data in the database must obey all specified business rules. In order to define a conceptual schema, a database administrator may interview perspective users, examine existing and proposed reports and data screens, and consider existing and proposed applications to identify the contents of a conceptual schema. A DBA describes the real-world objects, their relationships, and business rules using a special language called a conceptual database design language.

A conceptual database design language (CDDL) is a high-level language used by a DBA to describe a conceptual schema. In this chapter, the following four design languages will be evaluated:

- **English, or other natural languages,** are textual languages that the DBA and intended database users have in common. An example conceptual schema described in English is presented in Exhibit 1.
- **Entity-relationship diagrams** are a collection of graphical notations for describing conceptual schemas. First proposed by Peter Chen in 1976, they have become popular with many DBAs. A variation, called IDEF1X, was standardized by the military and is especially popular with defense contractors. Exhibit 2 illustrates entity-relationship diagrams for the conceptual schema shown in Exhibit 1.
- **SQL** is a formal computer language for creating and accessing a relational database. Exhibit 3 presents the SQL CREATE TABLE statements used to create a database that corresponds to the conceptual schema in Exhibits 1 and 2.
- **Relational diagrams** are a graphical notation that represents the objects and relationships expressed by SQL CREATE TABLE statements. Relational diagrams frequently appear in GUIs used by DBAs to define conceptual schemas for a relational database. Exhibit 4 shows the graphical notation describing the conceptual schema presented in Exhibits 1 through 3.

There are many other CDDLs, including the Universal Model Language (UML) and Bachman diagrams. However, the four languages identified above are the most popular with users of relational database management systems.

If the DBA designs the conceptual schema using notation other than SQL, it is necessary to convert the objects and relationships of the conceptual schema into the notation and format required by a relational DBMS. In most cases, the same software that DBAs use to create a conceptual schema can also be used to convert the schema into a relational database design.

The conceptual schemas shown in Exhibits 1 through 4 are designed to illustrate various features of the four design languages. However, the schemas do not contain all of the objects, relationships, and business rules of a real conceptual schema. Exhibits 1 to 4 illustrate that the same conceptual schema can be defined using any of the four popular CDDLs. Exhibit 5 presents the equivalent concepts and terminology used in entity-relationship diagrams and relational diagrams.

This evaluation will first present examples of how each of the four languages represent frequently occurring logical data structure concepts. In effect, these examples are mini-tutorials showing how to use each of the

Exhibit 12-1. Conceptual database design using english rules.

Every department has a name and budget.
No two departments have the same name.

Every employee has an employee identification, employee name, address, and
  social security number.
No two employees may have the same employee identification.
No two employees may have the same social security number.
Every employee must work in exactly one department.
Several employees may work in the same department.

Every project has a name, start date, and end date.
No two projects may have the same name.

Zero, one, or more employees may be assigned to a project.
An employee must be assigned to zero, one, or more projects.
An employee assigned to a project has a role.

Every dependent has a name and birthdate.
For a given employee, no two dependents may have the same name.
Some employees may have a policy that covers zero, one, or more dependents.
Each dependent must be covered by a policy of the employee for which they are
  listed as a dependent.

Every manager is also an employee.
Each manager has a bonus.

---

four CDDLs. Following the examples, the four languages will be evaluated
using several criteria.

EXAMPLE SCHEMAS USING FOUR DESIGN LANGUAGES

Entity Sets and Attributes

Basic to every conceptual database design language are the concepts of
entity and entity set. An entity is a representation of a real-world person,
event, or concept. For example, in Exhibits 1 through 4, the database may
contain Employee entities Jones, Smith, and Lewis, and the Department
entities Accounting and Sales. Each entity may take on a value for each of
its attributes. An attribute is a characteristic of an entity. An Employee
entity may have values <13, Jones, Seattle, 999-99-9999> for attributes
EmpId, EmpName, Address, and SocialSecurityNumber, respectively.

In order to organize the hundreds or thousands of entities in a database,
entities with the same attributes are grouped together as entity sets. An
entity set is a collection of homogeneous entities with the same attributes.

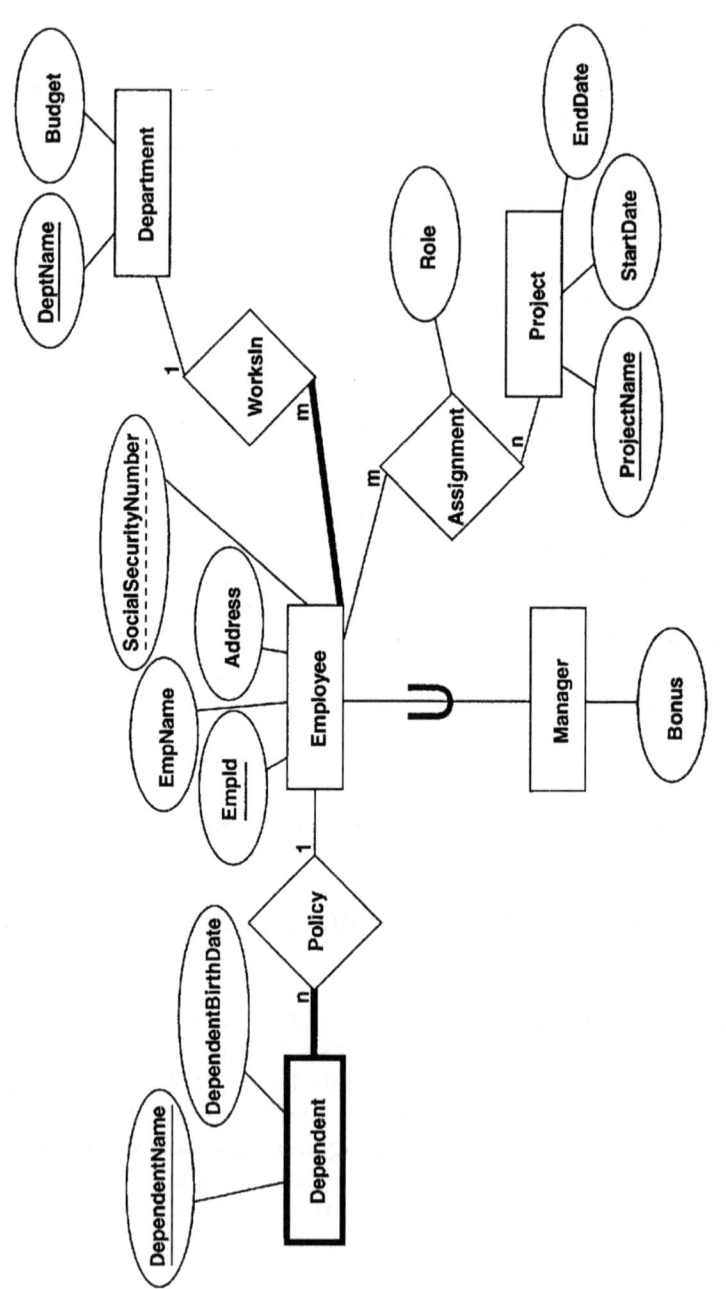

Exhibit 12-2. Conceptual database design using entity-relationship diagrams.

Exhibit 12-3. Conceptual database design using SQL syntax.

```
CREATE TABLE Department
    (DeptName                                    INTEGER,
    Budget                                       INTEGER,
    PRIMARY KEY (DeptName))

CREATE TABLE Employee
    (EmpId                                       INTEGER,
    EmpName                                      CHAR(20),
    Address                                      CHAR(40),
    SocialSecurityNumber                         INTEGER,
    DeptName                                     INTEGER,
    FOREIGN KEY (DeptName) REFERENCES Depart-
    ment,
    PRIMARY KEY (EmpId),
    UNIQUE (SocialSecurityNumber))

CREATE TABLE Project
    (ProjectName                                 CHAR(20),
    StartDate                                    DATE,
    EndDate                                      DATE,
    PRIMARY KEY (ProjectName))

CREATE TABLE Assignment
    (EmpId                                       INTEGER,
    ProjectName                                  CHAR(20),
    Role                                         CHAR(20),
    PRIMARY KEY (EmpId, ProjectName),
    FOREIGN KEY (EmpId) REFERENCES Employee,
    FOREIGN KEY (ProjectName) REFERENCES Project)

CREATE TABLE Dependent
    (EmpId                                       CHAR (20),
    DependentName                                CHAR (20),
    DependentBirthDate                           DATE,
    PRIMARY KEY (DependentName, EmpId),
    FOREIGN KEY (EmpId) REFERENCES Employee)

CREATE TABLE Manager
    (EmpId                                       INTEGER,
    Bonus                                        INTEGER,
    PRIMARY KEY (EmpId),
    FOREIGN KEY (EmpId) REFERENCES Employee)
```

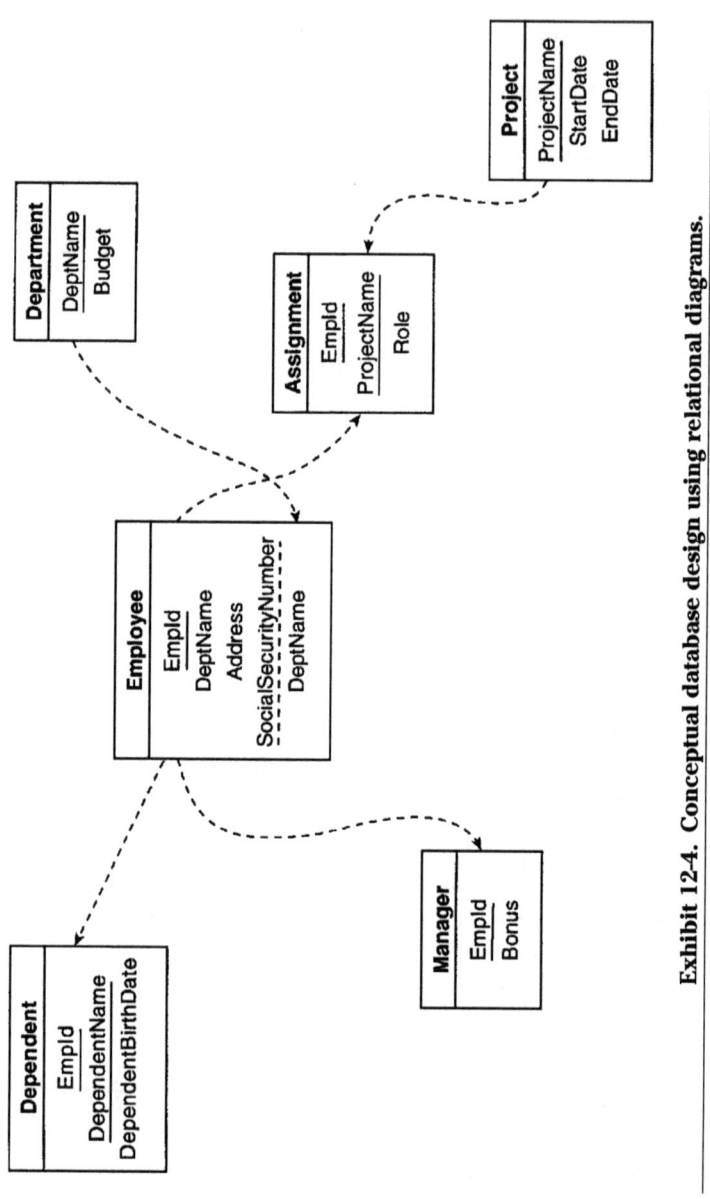

Exhibit 12-4. Conceptual database design using relational diagrams.

Exhibit 12-5. Equivalent Concepts and terminology between entity-relationship and relational diagrams.

Entity-Relationship Concepts	Relational Concepts
Entity set	Table
Entity	Row of a table
Attribute	Column of a table
Unique identifier	Primary key, candidate key
One-to-many relationship	Foreign key constraint
Many-to-many relationship	Two foreign keys referencing a linking table
Partial participation	No NOT NULL declaration in a relationship for a foreign key
Total participation	NOT NULL declaration in a relationship for a foreign key
Weak entity	Primary key is a composite key containing the primary key of another table
Class hierarchy	Two tables have the same primary key, one of which is the foreign key of the contained table

In the example above, the entities Jones, Smith, and Lewis are members of the Employee entity set, while entities Accounting and Sales are members of the Department entity set.

Exhibit 6 shows the Employee entity set described using each of the four design languages. The English text describes the Employee entity set as having four attributes: Employee Identification, Employee Name, Address, and Social Security Number. The entity-relationship diagram represents the entity set as a rectangle labeled Employee with its attributes shown as ovals labeled EmpId, EmpName, Address, and SocialSecurityNumber. Attribute ovals are connected to the entity that they describe. The SQL CREATE TABLE statement describes the same entity set as a table consisting of four columns. The relational diagrams illustrate the Employee table by showing a box with table name Employee at the top and column headings EmpId, EmpName, Address, and SocialSecurityNumber at the bottom of the box.

Key Constraint

Exhibit 7 extends the entity set presented in Exhibit 6 to include the concept of a key constraint, which is used to enforce uniqueness among entities in an entity set. A key constraint specifies that no two entities in an entity set can have the same value for the key attribute. (A key is a subset of the attributes in the entity set.) In English, a constraint is specified by a sentence in the form of "No two <entities> may have the same value for <attribute>" or "<attribute> uniquely identifies <entity>." With entity-relationship diagrams, the attribute name of the unique identifier is underlined. In SQL, the clause PRIMARY KEY <attribute> identifies the unique

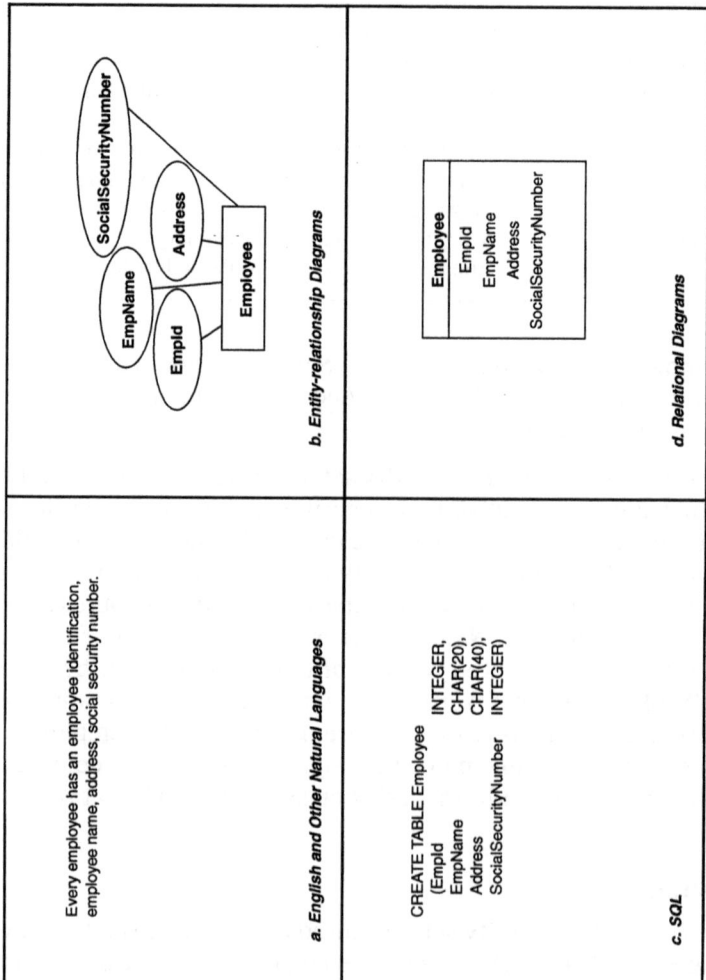

Every employee has an employee identification, employee name, address, social security number.

a. English and Other Natural Languages

```
CREATE TABLE Employee
    (EmpId                 INTEGER,
    EmpName               CHAR(20),
    Address               CHAR(40),
    SocialSecurityNumber  INTEGER)
```

c. SQL

b. Entity-relationship Diagrams

Employee
- EmpId
- EmpName
- Address
- SocialSecurityNumber

d. Relational Diagrams

Exhibit 12-6. Entity sets and attributes.

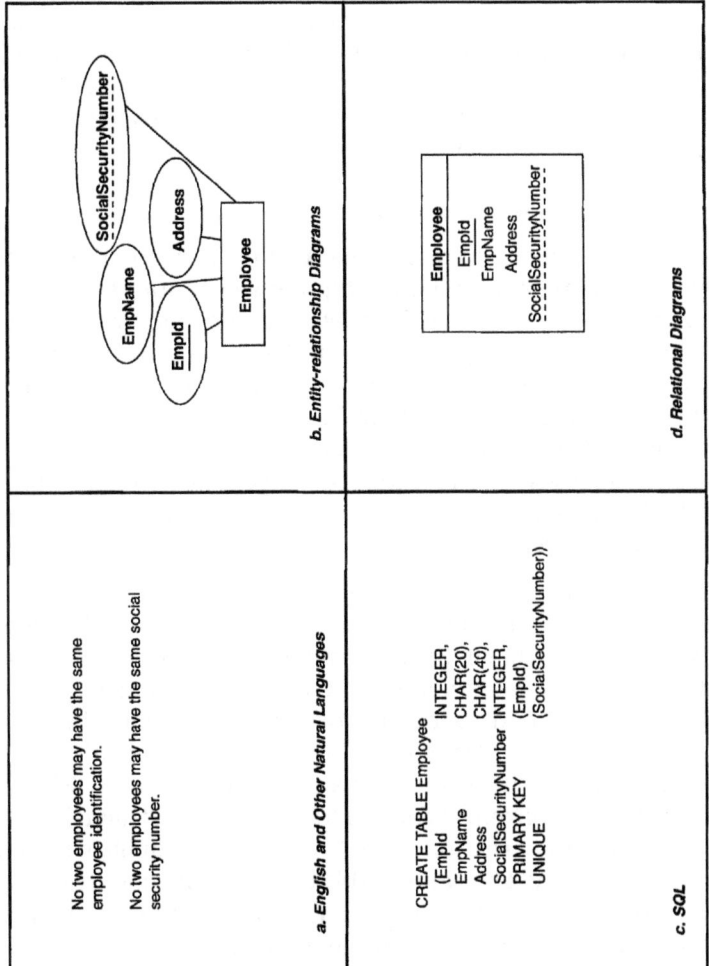

a. English and Other Natural Languages

No two employees may have the same employee identification.

No two employees may have the same social security number.

b. Entity-relationship Diagrams

c. SQL

```
CREATE TABLE Employee
    (EmpId               INTEGER,
    EmpName              CHAR(20),
    Address              CHAR(40),
    SocialSecurityNumber INTEGER,
    PRIMARY KEY          (EmpId)
    UNIQUE               (SocialSecurityNumber))
```

d. Relational Diagrams

Exhibit 12-7. Key contraints.

identifier. With relational diagrams, the name of the unique identifier is underlined.

In the example shown in Exhibit 6, there are two key constraints — Employee Identifier and Social Security Number. That means there are two English sentences: one for employee and one for social security number. In the entity-relationship diagrams, multiple key constraints are illustrated by underlining each key attribute by a different type of line. Relational DBMSs require exactly one primary key. The remaining unique identifiers are called candidate keys. Each candidate key is declared with the UNIQUE clause in SQL. With the relational diagrams, each unique identifier is under-lined with a different type of line, so they are not confused with other unique identifiers or the primary key.

One-to-Many Relationships

Exhibit 8 illustrates a one-to-many relationship between Department and Employee. A one-to-many relationship between entity sets A and B implies that zero or one A entity can be related to zero, one, or more B enti-ties. In Exhibit 8, a single Department can be related to one or more Employee entities. Each entity participates in, at most, one relationship. One-to-many relationships are important because they describe how enti-ties may relate to other entities. For example, a database containing Department and Employee entities alone fails to capture which employee works for which department. One-to-many relationships define these important types of associations.

With Exhibit 8, the English design language shows that one-to-many rela-tionships are expressed with sentences, such as "Every employee may work in zero or one department. Several employees may work in the same department." With entity-relationship diagrams, a one-to-many relation-ship is denoted as a diamond connecting two entity sets, with the "1" and "m" indicating the "one" and "many" entities in the relationship, respec-tively. The relationship name is shown inside of a diamond. In SQL nota-tion, a one-to-many relationship is called a foreign key constraint. The DBA specifies the primary key of the "one" (or A) entity as a column in the table of the "many" (or B) entity. The value of this extra column in the Employee table identifies the Department entity for which the Employee works. A special clause, called a foreign key, describes a business rule that implies the only values of the DeptName column in the Employee table may be val-ues in the DeptName column of the Department table. The relational dia-gram shows that the one-to-many relationship is represented by a dotted line from the primary key of the table representing the entity set A to the foreign key in the table representing entity set B. Thus, in this example, a dotted line goes from the DeptName column of the Department table to the DeptName column of the Employee table.

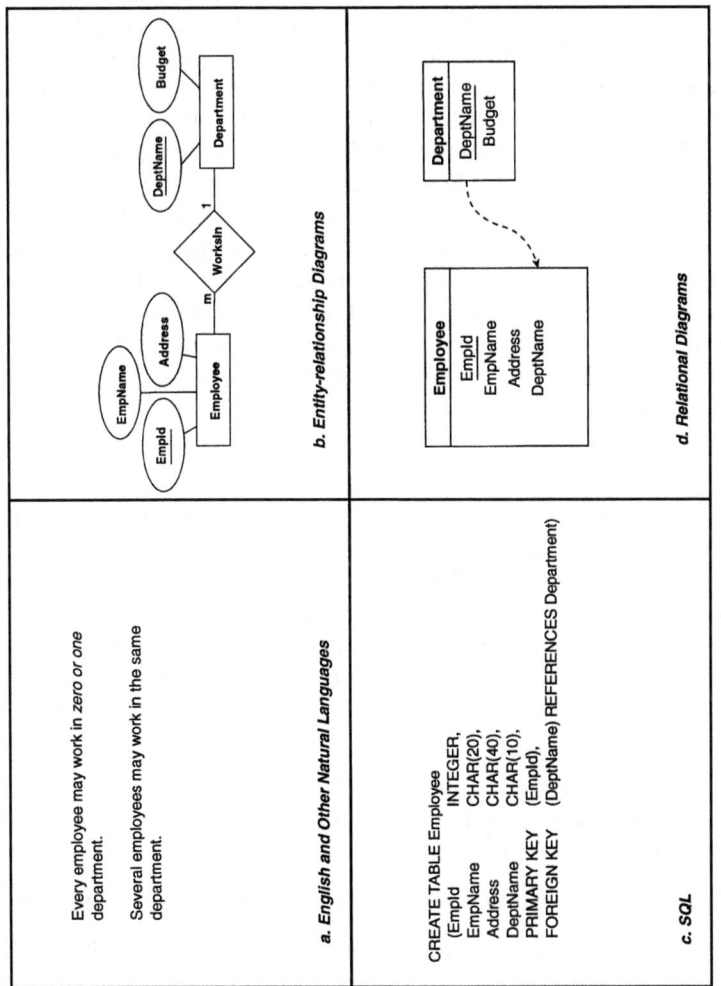

Every employee may work in *zero or one* department.

Several employees may work in the same department.

a. English and Other Natural Languages

```
CREATE TABLE Employee
  (EmpId        INTEGER,
   EmpName      CHAR(20),
   Address      CHAR(40),
   DeptName     CHAR(10),
   PRIMARY KEY  (EmpId),
   FOREIGN KEY  (DeptName) REFERENCES Department)
```

c. SQL

b. Entity-relationship Diagrams

d. Relational Diagrams

Exhibit 12-8. One-to-many relationship with partial participation.

If the entities on the B side of the relationship exist without participating in a relationship, then entity set B is said to have partial participation in the relationship. Exhibit 9 shows a variation in a one-to-many relationship where one of the B entities is required to participate in the relationship. This constraint often is referred to as total participation.

Exhibit 10 summarizes the English wording for partial and total participation of entities for both sides of a one-to-many relationship in the English CDDL. Total participation is denoted in entity-relationship diagrams with a thick line connecting the rectangle representing the entity — which must participate in the relationship — and the relationship diamond. In SQL, total participation is denoted by declaring the foreign key to be "NOT NULL." In Exhibit 9, the DeptName of the Employee is declared NOT NULL. This requires the Employee table to contain a value for the primary key of some Department record. This enforces the total constraint by requiring that each Employee works in some Department. As a comparison, Exhibit 9 shows that the DeptName of Employee has not been declared NOT NULL. This means that DeptName may be null, which in turn implies that the Employee does not work in any department. In relational diagrams, the words "NOT NULL" have been added near the relationship arrow to indicate total participation.

Many-to-Many Relationships

Exhibit 11 illustrates a many-to-many relationship between two entity sets. A many-to-many relationship implies that any number of entities from each of two entity sets can participate in a single relationship. Many-to-many relationships occur frequently in the real world. For example, pairs of entity sets — employees and projects, students and classes, and producers and suppliers — often are related by many-to-many relationships. There are two approaches for dealing with many-to-many relationships in the conceptual schema:

- explicit representation, as presented in entity-relationship diagrams
- implicit representation by two one-to-many relationships, as shown in SQL notation and relational diagrams

Using English, a DBA can describe a many-to-many relationship either:

- directly, by specifying the participation of each entity set within the relationship; or example, one or more employees may be assigned to one or more projects
- indirectly, by specifying two one-to-many relationships involving an induced entity set; for example, each employee is related to an Assignment, and each project is related to an Assignment

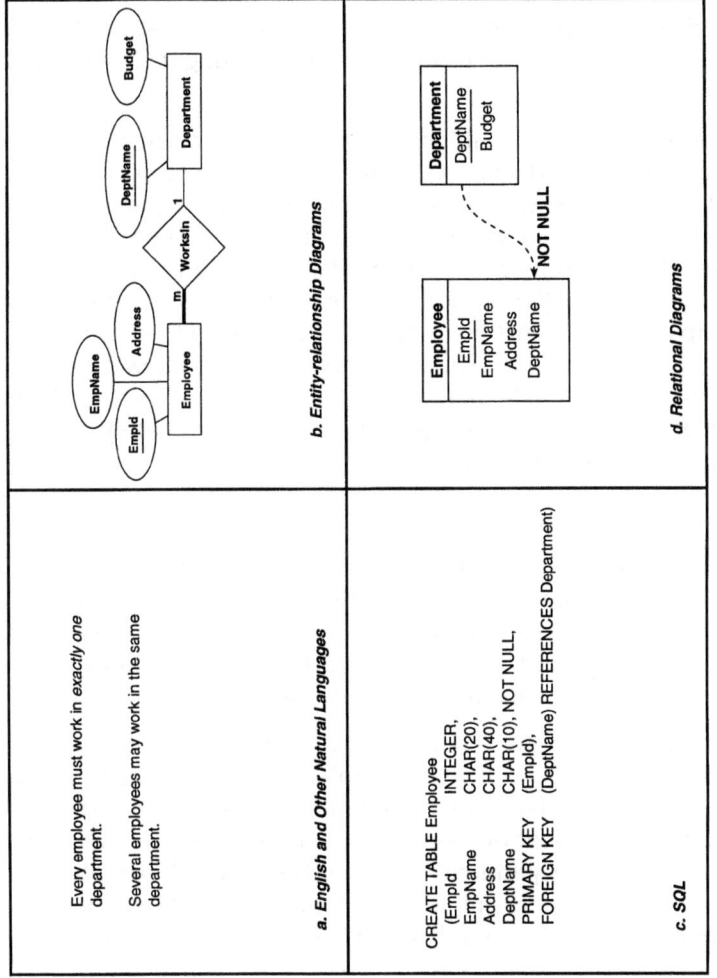

Every employee must work in *exactly one* department.

Several employees may work in the same department.

a. English and Other Natural Languages

```
CREATE TABLE Employee
   (Empld        INTEGER,
    EmpName      CHAR(20),
    Address      CHAR(40),
    DeptName     CHAR(10), NOT NULL,
    PRIMARY KEY  (Empld),
    FOREIGN KEY  (DeptName) REFERENCES Department)
```

c. SQL

b. Entity-relationship Diagrams

d. Relational Diagrams

Exhibit 12-9. One-to-many relationship with total participation.

EXHIBIT 12-10.   English wording for partial and total participation.

	One-side (A)	Many-side (B)
Partial	Zero or one	Zero or more
Total	Exactly one	One or more

In entity-relationship diagrams, an "m" or "n" is written on the sides of the diamond, which represents the many-to-many relationship. SQL always uses the indirect approach by using an induced linking table with two foreign keys.

As in one-to-many relationships, entity participation in many-to-many relationships can be partial or total. With English, the same words shown in Exhibit 10 can be used to specify partial or total participation in a many-to-many relationship. In entity-relationship diagrams, a thick line indicates total participation of entities with a relationship. Exhibit 12 presents a particular problem with SQL notation for a many-to-many relationship with total participation. SQL must use a TRIGGER command to specify the total participation constraint. Unfortunately, not all relational DBMSs support TRIGGER commands. Application developers who use these DBMSs must write applications to enforce total participation. Unfortunately, this makes applications more complex and difficult to write.

Weak Entities

Exhibit 13 presents a weak entity. A weak entity is an entity whose key values are unique among the entities participating within a single relationship, but not necessarily unique within the entire entity set. Weak entities occur when a compound attribute (an attribute containing multiple attributes) is replaced by an entity set and a relationship.

Two compound attributes — Dependent and EmpBirthDate — are illustrated in Exhibit 14. DBAs will seldom replace EmpBirthDate by an entity set related to Employee because BirthMonth, BirthDay, and BirthYear are not functionally dependent on one another. However, there is a functional dependency between DependentName and DependentBirthDate: given a Dependent's name, there is only one possible value for DependentBirthDate. Therefore, a DBA frequently can replace this compound attribute with a weak entity that participates in a total one-to-many relationship to Employee. (Note the similarity of this process to the process of normalization in relational database design.)

With the English CDDL in Exhibit 13, the DBA describes a weak entity that is related to another entity by a one-to-many dependent relationship. In the entity-relationship diagram, a thick line and a thick-lined rectangle denote the weak entity of the relationship. With SQL and relational diagrams, the

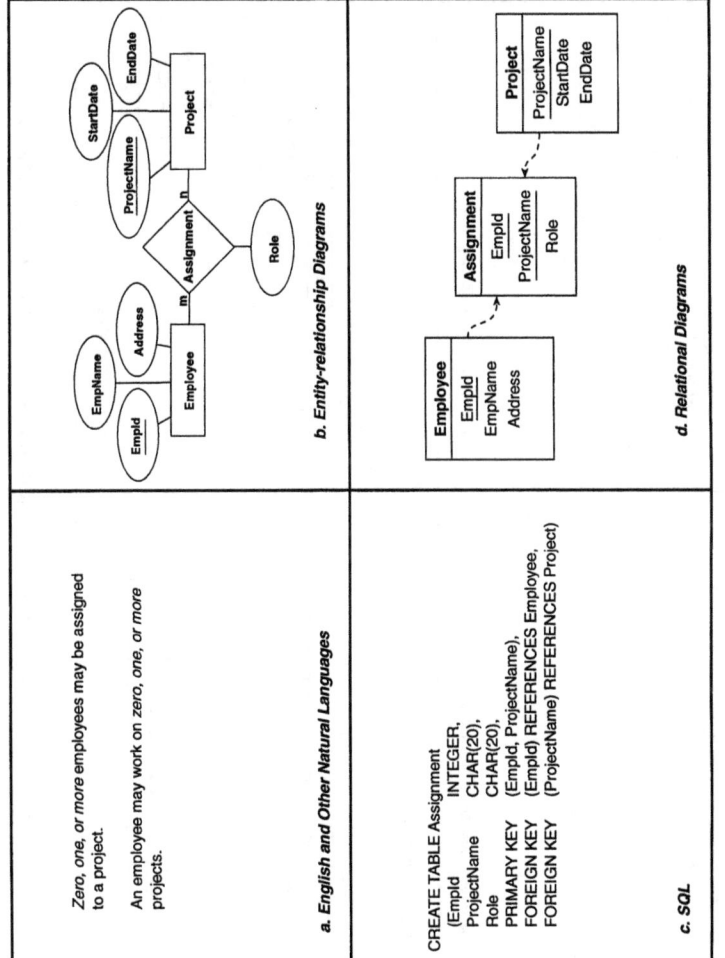

Exhibit 12-11. Many-to-many relationship with partial participation.

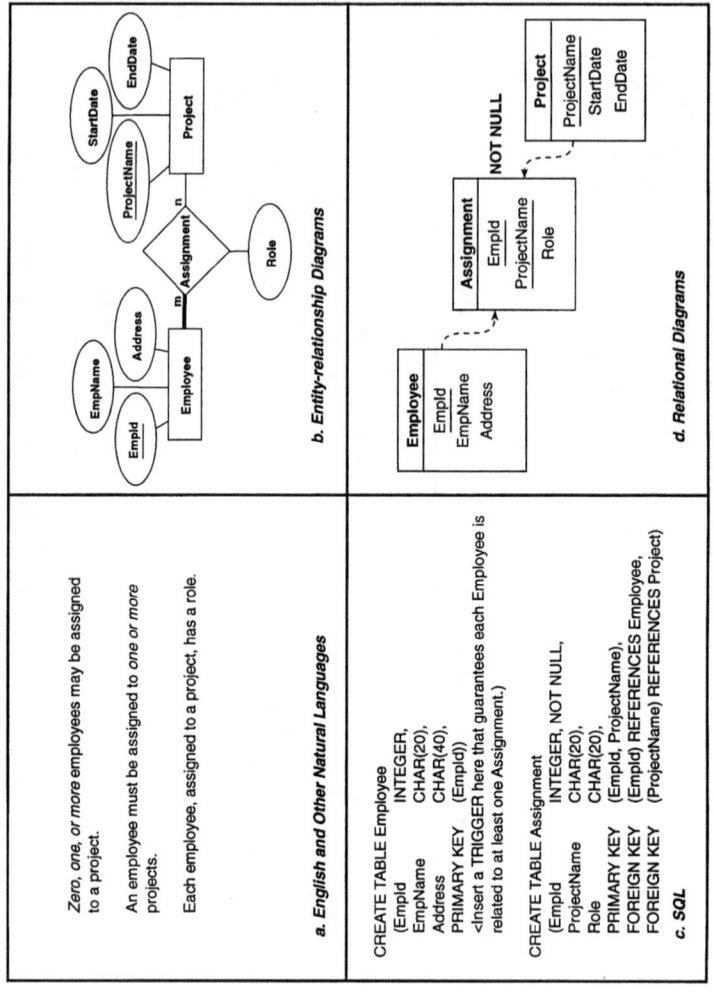

Exhibit 12-12. Many-to-many relationship with total participation.

Zero, one, or more employees may be assigned to a project.

An employee must be assigned to *one or more* projects.

Each employee, assigned to a project, has a role.

a. English and Other Natural Languages

```
CREATE TABLE Employee
  (EmpId        INTEGER,
   EmpName      CHAR(20),
   Address      CHAR(40),
   PRIMARY KEY  (EmpId))
<Insert a TRIGGER here that guarantees each Employee is
related to at least one Assignment.)

CREATE TABLE Assignment
  (EmpId        INTEGER, NOT NULL,
   ProjectName  CHAR(20),
   Role         CHAR(20),
   PRIMARY KEY  (EmpId, ProjectName),
   FOREIGN KEY  (EmpId) REFERENCES Employee,
   FOREIGN KEY  (ProjectName) REFERENCES Project)
```

c. SQL

b. Entity-relationship Diagrams

d. Relational Diagrams

Evaluation of Four Languages for Specifying Conceptual Database Designs

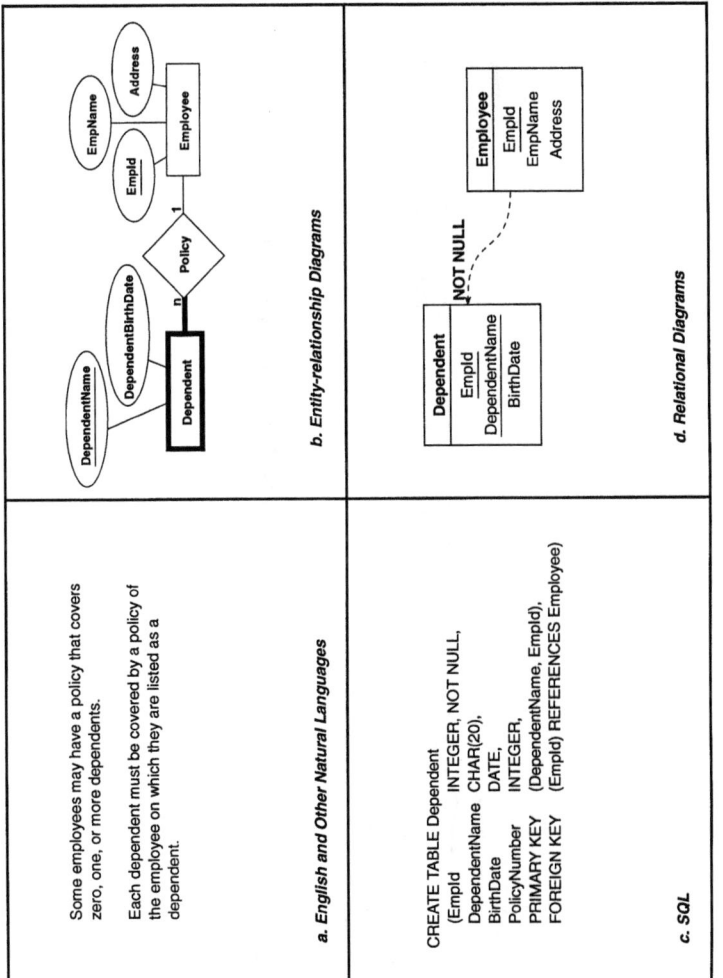

Exhibit 12-13. Weak entities.

187

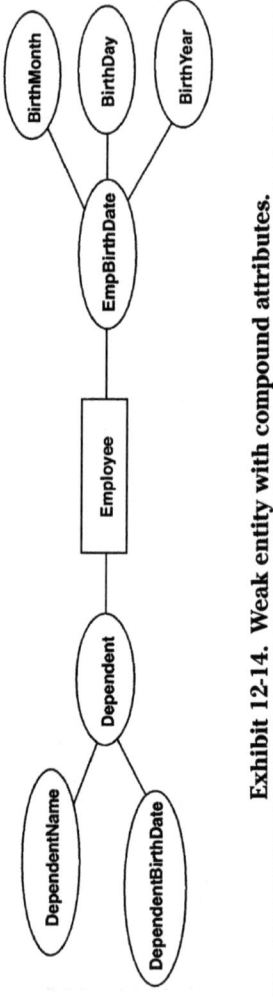

Exhibit 12-14. Weak entity with compound attributes.

primary key of the table corresponding to the weak entity is a combination of the key from the weak entity and the primary key from the related entity. The primary key from the related entity is also a foreign key.

Class Hierarchies

Exhibit 15 illustrates class hierarchy. A class hierarchy occurs when every entity in an entity set is also contained within another entity set. For example, every Manager is also an Employee. In this example, the Manager entity has an extra attribute, Bonus, that regular employees do not possess. Class hierarchies have become popular because of their use in object-oriented modeling, so DBAs familiar with object-oriented modeling concepts have begun to use entity set hierarchies in entity-relationship diagrams. Class hierarchies are a convenient way to represent:

- containment (every manager is also an employee)
- common attributes (every attribute of Employee is also an attribute of Manager; in object-oriented modeling terminology, this is called inheritance)

In Exhibit 15, the terms "is a" or "is also a" indicate containment in the English CDDL. The terms "have" or "also have" indicate additional attributes of the contained entity set. Entity-relationship diagrams use a "contains" symbol " ." A line with a " " denotes a hierarchical relationship diagram with the " " opening toward the containing entity. In SQL and relational diagrams, two tables of a hierarchy share a common primary key, which is also a foreign key in the "contained" table.

Exhibit 15 also shows one way to represent class hierarchies using relational diagrams. The contained entity set (Manager) has a foreign key to the containing entity set (Employee) and additional attributes (Bonus) not associated with the containing entity set. In order to retrieve all attributes associated with Manager, the Manager table must be joined with the Employee table.

EVALUATION OF FOUR DESIGN LANGUAGES FOR SPECIFYING CONCEPTUAL DATABASE DESIGNS

Exhibit 16 summarizes various criteria used to evaluate conceptual database design languages.

Sufficiency

Sufficiency implies that the entire conceptual schema can be described using a design language. In other words, the CDDL has all of the constructs needed to completely and adequately describe the conceptual schema.

All of the CDDLs contain language to describe entity sets and their attributes, keys, foreign keys, weak entities, and class hierarchies. English

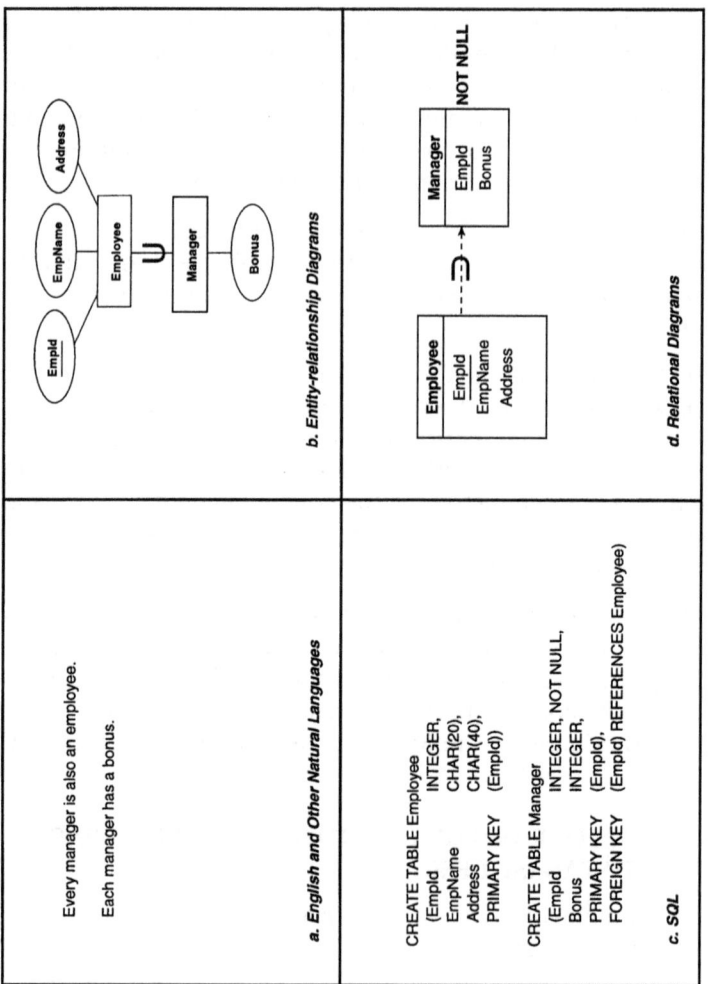

Every manager is also an employee.

Each manager has a bonus.

a. English and Other Natural Languages

CREATE TABLE Employee
(EmpId   INTEGER,
EmpName   CHAR(20),
Address   CHAR(40),
PRIMARY KEY   (EmpId))

CREATE TABLE Manager
(EmpId   INTEGER, NOT NULL,
Bonus   INTEGER,
PRIMARY KEY   (EmpId),
FOREIGN KEY   (EmpId) REFERENCES Employee)

c. SQL

b. Entity-relationship Diagrams

d. Relational Diagrams

Exhibit 12-15. Class hierarchies.

Exhibit 12-16. Summary of evaluation criteria for four conceptual database design languages.

Criteria	Conceptual Database Design Language			
	English	Entity-Relationship Diagrams	SQL	Relational Diagrams
Sufficiency	High	Medium	Medium	Low
Necessity	Low	Medium	High	High
Understandability and usability	Low	High	Medium	High
Consistency	Low	Medium	High	High
Software support	Low	Medium	High	Medium

rates high because it can be used to describe many constraints that cannot be described with the other conceptual database design languages. While entity-relationship diagrams cannot represent every possible rule, they can be used to specify many popular business rules. Entity-relationship diagrams are ranked medium. The SQL CREATE command must be augmented with TRIGGER commands to completely specify total participation of entity set within a many-to-many relationship. TRIGGER commands also enable DBAs to specify other business rules for which there is no corresponding notation in the entity-relationship and relational diagrams. Thus, SQL is ranked as medium. Relational diagrams do not have notation for TRIGGER commands, so they are given a low ranking.

Necessity

Necessity is defined to mean that each clause or concept of the design language is required to describe some conceptual schema.

Much of the syntax of English — and other natural languages — is not required to describe a conceptual schema. Therefore, it receives a low rating. Some DBAs feel that the entity-relationship diagrams contain too many concepts. Specifically, many-to-many relationships involving entity sets A and B can be replaced with a new, linking entity set related to each of A and B. Some DBAs argue that a one-to-many relationship set is itself unnecessary because it can be replaced by a foreign key constraint, as it is in SQL and relational diagrams. Likewise, the special hierarchical containment relationship can be replaced with a foreign key constraint. For this reason, entity-relationship diagrams are rated as medium. SQL and relational diagrams are rated high because of the small number of constructs, tables, keys, and foreign keys necessary to describe a realistic conceptual schema. None of these constructs can be removed from the conceptual database design language and still completely specify a conceptual schema.

UNDERSTANDABILITY AND USABILITY

Understandability and usability mean that the conceptual schema is easy to learn, easy to understand, and easy to specify.

At first glance, English — or some other natural language — would appear to be easy because no training is necessary to use it. However, natural language sentences frequently can be vague and imprecise. Because of the ambiguity and misunderstandings inherent in English and other natural languages, English has a low rating. The understandability of SQL is rated as medium because users must carefully study the SQL descriptions in order to visualize the conceptual model it describes. Entity-relationship diagrams and relational diagrams receive a high rating because it is possible to comprehend the significant aspects of a conceptual schema by quickly examining the diagrams. Once again, the saying, "a picture" — or more appropriately in this context, a diagram — "is worth a thousand words," holds true. Some DBAs rate the understandability of entity-relationship diagrams above relational diagrams because the relationships reflect more of the diverse structures of the conceptual schema than does the table-orientation of relational diagrams. On the other hand, the structure of relational diagrams is familiar to relational DBMS users who may become confused when dealing with the relationships of the entity-relationship CDDL.

Consistency

Consistency means that two DBAs will use the same constructs to describe similar concepts. English receives a low rating because there may be nearly an infinite number of ways to describe each and every business rule. Entity-relationship diagrams are rated as medium because it is possible to describe many-to-many relationships as two one-to-many relationships. It is also possible to describe an attribute of an entity set A as a weak entity set that is related to A. SQL and relational diagrams are the most consistent because they describe just a single type of thing — a table. Therefore, SQL and relational diagrams receive a high rating.

Note that there might be more than one way to represent a collection of attributes as tables. For example, a single table may contain all of the attributes or multiple tables each may contain some of the attributes. DBAs frequently use the process of normalization to break apart a table that represents multiple entity sets and structure the attributes into multiple tables. Normalization occurs regardless of which CDDL is used. The concept of normalization is orthogonal to the concept of consistency discussed here. DBAs should perform normalization, regardless of which CDDL is used.

Software Support

Software support implies that software exists to enable DBAs to enter a conceptual schema into the DBMS. Check the conceptual schema for missing or redundant expressions, and automatically create a conceptual schema for a relational DBMS.

While text editors exist for entering text describing a conceptual schema using English or some other natural language, it is not possible for a text editor to check for missing or redundant descriptions. Nor is it possible to automatically generate a relational conceptual schema from a conceptual schema expressed in English. Therefore, English is rated low. SQL editors and compilers enable DBAs to enter and check the completeness and redundancy of conceptual schemas and to create a relational schema for use by a relational DBMS. SQL receives a high rating. Graphic editors enable DBAs to draw entity-relationship diagrams and relational diagrams. Some specialized graphic editors may even be able to check for missing or redundant objects. Because these editors are not available for all relational DBMSs, entity-relationship and relational diagrams are given a medium rating.

Many vendors of relational DBMSs also supply graphical editors to compose entity-relationship and relational diagrams that automatically convert the diagrams into SQL before being processed by a DBMS. These include:

- 4Keeps: A.D.Experts; Ann Arbor, MI; www.adexperts.com
- DataModeler: Iconix Software Engineering, Inc.; Santa Monica, CA; www.iconixsw.com
- EasyCASE, Database Engineer, and EasyEr: Visible Systems Corp.; Bellevue, WA; www.visible.com
- ER/Studio: Embarcadero Technologies, Inc.; San Francisco, CA; www.embarcadero.com
- ERWin: Logic Works Inc.; Princeton, NJ; www.logicworks.com
- SilverRun Professional: SilverRun Technologies, Inc.; Woodcliff Lake, NJ; www.silverrun.com

One more step is necessary to create a working database. The DBA must create a physical schema to describe the data structures and access paths that the DBMS will use to access a database. (When purchasing schema design software, it is important to select product offerings that also enable DBAs to specify the physical schema.)

RECOMMENDATION

Entity-relationship diagrams should be used to define conceptual schemas. These diagrams directly represent many-to-many relationships, weak entities, and class hierarchies. While the relational database equivalent of these constraints can be represented using SQL or relational diagrams, the understanding inherent in these structures is lost when they are converted to their relational counterparts.

It is best to use a tool, such as a graphic editor, to capture entity-relationship diagrams and to generate the equivalent SQL notation. This enables the

DBA to easily update the entity-relationship diagrams and automatically generate the appropriate SQL to keep both the diagrams and the implemented schema synchronized.

If the entity-relationship design language is not suitable for the enterprise, then relational diagrams, followed by SQL, are recommended. English and other natural languages are not recommended because of their inherent vagueness and inconsistency.

Notes

The following sources are recommended.

Bachman, C. The Data Structure Set Model, *Proceedings of the ACM SIGMOD Debate on Data Models: Data Structure Set Versus Relational,* 1974. Edited by R. Rustin. Bachman diagrams were widely used to define schemas for hierarchical DBMSs.

Chen, P. The Entity-relationship Model: Towards a Unified View of Data, in *ACM Transactions on Database Systems,* 1(1), 9–36, 1976. The classic paper on conceptual database design languages that introduced entity-relationship diagrams.

Ramakrishnan, R. *Database Management Systems,* New York: WCB/McGraw-Hill, 1998. Chapter 14 provides an excellent tutorial of the entity-relationship conceptual database design specification language and how to map its constraints to SQL.

For a description of the Universal Modeling Language (UML), see: http://www.pfu.edu.ru/TeleSys/ Calypso/Docs/Uml/html/ot/uml/technical_papers/index.html.

Chapter 13
A Comparison of Three Systems Modeling Methodologies

Michael P. Kushner, Il-Yeol Song, and Kyu-Young Whang

OBJECT MODELING METHODOLOGIES ARE BECOMING INCREASINGLY POPULAR. There are many different methodologies available to model a problem. A question that arises for many analysts is how do these techniques differ. This chapter compares three object methodologies: entity-relationship (ER) modeling, Shlaer and Mellor's Information Modeling, and Rumbaugh's Object Modeling Technique (OMT). Two scenarios are used to illustrate the methodology's syntax and to aid in the analysis of the techniques.

DESCRIPTION OF THE METHODOLOGIES

Entity-Relationship Modeling

The Entity Relationship model was first proposed by Peter Chen in 1976 and has been expanded to include the concepts of participation constraints, generalization/specialization, and aggregation. The Entity Relationship model is primarily used to design databases. It emphasizes that the data model closely map to the real world scenario being modeled.

There are many variations of notations for an ER diagram. In this article Elmasri and Navathe's definitions and notations are used except for the notation for total/partial participation. The basic components of this model are the entity, its attributes, and the relationships between entities. An entity is a thing that independently exists in the real world; it is usually a noun. It is modeled as a rectangle with the entity name inside the rectangle (see Exhibit 1). Entities also require more than one attribute and more than one instance to be a meaningful entity type in an application domain.

0-8493-0882-8/00/$0.00+$.50
© 2001 by CRC Press LLC

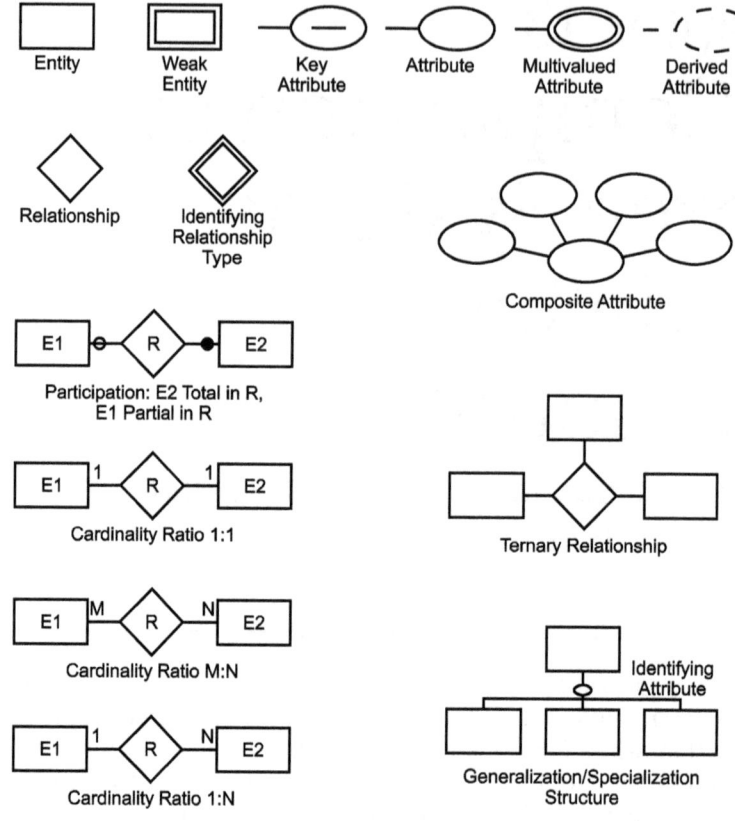

Entity · Weak Entity · Key Attribute · Attribute · Multivalued Attribute · Derived Attribute

Relationship · Identifying Relationship Type

Composite Attribute

Participation: E2 Total in R, E1 Partial in R

Cardinality Ratio 1:1

Ternary Relationship

Cardinality Ratio M:N

Identifying Attribute

Cardinality Ratio 1:N

Generalization/Specialization Structure

Exhibit 13-1. Diagram notation for the entity-relationship model.

An attribute is a property of an entity or a relationship; however, some models do not permit an attribute to a relationship. It is depicted as an ellipse that is attached to an entity. The name of the attribute is placed in the middle of the ellipse (see Exhibit 1).

Attributes can have many different roles. They can identify or describe. When an attribute identifies an entity it distinguishes that entity from the other entity of the same type. An example of this is a person's social security number. If it is assumed that all social security numbers are unique, then this attribute can be considered to be a primary key for this entity. A primary key uniquely identifies an entity. This attribute should not be null (this property is called entity constraint) or be changed often. It is represented as an attribute with the name underlined.

Attributes can be atomic, multivalued, composite, or derived. Anatomic attribute has a single value. The age of a person is an atomic attribute. A multivalued attribute can have several values. If a person speaks many

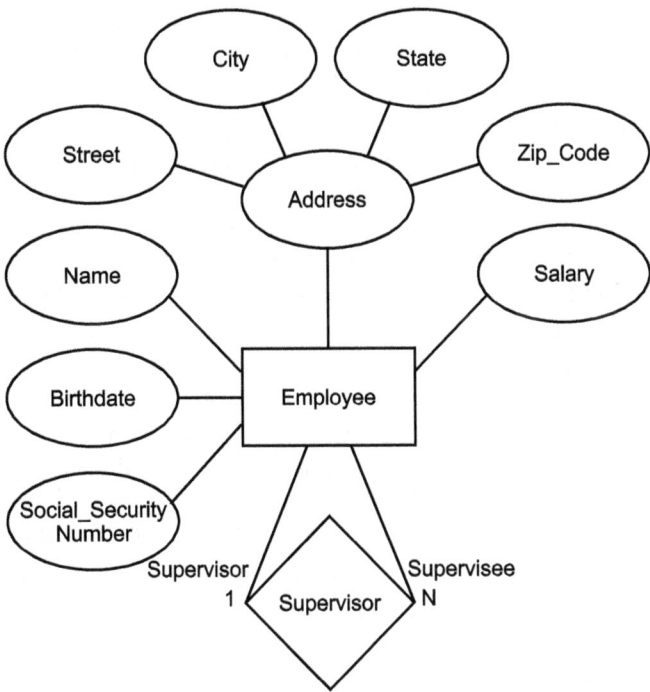

Exhibit 13-2. Entity-relationship model showing a unary relationship.

languages, the languages spoken by a person can be multivalued. An address is an example of a composite attribute, because it is composed of several more basic attributes. A derived attribute is one whose value can be calculated through the use of other attributes.

Entities that share the same attributes are grouped into entity types and are distinguished by the values of their attributes. For example, a company's employees would be grouped into an employee entity type.

The other basic component of an ER diagram is the relationship. A relationship is the association between entity types. It is represented by a diamond with lines connecting it to each related entity. The name of the relationship is written in the middle of the diamond (see Exhibit 1).

Relationships have three important properties: degree, cardinality, and participation. The degree of a relationship is based on the number of entities that are involved in the association. When an association occurs with only one entity it is called unary or recursive. Exhibit 2 illustrates such a relationship. The most common type of relationship is the binary type. This relationship has two entities involved in the association. All of the relationship in Exhibits 3 and 4 are binary relationships.

The cardinality of a relationship pertains to the maximum number of relationship instances that an entity can be involved in. The different levels of cardinality are: one to one (1:1), one to many (1:N), or many to many (M:N).

Relationships also use the concept of participation. Participation specifies the minimum cardinality. The minimum cardinality specifies whether any instance of one entity can exist without being associated with at least one member of another entity set. If it can, the participation is optional or partial; if it cannot, it is mandatory or total. In Exhibit 1, optional participation is represented by an open circle and mandatory is represented by a closed circle.

Another important concept in the ER model is the weak entity type. It is an entity that does not have its own unique identifier. The weak entity is depicted as a rectangle with double lines (see Exhibit 1). The relationship that associates the weak entity to its parent entity is called an identifying relationship and is modeled as a diamond with double lines (see Exhibit 1). An example of a weak entity type is an employee's dependents; a dependent cannot be identified without knowing the associated employee.

If entities have additional subgroups with important characteristics that require modeling, then a generalization/specialization structure is used. This structure is often known as a is-a relationship. An example of this structure is that an engineer entity is an employee entity. The employee entity is called a superclass and the other entities are referred to assubclasses. The subclasses have their own attributes plus they inherit all the attributes from their superclass.

The difference between generalization and specialization concerns how the structure is developed. Specialization is developed top-down whereas generalization is developed bottom-up. In specialization, an employee entity would be broken down into engineer, manager, and secretary entities. Using generalization, an analyst first develops engineer, manager, and secretary entities and then creates the employee entity. For ease of notation the term generalization is used in this article to refer to both specialization and generalization.

A constraint on the generalization structure is whether the entities are disjoint or if they can overlap. If the structure is disjoint, then an entity can only be a member of one subclass. If an entity can be a member of more than one subclass, then the structure is overlapping. The employee structure is disjoint because an employee is exactly an engineer, manager, or secretary.

Exhibit 3 presents an ER diagram of an accounting system. The diagram shows a Supplier, Account and Payment, Pay_Method, Check, Credit Card, and Cash entities. The Account has a single Supplier with total participation meaning that every account should have a responsible supplier. The Supplier entity charges many Accounts, with total participation. The Account has many Payment with partial participation. This means that an Account can

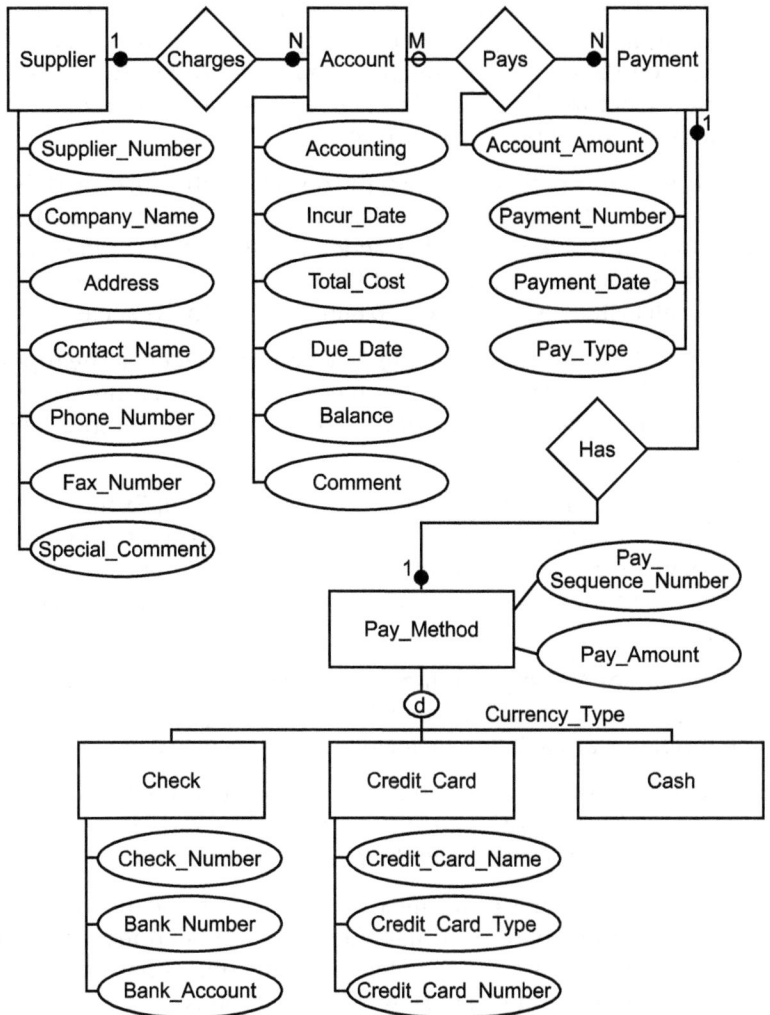

Exhibit 13-3. Entity-relationship model of an accounting system.

exist without being paid at a certain time. The Payment Pays many Accounts and its participation is total. The Pay relationship has attributes because of the M:N relationship between Payment and Account. There is a total one-to-one relationship between Pay_Method and Payment. The Pay_Method is the superclass for the Check, Cash, and Credit Card subclasses.

Shlaer and Mellor's Information Model

Shlaer and Mellor developed the Information Model in 1988 to help solve problems associated with software systems development. The Information

Model has been described as a thinking tool that uses graphical notation for describing and defining the vocabulary and conceptualization of a problem. It identifies what a problem is about and organizes these ideas into a format structure. This model can be regarded as a variation of the ER model discussed in the previous section.

The basic elements of this model are the object, its attributes, and the relationships between objects. The object is the basic part of the system. Shlaer and Mellor define an object as an abstraction of a set of real-world items such that all of the real-world items in the set-the instances-have the same characteristics and all instances are subject to and conform to the same rules.

An object is depicted as a rectangle. The name is placed at the top of the rectangle (see Exhibit 4). To identify objects, the Information Model uses five different categories-tangible things, roles, incidents, interactions and specifications.

A role is the part played by a person or organization. Examples of role objects include a doctor, a patient, a nurse, a department, an employee, and a supervisor. Sometimes role objects distinguish between different roles played by the same person. An example of this is an employee who is also a supervisor.

Another type of object is an incident. They are used to represent an occurrence or event-something which happens at a specific time. Examples of incident objects are a flight, an accident, or a service call.

The fourth type of object is the interaction object. Interaction objects can be compared to transactions or contracts. An example is a purchase which relates a buyer, a seller, and the purchase item.

The last type of object is a specification object. Specification objects frequently show up in inventory or manufacturing applications. An example of this type of object is a radio specification. This object has the specifications of the specific model. There would most likely be another object which describes each instance of a specific model of a radio.

The Shlaer and Mellor method specifies an object description, naming conventions, and methods to test if objects are valid. An object description is a short, informative statement that allows an analyst to tell with certainty whether a particular item is an instance of the object conceptualized in the information model.

Attributes are another important part of the Information Model. An attribute is defined as the abstraction of a single characteristic possessed by all the entities that were, themselves, abstracted as an object. An attribute is represented by a line item inside the object rectangle. The objective is a collection of attributes that are complete, fully factored, and mutually independent.

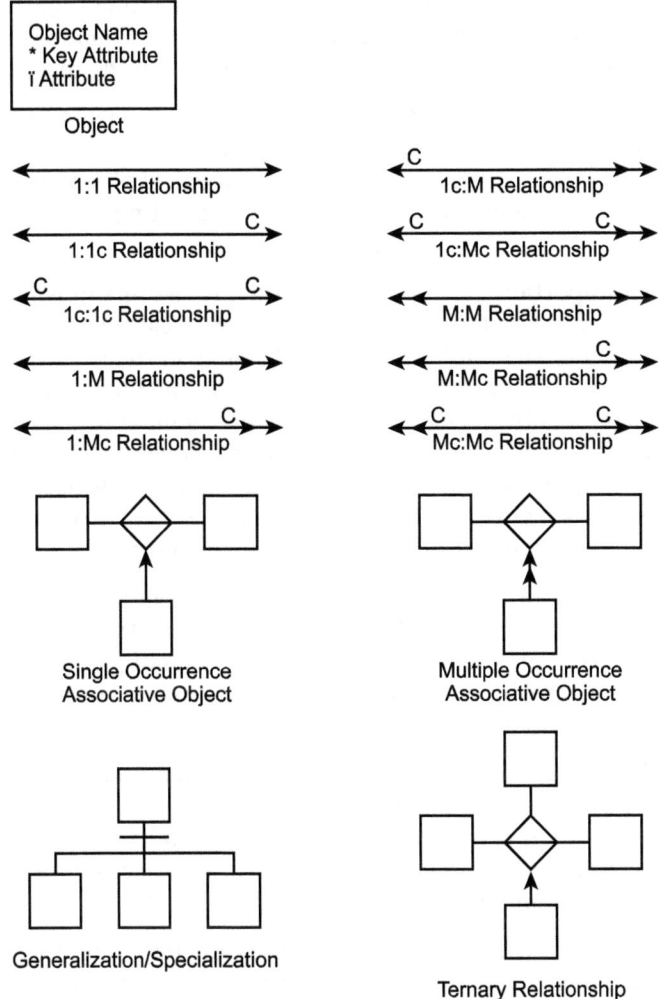

Exhibit 13-4. Diagram notation for shlaer and mellor's information model.

Different categories of attributes include descriptive attributes, naming attributes, referential attributes and identifier attributes. Descriptive attributes provide basic facts about each instance of an object. Examples are the salary and address of an employee object.

An identifier attribute is an attribute or combination of attributes that uniquely distinguishes one instance of an object from another. An identifier is sometimes called a candidate key. An example of identifier attributes are the state and title number for a car object. Neither attribute alone is sufficient to uniquely identify an instance of a car. Referential attributes are those that tie an instance of one object to an instance of another object. They are called foreign keys in a relational database. Neither the ER model nor Object Modeling Technique capture the referential attribute at the diagram level.

To describe an attribute the Information Model uses an attribute description. This is a short description that explains the significance of the attribute. The method also formalizes the concept of object mapping to a relational database table; the attributes of the object maps to the columns of the table.

The other important concept in this model is the relationship between objects. It is defined as the abstraction of a set of associations that holds systematically between different kinds of things in the real world. Examples include a person who borrows a book from the library or a research paper that has an author. Their relationships are similar to the ER model in that they include 1:1,1:N and M:M cardinality. However, the Information Model is different from the ER model because a diamond is used only when a relationship has its own attribute. When there are no attributes in a relationship, the two related entities are simply connected by a line.

Another important concept is the conditionality of a relationship. This concept is similar to the ER model's participation constraint. Relationships that are unconditional include every instance of an object in the relationship with another object. Conditional relationships optionally allow objects to participate in a relationship.

Cardinality is called multiplicity and is represented by a single arrow representing one and a double arrow representing many. The conditional constraint is depicted with a C on the conditional side(see Exhibit 4). Whenever a relationship has its own attributes, an object symbol is created and linked to the diamond.

Shlaer and Mellor have specific methods for implementing different types of relationships in a relational database. The implementation is based on the multiplicity and conditionality of a relationship.

Relationships can also show the association between subtypes and supertypes. This type of association is also known as generalization. This is a relationship in which distinct objects share common attributes. Exhibit 4 presents the notation for generalization and Exhibit 5 gives an example of generalization of the Pay_Methodobject.

Associative objects occur in many-to-many relationships where attributes are associated with a relationship. This type of object can be either a single or multiple occurrence. A single occurrence has one associative object instance associated with a single pairing of the two original relationship objects. A multiple occurrence form has many object instances

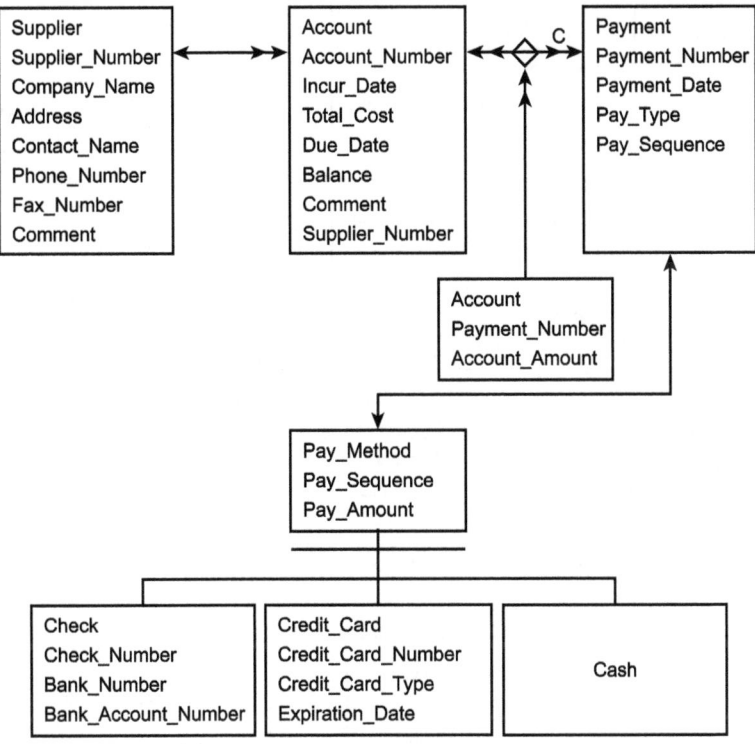

Exhibit 13-5. Information model diagram of an accounting system.

per associated pair. If an associative object can be thought of as a distinct object with an identifier then it can be modeled as a object. Thus, a ternary relationship would be created and it would still have the associative object which indicates the single or multiple occurrence form. Exhibit 4 gives an example of an associative relationship.

Exhibit 5 presents a Shlaer and Mellor information model of an accounting system. The diagram contains a Supplier, Account, Payment, Pay_Method, Check, Credit_Card, and Cash objects. The Account has a single Supplier with an unconditional relationship. The supplier object charges many Accounts and the relationship is unconditional. The object Account has a conditional relationship with many Payments. The Payment object is related to many Accounts and its relationship with the Account object is unconditional. The Pay relationship has a single occurrence of an associative object because of the Account_Amount attribute associated with the M:N relationship between Payment and Account. There is a mandatory one-to-one relationship between Pay_Method and Payment. The Pay_Method is the superclass for the Check, Cash, and Credit_Cardsubclasses.

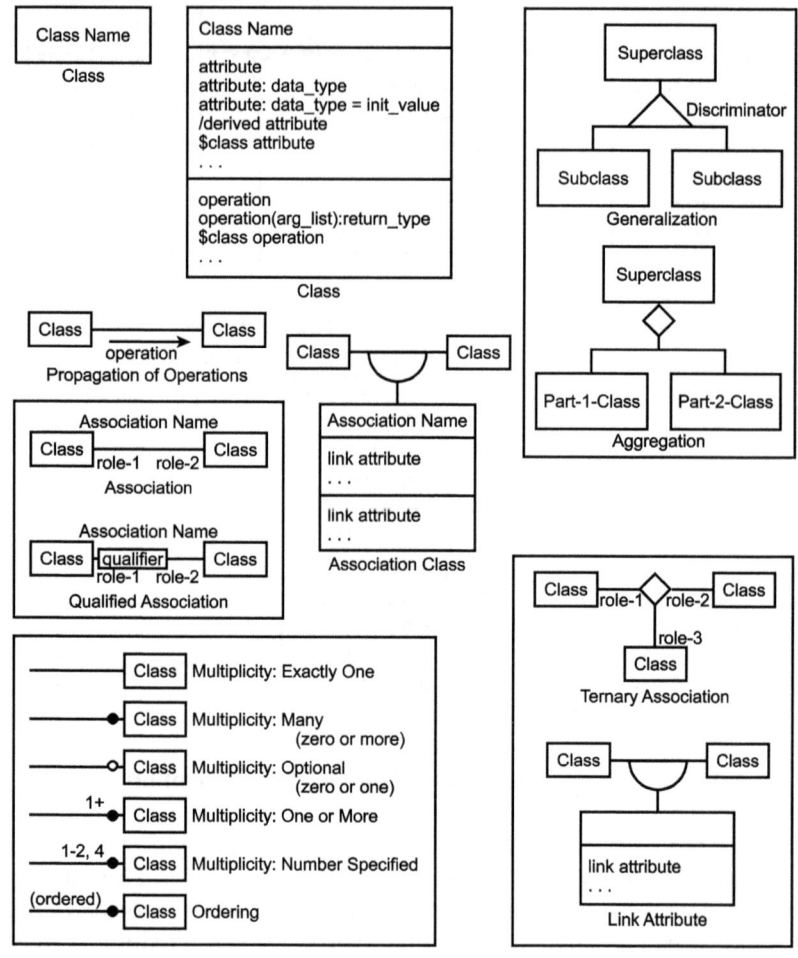

Exhibit 13-6. Rumbaugh's object model technique diagram notation.

Rumbaugh's Object Modeling Technique

The OMT (OMT) is used to develop software objects that have both a data structure and behavior. The object model shows the structure of a system in terms of objects, their attributes, their operations, and the relationships between objects. The goal in constructing an object model is to capture those concepts from the real world that are important to an application.

The basic element of the model is the object, which is represented by a box. The name of the object is placed at the top of the box (see Exhibit 6). An object is an abstraction of a real world entity that has definite boundaries and meaning. Objects that have similar attributes, operations, and relationships can be grouped together to form object classes. Each object in a class is distinguished by the value of its attributes.

In this model an attribute is a value held by an object. These attributes can be given a data type and default value if desired. Unlike in the Shlaer and Mellor model, object identifiers that do not have a real-world meaning to the system are not used as attributes. An example is an identifier number that is generated to make a person object unique. If this number is not used by the outside world, then the attribute should not be modeled. Such attributes as social security number and driver's license number can be modeled because they have meaning in the real world.

Attributes of an object are listed as line entries in the object box. They are written beneath the line drawn below the object name (see Exhibit 6).

An operation is a behavior associated with an object. This behavior can be an action performed by an object on another object or it can be a transformation that an object undergoes. These operations are available to all instances of a class and can apply to different classes. When the same operation is applied to different classes it is called polymorphic. An operation is implemented by a method. An example of a polymorphic operation is the opening of a file or a window. They have the same name — open — but they are applied to different classes and implemented by different methods. An operation is also listed as a line item in an object box. It is written beneath the line drawn below the list of attributes. Each operation can optionally have an argument list and result type (see Exhibit 6).

In an object model, relationships are known as links or associations. A link relates object instances, and an association relates object classes. These relationships can be reflexive (i.e., unary), binary, ternary, or of a higher order. The multiplicity (i.e., cardinality) of an object is determined by how many instances of a class relate to a single instance of another class. Multiplicity can be one to one, one to many (including zero), one to zero or one (i.e., optional), one to one or more, one to an exact number or a specific range. Exhibit 6 illustrates the syntax of links, associations, and multiplicity.

When objects in many-to-many relationships have attributes that cannot be associated with only one object, a link attribute is used. An example is shown in Exhibit 7 where the Account Payment objects have a link attribute for the amount of a payment associated with an account. If this attribute can have operations associated with it then it becomes a link object. Exhibit 6 shows the link attribute and link object notation.

A special type of association that shows a whole-to-part relationship is called aggregation. Aggregation is also called a part-of relationship. This type of association is used when the elements are intrinsically part of a whole. These objects may or may not have an independent existence in a system. This relationship is both transitive and asymmetric. Transitive

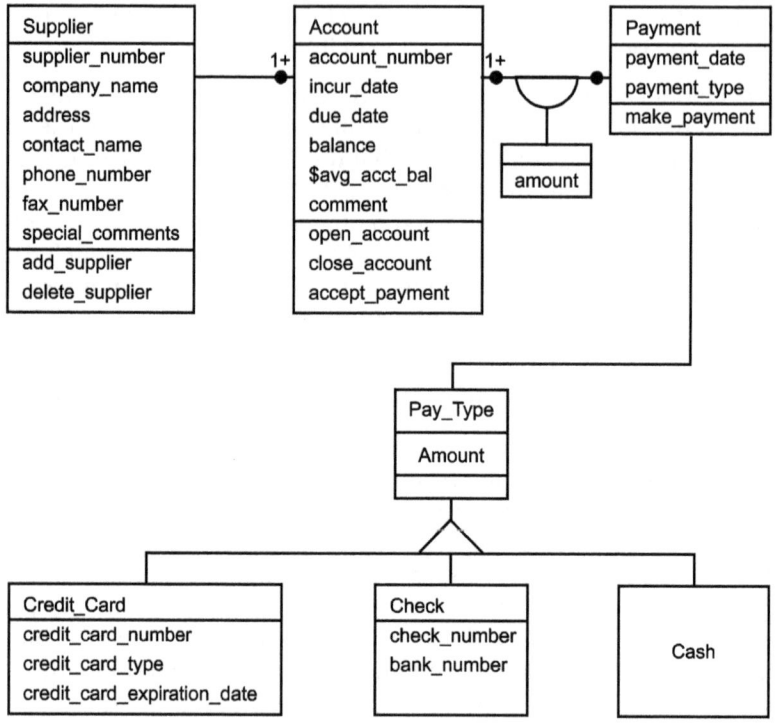

Exhibit 13-7. OMT diagram of an accounting system.

means if object A is part of object B and object B is part of object C, then object A is part of object C. Asymmetric means that if object A is part of object B, then object B is not part of object A.

Another important concept in the object model is generalization. In OMT, it is defined as the relationship between a class and one or more refined versions of the class. Generalization is also called an is-a relationship. An important property of generalization is inheritance. Inheritance is the sharing of attributes and operations among the classes in a generalization hierarchy. These features are inherited from a superclass by its subclasses.

Exhibit 7 illustrates these concepts in an OMT object diagram of an accounting system. The diagram contains a Supplier, Account, Payment, Pay_Method, Check, Credit_Card, and Cash objects. The Account must have a single Supplier. The Supplier object charges one or more Accounts. The Account object is associated with zero or more Payment objects. The Payment object pays one or more Accounts. There is a link attribute associated with the Account and Payment objects. This link attribute occurs because of the amount attribute associated with the many-to-many relationship between the Payment and Account objects. There is a one-to-one relationship between the Pay_Method and Payment objects. the Pay_Method object is the super-class for the Check, Cash, and Credit_Card subclasses.

COMPARISON OF THE MODELING METHODS

The three modeling techniques are somewhat similar-they all use the same basic elements: objects/entities, attributes, and relationships. When modeling the accounting system used as an example in this article, the three techniques produce essentially the same diagram; the only major difference is found in the notation. It is not true that this is the case for all applications, because there probably are certain scenarios where the models would look different.

The following sections compare the basic elements of these three modeling methodologies.

Entities and Objects

The most basic element of all three models is the object or entity. All three define this element in generally the same terms.

To help analysts determine valid objects, the Information Model methodology lists five different categories of objects: tangible items, roles, incidents, interactions, and specifications. This methodology also provides tests to determine the validity of an object. These tests include a uniformity test, more-than-a-name test, an or test, and a more-than-a-list test. All of these tests review the object definition or attributes to check the correctness and uniformity of an object.

OMT also provides guidelines for removing incorrect object classes. Invalid classes include those that are redundant, irrelevant, vague, attributes, operations, roles, and implementation constructs. In the Entity Relationship model a rule governing entities states that a valid entity must have at least one attribute and one instance.

An entity in the ER model and an object in the Information Model are very similar. An object in Object Modeling Technique has a major difference. An OMT object has operations defined for it. Defining operations for an object in a system can give an analyst greater insight into the use of the object in the system. The other models are strictly concerned with the data associated with the object or entity.

One special type of entity in the ER model is the weak entity type. This type is different from a normal entity in that it does not have an independent existence. The weak entity cannot exist without its parent entity. For example, an Employee_Dependent entity relies on an Employee entity for part of its unique identity. Although a unique attribute could be created for a weak entity, it should not be because of the strong bond between the entities. In the Information Model there is no way to show the strength of an association in a diagram. In OMT, however, there can be a qualified association, which enhances the identification of an association by attaching an identifying attribute to a dependent class.

Attributes

All three models use similar definitions for object and entity attributes. In the ER model, primary key are directly modeled, but foreign key are implicitly hidden in relationships (i.e., they are not explicitly shown on ER diagrams). In the Information Model, both primary keys and foreign keys (called reference attributes) are directly modeled and explicitly represented. If a unique key does not exist for an object, then one is created. A primary keys is annotated in an ER model with an underline and is annotated with a star in the Information Model.

OMT docs not use the concept of keys, because most object-oriented languages automatically generate implicit object identifiers. However, OMT does allow for these keys for Relational Database Management System.

The use of keys is an important difference among these models. Both the ER and Information models were developed on the assumption that a relational database is used to store the system's data. OMT does not make this assumption and does not stipulate any model. This allows the development of a more flexible model that can be implemented by any system.

OMT notation can more thoroughly define an attribute because it uses data types, default values, and class attributes. An attribute can optionally have a data type and default value optionally notated. This further definition of an attribute can give a quick understanding of an object and its attributes. When an OMT diagram is complicated by extra information, a simplified object diagram without the extra information can be shown.

Another special attribute only used in OMT is the class attribute. The class attribute is a value that only relates to the object class and not to any instance of that class. An example of a class attribute is the Average_Account_Balance attribute of the Account object class in Exhibit 7. This attribute is simply the average value of account balances for all instances of the Account object class. Because it is an average of all account balances, this attribute can only apply to the class and not to any individual object instance.

Both OMT and the ER model have notation for derived attributes but the Information Model does not. It is useful to know this type of information because derived attributes may affect final implementation of an attribute.

Another special type of attribute which differentiates OMT is the private attribute. A private attribute is one that can only be accessed by a class. This attribute type is not found in the other methodologies. Private attributes are used in the design phase of a project. They enforce a concept called information hiding. Information hiding is used to hide the details of the implementation of an object from the outside world. Information hiding also creates a clean interface that changes less frequently and is not affected by changes to the internal processing of the object.

Relationships

All three models describe relationships with basically the same approach. One difference is in OMT where it specifies different terms for the relationships between object classes and object instances. The relationship between classes is called an association and the relationship between instances is called a link.

All three use different notation and terminology to define the number of objects in a relationship. The ER model uses the terms cardinality and participation. The Shlaer and Mellor method uses the terms multiplicity and conditionality to refer to the number of objects used in an association. The term multiplicity is equivalent to cardinality in Elmasri and Navathe's ER convention. Conditionality in an information model is similar to participation in an ER model. The participation checks whether an entity can exist without being associated to another entity, but the conditionality concept checks whether all of the instances of one entity are mapped conditionally or unconditionally to another entity. The basic difference is in the notation that specifies participation and convention. Although the definition of conditionality is slightly different than that of participation the result is the same.

OMT uses the term multiplicity to represent both cardinality and participation as defined by the ER model. This is done by including zero in the cardinality (i.e., zero or one, zero or more, or one or more). Exhibit 6 presents all the OMT terms for multiplicity.

All three methodologies use different terminology and notation to describe the number of objects in a relationship. But the results of each notation is the same. Each method is successful at clearly displaying this information.

Each methodology also has special types of relationships. The ER model has relationship attributes, the Information Model has associative objects, and OMT has link attributes, link objects, ordering, qualifiers, and aggregation.

Relationship attributes, associative objects, and link attributes are all very similar. They occur in many-to-many relationships. An example of this is shown in the relationship between Account and Payment entities or objects in Exhibits 3, 5, and 7. The ER model and OMT notations are similar. The Information Model adds an extra dimension by indicating the number of occurrences of an attribute. A single arrow is used when there is only a single occurrence associated with a single relationship instance. A double arrow is used when multiple occurrences are associated with a single relationship instance. This gives added information that is not indicated by other models, but they can be simulated by ternary relationship in other models.

A qualifier and ordering constraint are used in OMT to further clarify an association. A qualifier can be used to reduce the multiplicity of an association. An ordering constraint which is shown at the many side of an association shows that the object requires a specific order to be a valid relationship. An example is the relationship between a Screen object and a Window object. There can be many windows on a screen but it is important to know which is the topmost window. To indicate this requirement an ordered constraint is placed above the relationship line next to the Window object.

Another special type of relationship that can be used in OMT is aggregation. Neither the Entity Relationship or Information models have this type of notation. This type of relationship shows the strength of a parts-whole relationship. An example is a Lamp object that is an aggregate of a Base, Body, Shade, and Bulb objects. Aggregation in a typical ER model is more limited, because it requires two entity types and one relationship to form a high-level entity.

To verify the relationship in ER and Information models a correlation table can be used. This is actually the implementation of a relationship. The table lists the instances involved in an association. By checking these instances the validity of an association can be confirmed. In OMT the following criteria are used for determining unnecessary or incorrect associations:

- associations between eliminated classes
- irrelevant or implementation associations
- actions
- derived associations

It is also recommended to break ternary relationships into binary relationships.

The generalization structure and approach used by all three models is very similar. Both the ER model and Object Modeling Technique allow the use of an attribute to distinguish the type of generalization. In the ER model this attribute is called a classifying attribute. In OMT it is called a discriminator. An example of this concept is shown in the Pay_Method generalization structures in Exhibit 3 and 7.

All these models consider disjointness constraints. If generalization is disjoint then each entity can only be a member of one subclass. If it can be a member of more than one subclass then the generalization has overlap. Elmasri & Navathe's convention shows this constraint in by placing a "D" for disjoint or "O" for overlap in the circle of the generalization symbol. Exhibit 3 illustrates the disjoint structure of the Pay_Method generalization.

The Information Model does not have any notation to indicate this constraint, but it is checked when producing an identifier for generalization.

CONCLUSION

Although the basic elements of the Entity Relationship model, the Information Model, and Object Modeling Technique are similar, there are major differences. Both the ER and Information models require the use of identifier attributes in the object or entity, but OMT does not. This identifier is only added during implementation if it is required. The Entity Relationship and the Information models are created with intention that a relational database will be used to implement the data. OMT does not force any implementation restrictions on the object model. This allows the model to be implemented by any type of system. Also, an OMT model is more complete because it shows not only the data associated with an object but also the processes that are performed on or by the object.

Another important difference concerns OMT's use of operations. OMT adds the extra dimension of operations to the objects, but the other models do not require them. The Information Model, however, captures operation information in later analysis phases by using the life cycle modeling technique.

Also, both the Information Model and OMT do not use any symbol for relationships when they do not have any attributes.

The Information Model is also clearly different from the other two models because it directly models a foreign key at the diagram level. This requires more effort at the modeling level and less effort during implementation.

The only major difference between the ER and Information models is in the use of single and multiple occurrence forms of an associative object.

The Information Model appears to be an updated version of the ER model and both are designed for implementation on a relational database. OMT has, however, is designed for object-oriented implementation. The differences between all three modeling techniques are summarized in Exhibit 8.

Bibliography

1. Chen, P.P. "The Entity Relationship Model-Toward a Unified View of Data" TODS 1, no. 1 (1976).
2. Elmarsi, R. and Navathe S.B. Fundamentals of Database Systems. Redwood City CA: Benjamin-Cumming s Publishing Co., 1989.
3. Rumbaugh, R. et al.Object-Oriented Modeling and Design. Englewood Cliffs NJ: Prentice Hall, 1991.
4. Shlaer, S. and Mellor S.J. Object-Oriented Systems Analysis-Modeling the World in Dat a. Englewood Cliffs: Yourdon Press, 1988.
5. Shlaer, S. and Mellor S.J. ="Object Lifecycles: Modeling the World in States. Englewood Cliffs NJ: Yourdon Press, 1992.

Exhibit 13-8. Summary of differences among the E-R, information model, and OMT systems modeling techniques.

Topic	E-R	Information Model	OMT
Entity	Entity	Object	Object
Operations	No	No	Yes
Primary Key	Yes	Yes	No
Foreign Key	No	Yes	No
Participation Constraint	Yes	Yes	Yes
Participation Notation	Look Here[1] (LH)	Look Across[2] (LA)	LA
Ternary Relationships	Yes	Yes	Yes
Cardinality Notation	LA	LA	LA
Multiplicity to Association Object	No	Yes	No
Attributes on Relationships	Yes	Yes	Yes
Relationship Qualifiers:			
Role	Yes	Yes	Yes
Ordering	No	No	Yes
Qualifier	No	No	Yes
Attribute Data Type	No	No	Yes
Default Value	No	No	Yes
Generalization Hierarchy	Yes	Yes	Yes
Aggregation	Yes (limited)	No	Yes

Notes

1. Look here (LH) notation is next to the primary entity in a relationship.

2. Look across (LA) notation is next to the secondary entity in a relationship.

Chapter 14
Building a
Data Model
Candace C. Fleming and Barbara von Halle

DATA MODELING IS A TECHNIQUE FOR CLEARLY REPRESENTING BUSINESS INFORMATION STRUCTURES AND RULES AS INPUT TO THE DATABASE DESIGN PROCESS. At the heart of data modeling is an appreciation of data as a valuable resource for a business organization. Data modeling is a philosophy (as well as a technique) for recognizing and documenting the fact that business information has an existence, independent of how it is accessed, who accesses it, and whether or not such access is computerized.

The following is a list of business facts that can be represented through a data model:

- Customers place orders.
- People eat ice cream cones.
- Some people pay bills on time.
- Some people do not pay bills on time.
- Some people do not pay bills at all.

These facts are true even if there is no current need to produce reports or answer queries about them. Recognizing such facts, identifying those that are significant to a user's business, and developing a corresponding data model enable the user to accommodate access requirements through database technology. Regardless of whether such facts (or some subset of them) become components of the actual database, a data model often can help people understand specific aspects of the business.

This chapter provides an overview of a methodology for logical data modeling.

DATA MODELING CHARACTERISTICS

Data modeling methodology has several important characteristics that contribute to its effectiveness. First, it is an entirely data-driven process (i.e., it is unbiased by particular information system requirements or technological considerations). A data-driven model facilitates greater stability and flexibility within subsequent database design. Second, the

0-8493-0882-8/00/$0.00+$.50
© 2001 by CRC Press LLC

methodology encourages comprehensive understanding of business information requirements by suggesting a cookbook-like approach complete with steps, rules, and implementation tips. It should enable even an inexperienced analyst to tackle complex design problems with confidence. Third, it facilitates effective communication among designers, developers, and users throughout the design process. The methodology relies heavily on diagramming techniques to illustrate information and relationships more clearly and concisely than textual descriptions alone can do. Finally, the methodology contributes to designing optimal databases using any database technology. In fact, because of the data-driven (technology-independent) nature of the methodology, a data model can be built even before deciding on a database environment.

Optimal database design is:

- *Correct* — It provides an accurate and faithful representation of the way information is used in the business.
- *Consistent* — It contains no contradictions in the way the information objects are named, defined, related, and documented.
- *Sharable* — It is accessible by multiple applications and users to meet varying access requirements.
- *Flexible* — It facilitates additions to reflect new information requirements, tweaking to accommodate strengths or weaknesses of a particular implementation approach, and modifications to respond to changes in business operations.

Many approaches and methodologies can be used for data modeling; some are more formal and more intimidating than others. The methodology described in this chapter is not so much formal as practica211 — that is, it is a simplified version of a rigorous, formal treatment. The combination of simplicity and practicality makes it effective for the modeling requirements of many business situations.

MAJOR CONCEPTS OF DATA MODELING

Exhibit 1 shows a very simple data model of Ron's Real Estate Business. Even knowing nothing about data modeling, by looking at Exhibit 1 it is obvious that:

- Ron deals with renters, properties (beach and mountain), and rental agreements. These seem to be the most important objects or concepts (or entities) in the exhibit.
- Renters rent rental agreements, and properties are rented to rental agreements. In addition, there are beach properties and mountain properties. The arrows reflect associations (relationships) between the boxes (entities).

- Ron is interested in selected details about each entity. For example, he tracks the name, address, telephone number, and maximum monthly rental amount of each renter. He is concerned with how many blocks away the beach is from a beach property, but not from a mountain property. These details are called attributes.
- Some attribute names appear above horizontal lines in the boxes (e.g., NAME in the RENTER box). These attributes appear to be the most important or most necessary details about the entity. In fact, these attributes must be present; for example, renters must have names but not always addresses, telephone numbers, or monthly rental amounts.
- Some attributes have names containing asterisks (e.g., RENTER*NAME, PROPERTY*STREET-ADDRESS, PROPERTY*TOWN-STATE-ADDRESS). These attributes seem to refer to other entities (or relate them to each other).
- The arrows are drawn with one or two arrowheads at one end and have no arrowheads at the other end. Arrowheads presumably carry some meaning.

Without any knowledge of data modeling, a lot of information can be obtained about Ron's business. Therefore, it is obvious that two benefits of the data modeling technique are that it is simple to understand, because it uses uncomplicated diagrams, and it expresses many facts precisely and unambiguously.

Entities and Relationships

The most important constructs within a data model are entities and relationships. An entity is a person, place, thing, or concept about which facts are to be recorded. Examples in Exhibit 1 are RENTER, RENTAL-AGREEMENT, PROPERTY, BEACH-PROPERTY, and MOUNTAIN-PROPERTY. A relationship is an association between two entities. Examples are RENTER rents RENTAL-AGREEMENT, PROPERTY is rented to RENTAL-AGREEMENT, and PROPERTY is of type BEACH-PROPERTY or MOUNTAIN-PROPERTY. In a data model diagram, entities are represented by boxes and relationships by arrows.

Entities have a number of properties. For instance, each entity has a name (e.g., RENTER) and a description (e.g., person who obtains the privilege of residing on a specific property according to the terms of a rental agreement). Entity sets (e.g., all renters) can be distinguished from entity occurrences (e.g., renter Harry Smith and renter Josephine Morgan). AU occurrences within an entity set have the same attributes or detailed information items (e.g., NAME, ADDRESS, PHONE-NUMBER, and MAX-MONTHLY-RENT-AMT-all of which are attributes of RENTER).

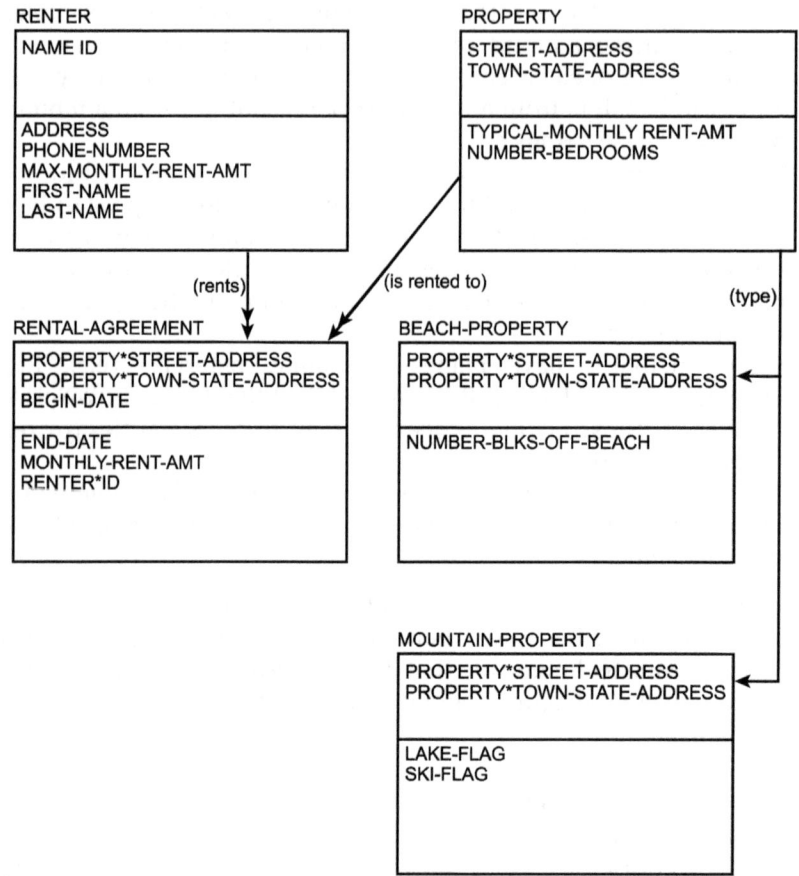

Exhibit 14-1. A data model for Ron's real estate business.

Attributes

More formally, an attribute is a fact or nondecomposable (atomic) piece of information describing an entity. Nondecomposable means that an attribute represents the smallest unit of information that will be referenced at one time.

For example, notice that a renter address is represented as one attribute (ADDRESS), but a property address is represented as two attributes (STREET-ADDRESS and TOWN-STATE-ADDRESS). This design enables the user to easily list all properties in a particular town and state; listing only those renters in a particular town and state may be more difficult.

A particular entity occurrence can be identified by the values of its attributes. For example, renter Harry Smith can be distinguished from renter Josephine Morgan based on values of their attributes as illustrated

Exhibit 14-2. RENTER sample value listing.

REENTER

NAME (UIX)	ADDRESS	PHONE-NUMBER	MAX-MONTHLY -RENT-AMT
Harry Smith	12 Oak Lane, Hopetown, NY 01111	212-984-3158	400
Josephine Morgan	5 Central Ave, Dallas, TX 75080	214-232-7990	650

in the sample value listing (sample entity occurrences with their respective attribute values) in Exhibit 2.

Typically, all of the attribute values are not needed to identify a particular entity occurrence. For example, a particular RENTER can be identified by an assigned RENTER-ID. This identifying attribute or set of attributes is known as an entity identifier. The entity identifier for PROPERTY is the combination of two attributes, STREET-ADDRESS and TOWN-STATE-ADDRESS. Both attributes are needed to identify a particular property, because multiple properties may have the same value for STREET-ADDRESS (in different towns) or the same value for TOWN-STATE-ADDRESS (with different street addresses). RENTAL-AGREEMENT has a primary key consisting of three attributes: PROPERTY* STREET-ADDRESS and PROP-ERTY*TOWN-STATE-ADDRESS (identifying the property) and BEGIN-DATE (identifying the rental period for that property). Entity identifiers are written above a horizontal line in the logical data model diagram (as in Exhibit 1) or on the far left above a primary key designation in a sample value listing (as in Exhibit 2).

Some assumptions about definitions of the attributes are made when choosing the entity identifiers. These definitions should be explicitly understood and recorded within the design documentation or data dictionary. A data dictionary is a manual or automated repository of information about information systems, databases, data models, users, and access authorizations. Assumptions about the model are based on naming conventions used in the data model diagram without referring to the data dictionary. All entity, relationship, and attribute names are composed of English words, are frequently and consistently abbreviated, and are usually connected by hyphens. Moreover, each attribute name includes one word (the class word) that indicates the nature of the data represented by the attribute (e.g., NAME, ADDRESS, NUMBER, AMOUNT, DATE, FLAG).

Some of the attribute names include the name of another entity as a prefix, followed by an asterisk-for example, RENTER*NAME, PROPERTY*STREET-ADDRESS, PROPERTY*TOWN-STATE-ADDRESS. These attributes are part of a foreign key-an attribute or set of attributes that completes a relationship by identifying the associated entity. The term *foreign* conveys the idea that the attribute belongs to or refers to another foreign entity. Thus, RENTER*NAME in RENTAL-AGREEMENT identifies which RENTER is renting the agreement; and PROPERTY*STREET-ADDRESS, PROPERTY*TOWN-STATE-ADDRESS in RENTAL-AGREEMENT identifies which PROPERTY is being rented. The use of an asterisk in Exhibit 1 is for illustration purposes only. Typically, attribute names do not contain an asterisk.

BEACH-PROPERTY and MOUNTAIN-PROPERTY share a special relationship with PROPERTY, designated by the squared-off arrow connecting the two to PROPERTY. BEACH-PROPERTY and MOUNTAIN-PROPERTY are each subtypes of PROPERTY, representing the same real-world object but having slightly different, more specific definitions and characteristics. They also contain the foreign key PROPERTY*STREET-ADDRESS, PROPERTY*TOWN-STATE-ADDRESS, identifying with which PROPERTY each is associated.

Some of the arrows in the diagram are double-headed, and others are single-headed. The double-headed arrow represents a one-to-many relationship; for example, one RENTER may rent many RENTAL-AGREEMENTs, and one PROPERTY may be rented through many different RENTAL-AGREE-MENTs (although not for the same week). A single-headed arrow represents a one-to-one relationship-for example, a PROPERTY is listed as a BEACH-PROPERTY or a MOUNTAIN-PROPERTY, but never as both.

A full data model consists of not only a diagram but specifications in a data dictionary. For example, although there may be multiple RENTAL-AGREE-MENTs for the same PROPERTY, they may not be for the same week; or, more generally, they may not be for overlapping time periods. As mentioned before, for two RENTAL-AGREEMENTs on the same PROPERTY (i.e., the same PROPERTY*STREET-ADDRESS, PROPERTY*TOWN-STATE-ADDRESS), the BEGIN-DATEs must be different (because PROPERTY*STREET-ADDRESS, PROPERTY*TQWN-STATE-ADDRESS and BEGIN-DATE constitute an entity identifier that uniquely identifies a RENTAL-AGREEMENT). However, a business rule involving END-DATE must also be specified. For example, when a new occurrence of RENTAL-AGREEMENT is inserted, the END-DATE must be later than the BEGIN-DATE. Moreover, the END-DATE must precede the BEGIN-DATEs of all existing RENTAL-AGREEMENTs having a BEGIN-DATE later than the new RENTAL-AGREEMENT's BEGIN-DATE for RENTAL-AGREEMENTs for the same property. Otherwise, the rental agreement is inappropriate and does not make business sense. A database implementation of the model should reject insertion of such an occurrence.

Such business rules are specifications that preserve the integrity of the data model by governing which values attributes may assume. True to the data-driven philosophy, business rules are identified without consideration for exactly how the system will produce reports or enforce edit criteria. For now, the data and all of its relevant rules are analyzed independently of information system requirements.

A data model, therefore, incorporates numerous rules about the integrity as well as the structure of information used within a business. Most of the rules conveyed by the data model diagram relate to structure. Other business rules specified within the data dictionary relate to integrity. For instance, the statement, RENTAL-AGREEMENT must be for a predefined PROPERTY but may be made by a RENTER who is not yet defined within the database, is a key business rule (governing valid relationships between primary and foreign key attributes). PHONE-NUMBER, a 10-digit numeric attribute, is a domain business rule (governing types and ranges of values that attributes may assume). The example discussed involving END-DATE is actually a type of rule called a triggering operation (governing general effects of insert, update, or delete operations on other entities or attributes). Structure and integrity within the logical data model are equally important. It is useless to understand the structure of information within the business without understanding rules pertaining to that information's integrity, and vice versa.

ROLE OF A THREE-SCHEMA ARCHITECTURE

At this point, there may be questions about the relationship of a logical data model (supporting one area of the business or one set of business functions) to an integrated model of information used throughout the business. Such an integrated model is frequently called a conceptual model or conceptual schema and is discussed in the following paragraphs.

In 1977, the American National Standards Institute (ANSI)/X3/SPARC Committee developed a set of requirements for effective database management systems (DBMSs). These requirements were specified in terms of a three-part framework for organizing data managed by a DBMS:

- *The external schema* — Data organization as viewed by the user or programmer.
- *The internal schema* — Data organization as viewed by the DBMS's internal access logic.
- *The conceptual schema* — An integrated view of all data used within the business.

Exhibit 3 illustrates the mappings among external, internal, and conceptual schemas.

The data modeling methodology described in this chapter is consistent with-and builds on-the ideas in the ANSI/X3/SPARC three-schema architecture. For example, the external schema for Ron's Real Estate Business is an organization of data requirements from the perspective of Ron, the owner. Yet another external schema could be described from the perspective of a property tenant. That external schema might include information about only one rental property because the tenant cares about only the one

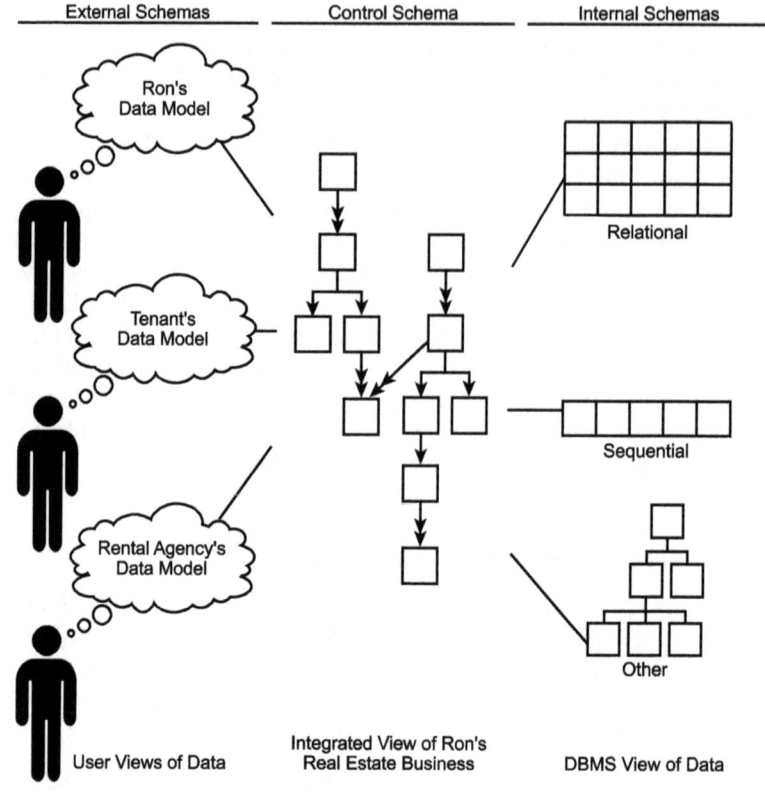

Exhibit 14-3. ANSI/X3/SPARC three-schema architecture.

property he or she is renting. It probably would include more details about that one property, such as days for garbage pickup and location of the nearest liquor store.

As the integrated view of all the business's data, the conceptual schema is a consolidation of all relevant data models. A conceptual schema can be developed as a prerequisite deliverable before implementing any databases. Or, more practically, a conceptual schema can evolve by consolidating data models as they are built. The conceptual schema will help ensure consistency of multiple data models, defined to support different user groups or different areas of the business. Existence of one (even evolving) conceptual schema will also aid in designing shared databases or internal schemas that support multiple external schemas. Finally, the conceptual schema will help ensure consistency across multiple database implementations or internal schemas (e.g., making use of different technological strengths). Thus, a user can maintain one view (one external schema) of the data regardless of underlying implementations (internal schemas).

This chapter has generalized the ANSI/X3/SPARC definition of a three-schema architecture: ANSI/X3/SPARC defined the three types of schemas in terms of how they should be supported within a given DBMS (e.g., a relational database product). The design principles of the three-schema framework are incorporated to produce data models and an integrated business conceptual schema that can be implemented through any (or, indeed, multiple) database technologies. Therefore, an architecture for DBMSs and also a specification for effective database design practices are borrowed from ANSI/X3/SPARC.

STEPS WITHIN LOGICAL DATA MODELING

The following list is a set of criteria for an optimal data model:

- *Structural validity* — Consistency with the way the business defines and organizes information.
- *Simplicity* — Ease of understanding even by users or by nontechnical professionals.
- *Nonredundancy* — Inclusion of no extraneous information and, in particular, representation of any one piece of information exactly once (this may be a subcriterion of simplicity).
- *Shareability* — Not specific to any particular application or technology and thereby usable by many.
- *Extensibility* — Ability to evolve to support new requirements with minimal impact on the existing base.
- *Integrity* — Consistency with the way the business uses and manages information values.

Satisfying these criteria requires more than assembling just any combination of boxes, arrows, and labels. Specifically, a set of rules and steps for applying those rules should be followed to ensure an optimal data model. Up to this point, this article has highlighted some of the rules, such as every entity should have a primary identifier and primary identifiers are unique. A sequence of steps for applying these rules is summarized as follows.

Building Skeletal User Views. Building a data model involves examining one activity or business function at a time. The information required by each function is individually modeled, and the individual models are then integrated into one composite model. The model or representation of information required by one business function is known as a user view. Building a user view begins with the following steps:

- Identifying major entities (significant objects of interest). (Step LDM1.)
- Determining relationships between entities. (Step LDM2.)

Adding Keys to User Views. The process continues with the addition of key detail information items and the most important business rules:

- Determining primary and alternate identifiers (identifying properties of entities). (Step LDM3.)
- Determining foreign keys (identifying properties of relationships). (Step LDM4.)
- Determining key business rules (rules that govern the effects of insert, delete, and update operations on relationships). (Step LDM5.)

Alternate identifiers are alternative choices of identifying attributes that (perhaps arbitrarily) are not chosen to be the primary entity identifier. For instance, if NAME is chosen as the entity identifier for the RENTER entity in Ron's Real Estate Business, SOC-SEC-NMBR (Social Security number) might be an alternate identifier.

Key business rules define conditions under which identifiers and foreign keys may be inserted, deleted, or updated. One insert rule and one delete rule are established for each relationship. The insert rule determines valid conditions under which the foreign key may be inserted or updated in an entity occurrence. The delete rule determines valid conditions under which the entity identifier referenced by a foreign key may be deleted or updated. These are the most frequently encountered and typically the most important constraints on insert, delete, and update operations. Because they define rules governing valid existence of particular entity occurrences, they are also called existence constraints.

Adding Detail to User Views. After identifying all key attributes (primary, alternate, and foreign keys), remaining nonkey attributes must be added-step LDM6. Nonkey attributes are the descriptive details that users naturally associate with the entities. For example, ADDRESS, PHONE-NUMBER, and MAX-MONTHLY-RENT-AMT are nonkey attributes in the RENTER entity. Each attribute is associated with the entity whose entire primary identifier is required to identify it. (The primary identifier may be a set of attributes.)

Validating User Views through Normalization. Step LDM6 relies primarily on an intuitive process of associating attributes with the seemingly proper entities. That process is then checked through a more structured, formal technique: validating normalization rules — step LDM7.

Normalization is a body of theory addressing analysis and decomposition of data structures into a new set of data structures exhibiting more desirable properties. Specifically, normalization increases the certainty of achieving an optimal data model. Each entity and its associated attributes are successively examined for structural redundancies or inconsistencies due to assignment of an attribute to the wrong entity (e.g., association of the customer credit rating with the ORDER rather than with the CUSTOMER entity). Such problems are eliminated by reassigning attributes to more appropriate entities or, in some cases, by decomposing entities into smaller, simpler entities. The result is a model that is at least structurally consistent.

Normalization does not ensure that the model correctly reflects the business meaning of data requirements. Therefore, normalization should be employed as a refinement technique (step LDM7) only after completing a thorough business analysis using the techniques in steps LDMI through LDM6.

Determining Additional Attribute Business Rules. Normalization also does not fully address business rules. These should be part of a data model to ensure that not only the structure but the values of the data correctly reflect business operations. Steps LDM3 through LDM5 already have uncovered the most significant business rules — those governing integrity of entity and foreign key attributes. At this point, two additional types of attribute business rules can be identified by:

- Determining domains (constraints on valid values that attributes may assume). (Step LDM8.)
- Determining triggering operations (rules that govern the effects of insert, delete, and update operations on other entities or other attributes within the same entity). (Step LDM9.)

The term domain includes data type, length, format or mask, uniqueness of values, null support (whether a value must be present), allowable values, default value if applicable, and business meaning. Domains verify whether values assigned to an attribute make business sense. They also help in determining when it makes sense to compare or manipulate values of two different attributes.

The term triggering operation refers to the most generalized form of business rule, encompassing domains and key business rules, as well as other attribute business rules. These elements reflect the user's understanding of all rules that make some sets of data values correct and others incorrect in the business world (e.g., for a given RENTAL-AGREEMENT, END-DATE must be later than BEGIN-DATE).

The intent in defining business rules is to clarify all data-driven constraints on the data values. In other words, those rules that always hold true are defined, regardless of any particular processing requirements. Because these rules are information system-independent, they are defined as part of the data design rather than as part of the information system design. If instead they are treated as part of the information system, they would have to be completely, consistently, and redundantly specified as part of every information system accessing the data.

Integrating User Views. The final logical design steps combine user views into one consolidated logical data model:

- Combining user views into one model. (Step LDMIO.)
- Integrating with existing data models. (Step LDM 1 1.)
- Analyzing for stability and growth. (Step LDMI2.)

In step LDMIO, user views defined for different business functions are combined; or perhaps different user groups are combined into one model. For example, one user view for Ron's Real Estate Business may be defined from the perspective of Ron, the owner, as illustrated in Exhibit 1. If Ron also uses rental agencies to assist him in locating potential renters, a different user view can be developed from the perspective of Clancey's Rental Agency, dealing with multiple property owners and additional rental properties. Thus, Clancey's user view includes additional entities, subtypes, relationships, attributes, and business rules. Presumably, in some areas, Clancey's and Ron's user views overlap; in some areas, they may even conflict. In step LDMIO, the overlaps are consolidated, any inconsistencies resolved, and new, inter-view relationships and business rules added to form one composite logical data model.

In step LDM11, this consolidated data model is examined in light of models developed for other purposes. Again, overlaps and some inconsistencies will be discovered. Most of these other models may already have been implemented as databases; thus, the models may not be able to be changed if errors or omissions are discovered. The objective here is to understand and document relationships (including inconsistencies) among the designs.

This can be accomplished by comparing and defining mappings among the data models, specifically through mappings to the business conceptual schema. The conceptual schema evolves by combining the data models and merging them two at a time, similar to merging user views. Then mappings are identified between each data model and the business conceptual schema, including:

- differences in names
- operations performed on the conceptual schema to obtain constructs within a particular logical data model
- interrelation of business rules

A business conceptual schema therefore allows multiple data models and multiple database implementations that are consistent with one another and with the business's overall operations as well as being representative of individual user perspectives.

Finally, in step LDM12, consideration should be given to future business changes that may affect the current data model. Those that are significant, imminent, or probable are incorporated into, or at least documented with, the data model. The goal is to maximize stability of the data model — to ensure that correctness and usefulness will necessitate few changes over a reasonable period. It is most important to incorporate any changes that affect the business conceptual schema, because these are likely to have a major influence on one or more individual logical data models.

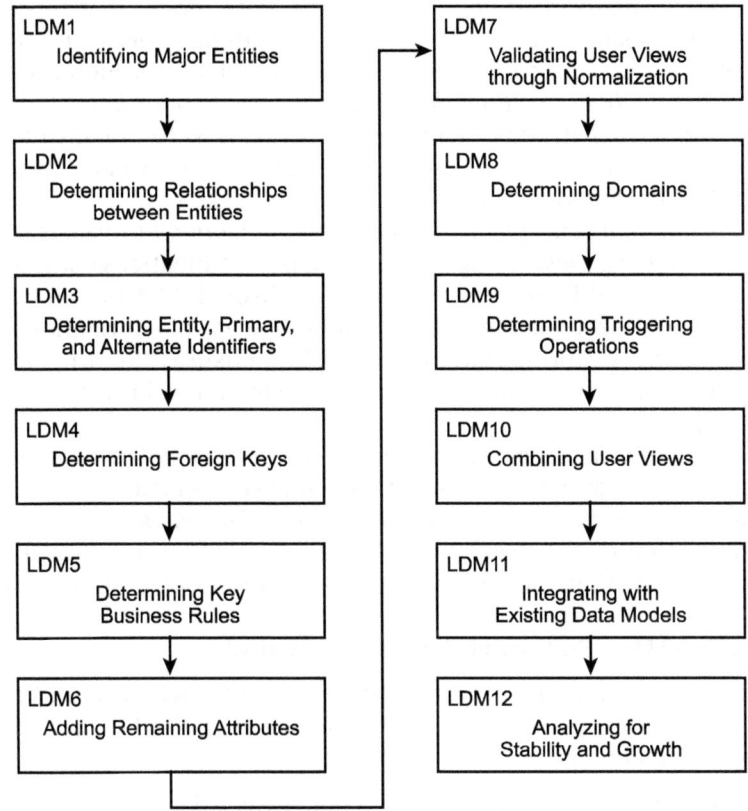

Exhibit 14-4. The data modeling process.

Exhibit 4 illustrates all the steps in the data modeling process, The result is a simple, clear, sharable, stable model exhibiting minimal redundancy and accurately reflecting both the structure and the integrity of information used within the business.

CRITICAL SUCCESS FACTORS IN DATA MODELING

For successful application of a data modeling methodology, the manager should:

- *Work interactively with the users as much as possible.* This will ensure that the manager and the users share an understanding of the information requirements.
- *Follow a structured methodology throughout the data modeling process.* Choose a methodology before beginning and stay with it.

- *Employ a data-driven approach.* Build a data model that represents how the business uses and manages information, unbiased by any particular processing requirements or technological considerations.
- *Incorporate both structural and integrity considerations in the data model.* Addressing structure alone might reveal how to organize records within a database but will not ensure that the data values accurately model business operations.
- *Combine both conceptualization and normalization techniques into the data modeling methodology.* Conceptualization identifies entities, relationships, and identifiers (steps LDM1 through LDM6) and ensures that the model on paper nub-represents the use of information within the business. Normalization (step LDM7) ensures that the model is structurally consistent and logical and has minimal syntactic redundancy.
- *Use diagrams to represent as much of the data model as possible.* Diagrams are clearer, simpler, and more concise than text.
- *Build a data dictionary to supplement the data model diagrams.* Diagrams cannot convey everything. Textual specifications of entity/relationship/attribute definitions and business rules are also needed.

BENEFITS AND APPLICABILITY OF DATA MODELS

Data modeling is a critical prerequisite to effective database design. Logical data modeling m also contribute to the success of other less obvious endeavors, including:

- *Assessing technological feasibility.* A data-driven data model represents data structures, relationships, and rules without any compromises to accommodate technological limitations. The degree to which a particular technological implementation can materialize all components of the data model provides an effective measure of the technology's optimality for related applications.
- *Assessing software packages.* In particular, the degree to which the database design of an application software package approximates the data model serves as one gauge of the package's ability to meet business requirements.
- *Assessing the impact of future changes.* A data model provides a clear picture of the underlying database design, unobliterated by technological detail. It therefore aids significantly in evaluating the effects of changes in business requirements or technology.
- *Facilitating end-user access to data.* A data model is a business representation of information structures and rules, and can be understood by users. It can provide these users with an intelligible map of their data within an end-user computing environment.

- *Facilitating a strategic overview of the business's information needs.* The data modeling process, minus some of its more detailed steps, can be employed to build a strategic data model or high-level representation of all the business's information requirements. A strategic data model can be thought of as a summarized version of the business conceptual schema. The strategic data model can assist in analyzing information interrelationships throughout the business. It therefore can contribute to more effective planning of database and application implementations. For example, it can aid in planning and relating detailed operational systems (those required to run the daily business) and summarized, executive decision-support systems.
- *Migrating data from one technology to another.* Databases can more easily migrate from one technology to a newer or more appropriate technology when a current data model exists. The model can be translated into a new database implementation. The data model can also be used to design extract procedures. If a data model does not exist, one should be built by treating the existing database as a user view and by working with users to discard unnecessary information requirements as well as add new ones.

SUMMARY

Data modeling is the first phase of an effective database design process. It is a technique for understanding and capturing business information requirements that must be met through a database implementation.

The data modeling process begins with the definition of a user view or representation of information requirements for one business function, user, or user group. It culminates in the integration of all user views into one composite data model. Multiple data models are related through their mappings to a business conceptual schema, an integrated data model representing all the business's data requirements at their most detailed level.

Development of data models is a critical component of a data-driven design philosophy. Success stories of database designs that were founded on data models and business conceptual schemas are increasing. The emergence of computer-aided software engineering (CASE) tools has made it possible to automate portions of the logical data modeling process. In addition, the dramatic surge and acceptance of commercial relational DBMS products have provided opportunities for designing databases that closely resemble data models. For all of these reasons, the benefits of a stable data model are perhaps more widely understood and more easily accomplished than ever before.

Chapter 15
Business Information Data Modeling

Deborah L. Brooks

TRANSLATING BUSINESS INFORMATION REQUIREMENTS INTO A DATA MODEL IS NOT ALWAYS A STRAIGHTFORWARD TASK. Certain business information does not always fit into the data model when standard data modeling rules and principles are used. The miles cannot adequately address derived, time-dependent, historical, and externally controlled business information. When faced with such problems, an organization must decide whether to leave these types of business information out of the data model or document them by other means. Before making any decisions, however, the goal of the data model should be reviewed.

A data model embodies a comprehensive understanding of the business information requirements; enables effective communication among designers, developers, and users; and forms the basis for designing correct, consistent, shareable, and flexible databases. An effective data model must reflect reality so that meaningful communication and a sound database design can be facilitated. All business information, regardless of its relative ease to model, should be included in the data model. If a business information requirement is ignored, it may render the data model incomplete and incorrect and may sabotage the subsequent database design.

DERIVED BUSINESS INFORMATION

Derived business information is usually avoided by most data modelers because of its tendency to become redundant. Instances do occur, however, when its inclusion in a data model is appropriate even though it may directly contradict the principles of proper data modeling. One of these circumstances is when the derived data elements represent a significant business meaning for users. For example, a data element for the total amount of an invoice represents the sum of the cost of all individual items ordered minus discounts and including applicable sales tax.

Although this data element is redundant, the concept of an invoice total amount may be extremely valuable to the user. Therefore, its inclusion in the data model represents completeness and promotes understanding and usually outweighs the data modeler's instinct to leave it out. The derived data element, however, must always be designated as such (perhaps with the letter d in parentheses) and the associated derivation algorithm must be documented in the repository, as follows:

```
ENTITY:            INVOICE                      CUSTOMER

DATA ELEMENTS:     INV-NBR                       CUST-NBR

                   CUST-NBR                      CUST-NM

                   INV-DT                        CUST-DSCNT-PCT

                   INV-TOT-AMT   (d)

DATA ELEMENT:      INV-TOT-AMT

DERIVATION:        SUM (UNIT-PRICE-AMT * UNIT-QTY)

                   -CUST-DSCT-AMT *

                   (SUM (UNIT-PRICE-AMT * UNIT-QTY)

                   -SALES TAX-RT *

                   (SUM (UNIT-PRICE-AMT * UNIT-QTY))
```

This documentation ensures that the dependency on the other data elements from which the information derives is not overlooked, which may result in inconsistent data values. This is particularly important because the dependency is often across rather than within entities, and therefore normalization does not detect, eliminate, or control the redundancy.

If derivation is performed outside the scope of the user's view, as is the case with externally controlled business information, the data modeler must decide whether the component data elements used in the derivation are available. If they are not, the data modeler has no choice but to include the derived business information in the data model. However, the data modeler must document the derivation from the other data elements that are outside the scope of the user view that is being developed. This facilitates the combination of user views to create a consolidated enterprise data model at a future date. If the derived data elements are available, the data modeler may still want to include the derived data element in the model if it is meaningful to the user. The elements should, however, be identified as derived and the derivation formula documented in the repository.

Summary-level entities in which all data elements are derived may occur when business information from outside the data model's scope is received at an aggregate level. The base or atomic data elements from which the aggregate data elements derive exist in another user view. These aggregate entities should be included in the data model because this is the level of business information that is relevant to the user view that is being developed.

Aggregate entities may also provide a bridge between an operational or a transaction-level user view and a decision support user view when they are consolidated into an enterprise data model. Aggregate entities that contain summarized business information from base data elements within the user view may be included in the data model. If the summary-level entity participates in relationships that the base entity does not, it should be included. For example, if the level of business information in the aggregate entity is appropriate to compare the base data elements of another entity (e.g., in an auditing system), the aggregate entity should be represented in the data model.

A data model promotes a comprehensive understanding of the business information requirements. If an entity of aggregate business information is meaningful to the user, and if the necessary understanding of the business information Requirements is likely to be impaired by its exclusion, it must be included in the data model. If these aggregate entities are used, however, the data modeler should designate them as such and should reference the base entity that is being summarized in the repository. Every data element in the aggregate entity, the base data elements from which they derive, and the associated algorithm must also be documented in the repository.

TIME-DEPENDENT BUSINESS INFORMATION

When a data model is created with no regard to the element of time, it assumes that the data element values always remain the same. The time-independent data model encapsulates the business information requirements at a single point in time and creates a static view. Therefore, a data model that attempts to depict a realistic view of the data elements must be able to accommodate change. A successful data model contains time-dependent business information so that it can represent the information's requirements over time, not just at a single point in time.

The element of time is incorporated into the data model when the data modeler identifies all data elements whose value can change at different points in time based on a predetermined policy. A policy is then determined internally, as in the case of the maximum percentage of salary contributions made to a retirement account that is matched by the employer, or externally, as in the case of tax or interest rates, by a governing body. The value of these data elements is set on a specific date or day and at a specific time. For example, tax rates are effective on the first day of the calendar year and the IRA interest rates are set each Monday at 10:00 AM. These time-dependent, policy-determined data elements are often used in the calculation of derived business information.

To add the dimension of time to entities, the data modeler can include an effective date as a component of the entity identifier. Examples of time-dependent entities are as follows:

ENTITY:	IRA INTEREST	FEDERAL TAX
DATA ELEMENTS:	IRA_RATE_EFF DT*	FED_TAX_YR*
	TERM_MONTH_NBR	BEG_ANNI_SALARY_AMT
	IRA-INTEREST-PCT	END_ANNI_SALARY_AMT
		FED_TAX_RT

In these examples, the data elements that are denoted by an asterisk provide the time component. The rate of interest for an IRA is determined by the term of the IRA (e.g., 6 months, 12 months, or 24 months) and the effective date of the interest rate. The federal tax rate applied to an employee's salary depends on the tax year, because tax rates are revised annually, and the employee's salary range. Without the two time-specific data elements-the IRA rate effective date and the federal tax year-the entities are still valid, but only for the current point in time. Any changes to these rates then requires coordination so that users know which business information they are working with. If the table containing the IRA interest rates is not updated in a timely manner, users may continue to use the old rates and may assume that the updates have been made. This assumption may exist because it is impossible to identify the time period for which the rate is applicable. Updates cannot be performed in advance of the rate change's effective date because the previous business information, which is still valid at the time, may be lost. In addition, any updates require the use of the business information to be suspended while updates are made.

Although planning for time-dependent business information in the data model is desirable because it provides long-term flexibility, it should also be noted whether the relationships between the entities are different when the data model is viewed at a certain point in time. For example, a current employee is assigned to many departments in the course of his or her tenure with the organization. In addition, a department may have many employees assigned to it. The current employee, the department entities, and the association entity—employee assignment—that are created to resolve this many-to-many relationship is formulated as follows:

ENTITY:	CURRENT EMPLOYEE	DEPARTMENT
DATA ELEMENTS:	EMPLOYEE_NBR	DEPT_NBR
	INTERNAL_TEL_NBR	LOCN_NBR
ASSOCIATIVE ENTITY:	EMPLOYEE ASSIGNMENT	
DATA ELEMENTS:	EMPLOYEE_NBR	
	DEPT_NBR	

One-to-many relationships exist between the current employee and employee assignment entities and between the department and employee

assignment entities. A current employee may, however, be assigned to no more
than one department at a time so that the static data model does not have the
associative entity employee assignment. Instead, a one-to-many relationship
exists between the department and current employee entities, as follows:

```
ENTITY:            CURRENT EMPLOYEE      DEPARTMENT
DATA ELEMENTS:     EMPLOYEE_NBR          DEPT_NBR
                   INTERNAL_TEL_NBR      LOCN_NBR
                   DEPT_NBR
```

How can the data modeler ensure that an employee who is assigned to
many departments is only assigned to one at any given time? The data model
should represent all business information requirements and a one-to-many
relationship cannot accomplish this. The employee assignment that is created to resolve a many-to-many relationship can represent all business information requirements by specifying the business rules that support these
relationships. So, although a one-to-many relationship between current
employee and employee assignment still exists, the organization can specify
a business rule to accommodate this time-specific restriction.

Another alternative to this situation is to add the element of time to the
entity identifier of the associative entity. A modified version of the
employee assignment entity may read as follows:

```
ASSOCIATIVE ENTITY:    EMPLOYEE ASSIGNMENT
DATA ELEMENTS:         EMPLOYEE_NBR
                       DEPT_NBR
                       EMPL_DEPT_BEG_DT
                       EMPL_DEPT_END_DT
```

When the start and end dates that an employee is assigned to a department are added, the time-specific nature of the relationship is clear. The
date modeler should create a business rule that specifies that the period of
time that these dates represent cannot overlap that of any other employee
assignment occurrence for this employee. In addition, the data modeler
should specify whether the number of occurrences that result when the
time component is introduced are fixed in number or variable. This information helps the data modeler to make decisions on how to implement
repeating groups. If the number of occurrences is fixed, the time-dependent
data elements may be implemented as columns instead of as rows.

HISTORICAL BUSINESS INFORMATION

Historical business information is a type of time-dependent business
information, but its focus is different. Time-dependent business information

accommodates future change so that business information requirements can continue to be met. Historical business information documents what has occurred to create a historical record. Time-dependent business information provides for the data model's future; historical business information documents the data model's past.

One form of historical business information is time-dependent derived information. This type of historical information exists when business information is derived at a particular point in time and the same value cannot be recreated at a different point in time using the same algorithm. One reason that the same value cannot be derived again is that the data element values used to derive the business information may change over time (e.g., the price of an item). For example, the tax rate used to compute the federal tax amount deducted from a paycheck changes over time. The tax rate for 1990 is different from the rate for 1991. As a result, it is not possible to recompute the same value for the federal tax deducted from a December 1990 paycheck in the month of January if no history of tax rates is kept.

If no history of the base data element values used to derive another data element is kept, and if historical business information is important to the user, the data modeler must find alternatives. One option is to add the derived data element to the entity so that recalculation at a later date is not required. The data modeler must also ensure that the data element is clearly identified as derived and that its derivation is documented in the repository, illustrated as follows:

```
ENTITY:            EMPLOYEE PAYCHECK      FEDERAL TAX

DATA ELEMENTS:     EMPLOYEF_NBR           BEG_ANNI_SALARY_AMT

                   PAYCHECK_ISSUE_DT      END_ANNI_SALARY_AMT

                   PAY_PERIOD_BEG_DT      FED_TAX_RT

                   BIWK_SALARY_AMT

                   FED_TAX_AMT  (d)

DATA ELEMENT:      FED_TAX_AMT

DERIVATION:        BIWK_SALARY_AMT * FED_TAX_RT that is
                   applicable for the annual salary
                   (BIWK_SALARY_AMT * 26 is between
                   BEG_ANNI_SALARY_AMT and
                   END_ANNI_SALARY_AMT)
```

If all other base data elements used in the calculation are present in the entity, another option is to add the missing data element to the entity so that recalculation is possible. In this case, the federal tax rate is included in the paycheck entity, as follows:

```
ENTITY:            EMPLOYEE PAYCHECK      FEDERAL TAX

DATA ELEMENTS:     EMPLOYEE_NBR           BEG_ANNI_SALARY_AMT

                   PAYCHECK_ISSUE_DT      END_ANNI_SALARY_AMT

                   PAY_PERIOD_BEG_DT      FED_TAX_RT

                   PAY_PERIOD_END_DT

                   BIWK_SALARY_AMT

                   FED_TAX_RT
```

This may be a problem, however, when the derivation algorithm is subject to change. If this occurs, having all the original values does not meet the user's business information requirements because the values do not yield the same result. If the data element is added to another entity, the data modeler should identify the element as redundant and document its source entity in the repository.

The ideal way to handle historical business information is to recognize that change occurs and to plan for it. The data modeler can deal with this by adding an effective date to the entity identifier of the entities whose occurrences may be time-dependent. This ensures that the value of the derived data element can be recalculated at any point in time and keeps redundancy and derived business information to a minimum. The following entry illustrates a scenario in which the year that the federal tax is applied is used to obtain the appropriate tax rate from the federal tax entity:

```
ENTITY:            EMPLOYEE PAYCHECK      FEDERAL TAX

DATA ELEMENTS:     EMPLOYEE_NBR           FED_TAX_YR

                   PAYCHECK_ISSUE_DT      BEG_ANNI_SALARY_AMT

                   PAY_PERIOD_BEG_DT      END_ANNI_SALARY_AMT

                   PAY_PERIOD_END_DT      FED_TAX_RT

                   BIWK_SALARY_AMT

                   FED_TAX_YR
```

Referential integrity must be maintained between these two entities to ensure that there is always an occurrence of the federal tax entity that corresponds to the federal tax year data element in the employee paycheck entity. If these standards are not met, recalculation is not possible.

Another reason to include historical business information in the data model is to fulfill a mandated requirement. A legal requirement or an organizationwide policy may stipulate that all business information that relates to specific transactions must be recorded in full at the time the transaction is issued, to serve as an audit trail. The business information requirement for an audit trail is not met by incorporating the ability to recreate any business information at a later time because this does not ensure the same result.

An employee payroll function illustrates such a situation. When an employee paycheck is issued, it may be considered an auditable event. Examples of derived amounts on a paycheck include FICA; federal, state, and local tax amounts, health insurance payments, and retirement account contributions. To create an audit trail, the data modeler must add a new entity that contains the employee's payroll history. Occurrences of this entity are created only when a paycheck is issued. This ensures that the issued transactions that require an audit trail are separated from those that are pending. AU calculated amounts are included as data elements of this entity. In addition, the data modeler can record all time-dependent, policy-determined data elements that are used in the calculations to support inquiry and dispute resolution requirements. This is particularly necessary when the time-dependent entities for the factors used to calculate the derived business information (e.g., tax rates and the dollar amount represented by each exemption) are not created.

A separate entity can also be created when there is a change in status of an entity's occurrence so that it no longer participates in existing relationships with other entities or now participates in a different set of relationships. For example, a retired employee receives Medicare benefits but does not receive a vacation allowance. A current employee is assigned to a department and a retired employee is not. In addition, different data elements may now be applicable. The current employee has an internal telephone number and the retired employee does not, but he or she always has a retirement date.

The definition of the entity may no longer apply to an occurrence that has undergone a time-dependent status change. The relationships it participates in are different and so are the data elements that describe it. As a result, it cannot be considered the same entity. A new entity-retired employee-should be created. The original employee entity should be renamed current employee to reflect its status because it no longer encompasses all employees, past and present. Because the entity identifier of the two entities is the same (i.e., employee number), however, and because they share many common data elements (e.g., employee name and date of birth), the creation of a supertype entity-employee-is created and the current employee and retired employee entities becomes its subtypes. The subtype entities are related to the supertype entity by a mutually exclusive (e.g., an employee can either be current or retired, but not both) one-to-one relationship. These three entities are formulated as follows:

```
SUPERTYPE ENTITY:    EMPLOYEE
DATA ELEMENTS:       EMPLOYEE_NBR
                     ACTIVE_STATUS_IND
                     EMPLOYEE_NM
                     BIRTH_DT
SUBTYPE ENTITY:      CURRENT EMPLOYEE       RETIRED EMPLOYEE
DATA ELEMENTS:       EMPLOYEE_NBR           EMPLOYEE_NBR
                     DEPT_NBR               RETIRE_DT
                     INTERNAL_TEL_NBR
```

The creation of these additional entities necessitates the maintenance of business information's referential integrity as defined by their relationships. As a result, business rules must be defined for the relationship between the supertype and subtype entities or for any relationships with other entities specific to one of the subtype entities. The same rules exist for the relationships that now apply to an entity that contains historical business information. All historical business information, corporately mandated audit trails, and time-dependent status changes are business information requirements and must be represented in the data model so that comprehensive understanding is achieved and documented.

EXTERNALLY CONTROLLED BUSINESS INFORMATION

All business information that is depicted in the data model may not originate in the organization where the data model is constructed. Because the focus of a data model may be an application, a function, a department, or an organization, external business information refers to any information that is not under the control of the area which constructs the data model. When modeling external business information, the data modeler is inclined to create entities for the business information that is received and not for context-giving entities. For example, when invoices are received from another organization, an invoice entity may be created. However, no invoice is created for the entities of the organization that renders the invoice, the billing account, or the products and services being billed. Only the entity identifier need be defined for contextual entities because their function is to provide a framework for the data model's more detailed entities.

Including the contextual entities makes the data model more understandable and extensible. In the future, it should be easier to increase the scope of a data model because the contextual entities may function as building blocks on which relationships to additional entities can be built. Additional data elements can also be added to these entities as necessitated by the business information requirements being modeled. This method transforms contextual entities -into detailed entities. In addition, contextual entities provide the opportunity to identify redundant data elements or incorrect relationships. For example, the billing account entity that resulted in the previously mentioned invoice may have direct relationships to a billing organization and a geographic region because of its data elements, illustrated as follows:

```
ENTITY:            BILLING ACCOUNT
DATA ELEMENTS:     BILLING_ACCT_NBR
                   BILLING_COMP_CD
                   REGION_CD
```

A billing organization's jurisdiction may, however, cross regional lines. If each region is associated with multiple billing organizations, the data model that depicts one-to-many relationships to the billing account entity from the billing organization and region entities is incorrect. The many-to-many relationship between the billing organization and the region entities must be resolved by creating an associative entity. This, in turn, creates a one-to-many relationship with the billing account entity, as follows:

```
ENTITY:            REGION:                 BILLING COMPANY
DATA ELEMENTS:     REGION_CD               BILL_COMP_CD
ENTITY:            BILLING JURISDICTION
DATA ELEMENTS:     BILLING_COMP_CD
                   REGION-CD
ENTITY:            BILLING ACCOUNT
DATA ELEMENTS:     BILLING_ACCT_NBR
                   BILLING_COMP_CD
                   REGION_CD
```

The relationship of the billing organization is now revised to an association with a single region, but that region can be associated with multiple billing organizations for geographic reporting purposes. There is no direct relationship between the region and billing account entities. If the contextual entities are not included in the data model, the redundant data element-region code-in the billing account entity cannot be uncovered. The fully normalized entities read as follows:

```
ENTITY:            REGION                  BILLING COMPANY
DATA ELEMENTS:     REGION_CD               BILL_COMP_CD
                                           REGION_CD
```

```
ENTITY:            BILLING ACCOUNT
DATA ELEMENTS:     BILLING_ACCT_NBR
                   BILLING_COMP_CD
```

One problem with externally controlled business information is that the same entity in two Organizations may not be consistently defined or have consistent entity identifiers. This occurs when the data models for each organization are constructed independently, with no overall coordination and resolution of differences by an impartial third party. TMs is less of an issue when the organizations are in the same industry, because of the establishment of data administration, which performs this coordination function. It is always an issue when crossing corporate boundaries, however, because each organization has its own version of the industry's vernacular.

An organization must understand what the business information that originates from an external organization actually represents. Only a subset of business information may be received based on some prespecified criteria. For example, the relevant business information from an external billing system are bills with a final status, all other statuses are not relevant. In addition, an aggregate level of the business information is of concern instead of a detailed level. For example, the relevant billing information for time-sharing computer services is the number of minutes used during each rate period, the applicable rate per minute, and the associated cost, not the detail on each individual access to the time-sharing system. By understanding the business information, the data modeler can create entities that capture these relationships in the data model, which improves its clarity and understandability. The determination of the specific business information that is received, as well as its derivation algorithm, can be documented in the repository.

The same entity identifier that the originating organization uses should be implemented whenever possible. The external organization has already determined an entity identifier and it should be used as long as it has all the properties of a proper identifier. This ensures that the same object is identified consistently across organizations. Unfortunately, entity identifiers under the control of an external organization are not always proper identifiers. The entity identifier may not be unique, always present, not null, and stable. In this case, a surrogate key may be used as the entity identifier and the original entity identifier data elements can be included as nonkey data elements in the entity. TMs resolves the entity identifier problem and maintains the ability to track entity occurrences across organizations.

Another consideration when dealing with externally controlled business information is how to physically define the data elements. The originating organization may define data elements as having a numeric physical domain. This is a problem when the business information is physically implemented as numeric and when the physical domain is changed to character at some later date. The existing database structures must be redefined, the business information must be converted, and all application programs that expect a numeric data type must be changed.

If all externally controlled data elements are defined as having a character physical domain to minimize the impact of future changes, however, calculations can no longer be performed. The physical domain should be chang6d to character if the data element is used as an identifier or indicator (e.g., customer number). The valid range of numeric values can be enforced through application logic. If the data element is a dollar amount or a numeric field that may be used in a calculation, the physical domain should not be changed. This approach prevents most conversion efforts because the numeric fields that are used as identifiers are the most likely ones to change to character.

Business information that originates from an external organization presents some unique challenges for the data modeler. This business information cannot be controlled and may cause problems for entity identifier definitions and data element physical domains. Understanding exactly which business information is received concerning its definition, level, and use and designing additional entities that create a context for it helps the organization to achieve a comprehensive data model.

SUMMARY

Some business information is easy to model and other information may be more difficult. Regardless of its difficulty to model, the data modeler must include all business information in the data model to be able to develop a data model that represents a comprehensive understanding of the business information requirements. To develop such a data model, the data modeler must have a thorough understanding of the business information and its meaning and with this knowledge, no business information is impossible to model.

Chapter 16
Making Data Models Readable

David C. Hay

ENTITY-RELATIONSHIP MODELS (OR SIMPLY DATA MODELS) ARE POWER-FUL TOOLS FOR ANALYZING AND REPRESENTING THE STRUCTURE OF AN ORGANIZATION. Properly used, they can reveal subtle relationships between elements of a business. They can also form the basis for robust and reliable database design.

Data models have gotten a bad reputation in recent years, however, as many people have found them to be more trouble to produce and less beneficial than promised. Discouraged, people have gone on to other approaches to developing systems — often abandoning modeling altogether, in favor of simply starting with system design.

Requirements analysis remains important, however, if systems are ultimately to do something useful for the company. And modeling — especially data modeling — is an essential component of requirements analysis.

It is important, therefore, to try to understand why data models have been getting such a bad rap. This author believes, along with Tufte, that the fault lies in the way most people design the models, not in the underlying complexity of what is being represented.

GOALS OF ENTITY-RELATIONSHIP MODELS

An entity-relationship model has two primary objectives:

- First it represents the analyst's public understanding of an enterprise, so that the ultimate consumer of a prospective computer system can be sure that the analyst got it right. Does the analyst really know the business? A properly drawn data model can provide a vivid answer to that question. To the user it addresses the question: "Is this what you want?"
- Second, it represents the fundamental architecture of an enterprise's data, and as such is an ideal starting place for database design. To be sure, the final structure of a database may differ from the data model for good and valid reasons, but the closer it remains to the original

structure, the more likely it is to be able to resist requirements for future changes. To the system designer and builder, it sends the message: "This (rigorously described) is what you are to build."

Because data modeling was created within the computer industry, the second objective has often taken priority. As drawn by systems engineers, data models tend to look like electronic schematics — to be read only by other engineers. The morass of boxes and lines makes them quite formidable to all but the most dedicated reader. Many data modeling conventions — and a great many data modeling practitioners — do not put enough weight on the importance of making the model accessible to the outside world. Indeed, some contend that the models cannot be made accessible to the outside world, so there is no point in even trying.

This article takes the position that not only is it possible to produce model drawings that can be understood by potential systems users, but it is the modeler's responsibility to do so. Some guidelines for producing model drawings follow.

There are two major issues in the readability of models. The first, and the one to be discussed most, is aesthetic. How is the drawing constructed and to what visual effect? The second is the way things in it are named. Are the words on the diagram helpful in divining its meaning?

AESTHETICS

Data modeling was originally an engineering discipline, not an artistic one. For this reason, most modelers pay less attention to aesthetics than they should. Part of the problem is the system of notation they use. Some notations lend themselves to improved aesthetics, while others produce drawings that are nearly impossible to read, regardless of what the modeler does. The rest of the problem is in the way the modeler does his work.

The aesthetic considerations to be discussed are:

1. The ordering or arrangement of symbols on the model
2. The number of symbols on the model
3. The number of symbol types there are
4. How the various layers of the model interact with each other

The modeler has control over the arrangement of the drawing, the number of symbols he uses, and the overall layering of the diagram. The system of notation chosen also affects layering, and determines the number of kinds of symbols that will be present.

Order

How the entities are placed on a page is critical to the viewer's ability to understand a diagram. Typically (especially if the model was produced via an automated tool), there is no rationale for entities' relative positions on a diagram. They wind up wherever it is convenient. In some cases, people will rearrange entities to minimize the crossing of lines, but this adds no semantic meaning to the picture.

This has the effect that as you look at a model drawing, you have no way to get a hold of its overall meaning. You see a random collection of boxes and lines. There is nothing in its overall shape to tell you anything about it.

A very powerful convention for positioning entities is to force all relationships to point in the same direction. Your author follows the "dead crow" rule, that all crow's foot toes should be be pointing either up or to the left. This has the effect of placing the reference entities — the entities describing tangible things in the business — on the lower right, and the transaction entities — those describing what the enterprise does — on the upper left. Others reverse the convention, pointing crow's foot toes south and east. Whichever convention is followed, anyone looking at a model following the dead crow convention can now quickly determine the subject (products, laboratory tests, etc.) and the elements of interest.

Too Many Symbols

The simplest way to improve the appearance of a model is to limit the number of figures (any two-dimensional graphic object) on any one drawing. Twenty seems to be about the maximum that is possible without making a drawing completely unreadable, and ten to fifteen is better.

The number of relationship lines present is less significant, and this will necessarily be a function of the number of things to be connected. The number of line segments can be reduced as well, by eliminating "elbows" in the line. A bent line after all is graphically two lines.

Too Many Symbol Types

Clearly the more different kinds of figures that are on the page, the more confusing the result will be. The question is, how many are needed? Each different kind of symbol is something new for the viewer to learn, and therefore is one more obstacle to understanding. One of the reasons models often become cumbersome is that too much is attempted with them. There is a limit to the amount of information that can be conveyed on one page.

As a minimum, the model needs symbols for:

- Entities
- The existence of relationships between pairs of entities
- Optionality: Must an occurrence of one entity have a corresponding occurrence of another, or not?
- Cardinality: May an occurrence of one entity have more than one corresponding occurrence of another, or not?

243

In addition, it is often necessary to represent sub-types of an entity — sets of occurrences that represent subsets of the occurrences of the entity. There is a question, however, as to how elaborate this representation should be. There also is a question of whether to represent attributes of an entity, and how. And finally, many notations — but not all — represent the elements that uniquely identify an occurrence of an entity.

A wide variety of data modeling techniques are being used today. The original notation was invented by Peter Chen. Among those most commonly used since Chen's work are James Martin's Information Engineering and IDEF1X[1]. The latter is the standard for the Federal Government. Also popular is Oracle's Oracle Method (formerly the CASE*Method)[2], and the Structured Systems Analysis and Design Method (SSADM)[3], which is particularly popular in Europe.

Lately, the object-oriented phenomenon has produced several techniques for drawing "object models" instead of entity-relationship (e-r) models. While object models do include descriptions of the "behavior" of each entity, they otherwise show exactly the same concepts as e-r models. Indeed, James Martin's "object diagrams," for example, are literally his entity-relationship diagrams renamed (although he does modify his sub-type notation somewhat).[4] Among the most popular object modeling techniques are those published by James Rumbaugh and his associates,[5] Sally Shlaer and Stephen Mellor,[6] and the team of David Embley, Barry Kurtz, and Scott Woodfield.[7] Ed Yourdon has also published a book on object modeling.[8]

A completely different approach to modeling data structure is presented in object-role modeling, formerly known as NIAM[9].

In this article, examples from many of these techniques will be presented. The principles discussed, however, apply to all of them.

Entities. Representation of the first concept is not controversial. A box, with rounded or square corners (or in some cases, an ellipse) can represent an entity. This is a thing of significance to the organization, about which it wishes to hold information. Entities are the primary objects on an entity/relationship diagram. Exhibit 1 shows some entities.

Be sure, however, that you are in fact modeling entities — things of significance to the business — and not just a database design. The concepts

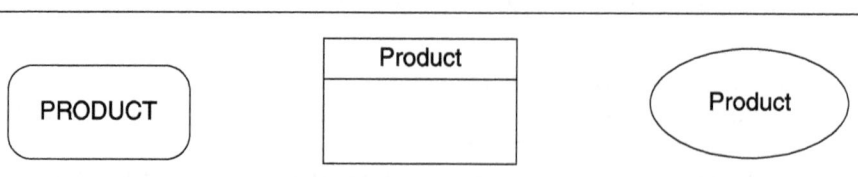

Exhibit 16-1. Entities.

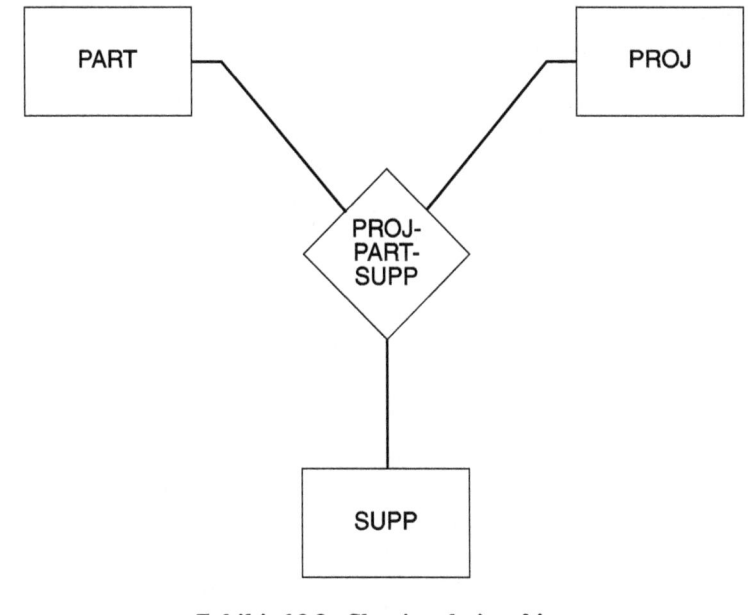

Exhibit 16-2. Chen's relationships.

and issues which go into database design are by and large not of interest to the general public.

Relationships. At its simplest, a relationship is represented in most techniques by a simple line connecting two entities. Optionality and cardinality are then shown as characteristics of the relationship by additional symbols. In those cases where a relationship itself has attributes and other relationships to it, many techniques endorse simply defining an entity to represent the relationship as itself being a thing of significance to the enterprise. A line item, for example, is essentially a relationship between an order and a product, but most approaches treat it as an entity in its own right.

Chen, on the other hand, adds a different symbol (a rhombus) in the middle of the relationship line, to allow him to show these entity-like characteristics, without losing the fact that it is something other than an entity that is being represented.

Exhibit 2, for example, shows the three-way relationship PROJ-PART-SUPP,[10] which is the fact that a PART is supplied to a PROJECT by a SUPPLIER. An alternative to this approach would be to replace PROJ-PART-SUPP with an entity of the same name. (Better yet, replace it with an entity that has a meaningful name, such as SUPPLY. See the discussion of names following.) This would mean the same thing, while eliminating the second symbol type. Chen would probably argue that this second approach camouflages the object's role as a relationship. The question to answer is: how important is that to

245

the viewer's comprehension of the model, and does the distinction have any effect on database design?

Optionality and Cardinality. The most direct way to approach optionality and cardinality is to simply place numbers by the target entity. The Chen, Coad/Yourdon, and several of the object-oriented techniques do this. "Must be at least one but may be any positive number" is shown by "1,m." "Must be exactly one" is shown by "1,1." "May be zero or any number" is shown by "0,m," etc.

This keeps the graphics simple and puts this information on a different graphic "layer" than the rest of the drawing. It means, for example, that the information must be processed by the left brain as data, rather than the right brain as a graphic experience. This makes the effect less powerful.

A small graphic symbol and its absence can also convey whether or not an occurrence of an entity may have more than one occurrence of a related entity. Another symbol or its absence can convey whether the upper limit of the relationship is one or more than one. As small symbols, these do not compete graphically with the overall presentation of entities and relationships. Typically, a crow's foot or its absence shows cardinality. The Oracle Method uses this convention. James Martin's Information Engineering uses the crow's foot for an upper limit of "many," but instead of just leaving it off for an upper limit of one, it adds an extra mark across the line.

There is less agreement on the representation of optionality. James Martin puts a circle next to the optional entity and a mark across the relationship next to a mandatory entity. ("One and only one" then winds up with two marks next to the entity.) The Oracle Method uses a dashed half-line for an optional relationship and a solid half line for a mandatory one. SSADM assumes that in most cases the many side is optional and the one side is mandatory, so it only adds a circle in the middle of the line for those cases where the one side is optional. It does not permit the many side to be mandatory.

Exhibit 3 shows the Oracle Method's treatment of optionality and cardinality, and Exhibit 4 shows James Martin's symbols. Martin's symbols are a bit more busy, but in both cases, if the symbols for the upper limit are known, the cardinality is known regardless of the optionality. Similarly, if you know the symbols for lower limit, you know optionality regardless of cardinality.

Shlaer and Mellor use a different set of graphics (Exhibit 5), but they also show consistency for all combinations of optionality and cardinality.

By far the most complex system of notation is also one that is widely used — IDEF1X. It is the standard for the U.S. Government and is common elsewhere as well. Unfortunately, it suffers from several problems that make it more complex than is necessary for the purposes we are pursuing here.

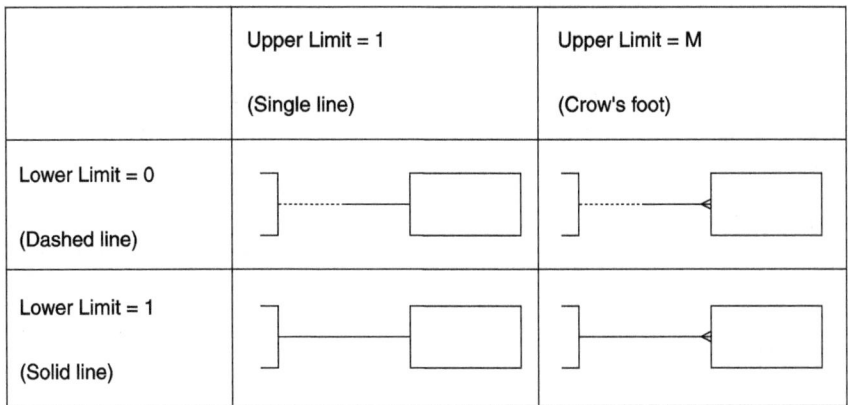

	Upper Limit = 1 (Single line)	Upper Limit = M (Crow's foot)
Lower Limit = 0 (Dashed line)		
Lower Limit = 1 (Solid line)		

Exhibit 16-3. Oracle method cardinaltiy and optionality.

Attributes. There is also a question of whether attributes must be shown, and if so, how.

The tidiest model clearly is one in which attributes are not shown. If the model is being presented to a group for the purpose of communicating the basic nature of the entities and relationships, it is better to leave them off. In your presentation of the model, describe enough of them to make clear the meaning of each entity, but they do not have to be on the drawing. Adding them as text inside the entity boxes does not have a serious impact on the overall readability of the model, however (as long as there aren't too many), so they can be included, if desired. Exhibit 6 shows this. Note that in this example, the attributes themselves have been flagged as to whether

	Upper Limit = 1 (Single line)	Upper Limit = M (Crow's foot)
Lower Limit = 0 (Circle)		
Lower Limit = 1 (Solid line)		

Exhibit 16-4. James Martin cardinality and optionality.

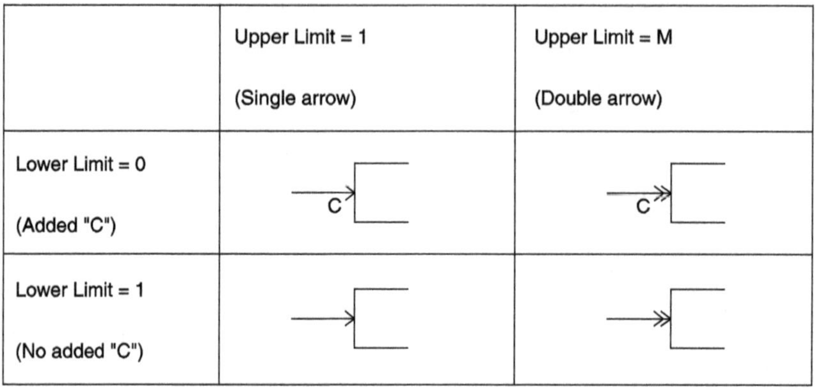

	Upper Limit = 1 (Single arrow)	Upper Limit = M (Double arrow)
Lower Limit = 0 (Added "C")		
Lower Limit = 1 (No added "C")		

Exhibit 16-5. Shlaer and Mellor cardinality and optionality.

each is mandatory (*) or optional (.). These additional symbols add information without cluttering the overall model.

Some techniques (object-role modeling and Chen) go a step further, however, by showing attributes in additional circles (or ellipses) on the drawing. Chen's notation is shown in Exhibit 7. This greatly increases the number of symbols that must be on a page, thus making the model more complex.

Object-role modeling takes the unusual approach of not distinguishing graphically between attributes and entities. This is based on the premise that the relationship between an attribute and an entity is conceptually the same as a relationship between two entities. While this also makes the model more crowded than the notation shown previously, the consolidation of entities and attributes actually reduces the number of kinds of symbols by one. The "not too many objects" rule still applies, though, and this will require the domain of each drawing to be smaller. Exhibit 7 shows an example using object-role modeling, where the relationships

PRODUCT
* ID
* Name
• Standard Cost
• Color

Exhibit 16-6. Attributes.

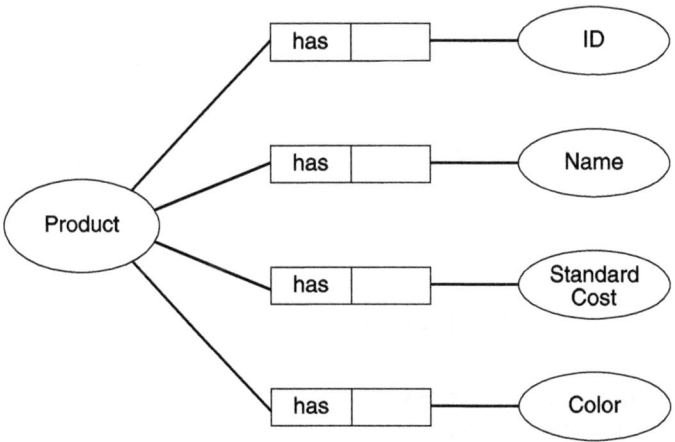

Exhibit 16-7. ORM attributes.

between an entity and its attributes have now been made explicit. "ID" and "Name" are shown to be mandatory by the dots on their relationships, next to PRODUCT.

The arrows under "has" in each relationship simply mean that PRODUCT can have only one value for each attribute — thus requiring the model to be in first normal form. This representation of uniqueness in ORM is difficult to master initially (it is another symbol, after all), but it does allow this technique to represent subtleties not available to conventional e-r modeling. It extends to the relationships between an entity and its attributes the same concepts of optionality and cardinality discussed earlier between entities themselves. The notation is the same whether the ellipses stand for entities or attributes: for cardinality, the presence of a double-headed arrow under the left side of the relationship means that only one occurrence of the object on the right may be applied to an occurrence of the object on the left. Without it, a PRODUCT could have more than one value for "ID." Similarly the dot or its absence represents optionality for both attributes and entities.

Subtypes and Supertypes. A subtype is an entity which represents a subset of occurrences of another entity — its supertype. An occurrence of the supertype is also an occurrence of one and only one subtype, and an occurrence of a subtype must also be an occurrence of the supertype. Some techniques take the Venn diagram approach of showing the subtypes inside the supertype. Exhibit 8, for example, shows Martin's Information Engineering notation for subtypes and supertypes. This has the advantage of compactness and of emphasizing the fact that an occurrence of the subtype is an occurrence of the supertype. The compactness allows the supertype and

249

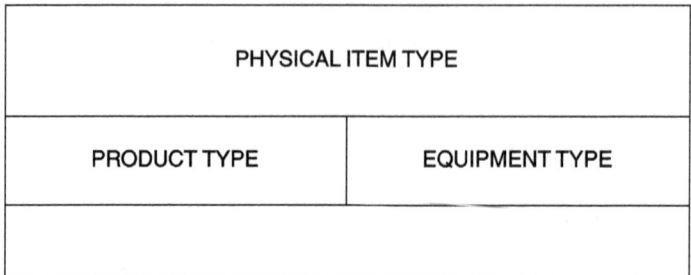

Exhibit 16-8. Compact substyles.

all its subtypes to count graphically as one object, making it easier to follow the "not too many objects" rule.

This has the disadvantage, however, of making it impossible to show the case where a subtype is of more than one supertype ("multiple inheritance" in object-oriented lingo). It is also not possible to show the case where a supertype has more than one set of non-overlapping subtypes ("orthogonal subtypes").

To represent these situations, it is necessary to show the subtypes outside the supertype entity with a relationship (often called an "isa" relationship) tying them together. While this does provide the added expressiveness, it has the disadvantage of adding objects to the diagram, and of reducing the clarity of the subtype concept. Exhibit 9 shows the example from Exhibit 8 in this external version, as specified by the object-modeling technique (described by James Rumbaugh and his colleagues). A similar approach is used by other object-modeling techniques and IDEF1X.

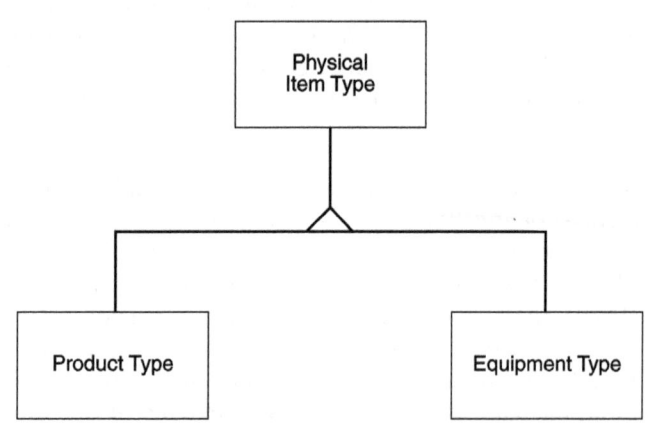

Exhibit 16-9. "ISA" relationships.

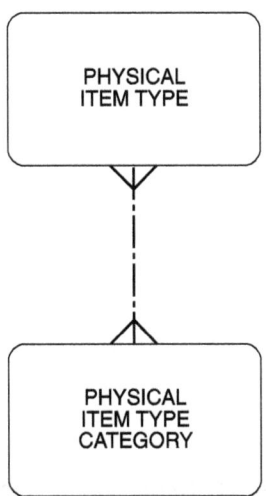

Exhibit 16-10. The category approach — unique identifiers.

Multiple inheritance is a bad idea; every example of multiple inheritance (and its complexity) could be eliminated by doing the model differently. Similarly, subtypes are reserved for the situation where the structure is fundamental, and in these cases it is highly unlikely that there would be more than one set of subtypes for a supertype. The other situations can be handled by defining a … CATEGORY entity, where each member of the entity may be (or must be) a member of one (or one or more?) … CATEGORY. For example, Exhibit 10 shows that each PHYSICAL ITEM TYPE must be in one or more PHYSICAL ITEM TYPE CATEGORIES. Examples of PHYSICAL ITEM TYPE CATEGORY could be "product type" and "equipment type," along with all the other possible subtypes.

Unique Identifiers. An additional concept that can be represented on a model is the set of attributes and relationships which uniquely identify an occurrence of an entity. Many of the notations do not include this information. Some, such as the Oracle Method, simply add a special symbol (such as the "#" in Oracle's case) in front of an attribute participating in the unique identifier, and place a symbol (in Oracle's case, an extra mark) across a relationship participating.

In Exhibit 11, COURSE's unique identifier, for example, is simply the attribute "ID." COURSE OFFERING's unique identifier is a combination of the attribute "Sequence" plus the relationship to COURSE. This means that when this model is implemented in tables, the primary key of COURSE ("ID") will become a foreign key in COURSE OFFERING. It and "Sequence" together will form the primary key of that table.

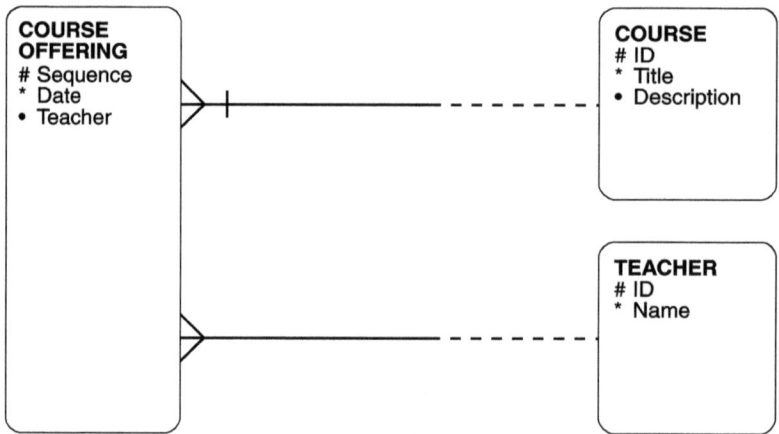

Exhibit 16-11. Oracle unique identifiers.

Note that COURSE OFFERING is also related to TEACHER, but this is not part of the unique identifier, so it does not have the short line crossing the relationship. Each line is partially solid and partially dashed, according to the rules for optionality described previously. (Each COURSE OFFERING *must be* related to one COURSE and to one TEACHER, but that each COURSE and TEACHER may or may not be related to a COURSE OFFERING.)

IDEF1X, on the other hand, takes a more dramatic approach. If a relationship participates, the entire line is changed from a dashed line to a solid line, and the entity box so identified is changed from having square corners to having round corners. The identified entity is considered to be conceptually different from those still having the square corners. It is called a "dependent entity." An example is shown in Exhibit 12. The relationship between COURSE and COURSE OFFERING is solid because it is part of COURSE OFFERING's unique identifier, while the relationship between TEACHER and COURSE OFFERING is dashed. The round corners for dependence happen if any of its relationships are identifying.

In addition, IDEF1X describes the unique identifier yet one more time by using the language of relational database design. Relationships are explicitly (if redundantly) shown as foreign keys, identified by "(fk)." The unique identifier is referred to as a "primary key" and is shown above the line in the entity box. If the relationship participates in a primary key, the foreign key implied by the relationship is shown accordingly.

This places great emphasis on the concept of dependence, but it is questionable whether this is either meaningful to any users viewing the model, or if it in any way changes the response of system designers, who only

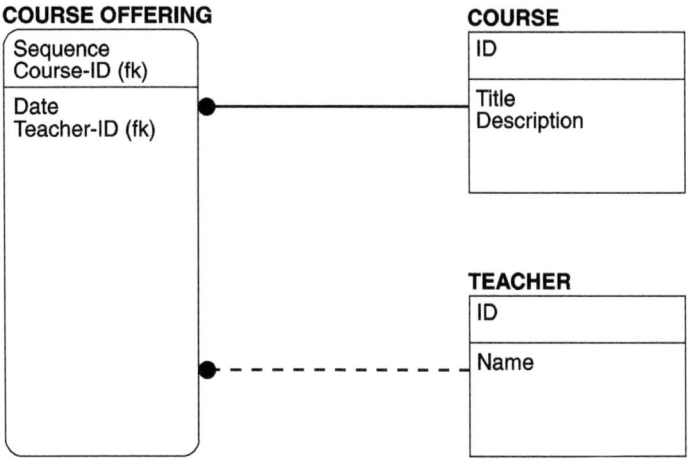

COURSE OFFERING

| Sequence
Course-ID (fk) |
| Date
Teacher-ID (fk) |

COURSE

| ID |
| Title
Description |

TEACHER

| ID |
| Name |

Exhibit 16-12. Unique identifiers in IDEF1X.

really need to know what the unique identifier (to be implemented as a primary key) is.

In summary, the following require additional symbols on the model, and it is not clear whether these are either required to make the model more effective in communicating with users, or useful in providing more information to system developers:

- A distinction between an objectified relationship and an intangible entity.
- Multiple inheritance of subtypes.
- Orthogonal subtypes.
- Attributes as alternatives to entities.
- Dependent entities.
- Database design references

By not seeking to add these concepts to the model, you can greatly reduce its complexity and make it more accessible to end users.

Bent Lines. Another way extra symbols get added to a diagram is unintentional: elbows in relationship lines. A corner is a shape, one that draws the eye to it as much as any other shape, but one that carries no semantic meaning. Moreover, when the relationship lines become too convoluted, they also create additional graphic figures on the page — figures which add clutter, but do not add information. In Exhibit 13, how many rectangles are there? How many of them have meaning? The one in the middle is clearly a distraction.

Even if crossed lines are avoided, ghost shapes are not. Where is the fifth rectangle in Exhibit 14?

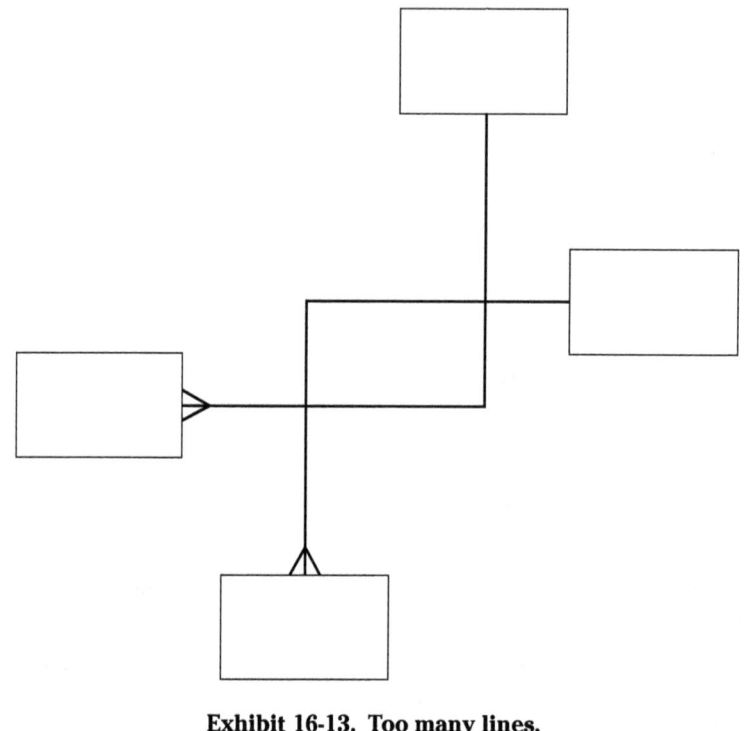

Exhibit 16-13. Too many lines.

The way to avoid bending lines, of course, is to stretch the entities as necessary. (CASE tools which do not allow this are particularly reprehensible.) Exhibit 15 shows how straighter lines give the entities much greater impact.

Layering. Edward Tufte has said that "among the most powerful devices for reducing noise and enriching the content of displays is the technique of layering and separation, visually stratifying various aspects of data ... the various elements of flatland interact creating non-information patterns and texture, simply through their combined presence."[11]

Tufte's idea of layering is that different kinds of information should be represented in sufficiently different ways that one can view only part of the picture at once, and easily ignore the rest. When attributes are represented as symbols in their own right, as in the Chen and the ORM techniques, they have the same status on the diagram as entities. Similarly Chen's relationship symbols make the viewer see a relationship as another object on the same level as an entity, even though semantically he specifically wants it to be considered as different from an entity. That means that the viewer must deal with entities, relationships, and attributes at the same time, with all competing for attention. The graphic distinctions between completely different kinds of information are small.

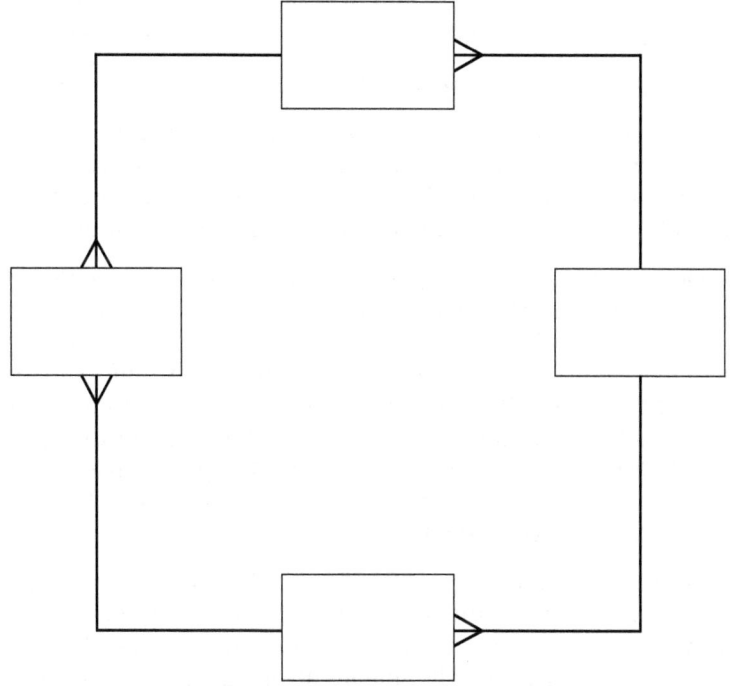

Exhibit 16-14. Hidden square?

There is a natural priority to the concepts discussed in this article. In working with a user to understand a business, it is most important to know what the entities are and whether the relationships among them are mandatory in either direction. That is, must an occurrence of one entity have

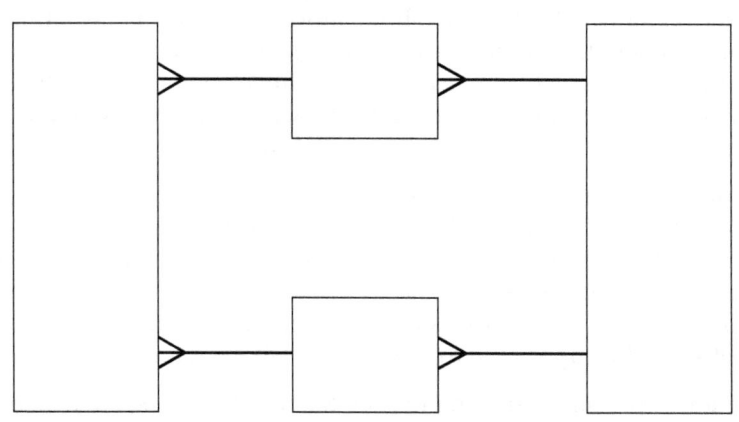

Exhibit 16-15. Straighter lines.

an occurrence of another? After that, it is important to ascertain whether an occurrence can have more than one occurrence of the other entity.

Of lesser interest are the specific attributes of each entity.

The lowest priority, and indeed something that probably will only be discussed with the user in special cases, is whether or not the identity of occurrences of an entity depends on occurrences of another entity. Where this is so, it is usually obvious and not something that requires discussion.

Because of these priorities, graphically, the most dramatic symbols should be the entities and relationships themselves, followed by those used for the cardinality and optionality questions, with perhaps an appended symbol for the unique identifier. In IDEF1X, unfortunately, the most dramatic feature is the least important one — the notation for unique identifier. This involves the relationship line, the shape of the entity box, and the definition of attributes. Among other things, the use of solid and dashed lines means that the unique identifier decision must be made first, in order to draw the model at all.

This issue of convoluted lines also goes to the point of layering as well. As shown in the example above, the use of many lines with elbows can interfere with the viewer's ability to pick out the entities. By restricting yourself to straight lines, even if it means stretching the entities, you focus the viewer's attention on the entities first. In stretching entities, by the way, you have the opportunity to make the most important entities larger, and the lesser entities smaller, further contributing to effective layering.

POOR NAMING

The hardest thing for technicians to do is to name things. Many of us got into computers, after all, because we didn't do all that well in English classes. But names are important. An entity is a thing of significance to the business, about which it wants to hold information. The name of that thing must be meaningful. It cannot be an acronym, or an abbreviation, or a table name. Unfortunately, too many analysts think they are providing table names for a database management system (with their attendant limitations on length), and the readability of the model suffers.

But one is looking for the names of things of significance to the business, not tables. In Chen's drawing (Exhibit 2), the entity names PROJ and SUPP are less than fully explanatory. Even worse, PART-PROJ-SUPP is not at all meaningful. Better would be something like SUPPLY, which at least conveys the idea that something is being supplied. Failure to name entities meaningfully makes it virtually impossible to understand what a data model is about.

Relationship names are even harder. Some techniques, such as SSADM and Yourdon's object-modeling technique, do not show relationship names at all. While it is true that this further simplifies the model aesthetically, it deprives the viewer of very important information about the model's meaning. Where they are used, it has become a convention to use verbs as relationship names, but unfortunately verbs, if not completely meaning-less, are often less than expressive of the full implication and meaning of the relationship. "Has" is the most commonly used relationship name, and it tells very little about the true nature of the relationship.

Moreover, when a verb is used, the relationship name often begins to look like a function name — which is the rightful topic of a different kind of model.

It is preferable to use prepositional phrases, since the preposition, after all, is the part of speech that specifically addresses relationships. The Oracle Method has a particularly clever way to do this, using a normal but highly structured sentence to describe an entire relationship. The relationship names are designed to fit into the following structure, reading the relationship in each direction:

> *Each*
> *<entity 1>*
> *must be*
> *[or]*
> *may be*
> *<relationship>*
> *one and only one*
> *[or]*
> *one or more*
> *<entity 2>.*

The sentence neatly captures not only the relationship itself, but also its cardinality and optionality. For example, in Exhibit 16, the relationship shown may be expressed by the two sentences:

1. Each ORDER may be composed of one or more LINE ITEMS."
2. Each LINE ITEM must be part of one and only one ORDER."

As described previously, the presence or absence of crow's feet dictates "one or more" (upper limit many) or "one and only one" (upper limit one).

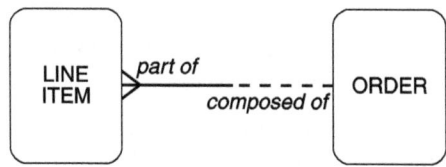

Exhibit 16-16. Oracle relationship names.

The solid line half means "must be" (lower limit one) and the dashed line half means "may be" (lower limit zero).

WHAT TO DO?

So, what is a person to do to make a diagram that is attractive and easy to read?

- Limit what you are trying to present to that which is meaningful and important to your audience. While it is desirable to present as much as possible, this exercise rapidly reaches the point of diminishing returns, where the addition of more information to the drawing actually subtracts from its overall effectiveness. Among other things, this means:
  — Using as consistent and spare a notation scheme as possible.
  — Limiting the number of objects appearing on a diagram.
- Arrange the diagram in a rational way.
- Make sure that your names are meaningful and clear.
- Use patterns that have been tested.

PRESENTING YOUR MODEL

As important as the construction of a model is, it is equally important to present it in a way that permits the viewer to ease his way into the concepts involved. Models can be presented in an understandable way if a few rules are followed.

First of all, be sure to begin the session with a careful and thorough explanation of just what the objectives are. One cannot build a system without the viewers' assurance that their business is understood. This technique is intended to show them what is understood, so that corrections can be made if necessary. The presenter is there to be wrong, since it is much cheaper for him or her to be wrong now, than it is to wait and be wrong in the design of a system. The presentation is in terms of the structure of their data, so by extension, it is really about the structure of their business. Admit that the technique is a bit arcane and point out that it examines business from a perspective which may be unfamiliar to them, so ask their indulgence.

Then, do not begin by presenting a completed model. Even the most artistic model is too frightening to see as a whole. Begin by presenting a slide with one entity. Discuss that entity. What does it mean? What are its attributes? Can you think of any examples?

Add another one, with a relationship between the two. Discuss the second entity. Then discuss the relationship. Is it true that it must be related to only one? Can a case ever be imagined where it is related to more than one? Then add a couple of more entities and relationships at a time, discussing each part thoroughly, until completing the page. Then build up the next drawing in the same way.

Where you have intersect entities, always present the reference entities first. There may even be a slide showing a many-to-many relationship. Discuss the need for attributes that apply to each occurrence of a pair. Then present the slide with the intersect entity.

In doing the presentation, be sure to have a marking pen handy. It will be amazing how quickly the audience becomes so involved that it tells you where the model is wrong. Listen. Where it is wrong (and it will be wrong), mark up the slide to demonstrate that someone is listening.

Notes

1. Thomas A. Bruce, *Designing Quality Databases: Practical Information Management & IDEF1X,* New York:Dorset House Publishing, 1992.
2. Richard Barker, *CASE*Method Entity Relationship Modelling.* Wokingham, England:Addison-Wesley Publishing Company, 1990.
3. Ed Downs, Peter Clare, and Ian Coe, *Structured Systems Analysis and Design Method.* Englewood Cliffs, NJ:Prentice-Hall, Inc., 1988).
4. James Martin and James J. Odell, *Object-oriented Methods.* Englewood Cliffs, NJ:PTR Prentice-Hall, Inc., 1995.
5. James Rumbaugh, Michael Blaha, William Premerlani, Frederick Eddy, and William Lorensen, *Object-oriented Modeling and Design.* Englewood Cliffs, NJ: Prentice-Hall, Inc., 1991.
6. Sally Shlaer and Stephen J. Mellor, *Object-oriented Systems Analysis: Modeling the World in Data.* Englewood Cliffs, NJ:Prentice-Hall, Inc., 1988.
7. David W. Embley, Barry D. Kurtz, and Scott N. Woodfield, *Object-oriented Systems Analysis: A Model Driven Approach.* Englewood Cliffs, NJ:Yourdon Press, 1992.
8. Edward Yourdon and Peter Coad, *Object-oriented Analysis.* Englewood Cliffs, NJ:Prentice-Hall, Inc., 1990.
9. Terry Halpin, *Conceptual Schema & Relational Database Design.* Sydney:Prentice-Hall Australia, 1995.
10. This example is from Chen, *op cit,* pp. 17–20
11. Tufte, *op. cit.*

Chapter 17
Integrating Process and Data Models in a Horizontal Organization

David C. Wallace

INFORMATION SYSTEMS ARE CREATED TO HELP ACHIEVE THE GOALS AND OBJECTIVES OF THE ORGANIZATION by integrating them with information technology. Information technology is an extensive concept in which all the new technologies from fax machines to multimedia devices to new computer hardware and software are grouped. To be an effective part of an organization, individuals must understand and use information technology within the organization.

Therefore, an organization that wishes to be successful must first develop a strategic plan, which involves a systematic way of integrating information systems and information technology. Currently, the IS field is focusing on developing both new methodologies and criteria for the evaluation and selection of appropriate methodologies. This is often completed without regard to new trends within the business and organization fields. When that happens, the new methodologies may not meet the needs of the business community and might produce systems that are flawed.

IS methodologies have largely ignored the recent trends within the business management area — the gap between research and practice. One of these major trends focuses on aligning organizational resources around essential processes, or *core processes*. This trend has been identified by F. Ostroff and D. Smith of McKinsey & Company as the horizontal corporation. M.A. Burns, Chairman of Ryder System Inc., states that the horizontal corporation concept is the wave of the future. From such large profit-centered organizations as General Electric, AT&T, Ryder, and Xerox to such small nonprofit organizations as the Police Department at Illinois State

0-8493-0882-8/00/$0.00+$.50

University, there is a movement toward the horizontal organization. L.A. Bossidy, chairman of Allied Signal Inc., sees a significant increase in productivity as more organizations restructure themselves around this concept.

In this paradigm, the organization restructures its goals and objectives around the essential processes that define the organization's existence and sequential survival. The result is the flattening of the organizational structure into essential processes — eliminating the traditional hierarchy of bureaucratic divisions, departments, or sections. This allows both profit and nonprofit organizations to be more responsive to their clients or customers. The traditional goals of profitability, market share, and shareholders' satisfaction will not be identified as goals, but as natural outcomes resulting from the emphasis on tying goals to an organization's essential processes.

Integrating recent trends in the business organization field with an effective IS methodology is a critical success factor for an organization. For a profit-centered organization, this will often provide the means to achieve competitive advantages in the market by: enhancing existing products and services, developing new products and services, changing the existing industry and its characteristics, and creating new industries and markets.

For a nonprofit organization, the ability to stretch shrinking resources to meet the demands of its constituents is critical to its success. As budget dollars for local, state, and federal agencies are cut, these agencies still find themselves responsible for meeting the requirements of their charters. They will also need to integrate their IS structures around proven trends within the organization field to achieve their maximum productivity. Therefore, it is important to develop IS methodologies that integrate these recent trends.

THE HORIZONTAL CORPORATION

The horizontal corporation is an approach for all types of organizations — public or private, profit or nonprofit, corporate or sole proprietorships, large or small. The prerequisites for this approach are to redefine corporate goals around strategic actions that will improve the organization's competitiveness, efficiency, or other strategic actions defined by the organization. One important goal for any organization is to focus on improvement.

To meet the challenges of competitive domestic and international markets or the demands for shrinking funding dollars, organizations must constantly review and improve their operations. The organization must know its markets and customers thoroughly to know what it will take to satisfy them. For nonprofit organizations, shareholders include the people they serve and the funding sources on which they depend. Once these corporate goals have been clearly identified, the organization should be able to identify key objectives that will help them achieve these goals (e.g., customer and supplier satisfaction). These key objectives are measurable and identifiable for reach process and should contribute to the organization goals.

The next step requires the organization to identify its essential processes. These processes can be characterized by mission-critical applications or core processes. The applications focus on the very purpose or meaning of the organization (e.g., the identification of new markets and new customers, retention of existing customers, and other critical applications). The very purpose or meaning criteria can be answered by focusing on the actions necessary to accomplish the corporate goals. The key objectives identified in the previous step should provide insight into the identification of the essential processes. For example, customer satisfaction can be achieved through customer support, new product development, and sales and fulfillment. The next series of steps involves the actual restructuring of the organization.

Multidisciplinary Efforts

Once the essential processes have been identified, the organization will restructure itself around these processes. Each process will have a manager who helps facilitate the coordination and communication within the process and with other processes. Each process should link related tasks to yield a product or service to a customer or user. Careful attention should be given to the elimination of tasks that do not support, in some way, the related objectives of the process. Such tasks or activities are a waste of time and resources.

Training, evaluating, and paying employees should be linked to the accomplishments of objectives of the essential processes. Each process is responsible for all tasks needed to produce the end-product or service. This requires each process to be multidisciplinary (e.g., finance, marketing, production, accounting, or sales). The intent is to localize the necessary tasks for an essential process to streamline operations so that the organization can react quickly to changing conditions. Ideally, each task should harmoniously fit together with the next to generate the end result, thereby eliminating layers of bureaucracy that tend to increase costs and delay actions. All essential processes should harmoniously fit together to achieve all strategic goals of the organization.

By eliminating layers of administration and bureaucracy, each process can focus on accomplishing its objectives and becoming better able to meet the constant challenges of a changing market. The upper-level support departments provide additional expertise (e.g., legal, technical, and administrative). Core knowledge and expertise will be provided by the essential process. The main purpose of flattening the organization structure into horizontal layers of essential processes is to allow the organization to function more efficiently and quickly.

Traditional organizational structures require much coordination across department boundaries where such functions as sales, marketing, management, and accounting are often housed. The larger, more complex organizations would often experience long delays and information failure (e.g., lost or misdirected paperwork) as information was passed from one functional area or department to another. By localizing the necessary tasks into one process, the organization can provide a seamless effort in which the amount of information interchange is kept to a minimum, thereby reducing delays and information failures. Companies that have moved toward the horizontal corporate approach have been able to reduce response time significantly and improve overall operating performance.

The horizontal concept is illustrated in Exhibit 1. The essential processes operate on a horizontal level using the multidisciplinary efforts within each process to accomplish their objectives. Each process is not a standalone entity, but is integrated into part of an entire picture in which each part communicates and coordinates with each other part. Realistically, special expertise and strategic direction are needed to monitor changing conditions in the markets and environments in which the organization must exist.

These strategic considerations should be accomplished at a higher level. The more operational and managerial considerations would be held at the process level. Downsized support departments (e.g., finance, legal, accounting, and marketing) will exist at the higher level within the organization to provide the expertise needed by the processes. Strategic direction will be provided by a high-level department. The responsibility for this department will be to provide strategic planning and direction for the organization. Exhibit 1 illustrates the relationship between the essential processes and the higher-level support departments. The interactions between the processes, between the support departments, and between the support departments and the processes are shown with double arrows.

Information, and the systems that support its capture, transformation, and dissemination, are strategic to the survival of the organization. To support horizontal organization adequately, IS personnel must incorporate a methodology that supports the horizontal approach. Without recognizing the recent trends in organizational structure and adopting methods to facilitate their integration, information system resources will not gain full management support and may lose their major impact on the organization.

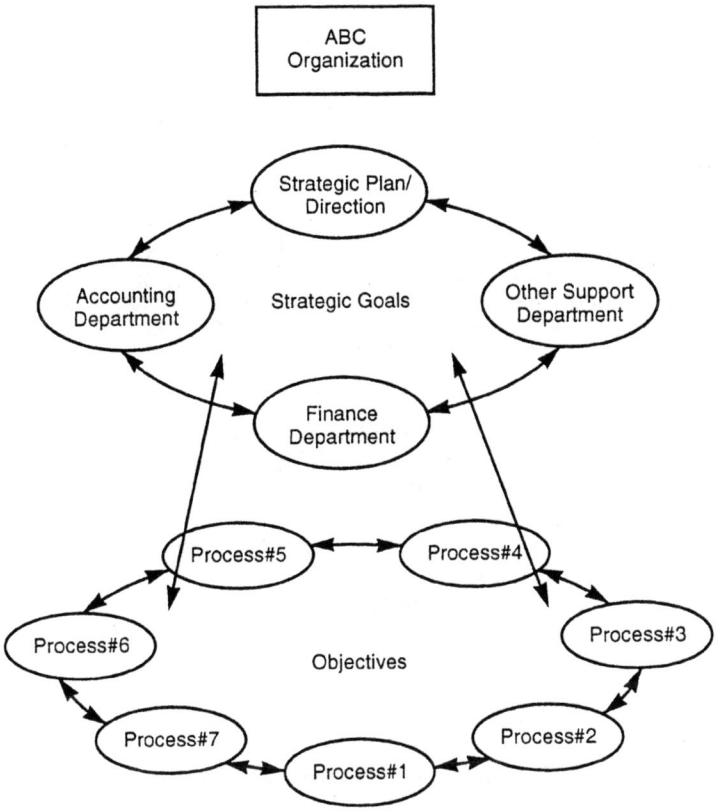

Exhibit 17-1. Horizontal organization structure.

IS METHODOLOGIES

Integrating IS throughout the organization is a key issue for senior management. Two popular methodologies that can be used to facilitate the integration of information systems within an organization are: a data-focused approach and a process-focused approach.

The Data-Focused Approach

The data-focused approach is currently the more popular methodology. Generally, data models are more stable reflections of how an organization uses data and establishes business rules within its various components. By focusing on the types of data and various attributes and classes they represent, a comprehensive, relational, or hierarchical model can be constructed to reflect their relationships within the organization. This model can serve

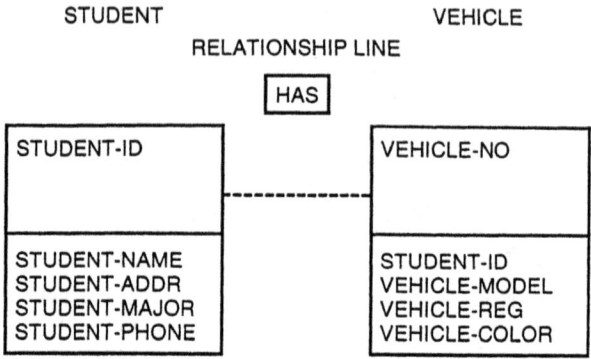

. DATA MODEL

INCORPORATED BUSINESS RULES, BASED ON THE
DATA STRUCTURE AND RELATIONSHIP LINE:

1. A STUDENT IS UNIQUELY IDENTIFIED THROUGH
   STUDENT ID.

2. A VEHICLE IS UNIQUELY IDENTIFIED THROUGH
   VEHICLE NO.

3. A STUDENT MAY HAVE ZERO OR MANY VEHICLES.

4. A VEHICLE CAN ONLY EXIST IN BUSINESS IF IT IS
   ASSOCIATED WITH ONE STUDENT.

5. A VEHICLE CANNOT BE ADDED UNLESS IT IS
   IMMEDIATELY ASSOCIATED WITH ONE STUDENT.

Exhibit 17-2. Data model with associated business rules.

---

to help simplify and reduce duplication of data, and validate business rules
governing relationships and dependencies. Data-focused models are powerful tools for data administrators, but offer little help for senior executives in
terms of IS planning unless they are properly presented (see Exhibit 2).

For nontechnical computer personnel, data-focused models are often
very difficult to comprehend and implement within an organization. Many
experienced IS managers and academics do not fully understand the data
modeling process and the related topics of object orientation for developing
information systems on the project level as well as on the corporate level.

The Process-Focused Approach

The process-focused methodology looks at IS as a series of related activities that transform data into information. The emphasis is on the processes or activities that comprise a particular information system. A model is
generated to reflect the hierarchical relationships of information systems
within an organization. Therefore, an information system like accounting

can be broken into basic processes (e.g., accounts payable, accounts receivable, payroll, and general ledger).

These processes can be further decomposed into smaller processes. For example, payroll can include the following related processes: generating payroll, generating quarterly payroll reports, generating year-end payroll reports, and updating employee records. Each of these processes can further be decomposed into smaller, related processes. The end result is the hierarchical process structure. Exhibit 3 illustrates this hierarchical relationship between the processes.

Each process has a set of objectives that supports the objectives of the next higher level process that in turn support the overall goals of the organization. Therefore, each activity or process can be justified by the objectives and goals of the organization. An organization model can be created to facilitate the process of evaluating activities within each information system, and to establish an effective decision support system for management. The evaluation process could be used to identify activities that are not contributing to the goals and objectives of the organization, and either eliminate or modify them. A recent study indicates that the process-focused approach remains (or is being reinstated) as the preferred IS planning tool.

The next important step for the process-focused approach is to integrate it into a corporate structure. Recent studies have indicated that senior IS managers and senior corporate management are looking for information technology that can be elevated to the organizational level.

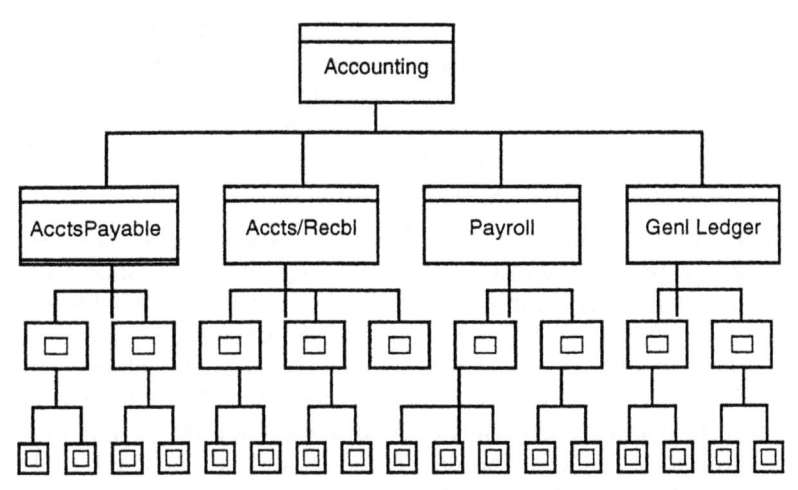

Exhibit 17-3. Simplified information systems structure.

Both process-focused and data-focused approaches have made significant effects on the project level where IS personnel have used each technique to develop information systems for specific applications. Yet, neither technique has made any significant effect on the corporate level. A methodology must be developed that can take the strengths of both process- and data-focused approaches and blend them into a corporate model — which can include the recent trends of the horizontal organization. This has been successfully accomplished in industry using the combination of the IDEF0 Activity Modeling and IDEF1X Data Modeling approaches, as well as through the Information Engineering Methodologies of J. Martin and C. Finkelstein.

INTEGRATING INTO THE HORIZONTAL ORGANIZATION

Integrating information systems technology into the corporate organizational structure requires the support of both senior management and lower-level personnel if it is to be successful. It must be a methodology that can be understood and communicated throughout the organization by both computer technical and noncomputer technical personnel to be effective. Since the horizontal organization concept uses multidisciplinary teams within each process, an effective IS methodology must be simple enough to communicate across disciplines and yet be effective in IS planning. Process-focused modeling relies on simple, easy-to-understand symbols that can be used across disciplines. This methodology must be easy and effective enough to be used by all levels within the organization.

Senior executives identified IS planning and information integration as a key issue for competition and survival in today's market. A process-focused methodology is compatible with modeling tasks and activities at the essential process level as well as strategic activities at the higher level. A process-focused approach has been recommended as an appropriate methodology for an organization structure. The data-focused approach is most appropriate for the data administrator. Therefore, an important consideration is to develop a methodology that can integrate the strengths of both process- and data-focused approaches within an organizational model.

With the growth in computer-aided modeling tools (e.g., CASE), the complex task of representing interrelated activities and their associated data components can be accomplished much more easily for both the process- and the data-focused methodologies. Detailed computer specifications can be generated to alleviate the problems of consistency at each level and between levels within each type of model hierarchy. The systems analyst must be very careful in choosing appropriate CASE tools to help facilitate the integration of process- and data-focused models. The CASE tool must be very easy to use and comprehensive enough to allow for easy integration between the two models.

Using Dynamic CASE Tools. The diagrams should have simple, easy-to-follow menus that allow the rapid development of each level of diagram. If the diagraming tool is difficult to use to create and modify different symbols, it becomes a more static tool with which systems analysts will tend to create models that they are reluctant to change. The tool should be aesthetically pleasing to view, and data flows should flow with arcs, straight lines, and right angles. Finally, the tool should be comprehensive enough to allow the systems analyst to move smoothly from the front-end stages (i.e., analysis and design) to the back-end stages (i.e., implementation and installation).

When users and systems analysts work with a CASE tool, the process should be a pleasing experience, thereby allowing the tool to be more dynamic or easily changeable. When the people who work with the model are glad that the model has been created and never have to touch it again, a static model has been created. If the model-creation process was a pleasing experience, they tend not to be bothered by changing it — this is a dynamic model. In the horizontal corporation, information systems change constantly as a result of changes in the competitive environment. Therefore, it is important that the model be a dynamic model capable of changing constantly.

By using simple, easy-to-understand symbols supported by a comprehensive data dictionary, a process model can be generated to represent detailed information processing as well as the more abstract decision-making at the higher level within the organization. The ultimate goal of integrating information systems methodologies into the horizontal organization is to develop a comprehensive organization model using a dynamic CASE tool that can handle constant changes. The major component of this model is a process-focused model supported by a data-focused model representing the higher-level support processes and the essential processes within the organization. This organization model can be used as a blueprint for the restructuring of the traditional hierarchical organization into the newer horizontal organization.

Data Structures. For organizations interested in developing a horizontal structure, the process-focused model can be used to reinforce and enhance communication, information flows, and coordination (i.e., exchanging of information) between the essential processes and the support departments. The data-focused portion of the integrated model supports the processes by ensuring that the data structures used (and perhaps created) by the processes are in their most logical formats. It will remove redundancy and simplify the actual data structures used within the organization.

Exhibit 4 represents the overview of this approach. In addition, more detailed discussions concerning process modeling techniques appear in

269

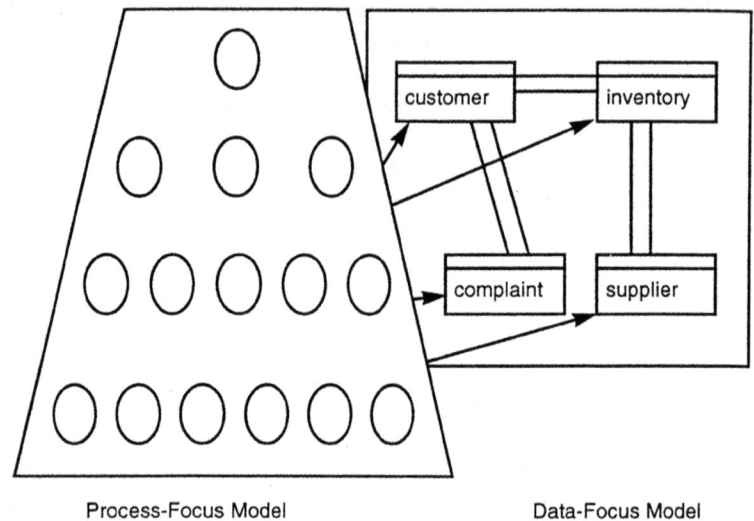

Process-Focus Model   Data-Focus Model

Exhibit 17-4. Simplified integration of process and data models.

McLeod's *Systems Analysis and Design: An Organization Approach* (The Dryden Press, 1994) and other comparable process modeling texts.

The arrows in Exhibit 4 illustrate the interaction or connection between the data structures in the process model and the data structure representation in the data model. Each access to a data structure in the process model is represented by either an object (e.g., customer) on the data model, or a relationship between objects (e.g., the connection between customer and inventory, or customer buys inventory). It is beyond the scope of this chapter to provide the detailed process of connecting the process-focused model to the data-focused model.

A possible connection can be established between the process and the data models. Once the process model has been developed, the principles of object orientation can be applied to the construction of a data model that will often provide better insight and use of existing data structures. If a particular data structure on the process model is not in its most logical format (redundancy with other data structures, transitive relationships or other problems associated related with data structures), the data model will show the changes and these changes will eventually be incorporated into the process model. Exhibit 5 illustrates the creation of a logical data structure model (entity-relationship diagram) and how it influences the changes in the process-focused diagram.

The original diagram accessed a complex data structure identified as a customer rental file. A normalization process generates a data model that

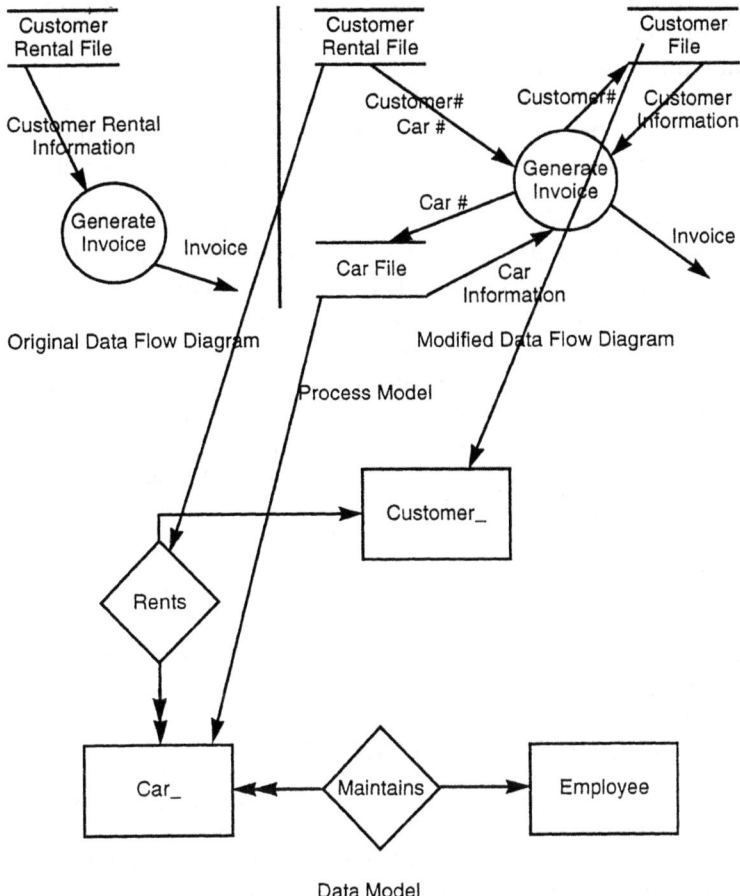

Original Data Flow Diagram

Modified Data Flow Diagram

Process Model

Data Model

Exhibit 17-5. Relationship between data and process models.

in essence created three entities (i.e., customer, employee, and car) with relationships between the objects where customers rent cars and employees maintain cars. The final result is that the process diagram is modified by the data model. The data model is a quality control mechanism that ensures that the data used in the organization are in the most logical format. When that format is assured, data can easily be shared throughout the organization to improve both coordination and communication between the essential processes and the support departments on the higher level.

Data can also be easily maintained, thereby ensuring data integrity. It is the business rules in the activities or processes within the organization that establish the relationships between the various data objects. As the process model is applied to the entire organization, the data model is also

271

extended to the entire organization (generally depicted by Exhibit 2). The end-product is an organization process model supported by an organization data model. The data administrator is responsible for maintaining the data model and coordinating with the various processes and support departments to ensure that changes in the process model are incorporated into the data model, subsequently modifying the process model.

Using the Internet. The Internet has grown at an astonishing rate over the past few years. Companies have been trying to integrate the Internet into their organizations to gain a strategic advantage with customers who now search the Internet for products and services. Developing applications of the Internet is an extension of the electronic data interchange (EDI) between customers and the company — except that the new EDI is open all year with customers all over the world. Now that companies can offer products or services that are bought over the Internet through the use of CGI programming techniques, the amount of overhead needed to maintain a sales operation has been dramatically reduced in may instances.

Understanding the relationship between home page development, CGI programming, network security, and Internet marketing strategies (such as listing the corporate home page on Yahoo, Lycos, WebCrawler, or Infoseek) is critical to the successful integration of Internet strategies into the process and data models of the organization.

CREATING A HORIZONTAL ORGANIZATION

To create a horizontal organization by integrating a process model and a data model, the organization will still have to identify the strategic goals of the organization and key competitive advantages (e.g., customer satisfaction and quality control issues) to achieve these goals.

These key competitive advantages will help the organization identify the core or essential processes necessary to achieve the goals. The next step is the restructuring of the organization. This involves establishing multidisciplinary teams centered around the essential processes. At this point, the teams will identify key objectives that will help them achieve the overall goals of the organization. Once the objectives have been identified, the essential process can be decomposed into several basic subprocesses that will allow the essential process to achieve its objectives. These subprocesses will often be multidisciplinary, involving accounting, finance, marketing, sales, production, and others.

After the essential processes and key subprocesses are identified, the organization should know what support departments are needed to provide more expertise for the essential processes. Of course, the standard support departments (e.g., legal, accounting, and other basic support functions) will probably be identified by both senior-level management and the essential processes. Each subprocess will be decomposed into smaller processes — each with its set of objectives (that support the objectives of its parent subprocess, as was mentioned earlier) — thereby creating a hierarchical information system model.

Again, the process of generating an IS model is not a disguise replacing one hierarchical structure with another. The process modeling concept is the identification of related activities or processes as a means of understanding the various multidisciplinary activities needed for incorporation into an essential process or support department. It shows how the activities within the organization interact, and not necessarily the lines of authority and responsibility often identified in the traditional hierarchical structure. Exhibit 2 shows the hierarchical nature of the process modeling method.

To facilitate the generation of an organization process model, a steering committee should be established at the highest level of the organization, to set such standards and guidelines as naming conventions for data elements and process identification. Each support department and essential process is responsible for developing its portion of the process model. Some overhead training will be needed to provide personnel involved in the development of the process model with basic information about process modeling. Experience has shown that a basic discussion (e.g., type of symbols, use of input data flows, processing, and output data flows) is necessary only to get nontechnical information personnel involved in the development process.

With the advance of group decision support systems (GDSS), a systems analyst can facilitate the decision-making processes used to generate the key objectives and the subprocesses. As each support department and essential process builds its respective model, the steering committee will provide guidance and coordination between all of these components. When each portion of the model (i.e., support departments and the essential processes) is completed, the steering committee will be responsible for bringing each portion together into an overall organization model.

Once the overall process model is created, the data administrator will be responsible for normalizing the data structures and subsequently for generating the data model. The series of steps used to generate the actual data model is beyond the scope of this chapter. But the general concepts of object-oriented analysis and design, along with the normalizing process, are used to generate this data model. Once the data model is completed, the process model must be modified to reflect the more logically created data structures. Exhibit 4 illustrates generally how data models on the project level change the process model. The same approach is used to develop data models on the organizational level and subsequent changes to the organizational level process models.

273

A CASE tool should be used to expedite the development of the subprocesses for the essential processes and for the support departments. The principles for selecting the appropriate CASE tool were discussed previously. In short, the CASE tool should be process oriented, with the ability to generate data models in support of the process models. The CASE tool should be powerful enough to handle complex organizations involving many levels. It should also be flexible enough to handle the dynamics of change. This decision must not be a trivial decision.

Building a dynamic process and data model is the salient consideration when deciding on an appropriate CASE tool. The methodology that supports the CASE tool is also important. The main point of this chapter is that the horizontal organization can be depicted by a process-focused model supported by a data model. Therefore, the use of a few simple, easy-to-understand symbols is necessary so that both technical and nontechnical IS personnel can use them appropriately.

Getting senior management to commit to a CASE tool and methodology is the underlying foundation of this approach. The use of the CASE tool must be a total effort by all personnel. The maintenance of the process model is the responsibility of each essential process and support department. With the help of the systems analyst component of each process, changes will be the constant force that drives the continual development of the process model. By incorporating users and IS personnel into the process model methodology, a common communication tool (e.g., CASE tool) can be used to help facilitate changes within the organization. Each person within the organization should be able to visualize his or her contribution to the organization and its goals by locating his or her process and its objectives in the process model.

SUMMARY

Incorporating the horizontal concept into today's organization is an important trend that will allow the organization to be more competitive in domestic and international markets for profit organizations and funding sources for nonprofit organizations. The horizontal organization will reduce the amount of bureaucracy that often generates information delays and failures. Organizations will need to be able to change quickly to meet the challenges of a volatile, competitive environment. IS methodologies should integrate recent trends to be successful and accepted by organizations. An effective approach would be to integrate the horizontal organization into an organizational process model supported by a data model. The process model should focus on the essential processes and the support departments in building its information system model.

The process model will help organizations move logically toward the horizontal organization by ensuring that the activities within each essential process and support department support overall the goals of the organization. The process model will also provide better coordination and communication throughout the organization by integrating the information used within it. The data model that supports the process model will ensure that the information is in its most logical format, thereby allowing the various components of the organization that need information to have it in a timely fashion. With the help of an effective, user-friendly CASE tool used as the common communication tool throughout the organization, the process model will become a dynamic tool for change.

Chapter 18
Avoiding Pitfalls in Data Modeling

Steven Cheung

DATA MODELS ARE USED TO IMPROVE THE LOGICAL DESIGN, ORGANIZA-
TION, AND IMPLEMENTATION OF A CORPORATION'S DATA. When developing such devices, however, the data modeler can encounter many obstacles. This article suggests ways to create a high-quality model while
avoiding the stumbling blocks.

CRITICAL CONSIDERATIONS TO IMPROVE DATA MODEL QUALITY

To help a data modeler produce a high-quality model, several critical
areas must be addressed. These areas — semantics, technique, completeness, and accuracy — and their considerations are discussed more thoroughly in the following sections.

Semantics

Semantics deals primarily with the proper identification and naming of
data modeling objects. A high-quality data model requires precision in the
choice of such names for objects as entity, attributes, and relationships.
A precise name conveys its meaning unambiguously, and difficulty in arriv-
ing at such a name might suggest a lack of understanding of the object's
definition. Semantics is particularly important in differentiating between a
concrete object and an abstract object. Throughout this article, examples
of proper semantics are discussed.

Technique

An important element contributing to the data modeling process is how
effectively the model reflects the business rules. Examples of a particular
business situation's being most effectively modeled by a particular choice
of modeling technique include the handling of the time dimension in data
modeling, the use of subtypes, and recursive relationships.

Completeness

A data model goes beyond an entity-relationship diagram, because it must encompass rigorous definition of data modeling objects-that is, entities, relationships, and attributes. Rigorous definition includes key attributes, domain rules, integrity constraints, algorithms for derived attributes, data type, and data format.

Accuracy

Finally, a data model has to be accurate in representing facts about business rules. In addition, it should be presented in a way that is clear, concise, smooth, and natural to allow users to verify it with ease.

Misrepresentation of facts could arise from a lack of understanding of techniques or from a misunderstanding of users' requirements. It is therefore important to provide a data model that is semantically precise, that uses the correct techniques, and is complete in its descriptions.

DATA MODELING

For the purpose of discussion, an arbitrarily selected data modeling notation-the crow's foot notation, as adopted by some of the Computer-Aided Software Engineering tools in the market today-is used. It should be pointed out that the same principles generally apply to other notations as well. Exhibit 1 depicts the convention of the syntax or notations used in this article.

Entity Type

An entity type is a person, place, thing, concept, event, or organization that has characteristics of interest to the enterprise. For the sake of brevity, the terms entity, attribute, and relationship as used in this article refer to entity type, attribute type, and relationship type.

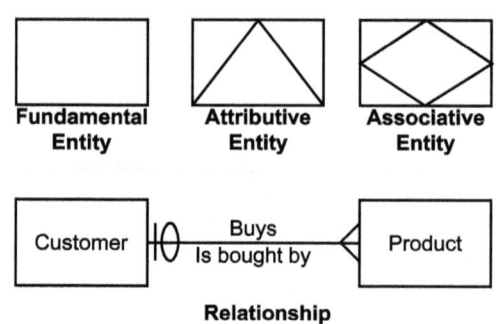

Exhibit 18-1. Data modeling notation conventions.

Entity Type Identification. One of the data modeler's first tasks is to identify entities. When considering candidate entities, the modeler should attempt to identify sample attributes, key identifiers, and entity instances.

Entities can be discovered by examining existing business documents, reports, screens, and file layouts and by interviewing users. Every effort should be made to discover entities for the application and to avoid relying on past requirements alone. In one situation, an auto insurance company found the discovery of the entity accident to be significant because the company had never tracked accident information before.

The model cannot be considered complete until all entities for a given business area have been defined. In addition, entities must be mutually exclusive in the sense that one entity should not contain an attribute that is also contained in another entity.

Imposter Entities. Entities named after a paper document are called imposter entities. Forms, reports, and similar paper documents employed by the business (e.g., a sales report or an address change form) are generally bad choices for entities because they have a high risk of not being mutually exclusive with other entities and because reports and forms typically incorporate information from several entities. One exception, however, is a purchase order. If a purchase order entity contains information regarding the purchase event and nothing more, it is a legitimate entity because an entity is needed to capture the purchase information. The fact that there is a paper form called purchase order can be deemed to be purely coincidental.

The pitfalls to avoid with imposter entities include accepting all forms and reports as entity names and rejecting the possibility of creating entities based on information on a form. In many situations, a paper form that records unique facts (e.g., airline tickets), particularly those with significant time reference, could generate acceptable candidate entities.

Concrete Versus Abstract Entity Types. In data modeling, it is common to encounter situations that require different levels of abstraction. For example, there is a difference between an entity representing an object and an entity representing a collection of similar objects (e.g., a tour group is a different entity from a tourist). An individual tourist is a concrete thing, whereas the tour group is abstract. The semantic aspect of this part of data modeling should not be overlooked.

To further illustrate the point, when a video tape is reserved at a store, the entity of concern is simply the movie title. When the tape is actually checked out, however, the entity is that one specific copy among several with the same title. This scenario can be modeled in one of two ways: with a single entity called video title, or with the entity video title together with an additional entity videocassette. A video store may carry 500 titles and have exactly two copies of each title. Using the video title entity allows the business to determine whether a given title is in its catalog but not whether a particular cassette has been returned. Using the video title entity together with the videocassette entity provides greater capability to answer business questions.

Mixing concrete and abstract objects is an easy trap to fall into, in part because in the English language, a given word can be used in more than one context. Some authors refer to the problem as modeling at different levels of abstraction. To differentiate the levels, the attributes associated with the proposed entities must be specified.

Relationship

A relationship is an association, of interest to the enterprise, that can exist between two entities. The specification of a relationship includes the names of the entities involved, the semantics of the relationship between them, and the cardinality and optionality involved. Relationship is an essential concept in data modeling because it is one of the key vehicles by which the business rules are represented.

Relationship Identification. The most common way to identify relationships is through business requirement interviews with users. Users could be asked directly about the relationship between entities and could be asked to define entities for the modeler as well-not only in terms of what the entity is but in terms of how it interacts with other entities. For example, a customer might be defined as a company or an individual that buys goods or services from the enterprise, on the basis of the terms and conditions covered in a master contract. Another way to discover relationships is to examine existing documents, screens, reports, and forms to uncover what some of the existing relationships are, on the basis of inferences that could be made from existing business practices. The pitfalls of missing relationships can be minimized by asking users what business questions must be answered in relation to two or more entities.

Misconstrued Relationships. It is a fallacy to think that, for example, because a physical purchase order form contains vendor name, vendor warehouse address, office address, product, and product price that the entities containing these data elements have to be directly related to the purchase order entity. It would be helpful instead to recognize that the physical purchase order form is really a data view, which is made up of the different entities (e.g., vendor, product, and address), as well as the purchase order entity itself. The various entities may be related, but all the entities are not by implication related directly to the purchase order entity itself.

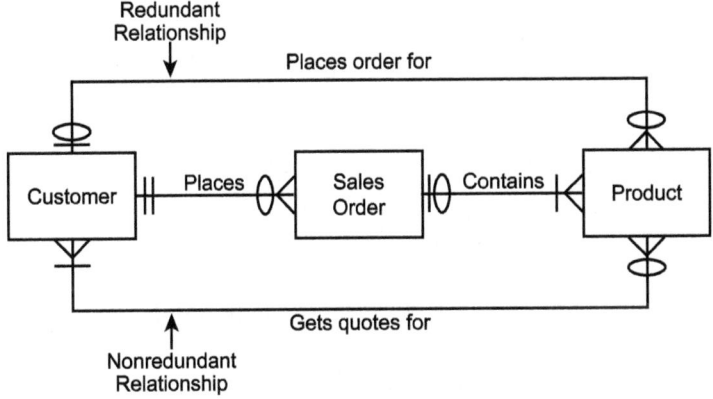

Exhibit 18-2. A redundant relationship.

Redundant Relationships. A relationship is redundant when its exclusion would not cause a loss in the representation of any business rules in the model. The diagram in Exhibit 2 contains a redundant relationship. In the exhibit, the relationship customer places order for product is clearly redundant. The relationship customer gets quote for product, however, is not necessarily redundant. The meaning of the relationships provides useful clues to help decipher whether a relationship is redundant. A more subtle clue is the cardinality.

The problems of redundant relationships are not as easy to identify because the modeler is generally reluctant to run the risk of missing significant relationships. Again, the modeler could ask users how effectively the relationship can help answer business questions, as is done with relationship identification.

Spurious Relationships. It is tempting to draw relationships between two entities that should not be related. What appears to be a significant relationship often does not even exist. Exhibit 3 illustrates such a case. In this exhibit, it might be a requirement that the data model shows the historical connection between the published market price and negotiated price. There may be a correlation between the two, but there is no real relationship needed to model this correlation. It would be incorrect to insert a relationship that directly links Published Market Price History and Negotiated Price History entities.

Spurious relationships happen occasionally, but they are not as common as redundant relationships. However, it is difficult to explain to users why a relationship is spurious without resorting to a technical data modeling discussion. One helpful approach is to avoid the discussion at a technical level and simply demonstrate to the users that their information needs can be met.

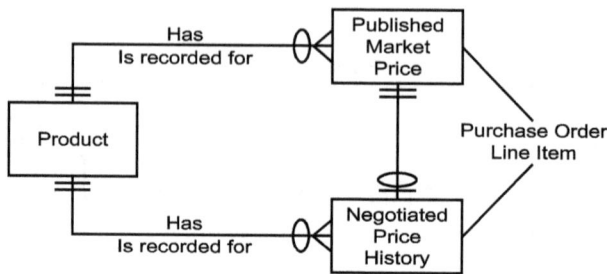

Exhibit 18-3. A spurious relationship.

Access Path versus Business Relationship. A problem can arise if relationships are created solely on an entity's access path as a substitute for relationships based on the true business rules. An example of this situation is illustrated in Exhibit 4A. It is not advisable to relate the Customer Account entity, the Service Address entity, and the Service Item entity to the Customer Bill entity as shown. The model is based exclusively on supporting the requirement for handling billing inquiries when it is commonly necessary to ascertain the service related to the bill, the account balance, the address the service was for, and the customer representative.

One of the dangers of modeling on the basis of access path consideration alone is that it can result in an unstable model. In the example, if the company decides to change the information displayed on a bill, the model would have to be revised. A better way to model this application is to model at the logical level and relate the Customer entity to the bill and the Account entity to the Customer as shown in Exhibit 4b.

The One-to-One Relationship (Except Supertype-Subtype). Occasionally, the relationship between two entities is such that the creation of an occurrence of one entity can bring about one and only one occurrence of another entity. For example, the relationship man marries woman (at least in a monogamous society) shows a one-to-one relationship. It could be suggested that instead of having one entity called man, and another entity called woman, it may be possible to have an entity called couple that includes the information for both. Before any conclusion is reached, however, two basic issues must be examined:

- Are there two significant concepts being represented? Does collapsing the two entities present the danger of losing sight of one or more major entities in the model?
- Should the model be more generalized to make the relationship one-to-many in anticipation of changes in business rules or incorporating the time dimension?

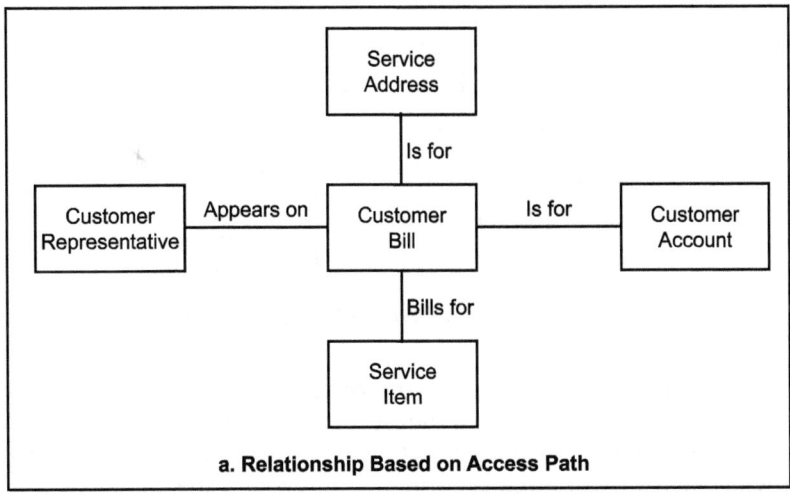

a. Relationship Based on Access Path

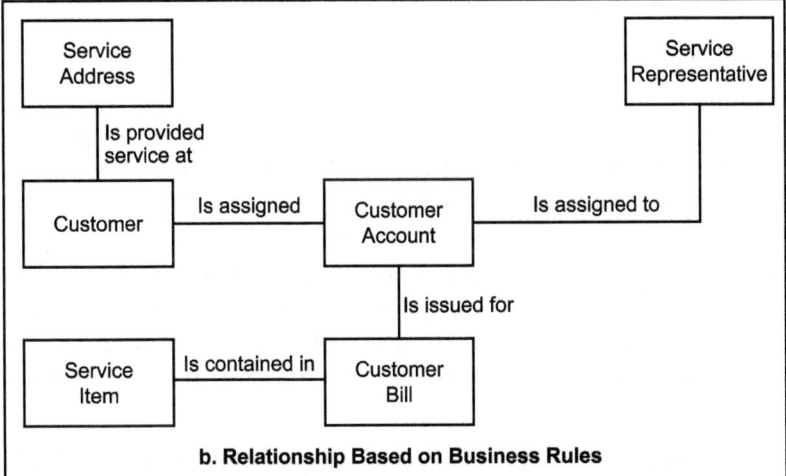

b. Relationship Based on Business Rules

Exhibit 18-4. Access path versus business rules relationships.

In the example of man marries woman, if a multicultural perspective is included, the relationship might no longer be one-to-one. The same is true if a time dimension is added.

Semantics in Relationship. Data modeling convention may require the modeler to name both directions of the flow in the relationship. It is easy to fall into the trap of semantic inconsistency between the two directions. The inconsistency can be eliminated with multiple relationships between a pair of entities.

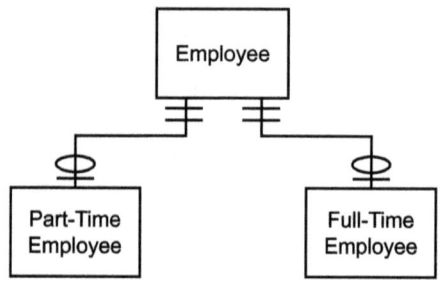

Exhibit 18-5. Supertype-subtype construct.

Assigning meaningful names to the relationships can be a challenge. There are some merits in using a thesaurus to find the right words or compiling a list of commonly used words to refer to as a relationship name. Having review sessions of a data model can improve the semantics if more users' opinions are solicited.

Entity Subtypes

An entity can be split into two or more subtype entities, each of which has unique attributes. An example of a supertype-subtype construct used in this article is shown in Exhibit 5. A subtype may have its own separate attributes and relationships. In addition, a subtype implicitly inherits all the key and non-key attributes of the supertype.

Two reasons prompt the creation of subtypes. First, a need for the subtypes to have separate relationships with other entities exists. Second, sufficient unique attributes at the subtype level justify its creation. In general, subtypes should not be created unless one-although preferably both-of the situations applies.

Multilevel Subtypes versus Orthogonal Subtypes. One or two levels of subtypes are sufficient to cover most needs. Subtypes that are several layers deep present a challenge in implementation. Often, a better method is to split the model along different subtyping criteria. This technique is referred to as orthogonal subtyping. For example, Exhibit 6a provides a workable alternative to the hierarchical subtyping represented in Exhibit 6b.

Single and Multiple Subtypes under One Supertype. Occasionally, a model can contain a supertype with just one subtype. This may be justified if the organization being modeled will be interested in other subtypes at a later date. Typically, a supertype has two or more subtypes associated with it. It should also be noted that the subtypes shown under a supertype do not have to be an exhaustive list of all the possible situations. It is best to ensure that subtypes are mutually exclusive if possible, to minimize the risk of duplicating data.

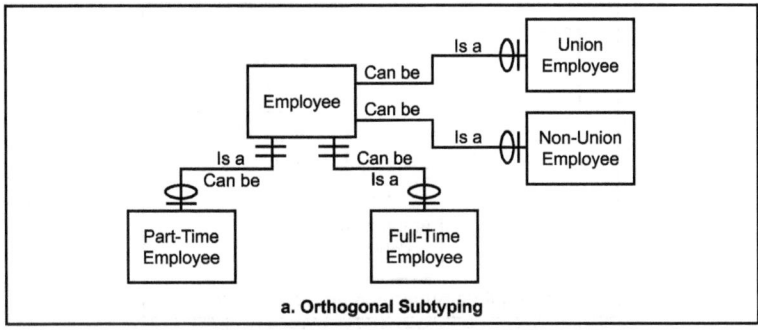

a. Orthogonal Subtyping

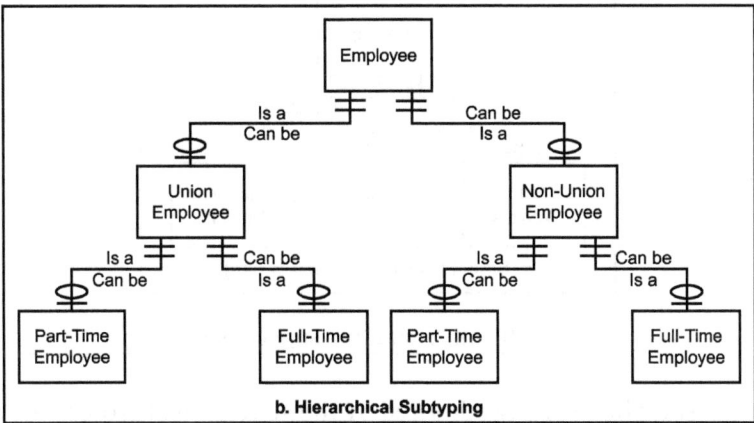

b. Hierarchical Subtyping

Exhibit 18-6. Hierarchical versus orthogonal subtypes.

Multiple Supertypes for One Subtype. A subtype that has multiple super-types at the same time is not recommended, because the subtype would inherit conflicting keys and attributes. In many situations, if it appears as though a subtype needs multiple supertypes, further analysis will show that a regular supertype-subtype construct will suffice, or that the alleged subtype has multiple roles instead.

In Exhibit 7a, it appears as though multiple supertypes are needed to accommodate the case of the amphibious vehicle. It is likely that an amphib-ious vehicle has unique properties of its own, however, different from both land and water vehicles, and could therefore possibly be modeled as another subtype (see Exhibit 7b). Another situation that might require two or more supertypes for a subtype probably arises because an entity is performing dif-ferent roles at the same time and not because an entity has the need to inherit properties from multiple entities at the same time.

The multiple supertype pitfall is more noticeable when the modeler assigns key and non-key attributes to the entities. The realization of

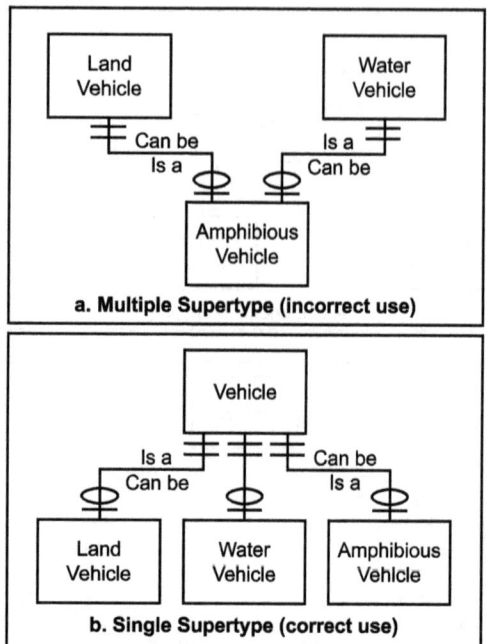

Exhibit 18-7. Multiple supertypes.

conflicting attributes being inherited by the subtype will prompt the modeler to address the problem. This is another reason why key attributes should be identified as soon as possible.

Omission of Supertype. Sometimes it is understood that two entities are subtypes of something of a higher order , but the business has no need to keep information about the entity at the generalized level (e.g., customer and vendors could both be people, but the company may have no desire to keep information about people in a generic way).

In other situations, however, the omission of the supertypes could cause problems. The examples in Exhibit 8b show a supertype engaged in an associative Entity Relationship. The omission of the supertype, as shown in Exhibit 8a, violates the cardinality rule of entities as parent of an associative entity. This rule states that an associative entity by definition has relationships with at least two other entities, and these relationships cannot be optional.

The example shown with the supertype omitted (Exhibit 8a) does not accurately represent the business rules because the cardinality of both of the relationships linking Project Assignment with Regular Employee and Seasonal Employee entities is optional. In this case, there is no guarantee

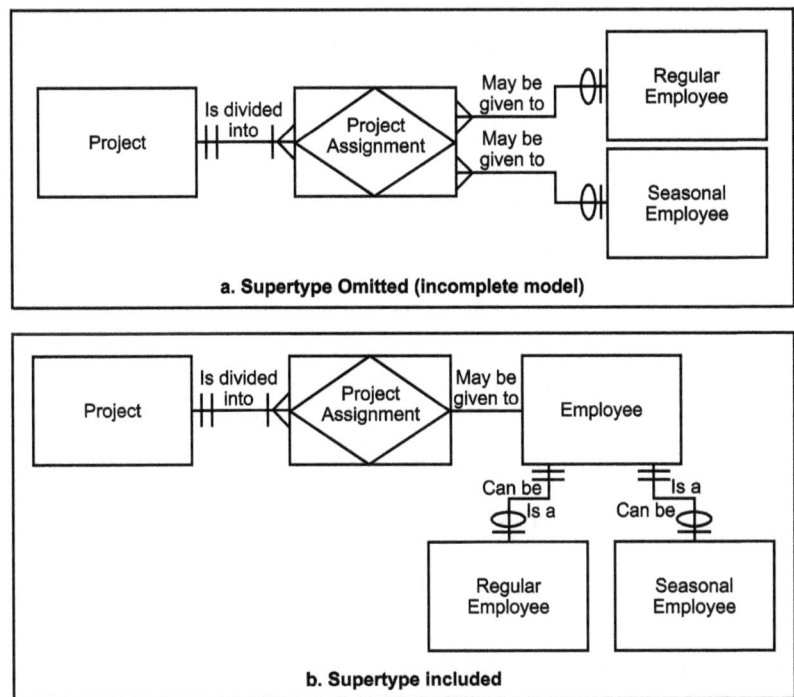

Exhibit 18-8. Omission and inclusion of supertype.

that any Employee occurrence must be the parent to the associative entity Project Assignment.

Entity Role in Data Modeling

A role entity is an entity playing a role that is a generalization of the role played by several other entity types. In Exhibit 9a, the Organization Unit entity serves as a role entity.

Use of Role Entity. A modeler may encounter situations in which confusion exists about whether to use the more generic role entity instead of specific entities. Referring to the examples in Exhibit 9, the modeler has the choice of modeling as in Exhibit 9b with existing concrete business terms (e.g., division, regional office, or department) or of using a more generic, more abstract entity named Organizational Unit, as in Exhibit 9a. The role entity form should be used when a structure is not very stable (e.g., the regional office is removed), when the structure contains too many levels, or when the number of levels is undeterminable.

The point is that even a model appears to reflect the business rules because it does not show all the business facts that are needed. The pitfall

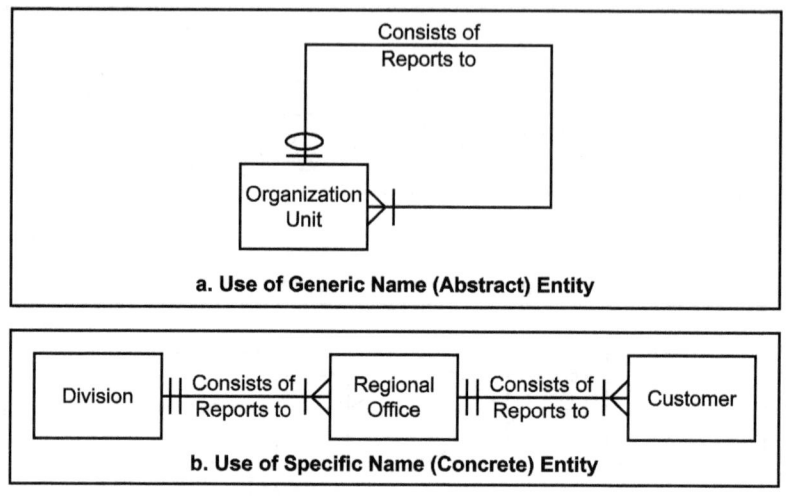

a. Use of Generic Name (Abstract) Entity

b. Use of Specific Name (Concrete) Entity

Note: Organization unit is a generic (role) name for a division, regional office, and department.

Exhibit 18-9. Role entity.

is that the modeler fills in the blanks for the missing supertype so readily in the mind that the missing supertype does not appear as a major omission.

Role Name. Multiple relationships between a pair of entity types often occur, as shown in Exhibit 10. In the example, the city that a person lives in may or may not be the same city that a person works in. The foreign key in the person entity should be qualified by the respective roles reflected in the relationships to show the distinction (e.g., work city and live city). A foreign keys is an attribute in one table whose values are required to match those of the primary key of some other table. It is the mechanism used to join tables in a relational database.

Role Entity. Exhibit 11 illustrates a situation in which a role entity should be used. Exhibit 11a depicts a situation in which teaching courses is an activity performed by employees and contractors. To model this situation more precisely, another entity. Instructor, is introduced to create a place for information that pertains to the instructor. Examples of such informa-

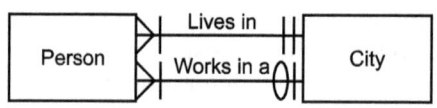

Exhibit 18-10. Role name.

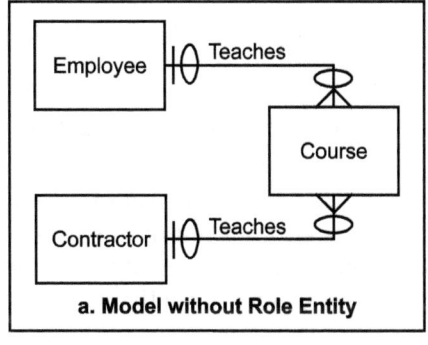

a. Model without Role Entity

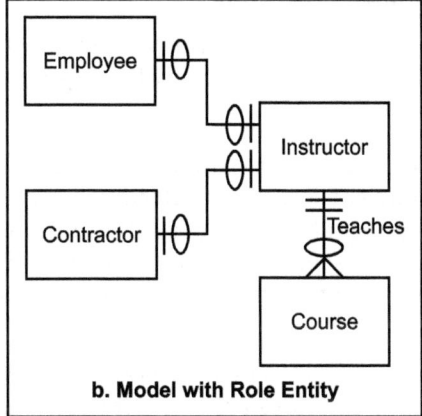

b. Model with Role Entity

Exhibit 18-11. Role entity.

tion include number of years of teaching experience and specialty. The alternative model is shown in Exhibit 11b.

One way to explain the role aspect is to rephrase the relationships depicted in the example as the following English sentences:

- The Employee acts as an instructor to teach a course.
- The Contractor acts as an instructor to teach a course.

In these sentences, the instructor entity is derived from the generalization of the action verb (or the semantics of the relationship) teach. This is the way the need for a role entity can be established.

In a supertype-subtype situation, on the other hand, the entity is derived by generalizing the noun (i.e., the entity name). For instance, in an earlier example, employee was a generalization for part-time employee and full-time employee.

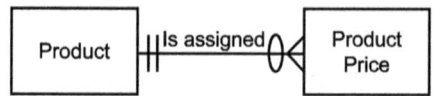

Exhibit 18-12. History information.

The problems that can occur in this aspect of data modeling do not necessarily arise because a role entity is not used in this example. It is important for a modeler to recognize the role concepts and decide whether there is enough information needed about the entity Instructor before creating it.

Time-Related Situations

In data modeling, time-related situations are encountered. The effects of time on entities and their relationships with other entities must be a concern of the data modeler.

History Information. History information is generally modeled as an attributive or dependent entity. An attributive or dependent entity depends on the fundamental entity it describes. Product price history, for example, is meaningless except within the context of the entity product. It is common to model such information as a one-to-many relationship as shown in Exhibit 12.

The most common issue is to consider how the current price should be dealt with. Two possible solutions are to use the same entity type for all the price information, whether current or history, or to make current price an attribute of the product entity. The choice is more one of practicality than of pure data modeling.

Effect of Time on Semantics and Cardinality. If the relationship between entity A and entity B viewed as a snapshot is one-to-many, over time the relationship may become many-to-many. An example of this situation is shown in Exhibit 13. In Exhibit 13a, an employee attends a meeting, and a meeting is attended by many employees. This is a one-to-many relationship, and as a snapshot of one point in time it reflects the fact that an employee cannot attend two meetings simultaneously. Over time, however, an employee may have attended many meetings. Exhibit 13b depicts the latter situation, in which both the cardinality and the semantics are different. In this case, the employee-meeting relationship is changed from attends to has attended, and is now many-to-many.

Which model is more accurate depends entirely on the business requirement. If the requirement is to track attendance for each meeting, the first model is adequate, and the second model is redundant. Conversely, if the requirement is to provide information on what meetings an employee has attended, the second option is more accurate. Problems arise only when

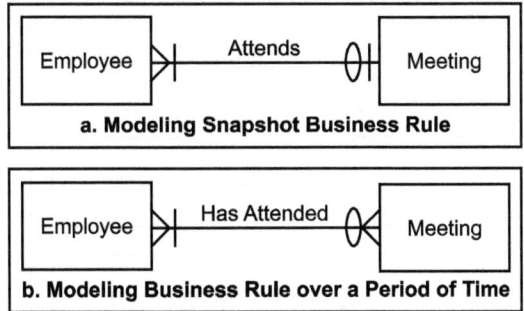

Exhibit 18-13. Time dimension affecting semantics and cardinality.

the modeler assumes certain time dimensions that differ from what the users have in mind.

Time as an Entity. In general, time is not modeled as an object in data modeling, but situations can arise in which time periods could be of interest and significance.[1]

For example, window periods allowed for different kinds of fish that sport fishermen can catch might necessitate the creation of an entity Time Period, as shown in Exhibit 14. This is based on the assumption that some special regulations are associated with each time period.

Cardinality and Optionality

Cardinality constraints represent the upper and lower bounds on the number of instances in one entity type with respect to instances of another type. It represents to what degree the relationship exists between two entities. The cardinality is commonly expressed as a qualifier for relationships such as one-to-one (1-1), one-to-many (1-m) or many-to-many (m-m) relationship. Note that the common use refers to the maximum cardinality (the upper bounds) only. Exhibit 15 illustrates the two types of cardinality, called maximum and minimum cardinality. Cardinality in this article generally refers to maximum cardinality, and optionality generally refers to minimum cardinality.

Cardinality and Telltale Signs of the Model. Critical examination of the cardinality of the entity-relationship model often highlights areas that

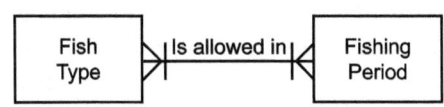

Exhibit 18-14. Time period as entity type.

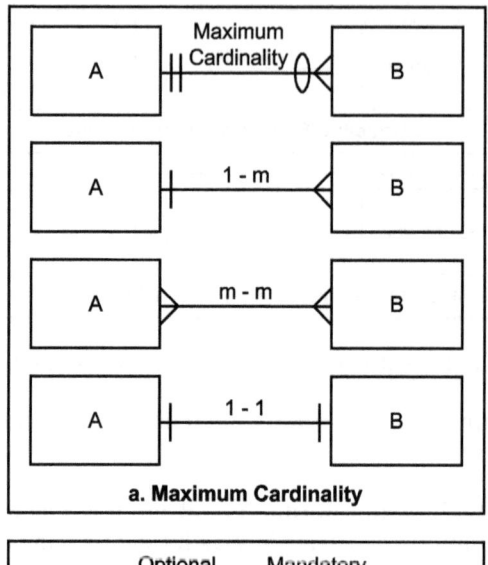

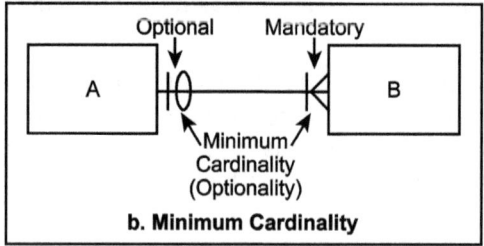

Exhibit 18-15. Cardinality convention.

might need clarification or more precise definitions of the users' requirements. The most common combination of maximum cardinality is one-to-many; a less common combination is many-to-many; and the least common combination is one-to-one. The use of the second combination requires resolution by way of an associative entity, and the use of the last one may require additional clarification or refinement.

There are specific areas in which cardinality should be reviewed. For example, the most generalized cardinality pair is the use of zero optionality on both ends of a many-to-many relationship. This trait falls into a one-size-fits-all pattern. This type of cardinality might require more specific details (see Exhibit 15a).

On the other extreme of the spectrum, the use of mandatory optionality on one-to-one relationships should also prompt more investigation. This pattern represents the most definitive and narrow cardinality. (see Exhibit 15b). It even appears questionable whether the two entities involved are part of the same entity or not.

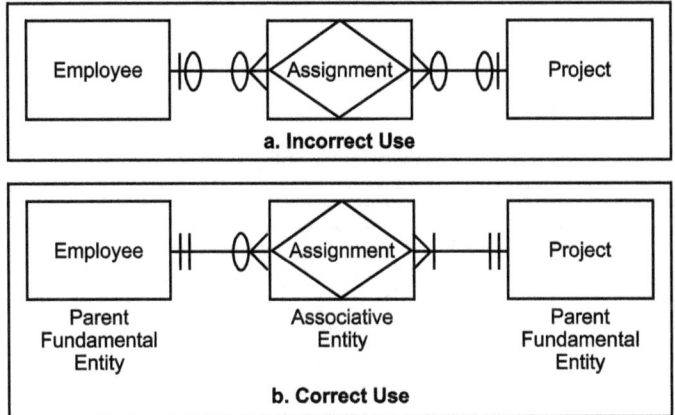

Exhibit 18-16. Associative entity and cardinality violation.

Between the two previous spectrums are several suspicious cardinality patterns. The use of mandatory optionality on many-to-many relationships, though theoretically possible, still implies a degree of mutual dependencies that may not map closely to business realities. In addition, another unlikely situation is the one-to-many recursive relationship with mandatory minimum cardinality.

It is useful in data model reviews to quickly look for telltale signs that indicate error conditions. Experience has shown that such signs help jump-start the review process to uncover the business issues lying beneath the surface rather than simply correcting cardinality errors.

Associative Entity and Relationships. An associative entity is an entity that is created when information is needed about a relationship or when representation is needed to resolve a many-to-many relationship between two entities. In this article, the entities through which the associative entity was created are called the parent entities of the associative entity.

Rules. Certain rules exist regarding the cardinality of entities involved in an associative entity situation. First, an associative entity exists because of other entities, and it does not exist without the relationship of at least two other entities (see Exhibit 16 for the correct use of cardinality). Second, an associative entity is used only to resolve many-to-many relationships; in fact, associative entities can be involved in any combination of cardinality as long as there is a need to keep information about the relationship. In the example shown in Exhibit 17, the attribute Sales Price of the painting could be an attribute neither of the Artist nor of the Live Model entity.

Third, if the identifiers of the two related fundamental entities do not provide uniqueness for the associative entity, the entity is still considered

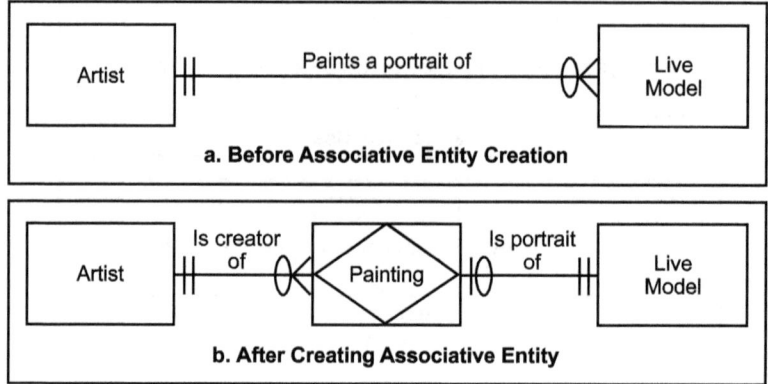

Exhibit 18-17. Associative entity created to keep information about relationship.

associative. The time aspect is implied and is often made part of the key to make the associative entity occurrence unique. Associative entities are often used to record information about a time-related event (e.g., shipment, assignment, and flight). Last, an associative entity may not have attributes of its own when it is created only for resolving a many-to-many relationship. Otherwise, there should always be attributes.

Associative entities are common in data modeling. In many situations, however, they create confusion for modelers and users alike. The most common pitfall is the incorrect use of cardinality for the parent entities of the associative entity. Another problem is the use of cardinality solely for resolving many-to-many relationships.

Recursive Relationship

A recursive relationship depicts a situation in which an entity has a relationship to itself. When the relationship exists, there is no stipulation whether the two entity occurrences are the same when they participate in the relationship. More often than not, the two entity occurrences are not the same (e.g., in an employee-supervises-employee relationship, it is reasonable to assume that an employee may not be allowed to manage himself or herself).

Recursive Relationship Patterns. The following examples illustrate some common types of recursive relationships. A bill-of-materials example (recursive) typically represents a many-to-many relationship and therefore, an associative entity must be present in the model to resolve the relationship. Exhibit 18 is a sample of a typical structure of bill-of-materials situations in which a part consists of part of a part.

Exhibit 19a shows the construction of a one-to-many scenario. The structure is one-to-many because an employee can report only to one

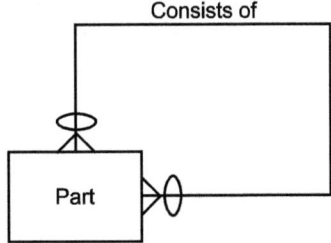

Exhibit 18-18. Recursive relationship example of a parts explosion.

supervisor, and one supervisor supervises many employees. Mandatory optionality, as shown in Exhibit 19b, must be expected because it implies that everyone has to work for somebody. That rule does not reflect reality, however, because senior-level employees do not report to anyone.

A Rationale for Recursive Relationship. In the earlier discussion of roles, a role entity was described as a more generalized entity. In Exhibit 8, a choice was given between the use of a generic name entity and the use of a specifically named entity. When a given occurrence of an entity could play different roles at different times or at the same time, however, the use of a specific name will not work. For example, it is not possible to replace the recursive model of the employee entity with a pair of entities like manager and subordinate, because the same person could play both roles at the same time.

NORMALIZATION

Normalization of data is a procedure used to ensure that a data model conforms to some useful standards. These standards are developed to avoid duplication of data and to minimize create, update, and delete anomalies of data.

The traditional approach has been to construct the model first and artificially normalize it afterward. In contrast, proper modeling practice will result in a naturally normalized model, at least to third normal form. The principle to remember is that a normalized data model is of high quality, and it is better to have quality built in than to have to add it later.

Proper data modeling practice includes the proper selection of entities, the proper placement of attributes in entities, the recognition of when it is necessary to make an entity of an attribute, the recognition of when to keep information about relationships, and last but not least, the proper identification of key attributes to ensure that all attributes depend on the whole key and the key alone.

In all situations discussed in this article, effective data modeling practice with normalization considerations produces models that require less

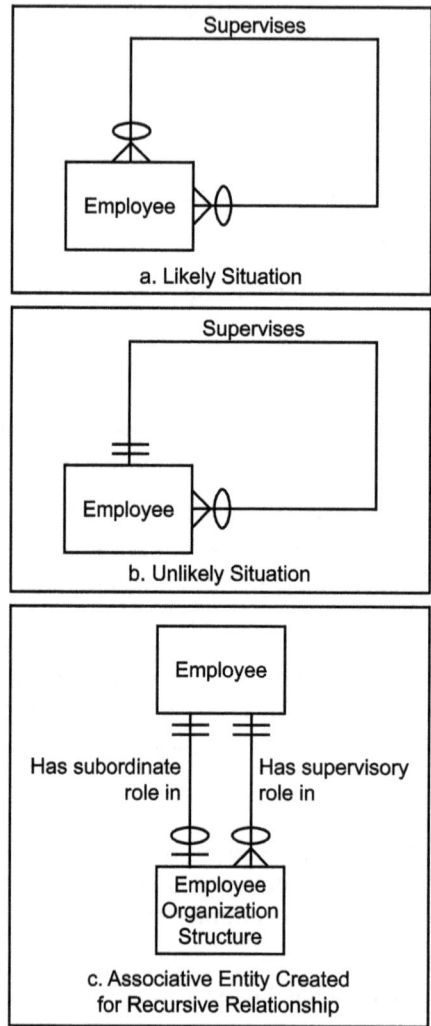

Exhibit 18-19. Recursive relationship-employee organization structure example.

rework. It is suggested, however, that the key attribute be identified as early as possible to allow the modeler to address related issues (e.g., supertype entities, subtype entities, associative entities, role names, and recursive relationships).

REFERENCE ENTITY OR MINOR ENTITY

Reference entities represent lookup tables used by a wide variety of applications. Examples include country codes, organization units, and color codes. These entities are also called domain tables because their attributes generally have well-defined domains (e.g., a state code table has 50 acceptable values).[2]

Domain is a set of allowable values for an attribute, and the domain table represents the home for the allowable values or combination of values. The domain table of valid city and state code addresses is a more elaborate form of domain because the table ensures that only legitimate value combinations are available.

Reference entities should be included as entities in the model, but all the relationships implied whenever an entity makes references to the domain table do not have to be shown explicitly all the time, from a practical view.

ATTRIBUTES

An attribute is a characteristic or property that describes an entity's value. A modeler must be aware of when to make an attribute an entity in its own right. The general rule is, an attribute becomes an entity if there is a need to break out a repeating group for normalization reasons or a need to keep more information about an attribute. For example, in a personnel application, spouse name is an attribute of employee, and if there is a need to keep information about the employee's spouse, spouse is an entity by its own right. Another consideration is that an attribute could potentially be an entity, but because the current business area does not need to know the additional information, it may stay as an attribute and may one day be changed into an entity when another business area comes along.

There is some latitude in this decision depending on a company's philosophy concerning the information resource management concept. For example, one company may find it acceptable to have the employee request an ID attribute on a work-order entity, whereas another company may want to create an employee entity with employee ID as a key attribute. In the latter approach, there is a relationship between the employee entity and the work-order entity, and therefore the employee ID is not an attribute of the work-order entity. The pitfall of not establishing major entities like employee in this example can result in more data inconsistencies and higher maintenance costs.

Derived Attributes

Many controversies are evolving around whether derived attributes should be included in a data model. The more fundamental question to ask is, What is derived data? For example, shoe size as an attribute is, by most people's standards, not derived data because few people know or care how it was derived. The business may not have a need to know either. Another example is inflation index information taken from a published source and used in an internal database. Clearly the data is derived, but it can be treated as though it is not, because the raw data is generally unavailable to begin with.

Forecast data is considered derived only if the forecast is done on a pure repeatable and mechanical basis with no judgment applied. Derived data in a data model is acceptable if the derivation is cumbersome and takes an unreasonable amount of historical data; if the value is derived for the first time and is later overridden with a different value; if the derivation algorithm changes over time, or the raw data needed to derive the data is changeable; or if the creation of it is temporary in nature to enhance the user's understanding.

COMPLETING THE DATA MODEL KNOWLEDGE BASE

Rigorous definition of data modeling objects is necessary before the modeling effort can be considered complete. The criteria for what is considered completeness in documentation are judged by the modeler. Entity documentation, for example, should include definition, purpose, synonyms, and volumetric and behavior rules. Behavior rules govern the change of an entity from one state to another-for example, the circumstances under which an unapproved Work Order becomes an approved work order.

Relationship documentation should include definition, create, update, and delete rules involving the pair of entities in the relationship. Attribute documentation should include definition, optionality of the attribute, uniqueness (e.g., key or non-key), default value, logical format, length, permitted value (domain), default value, and derivation rules.

CONCLUSION

This article has provided some critical quality considerations designed to assist in preparing a data model. The chart depicted in Exhibit 20 summarizes the obstacles that can beset even the most proficient modeler and suggests the steps that might be taken to remedy such situations.

A sound data model is achieved by the modeler after recognizing and avoiding the pitfalls that have been highlighted. The following list states fundamental principles that are important to keep in mind when creating high-quality data models:

- Modeling requires proper identification of the relevant data modeling objects and proper naming of those objects.
- Quality models require precise semantics and economical and nonredundant constructs.
- Abstract and concrete concepts should be modeled as different entities, and the distinction between the two must be made if the business requires it.

- Normalization is inseparable from effective data modeling practice.
- Quality must be built in with appropriate techniques, not added afterward.
- A complete data model goes beyond what is on an entity-relationship diagram; it requires copious definitions of business rules to support the diagram.
- The correctness of the model depends heavily on business context.

Notes

1. D. Tasker, Fourth Generation Data: A Guide to Data Analysis of New and Old Data (Englewood Cliffs NJ: Prentice Hall, 1989), pp. 167173.
2. W. Durell, "Dealing with Domain Tables," Database Programming & Design, April 1991.

Exhibit 18-20. Chart of pitfalls and remedies.

Modeling Areas	Possible Pitfalls	Plausible Causes
Entities	1. Missed entities	• Did not explore all possible avenues to capture them • Paid too close attention to existing systems rather than new requirements
	2. Imposter entities	• Confused with paper documents • Created just to appease users
	3. Modeled abstract concepts using concrete entities	• Wrong level of abstraction • Did not recognize that data modeling requires more precision than common use of English terms
Relationships	1. Unidentified relationships	• Did not explore all possible avenues to capture them • Paid too close attention to existing business rather than new requirements
	2. Misconstrued relationships (when the entity name coincides with document name)	• Did not differentiate document from entity in case of coincidence in entity and document name
	3. Redundant relationships	• Cannot tell whether a relationship is redundant • Indirect relationship was discovered before the direct relationship
	4. Spurious relationship	• Indirect or spurious relationship was discovered first and overshadowed the real relationship
	5. Access path serves relationship	• Physical design considerations overrides logical
	6. Inconsistent semantics in relationships	• Lack of user input as to which one of the two semantics is germane • Potentially, a new relationship could be useful
Entity Subtypes	1. Multilevel subtype going too deep	• Possible improper choice of subtyping criteria • Did not carefully assess the real need for further subtyping
	2. Multiple supertypes for one subtype	• Confused with role situation
	3. Omission of needed supertype	• Overlooked attributes that need to be stored in supertype
Role Entities	Failure to identify needed role entities	• Confused with supertype-suptype situations • Did not know of role concept
Time-Related Situations	Incorrect cardinality on time-related entities	• Model did not reflect the time dimension requirement-assuming snapshot when it is perpetual or vice versa

Exhibit 18-20. Chart of pitfalls and remedies. (*continued*)

Modeling Areas	Possible Pitfalls	Plausible Causes
Cardinality	Suspect cardinality	• Model too generalized • Model too specific and restrictive • Current requirements emphasis only, did not allow for future cases
Associative Entities	1. Restricting the use of associative entity by limiting it to resolving many-to-many relationships	• Lack of understanding of purpose of associative entities
	2. Syntax error in cardinality around rule associative entities	• Lack of understanding of syntax
Recursive Relationship	Recursive relationship with an impossible case	• Lack of validation of model
Normalization	Data Modeling practice without normalization consideration	• Not able to identify entities quickly upon seeing their attributes • Attributes are placed in wrong entities • Did not identify key early enough
Reference (minor) Entities	Stored minor entities in attributes of major entities instead	• Did not believe in the value of validation table
Attributes	One or more clusters of attributes not separated out as an entity when a major business entity can be created	• Did not model with normalization concept • Did not believe the current application justifies the creation of new entity (place holder)
Data Model Knowledge Base	Incomplete documentation	• Did not decide beforehand what to document • Information not available

Modeling Areas	Considerations	Remedies
Entities	• Completeness	• Conduct brainstorming sessions to generate brand new ideas • Use other data gathering techniques (e.q., JAD); interview can also be used as remedy or precaution
	• Accuracy • Semantics	• Identify entities that own attributes on paper document
	• Accuracy • Semantics	• Rigorous definition of an entity • Close examination of fitness of attributes to an entity
Relationships	• Completeness	• Validate business queries that must be answered against the relationships
	• Accuracy • Semantics	• Examine the data view that supports the information on a document

301

Exhibit 18-20. Chart of pitfalls and remedies. (*continued*)

Modeling Areas	Considerations	Remedies
	• Semantics • Completeness • Technique	• Use semantics of relationship to see whether redundancy occurs • Use cardinality pattern as a clue • Determine whether all business questions can be answered without the indirect relationship • Examine and determine whether any direct relationships have been missed
	• Accuracy • Semantics	• Review model for semantic soundness with users • Explore direct relationship first
	• Semantics • Completeness	• Create new relationship • Delete or reword inconsistent semantics
Entity Subtypes	• Technique	• Try orthogonal subtype • Cut subtype hierarchy layer after picking the most significant criteria first
	• Technique • Accuracy	• Try role entity concept • Remodel with one supertype and possibly multiple subtypes
	• Completeness	• Examine to see if supertype is needed for the current and possibly future applications
Role Entities	• Technique • Accuracy	• Apply generalization technique as described
Time-Related Situations	• Accuracy • Semantics	• Review semantics of relationship • Review cardinality in comparison with semantics of relationship • Validate the "time" requirement with users
Cardinality	• Semantics • Completeness • Accuracy	• Review with users on specificity and validate with business questions applied against the model
Associative Entities	• Technique	• Examine rules provided in article
Recursive Relationship	• Technique • Semantics	• Review and walk through
Normalization	• Technique	• Identify many entities as major or minor, significant or less significant, as early as possible • Put attributes to right entities
Reference (minor) Entities Attributes	• Technique • Semantics	• Examine the cost of eliminating an entity against future system maintenance cost

Exhibit 18-20. Chart of pitfalls and remedies. (*continued*)

Modeling Areas	Considerations	Remedies
	• Technique • Semantics	• Emphasize data normalization concept • Evaluate the benefit of creating place-holder entities
Data Model Knowledge Base	• Completeness • Technique	• Decide beforehand what needs documenting • Obtain more information through review

Chapter 19
The Politics of Entity Identifiers

Deborah L. Brooks

ENTITY IDENTIFIERS HAVE FAR-REACHING IMPLICATIONS FOR BOTH THE DATA MODEL AND PHYSICAL DATA BASE DESIGN. If an organization chooses an unsuccessful entity identifier, the results may be an inaccurate data model, data base design and application programming complexity, poor application performance, and the inability to establish a shared data environment. How can one distinguish a good entity identifier from a bad one and what should be done when one discovers an entity identifier problem? Before these questions can be addressed, the properties that the data element should possess or the data element sets that are being considered for the entity identifier must be reviewed.

ENTITY IDENTIFIER PROPERTIES

An entity identifier should be unique to be able to distinguish one entity occurrence from another. This is not possible if the entity does not contain a unique value for each occurrence. An entity identifier should also be explicit so that a value exists for every entity occurrence that is known when it is created, definite so that its initial value is not null, consistent so that each occurrence is associated with only one value of its identifier, and stable so that its value never changes or becomes null as long as that occurrence exists. An entity identifier must also be factless so that it identifies but does not describe the entity occurrence. A factless entity identifier is likely to be unique, explicit, definite, consistent, and stable.

In addition to these fundamental properties of an entity identifier, end-users should be able to access and understand the data elements and the elements should conform to any data base management system (DBMS) or installation-specific limitations. Whenever possible, an entity identifier should also be able to be controlled so that an identifier with all the correct properties can be assigned.

ENTITY IDENTIFIER PROBLEMS

Because the data elements that aspire to be entity identifiers must adhere to an extensive list of qualifications, many problems may occur during this process. These problems may result in volatile, denormalized, all-purpose, or nonuniversal or parochial entity identifiers.

Volatile Entity Identifiers

A volatile entity identifier is one whose value is subject to change, become null, or that comprises potentially non-key data elements. An example of a volatile entity identifiers is an addressee on an electronic mail system. Addressees can both send and receive electronic mail messages. The entity identifier comprises three data elements-the addressee's last name, first name, and middle name. This identifier reads as:

```
LAST_NM      CHAR (15)

FIRST_NM     CHAR (15)

MIDDLE_NM    CHAR (15)
```

Assuming that these three data elements guarantee uniqueness (which is possible, but highly unlikely), if any part of an addressee's name changes, a duplicate name may exist. For example, a woman marries and takes her husband's name. Either her husband's surname replaces her last name or it is appended to her name with a hyphen. The middle name may also be affected because she may take her maiden name as her middle name. This situation may compromise the entity identifier's uniqueness and stability. In addition, if the entity identifier becomes null, its consistency and explicitness are in jeopardy because a null does not signify a valid value.

Non-key entity identifier data elements affect the identifier's stability, consistency, and explicitness. The data administrator must update the data model and repository entries to reflect the data element's removal from the entity identifier. In addition, volatile entity identifiers may affect physical data base design and application programming by creating problems with the maintenance of referential integrity. If an entity has a relationship with other entities and the entity identifier of one occurrence of the entity changes, then the foreign key of all corresponding occurrences in the related entities must be changed to maintain referential integrity.

Joins and such operations as data element concatenation are also impacted by nulls. For joins, when null values are used, the results are unpredictable depending on whether the chosen relational DBMS treats all null values as equal or as distinct. It is questionable whether a query that joins two tables can return any matching rows at all or whether it may erroneously pair rows that are truly unrelated. When dealing with nullable entity identifiers it may not be possible to define a unique index on the entity identifier, depending on how the chosen DBMS handles the nulls. If one entity identifier data element is null (e.g., when someone does not have a middle name), a null column's concatenation with a nonnull column results in a null value unless the VALUE function is used as shown in the following WHERE clause:

```
WHERE ADDRESSEE NM =

FIRST_NM VALUE (MIDDLE_NM, '') LAST_NM
```

When business information is ordered, nulls either sort to the end or the beginning 4 the output list, depending on the chosen relational DBMS.

Denormalized Entity Identifiers

Another entity identifier problem occurs during the concatenation of multiple data elements into one denormalized entity identifier data element. Any entity identifier that is not randomly assigned has meaning built into its various substrings (e.g., for geographic location or type of account) and contains hidden denormalization. If any part of the entity identifier data element can potentially change or become null, it is much more difficult to deal with than if the data elements remain separate. For example, in the account number for a home telephone, the first three characters are the area code that identifies the state or geographic division where the phone is located. The second three characters identify the local exchange or geographic location within the area code. The next four characters are the number for the line and the final three characters contain a customer code that makes the account number unique in case the phone number is reassigned to a different customer. Here, the entity identifier customer account number actually comprises four atomic data elements, as follows:

```
Denormalized Entity Identifier:

Normalized Entity Identifier:

CUST_ACCT_NBR CHAR(13)           AREA_CD       CHAR(3)

                                 LCL_EXCH_CD   CHAR(3)

                                 LINE_NBR      CHAR(4)

                                 CUST_CD       CHAR(3)
```

Denormalized entity identifiers may have adverse effects on the accuracy of the data model. Because the entity identifier's component atomic data elements are not identified, undiscovered violations of a second normal form may exist. Any partial key dependencies that are left denormalized may introduce redundant business information into the data base structures that are designed from the data model.

307

In the previous example, the state in which a home telephone is located functionally depends only on the area code. Placing the data element for state in the customer account entity causes this business information to be replicated for every account that has this area code. It is more appropriate to create an entity for an area code that has the state as data element, make the customer account entity's area code a foreign key, and define an appropriate business rule to support referential integrity. Hidden denormalization can mask data model redundancy and can obscure entities and relationships, thus rendering the data model inaccurate and incomplete.

Because the entity identifier is not decomposed into its component atomic data elements, the business information is probably not well defined or understood and can hinder the establishment of a shared data environment. If the entity with the denormalized entity identifier is related to other entities by a 1:M relationship, the denormalized entity identifier is propagated to all related entities as a foreign key. This results in poorly understood business information throughout the shared data environment. In addition, it is difficult for the different business groups that participate in the shared data environment to reach an agreement on the meaning of the business information and to use it effectively.

In the example used earlier, if the entity identifier customer account number is not completely understood, different business groups may interpret it in different ways. The group that bills residential accounts attaches a different meaning to the customer account number than the group that markets commercial accounts. The commercial customer account number is composed differently from the residential customer account number — a 13-character sequentially assigned entity identifier is assigned for each discrete commercial customer. In both cases, the customer account number's physical domain is the same and it identifies a customer account, but its underlying meaning and logical domain differs. Therefore, two customer entities exist: one for residential accounts and one for commercial accounts. This fact is often obscured by the group data element in the entity identifier.

If an organization attempts to implement a shared data environment, denormalized entity identifiers may cause many problems. When denormalization is first discovered, the organization must mediate discussions between the participating business groups to determine the correct level of decomposition and to arrive at successful data element definitions. This task is more difficult when one or more business groups must redefine a key business concept in unfamiliar or less convenient terms. This situation may occur when organizations develop application-level data models without any overall coordination by the data administrator. If a system is implemented using a denormalized entity identifier, the data administrator must also ensure that both the group and atomic data elements are documented, as well as their derivations, so that the link between them is not lost. Therefore, denormalized entity identifiers increase the level of control and coordination that is required to maintain shared business information.

Denormalized entity identifiers also make it difficult to define indexes for the physical database designer. If the only basis for partitioning a data base table is the beginning substring of the group data element, the index definition syntax becomes involved when the highest index key value for each partition is defined. The remaining characters of each partition's highest index key value must be padded with either blanks or high values. For example, if a table was partitioned on area code, the index key value for the partition that contains the residential customer accounts for Virginia would have to be defined as either "703" or "703999999999." A denormalized entity identifier also does not allow the data base designer to define a clustering index on the area code, without the-rest of the group data element, in combination with any other column.

Programming a join between two tables is also difficult. If one table has implemented atomic data elements as the entity identifier and another table, sometimes from another application area, and has the foreign key represented by a group data element, problems may occur. When any one of the atomic data elements has a physical domain that is different from that of the group data element, such relational operations as joins are either impossible or perform poorly. Even if two columns have comparable but not identical data types, the comparison has to involve a data conversion.

Even if the physical domains are an exact match, the use of a group data element by one application and the atomic data elements by another complicates the join-structured query language (SQL). Joins must be established by the use of the scalar function SUBSTR for the column that contains the group data element or the concatenation operator for the columns that contain the atomic data elements, as shown in the following WHERE clauses:

```
WHERE SUBSTR (CUST_ACCT_NO, 1,3) = AREA_CD

WHERE CUST_ACCT_NO =

AREA_CD LCL_EXCH_CD LINE_NO CUST_CD
```

Similar to the comparison of columns, concatenation of columns can only occur if both are compatible strings. It is not possible to concatenate a character column with a decimal column, so the data administrator must ensure that the atomic data element columns are all of the same type as the original group data elements. If one atomic data element is null, concatenation of a nun column with a non-null column results in a null value and yields unpredictable results. If the group data element cannot be null, then a join on the column that contains the group data element and the concatenation of the columns that contain the atomic data elements may not return any matching rows for the row that contains the null-valued column.

If the procedure requires sorting, ordering, grouping, or range checking, a denormalized entity identifier may be a problem. It is impossible to define a substring of the group data element as the basis for a sort or order by, either alone or in conjunction with, another data element. Similarly, it is impossible to range check or group business information through a substring of the group data element.

The administrator must ensure that the physical domain of the foreign key matches that of the entity identifier to maintain referential integrity and enforce logical domains. If one application uses atomic data elements as an entity identifier and a subsequent application uses a group data element, referential integrity and logical domains must be enforced. This must occur through the application logic rather than the DBMS because of the difference in the physical domains of the primary and foreign keys. In addition, the string operators and data conversions that are required by the use of denormalized entity identifiers often preclude the use of an index to retrieve business information and delay the retrieval process stage that evaluates the selection criteria in the predicate.

If denormalized entity identifiers are discovered in data modeling, corrections can be made if the participating business groups are open-minded and committed to the data sharing process. To prevent denormalized entity identifiers, the business information must be understood by either the data modeler or someone involved in the data modeling process. Once the business information has been modeled, all entity identifiers should be carefully examined, especially those that may not be randomly assigned. The most knowledgeable members of the participating groups must be questioned as to their meaning and composition. AU identifiers should be assumed to be group data elements unless proven otherwise. If a denormalized entity identifier is found, the group data element should be decomposed into its component atomic data elements. AU non-key data elements must also be checked for violations of second normal form and entities and relationships should be created as necessary if any violations are found.

It is more difficult to correct denormalized entity identifiers if they are discovered after implementation. The entity identifier should be normalized and the data model and physical data base structures should be modified to reflect the normalization results. This usually means that the administrator must redefine existing tables, redefine indexes, and define new tables for the new entities that have been uncovered. It may also involve extensive programming changes. Depending on the extent of these changes, this alternative may not be feasible even though it is best for the organization if the application database structures are the cornerstone for future systems development.

All-Purpose Entity Identifiers

With an all-purpose entity identifier, either one data element or another can function as the entity identifier because values never occur simultaneously in both. Both data elements are layered on top of each other to create an entity identifier without a null component. The entity identifier of the facility entity can be either the department number or the location number, as follows:

```
All-Purpose Entity Identifier

Entity Identifier Data Elements

DEPT_LOCN_NBR           CHAR(5)          DEPT_NBR CHAR(5)

                                         LOCN_NBR CHAR(3)
```

The all-purpose entity identifier is created by taking the most forgiving data type (usually character) and longest length of the two data elements, calling it some combination of their names, and populating it with whichever value is present in each entity occurrence.

An all-purpose entity identifier is, in effect, a form of a denormalized entity identifi6'r because the identifier's data element actually comprises two data elements. Instead of denormalization through the data element concatenation, the elements are superimposed on one another. AU-purpose entity identifiers may also result in. an inaccurate data model, an unclear understanding of the business information, an increased burden for the data administrator, and difficulty in maintaining the cross-application referential integrity. The steps that can be taken to prevent denormalized entity identifiers, however, can also be used to prevent all-purpose entity identifiers.

It may not be physically possible to define a unique index on the all-purpose key data element if the range of values for the two original data elements overlap. Overlapping logical domains may also complicate range checking and prevent the data administrator from ordering or grouping department business information separately from location business information.

Nonuniversal or Parochial Entity Identifiers

An entity identifier that is not universally agreed on also poses a problem. These identifiers are nonuniversal or parochial and occur when the entity lifecycle phases occur in different functional organizations. For example, the planning department may identify a product by a different set of data elements than the manufacturing department, and so on through the warehousing, marketing, and sales departments. Even if a data element of the same name is used (e.g., product number) it may have different logical and physical domains, as follows:

PRODUCT_NBR	CHAR(6)	PLANNING
PRODUCT_CD	CHAR(2)	MANUFACTURING
MANU_ITEM_NBR	CHAR(8)	
STOCK_UNIT_CD	CHAR(10)	WAREHOUSING
PRODUCT_NBR	CHAR(12)	MARKETING

In addition, each department's definition of a product may differ. What the planning department defines as a product may be unbundled into multiple products or bundled with other products by the marketing department to maximize the number of market segments in which it can be sold. The planning department's product entity may be more of a product line, while the marketing department's product is a salable good or service. Therefore, the product entity is defined at different levels in different departments.

For this situation to occur, data models for each functional area must be developed independently, otherwise the discrepancies in entity definitions and identifiers should have been uncovered and resolved by the data administrator. However, the data administrator faces a monumental task when establishing a shared data environment. The administrator must consolidate the function-specific data models into an integrated enterprise data model and document all discrepancy resolutions in the repository. The results must then be socialized to all affected departments so that they can begin to use common names and entity identifiers to refer to common concepts.

It is impossible to enforce organizationwide uniqueness when each department operates independently when choosing an entity identifier. Allowing end users to access and understand the business information across departments is similarly impossible and prohibits any meaningful cross-departmental or historical tracking. Nor can the entity identifier be considered stable when it takes on different physical representations, values, and meanings that are department-specific. As a result, the administrator cannot establish or maintain cross-departmental referential integrity.

SOLUTIONS

When the entity identifier problems described here exist, there are several solutions that can be implemented to help correct these problem situations. The most common solutions include the use of surrogate keys, time stamps, surrogate key components, substitute keys, redundant business information, and application workarounds.

Surrogate Keys

Surrogate keys (i.e., artificial, meaningless arbitrary identifiers) are often proposed as an alternative when problems with entity identifiers occur. But which factors should the data modeler and data base designer consider to determine whether a surrogate key should take the role of primary identifier? Although other data elements that better fulfill the properties of an entity identifier, known as an alternate key, may exist, a surrogate key should always be considered. Because of the rapidly changing nature of business, any entity identifier that is not factless may sometimes become volatile. Before the decision to use a surrogate key is made, however, a number of other factors must be weighed.

The length of the entity identifier should be considered. Long entity identifiers have implications for direct access storage device (DASD) consumption to store the indexes that support the entity identifier and its occurrence in other tables as a foreign key. A long entity identifier also affects the processing time for such utilities as load, backup, and recovery and such operations as joins, scans, inserts, and deletes. A surrogate key, however, has the advantage of being relatively short by comparison. If the entity identifier is a composite or multicolumn key, all entity identifier columns must be specified to retrieve a row or to perform a join. If the administrator creates views to define selection or join criteria or creates synonyms for column concatenation, this situation may be avoided. All columns must also maintain referential integrity. A multicolumn entity identifier may be long, with all the concerns listed previously. A surrogate key is usually a single data element, which simplifies SQL statement coding and referential integrity.

Index limitations posed by the DBMS must also be considered. Limits on the length of an index or the number of columns it can reference may preclude the use of an index to enforce uniqueness. In this case, uniqueness is enforced through application logic and a surrogate key may provide an attractive alternative. The existence of any of the previously mentioned factors will tip the scales in favor of using surrogate keys. The following considerations may weight the decision in the other direction.

Installation-specific limitations also affect the decision to use surrogate keys, particularly when coupled with a requirement for end-user access by the original entity identifier instead of the surrogate key. The administrator may place a limit on the number of indexes that can be defined on a table. As more indexes are defined on a table, the amount of required DASD increases, as does the probability of locking problems; the processing time for inserts, updates, reorganizations, recovery, backup, load, and statistics-gathering; the object administration that creates the indexes; the probability of reaching a limit on the number of open data sets; and the complexity of table or partition recovery. If end users need access through the entity identifier and there is an installation limit on the number of indexes allowed, the use of a surrogate key may not be feasible.

The primary factor in determining whether to use a surrogate key is which organization owns the business information and assigns the entity identifier. If the entity identifier is assigned externally, a surrogate key may not be the appropriate choice because it may be impossible to consistently identify the same entity occurrence across organizational boundaries. If the entity identifier is assigned internally, the data base designers must decide whether to use surrogate keys based on a thorough analysis of the business information. An externally assigned entity identifier is not controllable, however, and may not prove to be factless and prone to volatility and other entity identifier problems. In this case, a surrogate key may be used internally, but the data administrator must maintain the identifier data elements and provide cross-organizational tracking.

Another reason not to use surrogate keys for externally controlled business information is when two self-contained systems with different entity identifiers are integrated and surrogate keys are already used by the target system. A cross-reference of the original entity identifier to the new surrogate entity identifier should be created to provide a bridge between systems, as required. If a surrogate key is assigned as the entity identifier, the end users must be immediately aware of the values. The original entity identifier data elements should be included as non-key data elements, and an index must be created if end-user access warrants it and installation limitations allow it.

After the decision to use surrogate keys is made, implications exist for different types of indexes. If the organization uses a random assignment algorithm for a surrogate key, it risks the possibility of duplicate values. This can be controlled through application logic that generates another value if a duplicate exists. A surrogate key may not be a proper basis for a clustered index because the values have no inherent business meaning. Although a unique index can be defined on the surrogate key, a clustering index on the original entity identifier or another attribute may better support access requirements. For example, a table that contains customer invoices is assigned a surrogate key for the invoice number instead of the original entity identifier of customer number and invoice date. However, the invoices are always retrieved either by customer number alone or in combination with the invoice date. A clustering index on customer number and invoice date fulfills the access requirement and provides fast response time because all customer invoices are physically stored together, thereby reducing the I/O to retrieve them.

When partitioning is required, the serial assignment of a surrogate key results in a skewed distribution of rows across partitions. The first partition is completely filled before any rows are inserted into the second partition. Because of the amount of activity in one partition, locking problems may occur. A modified serial assignment algorithm can resolve this problem. Instead of vertically filling each partition before going on to the next, the surrogate key values are assigned to insert one row into each partition before inserting a second. This horizontal assignment ensures a uniform distribution of rows across partitions and eliminates potential locking problems.

Time Stamps

If entity identifier problems prohibit the use of the original entity identifier and the surrogate key is not a viable alternative, other options do exist. A time stamp can replace the entity identifier or an entity identifier component. Except in the case of batched arrival, uniqueness is ensured. A time stamp is also meaningful if the arrival sequence is important to the entity. An example of an ATM transaction follows:

```
ACCOUNT_NBR      DEC(11)

ATM_NBR          DEC(7)

TRANS_TS         TIMESTAMP
```

A customer issues a transaction, which is represented by a transaction code, against the bank account with the use of a specific ATM. Because a single customer can do this multiple times in the course of one day, one transaction is distinguished from another through the addition of a time stamp, which records the precise time in which the transaction was executed.

A time stamp, however, is 26 bytes in length, which increases the size of the entity identifier and raises the issue of all the DASD, performance, and index limits that are included in the discussion on surrogate keys. The time stamp represents adding another column to the entity identifier so that the multicolumn entity identifier considerations also apply, However, this does not resolve the problems associated with externally controlled business information because the only controllable part of the entity identifier is the time stamp. In addition, clustering and partitioning indexes should not be defined on an entity identifier that consists of a time stamp alone. Locking problems could result because DB2 can attempt to add all inserts to the end of the table or partition, and this may cause contention for that physical space.

Surrogate Key Components

Although a surrogate key may not work as the entity identifier, it may be suitable as an entity identifier component. If the entity identifier data elements are not unique, the addition of a surrogate key in the form of a sequential counter may ensure uniqueness. This is commonly done for identifying invoice or order line items, as illustrated in the following configuration:

```
ORDER_NBR      DEC(11)

LINE_NBR       DEC(3)
```

Adding a sequential counter does not increase the overall length of the entity identifier by much, but it may be enough to raise the issues of DASD consumption, performance degradation, and installation-specific index limitations. If the business information originates from an external organization, the only part of the entity identifier that can be controlled is the sequential counter.

Substitute Keys

When substitute keys are used, the value of the entity identifier or its components is abbreviated or encoded to reduce its length. All substitute values are predetermined to represent a specific business meaning prior to their assignment as an entity identifier. This is unlike the surrogate key which has no inherent business meaning and whose value is determined when it is assigned. The abbreviations for airline carriers and airports are examples of substitute keys, as follows:

DCA - Washington/National	UA - United Airlines
DFW - Dallas/Fort Worth	US - USAir

An airline flight can be identified by the airport from which the flight originates, the airport where the flight terminates, the airline carrier, and the departure date and time. Without the use of substitute keys, the entity identifier would be 98 bytes in length, as follows:

ORIG_AIRPORT_NM	CHAR(30)
TERM_AIRPORT_NM	CHAR(30)
CARRIER_NM	CHAR(20)
DEPART_DT	DATE
DEPART_TM	TIME
Key Length:	98

When substitute keys for airports and airline carriers are used, the length of the entity identifier is reduced to 26 bytes, as follows:

ORIG_AIRPORT_CD	CHART(3)
TERM_AIRPORT_CD	CHAR(3)
CARRIER_CD	CHAR(2)
DEPART_DT	DATE
DEPART_TM	TIME
Key Length:	26

The key length is further reduced when a substitute key represents the originating and terminating airports and the flight's departure time, as illustrated by the following example:

FLIGHT_NBR	CHAR(4)
CARRIER_CD	CHAR(2)
DEPART_DT	DATE
Key Length:	16

These alternatives substantially reduce the entity identifier length. However, externally controlled business information is still an issue. Only the substitute key assignment can be controlled. The use of substitute keys with external business information may not be possible if volatility exists in the external business information. Valid substitute keys must be designated before assigning the substitute key to entity occurrences. If substitute keys are used, the model must contain entities to perform a cross-reference of the original value to its abbreviated or encoded value. Business rules must also be used to enforce the referential integrity between these reference entities and data entities must be established to ensure the use of only valid substitute keys.

Redundant Business Information

An alternative to dealing with denormalized and all-purpose entity identifiers is to introduce redundant business information. If some applications use denormalized or all-purpose entity identifiers and others do not, then the original application that contains the entity identifier problems can introduce redundancy. This is done by including component data elements as non-key elements in the table by using the group or layered data element as the entity identifier. Additional indexes that support joins and access requirements must also be defined, installation limits permitting. This approach avoids the complicated application programming that is required when substring and concatenation are used.

Drawbacks to this procedure include the administration of additional indexes and the need to keep the group values or layered data element and the component data elements in the table synchronized because data integrity must be maintained through application code. The introduction of redundancy may be justified, however, because it enables users to understand the data, which faci4tates data sharing and straightforward application programming.

Application Workarounds

Programming complexities can be mitigated by creating views for joins and selections that require the use of string operators. Even with application work-arounds, the performance problems and inability to perform such operations as joins and data element concatenation may still exist.

SUMMARY

Although entity identifier problems frequently exist, steps can be taken to ensure that these problems are eliminated whenever possible. Volatile entity identifiers can be prevented if the organization performs a stability analysis of the data model. It must also be determined whether any business changes, however unlikely, may result in an unstable, non-unique, or nun entity identifier. The organization must also realize whether any entity identifier data elements may become non-key. If these possibilities do exist, then an entity identifier must be chosen that can retain its entity identifier properties over time (e.g., a surrogate key). Although conducting a stability analysis does not guarantee that volatile entity identifiers do not occur, it lessens their likelihood.

Denormalized and all-purpose entity identifiers often occur when the organization does not have a thorough understanding of the business information and cannot spot denormalized or layered data elements. Following the steps to prevent denormalized entity identifiers that were mentioned earlier should prevent this. Denormalized, all-purpose, and parochial entity identifiers may occur when the administrator focuses solely at an application level during data model development. It should always be assumed that an application-specific data model is eventually consolidated into the enterprise data model. AU data elements should be defined at the atomic level and all principal entities should be included. The data administrator should review the application data model and, specifically, the entity identifiers to uncover any application-specific bias that may manifest itself as denormalized or all-purpose entity identifiers.

The best way to avoid entity identifier problems and to ensure that entity identifiers retain the properties necessary to implement correct, consistent, flexible, and shared databases is to thoroughly understand the organization's business information requirements and to model them correctly. The data base designer is then in a better position to make intelligent decisions about which solution to choose if an entity identifier problem exists.

Chapter 20
Practical Guidelines for Supertype and Subtype Modeling

Richard E. Biehl

WHEN DATA MODELERS DEFINE AN ENTITY, THEY DESCRIBE A SET OF ELE-
MENTS THAT SHARE COMMON CHARACTERISTICS DEFINED BY THE
ENTITY'S ATTRIBUTES AND THE RELATIONSHIPS THAT ASSOCIATE IT WITH
OTHER ENTITIES. In addition, when data modelers define a subtype entity,
they define it as a subset of the supertype entity instances. Supertype and
subtype modeling is based on basic set theory and many of its uses and
problems can be discerned by examining simple sets.

SIMPLE SETS

The starting point is always a base set, like the set of values that can
result from the roll of a pair of dice — $S_0 = \{2,3,4,5,6,7,8,9,10,11,12\}$. A subset
of S_0 might be the values that can result from rolling doubles (i.e., the same
value on each die) — $S_1 = \{2,4,6,8,10,12\}$. A subset of S_1 is created by including those values that can be achieved only through rolling doubles —
$S_2 = \{2,12\}$. There can be no members in S_2 that are not in S_1; nor can there
be members of S_1 that are not in S_0. The criteria for membership in the subset includes membership in the superset as well as additional criteria that
limit the subset to only the desired elements.

In data modeling, few entities are defined by simply listing every possible occurrence; they must be defined algebraically. The set that represents
dice rolls is defined as $S_0 = \{1<X>13\}$. The subset S_1 is defined as $S_1 = \{S_0\{X\},$
$Even(X)\}$. The subset S_2 cannot be defined by exclusive reference to the
superset S_1. The subset S_2 can only be defined by accessing knowledge outside of the set. In this case, the outside knowledge consists of the dice
structure and what combinations are possible when the two dice are
rolled. This set might be defined as $R = \{(1,1),(1,2),(1,3)...(6,6)\}$ or algebraically as $R = \{(X,Y),0<X>7,0<Y>7\}$. The set S_2 is actually an intersection of
sets S_1 and R and the value in S_1 can only be achieved by a single set

(e.g., X,Y) in R. Basic set theory does not, however, support the intersection of two sets of a different degree (e.g., [X] versus [X,Y]).

The definition of a detail subset may require the data modeler to extensively rethink the original superset definitions. This problem is inherent in basic sets-how to determine that the criteria for including a member in a set is complete and unambiguous for all occurrences. Godel's incompleteness theorem proves that no definition of a set is absolutely complete. The challenge is to provide a definition that is complete for all practical purposes.

ENTITY SETS

Membership in each set defined by an entity is determined by the unique attributes of the entity (i.e., algebraic variables) and the values that those attributes can take on (i.e., their domains). A subtype entity defines a subset of the set that is defined by the supertype entity. All the rigor and rules of set theory apply and all the inherent problems remain. Practical guidelines must be set up to ensure that subtype entities defined within project data models serve appropriate purposes and define useful entity subsets.

Arbitrary and indiscriminate subtype modeling leads to endless discussions that add little or no value to the project and may be counterproductive. Set theory illustrates that all sets have an infinite number of subsets, most of which contain no members. Subtype entity proliferation in a model without defined goals for the entities leads to cluttered model diagrams that may hide relevant business detail from the analyst. If the analyst examines the uses that subtype modeling serves, practical guidelines can be established to define when subtype modeling is appropriate and predict what impact entity subtypes may have on the application and data architectures of targeted application systems.

SUPERTYPE AND SUBTYPE MODELING

When subtype entities are included in the data model, several assertions are made that are less generic than those that are a part of set theory. Specifically, to claim that $ENTITY_1$ is a subtype of $ENTITY_0$ is to assert not just that the former describes a subset of the latter, but that each instance of the subtype entity corresponds to the same real world object as the corresponding instance of the supertype entity. This translates into a specific relationship description between the supertype and subtype entities (see Exhibit 1). Each instance of the subtype entity is one and the same with an

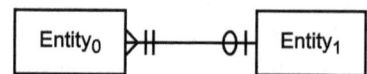

Exhibit 20-1. Generic supertype and subtype definition.

instance of the supertype entity. Because the converse is not always true, however, subtype modeling is often necessary.

Subtype Modeling Effects

A principal effect of a subtype entity is to constrain the cardinalities associated with a supertype's attributes and outbound relationships. Optional attributes of the supertype can become required attributes of the subtype or optional outbound relationships can become required. This provides more than just aesthetic value to the model; it emphasizes the optional nature of the involvement and may lead to a more precise model. In addition, many subtype entities consolidate several attributes and relationships to provide a single definition of the circumstances of their occurrence.

Subtype modeling effects are not limited to requiring certain properties that may otherwise be optional, although this is their most common use. The optional-to-required theory is a special case that constrains the minimum cardinality of an attribute or outbound relationship (e.g., from zero to greater than zero). This same theory can apply to all other properties that describe the involvement of an entity with other objects in the data model (i.e., maximum cardinality or average cardinality). In addition, other effects may restrict the domains that are applicable to supertype attributes. In this case, one or more supertype attributes are common to each of its defined subtypes, but the domain of values that can be taken on by the attribute is restricted for each subtype.

There is some controversy among data modelers as to whether constraining the domain of an attribute is actually the definition of a new attribute. Regardless of this controversy, subtype entities can still make context-sensitive, domains more precise in the model. It makes no difference whether the result is two different attributes with their own domains or one attribute with slightly differing domains based on context.

Subtype Modeling Uses

The common uses of subtype modeling on a project are status-based, the definition of how a single instance of an entity changes as it progresses through time, and type-based, the definition of how different instances of an entity vary. Both of these applications can combine the effects of attribute and relationship cardinality constraint with domain constraint.

In status-based subtype modeling, entity occurrences pass through several states as the organization processes them. Individual attributes and outbound relationships are optional or required based on the entity occurrence's state at a certain point in time. Optional attributes dominate entities in their earliest states; required attributes dominate in later stages. For instance, during order entry, the SHIPPED-DATE for an ORDER is not available and therefore is modeled as an optional attribute (see Exhibit 2). Similarly, the

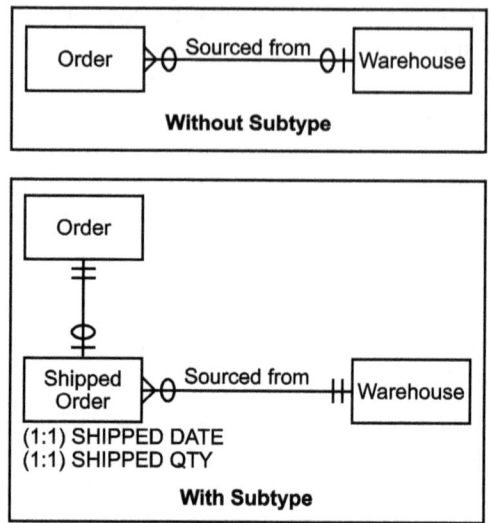

Exhibit 20-2. Status-based subtype.

SHIPPED-QTY is not available early in the life cycle of ORDER. Recently received may not have a WAREHOUSE assigned as a source point.

By defining a subtype entity (e.g., SHIPPED ORDER) these three optional properties are brought under a single definition that states when they are to be required. Both SHIPPED-DATE and SHIPPED-QTY are required attributes of the subtype and the outbound relationship to WAREHOUSE is now required. The warehouse assignment, shipment date, and shipment quantity are not optional for an order. What is optional is whether an order is shipped at all. Once shipped, the warehouse, date, and quantity are then required. When the subtype definition is added, the model is clarified (e.g., SHIPPED-DATE is never present without SHIPPED-QTY and supplemented with facts that are not present in the model without the subtype (e.g., the average cardinality of the subtype relationship represents the percentage of orders that are shipped).

In type-based subtype modeling, distinctions are made between different instances of an entity. Employees have an annual salary or an hourly rate based on whether they are exempt or nonexempt employees (see Exhibit 3). At the supertype level both attributes must be optional. When the data modeler uses subtype entities, each attribute can be required within a narrower context. Because an employee can be only one of these types, the subtype entities are exclusive and exhaustive. The modeler can also establish other subtype relationships for the same entity independent of other established subtype schemas. Each view serves an appropriate purpose if it continues to add to the model's precision. Entities are often combinations of both type-based and status-based subtype schemas.

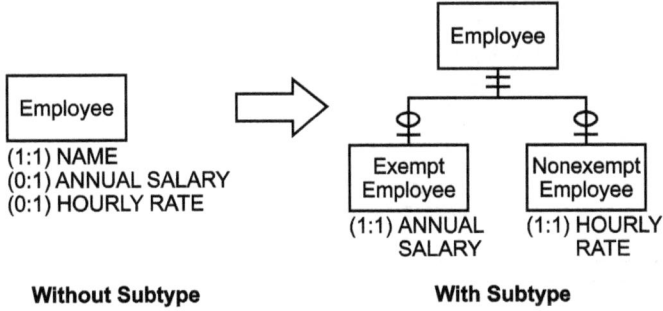

Without Subtype **With Subtype**

Exhibit 20-3. Type-based subtype.

An employee can either be active or retired. This subtype relationship is independent of the employee exemption theory. The relationship is exclusive because an employee cannot be both active and retired. To determine whether the subtype is exhaustive requires some analysis; the answer lies in the ultimate definition of the term "employee." Is a former employee that resigned still an employee in the sense being conveyed by the EMPLOYEE entity? What about an active or retired employee that dies? There are no a priori answers to these questions because they are the organization's issues, not data modeling issues.

Exhibit 4 presumes that each of these perspectives is required by the organization and must be included in the model. The INACTIVE EMPLOYEE subtype is introduced because the active or inactive subtype is exclusive and exhaustive. Subtype entities that represent retired, deceased, or resigned employees are not exclusive and, on further analysis, may not yet be exhaustive. Although it is not clear which subtype perspective is best, all required attributes of each subtype in Exhibit 4 must be treated as optional in the absence of subtype modeling. This action leads to increased ambiguity in the organization's business rules that govern employees.

Subtype Modeling Implications

The use of subtype modeling during a project carries implications for the data and application architectures that are chosen for the information systems implementation. For exclusive subtype relationships, a field is usually introduced into the physical data structure that represents which subtype involvement is appropriate for an instance of the entity. For status-based subtype entities, this field is often named STATUS-CODE. For type-based subtypes, it is often named TYPE-CODE. For nonexclusive subtypes, the modeler must identify a data condition for each particular subtype that determines a subtype's applicability to a particular instance (e.g., the employee is retired if RETIREMENT-DATE is not null). In the absence of a field-based criterion, the modeler must introduce and maintain a FLAG field to signal subtype use.

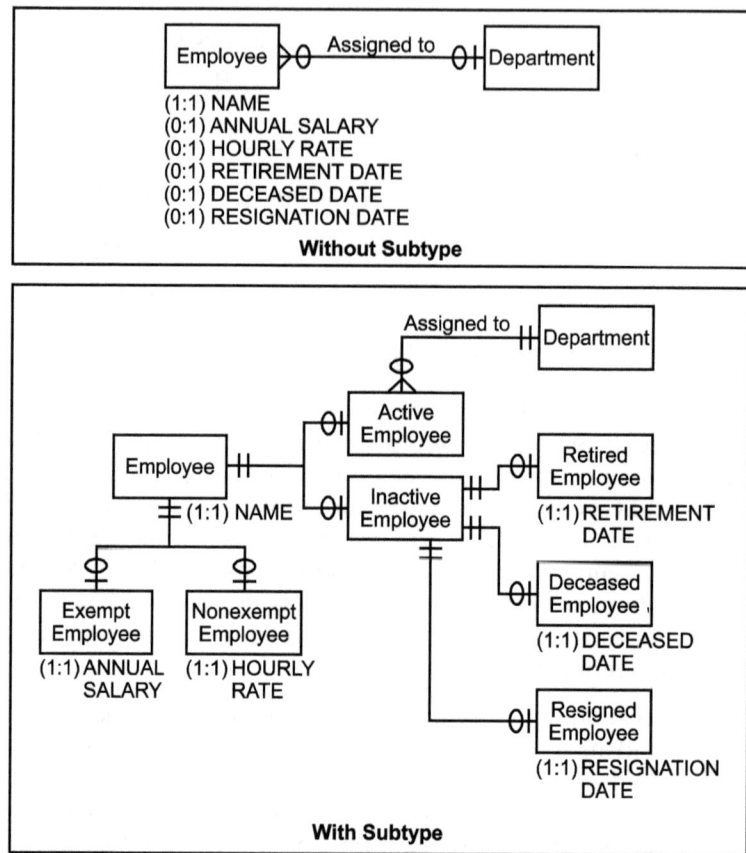

Exhibit 20-4. Reduced ambiguity through subtypes.

For exhaustive and exclusive subtypes, the subtype identifier can drive the application architecture. Because every instance must be one of the available subtypes, high-level conditional logic can be created to determine the appropriate processing for data records from the subtype identifier. If the subtype is not exhaustive, there may always be exceptions to any subtype-based driver logic.

APLLICATION PROBLEMS

Several problems typically arise when an organization implements basic subtype modeling to any project. Subtype theory provides a robust tool that defines and evaluates the intricate details that concern the way the model's information should be constrained based on the type of entity instances that are viewed. In practice, it is the extensive proliferation of this detail that may create potentially cumbersome data models that are unmanageable and unusable.

Object Proliferation

The greatest problem that data modelers immediately encounter when they conduct subtype modeling is object proliferation in the model diagrams and supporting documentation. A nontrivial diagram may contain several subtype entities for one supertype. Each of the supertype's attributes and outbound relationships may be replicated for each subtype entity to constrain the cardinality or domain. When a supertype entity has five attributes and is involved in three relationships, this means an additional 120 objects (i.e., subtypes, attributes, and relationships) in the data model. The model may now contain 60 new attributes; however, only five fields that correspond to the supertype's original five attributes may be implemented. The knowledge that the data modeler gains through subtyping adds precision to the defined use of the data but does not necessarily contribute any new data.

Although the data analyst may find these initial stages of subtyping to be cumbersome, further investigation often uncovers additional subtype-specific data requirements that may be overlooked without subtype modeling. This new information provides value to the project, but is only useful if analysts allow the number of entities, attributes, and relationships associated with the model to grow rapidly.

Arbitrary Decomposition

Another problem with subtype modeling is the selection of appropriate subtype perspectives. Subtyping is primarily a decomposing technique. Successful decomposition requires a clear and unambiguous criterion: Mixing the criteria within a single attempt at decomposition may lead to results that do not isolate subtype knowledge in a single location in the model but distribute it incorrectly across multiple points in the diagram. In addition, the selected decomposition criterion may not be relevant to the project. This results in the proliferation of subtype entities that contain no attributes and cannot participate in relation- ships because they do not require the constraint of any subtype involvements.

Conflicting Hierarchies

The decomposition associated with subtype modeling is hierarchical in nature. Subtype relationships that are more network-oriented are difficult to define when the data modeler uses techniques. Therefore, it may be difficult to provide for all known data constraints with current subtyping techniques.

List Variability

Subtype modeling is difficult to implement with subtype schemas that cannot be exhausted, either because the entire subtype list is unknown or because the list may grow over time to include undefined types. In this situation it is dangerous for an analyst to treat the subtype as exhaustive, but the analyst may be tempted to do so because of the scope of the known list. As a result, application systems may be developed that are highly oriented around the subtype and require major enhancements each time a new subtype is introduced.

PRACTICAL SOLUTIONS

Even with the existence of diagrammatic complexity, subtype modeling can be a viable tool in every modeling project. The less committed data modeler, however, may tend to abbreviate the modeling effort and include only rudimentary subtype modeling and not the level of detail and precision that is implied by the data itself. Guidelines are therefore needed to make necessary subtype modeling a practical option for all modelers and to promote consistency in the development of subtype schemas.

Goals

To develop practical strategies, subtype modeling must be viewed as a means to an end so that its goals can be better understood. If the data administrator understands why the data model should contain subtypes, then how to develop subtype models becomes clearer. Subtype modeling does not exist to articulate a list of the classes into which instances of an entity can be placed. This approach forces analysts to continually invent subtype schemas that add no real value to the model, yet contribute to the diagrammatic complexity that may prevent successful subtype modeling.

The purpose of subtype modeling is to define the detailed business constraints that are placed on the facts that are represented in the supertype-based model. This is the means to an end approach. The classes that an instance of an entity may fall into are listed explicitly. This helps the data modeler understand the differences in how the data that relates to the instance is presented and used. If no differences are discerned, the subtype is not useful. This approach results in a single goal that must be satisfied to include a subtype entity in a model.

This goal states that a subtype entity may be included in a data model if and only if it contains at least one property (attribute or outbound relationship) with a cardinality different than that defined when the property is created for the supertype entity directly. This goal reduces the number of superfluous subtype entities that are defined on a typical project and ensures that the defined entities continue to provide their intended value.

The Entity Constraint Matrix

Another step that can be taken to develop practical subtype modeling strategies is to remove entity-relationship diagramming complexity as a central issue. Subtype modeling problems often concern the excessive

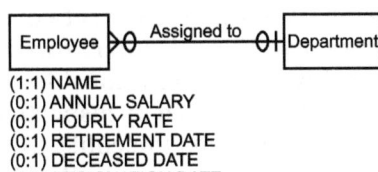

(1:1) NAME
(0:1) ANNUAL SALARY
(0:1) HOURLY RATE
(0:1) RETIREMENT DATE
(0:1) DECEASED DATE
(0:1) RESIGNATION DATE

	ANNUAL SALARY 0:1	HOURLY RATE 0:1	RETIREMENT DATE 0:1	DECEASED DATE 0:1	RESIGNATION DATE 0:1	Assigned to DEPARTMENT 0:1
EXEMPT	1:1	0:0				
NONEXEMPT	0:0	1:1				
ACTIVE			0:0	0:0	0:0	1:1
INACTIVE						0:0
RETIRED			1:1		0:0	0:0
DECEASED				1:1		0:0
RESIGNED			0:0		1:1	0:0

Exhibit 20-5. Employee entity constraint matrix.

number of additional entities and relationships that are required in typical entity-relationship diagrams. An alternative is to diagram only the supertype entity as part of the entity-relationship model and to include an entity constraint matrix as part of the model's documentation. An entity constraint matrix can be created for any entity in the entity-relationship diagram. The columns in the matrix are the outbound properties associated with the supertype entity and the rows are the various subtypes that are analyzed. By drawing the entity constraint matrix the modeler asserts that the entity is a supertype without the need to clutter the entity-relationship diagram with all the subtyping details.

Exhibit 5 illustrates an entity constraint matrix for EMPLOYEE. The six columns correspond to the six properties of the EMPLOYEE entity that can be constrained. Properties that are required singly (e.g., [1:1] NAME) cannot be constrained and do not appear in the matrix. The matrix rows are the seven subtypes that are defined for EMPLOYEE. The matrix cells represent additional constraints placed on the model whenever the subtypes are referenced. The data modeler can describe all of the matrix's information by using traditional entity-relationship diagramming techniques. The entity constraint matrix can capture these facts in a less cumbersome way and can avoid the pitfalls associated with traditional subtype modeling by using entity-relationship diagramming. The object proliferation problem still exists, but the diagrammatic complexity associated with that proliferation is eliminated.

The entity constraint matrix also avoids the arbitrary nature of decomposition. Each row specifies the rule necessary to create a subset. These subsets contain all members in the original set constrained by any non-blank cells in the selected row. This selection process may even be represented in a context-sensitive, entity-relationship diagram. In addition, decomposition criterion can be revealed by inspecting the contents of the constraint cells. Every row constrains the entity to its subtype members and many also constrain other matrix rows. An INACTIVE EMPLOYEE is an EMPLOYEE that cannot be assigned to a department. Any other row that provides for the same constraint represents a subset of EMPLOYEE as well as INACTIVE EMPLOYEE. Through this criteria, RETIRED EMPLOYEE, DECEASED EMPLOYEE, and RESIGNED EMPLOYEE are all subtypes of INACTIVE EMPLOYEE. These subtype hierarchies can now be constructed mechanically from the matrix without relying on the data analyst to intuitively spot them.

The problem of conflicting hierarchies, or the need to support rule networks, is also addressed by the entity constraint matrix. Any two matrix rows that do not contradict each other may be combined into a new subtype that might not have been obvious if modeled hierarchically. For example, an ACTIVE EXEMPT EMPLOYEE combines the constraints of both the ACTIVE EMPLOYEE and EXEMPT EMPLOYEE rows. A RETIRED ACTIVE EMPLOYEE entity is not possible because of contradictions in the RETIREMENT DATE attribute and ASSIGNED DEPARTMENT relationship constraints. Any experienced data modeler can define the combinations that are created by this matrix analysis. As a mechanical process, however, entity constraint matrix analysis ensures that all combinations, both valid and invalid, are defined.

The matrix also helps alleviate some list variability problems. Short of mathematically exploding the rows of the matrix to represent every permutation of constrainable properties, nothing can guarantee that a subtype list is exhaustive. One test that the modeler can perform on the matrix is to inspect each column to ensure that at least one row makes the property required.

There is no mandate in data modeling that every attribute or relationship be required in some context, but the modeler must ensure that only fairly trivial properties are truly universally optional. For those nontrivial properties in the matrix that remain completely optional, a new row that makes the property required can be created. The analyst's investigation should reveal what this row might mean to the organization if, in fact, an additional subtype is discovered. If not, the newly created row may be discarded.

The entity constraint matrix is continually inspected for insights into the organization's data. For example, by looking at the affinities shared by the matrix's rows and columns, the modeler can discern the independence of the various subtype schemas. In the matrix in Exhibit 5 the exemption of an employee is independent of whether an employee is active. This can be seen by noting that the two schemas constrain completely different properties in the matrix. Unfortunately, not all independent schemas are as obvious. For example, it is a mistake to perceive the INACTIVE EMPLOYEE subtype as containing a single additional subtype schema that is represented by the RETIRED EMPLOYEE, DECEASED EMPLOYEE, and RESIGNED EMPLOYEE subtypes. The properties constrained by the RETIRED EMPLOYEE and RESIGNED EMPLOYEE subtypes are the same, while the DECEASED EMPLOYEE subtype constrains other properties. There are two different subtype schemas at work here and they must not be arbitrarily combined because such a combination may contradict business information that has not yet been discovered.

Metadata Tables

The list variability problem that cannot be addressed by the entity constraint matrix is one of inexhaustability. Many projects encounter business areas that have subtype lists which are not fixed over time. A requirement often exists to be able to add additional subtypes or remove existing subtypes after the implementation of a system. For these projects, applications must be written that are table-driven. Other applications may be able to list all valid subtypes, but the list and its associated entity constraint matrix is so complicated that a table-driven approach is the only viable application architecture.

Some of these situations arise within the set of subtype schemas and do not require the entire application to be written in a table-driven format. Examples of these situations are found through the nesting of exclusive subtype schemas within the entity constraint matrix. In Exhibit 5, the ACTIVE EMPLOYEE and INACTIVE EMPLOYEE schema is exclusive (e.g., the ASSIGNED DEPARTMENT properties are contradictory). Within the INACTIVE EMPLOYEE schema, the exclusive schema for RETIRED EMPLOYEE and RESIGNED EMPLOYEE exists. This exclusivity may remain hidden if the DECEASED EMPLOYEE subtype is not isolated as a different subtype schema. It is still not clear, however, whether the subtypes of INACTIVE EMPLOYEE are exhaustive. If they are not and an exhaustive list cannot be discovered during analysis, then this subtype schema should be physically implemented using a logical table of reasons of inactivity. Rather than implementing the RESIGNATION DATE and RETIREMENT DATES fields (i.e., the exclusive subtype option), the physical application should implement INACTIVE DATE and INACTIVE REASON CODE fields. The reason code domain might initially be resigned and retired, but may be expanded in the future without substantive changes to the production application.

On some projects, the subtype schema's ambiguity exists at the highest supertype level. Application models that do not exhaust the list of major subtypes before implementation are prone to major enhancement activity

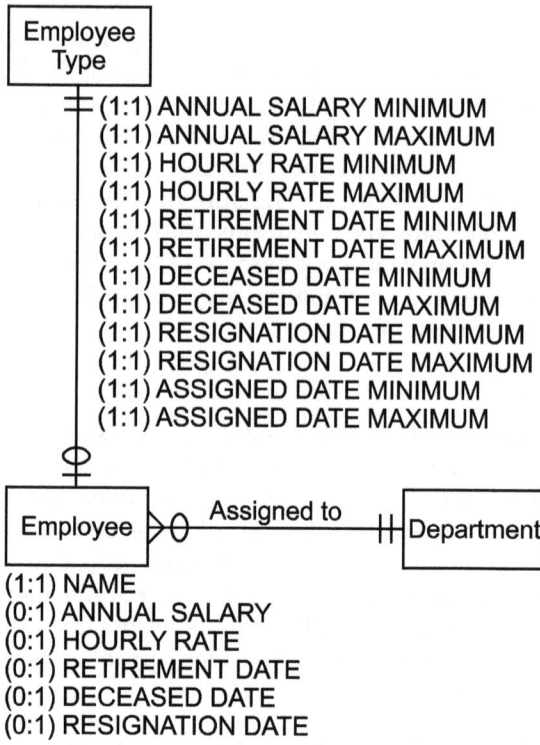

Exhibit 20-6. Metadata table approach.

after implementation. In these cases, the entity constraint matrix provides the alternate data architecture that the modeler can then implement with a table- driven application development strategy for the entire system. For the project data model this means that no subtype entities are included in any data diagrams. Instead, the entity-relationship diagram is modified to include a type entity for the supertype (see Exhibit 6). Attributes of the type entity represent the values in the cells of the entity constraint matrix. The application system dynamically interrogates the metadata table and handles instances of the supertype entity according to the constraints found. Performance considerations are potential concerns because of the implied additional input-output that the applications require. The modelers must develop maintenance capabilities for the physical metadata tables and procedures to ensure that their contents are valid. In many cases the benefits of additional flexibility that exist for the organization far outweigh these concerns. An automated link between the entity constraint matrix and the table that implements it is highly desirable.

Such approaches to subtype modeling as goal orientation, entity constraint matrix, and metadata tables offer incremental payback to any data-oriented projects that adopt them. Larger, more complex modeling efforts will experience the greatest benefits. An organization's most complex entities are usually the type of entities that can be most helped by these approaches (e.g., PRODUCT, CUSTOMER, and ORDER).

SUMMARY

The goal-oriented approach to supertype and subtype modeling requires that IS management articulate a clear vision of the types of applications that must be built in the future. Data administration managers should establish a data architecture that can articulate the goals that must be achieved by subtype modeling. Performance, security, and control thresholds must be established to determine which modeling approaches are appropriate on a project-by-project basis. Application development managers must establish an application architecture that can determine the situations that require tabularization. Finally, business and applications analysts must be trained in the proper techniques necessary to put these architectures into practice.

Section V
Performance Design and Development

THE LOGICAL DATA MODEL IS TRANSFORMED INTO THE PHYSICAL DATA DESIGN, WHICH IS THEN IMPLEMENTED UNDER A SPECIFIC DATABASE TECHNOLOGY. Significant database performance improvements can be gained by manipulating the physical database design. Application performance can be optimized using a number of extensions and components, such as indexes, triggers, and stored procedures against the database. Techniques, such as transactional analysis, provide an opportunity to denormalize or modify the physical implementation of a database design. Opportunities to improve database performance also exist at the application, architecture, and operations levels. This section contains the following chapters.

Chapter 21, "Physical Database Design," shows how to use transactional analysis, anticipated workload, and a relationship schema to construct a physical database. This chapter also examines methods of fine-tuning the physical database design to improve application performance.

Chapters 22 and 23 demonstrate how to transform a logical data design into a physical, distributed database. This includes a discussion of management and implementation issues commonly encountered during this transformation process.

Chapter 24, "Relational Database Design Using Semantic Objects," provides an approach for building a physical database design based on available semantic objects.

Chapter 25, "Component Design for Relational Databases," describes a twist on relational-to-object impedance matching, which can also be referred to as a data-component approach. This involves leveraging the advantages of having a component take responsibility for updating data, while providing relevant inquiry functions. This results in improved application performance.

Chapter 26, "Designing Relational Databases," shows how to transform a data model into a relational database. This chapter provides a methodology that examines how to transform every logical construct to a physical implementation.

Chapter 21
Physical Database Design
James A. Larson and Carol L. Larson

CREATING A PHYSICAL DATABASE DESIGN CAN BE A COMPLEX AND DIFFICULT TASK. This article presents a four-phase methodology for selecting primary search keys and the corresponding files structure for each table, determining how to support join operations, selecting secondary search keys and appropriate supporting access methods, and identifying and supporting composite search keys and structures. The database administrator (DBA) may need to fine-tune the physical database design as DBMS usage requirements change.

STAGES OF A DATABASE LIFECYCLE

Exhibit 1 illustrates the lifecycle of a database that consists of several stages leading to database usage. While Exhibit 1 presents each stage as desecrate, in reality, database administrators (DBAs) frequently revisit and revise decisions made in earlier stages as they proceed with later ones. Briefly, the individual stages are:

- **Conceptual schema design.** The DBA interviews prospective users and considers the proposed database applications to create a conceptual schema design. The conceptual schema describes the entities and their relationships that will be represented in the database.
- **Relational schema design.** If the DBA designs the conceptual schema using notation other than the relational data model, then this stage is necessary to convert the objects and relationships of the conceptual schema into the notation and format required by a relational DBMS.
- **Schema refinement.** The DBA examines business rules describing the constraints on the data values in the database. The DBA structures the relational tables in such a manner that updating the tables will not result in update anomalies. However, if the database is never modified — as with data warehouses — or is seldom updated, then this stage can be skipped.

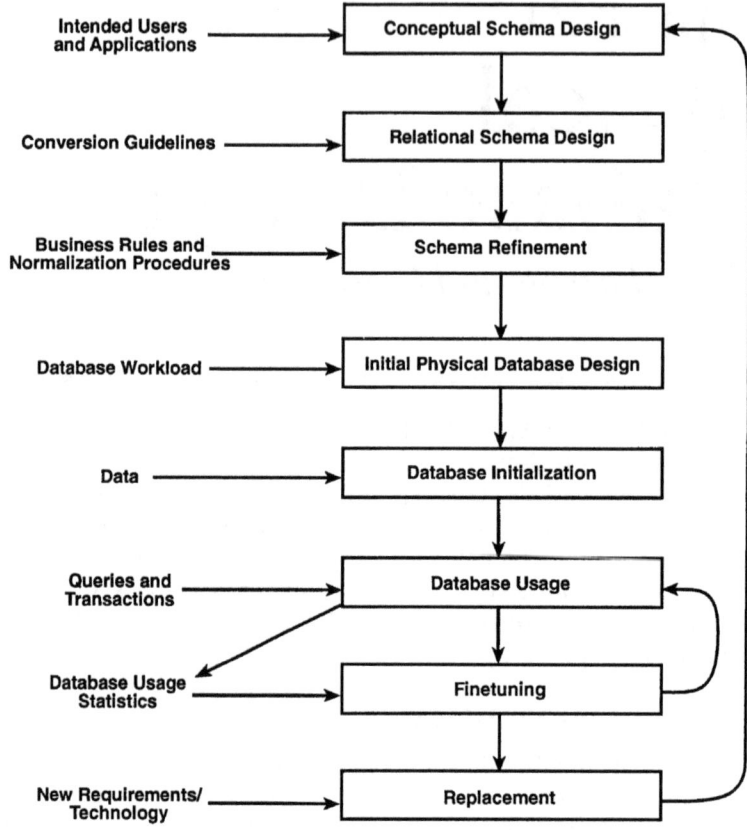

Exhibit 21-1. Lifecycle of a database.

- **Initial physical database design.** The DBA examines the proposed database workload and determines how to physically represent each table in the database. The DBA also determines if extra indexes will be useful to make the DBMS more efficient as it processes the queries and transactions in the workload.
- **Database initialization.** The DBA uses utility programs to capture, reformat, and load data into the database.
- **Database usage.** Users submit queries and transactions to the database to obtain data needed to perform the users' every-day work functions.
- **Database fine-tuning.** As new uses for the database emerge, the workload will change. To optimize the execution of the DBMS with respect to the new workload, the database administrator should modify the initial physical database design by creating new tables, deleting existing indexes, creating new indexes, and modifying views.

• **Replacement.** There comes a time when the DBMS is not able to support new requirements of the enterprise in which it is used. New technology may enable new DBMSs to better serve the enterprise. When the benefits of the new DBMS outweigh the costs of converting the old database to the new DBMS, the old DBMS is replaced and the database lifecycle begins again.

INITIAL PHYSICAL DATABASE DESIGN METHODOLOGY

Creating the initial physical database design is an important stage in the database lifecycle. The DBA determines the physical data structures for representing data so that the DBMS efficiently processes queries and transactions in the workload. The basic methodology for creating the initial physical database design consists of four phases:

1. For each table in the relational schema, determine the primary search key, determine the appropriate file structure, and choose the primary access method for accessing that file.
2. For frequently joined tables, determine how to support the join operation.
3. For each file, identify additional search keys and determine the appropriate physical structures for supporting them.
4. For each file, identify multi-attribute search keys and determine the appropriate physical structures for supporting them.

To illustrate each phase of the initial physical database design process, a simple relational database — which consists of two tables, Employee and Department — will be used. Exhibit 2 illustrates the relational schema for these two tables. The Employee table has four columns with the EmpId col-

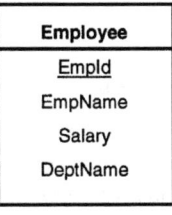

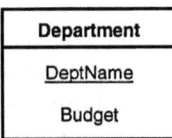

Exhibit 21-2. Example of a relational schema.

Exhibit 21-3.   Seven important queries and their relative frequency of execution.

Query Number	SQL Query	Relative Frequency of Query Execution
1	Select * from Department where DeptName = "Accounting"	25 percent
2	Select * from Department where DeptName = "Sales" or DeptName = "Production"	5 percent
3	Select * from Employee, Department where Budget = 200,000 and Employee.DeptName = Department.DeptName	15 percent
4	Select * from Department where Budget = 500,000	5 percent
5	Select * from Department where 100,000 < Budget and Budget < 500,000	15 percent
6	Select * from Employee where EmpName = "Jones"	20 percent
7	Update Employee	15 percent

umn as the primary key. The Department table has two columns with Dept-Name as the primary key. In addition, assume that the example workload consists of the six representative queries presented in Exhibit 3. A representative query is a query that is representative of homogeneous class of queries. For example, Query 6 is representative of queries in the form:

Select <attribute list> from Employee where EmpName = <some name>

Also assume that while updates to the Employee table are 15 percent of the workload, updates to the Department table are not significant because they seldom occur.

With the relational schema and the anticipated workload in place, the DBA is ready to begin performing the four phases in the initial physical database design process.

Phase 1: Determine File Structures

Most DBMSs support three basic file structures: heap files, sorted files, and hashed files. Each of these structures organize multiple data pages. A data page is a unit of data that is transferred between disks and main memory and usually contains several database records. DBAs design physical databases so the number of data pages being transferred is minimized for frequently performed queries.

Two of the three basic file structures involve a search key. A search key is one or more columns of a table that are frequently used to access records of the file. Often, but not always, the most frequently used search key is the primary key of the table. DBAs design physical databases to efficiently access database tables using search keys. Some tables have multiple search

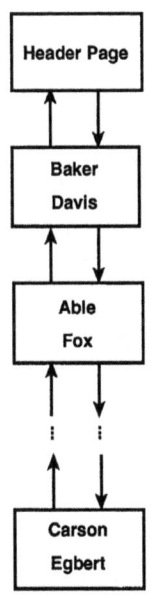
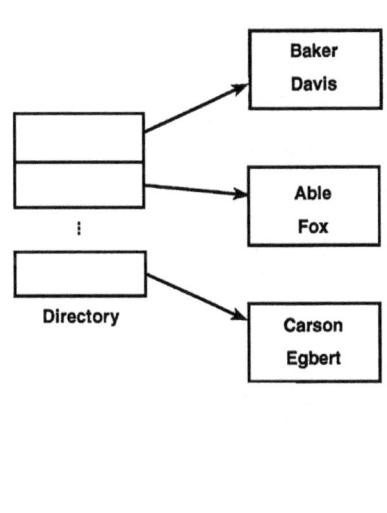

a. Doubly-linked List of Data Pages   **b.** Directory With Pointers to Data Pages

Exhibit 21-4. Alternative heap file organizations.

keys. The most important search key is called the primary search key. The remaining search keys of a table are called secondary search keys.

It is important that the DBA understands the basic mechanisms of the three widely used file structures, as well as their strengths and weaknesses, so the database being designed will fit the needs of the users.

Heap Files. A heap file maintains an unsorted list of records in a file. Two popular approaches for implementing the Employee table as a heap file are illustrated in Exhibit 4. Heap files are implemented using a doubly linked list of data pages, each containing one or more records. For simplicity purposes, only the value of the EmpName search key is shown for each record. A new record can be inserted into any data page that has room to store the record, or a new data page can be inserted into the doubly linked list with the new record stored in the data page.

Alternatively, a directory contains pointers to every data page. A new record is inserted into any data page that has room to store the record, or a pointer to a new data page can be inserted into the directory with the new record stored in the new data page.

Heap files are efficient when every record in a file must be accessed. However, they are not efficient when retrieving a record with a specific

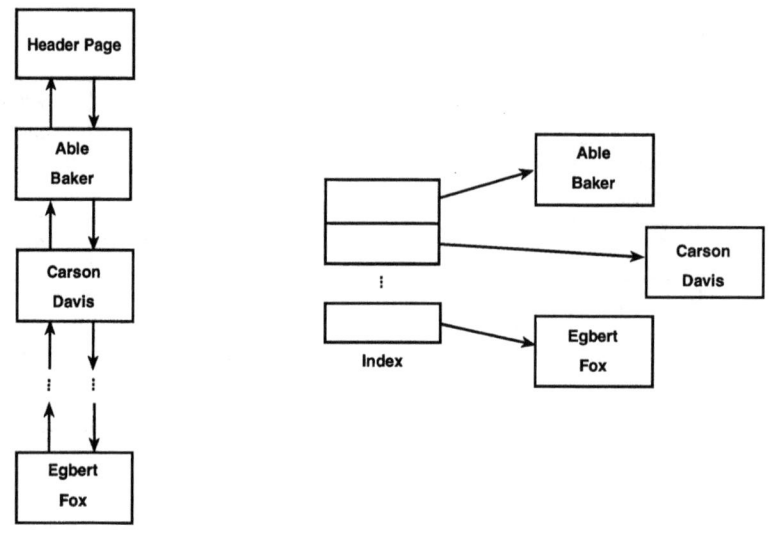

a. Doubly-linked List of Data Pages   **b.** Index With Pointers to Data Pages

Exhibit 21-5. Alternative sorted file organizations.

value for the search key or retrieving records within a specific range of values for the search key. This inefficiency occurs because files must be scanned sequentially to locate any specific value or specific range of values. On the average, half of the records in a heap file must be accessed to locate a specific record.

Sorted Files. A sorted file maintains a list of records sorted by the values of the primary search key. The two approaches for implementing the Employee table with primary search key EmpName as a sorted file are presented in Exhibit 5. Again, for simplicity, only the value of the EmpName search key is shown for each record. When using the doubly linked list of data pages, a new record must be inserted into the appropriate data page so the sorted order of records is maintained. Alternatively, an index may contain pointers to every data page. Again, a new record is inserted into the appropriate data page so the sorted order of records is maintained. If there is no space for a new record in the existing data page, a new data page is created and linked into the appropriate position within the doubly linked list.

Sorted files are efficient when:

1. Records need to be accessed in the sequence of the search key. For example, if the Employee file is sorted by EmpName, then the sorted file would be efficient for the representative Query 6.

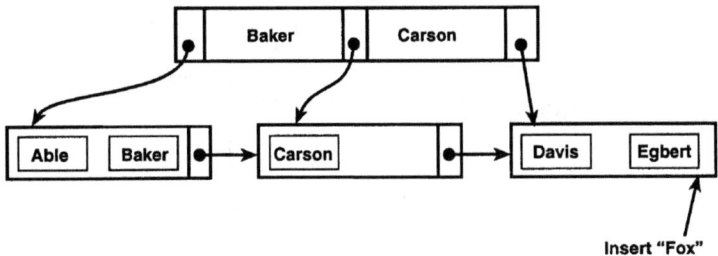

a. B+ Tree Before Inserting a Record for "Fox"

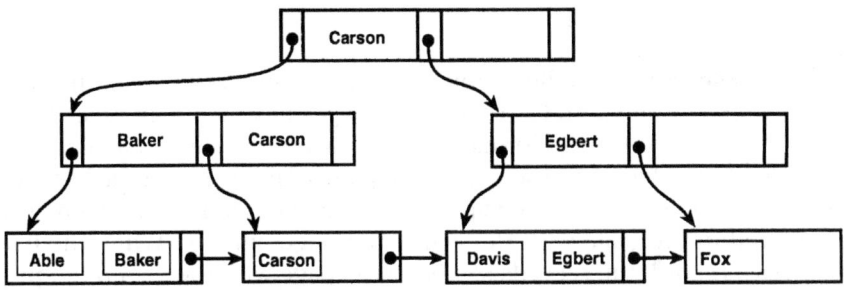

b. Reorganized B+ Tree After Inserting a Record for "Fox"

Exhibit 21-6. B+ tree.

2. Records need to be accessed within a prescribed range of values of the search key. For example, if the Department file is sorted by Budget, then the sorted file would be efficient for Query 5. The DBMS would locate the first record with a value for Budget less than 100,000, then retrieve records sequentially from the sorted file until it encounters a record with a value for Budget equal to 500,000.

The DBA can use alternative tree structures to organize a sorted file. The Indexed Sequential Access Method (ISAM) was used for many years as a tree index structure, but has been replaced by the more popular B-tree and its variation, B+ tree. B+ trees are used because they are dynamically self-organizing. All searches of the B+ tree access the same number of internal branch points, even if the number of records in the indexed file grow. Exhibit 6a illustrates a B+ tree before an insertion, which results in the reorganized tree shown in Exhibit 6b. In the reorganized tree, the overall tree

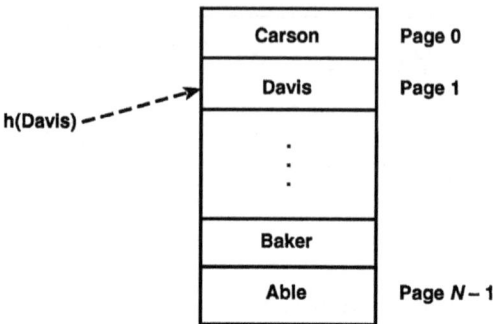

Carson	Page 0
Davis	Page 1
.	
.	
.	
Baker	
Able	Page N-1

Exhibit 21-7. Hashed file.

depth is increased with every leaf of the B+ tree guaranteed to be the same distance from the root of the tree.

Hashed File. A hashed file enables access to any record given the value of its search key. In Exhibit 7, there are N pages in which data records can be stored. By performing a transformation — often called a hashing function — on the value of the search key, a page number is generated where the page number is in the range $[0, N - 1]$. When the user inserts a record, it is stored in the page with the generated page number. When the user retrieves a record, the records stored in the page with the generated page number are retrieved.

Hashed files are efficient when retrieving records that match the selection criteria exactly. For example, consider the SQL request:

Select * from Department where DeptName = "Accounting"

Applying the hashing function to the value for "Accounting" would generate the page number for the data page containing the record for the department with DeptName = "Accounting," which would be retrieved quickly. Unfortunately, hashed files do not lend themselves to range searches, such as Query 5.

Choosing Primary Search Keys and File Structures. While a table may have multiple search keys, the primary search key is used to determine the file structure for the table. To choose a file structure for each table in a relational database, the DBA performs the following calculations: For each table in the relational database, examine the workload for queries and transactions that access the table. Let:

- HEAP be the sum of the weights associated with queries and transactions that scan the entire table.

Exhibit 21-8. Relational tables and search key analysis.

Table	Search Key	Use	Queries	Weight
Department	DeptName	Equality match	1, 2, 3	45
Department	Budget	Equality	3, 4	20
Department	Budget	Range	5	15
Employee	DeptName	Equality match	3	15
Employee	EmpName	Equality match	6	20

For each potential search key, let:

- SORTED be the sum of the weights associated with queries and transactions that access the table in sequence by the search key or involve a range query involving the search key.
- HASHED be the sum of the weights associated with queries and transactions that access the table by matching values with the search key.

For each table, choose the search key with the largest value for HEAP, SORTED, or HASHED. This search key is the primary search key. Then choose the corresponding file structure to represent that table in the database.

For example, examining the queries presented in Exhibit 3, two search keys (DeptName and Budget) exist for the Department table and two search keys (EmpName and DeptName) exist for the Employee table. Exhibit 8 presents an additional analysis of Exhibit 3.

In the Department table, the DeptName search key is used more frequently than the Budget search key. The DBA chooses DeptName to be the primary search key for the Department table. Because the DeptName search key is always used for equality matches, the DBA selects a hashed file structure to represent the Department table.

In the Employee table, the EmpName search key is used more frequently than the DeptName search key. The DBA chooses EmpName to be the primary search key for the Employee table. Because EmpName is always used for equality matches, the DBA selects a hashed file structure to represent the Employee table.

Phase 2: Facilitate Frequent Joins of Two Tables

Joining of two tables is a potentially expensive operation that matches records from two tables with identical values for corresponding columns. In order to improve the efficiency of frequently executed joins, the DBA may elect to perform any of the three following tasks.

1. Denormalize the tables to be joined.
2. Build a hierarchical structure to facilitate the join.
3. Build an index to facilitate the join.

Denormalization. During the schema refinement stage in the database lifecycle, the DBA examines the database tables to determine if they should be vertically partitioned into two or more tables to avoid update anomalies. This process, called normalization, can result in multiple tables replacing a single table. If two tables are frequently joined in the workload, the DBA might decide to denormalize them. Denormalization is the process of replacing multiple tables with a single table in the relational schema. During the initial physical database design stage, the DBA reexamines the decision to normalize and weighs the benefits of normalization, which avoids update anomalies, against the cost of performing frequent joins among the normalized tables.

As a general rule, if users always access two tables together, the tables should be denormalized by joining them into a single table. For example, suppose a DBA decides that a zip code functionally determines the city and state: given a value of zip code, there is one and only one possible value for city and one and only one possible value for state. In the schema refinement stage, the DBA normalizes the address table into two tables: one table containing the street address and zip code, and the second table containing the city, state, and zip code. However, the user always accesses the street address, city, state, and zip code at the same time. There should never be a record in the table containing the street address and zip code without a corresponding record in the table containing the street address, city, state, and zip code. In this case, the DBA should denormalize the two tables during step 2 of the initial physical database design phase.

Hierarchical Files. Table A is dependent on table B if table A is accessed only when table B is accessed. For example, suppose there is a third table, EmpDependent, that contains information about an employee's dependents. The EmpDependent table is dependent on the Employee table because no query ever accesses the EmpDependent table without also accessing the Employee table. Note that some employees may have no dependents, while others may have multiple dependents. The DBA determines that the Employee and EmpDependent tables should not be denormalized because there are many queries that access the Employee table without accessing the EmpDependent table.

Dependent tables are candidates for representation by hierarchical file structures. Exhibit 9 illustrates a hierarchical file structure that facilitates the joining of the Employee and EmpDependent tables. Each Employee record contains pointers to the records of dependents supported by the employee. The DBMS joins the Employee and EmpDependent records by accessing the Employee records one at a time. For each Employee record, the DBMS follows the pointers to retrieve the records of the employee's dependents. This results in an efficient join operation.

Employee Files   **EmpDependent Files**

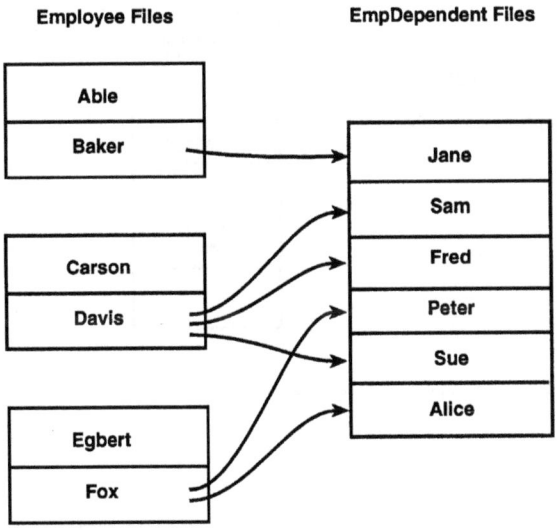

Exhibit 21-9. Hierarchical files.

Indexes for Joins. Query 3 joins the Employee and Department tables and should be executed according to the following steps.

1. Select the rows of the Department table where Budget = 200,000
2. Select the rows of the Employee table for which the value of Dept-Name matches the value of DeptName in one of the rows selected in step 1.

Step 2 executes faster if DeptName is a secondary search key of the Employee table.

Phase 3: Identify And Implement Secondary Search Keys

Secondary search keys are useful in two general situations:

1. Frequently executed queries involve conditions in which a column of a table matches a specific value and the column is not part of the primary search key. For example, in Query 3, Budget is a secondary search key for the Department table.
2. Frequently executed queries require that tables be joined on columns that are not part of the primary search key. In this case, Dept-Name in Query 3 is the secondary search key in the Employee table.

Either hashed indexes or tree indexes can be used to support secondary search keys. (Technically, hashing is not an index structure. But because it is used to provide fast access to individual records given a value of a search key, hashing is often used instead of a tree index.)

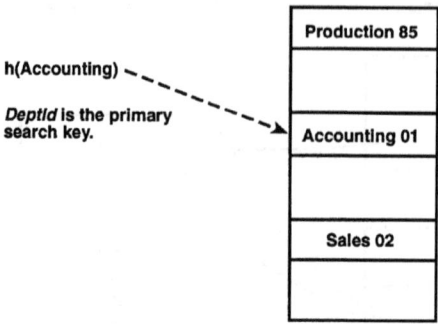

a. *DeptName* Is the Primary Search Key Used For a Hashed File

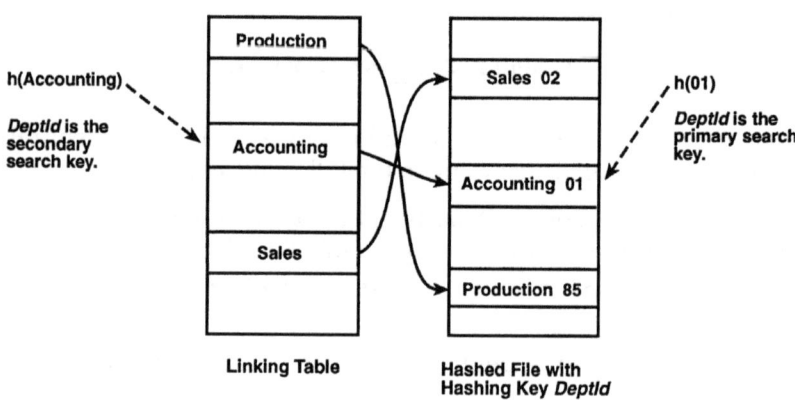

b. *DeptName* Search Key Is Different from the Hashing Key of a Hashed File, Which Requires a Linking Table

Exhibit 21-10. Hashing search keys.

Hashed Index. A hashed index works basically the same way as a hashed file. A hashing function is applied to the value of the search key to calculate the number of the data page for the search key value. As illustrated in Exhibit 10a, if the search key is the same as the primary search key used for a hashed file, then no additional structure is needed. However, if the search key is different from the primary search key used for the hashed file as shown in Exhibit 10b, then a linking table is needed to relate the address calculated by the hashing function and the actual data page used by the underlying hashed file. Exhibits 10c and 10d show that a linking table is needed to relate the address calculated by the hashing function with the actual data page used by the underlying sorted or heap file.

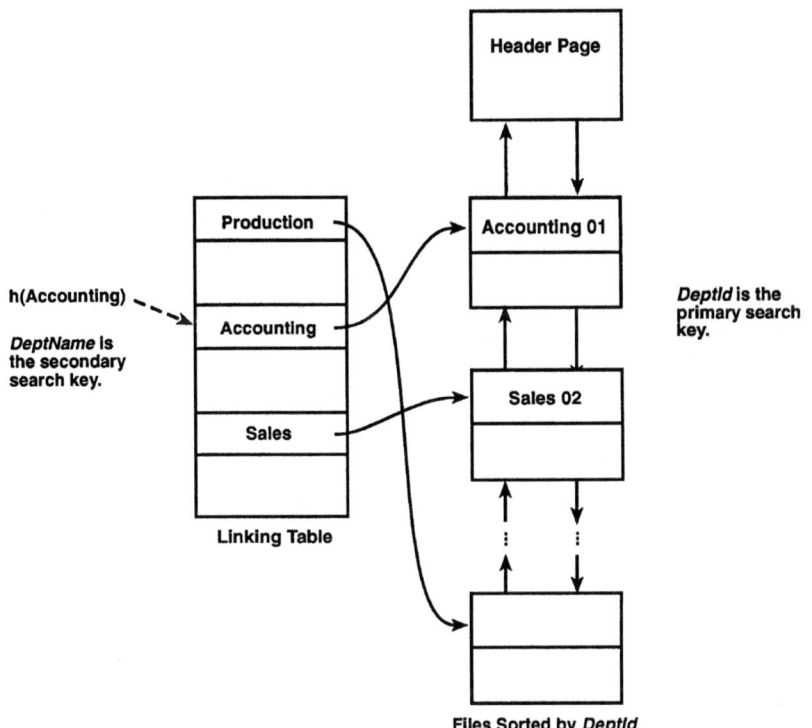

Files Sorted by *DeptId*

c. *DeptName* Search Key and a File Sorted by *DeptId* Require a Linking Table

Exhibit 21-10. Hashing search keys. (*continued*)

Tree Index. Rather than using a function to calculate the data page address, a tree index can be used to map a value of a search key to a data page. The tree index does not require a linking table if the search key is the primary search key used to order the file. However, a linking table is required if the file is a heap or hashed file, or if the secondary search key is different from the primary search key used to sort the file.

Hashed or Tree Index. The choice between using a hashed or tree index is determined by the number of matching requests as compared to the number of range requests. For example, consider Queries 4 and 5 from the workload in Exhibit 3:

- Query 4: Select * from Department where Budget = 500,000
- Query 5: Select * from Department where 100,000 < Budget and Budget < 500,000

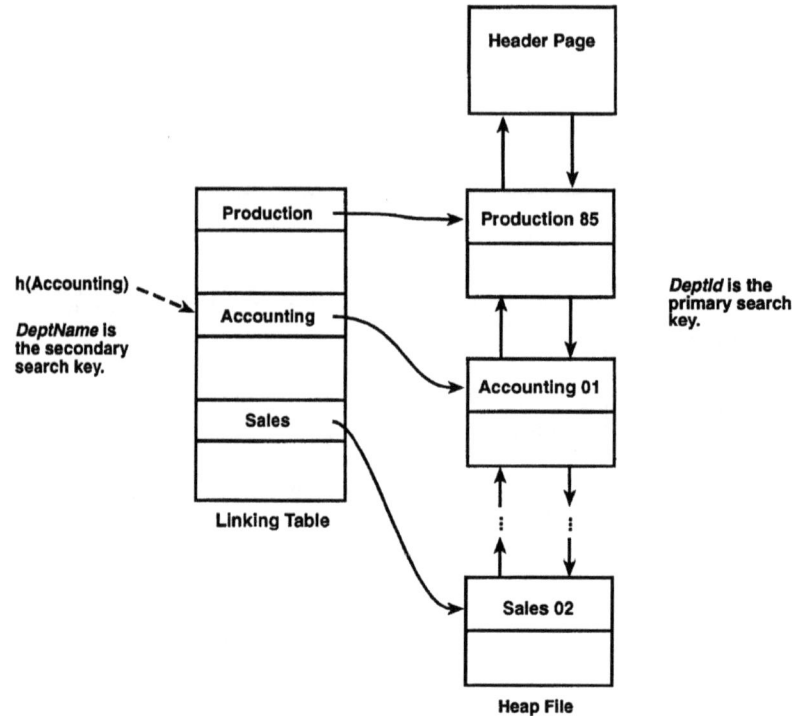

d. *DeptName* Search Key and a Heap File Require a Linking Table

_____

Exhibit 21-10. Hashing search keys. (*continued*)
_____

Query 4 is an equality match on the Budget, while Query 5 is a range query over DeptName. The DBA should create an index on Budget to support the secondary search key Budget. Because Query 5 is executed more frequently than Query 4, the DBA should create a B+ tree rather than a hashed index to support the secondary search key DeptName because hashed indexes do not support range queries. A linking table will be needed because there already is an index file structure for Department.

Phase 4: Build Composite Indexes

A composite index is an index built on a composite search key containing more than one field. Composite search keys can be useful if queries, such as the following, are executed frequently:

Select * from Project where 8/9/98 < StartDate and EndDate < 9/9/99

The DBA creates a composite tree index <StartDate, EndDate>. Then, the DBMS can use the index to locate addresses of records by examining one

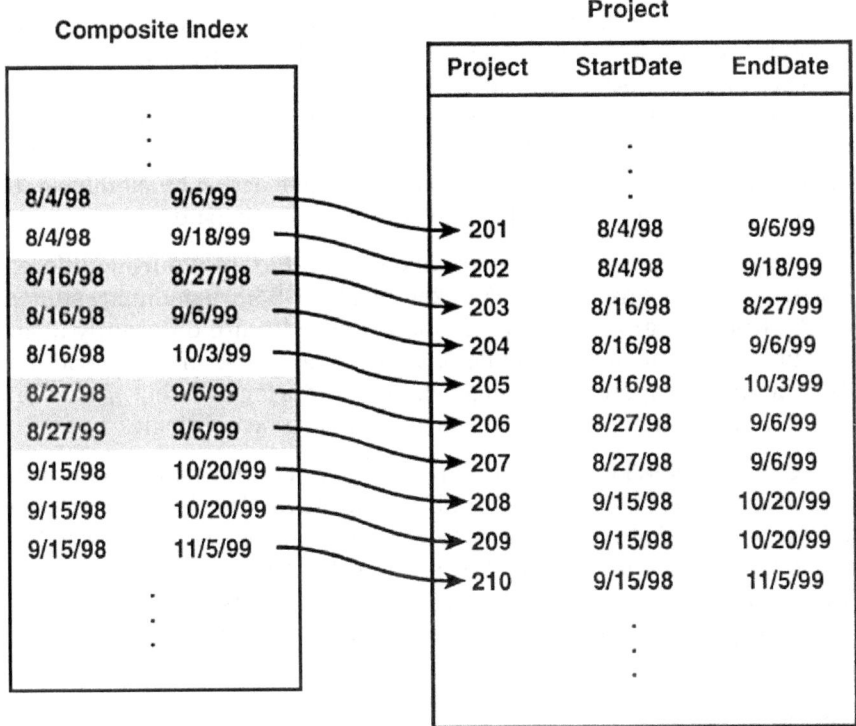

Exhibit 21-11. Composite index with highlighted data that satisfies the condition 8/9/98 < StartDate and EndDate < 9/9/99.

index structure. Exhibit 11 presents a composite index. The DBMS uses the composite index to locate projects quickly with 8/9/98 < StartDate and End-Date < 9/9/99.

An alternative approach is to create tree indexes on both the StartDate and EndDate. The DBMS can:

- use the StartDate index to create the set of addresses that satisfy 8/9/98 < StartDate
- use the EndDate index to create the set of addresses that satisfy End-Date < 9/9/99
- sort both sets and then identify addresses contained in both sorted sets
- finally, retrieve the records that satisfy both criteria

DATABASE FINE-TUNING

Physical database design is never complete as long as the database is in use. After the initial physical database design is complete, the DBA loads the database and users begin to access the data. When using a new DBMS, users will discover new methods of using data to facilitate their work tasks in ways the DBA did not anticipate. The DBA may find it necessary to modify the physical database design. In order to keep the DBMS working at near-optimal performance, the DBA needs to add and remove search keys, change index structures, and evolve the database. The DBA should monitor the DBMS activity to detect inefficiencies and take corrective action by modifying the physical data structures to reflect the new and unanticipated uses.

In many enterprises, DBMSs are accessed differently during different phases of their business cycle. For example, the DBMS maintaining student registration and grade information is accessed quite differently at the beginning of a term, in the middle of a term, and at the end of a term. The DBA should anticipate the changes in access during different processing phases and may adjust physical access structures accordingly.

Most major DBMS vendors provide a variety of performance-monitoring tools to assist the DBA in understanding how the DBMS is being used. Some of these tools and utilities are able to suggest changes to the physical database design and, with approval from the DBA, automatically implement those changes. However, the self-organizing DBMS is still in the distant future. Until then, the DBA will play a critical role in providing high performance for modern DBMSs.

CONCLUSION

In order to develop a good initial physical database design, the DBA must understand the anticipated workload of the DBMS, which includes the relative frequencies of queries and updates, as well as the properties of the various access methods and index structures available within the DBMS.

The DBA can use the four-phase procedure outlined in this article for designing an initial physical database. However, the method should be modified and extended appropriately to include any special data structures supported by the DBMS being used by the enterprise.

However, the DBA still is not finished after completing the initial physical database design. The DBA should monitor DBMS activity and modify the physical design when new queries and transactions adversely affect the DBMS performance.

Notes

1. Elmasri, R. and Navathe, S. *Fundamentals of Database Systems,* 2nd ed., Reading, MA: Addison-Wesley, 1994. Contains chapters on record storage and primary file organizations, index structures for files, and a short section on physical database design guidelines.
2. Ramakrishnan, R. *Database Management Systems,* New York: WCB/McGraw-Hill, 1998. Contains chapters on files, file organizations and indexes, tree-structured indexing, hash-based indexing, and physical database design and tuning.

Chapter 22
Design, Implementation, and Management of Distributed Databases — An Overview

Elizabeth N. Fong, Charles L. Sheppard, and Kathryn A. Harvill

A DISTRIBUTED DATABASE ENVIRONMENT ENABLES A USER TO ACCESS DATA RESIDING ANYWHERE IN A CORPORATION'S COMPUTER NETWORK, WITHOUT REGARD TO DIFFERENCES AMONG COMPUTERS, OPERATING SYSTEMS, DATA MANIPULATION LANGUAGE, OR FILE STRUCTURES. Data that is actually distributed across multiple remote computers will appear to the user as if it resided on the user's own computer. This scenario is functionally limited with today's distributed database technology; true distributed database technology is still a research consideration. The functional limitations are generally in the following areas:

- transaction management
- standard protocols for establishing a remote connection
- independence of network topology

Transaction management capabilities are essential to maintaining reliable and accurate databases. In some cases, today's distributed database software places and responsibility of managing transactions on the application program. In other cases, transactions are committed or rolled back at each location independently, which means that it is not possible to create a single distributed transaction. For example, multiple site updates require multiple transactions.

0-8493-0882-8/00/$0.00+$.50
© 2001 by CRC Press LLC

TODAY'S TECHNOLOGY

In today's distributed database technology, different gateway software must be used and installed to connect nodes using different distributed database management system (DBMS) software. Therefore, connectivity among heterogeneous distributed DBMS nodes is not readily available (i.e., available only through selected vendor markets).

In some instances, distributed DBMS software is tied to a single Network Operating System. This limits the design alternatives for the distributed DBMS environment to the products of a single vendor. It is advisable to select a product that supports more than one Network Operating System. This will increase the possibility of successfully integrating the distributed DBMS software into existing computer environments.

In reality, distributed databases encompass a wide spectrum of possibilities including:

- remote terminal access to centralized DBMSs (e.g., an airline reservation system)
- remote terminal access to different DBMSs, but one at a time (e.g., Prodigy, COMPUSERVE, and Dow Jones)
- simple pairwise interconnection with data sharing that requires users to know the data location, data access language, and the log-on procedure to the remote DBMS
- distributed database management with a generic Data Definition Language and a Data Manipulation Language at all nodes
- distributed update and transaction management
- distributed databases with replication that support vertical and horizontal fragmentation
- "true" distributed DBMSs with heterogeneous hardware, software, and communications

The definition of distributed DBMSs lies anywhere along this spectrum. For the purpose of this chapter, the remote terminal access to data as discussed in the first two bullets in the preceding list is not considered a distributed DBMS because a node in the distributed DBMS must have its own hardware, central processor, and software.

MANAGEMENT MOTIVATION

Some of the problems that currently frustrate managers and technicians who might otherwise be interested in exploring distributed database solutions include:

- A distributed database environment has all of the problems associated with the single centralized database environment but at a more complex level.

- There is a lack of basic step-by-step guides covering the analysis, design, and implementation of a distributed database environment.

A distributed database management system offers many benefits. However, there are also many architectural choices that make the application design for distributed databases very complex. To ensure an effective and productive distributed database environment, it is essential that the distributed environment be properly designed to support the expected distributed database applications. In addition, an effective design will depend on the limitations of the distributed DBMS software. Therefore, implementing today's distributed database technology requires identifying the functional limitations of a selected commercial product. Identification of these limitations is critical to the successful operation of an application in a distributed database environment.

DISTRIBUTED DATABASE DEVELOPMENT PHASES

Effective corporationwide distributed database processing is not going to happen overnight. It requires a carefully planned infrastructure within which an orderly evolution can occur. The four major development phases are: planning, design, installation and implementation, and support and maintenance.

The Planning Phase

The planning phase consists of the very high-level management strategy planning. During the planning phase, an organization must consider whether it is advantageous to migrate to a distributed environment. This chapter assumes that migration to a distributed environment is desirable and feasible and that the corporate strategy planning issues and tasks have been identified. The result of this phase is the total management commitment for cost, resources, and a careful migration path towards a distributed database environment.

The Design Phase

The design phase is concerned with the overall design of the distributed database strategy. The overall design task involves the selection of a distributed DBMS environment in terms of the hardware, software, and the communications network for each node and how these elements are to be interconnected. The design of the distributed database environment must incorporate the requirements for the actual distributed database application. The overall design divides into two main tasks: the detailed design of the distributed database environment and the detailed design of the initial distributed database application. In certain cases, the initial application may be a prototype that is intended to pave the way for the full-production distributed database application.

The Installation and Implementation Phase

This phase consists of the installation and implementation of the environment that provides basic software support for the distributed DBMS application. The task of developing the distributed database application could occur in parallel with the installation of the environment.

The Support and Maintenance Phase

The support and maintenance phase consists of support for the distributed DBMS environment and the support and maintenance of the application. Although these support and maintenance tasks can be performed by the same people, the nature of the tasks and responsibilities are quite distinct. For example, the distributed application may require modification of report formats, while the distributed environment may require modification to add more memory.

CORPORATION STRATEGY PLANNING

The main task during the strategic planning phase is to obtain the commitment of senior management. The measure of this commitment is the amount of resources — both personnel and equipment — necessary for the development of a distributed DBMS. The factors that must be considered during the strategy planning phase are as follows:

- What are the objectives of the organization's next five-year plan?
- How will technological changes affect the organization's way of doing business?
- What resources are needed to plan for the development of, and migration to, a distributed DBMS?
- What tools or methods can be employed to develop and implement the plan?
- How will outcomes be measured relative to the impact on the organization's competitive position?

The corporate strategy plan must include detailed specifications of the total system life cycle. It must also include a realistic timetable of schedules and milestones. Important consideration must be paid to the allocation of cost for new acquisitions, training of personnel, physical space requirements, and other tangible items.

During the strategic planning phase, information must be gathered on the organization's business functions and goals, related constraints and problem areas, and the organization's user groups. Only after the needed information has been gathered is it possible to develop high-level information categories and their interrelationships.

The process of developing the distributed database plan is iterative. The activities involved are often performed by data administrators or information resource managers. Although these individuals often have the vision to recognize the long-term benefit of a distributed DBMS environment to an organization, they must rely on the participation and input of those in the organization who are directly involved with the business functions and use information to make decisions and manage operations. There must be considerable interaction among many different people in the organization, each of whom provides feedback to validate and refine the plans.

Strategic planning must first provide a sufficient justification for the expenditure of resources necessary to migrate to a distributed environment. Only after this justification has been accepted and fully approved by senior management can the task of initiating projects to design, develop, and implement a distributed DBMS environment and applications start.

OVERALL DESIGN OF DISTRIBUTED DATABASE STRATEGY

A distributed database environment consists of a collection of sites or nodes, connected by a communications network. Each node has its own hardware, central processor, and software which may, or may not, include a database management system. The primary objective of a distributed DBMS is to give interactive query users and application programs access to remote data as well as local data.

Individual nodes within the distributed environment can have different computing requirements. Accordingly, these nodes may have different hardware, different software, and they may be connected in many different ways. Some of the variations possible in the distributed database environment are discussed in the following sections.

Client/Server Computing

The most basic distributed capability is Remote Database access from single users at a node. A node may be a mainframe, a minicomputer, or a microcomputer (personal computer). The node that makes the database access request is referred to as a client node, and the node that responds to the request and provides database services is referred to as the server node. The association is limited to the two parties involved — the client and the server.

Exhibit 1 represents several different configurations available under a client/server computing environment. The following are descriptions of the different configurations shown in the exhibit.

Client Single User Node. The operating environment of an individual node can be single-user or multiuser, depending on the operating system of that node. In a single-user operating environment, a node can be only a client. Such a node may or may not have databases. For non-database client nodes, the software typically consists of front-end application programs

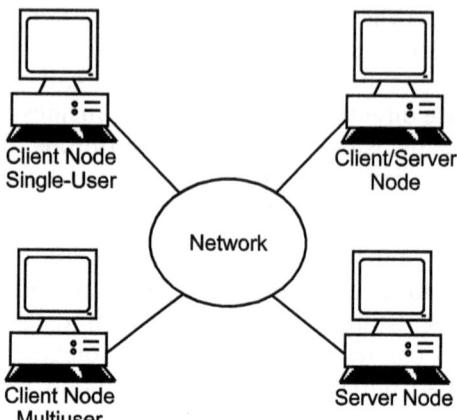

Exhibit 22-1. Client/server computing.

used to access remote database server nodes. This front-end software is generally in the form of end-user interface tools (e.g., a query language processor, a form processor, or some other application-specific program written in a third-Generation Language).

The front-end software formulates and issues user requests. It processes user requests through its established links with appropriate communications software. The front-end software only captures a user's request and uses communications software to send that request to a remote database node requesting its database management system to process the request. In addition to the capabilities outlined, single-user nodes with databases allow local data to be included in the same query operations specified for remote data. Therefore, operationally, the query results will appear as if all data is coming from a single central database.

Client Multiuser Node. The functional capabilities outlined for the client single-user node are expanded in the client multiuser node, because of the presence of a multiuser operating system at the user node. Such a configuration generally has several user processes running at the same time. At peak use time, the presence of several user processes can cause slower response time than is experienced in a client single-user node. The client multiuser node is more cost-effective, however, because it can allow multiple remote database accesses at different sites by different users at the same time. This is made possible through an identifiable list of remote server node locations. In addition, as with the client single-user node, the client multiuser node can include local database accesses in conjunction with accessing remote database.

Server Node. The server node is capable of providing database services to other client requests as well as to itself. It is a special multiuser node that is dedicated to servicing Remote Database requests and any local processes. This means that incoming requests are serviced, but it does not originate requests to other server nodes. The functional capabilities of a server node are as follows: this node must be included in the server list of some remote client node, there must be an operating DBMS, and there must be a continuously running process that listens for incoming database requests.

Client/Server Node. A node with a database can be a client as well as a server. This means that this node can service remote database requests as well as originate database requests to other server nodes. Therefore, the client/server node can play a dual role.

Homogeneous Distributed DBMS Environment

A completely homogeneous distributed DBMS environment exists when all the nodes in the distributed environment have the same DBMS but not necessarily the same hardware and operating system. However, the communication software for each node must use the same protocol to send or receive requests and data.

Design and implementation of a homogeneous distributed DBMS environment need involve only a single vendor. Any database request issued at a client node does not require translation, because the database language and data model are the same across all nodes in the network.

Heterogeneous Distributed DBMS Environment

In a truly heterogeneous distributed DBMS environment, the hardware, operating systems, communications systems, and DBMSs can all be different. Different DBMSs may mean different data models along with different database languages for definition and manipulation. Any database request issued at a client node would have to be translated so that the server node responding to the request would understand how to execute the request.

Various degrees of heterogeneity can exist. For example, within the distributed environment, different DBMSs can still be compatible if they all support the relational data model and understand SQL, a relational query language that is an American National Standards Institute and International Standards Organization standard. Presently, however, even among SQL conforming systems, there is no general communications software that will accept generic SQL statements from any other SQL conforming DBMS. This is an area in which the pending remote data access (RDA) standards are needed.

DISTRIBUTED ENVIRONMENT ARCHITECTURE

The design of a distributed database environment can be evolutionary — by incremental interconnection of existing systems, or by developing a totally new distributed DBMS environment using the bottom-up approach.

Some of the design issues in adopting either approach are described in the following sections.

Interconnection of Existing Systems

Not all organizations have the luxury of developing the distributed database environment from scratch. Already existing database management applications are costly investments that are not likely to be replaced all at once by new distributed systems. The existing environment, including hardware, software, and databases, can be preserved by providing a mechanism for producing federated systems (i.e., systems composed of autonomous software components).

The federated approach is a practical, first-step solution toward a distributed database environment. It accommodates a legacy of existing systems while extending to incorporate new nodes. Therefore, it is important to select distributed DBMS software that supports existing computing hardware and allows for expansion. Within a federated system, pairs of nodes can be coupled in ways that range from very loose (i.e., each node is autonomous) to very tight (i.e., each node interacts directly with the other). The various forms of coupling affect the design, execution, and capability of the distributed applications.

The mode of coupling affects the number of translations required to exchange information between each site. Zero translations are needed when both components use the same representations. Some systems may choose to translate the data produced by one site directly to the format required by the other site. A more common method is to translate the data into a neutral format first, and then translate into the target format.

Loose Coupling. Loosely coupled systems are the most modular and in some ways are easier to maintain. This is because changes to the implementation of a site's system characteristics and its DBMS are not as likely to affect other sites. The disadvantage of loosely coupled systems is that users must have some knowledge of each site's characteristics to execute requests. Because very little central authority to control consistency exists, correctness cannot be guaranteed. In addition, loosely coupled systems typically involve more translations that may cause performance problems.

Tight Coupling. Tightly coupled systems behave more like a single, integrated system. Users need not be aware of the characteristics of the sites fulfilling a request. With centralized control, the tightly coupled systems are more consistent in their use of resources and in their management of shared data. The disadvantage of tight coupling is that because sites are interdependent, changes to one site are likely to affect other sites. Also, users at some sites may object to the loss of freedom to the central control mechanisms necessary to maintain the tight coupling of all the systems.

Cooperation Between Sites

For a truly distributed DBMS environment, a variety of methods are available to specify cooperation between sites. One way of classifying the distributed environment is to define the amount of transparency offered to the users. Another way is to define the amount of site autonomy available to each site, and the way sites interact cooperatively.

Degrees of Transparency. Transparency is the degree to which a service is offered by the distributed DBMS so that the user does not need to be aware of it. One example of transparency is location transparency, which means users can retrieve data from any site without having to know where the data is located.

Types of Site Autonomy. Site autonomy refers to the amount of independence that a site has in making policy decisions. Some examples of policy decisions include ownership of data, policies for accessing the data, policies for hours and days of operation, and human support. In addition, all modifications to the site's data structures must be approved by the cooperating federation of data administrators.

Interconnection of Newly Purchased Systems

An organization will have much more freedom if it decides to establish a distributed database environment from scratch. Currently, vendors are offering homogeneous distributed DBMSs with a compatible family of software. This approach, however, can lock the organization into a single vendor's proprietary distributed database products.

Other approaches in selecting distributed architecture choices are as follows:

- Identical DBMS products at each node, with possibly different hardware environments but a single proprietary communications network to interconnect all sites.
- Standard conforming DBMS products at each node that rely on standard communications protocols.
- Different DBMSs, using the same data model (e.g., relational), interconnected by a single or standard communications protocol.
- Different DBMSs, using different data models (e.g., relational or object-oriented), interconnected by a single or standard communications protocol.

Some distributed DBMS vendors offer a bridge (gateway) mechanism from their distributed database software to any foreign distributed database software. This bridge (gateway) may be obtained at additional development cost if it has not already been included in the vendor's library of available software.

In the design of a totally new distributed DBMS product, it is advisable to consider a mixture of standard conforming DBMSs and communications protocols. Because the technology and products are changing quickly, the designed architecture must be continuously reviewed to prevent it from being locked into an inflexible mode.

CONSIDERATION FOR STANDARDS

As the trend towards distributed computing accelerates, the need for standards, guidance, and support will increase. Application distribution and use will be chaotic unless there is an architectural vision and some degree of uniformity in information technology platforms. This is particularly true in client/server and workstation environments. To achieve this goal, a systems architecture incorporating standards to meet the users' needs must be established. This architecture must isolate the application software from the lower levels of machine architecture and systems service implementation. The systems architecture serves as the context for user requirements, technology integration, and standards specifications.

The benefits of standardization for both the user and the vendor are many. The number and variety of distributed DBMS products is increasing. By insisting that purchased products conform to standards, users may be able to choose the best product for each function without being locked into a specific vendor. Therefore, small to midsized vendors may effectively compete in the open marketplace. For effective planning and designing of a distributed DBMS environment, it is important for the designers to consider what standards already exist and what standards will be emerging to be able to incorporate standardized products.

There are many areas of a distributed DBMS environment in which standards should be applied. Some of the standards relevant to the design of a distributed DBMS include: communications protocols, application programming interfaces, data languages for DBMSs, data representation and interchange format, and remote data access.

Communications protocol standards are necessary so that systems from different products can connect to a communications network and understand the information being transmitted. An example of a communications protocol standard is the Government Open Systems Interconnection Profile (GOSIP).

The application programming interface standard is directed toward the goal of having portable applications. This enables software applications developed in one computing environment to run almost unchanged in any other environment. An example of an application programming interface standard is the Portable Operating System Interface for Computer Environments (POSIX).

362

The data languages commonly supported by a DBMS are the Data Definition Language, the Data Manipulation Language, and the data Control Language. An example of a standard data language for the relational DBMS model is SQL.

To exchange data among open systems, a standard interchange format is necessary. The interchange format consists of a language for defining general data structures and the encoding rules. An example of a standard data interchange language is Abstract Syntax Notation One (ASN.1).

An important standard for the distributed processing environment is the remote access of data from a client site to a database server site. A specialized remote data access protocol based on the SQL standard is currently under development.

CONCLUSION

To start the overall design process, a review of the organization's existing facilities should be conducted. This review is done to determine whether the new distributed database environment can use some or all of the existing facilities. In the decision to move into a distributed environment, requirements for additional functionalities must be identified. Such organizational issues as setting up regional offices may also be involved. The distributed architecture must take into consideration the actual application to be operating and the characteristics of the user population and the workloads to be placed on the system. Such an architecture must also incorporate standardized components.

Chapter 23
Detailed Design and Application of Distributed Database Management Systems

Elizabeth N. Fong, Charles L. Sheppard, and Kathryn A. Harvill

THE DETAILED DESIGN AND INSTALLATION OF A DISTRIBUTED DATABASE ENVIRONMENT DEALS WITH A WIDE RANGE OF ISSUES. Because so many people will ultimately benefit from or be affected by the distributed database management system (DBMS), the selection of the most appropriate hardware and software for an organization's specific needs is paramount. In addition, once the new system is in place, continuous support is needed to ensure that any problems are handled quickly and that new needs are addressed as they arise.

HARDWARE DESIGN

The hardware design issue is centered on the client/server model. The node with the fastest or most powerful computing power is generally assigned the role of server. As server, it handles most of the processing and data storage. The two important aspects to be considered in choosing server nodes are processing power and storage capacity.

The processing power of a server is critical to the response time available to queries (i.e., servers should not be allowed to become bottlenecks of the distributed database community). Another concern related to the server's processing power is the fact that other processes may be competing for processing time other than database requests. Therefore, an excessive amount of processing traffic on a server can cause monumental performance problems in the distributed database community.

The other issue for a server node is its storage capacity. This is critical because the server maintains the central repository for data in the distributed database community. This central repository may be concentrated locally in this one server node or it may be spread across several other remote server nodes.

As compared with the server node, the client node can be limited in its amount of processing power and storage capacity. Client nodes are typically smaller desktop microcomputers or workstations. The exception to this rule occurs when a node acts as both a client and a server. Other issues that can dictate the amount of processing power and storage capacity on the client node are the amount of data redundancy kept on the node and the storage requirements for its application software.

SOFTWARE DESIGN

For most commercially available distributed DBMSs, the software consists of a family of products that are available on a variety of hardware platforms. A typical family of products might include:

- The basic DBMS and its active data dictionary.
- The communications software that is coupled with the DBMS .This software may be available with various levels of capability. For example, the minimal capability would be a protocol for remote data access. The next level of capability would be a gateway for remotely accessing foreign databases or files. (Foreign databases are databases established by other brands of DBMS software.) The truly distributed functional capability would be a communications software product that supports location transparency data accesses and concurrence control. It would also include such features as a two-phase commit protocol for ensuring data consistency.
- Some distributed DBMS vendors also offer additional software utilities (e.g., fourth-generation languages, Query-By-Forms or Query-By-Example, fancy report writers, and DBA tools for monitoring activities).

One of the first decisions the organization must resolve is the make-or-buy decision. To be practical, unless the application is so unique that none of the commercially available distributed DBMSs will suit the needs, it is advisable not to build a home-grown distributed DBMS. Once the organization decides to buy, a survey and feature analysis of the market must be performed. The selection criteria must also take into consideration the amount and the types of software packages that will also be operating within the same platform.

The family of software packages used in a distributed database environment is configured according to the role of each node in the network. For a client node without a database server service, minimum software packages are required (e.g., the communications software and software application tools or languages such as Formula Translation or C). The communications software allows requests to be sent and received by the application software. For a database server node , the minimum software packages must have not only the communications software and the application tools but a DBMS. For a value-added multiuser operating system environment, a full family of software tools can be configured including fourth-generation languages, two-phase commit protocol, database administrator monitoring tools for tuning, and communications tools for monitoring database requests and traffic within the network.

COMMUNICATIONS NETWORK DESIGN

The linking of computers that are geographically dispersed is accomplished by the communications network. The basic function provided by the communications network is to allow a process running at any site to send a message to a process running on another site of the network. When the communications network is selected or designed, the following factors should be considered: cost, reliability, performance, and Open Systems Interconnection (OSI). These topics are discussed in the following sections.

Cost

The cost of transmitting a message is usually computed by an algorithm defined by the system administrator. In general, the cost is proportional to the length of the message and the distance between the source host and the target host. There is always a trade-off between the cost of local data storage and the cost of transmitting that data.

Reliability

The probability that the message is correctly delivered at its target destination is an important factor to be considered. Reliable transport service with error correction and error detection is currently provided by most communications software.

Performance

A critical issue in measuring the performance of a network is the amount of time it takes to deliver a message from its point of origin to its destination. The time required to deliver a message depends on such factors as the amount of traffic on the network, the bandwidth and the capacity of the communications line, how efficiently the communications software can perform optimum routing algorithms, and the mixing of a local area network (LAN) with a wide area network (WAN).

Open Systems Interconnection (OSI)

Standard communication protocols are necessary to allow interoperability among a variety of computer systems without regard to differences in equipment. As of August 15, 1990, it is mandatory that federal agencies acquire computer network products and services that are in accord with the Government Open Systems Interconnection Profile (GOSIP).

DESIGN REVIEW

The result of the overall design of a distributed database strategy is the determination of the distributed database architecture. Alternatives include the client/server model, the homogeneous DBMS environment, and the truly heterogeneous distributed DBMS environment. Establishing site requirements involves identification of the hardware, software and communications networks for each site.

Hardware and software configurations must be identified for each site in the distributed database environment. Decisions on hardware must take into consideration the use of existing hardware as opposed to acquiring new hardware. The selection of distributed DBMS software and communications software must depend on the hardware platform supported. For Commercial Off-The-Shelf software to be used, an analysis must incorporate supporting hardware considerations. These hardware and software decisions must be made in a closely integrated manner. For example, it is useless to select one type of hardware if the desired software cannot function on that particular hardware.

The feature analysis performed for the selection of the products (e.g.,a DBMS) involves identifying the features required for the application, comparing the required features against the features offered by the contending products, and making the best final selection decision.

INSTALLATION OF A DISTRIBUTED DATABASE ENVIRONMENT

The technical activities performed during the installation phase involve the actual implementation and testing of hardware, software, and communications software for each node of the distributed database environment. Detailed engineering and physical tasks of running cables and establishing hardware configurations are not described in this chapter.

HARDWARE INSTALLATION

Installing a mainframe is quite different from installing a microcomputer. If existing hardware is to be employed as a node within the distributed database environment, additional hardware modification may be required. Information on any additional hardware modifications can be determined from the distributed DBMS technical requirements as specified by its vendor. For example, technical knowledge is required to add any needed additional random access memory (RAM), communications cards, and communications lines.

The addition of RAM may take the form of installing memory chips into a memory board or purchasing a memory board with the memory chips already installed. The appropriate existing memory cards must be identified and extracted from their position in the computer's chassis or cabinet. Any new card or existing cards with the required added memory must then be installed in the computer chassis. Depending on the targeted computer, switches or jumpers on the memory cards may have to be set for proper recognition of the added memory.

After any required memory has been added, diagnostic software should be run to confirm that the computing software recognizes this additional memory. In most computers, built-in firmware will check for the existence of the additional memory during the initial boot process of the computer.

To establish a connection among computers targeted as nodes in the distributed database environment, a communications card must be present in each computer. The features required for a communications card should be confirmed by the vendor of the candidate distributed DBMS software. It is advisable to purchase the compatible communications card used by the vendor in developing the software. The brand of the communications card and the computing platform will determine any extras that are required to connect to a network. For example, on personal computers, the communications cards generally allow either an external transceiver connection (i.e., a thick-net cabling connection) or connection to its built-in transceiver (i.e., a thin-net cabling connection). In the first case, an external transceiver must be purchased in addition to the communications card. In the second case, only thin-net cabling is required. On workstations and other larger computing platforms, the first case is generally the only option.

After the communications card has been installed, the following tasks must be performed:

- running the hardware diagnostic software
- testing the remote connectivity capability

Running the hardware diagnostic software verifies system recognition of the newly installed communications card. Proper recognition by the system means that the communications card is linked to an acceptable (non-conflicting) address and its features have been recorded by the system.

It is highly desirable to confirm remote connectivity before attempting to install the distributed DBMS software. This eliminates having to consider local hardware communications problems should connectivity problems arise after installing the software.

NETWORK COMMUNICATIONS SOFTWARE INSTALLATION

The primary task of the network communications software installation involves the establishment of specific communications parameters. These parameters are generally specified during the initial setup process and are contained in various special parameter files. The names and locations of these files are known to the communications software. For example, one such parameter file is generally called a HOST file. This file usually contains specific internet addresses and associated logical names for locating nodes that are on the LAN and the related WAN.

In addition to the HOST file, a SERVICES file generally contains the address of the communications port to be used by the distributed DBMS's communications software. Therefore, when the installed network communications software reads the SERVICES file, the designated communications port is reserved as a communications link to the distributed DBMS's communications software.

It is critical that the distributed DBMS communications software and the installed network communications software for the operating system have the same protocol. For example, if the network communications software uses the TCP/IP protocol, the distributed DBMS communications software must know how to package communications requests accordingly. If the network communications software uses GOSIP, the communications software requests must be packaged according to the appropriate layers of the ISO/OSI seven-layer model.

DBMS COMMUNICATIONS SOFTWARE INSTALLATION

The DBMS kernel must be installed before installing the distributed DBMS. Installation of the DBMS kernel and its support software (e.g., fourth-generation languages, report writers, forms processors, and graphics packages) follow the same general procedures:

- *Preparation.* This task requires super user authority to first allocate memory space. A separate directory is generally established in preparation for loading the software.
- *Loading.* The initial parameter file is loaded into the memory.
- *Configuration.* The configuration of the shared memory is adjusted in accordance with the requirements of the chosen architecture.
- *Compilation.* The loaded software, in source form, is compiled to create an absolute module ready for execution.

- *Testing and verification.* The software is executed to test and verify it for correctness.
- *Cleanup.* This procedure deletes any unwanted files.

After the DBMS kernel and its support software have been individually installed, a set of logical definitions must be identified that will delineate local and remote data to the DBMS kernel. It is through this association that the support software is capable of transparently accessing data throughout the global distributed DBMS scheme.

Depending on the design considerations, each node may have a different set of software support requirements. Therefore, the installation includes only those support packages as required.

INSTALLATION REVIEW

After the decision has been made regarding the equipment necessary for each node , the acquisition process should begin. The plan for installation should be coordinated so that each node is installed and checked out, followed by the installation of the networking between nodes. The installation phase requires highly skilled technical engineers and system programmers.

SUPPORT FOR THE DISTRIBUTED DATABASE

The final stage of design and implementation occurs when the distributed environment and the distributed application system are ready to be released for real operational use. It is at that time that the support and maintenance tasks begin. In practice, the support for the distributed database environment and the support for the application are typically performed by the same team of system programmers and database administrators. Some organizations, however, may prefer to separate the tasks of supporting the environment and supporting the applications.

Overall system management and support for the distributed database environment involves a team of database administrators. If the distributed environment includes several locations that are physically separated, it is desirable to have a local database administrator and a network data manager at each location. The network data manager is sometimes referred to as the global database administrator. The local database administrator manages the local node support activities. The global database administrator coordinates the communications activities and provides services to other distributed nodes.

TUNING FOR BETTER PERFORMANCE

One of the main tasks involved in supporting the distributed database system is monitoring the traffic within the network and tuning the network systems for better performance. Various tools are supplied by DBMS vendors for gathering system statistics. Tuning a distributed environment is much more complex than tuning a centralized system because not only must monitoring be conducted at each local node, it must also be performed at the network interface level across the entire distributed environment.

BACKUP, RECOVERY, AND SECURITY PROTECTION

When the distributed DBMS system and the network software encounter system failure (e.g., hardware or network problems), the prompt restoration to proper functioning is a crucial task to ensure that reliable service is provided to the users. Providing both physical security and software protection against unauthorized users are two of the support activities to be performed by the local and global database administrators. Because security is an extensive and complex subject, it is beyond the scope of this chapter except to say that security requirements must be considered at every step in the development of a distributed database system.

USER TRAINING AND RESOLVING PROBLEMS

Another important task for the support phase is to provide users with adequate training on the use of the distributed database system. This task could also include assigning user account and password numbers and allocating working and permanent storage.

When DBMS vendors put out new versions of their software, it is the responsibility of the local database administrator to install the new version. When problems are detected, the support staff must verify and isolate the problem. The problem should be either fixed or reported to the appropriate vendors.

SUPPORT REVIEW

The support task is of a continuous nature. Therefore, one or more permanent system programmers or engineers should be on duty at all times. The skills of the support team members and the size of that team will depend to a large extent on the size and nature of the distributed database environment and the applications.

CRITICAL SUCCESS FACTORS

The development of a distributed database environment and of distributed applications are successful only when each phase of the development is carefully planned and executed. The success of the development of a distributed environment and distributed applications is difficult to quantify. Different measures are appropriate for different application areas. Some commonly perceived measures of success include:

- adequate performance of the overall distributed DBMS applications

- greater user satisfaction with the newly installed distributed application than with the previous non-distributed application
- lower costs for resources and better efficiency in the processing of data with the distributed applications
- improved maintenance of the Distributed Database System and the distributed data administration procedures

FUTURE ISSUES

The development of such a project from conception to operation requires a long time span. Some large-scale distributed environments and applications could take more than two years to complete. During the two-year development period, however, distributed database technology and the organization's requirements are likely to be changing. This situation does, of course, present the possibility of having an obsolete system on completion. A few observations follow:

- The technology of the truly distributed, all-powerful, all-embracing data model and language to provide transparent accesses to separate databases and computers is still not as mature as might be expected. All the present distributed environments in support of operational distributed database applications are either homogeneous or federated with translation mechanisms.
- Issues of access control, concurrence control, schema and transaction management, performance, capacity growth, and support for complex environments are still in the research stage. In practice, distributed data processing is still partly a learning process.
- In current practice, users depend increasingly on single vendors to supply the DBMS and communications products. Some very difficult decisions must be made by system designers to achieve the best balance of functional ability, performance, and vendor independence. The use of standard products alleviates the vendor dependence problem.
- In the near term, the release of an RDA/SQL standard will provide technical specifications on how to package SQL network service requests. These packages contain service elements for association control, which includes establishing an association between the client and server remote sites and managing connections to specific databases at the server site; the transfer of database operations and parameters from client to server, and the transfer of resulting data from server to client; and band transaction management, which includes capabilities for both one-phase and two-phase commit. The introduction of the RDA/SQL standard will pave the way for wider interoperability among heterogeneous distributed DBMS nodes supporting SQL data languages.
- The migration from a centralized environment to a distributed environment requires careful planning. A more important consideration is that data sharing and resource consolidation requires cultural changes.

Some of the open questions as listed previously cannot be answered until more experience is gained and documented. The lessons learned in such a project are valuable. The authors of this chapter would welcome any further guidelines and comments on the development of a distributed database system.

CONCLUSION

After a detailed design of the distributed environment has been performed, the results include a high-level specification of the hardware, DBMS, communications, and other support software configuration for each site participating in the distributed DBMS. Similarly, after the installation phase, the result is a distributed environment that is properly installed and functioning. Finally, supporting the environment and its applications yields a distributed database environment that is properly maintained and fully operational.

Chapter 24
Relational Database Design Using Semantic Objects

Jong-Sung Lee and Bo Kai Wong

IN THE INITIAL STAGES OF DATABASE DESIGN, DATABASE DESIGNERS DEVELOP A CONCEPTUAL SCHEMA AS A BASIS FOR USERS TO EXPRESS THEIR DATA NEEDS. The conceptual schema can be modified after receiving user feedback. The conceptual schema is then transformed into the logical schema.

The conceptual data model called the semantic object can be used to build the conceptual schema. This chapter shows how the conceptual schema presented in semantic objects can be easily converted into the logical schema presented in the relational data model, which is the most common logical data model.

SCHEMAS

A data model is a set of concepts that can be used to describe the whole structure of a database, which is called the schema. In the process of database design, a schema is represented in three levels of data models: conceptual, logical, and physical data models.

The schema presented in a conceptual data model can be understood by users as well as database designers. Database designers transform this conceptual schema into the logical schema (i.e., the schema presented in a logical data model, of which there are three traditional types — hierarchical, network, and relational model). The database designers then adapt the logical schema to the physical schema, which is a schema presented in a physical data model. The physical schema should meet all the requirements of a specific database management system (DBMS).

0-8493-0882-8/00/$0.00+$.50
© 2001 by CRC Press LLC

Conceptual Schema

One major goal of database design is to meet users' needs of data. Users should be given opportunities to express their needs of data in the so-called miniworld, which is the part of the real world to be represented in the schema. However, often users are unable to articulate their needs to the database designers because the terminology and concepts the designers use are alien to users. The idea of the conceptual schema was introduced for this reason — to help users understand database design concerns.

The conceptual schema provides concepts of database structure that are easy enough for users to comprehend. Thus, users can give their feedback by examining the conceptual schema. The conceptual schema may then be modified according to the users' feedback and converted into the logical schema.

Because the most common data model used to build a logical schema is the relational data model, it is used as the basis for the discussion in this chapter. The process of developing a conceptual schema and transforming it into a relational schema is termed relational database design. In this context, a conceptual data model is effective and efficient if it can be easily understood by users and transformed into the relational data model.

The primary conceptual data model has been the entity-relationship (E-R) model. Although the E-R model has been used widely to present the conceptual schema for the miniworld, it includes some artificial elements. As a result, there is a considerable gap between users' concepts of data and those that the E-R model provides.

Introducing the Semantic Object

Accordingly, the conceptual schema presented in the E-R model could not serve as a convenient basis for users' feedback. A new conceptual data model called the semantic object has been advanced to describe the conceptual schema in the way that is even closer to the users' direct perception of the miniworld.[1]

The semantic object represents an entity and its relationship with other entities as a user sees them. As shown in Exhibit 1, the semantic object called DEAN represents the properties of an entity called Dean and its relationship with the College entity by simply including it as a property. Thus, there is no artificial element in the semantic object.

By comparison, the E-R model, as seen in Exhibit 2, uses a separate relationship type called College-Dean to represent the Dean entity and the College entity. This relationship type is an artificial element. Therefore, the E-R model represents entities in more complicated ways than the semantic object does.

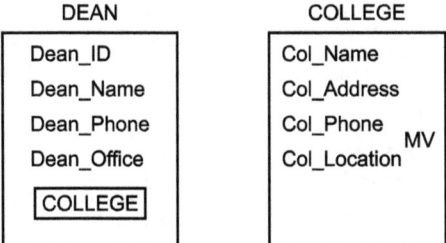

Exhibit 24-1. Examples of the semantic object.

The semantic object can be used as a conceptual data model in relational database design. The rest of this chapter explains:

- How the semantic object can be modified and used to build a conceptual schema.
- The rules for converting the conceptual schema presented in the semantic object into the relational schema.
- The reasons why the semantic object is the most user-oriented conceptual data model.

BUILDING A SCHEMA IN THE SEMANTIC OBJECT: A SAMPLE DATABASE

A simple database called UNIVERSITY is used as an example database to help explain how to use the semantic object to build a conceptual schema. The miniworld for which the example schema is designed describes a university as follows: A college has a dean and many departments. A college can have one or more telephone numbers. A department has multiple professors, students, and classes and offers many courses. A course has one or more sections. A section is a class. A section has a unique call number called a section number. A professor can advise one or more students and teach one or more classes. A professor has only one personal computer. A student can take one or more classes, and a class consists of multiple students.

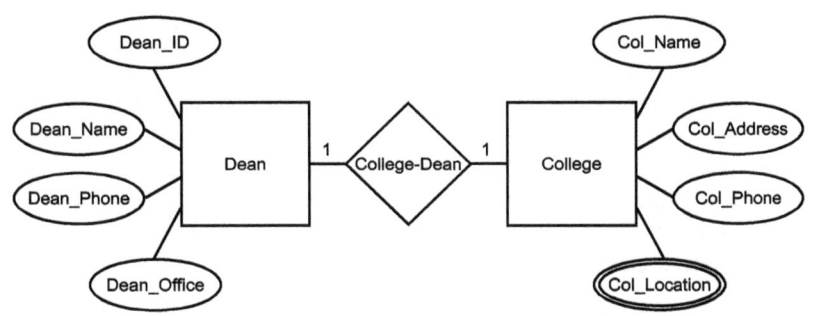

Exhibit 24-2. An example of the entity-relationship model.

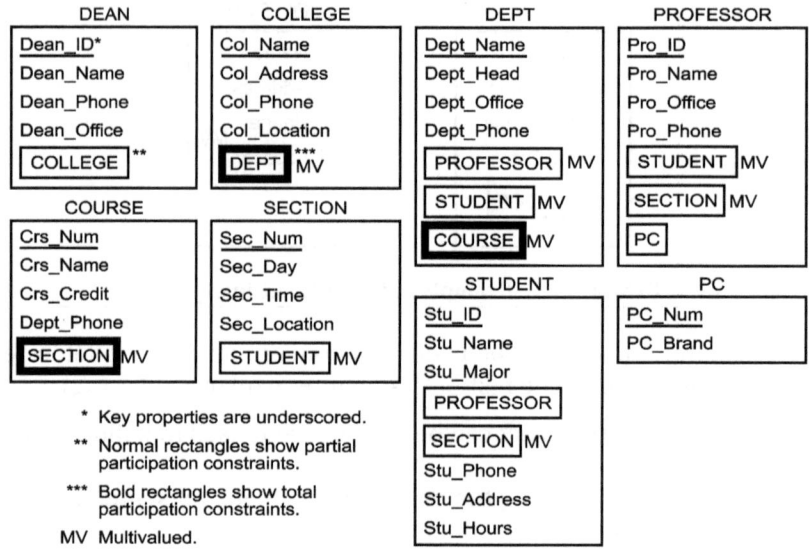

Exhibit 24-3. University schema in semantic objects.

An entity is something that users perceive as an independent unit in the miniworld. To build a conceptual schema, a semantic object is defined for each entity in the miniworld. In the example database, there are eight entities — that is, dean, college, department, professor, course, section, student, and personal computer. One semantic object is defined for each of these eight entities. These semantic objects are presented in Exhibit 3.

Properties and Object Properties. A semantic object has one or more semantic object instances. In this example, PROFESSOR is a semantic object and Professor J. Doe is a semantic object instance.

Each semantic object includes the properties that describe the semantic object. Properties may be single-valued or multivalued. A property or a combination of properties that uniquely identifies the semantic object is the key. The key is shown by underscoring it as shown in Exhibit 3.

A property is single-valued if it has only one instance for one instance of the key. Most of the properties in the example database are single-valued properties. A property is multivalued if it can have more than one instance for one instance of the key. In the example database, the semantic object called COLLEGE has a multivalued property called Col_Phone. Because a college can have more than one phone number, Col_Phone can have more than one instance for one instance of a college name.

A property may also be another semantic object. In the example database, all the semantic objects except PC have other semantic objects as properties. These properties, called object properties, are shown as rectangles in Exhibit 3.

Participation constraints are also shown in Exhibit 3 through the use of a bold rectangle and a regular rectangle. The bold rectangle shows total participation. The regular rectangle indicates partial participation. A semantic object that an object property presents in a bold rectangle cannot exist without the semantic object that contains it. For example, as shown in Exhibit 3, the DEPT semantic object cannot exist without the COLLEGE semantic object. The semantic object that an object property presents in a regular rectangle can exist with or without the semantic object that contains it. In the example database, the semantic object called COLLEGE is presented as an object property in a regular rectangle in the semantic object called DEAN. Therefore, the COLLEGE semantic object can exist with or without the DEAN semantic object.

The object properties can also be single-valued or multivalued. An object property plays the role of connector between the semantic object that includes it and the semantic object that it represents.

Types of Semantic Objects. Semantic objects are divided into different types for the purpose of transforming them into relations or other conventional logical data models.

Simple Semantic Object. A semantic object that contains only single-valued, nonsemantic object properties is called a simple semantic object. The semantic object called PC in the university schema is an example of a simple semantic object.

Composite Semantic Object. A semantic object that contains one or more nonobject multivalued properties is called a composite semantic object. The COLLEGE semantic object in the university schema is a composite semantic object, though it is also a compound semantic object.

Compound Semantic Object. A semantic object that includes at least one object property is called a compound semantic object. In this case, relationships between two or more semantic objects are established with a compound semantic object. All the semantic objects except the PC semantic object in the university schema are compound semantic objects. The relationship status between semantic objects of the compound type may be one-to-one (1:1), one-to-many (1:N), or many-to-many (M:N). What determines the relationship status is explained in the next section.

Typically a semantic object may belong to one or more semantic object types. For example, a semantic object may be a composite type and a compound type at the same time, as in the case of the COLLEGE semantic object in the sample database of Exhibit 3.

Exhibit 24-4. Rules applied to conversion of semantic object into relations in the university schema.

Semantic Objects (in Exhibit 3)	Rules	Pertinent Relations (in Exhibit 5)
DEAN	3	DEAN, COLLEGE
COLLEGE	2, 3, 4	COLLEGE-PHONE, COLLEGE, DEPT
DEPT	4	DEPT, PROFESSOR, STUDENT, COURSE
PROFESSOR	3, 4	PROFESSOR, SECTION, STUDENT
COURSE	4	COURSE, SECTION
SECTION	5	SECTION, ENROLL
STUDENT	5	STUDENT, ENROLL
PC	1, 3	PC, PROFESSOR

TRANSFORMING THE SEMANTIC OBJECT INTO THE RELATIONAL MODEL

There are some basic rules to convert semantic objects into relations by dividing semantic objects into several different types and then transforming these different types of semantic objects into relations.[2] These rules can be used as a guideline, but they have limitations — many semantic objects are not, after all, classified as only one specific type.

Although this discussion on transforming the semantic object into the relational model is based on these basic rules, the recommendations have expanded to semantic objects that are a mixture of more than one semantic object type.

Five rules can be applied to the conversion of semantic objects into relations. Any combination of these rules can be applied to one semantic object. All of the following five rules should be checked one by one for each semantic object and all the relevant rules should be applied. In the sample database in Exhibit 3, there are eight semantic objects. Rules that are applied to each of these eight semantic objects and the pertinent relations are shown in Exhibit 4.

The university schema presented in semantic objects in Exhibit 3 is converted into the schema presented in the relational models in Exhibit 5. To simplify the comparison of the semantic object with the relation, the same names are used for the semantic object and the relation that presented the same entity. The same names are also used for the properties of the semantic object and the attributes of the relation.

Rule 1. For each semantic object containing only single-valued nonobject properties, a single relation is defined that has all the properties as attributes and possibly one or more foreign key, depending on the inclusion of this semantic object in other semantic objects. In this case, the

Exhibit 24-5. University schema in the relational data model.

DEAN (Dean_ID,* Dean_Name, Dean_Phone, Dean_Office)
COLLEGE (Col_Name, Col_Address, Col_Location, Dean_ID)
COLLEGE_PHONE (Col_Name, Col_Address, Col_Location, Dean_ID)
DEPT (Dept_Name, Dept_Head, Dept_Office, Pro_Phone, Col_Name)
PROFESSOR (Pro_ID, Pro_Name, Pro_Office, Pro_Phone, Dept_Name, PC_Num)
COURSE (Crs_Num, Crs_Name, Crs_Credit, Dept_Name)
SECTION (Sec_Num, Sec_Day, Sec_Day, Sec_Time, Sec_Location, Crs_Num, Pro_ID)
STUDENT (Stu_ID, Stu_Name, Stu_Major, Stu_Phone, Stu_Address, Stu_Hours, Dept_ID, Pro_ID)
ENROLL (Stu_ID, Sec_Num)
PC (PC_Num, PC_Brand)

* Key attributes are underscored.

semantic object is a simple type. The key property of the semantic object becomes the key attribute in the relation. In the sample database in Exhibit 3, the semantic object called PC is a simple type. The PC relation is defined for this semantic object as shown in Exhibit 5.

Rule 2. For one or more multivalued nonobject properties of a semantic object, a relation is defined that includes all the multivalued nonobject properties and the key property as attributes. This type of semantic object is a composite type. The key of this relation is the combination of the key property and all the multivalued nonobject properties. In Exhibit 3, the COLLEGE semantic object is a composite type because it has a multivalued nonobject property called Col_Phone.

A relation called COLLEGE_PHONE is defined to include the multivalued nonobject property and the key property of the COLLEGE semantic object as shown in Exhibit 5.

Rule 3. For each of two semantic objects in which the first semantic object contains the second semantic object as a single-valued object property (it does not make a difference whether or not the second semantic object contains the first semantic object as a single-valued object property), relations that include all the single-valued nonobject properties as attributes are created. Furthermore, either one of the two relations should have the foreign key from the other relation and possibly, depending on the application of other rules, other foreign keys as well.

In this case, the first semantic object containing the second semantic object as a single-valued object property is a compound type in 1:1 relationship with the second semantic object. In the schema illustrated in Exhibit 3, the semantic object called DEAN is a compound type that is in

1:1relationship with the semantic object called COLLEGE. For these two semantic objects, two relations called DEAN and COLLEGE are defined as shown in Exhibit 5. The attributes of these two relations are all the single-valued nonobject properties from the respective semantic objects. The COLLEGE relation also has a foreign keys called Dean_ID from the DEAN relation. The semantic object called PROFESSOR is also a compound type in 1:1 relationship with another semantic object called PC. The corresponding relations are shown in Exhibit 5.

Rule 4. For two semantic objects in which the first semantic object contains the second semantic object as a multivalued object property, regardless of the inclusion of the first semantic object in the second semantic object as a single-valued object-property, two relations are created. In this case, the first semantic object is a compound type in 1:N relationship with the second semantic object. The relation defined for the first semantic object contains attributes derived from all its single-valued nonobject properties and possibly, depending on the application of other rules, foreign keys. The relation defined for the second semantic object includes attributes derived from all its single-valued nonobject properties, a foreign keys from the first semantic object, and depending on the application of other rules, other foreign keys. In the university schema shown in Exhibit 3, the semantic object called COLLEGE is a compound type that is in 1:N relationship with the semantic object called DEPT. For the COLLEGE semantic object, the COLLEGE relation is defined to contain all the single-valued nonobject properties as its attributes as shown in Exhibit 5. For the DEPT semantic object, the DEPT relation is defined to contain all the single-valued nonobject properties as its attributes plus a foreign keys called Col_Name from the COLLEGE semantic object. All the other semantic objects that belong to this case and accordingly applied this rule are shown in Exhibit 4.

Rule 5. For two semantic objects in which the first semantic object contains the second semantic object as a multivalued object property, two relations for these two semantic objects are defined — as well as a third relation comprising foreign keys from the two semantic objects. Each one of the two relations for the two semantic objects includes all its single-valued nonobject properties and, depending on the application for other rules, foreign keys. These two semantic objects are compound types in M:N relationship.

In the example database shown in Exhibit 3, the two semantic objects called SECTION and STUDENT are compound objects in M:N relationship. Thus two relations (i.e., SECTION AND STUDENT) as well as the third relation (ENROLL) are defined as in Exhibit 5. The attributes of these three relations that are defined according to the previous rules are also shown in Exhibit 5. The attributes of the ENROLL relation are foreign keys from the two semantic objects.

USER ORIENTATION OF THE SEMANTIC OBJECT

The major characteristic of the semantic object when used to present a conceptual schema is its user orientation. This characteristic is manifested in two aspects of the semantic object.

First, the semantic object naturally presents the entities of the mini-world by including other entities directly. For example, the PROFESSOR semantic object in the university schema includes three entities called STUDENT, SECTION, and PC. Traditional conceptual data models such as the E-R model cannot present an entity in terms of its own properties. This aspect of the semantic object allows the semantic object to depict entities as they are naturally perceived in the miniworld.

Second, relationships between entities are naturally and implicitly presented. A database is conceptually an integration of related entities of the miniworld. Each entity is represented by a semantic object. This means that semantic objects in the miniworld are related to each other. The relationship structure can be constructed from a relationship between two semantic objects called a binary relationship. Thus, however complicated the relationship structure is, it is eventually decomposed into binary relationships.

If a schema is built in semantic objects, binary relationships are presented implicitly and naturally without any artificial components. Specifically, a semantic object included in another semantic object plays the role of a pointer to establish a binary relationship between the two semantic objects. In the university schema, the object property called STUDENT included in the PROFESSOR semantic object establishes a binary relationship between the two semantic objects. Other conceptual data models need artificial elements to show binary relationships. For example, the E-R model uses an artificial element called the relationship type to present a binary relationship.

Thus, with the natural presentation of entities and binary relationships, the semantic object makes a schema closest to the miniworld. Because the miniworld for which the schema is designed is the users' functional area, they are already familiar with the miniworld. A conceptual schema that is closest to the miniworld should serve as the best basis of users' feedback in database design. Consequently, the semantic object is the most user-oriented conceptual data model.

CONCLUSION

Users are the best people to specify data requirements, but they must be able to express their needs of data in the initial stage of database design. A conceptual data model is used to build a conceptual schema that both users and database designers can understand. The conceptual schema is then transformed into the logical schema that is presented in a logical data model. In this context, the conceptual schema should be close to the users' perception of the miniworld and easily converted into the logical schema (which, for the sake of this discussion, is the relational data model).

In traditional conceptual data models, a gap exists between the conceptual schema presented in them and users' direct perception of the miniworld. A new conceptual data model called the semantic object, with its user orientation, should narrow this gap and serve as an excellent basis of users' feedback in designing a database.

Although there were some limitations of the semantic object, they were overcome by modifying the semantic object. The rules applied to convert the conceptual schema presented in semantic objects into the logical schema presented in the relational data model are also simple.

Thus the semantic object can be used to build the conceptual schema that meets the two needs of the conceptual schema — that is, user orientation and easy conversion into the relational schema. This conceptual data model is recommended as an effective and efficient tool in relational database design.

Notes

1. M. Hammer and D. McLeod, "Database Description with SDM: A Semantic Data Model," *ACM Transactions on Database Systems* 5, no. 6 (September 1981); D. Kroenke, *Database Processing,* 4th ed (Science Research Associates, 1992).
2. Kroenke, *Database Processing*

Bibliography

1. Lee, J., and Hughes, C. "The Object Diagram: A Tool for Effective Database Design." Database Management 17, no. 2 (March 1992).

Chapter 25
Component Design for Relational Databases

Ashvin Iyengar

INTRODUCTION

COMPONENT-BASED OBJECT-ORIENTED ARCHITECTURES are becoming increasingly popular in building industrial strength applications. However, relational databases are not going to be replaced by object databases in the foreseeable future. This paper explores the ramifications of component-based designs on data management and offers strategies which could be deployed in the use of relational centralized databases with object-oriented component-based application architectures.

WHY RELATIONAL DATABASES ARE HERE TO STAY

From a pure application design perspective, object-oriented databases would be much more suitable for use with object-oriented component-based application architectures. However, the business realities are more complex and include the following considerations:

- Object-oriented databases are not mature enough to be entrusted with the job of managing large corporate data;
- It is more difficult to find professionals with experience in administration as well as the design of object-oriented databases;
- The vast majority of corporations are currently using relational databases to manage business information; and
- Most current live applications have been designed and developed to work with relational databases.

MOVING TOWARDS A COMPONENT-BASED ARCHITECTURE STANDARD

The subject of object-oriented design and programming involving relational databases has been well explored. More often than not, the data model is constructed using pure relational database modeling techniques with little if any consideration for object-oriented design techniques. This necessitates the use of impedance matching techniques to allow object-oriented applications to interact with relational data models.

Application architectures are becoming increasingly component based to satisfy the need for flexible as well as manageable systems. The effort to move away from large monolithic applications has been underway for a number of years. This has resulted in the adoption of client-server based architecture as the de facto standard in the industry. However, with lack of proper design, client-server architectures became just as monolithic as mainframe applications and thus inherited all the maintenance problems associated with large monolithic applications. Object-oriented design techniques and multi-tiered architectures were adopted in order to solve this problem. Component design is a natural step in the evolution of application architectures since it combines the principles of object-oriented design with multi-tiered application architecture. In addition, industry-wide acceptance of the incremental and iterative software development methodology over the old waterfall development methodology has provided an additional thrust towards component-based design.

Some of the other factors contributing towards making component-based application design the de facto standard are:

- the maturing of technologies like DCOM (distributed component object model) and CORBA
- the plethora of new technologies encouraging the design and deployment of components over the Web (e.g., JavaBeans)
- the ability to design, develop, and deploy components using high level, widely used applications like Visual Basic
- the potential for using third-party components along with in-house applications in order to fulfill specific needs (e.g., a professional third-party charting component)
- the resulting relative ease of component replacement

BACKGROUND OF MULTI-TIERED ARCHITECTURES

The current thrust is towards the use of distributed, component-based application architectures. The ever-increasing need to deploy applications over the Web and the resulting security considerations have led to a n-tiered architecture, using, at the very least, three distinct tiers.

- Web server
- Application server
- Database server

Whereas, a number of studies have shown that pure object-oriented applications are difficult to design and develop and that the payoffs information technology (IT) executives had hoped for in terms of reuse are seldom realized, multi-tiered architecture is here to stay. Three-tiered architecture is, in fact, the industry standard and a wide variety of application development environments from Smalltalk to Visual Basic support and encourage the use of this standard architecture.

In general, a three-tiered architecture has the following layers:

- Interface layer
- Business layer
- Data layer

The driving force behind three-tiered architecture is the need to support both flexibility and robustness in applications. De-coupling the interface layer from the database offers the advantage of changes in the database that need not affect the interface layer directly, thereby isolating the effects of a change in either layer. The interface layer describes how the application interacts with the outside world. If the outside world is comprised of end users, then the interface layer refers to a user interface. Alternatively, if it is comprised of client applications, it refers to an applications interface.

Arguably, the main payoff involved in object-oriented architectures is not reuse but rather change management. Effective change management is also the goal of three-tiered architectures. Since three-tiered architectures are easier to implement with object-based (if not object-oriented) systems, new life has been extended to object-based systems. In this article, a distinction is being made between object-oriented and object-based systems. Object-based systems implement classes and objects, but do not permit other aspects of object-oriented programming like inheritance and polymorphism. So whereas the three pillars of object-oriented programming can be said to be encapsulation, inheritance, and polymorphism, object-based programming concerns itself with mainly encapsulation.

A leading example of an object-based application development is Visual Basic. Visual Basic is to the client-server world what Cobol is to the mainframe world. Since classes in Visual Basic are implemented using DCOM (distributed component object model), it is extremely easy to develop and deploy components using Visual Basic.

An object-based component can be described as a set of objects collaborating to provide a common functionality and implementing a common interface. Thus, an object-based component improves the encapsulation aspect of object-based applications. By virtue of this it also increases the flexibility as well as robustness of an object-based application, since changes to the component are isolated.

It has already been argued that the main thrust towards three-tiered architecture is coming from a need for effective change management. Change management, as used in this paper, encompasses the concepts of flexibility and robustness. It has also been argued that object-based applications by virtue of their support for encapsulation are a natural choice for the implementation of business solutions with underlying multi-tiered architectures. Since a component-based architecture enhances the ability of multi-tiered architectures to deliver on its promise, it would be logical to conclude that component-based multi-tiered architectures are here to stay.

So the prevalent application development environment can be said to have the following features:

- Multi-tiered architecture
- Relational databases
- Object-based applications
- Component-based application architecture

APPLICATION ARCHITECTURE EXAMPLE

Now this article will take an example where a set of three tables provides a certain functionality (e.g., hold information pertaining to interest rates in a portfolio management system) and three discrete applications that interact with these three tables. It will start with a simple two-tiered application architecture example and note the problems in the chosen context.

Then it will move to a more object-oriented version of the same problem and again note the problems with the approach. Finally, it will illustrate a solution to the same problem using a data-component approach.

In Exhibit 1, Application A1 is responsible for displaying and maintaining information in M1 (the set of tables T1, T2, and T3 constituting a sub data model). Applications A2, A3 use the information in M1 to do their processing. Note that Application A1 interacts with all the tables in M1, whereas Applications A2, A3 interact with only T3.

The shortcomings of two-tiered applications have already been noted. In this case, the tight coupling between the applications and the data is obvious, and consequently, flexibility is severely compromised. Also, there are three different applications interacting with the same data and consequently, complexity is increased since a change in data storage/design would necessitate change to all the client applications.

To make this design more object-oriented, now move to Exhibit 2 which illustrates a three-tiered object-oriented architecture. Applications A1, A2, and A3 contain their own relational to object mapping layer (also known as impedance matching layer). Now consider that new business rules necessitate a change to M1. M1 is a sub data model corresponding to functionality F1 (e.g., performance history of various investment options in a portfolio management system). If the new data model involves changing the way

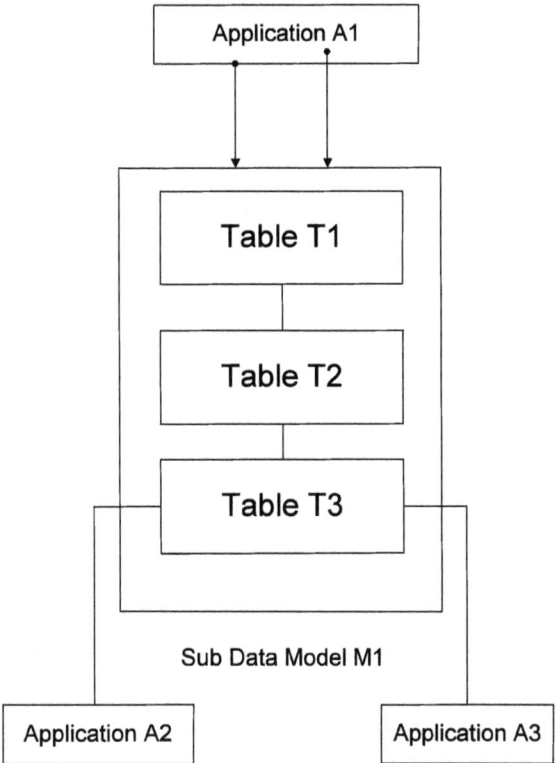

Exhibit 25-1. Two-tier application architecture.

information is represented in T3, then all applications involving T3 (in this case Applications A1, A2, and A3) have to be updated. In addition to requiring duplication of effort this design increases the risk of application malfunction, since it is possible to miss updating an application which needs updating. Also note that even aside from complicating change management, this design involves duplication of effort in terms of data access as well as relational to object mapping.

In order to solve the above-mentioned problems, modify the design to produce a more object-oriented approach by introducing components. Exhibit 3 introduces a component C1 that encapsulates sub data model M1. This makes C1 a data-component. Consequently, to the methodology illustrated in Exhibit 3 is referred to as the data-component approach.

ADVANTAGES/FEATURES OF THE DATA-COMPONENT APPROACH

The data-component approach, as illustrated in Exhibit 3, offers the following features and advantages:

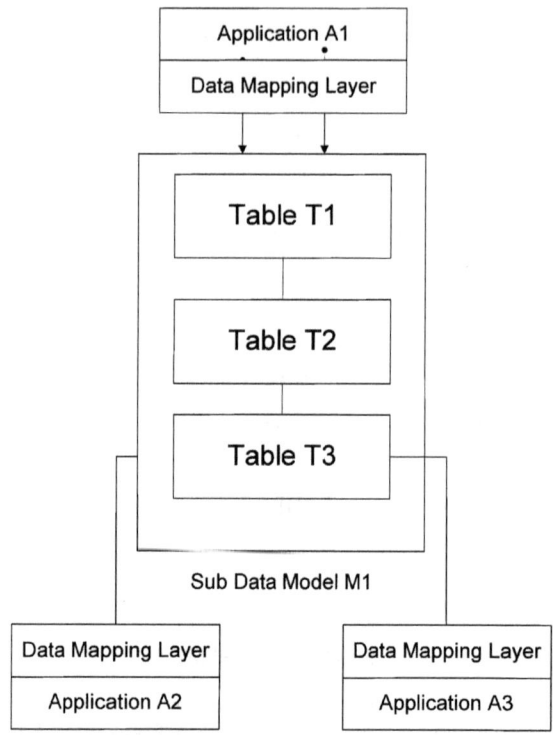

Exhibit 25-2. Three-tier application architecture with data-mapping layer.

- Applications do not access the tables directly but use the interface functions provided by the interface layer in C1.
- Satisfies an important OOD (object-oriented design) requirement: keep function and data together.
- Eliminates redundant data access as well as data mapping.
- Separates the GUI from the business logic — an important requirement of three-tier client server computing.
- Allows implementation of n-tiered architecture since C1 can be deployed on an application server.
- Provides much better change management (which as elaborated before, is an even greater benefit of object-oriented development than reuse), since changes in the data model no longer affect client applications directly. The only time the client applications are affected is when changes to the data model/functionality affect the interface between C1 and the client applications.
- Allows implementation of multiple interface or different views of data thus adding a new twist to the classic MVC (Model View Controller) object-oriented architecture.

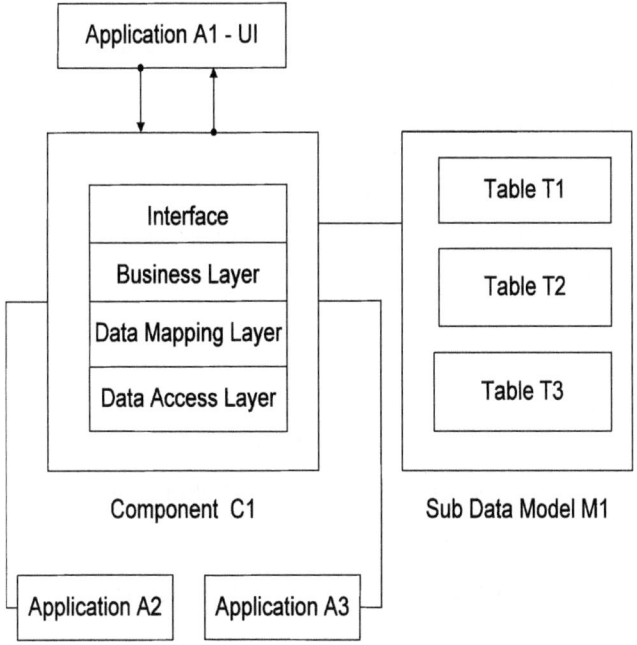

Exhibit 25-3. Application architecture example using data-component approach.

- Provides data source independence, since changing the source of the data will affect only the data access and data mapping layers of the component and the client applications will be insulated from any such change.
- Reduces the effort involved in allowing new applications to access the data.

DISADVANTAGES/LIMITATIONS OF THE DATA-COMPONENT APPROACH

The data-component approach as illustrated in Exhibit 3 has the following possible disadvantages or limitations:

- If used indiscriminately, this approach could lead to a proliferation of components thereby increasing the number of applications.
- Large applications using a large number of components could experience performance degradation, especially while loading the application.
- Each component will possibly have registration requirements, so the task of installing and distributing applications will be more complex.
- This approach deals primarily with discrete, non-overlapping use cases. Overlapping use cases will create additional complexities that have not been addressed in this approach.

391

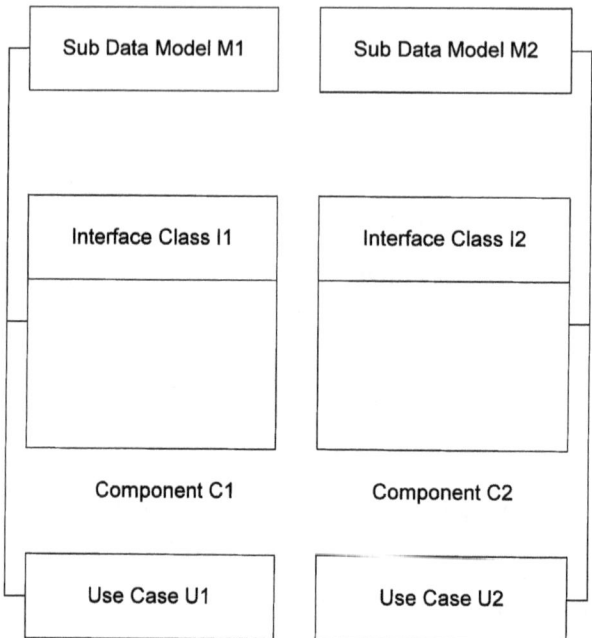

Exhibit 25-4. One-to-one component to subdata model example.

DATA-COMPONENT GRANULARITY CONSIDERATIONS

To prevent proliferation of components, the granularity of the components can be increased. For example as shown in Exhibit 4, use case U1 and U2 use sub data models M1 and M2 correspondingly.

Instead of having components C1 and C2 that correspond to use cases U1 and U2, if U1 and U2 are closely related, a single component C (with interfaces I1 and I2) can serve U1 and U2, as illustrated in Exhibit 5.

The same exercise of combining related use cases into components could be carried out through the application design space thereby bringing component proliferation under control.

IMPLEMENTATION OF THE COMPONENT-BASED DESIGN USING MICROSOFT'S ARCHITECTURE

Even though the component technology war between CORBA and DCOM is far from over, the fact remains that DCOM (in some form) has been around longer and is used widely in the industry. It also has, arguably, more opportunities to mature into a stable industrial strength technology. Consequently, Microsoft's DCOM platform is discussed in the implementation of the data-component approach illustrated in Exhibit 3.

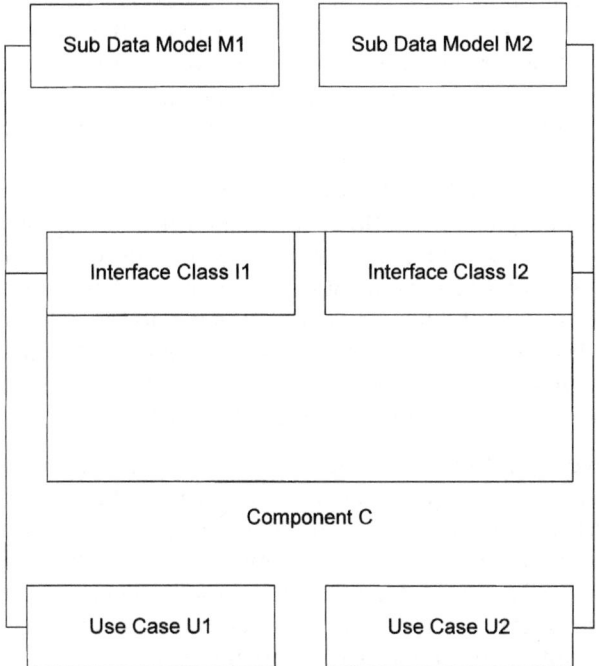

Exhibit 25-5. One-to-many component to subdata model example.

In Microsoft's DCOM technology there are two main types of components:

1. ActiveX Exe
2. ActiveX DLL

The difference between the two types of components is that the ActiveX Exe is an out-of-process component while the ActiveX DLL is an in-process component. In-process components usually offer significantly better performance than out-of-process components. However, in-process components and their client applications must reside on the same physical machines. With out-of-process components there is no such restriction, therefore out-of-process components offer greater flexibility in terms of deployment at the cost of application performance.

The choice between in-process and out-of-process components would therefore depend on the physical architecture. Note that three-tier software architectures can be deployed using two-tier physical architectures. In a two-tier implementation, the database runs on a database server and the user interface layer as well as the business layer runs on the client desktops. This kind of implementation is also called fat-client, since most of the applications are deployed on individual workstations. Whereas this might be sufficient for a small shop, for larger shops, distribution as well as maintenance of all the various components on individual workstations can prove to be a daunting as well as error-prone task. For this reason, larger shops may prefer to implement a physical three-tier architecture which would involve client workstations interacting with an application server which in turn would interact with a database server. While this approach alleviates some of the distribution problems inherent in the two-tier architecture, a new problem is created with multiple workstations accessing the same application on the applications server concurrently. Clearly, it would be counter-productive to start up a new copy of the application for every workstation that needs it. Therefore, some sort of a queuing solution is inevitable. It is in this respect that the DCOM architecture is yet to mature. Microsoft's solution to the problem involves use of MTS (Microsoft's transaction server), but that may not be a universally viable solution for every situation.

It is also worth noting that even though it is technically easy to convert an ActiveX DLL to an ActiveX Exe, there are other considerations involved which might necessitate knowledge of the physical architecture in advance. The main consideration is network traffic. With out-of-process components, performance requirements usually dictate the use of fewer but longer messages, whereas with in-process components, frequencies of messages do not result in performance penalties.

If the generic architecture example illustrated in Exhibit 3 were to be implemented on a Microsoft platform, the following notes may apply:

- The interface layer of component C1 interfaces with Applications A1, A2, and A3. Since A2 and A3 are inquiry-only applications, they can share a common interface. So, we would have two interface classes, I1 and I2. I1 will implement the interface needed for A1 and I2 would implement the interface needed for Applications A2 and A3. In some cases, classes I1 and I2 could be implemented in a separate ActiveX DLL. This has the advantage of providing de-coupling between the client and server applications. In practice, this has to be weighed against the cost of distributing this additional component. There will also be a minor performance penalty involved in separating the interface classes in a separate component, since an additional program will have to be loaded.
- Another factor to be considered while designing the interface layer is the number of parameters needed for the component to query and present the information. Assume for starters a method M1 in component C1, where the number of input parameters is n and the method returns only one value. A change in the input parameters would entail changing method M1 and therefore changing the interface. Therefore, except for trivial methods, it would make sense to encapsulate the data flowing between the component and its client applications, in

classes. In this example a class C1M1 would contain all the input parameters as well as result values for method M1 in Component C1. M1 now would be passed a reference to object OC1M1 (corresponding to class C1M1). With this approach, if method M1 were to need a new input parameter or need to return an extra result value, the interface would remain unchanged and changes would be restricted to class C1M1 and its usage.

- The business layer of the component should contain most of editing rules and the business logic. Including the editing logic in the business layer of the component goes a long way towards ensuring data integrity since applications that update the data maintained by the component have to use the interface layer of the component. Note that the business layer is not exposed directly to the outside world. External applications can only use the methods exposed by the interface layer, which in turn will interact with the business layer. Also, since the interface layer does not directly interact with the data layer of the component, the business layer has a chance to enforce its business rules and ensure logical integrity.

- The data layer of the component typically consists of two internal layers namely a relational to object mapping layer and a data access layer. The data access layer is responsible for the actual interaction with the database. The data mapping layer is responsible for mapping relational data into objects. Each record in a relational database is essentially an array of values. If a query returns more than one record (a RecordSet in Microsoft-speak), then we are dealing with a two-dimensional array. The data-mapping layer typically converts a single record to an object and a RecordSet to a collection of objects. Also, for persistent data, the object in the data mapping layer must know how to access the objects in the data access layer in order to store updated data. It is also worthwhile noting that the data access layer could be implemented as a separate component in itself. That way multiple applications can use the data access layer to manage their interactions with the physical database.

Following are examples of the architectures discussed in this paper:

1. The business layer has classes B1 and B2 that correspond to the interface layer classes I1 and I2. B1 and B2 interact with classes R1,R2,..., RN which implement various business rules. B1 and B2 also interact with corresponding classes DM1 and DM2, which belong to the data mapping layer of the data layer. DM1 and DM2 in turn interact with classes DA1, DA2, and DA3, which access/update data in Tables T1, T2, and T3.

2. Instead of having separate classes B1 and B2, depending on the application, a single class B may suffice.

3. Again, depending on the application, a single class DA may provide the functionality provided by DA1, DA2, and DA3.
4. Note that DM1 and DM2 provide the business view of the data model and this case is basically driven by the choice of B1 and B2 as the business classes. Depending on the requirements, classes DM1, DM2, and DM3 could correspond to DA1, DA2, and DA3 or any other combination that makes sense.
5. Note that classes DM1 and DM2 could create and return a variety of object. For example, object O11 might correspond to a specific record in the table T1. Object O12 might correspond to a collection of records. Alternatively, O12 may be implemented as an object containing a collection of O11 objects. Similarly, objects O21 through O2N might correspond to Table T2. Alternatively, O21 through O2N might correspond to data linked between Tables T2 and T3 if appropriate.

The possibilities are endless. The examples listed previously illustrate some of the considerations that might come into play during the design of the component. To reiterate one of the main points in this article, effective change management, assume that a change is to be made to this design. Instead of accessing data in Table T2 and T3 directly, applications must use a View instead. In this case, only relevant classes in the data access layer and maybe the data mapping layer will need to be changed. All other classes in the business and the interface layer of the component can remain unchanged. Also, the client applications using the component remain unaffected. Thus use of a multi-tiered component-based architecture has provided for flexibility (providing ease of change by restricting the area of change) as well as robustness (limiting the scope of the effect of change).

DATA-COMPONENT MINING

Data-component mining is the process by which an existing data model can be analyzed and broken up into sub data models with associated data-components. One approach to component mining is to study the data model to identify loosely coupled sets of entities. Each such set of entities can be called a sub-data model. Each sub-data model is a good candidate for a component and more so if the sub-data model is used by more than one application. Use cases have become a standard way to defining requirements/functionality in object-oriented design. A list of existing as well as future use cases can also provide a valuable perspective during data-component mining design. Related use cases can be combined to help identify sub-data models and consequently corresponding data components.

For example, in a portfolio management system, analysis of the ERD (entity relationship diagram) of the data model might suggest that the set of entities containing historical performance data could constitute a sub-data model M1. Similarly, the set of entities pertaining to investment choices in a client's portfolio could constitute another sub-data model M2. There is now a potential use for two data components: C1 corresponding to model M1 (historical performance data) and C2 corresponding to model M2 (client's investment choices). Alternatively, it could start with use cases. For example, consider the following use cases:

- U1 — Provide inquiry of client's investment elections.
- U2 — Provide investment election change update/change.
- U3 — Provide inquiry of investment performance data.
- U4 — Provide update of investment performance data.
- U5 — Calculate portfolio values for a given client.

U1 and U2 deal with the same information (a client's investment choices). Similarly, U3 and U4 deal with the same information (investment performance data). U5 deals with the client's investment choices as well as investment performance data. Since investment performance data is independent of a client's investment choices, the entities in the data model corresponding to investment performance data, can be said to be loosely coupled with the entities pertaining to client investment elections. Therefore, investment performance data as well as client investment choices are both candidates for sub-data models with corresponding data components. The implementation of U5 would then involve use of both data components.

CONCLUSION

The data component approach to data management can be valuable in an environment involving object-oriented applications and relational databases. The primary advantage provided by this approach is ensuring that the application responsible for updating information is responsible for providing inquiry of the same information, thereby providing for superior change management. This approach can be used in any environment that allows development of component-based applications.

Chapter 26
Designing Relational Databases
Candace C. Fleming and Barbara von Halle

RELATIONAL DATABASE DESIGN IS A PROCESS FOR TRANSFORMING A DATA MODEL INTO A RELATIONAL DATABASE. A data model is a disciplined map of data requirements. It is disciplined because it depicts the data in a simple, stable, and minimally redundant form, unbiased by information system processing requirements or technological considerations. A complete data model defines the following elements:

- *Entities.* Major objects of interest to the user.
- *Relationships.* Associations between the entities.
- *Attributes.* Detailed information items describing the entities.
- *Business rules.* Guidelines governing the relationships and the values that the attributes can assume.

A relational database design should preserve the stability and shareability that are inherent to a good data model. The challenge is to design a relational database that also offers acceptable performance and achieves its design functions.

This chapter describes a relational database design methodology that addresses the implementation of each construct of the data model. The relational design methodology addresses the implementation of both structural constructs (i.e., entities, relationships, and attributes) and integrity constructs (i.e., business rules — including entity identifiers, foreign keys, domains, and other data model constructs). This scope may be significantly broader than that traditionally defined for database design. Relational database technology encourages a broader perspective because the underlying relational data model incorporates structure and data integrity rules in the data definition.

Addressing data integrity as part of database design rather than information system design means enforcing business rules independently of any particular information system. Some rules can be enforced by built-in relational DBMS facilities, such as data type specifications in the database definition. Frequently, however, other business rules will require developing code — for example, to enforce a rule about the relationship between two attributes or to enforce range checking. The methodology in this article addresses the enforcement of all business rules that are not information system-specific as part of the database design process, even if they must be implemented through code.

There are four benefits of this data-driven approach:

- *Data integrity.* Enforcing business rules through one integrated approach results in a database that is less vulnerable to contamination
- *Productivity.* Using a data-driven approach enables enforcement of business rules completely and consistently yet with minimal overhead. Specifically, each business rule is defined and possibly implemented only once for the database, rather than once per application.
- *Maintainability.* Because the rules have been defined and implemented consistently, changes in business rules can be accommodated quickly and easily as the business evolves.
- *Evolution.* As relational DBMS products provide better automated facilities for enforcing business rules, it is easy to migrate from this consistent, integrated implementation approach to take advantage of new facilities.

In the end, the success of relational databases is measured by how easily they accommodate a multiplicity of needs: different types of users, various access patterns and requirements, and changing business and technological issues. The databases are more likely to support these various needs if the database design is founded on a data-driven philosophy.

MAJOR CONCEPTS OF RELATIONAL DATABASE DESIGN

The major components of a data model are entities, entity identifiers, foreign keys, attributes, relationships, and business rules. An entity identifier is an attribute or set of attributes that identifies a particular entity occurrence. For example, Exhibit 1 depicts a data model as a real estate business in which RENTER-11) is the entity identifier because a given renter can be identified by his name. A foreign key is an attribute or set of attributes that completes a relationship by identifying the associated entity. For example, in Exhibit 1, RENTER*ID is a foreign key in RENTAL-AGREEMENT that identifies which RENTER is a party to the agreement.

Major constructs of the relational data model are relational tables (i.e., sets of rows and columns typically containing data describing some object — much like entities), primary keys, foreign keys, columns (which are much like attributes), and integrity rules (i.e., entity, referential, and domain integrity rules — much like business rules in your logical data model). It is no coincidence that data modeling terminology resembles relational model terminology because the concepts themselves are similar.

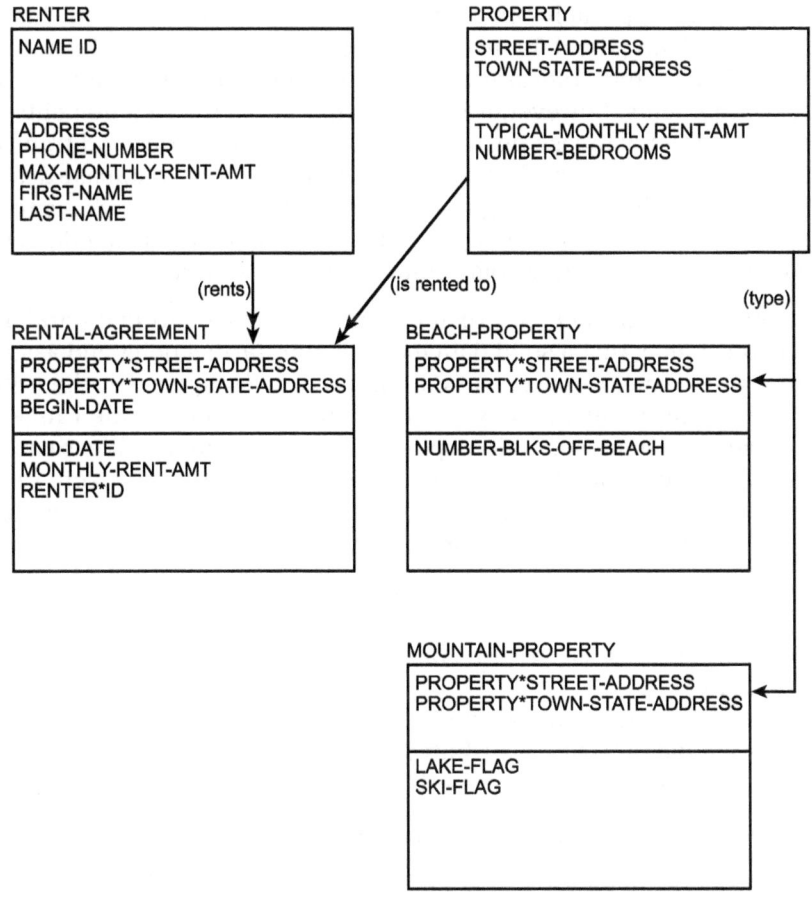

RENTER

NAME ID
ADDRESS PHONE-NUMBER MAX-MONTHLY-RENT-AMT FIRST-NAME LAST-NAME

PROPERTY

STREET-ADDRESS TOWN-STATE-ADDRESS
TYPICAL-MONTHLY RENT-AMT NUMBER-BEDROOMS

(rents)   (is rented to)   (type)

RENTAL-AGREEMENT

PROPERTY*STREET-ADDRESS PROPERTY*TOWN-STATE-ADDRESS BEGIN-DATE
END-DATE MONTHLY-RENT-AMT RENTER*ID

BEACH-PROPERTY

PROPERTY*STREET-ADDRESS PROPERTY*TOWN-STATE-ADDRESS
NUMBER-BLKS-OFF-BEACH

MOUNTAIN-PROPERTY

PROPERTY*STREET-ADDRESS PROPERTY*TOWN-STATE-ADDRESS
LAKE-FLAG SKI-FLAG

Exhibit 26-1. A data model for ron's real estate business.

This similarity enables at least the initial steps of relational design to be a straight-forward process.

An intuitive first attempt at a relational database design to support Ron's Real Estate Business (depicted in Exhibit 1) would probably include five tables, one for each entity in the data model: RENTER, PROPERTY, RENTAL-AGREEMENT, BEACH-PROPERTY, and MOUNTAIN-PROPERTY. The RENTER table would then have four columns representing NAME, ADDRESS, PHONE-NUMBER, and MAX-MONTHLY-RENT-AMT. The values of these columns should comply with the integrity rules identified in the logical data model. Some implementation mechanisms for enforcing those integrity rules include using a DBMS to specify NOT NULL and create a unique index on entity identifier columns, and enforcing other domain rules (such as data type or even default value) through the data definition language.

An intuitive approach can accomplish the first of two major design phases: translating the data model into a preliminary relational database design. When merely translating the data model into corresponding relational components, however, it is important that all the requirements be satisfied. A good database design will make all user queries and transactions feasible and efficient. The second phase of relational database design — tuning the preliminary design — addresses these concerns. Some techniques used to speed processing of particular data requests include defining indexes and duplicating some columns in two or more tables.

An intuitive approach can result in an excellent relational database design, presuming that a solid data model is the starting point and assuming that processing requirements are not overly complex. On the other hand, an intuitive design may not be sufficient given a wide range of requirements or implementation options. Therefore, intuitive ideas can be reinforced by following a more rigorous and systematic approach, referencing technical guidelines and organizational standards for each step. Some key questions to consider are:

- Should entities always be translated directly to tables on a one-to-one basis?
- How are names assigned to tables and columns for clarity and for usability?
- How are business rules enforced?
- How should tables be distributed among multiple databases?
- How and when should space utilization be calculated?

STEPS IN RELATIONAL DATABASE DESIGN

The relational database design methodology described in this chapter begins with a data model and outlines 13 steps for building and tuning a corresponding relational database design. Each step is numbered using the convention RDN where RDD denotes relational database design and n denotes the step number.

Translating the Logical Data Structure

Database design begins with the translation of the data model. Initially, this process occurs independently of any investigation of access patterns, transaction volumes, or even security requirements. The first steps are:

- Identifying tables — step RDD1.
- Identi4dng columns — step RDD2.
- Adapting data structure to product environment — step RDD3.

Translating the Logical Data Integrity

The second component of the translation process is to enforce the data integrity constraints or business rules. The necessary steps are:

Exhibit 26-2. RENTER relational table.

RENTER

NAME (UIX)	ADDRESS	PHONE-NUMBER	MAX-MONTHLY -RENT-AMT
Harry Smith	12 Oak Lane, Hopetown, NY 01111	212-984-3158	400
Josephine Morgan	5 Central Ave, Dallas, TX 75080	214-232-7990	650

- Designing for business rules about entities — step RDD4.
- Designing for business rules about relationships — step RDD5.
- Designing for additional business rules about attributes — step RDD6.

The relational design should include optimal mechanisms for enforcing business rules; it is important to consider ways to supplement the built-in features of the product, weighing the advantages and disadvantages of each option. ANSI SQL can be a useful tool for gaining insight into how the relational DBMS may evolve. Such insight can assist in choosing implementation options that will not hamper the exploitation of technological advances as they occur.

Exhibit 2 continues the real estate example and illustrates a relational table for RENTER. Various codes positioned below each column name designate the use of implementation options, selected now or in later design steps. For example, (UIX) beneath NAME indicates the implementation of a unique index on the NAME column. When translating the RENTER entity to this relational table, it is important to choose an appropriate table name, column names, data types, and validation checks.

TUNING THE DESIGN BY ESTABLISHING STORAGE-RELATED ACCESS MECHANISMS

The final step is to tune the relational design. Tuning efforts are primarily concerned with facilitating specific access requirements. Frequently, proper tuning can make a successful relational database implementation. Tuning options should be applied in a deliberate sequence — the sequence that maximizes benefits and minimizes visibility to users. In particular, when tuning a design to accommodate new requirements, it is critical to minimize potential problems for existing users.

Initial tuning efforts should address the effective use of the access mechanisms provided by the relational DBMS. Techniques include the use of scans, clustering, hashing, and indexes. There are several reasons to begin with access mechanisms.

Access mechanisms in relational products should be transparent to users. Users should never need to specify through language syntax which access mechanisms the relational DBMS is to use in satisfying a given query. That decision is left to the product's optimizer. Thus the designer can introduce changes in the access mechanisms without necessitating changes in application code or in users' use of SQL or other commands.

The designer must become familiar with the performance benefits and implications of various access mechanisms. Particularly during an initial design project using a new product, it is important to experiment with access mechanisms early so that the design can leverage the performance strengths and weaknesses of the product. It is also necessary to understand the performance limitations of the facilities in the DBMS before modifying the design.

Access mechanisms rely on and benefit from the choice of storage options for each table. The necessary steps are:

- Tuning for scan efficiency — step RDD7.
- Defining clustering sequences — step RDD8.
- Defining hash keys — step RDD9.

To apply these steps to Ron's Real Estate Business example, it is necessary to understand more about his processing requirements. Some of Ron's requirements are that:

1. When a renter's name is given, the address is returned.
2. When a renter's name is given, the telephone number is returned.
3. When a monthly rental figure is given, the names of all potential renters willing to pay that rent are returned.
4. All properties with all associated detail information are listed.
5. Properties that will be vacant as of a specific date are listed in descending order by monthly rental amount.

Alternatives exist for optimizing cost and performance trade-offs for each of these requirements. Because requirements 1 and 2 involve direct random access to individual rows, hashed access may be the most efficient alternative. Requirement 3 involves a qualification on a range of values (i.e., which renters are willing to pay maximum monthly rental amounts equal to or greater than some specified figure.) Storing RENTER rows in sorted sequence by MAX-MONTHLY-RENT-AMT may accelerate the processing of this requirement. Because the RENTER table cannot be both hashed and clustered, however, compromises must be made. The speed with which the DBMS can scan the entire table and the table can be sorted must be examined. The relative importance of each requirement and its performance objectives and constraints must be weighed.

Requirement 4 entails joins of PROPERTY with BEACH-PROPERTY and PROPERTY with MOUNTAIN-PROPERTY. Some relevant questions to consider are: can the speed of access be increased by storing the rows in sequence by primary key? Are the tables small enough to rely on internal DBMS scanning and sorting? Will indexes help?

Requirement 5 involves scanning the RENTAL-AGREEMENT table. The important questions here are: will physically storing the rows in a particular sequence (with or without an index) speed up access? Which sequence (END-DATE, BEGIN-DATE, or a concatenation of both dates) is best? Should the rows be stored in ascending or descending order, or is it better to store the rows in sequence by MONTHLY-RENT-AMT?

Tuning by Adding Indexes. The final access mechanism can be used in combination with the first three storage-related access mechanisms to tune for a mix of user requirements: adding indexes — step RDD10. Indexes usually are optional access mechanisms that can complement scanning, clustering, or hashing. Indexes can significantly increase the ratio of rows returned to rows searched in order to satisfy a query by enabling direct access to individual rows, thereby eliminating table scans; reducing the span of rows searched when a scan is required; avoiding a sort of table rows (most useful when a small percentage of rows is required in sorted order); and eliminating table access altogether if required columns are stored as part of the index.

Indexes can be helpful in the implementation supporting Ron's Real Estate Business. Indexes on the primary key of PROPERTY and on the foreign (also primary) keys of BEACH-PROPERTY and MOUNTAIN-PROPERTY would facilitate the required join to produce a list of all properties with all details. For time requests, indexes can help the DBMS scan the RENTAL-AGREEMENT table. Building an index on BEGIN-DATE, on END-DATE, or on both dates could improve access time.

If Ron is unsure of other processing requirements, a good tuning might proceed by assuming that he will need to join tables, most likely by primary-to-foreign key reference paths. An index on each foreign key might be helpful as well. When a given foreign key is a component of a primary key (e.g., PROPERTY*STREET-ADDRESS and PROPERTY*TOWN-STATE-ADDRESS in the RENTAL-AGREEMENT table) and that primary key already has an index on it (e.g., to enforce uniqueness), the primary key index may also be used to facilitate foreign key access. Other possibilities include altering the sequence of columns in the index or a new index built solely on the foreign key.

Tuning by Introducing Controlled Data Redundancy

The next group of tuning techniques involves altering the relational database structure to accommodate functional and performance requirements. Changing the database structure raises two important issues. First, it introduces deviations from the stable logical data model; these deviations frequently add complexity or detract from flexibility. Second, structural database changes, although implemented for tuning purposes, are nevertheless visible to users. For example, if a column is duplicated in another table to avoid joining the two tables, users and programmers must know that the column appears in both tables and, specifically, that a join is no longer necessary. Obviously, such tuning efforts will affect the command syntax for users and within programs.

These two issues are significant, and they discourage extensive structural modifications. It is imperative that such design changes are justifiable and that data integrity is still adequately addressed (not unintentionally sacrificed).

The most straightforward way to modify a structure is to add duplicate columns or rows by adding duplicate data — step RDD11. Duplicate data can take any of several forms. For example, additional columns can be exact copies or derivations of other columns, repeating columns that represent multiple occurrences of the same attribute, or shorter contrived columns that replace unwieldy primary or foreign keys. Finally, extra columns or rows can facilitate such functional requirements as the outer join.

Suppose a frequent online query in Ron's Real Estate Business involves retrieving the address of a rental property with the name and telephone number of the current renter. This query requires a join of the RENTER and RENTER-AGREEMENT tables. One option for eliminating the join, and thereby improving the performance of this query, is to duplicate the renter's PHONE-NUMBER in RENTAL-AGREEMENT. However, the cost associated with the data redundancy is high. Extra storage is required to store each PHONE-NUMBER once for the associated RENTER plus once for each related RENTAL-AG REEMENT. Additional business rules are required to ensure synchronization of the duplicate data whenever PHONE-NUMBER is updated. Finally, user queries must know when accessing PHONE-NUMBER from RENTAL-AGRFEMENT is more efficient than accessing PHONE-NUM-BER from RENTER, and vice versa. The database designer must weigh these costs against the performance benefits.

Tuning by Redefining the Relational Database Structure

There are two ways to redefine the original tables and columns:

- Redefining columns — step RDD12.
- Redefining tables — step RDD13.

Long textual columns are candidates for redefinition into one or more shorter columns. Moreover, foreign keys are sometimes redefined to reference alternate rather than primary keys. There are many motivations and techniques for eliminating, duplicating, segmenting (or splitting), and combining tables. The result is a database design in which the tables no longer correspond in a one-to-one manner to the entities of your logical data model.

The most active properties in Ron's Real Estate Business, for example, are his beach properties. Thus when Ron needs information about properties, he usually joins the PROPERTY table with the BEACH-PROPERTY table. As his business grows and the number of properties increases, he discovers that performance of this join degrades in spite of placing indexes on foreign keys and storing rows in foreign-key sequence. A designer may decide to combine the PROPERTY table with the BEACH-PROPERTY table to avoid this join because the only reason to join these tables is to determine how far the properties are from the beach. The resulting PROPERTY table would have five columns instead of four and the BEACH-PROPERTY table would no longer exist.

However, there are some negative implications of this action. Specifically, the PROPERTY table would become larger (i.e., it would include one more column for each row). Combining these two tables would increase the occurrences of nulls, because rows representing mountain properties have no value for the new attribute NUMBER-BLKS-OFF-BEACH. The relational database would no longer be consistent with the logical data model, which has five entities but four tables. Enforcement of business rules pertaining to property deletions would be more complex in that deleting a beach property requires a deletion of only the PROPERTY table, whereas deleting a mountain property requires the deletion of both the PROPERTY and the MOUNTAIN-PROPERTY tables. Users would have to recode existing commands that reference the BEACH-PROPERTY table so that the commands refer to the PROPERTY table. Exhibit 3 depicts all 13 steps in the relational database design process.

CRITICAL SUCCESS FACTORS FOR A RELATIONAL DATABASE DESIGN METHODOLOGY

There are many ways to go about designing relational databases in addition to the steps described in this chapter. At the very least, a designer will want to supplement these steps with product-specific techniques for the environment and with other practical tips learned through experience.

In applying, developing, or adapting a relational database design methodology, it is important to ensure that the design approach:

- *Provides a step-by-step procedure.* The design methodology should include guidelines to assist a novice designer and should supplement them with organizational standards addressing naming conventions, documentation, and resource utilization. It should also provide a list of contacts for education and support.

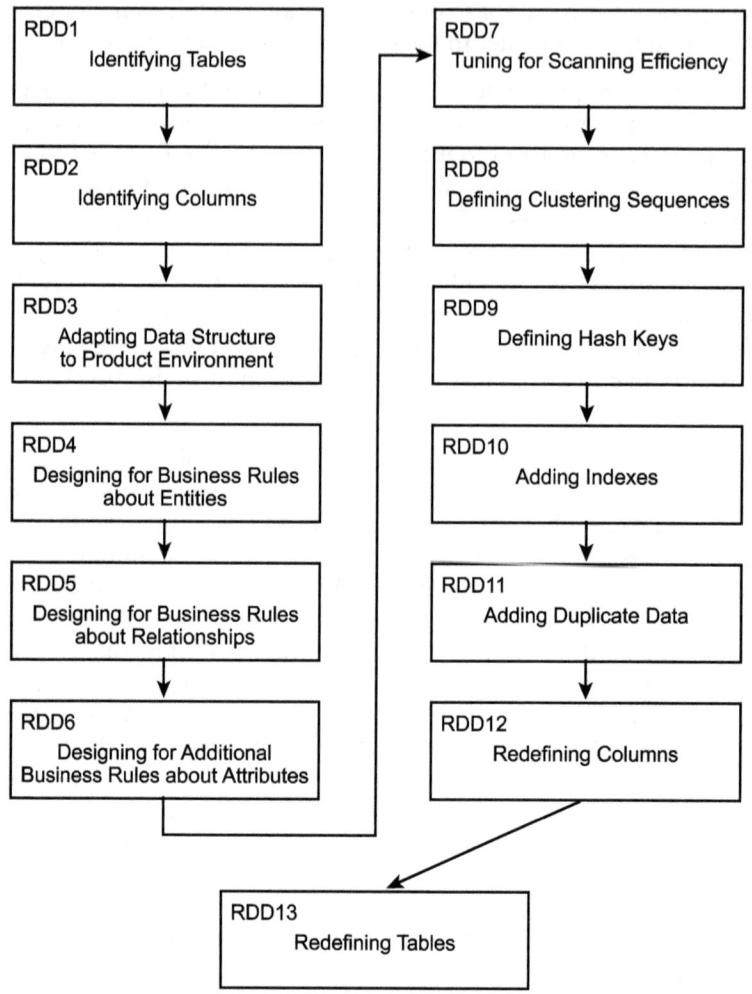

Exhibit 26-3. The relational database design process.

- *Evaluates roles and responsibilities carefully.* In some cases, people with little database design experience may develop initial relational database designs. These people will need exposure to concepts, a methodology, and access to more experienced designers. The more experienced designers should critique and tune preliminary designs and choose among proposed design alternatives.
- *Clearly distinguishes between generic and product-specific design techniques.* This allows the methodology to span product environments. Most organizations host a set of relational products. For each generic design step, the designer can add guidelines or implementation tips that address product-specific options.

- *Provides a data dictionary.* The dictionary should capture definitions for the relational database and related objects and should provide a cross-reference from the logical data model to relational constructs.
- *Bases the methodology on a logical data model.* Designers will not automatically build logical data models first. Therefore, a logical data model must be made as a prerequisite, if only by using terminology in the relational design steps that demands the application of logical data modeling concepts.
- *Provides for database design reviews.* Checkpoints must be established throughout the design process that allow or require designers to solicit opinions and insights from other people. Design review sessions should be supported with design documentation produced by the data dictionary or relational DBMS, and standard forms (preferably computer-based) containing additional relevant design information must be used.
- *Includes both structural and integrity considerations in the relational database implementation.* Business rules should be enforced as part of an integrated data-driven process rather than by individual applications or users. Standards for enforcing these rules must be defined in a controlled and integrated fashion within the environment.
- *Uses a database diagramming technique to illustrate the relational database design.* Similarities in diagramming constructs should be used to convey similarities between the logical data model and the relational database design. In addition, the use of tuning techniques, such as indexes, hashed access, and duplicate data, should be conveyed in the relational diagram.

BENEFITS AND APPLICABILITY OF A RELATIONAL DATABASE DESIGN METHODOLOGY

A relational database design methodology provides several benefits. It promotes early usability of a new relational DBMS or related product, especially by encouraging development of prototypes. It removes fear and doubt in the minds of first-time designers. It communicates common and proven approaches for solving functional and performance challenges. It promotes consistent documentation and effective communication of design alternatives and justifications.

Moreover, a relational database design methodology is applicable under many circumstances. A few examples are:

- *Developing preliminary or prototype databases.* In this instance, the designer will probably need only to translate the logical data model and choose access approaches. Many technical and product-specific steps can be omitted.

- *Developing production databases.* The designer will need all steps of a relational database design methodology, with additional product-specific techniques.
- *Assessing the maturity of relational DBMS products.* A designer can evaluate a DBMS by considering how effectively each step of a design methodology can be performed using that DBMS for a given set of user requirements. Compare multiple DBMSs by determining which products require the most work (e.g., the most customized code). This comparison will indicate which products enable maximum satisfaction of design requirements and with what degree of ease.
- *Evaluating the applicability of automated design tools.* A designer can evaluate a design aid by analyzing the degree to which it automates the steps and guidelines of a relational database design methodology. The methodology should provide an effective benchmark of the product's ability to meet design needs.
- *Establishing a basis for database design reviews.* When a standard step-by-step design process is used, database design reviews are more straightforward because all participants are grounded in common design approaches and goals.

SUMMARY

Relational technology can be an important asset to an organization, especially if it is used to build relational databases that serve a variety of business needs. To be used most effectively, relational technology requires a data-driven design approach.

This chapter describes data-driven relational database design as composed of two phases. The first, translation of the data model, preserves the logical structure and integrity of the data. The second phase, tuning, refines a preliminary relational design to accommodate performance and functional objectives.

A relational database design methodology should consist of step-by-step procedures and supporting rules. Use of these steps and guidelines will increase the productivity of relational database designers. In addition, it may assist them in avoiding disasters and less severe (albeit more common) errors. A methodology should encourage use of consistent and proven approaches for resolving technical issues. It also should suggest practical techniques for meeting functional and performance challenges posed to the relational database products of today and tomorrow.

Section VI
Database Integrity and Quality

DATABASE INTEGRITY REFERS TO THE CORRECTNESS OF THE DATA STORED IN THE DATABASE STRUCTURE OR COLLECTION OF STRUCTURES. Data values at the atomic level must be correct, as must data values related to other data values (e.g., referential integrity). Data can be corrupted by many events; for example, by users accessing data or as the result of a failed operation that does not have an accurate transaction rollback procedure. External factors such as disasters, viruses, and hackers can also corrupt data. Maintaining the integrity of a database requires an end-to-end approach within an organization. Quality is an ongoing process that assists in ensuring database integrity. It can be a set of procedures or checks that are followed to develop a database and to manage ongoing operations.

Database intergrity and quality are clearly important to the value of a database and in some cases may overshadow other features. This section examines approaches and tools for ensuring referential data integrity and quality. This section contains the following chapters.

Chapter 27, "What Is Wrong with My Data?," examines approaches for correcting "bad" data so that organizations can fully realize the potential of the systems that are being developed.

Chapter 28, "Referential Integrity for Database Design," defines referential integrity, describes its limitations with examples, and then proposes methods of overcoming its limitations. Attribute referential integrity is discussed as it applies to entity-relationship and relational data models.

Chapter 29, "Data Quality: An Architectural Solution," discusses the process of integrating data from multiple data sources into a data warehouse, while maintaining data quality. This chapter provides advice on resolving such problems as caused by extracting data from multiple inconsistent data sources or integrating data stores that utilize different types of data models.

Chapter 30, "Ensuring the Integrity of the Database," provides an approach that is based on organizational checks and balances, data access security, and programmed integrity tests. The approach includes a discussion of issues relevant to distributed data sources. This chapter also examines some sample tools and repositories.

Chapter 27
What's Wrong With My Data?

Jeffery Feldman

YOU HAVE PROBABLY HEARD THE EXPRESSION, "GARBAGE IN, GARBAGE OUT." A computer system utilizing the most technologically sophisticated architecture, elegant user interfaces, and intuitive report generation capabilities, can be rendered nearly useless if the data it relies upon is fundamentally flawed. While investigating and correcting "bad" data may be among the least glamourous tasks to perform, it is absolutely critical if organizations are to realize the full potential of the systems they have developed (often at a considerable cost in time, resources, and dollars).

This paper illustrates a variety of potential quality problems that could be present within the files and databases of any organization. These problems will be especially evident in older legacy systems, although not necessarily restricted to older systems by any means. Knowing the possible issues is the first step towards addressing them. Further steps would include taking action to correct the data, and (perhaps even more importantly) taking action to correct the processes that led to flawed data being stored in the first place. This paper focuses on describing those possible flaws.

WHY SHOULD I CARE?

Perhaps you are not quite convinced that data integrity should be a major concern, or at any rate not for the applications you are dealing with. After all, the existing systems are running just fine with the current data, aren't they? And any required data cleansing can be done at some point in the future, when time and resources become more available.

Well, maybe. Much depends on just how the data is being used, and on the organization's tolerance for risk. Let us say, for example, that the only use of the data is to support a company-internal management information system, and that about 5 percent of the data is known to be in error. A cost-benefit analysis that compares the effort required to correct the data vs.

the increased value of the system to its users might well conclude the 5 percent error rate is acceptable.

On the other hand, what if that error rate was actually 30 percent? Or what if the application in question was sending bills to your customers? It is unlikely that faulty data could be tolerated for long in either situation.

Just because existing systems can use a particular set of data, that does not necessarily imply ease-of-use for a new system — among other things, there may be a great deal of hard-coded logic in the old systems that allows them to bypass problems in the raw data. And there are a host of potential new problems once you start merging data from several different existing systems in order to feed your new system.

And postponing the cleansing effort is generally inadvisable. The initial data propagation/transformation efforts can require significant revision and re-execution. Considerable additional effort and cost may be needed to repair data, to make it accessible, and to prevent continued corruption. However, once the users have started to access the system, its credibility (and your own) are on the line. There may not be any funds available for continued work if the system's users are not satisfied with the initial release. And does time and additional resources ever *really* become easier to get onto a project at a "later date"?

Potential Impacts

Some potential impacts of unreliable data include the following:

- *Increased Cost of Database Marketing.* Poor quality data affects direct-mail, telemarketing, and marketing collateral costs. A large automobile manufacturer purged its customer files and cut direct-mail costs by U.S. $500,000 the first year, and lowered the costs of managing this data long term.[1]
- *Increased Operational Costs.* The time that resources must spend to detect and correct errors can be very significant. One estimate for the cost of poor data quality is 8 to 12 percent of revenue; for service organizations, a "good working estimate" might be 40 to 60 percent of expenses.[2] There is also a related negative impact on employee morale.
- *Lowered Customer Satisfaction.* Multiple mailings sent to the same customer can be annoying, they can cause the customer to question your enterprise's competence, and can harm the customer relationship. This is especially true if the information within a given mailing or statement pertaining to a customer is incorrect.
- *Reduced Use of System.* If the believability and/or the objectivity of the data comes into question, then the resulting poor reputation will cause reduced use of the system and underlying databases.[3] Considering the effort and cost of developing these systems, anything impairing their value or use is clearly counterproductive.

- *Risk to Health/Safety.* The quality of data in (for example) medical records is clearly of major importance, as the diagnosis and procedure must be recorded correctly. Other examples of critical systems include those controlling aircraft movement and traffic signals, chemical plants and nuclear reactors, jail security, and many others.

WHAT PROBLEMS MIGHT THERE BE?

Let us take the following as our working scenario: a new data warehouse is being constructed, and the data from several operational legacy systems/databases will be used to populate it. These legacy feeder systems will remain in production for some time. We are therefore concerned with the quality of the available data not only for the purpose of the initial load of our data warehouse, but also because any problems that currently exist will continue to contaminate our data until they are fixed. This is a hypothetical but common situation, and provides the context for further discussion.

Potential Problems

Missing Data

In Exhibit 27-1:

- Lee does not have a *Smoker* status code/flag, while Frank does not have a value in the *Sex* field. The degree to which either is an issue will depend upon whether they are mandatory fields or not. If one or the other is mandatory, how will you go about getting that information?
- Record 525 is not present. Does this indicate a deletion, or a problem with missing records in this particular file?
- Smith and Yu have a zero *Age*. Either they are less than a year old, or 00 is the default or dummy value given to the *Age* field. Do the business rules help you to determine which is which? If 00 is the dummy value, then this data is missing.
- There is another kind of missing data — data that is needed by the new application, but was not captured by any of the older feeding systems. If you are fortunate, it will be possible to derive the new value by manipulating the old data. Otherwise, the effort to capture and record new information can be considerable.

Exhibit 27-1. Example of missing data.

Identifier	Last Name	Sex	Age	Smoker
523	Smith	M	00	N
524	Jones	F	23	Y
526	Lee	M	42	
527	Frank		17	Y
528	Yu	M	00	N

Redundant Data with Inconsistencies

In Exhibit 27-2:

- Our hypothetical data warehouse draws information from both Files "A" and "B" (assume each has unique fields of interest not displayed in the above example). Because each file was developed and used separately by different divisions of the company, redundant information is stored. Which will you use as your primary source for those fields available from both?
- Note that the information for Jones is not consistent. Is it safe to assume that File "A" has more recent information, and therefore that Jones took up smoking at age 23? Regardless of the answer, how do we account for the difference in *Sex* for Lee?
- Data File "B" has a record 525 not present in File "A." Should we then merge the records from the two files to get a complete set? Or perhaps File "B" is out of date, and the record should have been deleted from File "B" as well? This is another illustration of inconsistency.

Exhibit 27-2. Example of redundant data.

Data File "A"				
Identifier	Last Name	Sex	Age	Smoker
523	Smith	M	00	N
524	Jones	F	23	Y
526	Lee	M	42	
527	Frank		17	Y
528	Yu	M	00	N

Data File "B"				
Identifier	Last Name	Sex	Age	Smoke
523	Smith	M	00	N
524	Jones	F	22	N
525	Samuelson	M	54	Y
526	Lee	F	42	
527	Frank		17	Y

Different/Changing Business Rules or Logic

In Exhibit 27-3, our hypothetical data warehouse draws information from both Files "A" and "C":

- Notice that Lee's *Smoker* status is "Y" in File "C." This is a result of a business rule in the application logic which says "Unless the individual specifically indicates that they are a non-smoker, give them the

smoker code." That rule is not present in the application producing File "A," causing the discrepancy.

- Is there disagreement on Smith's age between the two files? No, it's just that the dummy value for File "C" happens to be "99" rather than "00."
- Is File "C" missing more data for Frank than File "A"? Yes, but it's intentional — the logic for File "C" refuses to store values for *Age* and *Smoker* unless all mandatory fields (including *Sex*) are completed.
- Note that these types of inconsistency can appear within a single file just as easily as between files, if the business rules/application logic changes over time.

Exhibit 27-3. Example of different logic.

Data File "A"				
Identifier	**Last Name**	**Sex**	**Age**	**Smoker**
523	Smith	M	00	N
524	Jones	F	23	Y
526	Lee	M	42	
527	Frank		17	Y
528	Yu	M	00	N

Data File "C"				
Identifier	**Last Name**	**Sex**	**Age**	**Smoker**
523	Smith	M	99	N
524	Jones	F	22	N
525	Samuelson	M	54	Y
526	Lee	F	42	Y
527	Frank			

Missing/Non-Unique Primary Key

In Exhibit 27-4, our hypothetical data warehouse draws information from both Files "A" and "D":

- Data File "D" does not have the "Identifier" field, and in fact does not have a unique primary key. If we assume File "A" doesn't have the *First Name* field, then will you match record 523 with Fred Smith or with Sid Smith? Which File "D" record will you match record 528 with?
- At first glance, record 526 might seem an easy match. But can we really assume 536s Lee is the same person as File "D"s Tom Lee?
- The bottom line here is that the lack of a primary key can be a major obstacle to accessing the data you need, even when the data is present in the files themselves.

Exhibit 27-4. Example of primary key problems.

Data File "A"				
Identifier	**Last Name**	**Sex**	**Age**	**Smoker**
523	Smith	M	00	N
524	Jones	F	23	Y
526	Lee	M	42	
527	Frank		17	Y
528	Yu	M	00	N

Data File "D"				
Last Name	**First Name**	**Department**	**Yrs Employed**	**Salary**
Smith	Fred	40	2	50000
Smith	Sid	40	3	75000
Lee	Tom	30	3	60000
Yu	Robert	50	1	45000
Yu	Ted	30	6	80000

Non-Standardized and/or Multi-Element Fields

In Exhibit 27-5:

- Do all these people work for the same company? If there were 5,000 records to look at instead of just five, would you be able to identify the variations? Company names have not been standardized, and this is just a flavor of the possible result.
- In the *Name and Title* field there is an even worse lack of standards. Some titles are spelled out in full ("Vice President"), others are abbreviated ("Sr V.P.") Some names are accompanied by designations ("Mr."), others aren't. And do we include the department or division ("I.S."), or don't we?
- The positioning of the information in the *Name and Title* field is also inconsistent, with some last names first, some first names first, one title (marketing representative) preceding the name while the others follow the name, and so on.
- In fact, there are several individual elements contained within the *Name and Title* field, which is a large part of the problem. These elements include the First Name, Last Name, Initial (if any), Designation (e.g., Mr., Dr.), Title, the Department (e.g., I.S., Operations), and even in one case Degrees (B.Comm.)
- The individual elements within *Name and Title* are almost impossible to work with as they are now. Even a simple alphabetical report sorted by last name could be impractical. Clearly, separate fields for separate elements makes life much easier.

Exhibit 27-5. Example of non-standardized and multi-element fields.

Name and Title	Company
George Taylor, B. Comm., Vice President	DEC
Levi, Dr. Harold P. Sr V.P.	Digital Equipment
Marketing Representative Tim Hanlon	Digital
O'Leary Don, Operations	Digital Corporation
Mr. E. Rourke, Mgr I.S.	Dec Corp

Invalid Values

The constraints defining what constitutes a "Valid" value for any given field should be clearly defined within each database or file, as it will be different in every case, and can even change for the same field over time.

In Exhibit 27-6:

- If the only valid values for *Sex* are "M" or "F," then records 524 and 527 have invalid values. In the case of Jones, we know what was meant. In the case of Frank, however, the "N" might be a keystroke error, or it might mean "Not Known," or anything. Thus without the proper edits, coded values can easily become corrupted.
- Age should always be numeric, which makes Lee's age invalid as entered (what if we tried to add or subtract from it!) Also it is clear that Yu's age cannot be correct. The first problem illustrates that it is possible to get character data where numeric data is desired (and vice-versa), the second illustrates that without edits values can be entered outside of the acceptable range or domain for that field.
- Which Social Insurance Numbers are valid? Certainly Lee's and Yu's are not valid, and depending on our formatting rules Jones' may or may not be OK as is. Text fields are often the most difficult to validate, which is why when there is a choice (such as with SIN) it is generally better to look for alternatives.

Exhibit 27-6. Example of invalid values.

Identifier	Last Name	Sex	Age	SIN
523	Smith	M	00	143-476-987
524	Jones	Female	23	547198234
526	Lee	M	Forty-two	657-432-89
527	Frank	N	17	654-975-298
528	Yu	M	222	674-A27-897

Incorrect Values

In Exhibit 27-7, our hypothetical data warehouse draws information from both Files "D" and "E":

- Although the *Avg Salary* should have been the result of dividing the *Total Salary* by the *Total Staff*, somehow a mistake was made for Department 40, as 125000/2 = 62500, not 65000. Derived or calculated data can be in error within the same record, or file.
- Although the *Total* columns in File "E" were intended to sum the data of File "D," a calculation mistake was made in the *Total Years* (of experience) for Department 30 (should be 9, not 8). Thus derived or summary data in one file can also be incorrect based upon the data in a completely different file.
- These types of erroneous values can easily corrupt other results — For example, there may be a field in a third file containing the difference in average wages between men and women. Depending upon whether File "E" is used for source data (*Avg Salary*), the resulting calculation may be accurate, or not.

Exhibit 27-7. Example of incorrect values.

Data File "D"				
Last Name	First Name	Department	Yrs Employed	Salary
Smith	Fred	40	2	50000
Smith	Sid	40	3	75000
Lee	Tom	30	3	60000
Yu	Robert	50	1	45000
Yu	Ted	30	6	80000

Data File "E"				
Department	Total Years	Total Salary	Total Staff	Avg Salary
30	8	140000	2	70000
40	5	125000	2	65000
50	1	45000	1	45000

Referential Integrity Violations

Referential integrity is a constraint to ensure that relationships between rows of data exist, and in particular that one row of data will exist if another does (generally in different tables).

In Exhibit 27-8, our hypothetical data warehouse draws information from both Files "A" and "F":

- Although Data File "F" has *Identifier* as a key, unfortunately it is not unique, as can be seen from the two 523 rows. While under some circumstances this would boil down to a primary key issue (possibly combined with a missing, invalid, or redundant data issue), in this particular case it appears we should be consolidating the data in the two rows.
- There is no entry in File "F" corresponding to record 526 from File "A." This is a clear violation of referential integrity, as Lee must (at the very least) have a current-year salary recorded.
- Record 525 in File "F" has no corresponding entry in File "A," so just who is this a salary record for? This is an example of an "orphaned" record (does not have a "parent" record).

Exhibit 27-8. Example of referential integrity problems.

Data File "A"				
Identifier	**Last Name**	**Sex**	**Age**	**Smoker**
523	Smith	M	00	N
524	Jones	F	23	Y
526	Lee	M	42	
527	Frank		17	Y
528	Yu	M	00	N

Data File "F"				
Identifier	**Current Salary**	**Yr-1 Salary**	**Yr-2 Salary**	**Yr-3 Salary**
523	0	0	55000	45000
523	75000	65000	0	0
524	63000	58000	53000	50000
525	53500	48800	45000	42300
527	51800	47700	43500	40200
528	45000	45000	38500	37500

Special Case: Dates

Dates can be tricky to work with for a number of reasons:

- Many possible representations, including:
  — Multiple date formats (e.g., YYDDD, CCYYMMDD, DDMMYY)
  — Multiple internal storage options, depending on language, OS, etc.
  — Dates are often stored in pure numeric fields, or within text fields

- There are a large number of ways default or dummy dates have been established, some of which can be quite confusing:
  — Is 99365 (Dec 31, 1999) a dummy value, or a legitimate date?
  — How about 010101 (Jan 1, 2001)? 999999?
  — If your programs run across 000000 in the Year 2000, what action will they take? What action should they take?
- The Year 2000 itself will cause many of the existing dates and formats to become unacceptable, whereas up to now they may have worked just fine.
  — Two-digit years will need to be accompanied by two-digit century values, or
  — Some interim solution based (for example) on sliding date windows will need to be adopted, or
  — A business decision to accept the risks and potential consequences of inaccurate processing will need to be made by the enterprise.

Special Case: Addresses

Addresses can be complicated to work with because they routinely combine many of the issues we've described into just a few fields, with the resulting combination being particularly challenging to unravel and/or to correct. These problems can include:[4]

- No common customer key across records and files
- Multiple names within one field
- One name across two fields
- Name and address in same field
- Personal and Commercial names mixed
- Different addresses for the same customer
- Different names and spellings for same customer
- "Noisy" name and address domains
- Inconsistent use of special characters
- Multiple formats within disparate data files
- Legacy data buried and floating within free-form fields
- Multiple account numbers blocking a consolidated view
- Complex matching and consolidation
- Data values that stray from their descriptions and business rules.

CONCLUSION

Knowing your enemy is the first step towards defeating him. In this case the enemy is "bad" data, and this paper has illustrated several ways in which poor-quality data can be present in your files. The task for you, the reader, is to use the examples provided and apply them to your own specific systems and databases. Assess the severity of the situation, evaluate the cost-effectiveness or desirability of taking corrective action, and proceed accordingly.

Notes

1. Brethenoux, E. "Data Quality — The Missing Link in Data Mining." GartnerGroup (October 29, 1996).
2. Redman, T.C. The Impact of poor data quality on the typical enterprise. *Communications of the ACM* (February, 1998).
3. Strong, D.M., Lee Y.W., Wang R.Y. Data quality in context. *Communications of the ACM* (May, 1997).
4. "The Five Legacy Data Contaminants you will Encounter in your Warehouse Migration." White paper provided by *Vality Technology Incorporated*. Obtained from http://www. datawarehouse.com

Other helpful sources include:

Zimmer, M. Data conversion: doing it right the first time. *Handbook of Data Management 1999.* S. Purba, Ed. 1999. Auerbach Publications, Boca Raton, FL.

Customer Data Quality. White paper provided by *i.d.Centric*. Obtained from http://www. idcentric.com

Chapter 28
Referential Integrity for Database Design
Bonn-Oh Kim

MAINTAINING THE INTEGRITY OF DATA is one of the most critical issues involved in designing in database systems. In relational database systems, there are four common integrity constraints:

- The key constraint, which states that the values of a primary key must be unique, so there should be no duplicate primary key values.
- Entity integrity, which indicates that a primary key of a relation cannot take null values.
- Referential integrity, which is a constraint to ensure the existence of a tuple of a relation that is referenced by a tuple in another relation.
- Semantic integrity, which states that data in the database systems should be consistent or semantically correct.

A relational database is commonly considered to have referential integrity if there are no unmatched foreign key values. This definition is incomplete because attributes other than a foreign key also require data consistency with other relations. It is also limiting when designing an entity-relationship (E-R) model or relational model because referential integrity is indirectly represented via the foreign key concept.

This chapter discusses attribute referential integrity (ARI), an expanded concept that allows referential integrity to be specified on any attribute of a relation. It also explains the specifications of the new referential integrity constraint on the E-R and relational models. Methods of enforcing the referential integrity constraint are also suggested.

Discussion of the integrity issues is restricted to the relational model, although other data models such as the network or hierarchical model share the same concerns.

THE COMMON DEFINITION OF REFERENTIAL INTEGRITY

Referential integrity in the relational model is defined in various ways. Some definitions assert that to maintain referential integrity, the database must not contain any unmatched foreign key values; others assert that referential integrity is defined only between foreign and primary key relations. However, there is no theoretical reason to specify the referential integrity constraint only on the foreign key. Specifying referential integrity on any attribute of a relation should be possible.

In designing relational database systems, the E-R model can be used as a conceptual tool for specifying data requirements. This practice is widely accepted and supported by various computer-aided software engineering (CASE) tools.

In the E-R model, however, referential integrity is not explicitly represented, although it can be specified on a relationship among entity types. In the E-R model, referential integrity is implicitly represented on a relationship type between the participating entity types. It becomes explicit only after the E-R model is converted into the relational model. That is, referential integrity can be explicitly specified using structured query language (SQL) statements when creating tables.

LIMITS OF THE COMMON DEFINITION OF REFERENTIAL INTEGRITY

The commonly accepted definition of referential integrity is inadequate for representing the referential integrity constraint on attributes that are not a foreign key, as the following example illustrates.

A Sample Case: The Car Rental Company

A small car rental company wants to implement a database system for retaining information on vehicles and rental packages, represented by the objects VEHICLE and RENTAL_PACKAGE, respectively.

For VEHICLE, they would like to retain vehicle identification numbers (VehID#), makes (Make), and vehicle types (VehTypeName). Regarding RENTAL_PACKAGE, the package identification number (PackageID#), rates (Rate), and vehicle types (VehTypeName) need to be retained.

Information on vehicle types in both VEHICLE and RENTAL_PACKAGE should be consistent. RENTAL_PACKAGE is the primary source for information on the vehicle types. In other words, all the vehicle types shown in VEHICLE.VehTypeName should exist in RENTAL_PACKAGE.VehTypeName.

Exhibit 1 shows an E-R model for the above case. In the exhibit, the referential integrity constraint on VehTypeName between RENTAL_PACKAGE and VEHICLE is maintained by creating a new entity type (VEHICLE_TYPE) and two one-to-many relationships between VEHICLE_TYPE and RENTAL_PACKAGE, and VEHICLE_TYPE and VEHICLE.

Exhibit 2 shows a relational model converted from the E-R model in Exhibit 1. In these models, the referential integrity constraint of the vehicle

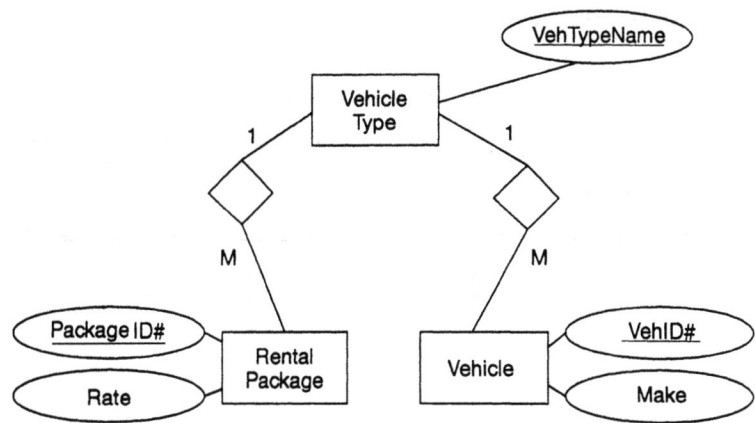

Exhibit 28-1. An example of a conventional E-R model.

type information is maintained by specifying a foreign key on VehTypeName on RENTAL_PACKAGE and VEHICLE, respectively.

Even though the models shown in Exhibits 1 and 2 appear to efficiently maintain referential integrity using the foreign keys, they actually incur unnecessary computational costs. That is, an entity type of VEHICLE_TYPE in Exhibit 1 and a relation of VEHICLE_TYPE in Exhibit 2 are created solely for maintaining and enforcing the referential integrity constraint of the vehicle type information.

Unless there is a need to retain more information (i.e., other attributes) in VEHICLE_TYPE, this way of implementing referential integrity is redundant and computationally expensive. Costs for creating and maintaining a unary relation (in the previous example, it is VEHICLE_TYPE) can be eliminated by directly defining the referential integrity between two relations (i.e., VEHICLE and RENTAL_PACKAGE). The following section discusses more direct and explicit representations of referential integrity to remedy this type of anomaly.

ATTRIBUTE REFERENTIAL INTEGRITY (ARI)

Referential integrity is an issue, not only in the context of referencing foreign keys and referenced primary keys. There is also a need to extend and generalize the concept of referential integrity beyond the current definition.

This section defines extended referential integrity and proposes a notation for the E-R model. Unlike the conventional definition of referential integrity, a foreign key is not a part of the definition. This expanded version of referential integrity is referred to as *attribute referential integrity*.

DATA INTEGRITY AND QUALITY

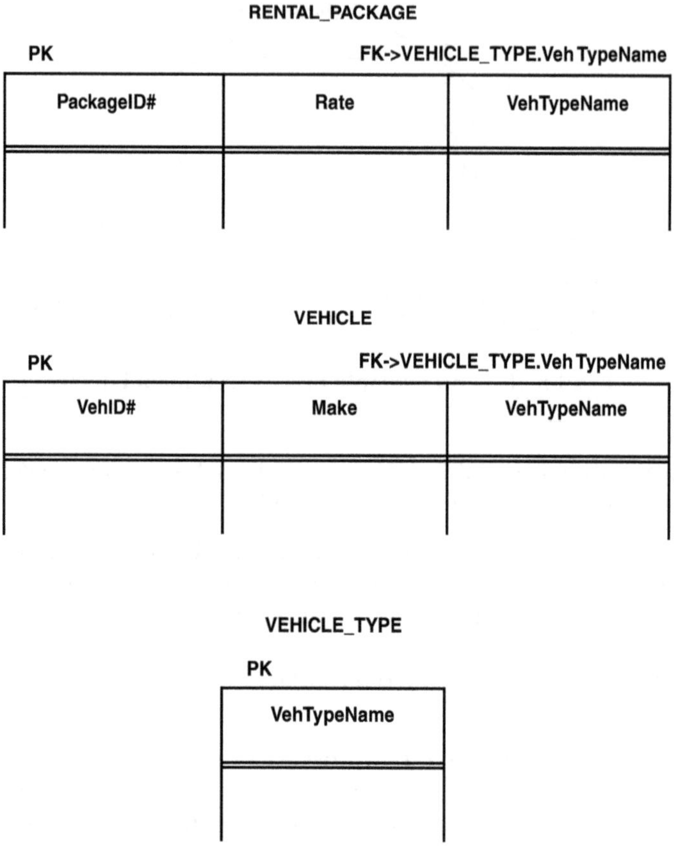

RENTAL_PACKAGE

PK   FK->VEHICLE_TYPE.Veh TypeName

PackageID#	Rate	VehTypeName

VEHICLE

PK   FK->VEHICLE_TYPE.Veh TypeName

VehID#	Make	VehTypeName

VEHICLE_TYPE

PK

VehTypeName

Exhibit 28-2. A relational model generated from the E-R model in Exhibit 11-1.

Attribute referential integrity ensures that a value appearing in the referencing attribute of one relation appears in the referenced attribute of the other relation, where these two relations are not necessarily distinct, and referencing or referenced attributes can be a combination of multiple attributes. The following section provides the formal definition.

The Formal Definition of Attribute Referential Integrity

r1 (R1) and r2 (R2) are relations of a schema R1 and R2, respectively. A subset α of R1 is a referencing attribute referring to a referenced attribute β in relation r2 if it is required that for every tuple t1 in r1, there must be a tuple t2 in r2 such that t1[α] = t2[β]. Requirements of this form are called the *attribute referential integrity constraint*. This can be written as $\prod \alpha_\alpha(r1)\prod_\alpha$

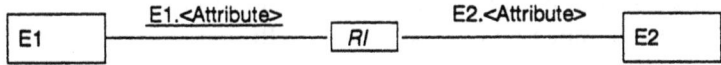

Exhibit 28-3. Proposed notation for attribute referential integrity.

(r2), where Π is a projection operation in the relational algebra. For an attribute referential integrity constraint to make sense, either $\alpha = \beta$ or α and β must be compatible sets of attributes.

The E-R Model

Exhibit 3 shows a proposed notation for attribute referential integrity on the E-R diagram. RI in the small rectangle indicates that the participating entity types E1 and E2 contain the attributes whose referential integrity should be maintained.

On the line between the RI rectangle and the participating entity types, the referential relationship is represented (i.e., the referencing or referenced attribute is specified), where an underlined attribute represents a referenced attribute. As defined, the referenced attribute contains a superset of all values appearing in the referencing attribute.

Exhibit 4 shows an example of a new E-R model for the previous example. Unlike the first example, there is no need to create a new entity type solely for representing the referential integrity constraint. On the entity types RENTAL_PACKAGE and VEHICLE, the vehicle type attribute (VehTypeName)

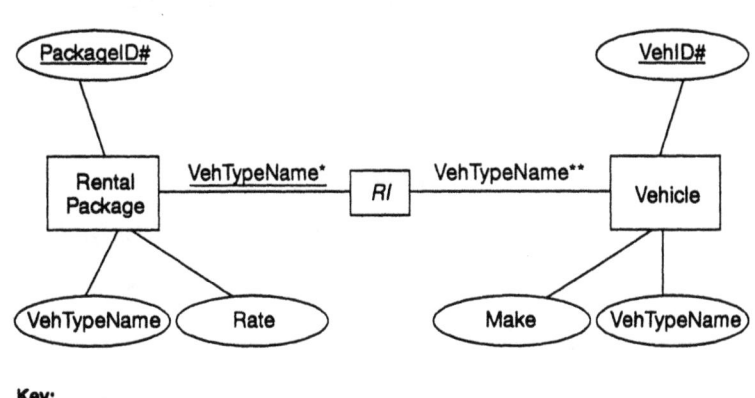

Key:
* Referenced attribute
** Referencing attribute

Exhibit 28-4. An example of the extended E-R model.

is included instead of separately creating an entity type VEHICLE_TYPE as in Exhibit 1. On the lines emanating from the RI rectangle, a referenced attribute (RENTAL_PACKAGE.VehTypeName), and a referencing attribute (VEHI-CLE.VehTypeName), are specified explicitly; whereas, in Exhibit 11-1 this referential integrity is implicitly represented via the foreign key concept.

The Relational Model

The ARI constraint can be directly represented on the referencing attribute of a relation by specifying a referenced attribute of the other relation. A notation representing this is:

ARI(<referencing attribute>) → <referenced attribute>

For example, Exhibit 5 shows a set of relations generated from the E-R model shown in Exhibit 4 . By specifying the attribute referential integrity constraint directly on VEHICLE.VehTypeName, there is no need to create a new relation of VEHICLE_TYPE because no foreign keys are involved to specify the referential integrity constraints as in Exhibit 2. Instead, the referential integrity constraint on VehTypeName can be directly and explicitly specified on the referencing attribute, VEHICLE.VehTypeName, referring to the referenced attribute, RENTAL_PACKAGE.VehTypeName.

RENTAL_PACKAGE

PK

TermID#	Rate	VehTypeName

VEHICLE

PK   ARI->RENTAL_PACKAGE.VehTypeName

VehID#	Make	VehTypeName

Exhibit 28-5. A relational model generated from the E-R model in Exhibit 11.4.

432

The conventional referential integrity constraint on the foreign key can be specified using SQL when defining a relation. In this relational model (or SQL based on it), there is no direct way of specifying the attribute referential integrity constraint. However, it can still be specified in the database designer's data dictionary and implemented using a procedural language. Future versions of SQL will include the specifications of the attribute referential integrity constraint on the non-foreign key attributes.

Following is the suggested syntax for specifying the ARI constraint:

```
CREATE TABLE <TableName>

    (<Attribute List> ; This attribute list must include
    the referencing attribute.

ATTRIBUTE REFERENTIAL INTEGRITY: <Referencing
Attribute>

REFERENCES <Referenced Attribute>)
```

The relational model shown in Exhibit 5 can be written as follows:

```
CREATE TABLE RENTAL_PACKAGE

    (TermID          #INT,

    RateDECIMAL      (3,1),

    VehTypeName      CHAR(20));

CREATE TABLE VEHICLE

    (VehID#          INT,

    Make             CHAR(20),

    VehTypeName      CHAR(20))

ATTRIBUTE REFERENTIAL INTEGRITY:

    (VehTypeName) REFERENCES RENTAL_PACKAGE
    (VehTypeName));
```

ENFORCING THE ARI CONSTRAINT

Enforcement of the referential integrity constraint on the foreign key can be conducted in three ways: restriction, cascading, and nullification (i.e., setting to a default value). The attribute referential integrity constraint can be enforced in a similar manner.

First, the delete or update operation on the referenced attribute can be restricted to the case where there are no matching values in the referencing attribute. Second, the delete or update operation on the referenced attribute cascades to delete or update the matching values in the referencing attribute. Finally, the referencing attribute value is set to null or a default value if a matching value in the referenced attribute is deleted or updated.

These three enforcement schemes are not, however, implemented in current database management systems (DBMSs). The attribute referential integrity constraint should be enforced by writing an application program on the database or attaching a procedure (i.e., trigger) to a referenced or referencing attribute.

SUMMARY

Specifying the attribute referential integrity has major advantages in database systems design. An E-R and relational model for a problem domain can be built compactly by dispensing with an entity type and a relation created solely for specifying the referential integrity constraint of a foreign key. Also, the referential integrity constraint of an attribute can be specified directly and explicitly without using foreign keys.

Using the attribute referential integrity concept, a referential semantic constraint can be explicitly represented in the E-R and relational models. In the current DBMS environment, this new integrity constraint can be implemented by writing an attached procedure on a referenced or referencing attribute. In the future, CASE tools and DBMSs will be able to represent the attribute referential integrity constraint.

Chapter 29
Data Quality: An Architectural Solution

Sriram Pidaparti

As CORPORATIONS EMBARK ON DATA WAREHOUSING EFFORTS, they are unearthing integrity and accuracy problems associated with the operational data. Another major challenge that has emerged is the integration of disparate operational data. This problem is characterized by inconsistent data models, disparate data structures, and poor quality of data that is fundamental to an organization — such as customer data, vendor data, and product data.

It is not uncommon to find a situation in which there are six different descriptions for the same product or four different data structures for customer name and address data. Such situations are common because of:

- Multiple transactional systems that have their own versions of the data stores (both structures and data), for example; different versions of customer data in order processing and billing systems.
- Package installations, business mergers, and acquisitions that incorporate new and different versions of data.
- Multiple instances of the same application used and extended differently in different geographies or departments.
- Different business units that have adopted their own definitions and standards for foundation databased on the belief that their business is different from the other business units.

Addressing these data quality issues at the enterprise architecture level is essential to finding an effective long-term solution. This chapter proposes that the corporate information factory be extended to include a construct called the foundation data store (FDS). The following sections define the foundation data store, describe how it fits into the corporate information factory, and suggest possible implementation approaches.

FDS OVERVIEW AND BENEFITS

Organizations have foundation data whether or not they design and implement it as a separate data store. Some organizations implement reference files/databases (also known in some companies as pillar databases, subject databases, and master databases) for foundation data. The foundation data store is a mechanism to formalize this practice into an architectural construct like the operational data store and data warehouse. The term *foundation data store* is used in this chapter because it appropriately reflects the architectural placement and importance of this data store.

The FDS contains relatively nonvolatile information that is traditionally found in a master file (e.g., customer data, vendor data, organization structures, and product data). This information can be viewed as a centrally maintained or authenticated data store that operational systems would use instead of creating and maintaining their own unique versions of the foundation data.

The information content of the FDS is based on standards for common data definitions, structures, and values. The commonality depends on how diverse an organization is; for example, the more diverse the organization, the less the commonality of data. An example of a high-level, entity-relationship (ER) diagram for a foundation data store is shown in Exhibit 1.

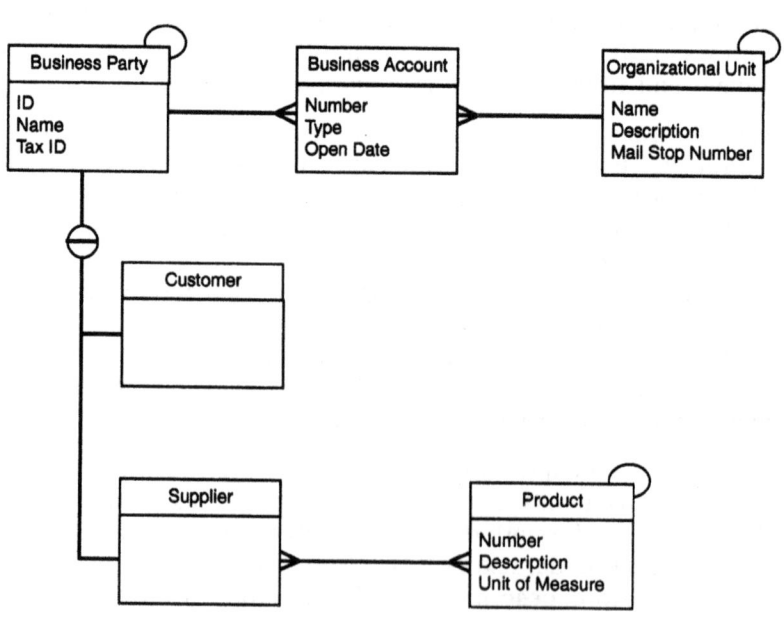

Exhibit 29-1. Sample ER diagram for foundation data store.

The FDS data model is only a part of the enterprisewide logical data model; otherwise, it would not contain all the entities and relationships. For example, an enterprise-level data model may have an associative entity called Order that connects the Customer and Product entities, but that entity belongs to the order processing transactional application data model rather than the foundation data model.

It is also possible that only certain attributes of an entity may belong to the FDS data model; for example, a business account balance does not necessarily have to be a foundation data attribute. The major entities of the foundation data store usually translate into dimensions in the informational processing world.

In addition to easier data integration and improved operational data quality, the foundation data store implementation offers the following benefits:

- Reduced effort in developing data warehousing applications because of easier integration of data.
- Better customer service because of data quality improvements.
- Cost savings because of centralized data maintenance and efficient external data vendor management.
- Improved decision-making because of more accurate information.
- More efficient transactional applications development because of reuse and avoidance of duplication of efforts.

FOUNDATION APPLICATION FRAMEWORK

The application or system that updates the foundation data store is primarily a data maintenance application. Therefore, it would not possess the complex processing logic of a transactional application such as an order processing system, production scheduling system, or trading system.

The framework shown in Exhibit 2 is a useful reference for administrators creating a new transactional application or reengineering a legacy ap-

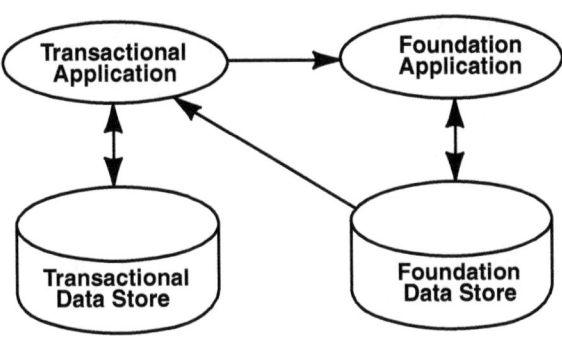

Exhibit 29-2. Framework for transactional and foundation applications.

	Transactional	Foundation
System Examples	Order processing system Billing system Equities trading system	Customer maintenance Product maintenance Vendor maintenance
Data Entity Examples	Order, invoice, shipment Payment, cash flow	Customer, product, vendor
Volatility	Very volatile	Relatively stable
Volume of Data	Large to very large	Small to large
Key Characteristic	Performance is most critical	Availability is most critical
Application Processing	Process/workflow intensive	Data intensive Mainly limited to table maintenance

Exhibit 29-3. Differences between transactional and foundation applications.

plication. Architectural separation of foundation and transactional applications along with their data stores is recommended. The demarcation of update responsibilities is very clear — the transactional application updates its transactional data and the foundation application updates the foundation data store. Access to the foundation data store is critical to the transactional application. Administrators usually need to be able to join data within two data stores. Technology solutions such as gateways make this possible, even across heterogeneous database environments.

The foundation application should be a centrally developed application deployed in a distributed fashion. The purpose of the interaction between foundation and transactional applications, as shown in Exhibit 2, is not only to give the transactional application user access to the foundation application, but to make it appear seamless to the user. For example, to create a new customer entry while taking an order, the customer service representative does not have to log into the foundation application. Exhibit 3 shows the differences between transactional and foundation applications.

FDS AND THE CORPORATE INFORMATION FACTORY

Inmon, Imhoff, and Battas, in their book *Building the Operational Data Store* (New York: John Wiley & Sons, Inc., 1995), proposed a common architecture called the *corporate information factory* that includes the operational data store (ODS), data warehouse, and legacy applications (see Exhibit 4). They describe the flow of data within the corporate information factory as follows:

1. Raw, detailed data is put into the corporate information factory by means of data capture, entry, and transaction interaction with the older legacy applications.

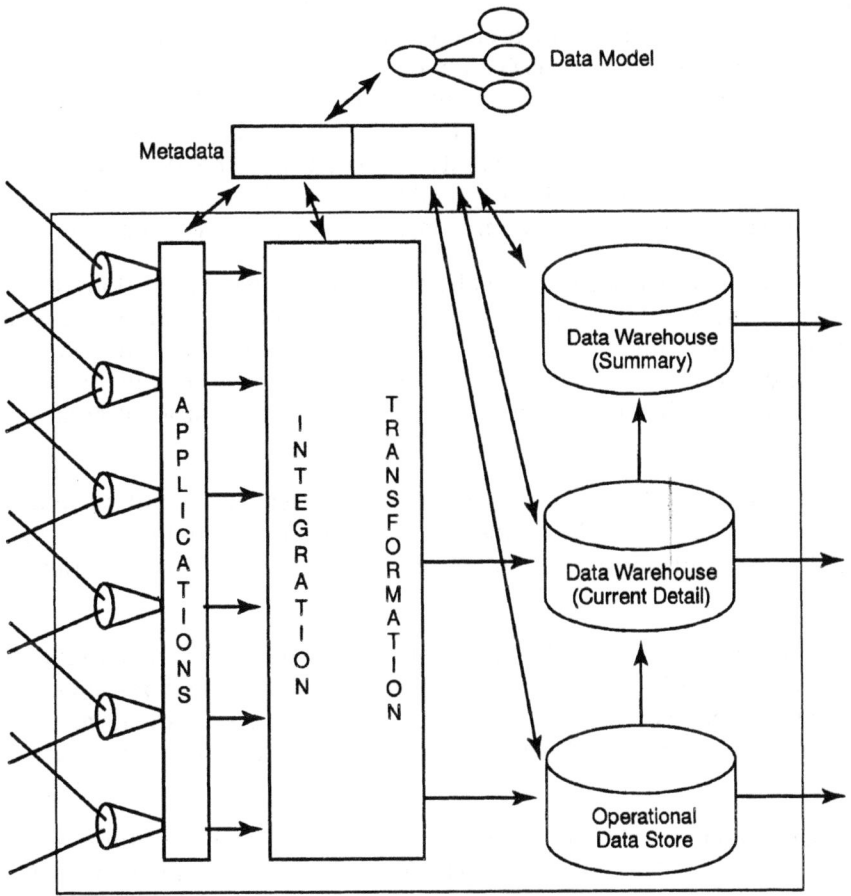

Data Model

Metadata

APPLICATIONS

INTEGRATION

TRANSFORMATION

Data Warehouse (Summary)

Data Warehouse (Current Detail)

Operational Data Store

Note: Bulk storage not shown.

SOURCE: Inmon, Imhoff, and Battas, *Building the Operational Data Store* (New York: John Wiley and Sons, Inc., 1995).

Exhibit 29-4. Corporate information factory.

2. The raw, detailed data are integrated and transformed and then passed into the operational data store or the current detail level of the data warehouse.

3. As the refined data passes out of the operational data store, this data goes into the current level of the data warehouse.

4. Once the refined data is summarized, the data passes from the current detail level of the warehouse into the summarized level of data in the data warehouse.

The corporate information factory can be extended to include the foundation data store as an integral architectural construct within the framework, as shown in Exhibit 5. The FDS functions as the official source (i.e., system of record) for an organization's foundation data. It maintains and supplies such data to transactional applications, the ODS, and data warehouse. The FDS also collects and conditions external data before that data can be used by an organization. The following sections discuss how the foundation data store relates to the other components of the corporate information factory.

Transactional Applications. Ideally, the transactional applications should not have their own versions of the foundation data, but should access the centrally maintained data store. In another possible configuration, the transactional application could make changes to a local copy of the central store, and the changes would be applied to the central store after authentication.

Integration and Transformation Layer. The implementation of the foundation data store makes the application component more integrated, which leads to a relatively simple and straightforward integration and transformation layer.

Operational Data Store. An ODS application usually uses the current version of the foundation data store. Therefore, ODS applications should be able to directly access the central foundation data store. An alternative is to replicate a subset of the central foundation data store into the ODS environment.

Data Warehouse. The major entities of the foundation data store become dimensions in a data warehouse. The data warehouse contains the historical snapshots of the foundation data store. The detail contained in the warehouse should reference the appropriate snapshot of the foundation data.

While doing comparative and trend analyses, users should be alerted if different summarization algorithms are used for different time periods. For example, if organizational hierarchy is one of the foundation data entities, the results of summarization would depend on the hierarchy that is used in the summarization process. Users should be given an option to view the history based on either the same hierarchy for all time periods or different hierarchies for different time periods.

Data Model. Design and implementation of the foundation data store should be based on a solid logical data model that is an integral part of an enterprise data model. In the case of foundation data, translation from the logical model to the physical design is relatively straightforward, unlike the

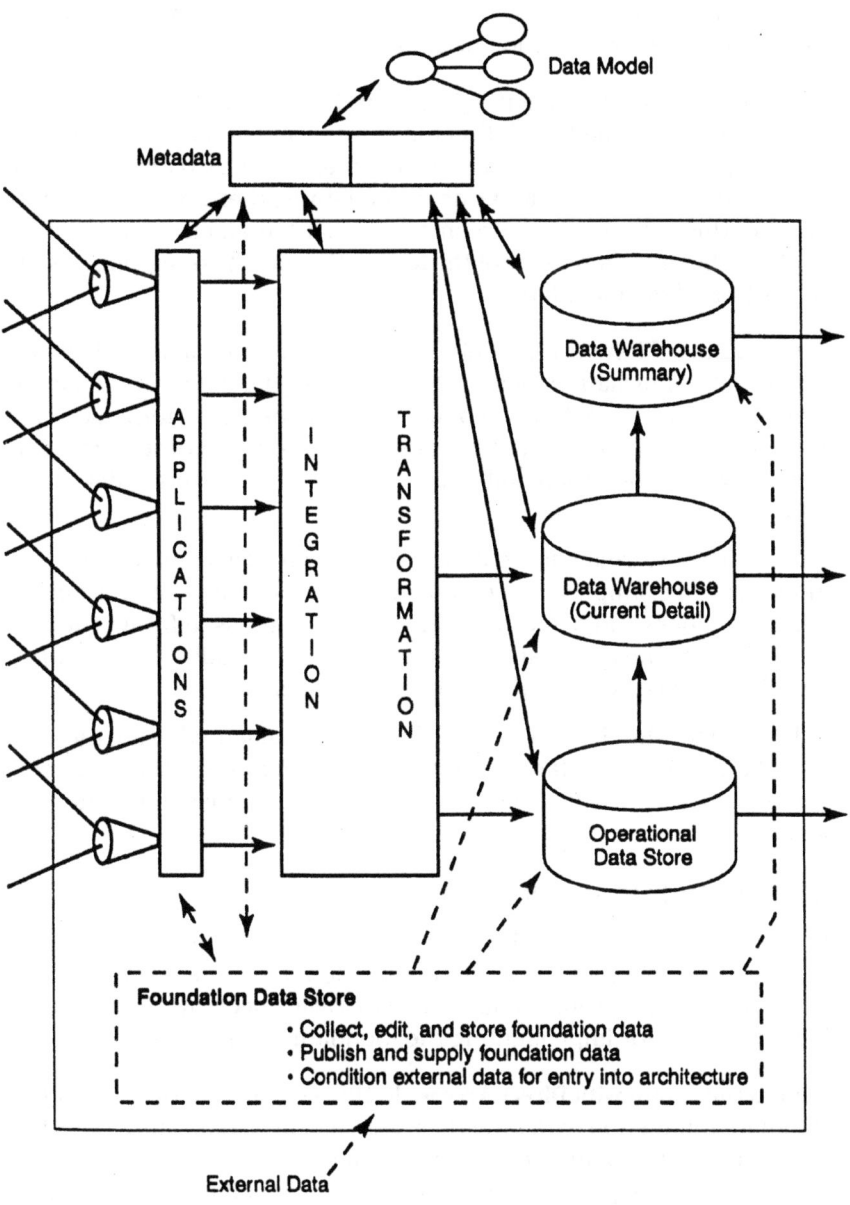

Metadata

Data Model

A
P
P
L
I
C
A
T
I
O
N
S

I
N
T
E
G
R
A
T
I
O
N

T
R
A
N
S
F
O
R
M
A
T
I
O
N

Data Warehouse
(Summary)

Data Warehouse
(Current Detail)

Operational
Data Store

Foundation Data Store
• Collect, edit, and store foundation data
• Publish and supply foundation data
• Condition external data for entry into architecture

External Data

Notes: Bulk storage not shown.

For the sake of clarity, the flows from external data
to the other components of the architecture are not shown.

Exhibit 29-5. FDS as a component of the corporate information factory.

441

design of data warehouse databases or transactional databases that may require a lot of denormalization or summarization.

Metadata. The metadata generated from the data model is used as a basis for the design of the foundation data store. One of the first steps in implementing a foundation data store is documenting the existing foundation data and developing the standards. Metadata is, therefore, a natural by-product of this process. In an organization that has an efficient FDS implementation, the data dictionary of the foundation database supplies a significant portion of the metadata.

External Data. There is a potential need for external data at all levels of the corporate information factory. For example, the data warehouse may contain external information to compare the historical performance of the organization with an external benchmark. Similarly, an order processing system may have electronic data interchange-related external data that is unique to that application.

Some of the external data that an organization uses is foundation information. Typical examples include financial product information from market data providers and name and address lists purchased from vendors. It is essential that the external data be conditioned to adhere to standards before that data is stored in the foundation data store.

External data should also be modeled and documented using the enterprise data model and metadata for it to be appropriately classified and integrated with the internal data in the data warehouse and other data stores.

FDS IMPLEMENTATION STRATEGIES

Implementing the foundation data store requires careful planning and commitment from all levels of an organization, including senior management, business user groups, and IS. The following sections discuss potential architectures for implementing the foundation data store.

Central Data Store with Direct Access. In this strategy, all the applications that require foundation data directly access a central data store. This technically simple solution provides the best data quality. However, it is vulnerable to performance problems and a single point of failure. In addition, this solution does not allow the creation of new foundation data or changes to be made to existing foundation data. Exhibit 6 shows a central data store with direct access.

Central Data Store with Replicated Copies. In this architecture, a subset of the central data store is replicated to allow local applications to access foundation data more rapidly. This solution provides better performance,

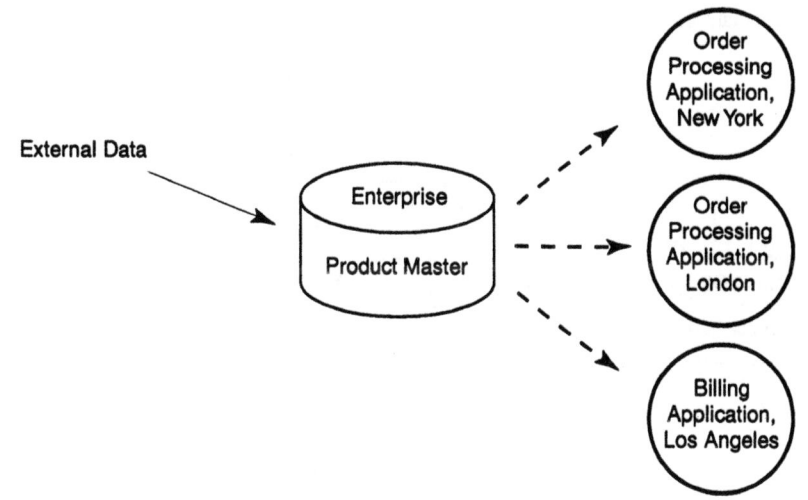

Exhibit 29-6. Central data store with direct access.

but is more complex technically and does not allow create and update functions to be performed. Exhibit 7 shows a central data store with replicated copies.

Central Authentication. Central authentication allows individual business units or local offices of an organization to create new foundation data and make changes to existing foundation data. The additions and changes

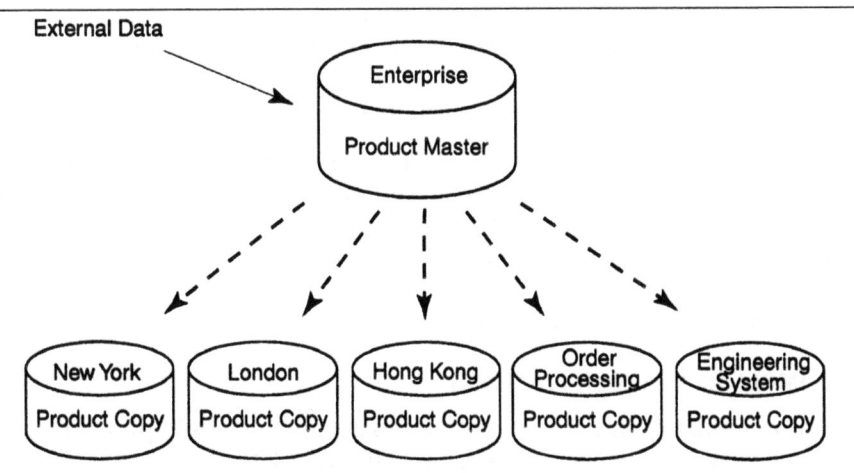

Exhibit 29-7. Central data store with replicated copies.

443

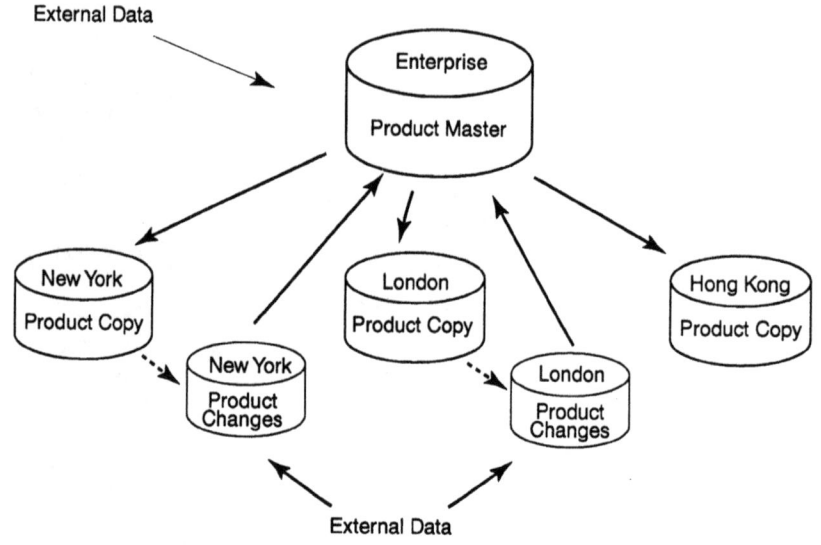

Exhibit 29-8. Central authentication.

are recorded locally in a database separate from the official replicated copy of the central store. The new and changed data is transferred to a central data store where the additions and changes are authenticated. The authenticated data are transmitted to all the users who requested it. This strategy reduces bottlenecks, but is the most complex technically. Central authentication is illustrated in Exhibit 8.

Consolidated Reference. This strategy is used primarily to implement consolidation standards for reporting and informational processing purposes (see Exhibit 9). Although it is a necessary step for data warehousing initiatives, it does not solve data quality problems in the operational systems.

Consolidated reference is a valid short-term strategy for organizations with urgent data warehousing project commitments and limited resources. A long-term solution to operational data problems, however, would be to implement the central foundation data store, which is the official source for the foundation data. Consolidated reference can be viewed as an intermediate step to implementing the foundation data store.

FDS IMPLEMENTATION FACTORS

An organization must choose the most appropriate implementation strategy based on its own context and situation. Although various factors influence FDS implementation in an organization, the solution depends on the organizational structure, number of database platforms, number of physical databases, number of geographic locations, and volume of data.

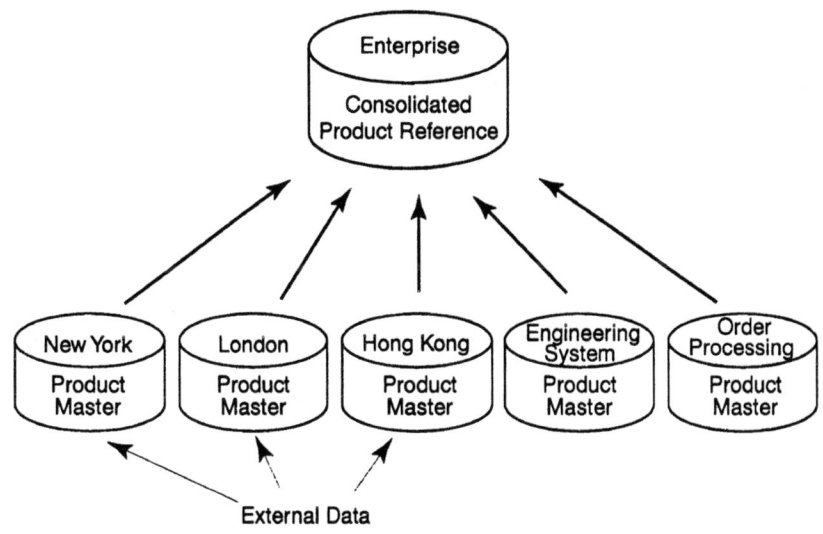

Exhibit 29-9. Consolidated reference.

An organization with a decentralized management philosophy may prefer central authentication rather than a central store with direct architecture, as with an organization that does not have a very strong WAN infrastructure. A company that has several transaction systems on various DBMS platforms requires a well-planned technical architecture involving gateways and message queues.

Although it is desirable, it is not necessary to have the same implementation strategy for all of the foundation data. For example, for a particular organization, a central data store with direct access may be more appropriate for vendor data, whereas central authentication may be more appropriate for customer data.

SUMMARY

A foundation data store should be chosen based on organizational structure, number of database platforms, number of physical databases, number of geographic locations, and volume of data. Although it is more manageable, it is not necessary to implement the same strategy for all the foundation data. For example, a central data store with direct access may be more appropriate for vendor data, whereas central authentication may be more appropriate for customer data.

The foundation data store is presented as an architectural component of the corporate information factory. Finding the appropriate implementation strategy and addressing the data quality issues are critical to the long-term success of an organization's data warehousing initiatives.

Chapter 30
Ensuring the Integrity of the Database
William E. Perry

A DATABASE IS A REPOSITORY FOR DATA, BOTH BETWEEN AND DURING PROCESSING. In traditional business systems, transactions constitute an organization's data. Data can include such items as product prices, messages, status of processing, and error or diagnostic data. Data can also be processing modules, or objects. When stored in a CASE technology environment, databases are often referred to as repositories. This chapter considers all of these database environments.

In a database environment, data management is separate from data processing. Data management functions that were performed by application programmers in non-database systems may now be performed by people independently of the application project team. Therefore, the application project team, and thus the user, must rely on the integrity of data managed by others.

A database environment in its simplest from (i.e., in which a single application or a series of closely related applications is the only user of the database) is not much more complex than an environment in which some other indexed access method is used. This type of environment may not pose any more integrity problems than a non-database environment.

A more sophisticated database, however, can involve multiple users. A loss of integrity in this type of database environment can be catastrophic to the organization as a whole.

The increased use of microcomputers has created a need for vast amounts of data. Much of that need is satisfied by downloading segments of data from corporate databases. This poses a new audit risk because many microcomputer users are unskilled in data integrity and methods of ensuring integrity.

The way that computer systems are constructed is changing radically. Computer-Aided Software Engineering (CASE) technology has introduced an engineering discipline into system development. One of the key concepts in

CASE is the repository, a database that stores system components (subroutines or modules) until they are assembled into programs. IBM's Application Development/Cycle (AD/Cycle) is a CASE methodology that improves the quality and productivity of new computer systems. Its repository contains subroutine and design specifications generated during system design; these are later tied together and implemented to build the system.

Data stored in a repository differs from that stored in a traditional database. Although the database typically contains business transaction data (e.g., accounts receivable and payroll), a repository contains data that defines data elements, processing modules, and their relationship. Despite this fundamental difference, the risks associated with repositories and traditional databases are similar; therefore, the concepts presented in this chapter are applicable to both. The chapter explains how to audit a traditional database and describes how the same approach can be used to audit a repository.

CUSTODIAL RESPONSIBILITY

Databases are usually managed by a database administration (DBA)function. In large organizations, this may be an independent group staffed by many individuals; in smaller organizations, however, the function may be performed on a part-time basis by a systems programmer or by computer operations personnel. In a client/server environment, the server facility has data management responsibility.

Although the DBA function is responsible for safeguarding the data delivered to the database, it cannot assume responsibility for the accuracy, completeness, and authorization of transaction that access the database. Thus, the responsibility for ensuring the integrity of a database is a custodial responsibility. This responsibility is fivefold:

- To safeguard the data delivered to the database.
- To protect the system from unauthorized access.
- To ensure that the database can be reconstructed in the event of technological problems.
- To establish an organization structure that provides necessary checks and balances.
- To provide and users with controls that ensure the integrity of actions and reports prepared using all or parts of a database.

DATABASE INTEGRITY CONCERNS

Databases involve several audit concerns. They include:

- *More reliance on integrity.* Users often do not enter their own data and thus rely on others for ensuring integrity. In addition, multiple users may access the same data element, thereby increasing the magnitude of problems should data integrity be lost.

- *Data managed independently of programs.* The people who use data are normally not those who manage it.
- *Complexity of database technology.* To be effective in designing, operating, and using databases requires different(sometimes higher-level) skills from those required for non-database technology.
- *Concurrent use of data.* Two or more users can access and use the same data item concurrently. Without proper controls, improper processing of data may occur.
- *Complexity of database structure.* There are three general types of data structure: hierarchical, network, and relational. All three types currently require a series of indexes and pointers that permit users to view the data from their individual perspectives. The more options available to the users, the greater the complexity of the data structure. In complex data structures, it is not uncommon for half of the total space allocated to the database to be used for indexes and pointers. The addition, deletion, and modification of data can literally require hundreds of these indexes and pointers to be changed. Improper data structure can thus make a database unresponsive to user needs.
- *Complexity of database recovery procedures.* The sophisticated use of databases can involve multiple users accessing, modifying, entering, and deleting data concurrently. Some of these processes are complex and occur in stages. Thus, at any time, various transactions are in various stages of processing, making database recovery difficult.
- The database environment can fail for a variety of reasons, including hardware failure, application system failure, operating system failure, database management system (DBMS) failure, loss of integrity of database, and operator failure. Adding to the complexity of recovery is the size of the database and the time required to recover. In large, sophisticated databases, recovery may require many hours or even days.
- *Extensiveness of backup data.* Databases can encompass many billions of bytes or characters of data. Stored on magnetic media, such data is often susceptible to loss. Thus, two factors must be considered in providing database backup. The first factor is the time frame in which recovery must occur. (The need for quick recovery requires frequent copies of the database.) The second factor to be considered is the volume of data in the database. (Large databases require large amounts of time to copy.)
- *Nonstandard DBMSs.* The file structure, access methods, and operating characteristics of DBMSs can vary from vendor to vendor and even within a single vendor. Because there is little uniformity between the operation of various databases, it is not always possible to pull out one database and plug in another. Individuals trained in one DBMS sometimes require additional training to deal effectively with another. The lack of standardization creates difficulties for auditors who have audit responsibilities for DBMSs from more than one vendor.

- *Segregation of new responsibilities.* Managing data independently of the application system requires a new organizational structure. In this reorganization, responsibilities should be adequately segregated to ensure the appropriate checks and balances in the database environment.
- *Increased privacy risk.* The concentration of personal data in a single place increases concern over privacy. This concern involved the accessibility of online database information and the fact that a greater concentration of data about an individual permits more analysis at a given time.
- *Increased security risk.* The greater concentration and accessibility of data in a database increases the need for security over that data. Although it is possible to intermix data of different security classifications, this should not be done in a way that gives users access to more data than they need.
- *Improper use of data by microcomputer users.* Improper processing of interpretation by microcomputer users of downloaded data from corporate databases can result in inconsistent reports, improper management actions, and misuse or loss of funds due to misinterpretation of data. For example, erroneously assuming that monthly data is weekly data and ordering inventory accordingly can result in the misuse or loss of funds.
- *Portability risk between multiple processing platforms.* In client/server environments and some CASE technology environments, various processing platforms are used (i.e., hardware and software from different vendors or different hardware and software from the same vendor). Data moving from one platform to another can be inadvertently altered unless adequate controls are in place. Field lengths may be changed, or data elements lost in movement.

THE DATABASE CONTROL ENVIRONMENT

Before conducting an internal control review, the auditor must understand the control environment in which the database operates. Such an understanding is also helpful in conducting tests of the control environment. The database control environment is illustrated in Exhibit 1.

The center of the control environment is the DBMS. As the name implies, it manages the environment, as opposed to reading and writing data to the database. In this management process, the DBMS interfaces with the operating system to perform the actual read and write instructions to the disk file. The users' interface to the DBMS is through their application program, or both. (Most DBMSs come with a query or interrogation language utility.)

There are three categories of database users. The first category includes users who need data for day-to-day operation. Second are the systems analysts and programmers who build and modify computer applications.

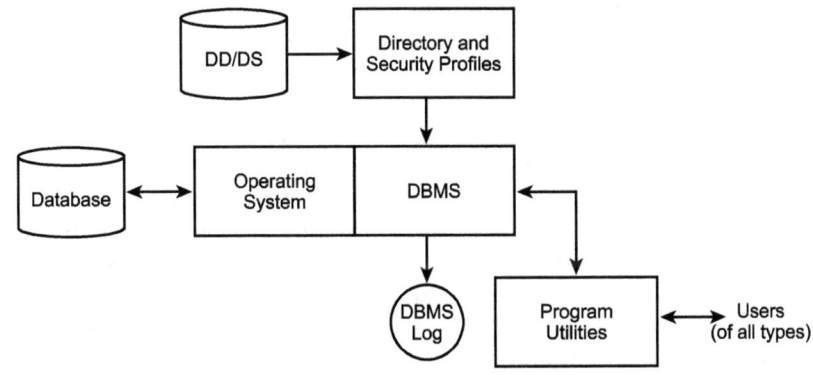

Exhibit 30-1. Database control environment.

Third are such technical personnel as operators, database administrators, and systems programmers who keep the database operational.

The DBMS has two components-the directory (including security profiles) and the DBMS log-that are crucial for control. The directory may be generated from a data dictionary or may be incorporated directly into the DBMS. The purpose of the directory is to match data on the database with user needs. The security profile defines access to data. The DBMS log is used to record events in the database; such information is used primarily for database recovery.

PLANNING CONSIDERATIONS

Because of the technical complexity of the database environment, the following considerations should be included in the audit planning process:

- *Use of database utilities.* Whether the use of database utilities affects the auditors independence in verifying the integrity of the database should be considered. These tools are quite powerful and can provide capabilities unavailable with other tools.
- *Depth of technical involvement by auditors.* Although databases are relatively easy to understand conceptually, they can be very complex technically. One organization estimated that a skilled systems analyst would require three months of training to use its database effectively. The auditor needs to develop a comparable level of skill to correctly assess the technical components of a database technology.
- *Database audit tools.* Of the database audit tools and the techniques available to auditors, the most prominent audit technique is called conversion to a flat file. With this technique, the data on the database is converted to a sequential file and then evaluated independently, through the use of audit software.

451

- *Skill of the auditor.* Effective auditing in a database environment requires skills that most auditors do not have. Unless the auditor understands database risks, concepts, and approaches, the auditor can neither access the adequacy of control nor obtain and evaluate the new forms of evidence available in a database environment. At a minimum, the auditor must understand the concepts of terminology of database technology.
- *Scope of the audit.* The database is normally independent of the applications that use that data. Thus, the database should be audited first, and the applications that use the data audited second. After the database is audited, conclusions of that audit can be applied to all of the application audits that follow. The integrity of the application normally depends on the adequacy of the controls in the database. Thus, without evaluating the database the auditor may not be able to conclude that controls in a specific application are effective.
- *Lack of standard audit approach.* There is no generally accepted approach to auditing databases; therefore, auditors must develop new audit approaches and identify audit tools that aid in the verification of database integrity.

AUDIT OBJECTIVES

The audit of database integrity is, in large part, an audit of the custodial responsibility of the group administering the database. Thus, the audit objectives addressing data integrity address he custodial aspects of data integrity. For example, accuracy deals with the ability to retain and return data accurately, as opposed to ensuring that the data included in the transaction is accurate from a business perspective, the following objectives are both operational and financial and encompass the concerns associated with ensuring database integrity.

Balancing of Data Items. The auditor should verify that the individual groupings of data balance to the control totals for those groupings. The data in a database belongs to, and is used by, multiple users, In the more sophisticated DBMSs, the access path to retrieve data can be created dynamically. Even with less sophisticated DBMSs, the DBA may not know how individual users use and control data. Therefore, the database controls may not maintain totals on groupings of data used by applications. The database system normally keeps counts of items in various paths and of total data items or segments within the database, which the auditor can use when balancing data items.

Accounting Period Cutoff Procedures. Because data need not be entered tin the database on the effective data of the transaction, the auditor should verify that data is properly identified so that users will include it in the proper accounting period. For example, in many banking systems the depositor can request the transmittal of funds up to 30 days before the execution date of that transaction. Those unexpected transactions that reside in the database must be properly handled.

Completeness of the Database. The auditor should endure that all data entered into the database is retrievable. The complexity of retrieving data depends on the data structure; that is, the more complex the structure, the greater the number of indexes and pointers required in the database. If these indexes or pointers are no constructed and used properly, the DBMS may inform a user that all of a grouping of data has been delivered, while in face it has not.

Recovery of the Database. The auditor should verify that the integrity of the database can be restored in the event of problems. This is one of the most complex tasks in a database, the organization may not have developed or practiced the procedures for some of them.

Reconstruction of Processing. The auditor should verify that the process creating the current status of data in the database can reconstructed. This audit objective is particularly important in an online environment because processing can occur in an interactive mode and involve multiple users. In such a situation, no single application may have an audit trail capable of reconstructing all of the processing.

Adequacy of Service Level. The auditor should verify that the service level provided by the database is adequate to meet the needs of all users. With multiple users vying for a single resource, one user may monopolize too large a segment of the database capacity. In addition, a poorly constructed data structure or an inadequate computer capacity can lead to the degradation of service levels. In a non-database environment, service usually degrades slowly. Because of the complexity of data structure in a database, environment, however, degradation can occur quickly. It is not uncommon, for example, for response rates to double in a few hours or days.

Access to Data is Restricted to Authorized Users. The auditor should verify that access to data is restricted to those individuals and programs authorized to access that data. Access controls should apply to end users, computer operators, DBAs, database technicians, vendor personnel, and other individuals using the system; no one should be excluded to access controls. These controls can be as restrictive as the organization or the DBMS permits.

The Data Definitions Are Complete. The auditor should verify that data Definitions are complete. Database users may depend on these definitions for the correct interpretation of the data. When the definitions do not contain the needed information, erroneous decisions may be made or the data may be modified in a manner unfamiliar to the other users of the data. From an audit prospective, a complete definition includes the name of the individual responsible for that data element, the data validation rules, where the data originates, who uses the data, and what individuals and programs have access to that element.

Security is Adequate. The auditor should verify that the security procedures are adequate to protect the data. Control over access to data is only one aspect of security. Adequate security includes protection from physical destruction, fraud, and embezzlement and from such acts of nature as floods.

Individual Privacy is Protected. The auditor should verify that procedures are adequate to ensure that data about individuals is protected according to law and good business practice and that the data is destroyed at the appropriate time. Privacy requirements are defined in federal and state laws. In addition, many organizations assume a moral obligation to protect information about their employees and customers.

Data Items Are Accurate. The auditor should verify that the accuracy of individual data items in the database is protected. With multiple users accessing data concurrently, two users can update the same data items concurrently, resulting in the loss of one of the updates. In addition, procedures should protect against loss of accuracy in the case of hardware or software failure.

Downloaded Data is Properly Utilized. The auditor should verify that there are controls, procedures, and training sessions to assist end users with ensuring the integrity of downloaded database data. Users should have a means to validate the integrity of data received and instructions for applying the validation method. End users should also be instructed on adequately protecting data from unauthorized access.

Assignment of Responsibilities is Adequate. The auditor should verify that no individual can cause and conceal a problem. Segregation of duties should be sufficient to prevent this.

Multiple platforms Are Compatible. The auditor should verify that the interfaces between platforms have been tested and are working. The risk of incompatible platforms is closely associated with the client/server environment. Software currently under development for managing client/server systems should deal with these problems better then today's software does. However, until these systems are available, the auditor should address the risk of incompatible platforms.

INTERNAL CONTROL REVIEW

To ensure that these objectives are met, the auditor should review internal controls and conduct tests on the basis of the results of this review.

These tests should indicate whether internal controls are effective and whether they verify the integrity of data within the database environment.

For the database integrity audit, the auditor should be concerned about the custodial, security, and organizational controls over the database. Exhibit 2 lists the internal control questions recommended for assessing these controls. The auditor can access the adequacy of internal controls by applying information obtained from these questions. If the controls are strong, the auditor can perform minimal tests. The assessment is therefore important in determining the scope of the audit tests.

AUDIT TESTS BY OBJECTIVE

After the adequacy of the internal controls have been assessed, the auditor must design tests to verify the integrity of the database and to help achieve the stated audit objectives. Descriptions of these test follow. (Exhibit 3 presents a check list of audit tests with there corresponding audit objectives.)

Review the Data Dictionary. Information about responsibility, verification, and access to key data elements must be extracted from the data dictionary. The auditor does this by examining data dictionary printouts or by analyzing the information in an automated data dictionary, using audit software. The test should then verify whether all needed information is contained in the data dictionary, whether it is correct, and whether the information can be used to perform other audit tests.

Verify the Database Pointers. It should be determined whether the pointers and indexes in the database are complete. Utility programs, commonly called database verifiers, can be used for this purpose, These verifiers, which may run for several hours or even days in large databases, verify that all access paths are complete and that all data in the database can be accessed by at least one data path.

Review the Vendor Documentation. DBMS vendors supply information on achievable ranges of performance for their DBMS as well as on operational and recovery procedures. This information can be used to assess actual service levels and to determine whether organizational recovery and operational procedures are adequate.

Test the Password Procedures. The auditor should verify that password procedures are adequate and that the procedures are enforced in the operating environment. When used, passwords can restrict data access to authorized individuals. By operating a terminal, the auditor can access the adequacy of password procedures by attempting to enter invalid passwords, by using valid passwords for invalid purposes, and by discovering passwords through repetitive attempts.

Exhibit 30-2. Internal control questionnaire.

Question Number	Question	Response Yes	No	NA	Comments
	Traditional Database Control Concerns				
1.	Is the database managed independently of the application programs that use that database?				
2.	Is the operation of the database organizationally separate from the administration of the database?				
3.	Is the definition of the data organizationally separate from the application systems that use that data?				
4.	Is the data policy of the organization established by senior management (i.e., normally done through a data administrator)?				
5.	Is one individual responsible for the accuracy, completeness, and authorization of each data item used in the database?				
6.	Is each programmer's knowledge of the database restricted to his or her view of the data in the database?				
7.	Is each data entity (called segments and elements in various DBMSs) password protected?				
8.	Is the database administration function restricted from accessing data in the database?				
9.	Are technical interface personnel restricted from accessing data in the database?				
10.	Can data be deleted only by application programs (i.e., administrative and technical personnel cannot delete data through procedures such as reorganization)?				
11.	Are counts of each different kind of data entity (e.g., segments, elements) maintained?				
12.	Is the completeness of the pointers verified immediately following each database reorganization?				
13.	Are database reorganization controls sufficient to ensure that the completeness and accuracy of data are maintained during the reorganization process?				
14.	Do users maintain independent control totals over data used in financial and other key applications?				
15.	Is sufficient backup data maintained to recover the database within the specified time interval?				

Exhibit 30-2. Internal control questionnaire. (*continued*)

Question Number	Question	Response Yes	No	NA	Comments
16.	Are standards established for database performance levels?				
17.	Can each data item be associated with the accounting period in which it belongs?				
18.	Is sufficient information maintained in the DBMS log to reconstruct transaction processing?				
19.	Is a log maintained of invalid attempts to access data and other potential security violations?				
20.	Is follow-up action taken on potential security and access violations?				
21.	Are mechanized tools (e.g., database modeling programs) used by the database administration function to aid in optimizing database performance and need satisfaction?				
22.	Is data defined in a data dictionary?				
23.	Is the data dictionary integrated into the DBMS so that the definitions and access rules can be enforced?				
24.	Are all adjustments to data in the database made through application systems, and not entered directly by technical or administrative personnel?				
25.	Are controls included with downloaded data to enable users to verify the integrity of the data?				
26.	Are end users trained in exercising data integrity controls, and do they use those procedures?				
27.	Are the CASE tools compatible?				
28.	Has a plan been developed to integrate all of the applications that will use the repository?				
29.	Do all of the applications using the repository employ the same definition for the data included in the repository?				
30.	Have standards been established to ensure that all hardware components to the client/server system are compatible?				
31.	Have standards been established to ensure that all software packages for the client/server system are compatible?				
32.	Are all databases under the control of the server facility?				
33.	If there are multiple databases, are common data definitions used throughout all of them?				
34.	Does the server facility perform the DBA function?				

Audit Objectives	Review Data Dictionary	Verify DB Pointers	Review Vendor Documentation	Test Password Procedures	Analyze DBMS (Query/Utilities)	Analyze DBMS Log	Analyze Security Log	Perform Disaster Test	Verify Details to External Control Totals	Review DB Operational Procedures	Count/Foot Database	Verify Ent-User Control over Downloaded Data	Platforms are Compatible
The detailed data items balance to the control totals.					✔				✔		✔		
Data is recorded in the proper accounting period.					✔								
The database is complete.		✔							✔		✔		
The database can be recovered.			✔					✔		✔			
Processing can be reconstructed.						✔	✔						
The service level is adequate.			✔				✔						
Access to data is restricted to authorized users.	✔			✔								✔	
The data definitions are complete.	✔											✔	
Security is adequate.				✔			✔			✔		✔	
Individual privacy is protected.							✔			✔		✔	
Data items are accurate.					✔					✔	✔	✔	
Assignment of responsibilities is adequate.	✔									✔		✔	
Downloaded data is properly utilized.												✔	
Verify that multiple platforms are compatible.													✔

Exhibit 30-3. Audit tests by objective.

Analyze the DBMS. Query languages and other utilities that search and print selected data items can help the auditor verify database integrity. query language contain most of the facilities found in an audit software language, and in some cases, they contain additional capabilities. The one audit software feature usually not found in query language is statistical sampling.

Analyze the DBMS Log. The DBMS log contains the equivalent of a motion picture of the activities occurring in a database operation. Although this log is typically used to help recover database operations, it also contains information that can be valuable for audit purposes. The auditor can use this information to reconstruct Transaction Processing as well as to analyze the types of activities that occur during database operations.

Analyze the Security Log. The security log records who accessed what item in the database. In addition, the security log should list the frequency and type of invalid accesses that were attempted. The auditor can sort this log by individuals accessing data to determine what data they accessed, or by key data items to determine who is accessing key data items. This information can be used for both security and privacy analyses.

Perform a Disaster Test. The auditor can simulate a disaster to verify whether operations personnel can recover the database and substantiate processing, should a real failure occur.

Verify Details to External Control Totals. Using the audit software or DBMS utilities, the auditor can accumulate the value of detailed data elements and then verify the accumulated total to that maintain independently by the application systems.

Review Database Operational Procedures. The auditor should determine whether the organization has procedures for designing, organizing, reorganizing, recovering, and performing other operational activities related to the database. The procedures should then be reviewed to determine if they are adequate and if actual procedures match the documented ones.

Verify Database Control Totals. A total of the number of data entities (e.g., segments or items)within the database should be accumulated and verified to the accounts maintained by the DBA. If the DBA function also maintains hash total or other accumulated totals, the auditor can verify those totals by using audit software or database utilities.

Verify End-User Control over Downloaded Data. The methods for controlling downloaded data should be determined, and the use of those controls at the end users' sites should be verified. The auditor should determine whether reports and decisions made by end users on the basis of downloaded data are consistent with the content of that data.

Verify Platform Compatibility. This test is normally too complex for the auditor to perform, but the auditor should verify that platform compatibility tests have be performed. The auditor can review the test plan and test results to verify compatibility.

Many audit software languages can not access a database. In such an environment, the auditor must either use database utilities or have the DBA function convert the database to a file that can be accessed by the auditor.

AUDITING A CASE TECHNOLOGY REPOSITORY

The major component of a CASE environment is the repository, where all common data and processing modules are stored. The upper CASE tools specify the attributes of the repository. The lower CASE tools use the repository to produce operational code. The repository is similar to the database in that the major components of the database are also components of the repository and the risks associated with loss of integrity are similar.

Traditional databases and repositories differ in the following ways:

- Databases contain transaction data, where as repositories contain data about the processing characteristics of data.
- Databases are subject to more financial risk, where- as repositories are subject to more processing integrity risks.
- Errors and manipulation of databases pose an immediate threat, whereas errors and manipulation in repositories can usually be detected during testing and evaluation.
- Improper or unauthorized processing is a greater risk in a repository then in a database because once such processing is introduced into the production environment, it can occur repeatedly over long periods of time.
- Repository problems can lead to loss of processing integrity, whereas database problems lead to loss of data integrity.

A CASE environment can be audited using the database integrity audit program presented in this chapter, but the auditor must follow the three-step process described in the following sections.

Step 1: Define Repository Characteristics

The auditor should first determine what type of database is used in the repository (i.e., traditional or unique database architecture). In addition, the auditor should establish the following:

- The repository's size.
- The indexing method used to access repository data.
- How the repository is secured.
- How the repository is used (i.e., is the primary purpose to reuse already developed capabilities throughout the organization?)
- Who generates, maintains, and controls the repository.

Step 2: Review the Database Integrity Program

On the basis of the information contained in step 1 and the similarities and differences between databases and repositories listed in this repository audit section, the audit program presented in this chapter should be reviewed to determine whether the differences between a database and a repository would alter the audit approach. For example, when reviewing the section on database integrity concerns, the auditor should evaluate each concern by asking the following questions:

- Is this concern affected by a difference between databases and repositories? For example, a concern regarding loss of data affects both databases and repositories, whereas a concern regarding the integrity of financial data involves only databases.

- Is this concern affected by the repository's architecture or structure? For example, if the architecture's naming or selection capabilities are limited in their ability to differentiate among program modules with similar names, an incorrect module may be selected.

Step 3: Modify the Audit Program

The audit program should be modified on the basis of conclusions drawn in step 2. For example, if a risk is increased because of a difference between databases and repositories, the audit program should be adjusted.

CASE software tools are usually available with repositories. The auditor may be able to use these tools to access the repository, list data contain in the repository, or perform repository analyses.

AUDITING CLIENT/SERVER DATABASES

Client/server databases and traditional databases are similar in the following ways:

- Both contain data.
- Both use the same basic storage and access approaches.
- Both contain indexes to access their data.
- Both are accessed by multiple users.

Traditional databases and client/server databases differ in the following ways:

- Transactions updating client/server databases move between multiple platforms, subjecting the data to greater processing integrity risks.
- Uses of data in a client/server system are less predictable then in a traditional database environment.
- Because testing methods in client/server systems are not as sophisticated as those in traditional database systems, they subject data integrity to more risks.
- Management of the server component of client/server systems may be less sophisticated in data processing technologies than in a traditional database environment.

A client/server environment can be audited using the database integrity audit program presented in this chapter, if the following four steps are added.

STEP 1: Define Client/Server Technology/Platforms

The auditor should determine the variety of platforms and technology used in a client/server environment. The more diverse the environment, the greater the risk to process integrity. Therefore, the auditor must establish the following regarding the client/server environment:

- The hardware vendors involved.
- The software vendors involved.
- An inventory of hardware platforms.
- An inventory of software systems.
- An assessment of the incompatibility of the platforms (The auditor may need to perform this step with the manager of the client/server environment.)

STEP 2: Review the Potential Usage of Data by Clients

The auditor should identify the potential uses of data in a client/server environment by talking to a representative number of system clients. The objective of this step is to determine the level of risk to data integrity due to the high-risk usage of data. To perform this step the auditor should ask the following questions:

- Will the client add, delete, or modify data before producing reports that may need to be reconciled by other uses of data from the same database?
- Is the client processing data with unproven software and then using the results to make business decisions?

STEP 3: Determine the Number of Databases in a Client/Server Environment

Having a single database in a client/server environment involves a similar risk relationship as with a traditional database. If additional databases exist, the auditor should ask the following questions:

- Will the databases be used independently or with one another? (If used together, the data integrity risk is increased.)
- Are the additional databases subsets of the main database? (If so, the auditor should explore how the integrity of the extracted database will be maintained.)

STEP 4: Modify the Audit Program

The audit program should be modified on the basis of conclusions drawn in steps 1 through 3. If multiple platforms pose additional risks, user processing characteristics pose additional risks, or multiple databases exist, the audit program should be adjusted.

The auditor should view himself or herself as a client of the client/server system. In this way, the auditor can perform the needed audit processing to evaluate the client/server risk.

RECOMMENDED COURSE OF ACTION

The proper functioning of application systems in a database environment depends on the ongoing integrity of the database. Without verifying the integrity of the database, the auditor may be unable to rely on data used by an application. It is therefore recommended that the auditor verify the integrity of the database before auditing individual applications that use that database. This chapter has provided an approach to verifying the integrity of the database, using several automated audit approaches.

Section VII
Distributed Databases, Portability, and Interoperability

THIS SECTION FOCUSES ON IMPLEMENTING AND MANAGING DISTRIBUTED DATABASES THAT SUPPORT A DIVERSE SET OF WEB-BASED APPLICATIONS. Web-based applications can support tightly coupled data sources or databases; however, they must also have the capability to support data in an expanded virtual architecture. This virtual environment can encompass logically and highly geographically separated data sources.

Portability and interoperability issues are also relevant to a discussion of distributed databases. Portability refers to the migration of solution components (e.g., business rules, data) to another architecture. Portability can be measured in terms of a degree of effort to complete the migration. Consequently, portability can be described as highly portable or not very portable, or some description in between. Highly portable applications are generally divided into components, layers, or tiers that rely on middleware (or APIs) to hide technical details. This allows them to be moved from one architecture platform to another with minmal work. Web-based applications should be designed to be highly portable.

Interoperability refers to an application's ability to support more than one architecture platform at the same time. Web-based applications must clearly be developed with this perspective in mind. A user can have any combination of hardware, browser, and operating system. Interoperability requires an application to be developed with this flexibility in mind. This section contains the following chapters.

Chapter 31, "Data Communications Requirements of Distributed Database Systems," identifies standard communication protocols for distributed databases. These protocols support a standard format for data transfer between a network of distributed databases.

Chapter 32, "Managing Multiple Databases Across Heterogeneous Hardware and Software Systems," describes procedures to connect disparate databases or data sources. This is an example of interoperable systems, and offers an alternative to porting applications to a new environment.

Chapter 33, "Providing Access to External Databases," describes standard interfaces and approaches for facilitating access to databases, especially those outside the boundary of an application.

Chapter 31
Data Communications Requirements of Distributed Database Systems

Dave Brueggen and Sooun Lee

THE FAST PACED, RAPIDLY CHANGING ENVIRONMENT OF INFORMATION RESOURCES HAS CAUSED COMPANIES TO LOOK BEYOND TRADITIONAL APPROACHES TO DATABASE MANAGEMENT. As companies move into new markets and geographic locations, it has become increasingly difficult and costly to access data in a traditional centralized database environment. Users need systems that transcend the usual barriers by making all information sources available to all users in real time.

Distributed databases represent a way of overcoming these barriers, by allowing access to databases in physically separate areas; corporations and their users are thus provided with a flexibility not attainable in centralized database environments. Key to distributed databases are the data communications facilities and networks that underlie them. They provide the vital link needed between users and databases in different locations.

DISTRIBUTED DATABASES

Large centralized computer systems have traditionally been the mainstay of large corporations. Centralized databases developed as a result of large-scale computing systems. Under this configuration, all processing, storage, and retrieval of data is done at a central site.

The growth of distributed databases has paralleled the growth of relational database technology. Because data is stored at separate sites, the need to move groups of data is critical. Relational technology is ideally suited for this task because queries can be expressed in a nonprocedural mathematical form that can be transformed into other equivalent queries.

0-8493-0882-8/00/$0.00+$.50
© 2001 by CRC Press LLC

Also, the ease of use of relational designs is better suited to the growing number of end users manipulating data.

Because distributed database management system (DBMS) technology is still in its youth, determining an exact definition of its composition and functions has been difficult. A distributed database has been described as a collection of data distributed over different computers of a computer network. Each site of the network has autonomous capabilities and can perform local applications. Each site also participates in the execution of at least one global application, which requires accessing data at several sites using a communications subsystem.

Key to this definition is the ideal that data be located in physically separate sites, close to the users who are actually manipulating the data. Users have access to data at each site through a communications network linking the sites. Managing the distributed database is a distributed DBMS, which monitors such functions as query optimization, concurrence control, and transaction handling.

Implementing Approaches

Three approaches can be used in implementing a distributed database, and the adoption of each approach presents a unique data communications requirement. The first approach is fragmentation, which deals with how a table is broken up and divided among different locations. Horizontal fragmentation breaks a table into rows, storing all fields (i.e., columns) within the table at a separate location but only a subset of its rows. Vertical fragmentation stores a subset of a table's column among different sites. Mixed fragmentation combines both vertical and horizontal fragmentation. With fragmentation, only site-specific data is stored at each location. If data is needed from other locations, the distributed DBMS retrieves it through a communications link.

The second approach is replication, which stores copies of the total file around the network. Replication achieves maximum availability as all data is stored in every location. It is also used to provide backup copies of data in case a particular network node fails.

The third approach — allocation — is a combination of replication and fragmentation. With allocation, records are stored at the nodes exhibiting the highest use of that data, thus maximizing local processing. The degree to which these three approaches are combined to form a distributed database structure is a critical factor in determining the data communications requirement for any distributed DBMS.

Another key feature of a distributed DBMS is the notion of transparency. Performance transparency means that a query can be made from any node in the distributed DBMS and runs with performance comparable to that of a centralized DBMS. Performance transparency depends on a distributed query optimizer — which finds a heuristically optimized plan to execute the command — and the network equipment over which data is transferred. This issue is also closely related to the determination of the data communications requirements of distributed DBMSs; three approaches to this issue are presented further in this chapter.

PROS AND CONS OF DISTRIBUTED DBMSS

Distributed DBMSs have several advantages over conventional DBMSs, including the following:

- A distributed DBMS reflects the changing structure of the organization. Organizations today are characterized by a decentralized structure spread across many geographic locations. The modular implementation of distributed databases allows data to change as the organization changes. Incremental growth and upgrades are made easier. Whereas changing the structure of the data in a centralized system necessitates taking down the system, adding new nodes to a distributed system has minimal impact.
- Because a majority of processing is done at the local level, faster response time can be achieved. Also, by locating data near its users, communications overhead can be reduced. In a centralized database environment, communications overhead is the key determinant of response time.
- In a distributed environment, greater reliability and availability can be achieved. In a centralized environment, failure at the central site would cause total system failure. If data is distributed, processing can continue after a failure, saving valuable time and money.
- In full replication mode, a Distributed Database System supports disaster recovery by locating data at physically different sites.
- With the workload distributed to different sites, the system workload becomes better balanced. Shifting the workload to a smaller system makes economic sense because computing on a mainframe can cost more than $100,000 per million instructions per second (MIPS).

Despite the numerous advantages of distributed database system, there are several problems inherent to having data located at multiple sites. Most of these problems stem from transparency issues discussed earlier. Among them are the following:

- Because data is no longer in a centralized environment, security becomes a greater issue. Security must be addressed consistently at each site.
- The high cost of communications equipment, dedicated lines, or network access needed to move a large amount of data between multiple sites.

- The complexity involved in managing transactions flowing between different sites.
- Communications delays caused by insufficient capacity during peak time loads.
- Managing data consistency and concurrency control between sites.

These obstacles explain why there are no true distributed database products. The remainder of this chapter addresses communications problems and requirements of distributed database system.

DATA COMMUNICATIONS REQUIREMENTS

A model of the decision-making steps for determining distributed database communications requirements is shown in Exhibit 1. The first step in this process is to choose the applications that the data communications networks will support. Determining a single set of communications requirements for all distributed DBMSs is difficult, because architectures and features depend on whether they are aimed at high-volume, online transaction environments or decision-support and revenue-generating applications. Each of these environments requires different network characteristics, depending on the number of distributed queries or updates made and the level of fragmentation and replication. Because of the complexity and difficulty of establishing the relationships between these factors and data communications requirements, detailed discussion of this matter is not provided in this chapter. Once the type of application has been identified, performance considerations can be evaluated.

PERFORMANCE CONSIDERATIONS

To provide an adequate level of performance, efficient response time is critical. Response time consists of processing time and transmission time. In a distributed environment, transmission time has a large impact on response time. The first step in evaluating network performance is to set response time objectives. If data is fully replicated or is fragmented at many sites requiring frequent accesses between sites, a low response time is difficult to achieve. For systems that have low fragmentation and do not replicate data fully, response time is not as critical. Once response time objectives have been determined, factors that directly affect performance (e.g., propagation delay, network capacity, media, and communications equipment) should be examined.

Propagation delay is perhaps the most significant obstacle to distributed DBMSs. Low delay is especially critical in systems that replicate data at different locations, or in situations in which a query is made that brings together fragments from several databases. Circuit propagation times of 20 milliseconds or more will cause throughput delays for data. With fully replicated systems, any update made at a local level must be propagated to

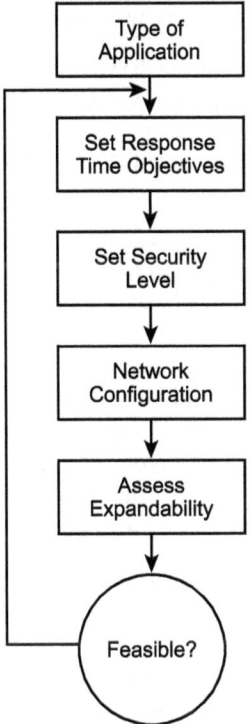

Exhibit 31-1. Steps for determining database communications requirements.

the central site to maintain the integrity of the database. If updates are made frequently, the network can become congested, further increasing response time.

If a network does not have the capacity relative to the amount of data it carries, the network will become congested, and response time will increase. When evaluating network capacity, the number of current locations over which data will be distributed should be considered. In addition, future locations should be accounted for as well as the number of users at each location. Users should be classified as to the type of data they can access. Those that have rights to update or query information at remote nodes will have a direct impact on the amount of traffic generated on the network. By identifying the type and frequency of remote queries made at each node in the network, the total network capacity can be determined.

The media used to transfer data affects both capacity and performance. A chart showing different media available for different network configurations appears in Exhibit 2. The choices here include twisted-pair, coaxial cable and fiber optics, as well as radiated signal from microwaves and broadcast signals from satellites. For high-end performance, fiber optics

Exhibit 31-2. Network media configurations.

	Configuration	Medium
Long Distance	Wide Area Networks	T1, T2, T3, T4 Lines
	Mainframe	Satellite
	Minicomputer	Microwave
	LANs	Leased Lines
		Switched Lines
Short Distance	Interconnected	Fiber Optics
	Local Area Networks	Coaxial Cable
	Twisted Pair	

should be employed. Fiber has the highest data rate (1,000M b/k and higher) and the lowest error rate; it also allows the greatest bandwidth. It is the most costly of the three, however. Coaxial cable has a high data rate (500M b/k and higher) but is bulky and easy to tap. twisted pair has the lowest data rate but is relatively cheap and not as bulky as coaxial cable.

Microwave transmission allows data to be transferred to locations at which running cable would normally be difficult (e.g., in crowded metropolitan areas). Microwave transmission rates can reach 45M b/s. Microwave transmission also has several disadvantages: microwave relay stations have a line of sight limitation of 30 miles and are susceptible to interference from other radio waves and weather. Satellites, while allowing significant flexibility in terms of location, introduce significant propagation delay because signals have to be relayed 22,300 miles above the earth.

Other media choices for long-distance communications include switched connections, leased lines, and high capacity T1, T2, T3, and T4 lines. Of these, only conditioned leased lines and high-capacity lines provide the performance and capacity needed for highly replicated or fragmented distributed DBMS applications. T1, T2, T3, and T4 lines have respective transfer rates of 1.5, 6.3, 46, and 281M b/s. Because these lines have a large bandwidth, they can be broken down into several lower-speed channels, increasing network capacity.

Other communications equipment (e.g., modems and multiplexers) can affect network performance. Multiplexers allow two or more simultaneous transmissions over a single communications circuit, thereby saving communications costs. Multiplexers can introduce delay, however, as they switch a circuit from a channel interface to an internodal link or bypass a circuit from one internodal link to another. A network with as few as five nodes may cause circuit delay if data must traverse many nodes to complete the transmission path. There are devices available (e.g., echo cancelers) to compensate for such delays. High-speed digital modems can also be used to guarantee maximum throughput on the line.

Another issue affecting network performance is compatibility among different vendors' networks. If network protocols are different, gateways must be used to translate messages across networks. Gateways handle any conversions necessary to go from one set of protocols to another, including message format conversion, address translation, and protocol conversion. Protocol conversion increases processing overhead, further reducing throughput and performance.

In a distributed environment, high availability requires that all necessary components be operational when they are needed. Availability is measured in Mean Time Between Failures and mean time between repair. The level of availability is guided by the level of replication and the number of nonlocal queries made. If data is manipulated on a local level and updates are done in batches, availability may not be a critical requirement. Data availability becomes an issue when data is not replicated between sites, and there are frequent queries or updates of nonlocal data. Maximum availability requires that data be fully replicated at all sites. In such a case, if a network node failed, processing could continue until the failed node is recovered.

SECURITY CONSIDERATIONS

In a distributed database environment, data becomes more vulnerable because it exists in more than one location and is transferred by a communications network. Data traveling over communications circuits is especially vulnerable to tampering. Areas in which data may be tampered with include the media itself and the hardware involved in transmitting the data.

At a local level, twisted-pair and coaxial cable are very easy to tap. Fiber, on the other hand, is very difficult to tap. When communicating over longer distances, microwave and satellite communications are very insecure. Because they employ broadcast media, anyone with the proper receiver can intercept the signals. Encryption can be used to ensure that if the data is intercepted, it will not be in a readable form. Although such precautions virtually guarantee security, there is a performance trade-off in the overhead required to first encrypt, then decrypt the data. In highly fragmented or fully replicated databases, the additional overhead may affect system performance.

The network manager must also take actions to protect the data communications equipment used to transfer the data. This includes actions to ensure the physical security of communications equipment (e.g., modems, encryption devices, earth stations for satellites or microwave, and any other key equipment).

NETWORK DESIGN CONSIDERATIONS

Distance is the major determinant of the network configuration chosen. Several configurations are available. If the distance between sites is short, a local area network (LAN) configuration can be used. The high throughput and low cost of LANs make them an attractive alternative for a communications network for distributed databases. Speeds of as high as 100M b/s are attainable on LANs using a fiber-optic backbone.

A single LAN often will not reflect the geographic distribution of an organization. One way of extending the distance over which a LAN may be used is to employ repeaters, which strengthen and relay messages across a network. The disadvantage of configurations that use repeaters is that as new nodes are added, network performance decreases.

Another way of extending the physical distance of a network is to use a bridge to connect two or more LANs. Unlike repeaters, bridges filter traffic between networks, keeping local traffic local while forwarding only traffic destined for other networks. In this configuration, data would be distributed between two or more LANs connected by a bridge.

If several LANs are involved, brouters may be used. Brouters — a type of smart bridge — not only filter data but perform routing functions as well. By deciding which route data will take through the network, brouters minimize traffic and increase throughput.

Employing any of the previously described devices allows network designers to extend the distance of a network. In essence, it enables them to create a Wide Area Network using several LANs. But this strategy could not be employed over extremely long distances such as between cities. In these situations, wide area network (WAN) using leased lines would be chosen. For maximum throughput, a network employing a high-speed service (e.g., T1, T2, T3, or T4) could be used. Because cost increases with performance, careful consideration should be paid to the level of service desired.

In a wide area network (WAN) configuration, leased T1 lines would act as a backbone for LANs at different physical locations. Using a LAN at each physically distinct site would provide cost and performance advantages, because most data would be manipulated at a local level. Accessing data on high-speed LANs allows maximum performance. Using a T1 line also allows voice to be run along with data, further increasing savings. Although performance does not match that of a LAN configuration, an acceptable level of throughput can be achieved.

NETWORK EXPANSION CONSIDERATION

As organizations grow and change, data requirements at new and existing sites also change. The communications networks and hardware that support distributed databases should be capable of changing along with the data they support. To assess possible changes in data communications requirements, network managers should have a thorough understanding of the company's business and strategic goals. Equipment bought today should provide a basis for the expanding technology of tomorrow.

Equipment based on Open Systems Interconnection (OSI) provides this flexibility. OSI represents a group of international architectural standards for data communications. It is meant to be a step toward truly open systems. A common OSI architecture enables networks built by different vendors and based on separate technologies to be connected across wide geographic areas. This will become more important as LANs play a larger role in processing at a local level. The effect of OSI on network expansibility will be a phasing out of equipment based on proprietary technology.

CONCLUSION

This chapter has focused on data communications issues of distributed databases. There are still many communications as well as other problems that must be addressed before true distributed databases can become reality. Key to this will be further technical advancement of high-speed communications on local and wide area networks.

In the near term, distributed DBMSs will be used only for decision support applications that are not highly fragmented or are fully replicated. Key to this will be to keep data access on a local basis, therefore taking advantage of savings in communications and computer resource costs. As communications technology continues to improve, distributed DBMSs will support more online, baseline applications. If distributed DBMSs are part of a company's long-term planning horizon, data managers should begin to analyze their current communications networks to avoid costly changes in the future.

Chapter 32

Managing Multiple Databases Across Heterogeneous Hardware and Software Systems

James Woods

A FUNCTIONAL BRIDGE BRINGS TRANSACTIONS FROM ONE DATABASE TO THE OTHERS, so that there is a single update path for all data items. The databases, though physically separated, thus function as one. This chapter reviews, step-by-step, the planning and design decisions related to the communications infrastructure and the designation of the database master. The techniques recommended will work with two or more separate databases.

THE GOAL: A SINGLE FUNCTIONAL DATABASE

Corporate IS management is often challenged when it finds that it must control multiple databases that may reside on separate and disparate systems. However, the cost of not harnessing these multiple databases into a coherent whole is very high.

First, there is the problem of data redundancy. The data that designates a single fact is represented multiple times in the organization. Apart from the obvious storage requirement considerations, there is the problem of inconsistent information. Because the databases each have their own update paths, the data items are likely to have conflicting values. Even if the updates pass along the same value to each data item, it will most likely not be in the same time frame. This leads to information that is out of sync with the other data items. However, more than just one data item is involved in this problem; the problem is widespread — probably tens or hundreds of data items. Some of those items will be used for critical business decisions.

When the information is summarized and reported to top management, conflicts in the information will become obvious, though it will not be obvious which specific data items differ, only that the information from one department does not square with another. Confidence levels in the integrity of all the databases will drop and the decision support results will be minimized.

Although a single, central database is preferable, the reality is that multiple databases exist. They come into existence for any number of reasons:

- *Independent purchases.* A user department buys and uses a separate system because it believes that is the best answer to its needs or that IS cannot address its informational requirements within an acceptable time frame.
- *Legacy systems.* The system has been in place for some time while IS attended to more urgent matters. Eventually, the need for some form of technical management of the data becomes evident.
- *Acquisitions.* The company has just acquired a new division that has its own database system.

All the problems cited can be avoided if the databases, although physically separate (and possibly residing on different hardware and software platforms), are made to function as a single database. In other words, the update path for one database is the update path for the others. This minimizes all the problems except for data redundancy. Exhibit 1 illustrates, from a user's perspective, how multiple databases can be physically separated yet conceptually linked together.

The remainder of this chapter addresses how to build the bridge from one database to another so that they function as one. Although the scenario described thus far considers two databases, more may be involved. The techniques suggested in this chapter will also work with multiple separate databases.

THE MANAGERIAL CHALLENGE

Although there are substantial technical considerations, the primary challenge is managerial. The reasons are threefold:

- *Departmental and functional areas will cross in the formation of the solution.* Without senior management involvement, turf lines may be drawn and the entire project risks becoming mired in political infighting.
- *The lack of detailed data definitions can cause the cost of the project to go up and the effectiveness of the solution to go down.* This activity is

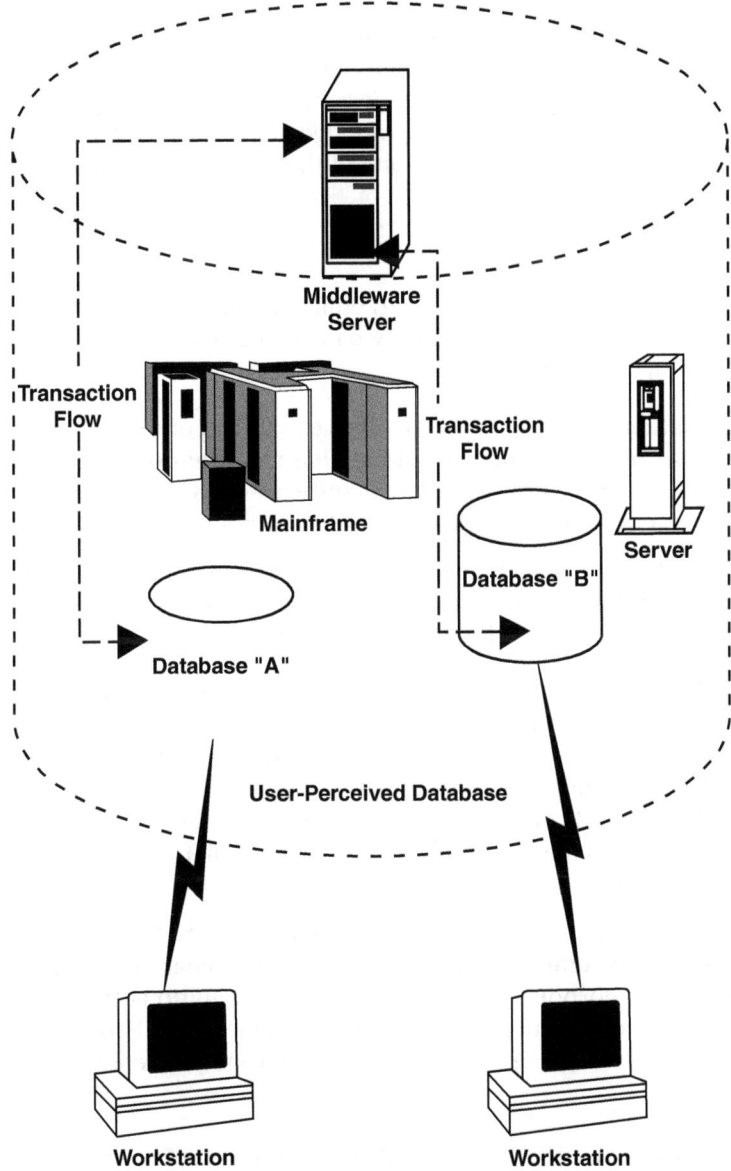

Exhibit 32-1. Physically separated but conceptually linked databases (user's perspective).

not primarily technical but rather managerial. The organization must decide who has what rights to the data and what, exactly, the data represents. As any database administrator can attest, this activity can be hampered by departmental disputes. Senior management support

481

and involvement can help minimize these disputes. An attempt to harness two (or more) databases without a serious data definition effort will produce enough confusion to endanger the entire project.
- *Because the ramifications of project failure can materially affect the organization's bottom line, senior management must be involved.* Management must recognize data as one of the most important assets of the organization.

EVALUATING ALTERNATIVES

Early in the project, alternatives to building a functional bridge might be evaluated. The alternatives fall into two main classes: incorporation versus consolidation of databases.

Incorporation. This technique involves expanding one database to cover the functions of the second. Data items that represent those not currently in the main database are added. New software must be created that provides the functional capabilities of the old system.

Although neither a small nor simple project (depending on the complexity of the replaced system), incorporation of databases does have the advantage that it eliminates the data redundancy problem.

Consolidation of Databases. This alternative involves combining the two databases on the same platform. The databases remain separate but reside on the same hardware and under the same software. A functional bridge must still be built, but the communications aspect is greatly simplified and replaced by internal computer processes. However, as in the incorporation technique, the replaced system's functional capabilities must be replaced with new software.

In each of the alternatives, considerations should be given to the current system load, the number of added users to the primary database, among other factors. Incorporation is technically less ambitious than consolidation and is therefore the preferred of the two methods. However, both of the alternatives are generally more expensive to implement than the functional bridge.

THE FUNCTIONAL BRIDGE SOLUTION: STEP BY STEP

A functional bridge is a method to bring transactions from one database to the other so that there is a single update path for all data items.

Planning the Functional Bridge

The first step, of course, is to plan the bridge. There is a great deal more documentation and planning work required than technical implementation effort in building the bridge. If inadequate planning is performed, it is almost certain that no amount of technical prowess will compensate. There are two main initiatives in the planning phase of the functional database bridge:

- *Evaluations of the existing communications infrastructure, available expertise, and commercial middleware.* These evaluations are primarily technical in nature, although management will have some influence because new capabilities may be indicated. For example, if the current communications infrastructure is deemed inadequate, management must approve the building of the new abilities.
- *Designations of master databases, update frequency, and data ownership.* These designations, although influenced by technical considerations, are primarily management decisions and represent points that could materially alter business practices.

Evaluating the Communications Infrastructure. An evaluation of the existing communications infrastructure should establish the following information:

- *The available communications paths between the databases.* This may be a LAN, WAN, T1 line, batch tape, queuing system, or any other way to move the information between systems.
- *The security of the communications paths.* Because there will now be transaction flow from one database to another, security considerations are important. For example, if the proposed communications channel is a T1 line from another city, it can be considered secure. If, however, the proposed channel is over a UNIX system that is connected to the Internet (without a firewall), then steps should be taken to qualify all incoming transactions before an update (or any other action, for that matter) is applied.
- *The stability of the communications paths.* How reliable is the channel? How often does it go down?
- *The current load on the communications channel.* Is there enough bandwidth to accommodate the new transaction load? This evaluation necessitates an estimate of transactions per unit time.
- *Failure analysis of the communications channel.* What are the ramifications if the communications carrier should fail? And how long can that failure continue before there are serious ramifications?
- *Communications protocols.* Some smaller (or older) systems do not natively possess modern communications protocols. The choices in this case are either to custom-build an interface to the database, perhaps with vendor assistance (though adding a modern communications protocol to a system can be complicated), or to drop back to a less ambitious communications protocol — for example, batch tape transfer instead of TCP/IP transfer.

Designation of the Database Master. With multiple databases, one database must be considered the master database. That is, the values of the data items in the master database are considered to be the final word. This designation as master, however, is on a data basis. For example, the database on the corporate mainframe may be considered the master for customer name and address, whereas the shipping database (which also contains the customer name and address) is considered the master for the shipping date for a customer's order.

In the determination of the master database, the following criteria should be considered:

- *Stability.* How stable is the database? How much maintenance is required?
- *Vendor support.* How effective is the vendor support for this system/database? How promptly does the vendor respond to support calls?
- *In-house expertise.* Who within the organization knows the system/database well enough to answer routine questions and solve performance problems?
- *Available consultant expertise.* If in-house expertise does not exist or should disappear, is there a pool of consultant expertise upon which to draw?
- *Volume of data.* What is the current volume of data on the database? If data fields are added, what are the ramifications?
- *User load on the host system.* How will the transactions affect system performance? Batch updates, for example, can almost negate online response while it is running. Again, an estimate of transaction volume should be made.

Making Critical Design Decisions

Overall Data Architecture. The design phase of the project should not be entirely end-user driven. The end-user maintains a biased view of the data and often requires data items that are actually derived information and not necessarily stored as fields (e.g., average customer order size). A database administrator (DBA) view, in this case, is required.

The DBA should obtain information about the data items in question from the end-users because they know the data. However, the DBA should then take that information and put it into the context of the overall database structure.

For example, the users tell the DBA about a data item called Last_Contact. The DBA is required to find out the context of this field (i.e., contact by whom?). This may be different from the data item in the main database with a similar name.

484

Database Linkage. A determination should be made of how tightly linked the databases are — that is to say, how often should the cross-communications occur? This factor is, of course, substantially affected by the communications infrastructure available.

Insofar as technically possible, this consideration should be made for business reasons. The update frequency of names and addresses will likely require no more than a batch update, whereas the update frequency of a medical chart location (in a hospital), for example, would require nothing less than a real-time update. The creation of additional communications ability may legitimately be driven by this design decision.

Data Item Map. The organizational aspects of generating the data definitions required for building the functional bridge were mentioned previously. The actual elements of that definition include:

- The name of the data field in both databases.
- The form of the field in both databases.
- The source of the data. It is not unusual for essentially different data to have the same or similar names across databases.
- The update path of the data. Where does the data originate? Is it original data (i.e., someone keys the data) or is it derived from other items in the database? Who audits the data, and who has the authority to change it?

Update Paths. The data definitions now become an essential ingredient to the design of the update paths. Without the documentation of the existing update paths for each data item involved, and the proposed new update paths, it will be impossible to create an effective transaction flow between the databases.

Changes in the update paths will undoubtedly change departmental procedures. This requires the full cooperation of that department's management and, of course, senior management support.

Communications Back-flow. In some cases, it will be necessary to send transactions in more than one direction. Communication in two or more directions is termed back-flow.

For example, names and addresses may originate in the corporate mainframe and it is considered the master. However, there could be a requirement that the data be updated from the satellite database at a customer service center, for example. Transactions must flow from the master to the satellite for a new customer, but also flow from the satellite to the master to ensure quality customer service. Again, these are not technical decisions (although they have technical ramifications). These decisions should be made for business reasons, not solely technical ones.

Ensuring Positive Feedback. No communications path is error free or fully functional 100% of the time. Good communications design requires a positive feedback. The receiving system must tell the sending system that the data it received was acceptable. This requirement is different from the standard acknowledgement/negative acknowledgement (ACK/NAK) code of a communications systems protocol. This feedback is done at the data application level. It must be known not only that all the bits of the address were received (ACK/NAK), but also that the customer number pointed to a real existing customer.

Sometimes, the positive feedback and the back-flow communications can be combined, thus reducing the network traffic. For example, a medical master database that is adding a new patient sends a transaction giving the demographic data. The satellite database reports back the local contract number assigned to the patient, which is added to the master as an alternative key. Thus, both functions are served with a single transaction.

Preventing Feedback Loops. Like a public address system, transaction systems can suffer from feedback. Transactions are usually triggered when a data field is updated. When this transaction arrives at the satellite database, the associated data field is updated as well. If the satellite database also reports changes in the data item, it would, of course, send a transaction to report the change just made. The result is a feedback loop that causes an endless chain of updates.

To avoid feedback loops, the triggering mechanisms must be aware of the source of the update. If the update came from the master database, the satellite database must recognize that fact and prohibit the change from being reported back to the master database.

Split Transactions. Occasionally, more than one satellite database must be updated with the same data from the master. It is good design to split the transaction rather than have the master send two transactions. Middleware software is usually used in this case. The transaction is received by the software and two (or more) transactions are forwarded to the satellite databases. The transactions may not have the same format (or even the same communications protocol), even though they convey the same information.

Recovery. What happens if the satellite system sends a transaction and the communications channel is down? An important feature of the network should be that it is not possible to lose a transaction. Therefore, if the communications channel is down, the software must wait and retry the transaction later. This recovery feature is inherent in some middleware and some gateways. Regardless of where it exists or whether it was bought or built, it must be present in the functional bridge in order to have a reliable communications path.

Common Ground: Constructing the Bridge

Once the above design has been completed, the actual bridge can be constructed. The bridge consists of five parts: transactions, transaction carriers, gateways, middleware, and trigger events.

Transactions. At this stage of design, the data required and the associated update paths should be fully known and documented. Because multiple transaction systems are not unusual, the content of the transactions must be designed so that coherent sets of information are available during update.

Transaction Carriers. This is the protocol of the transactions. There are multiple levels of the communications protocol. The low level is usually handled by the software employed (multiple communications protocols could be involved, however, and ways of translating one protocol to another may be required). On another level, the transaction must have ways of identifying itself to the update software. This requires transaction identification within the transaction itself. Routing information may also be required for complex environments.

Gateways. The software that actually updates the database is typically known as a gateway. In some database systems, the gateway comes as an internal part of the database itself; with others, it must be added.

In extreme cases, it will be necessary to create the gateway. This kind of gateway is likely to be the most difficult to test and debug, since all combinations of data must be tested — a substantial task even for a moderate set of transactions.

Middleware. Early in the project, evaluations of existing commercial middleware should be undertaken. There are several products on the market with a range of capabilities, some better than others. This software can substantially reduce the technical development and support aspect of the project and provide significantly better control than could (or would) be produced in-house.

Middleware is a generic name that refers to software that accepts and sends transactions between disparate clients and servers, usually converting communications protocols along the way. Better commercial versions also offer transaction reformatting and splitting.

Middleware is very effective in larger client/server systems, but requires an initial commitment to infrastructure creation. Middleware capabilities range from basic queuing support to full distributed computing management environments.

The control and statistical aspects of the software are also important because these features give the user the ability to shut down portions of the network and to keep track of the number, size, and status of the transactions.

Trigger Events. These are the events that cause a transaction to be sent or received. The trigger can be as simple as a command at the console (in the case of batch), the act of receiving a TCP/IP transaction, or a relational database stored procedure designed to act as a trigger.

In any case, the trigger event controls the flow of transactions over the bridge. Usually, these triggers must be coded in the database itself because it is at that point that the transaction originates.

SUMMARY

This chapter presents an overall view of the elements required for the successful management of multiple databases. The recommended approach is the construction of a functional bridge that allows the multiple databases to function as a single database.

The construction effort is largely one of management and definition, rather than a challenge of technical implementation. Failure to implement an integration strategy, such as a functional bridge, for databases that contain related data will inevitably result in inaccurate information being supplied to the organization's management.

Chapter 33
Providing Access to External Databases

Gilbert Held

OVER RECENT YEARS, AN INDUSTRY HAS ARISEN OF MORE THAN ONE HUNDRED FIRMS PROVIDING ACCESS TO COMPUTER-BASED INFORMATION. Some information providers, such as Down Jones, provide access to a wide range of financial information; others specialize in a narrow field of information, such as library book purchases, home construction permits, and department store sales. Thus, the first in developing an effective external information access strategy is to define an organization's external information needs. The next step is to select the appropriate external database sources.

DEFINING DATA NEEDS

In evaluating the data needs, the database manager should distinguish between user requests for information and for data. In this context, information is derived or formatted from raw data, and data is the raw element from which information is derived. Some users may need raw data that is not available internally; others may need only the derivations or formatted versions of data elements that are readily available internally.

New raw data elements should be acquired; however, information alone does not justify its purchase. Instead, if possible, existing data elements should be formulated to meet requests for information. For example, demographic reports are often aggregated into information as statistics are summarized and listed in categories (e.g., men or women of 25 to 49 years of age). If internal users decide they need more finite data concerning age brackets, their organization can comply by reformatting its existing data.

SELECTING EXTERNAL SOURCES

Although it may appear easy to decide which databases must be accessed to obtain required external information, providing this access in a cost-effective manner can be difficult. Several information providers may offer access to required information. One information access provider may

0-8493-0882-8/00/$0.00+$.50
© 2001 by CRC Press LLC

offer significant economic advantages over others. Many employees are unaware of this and select an information provider without researching sources. In addition, there may be significant differences in the manner in which the providers offer access to external database information. This fact can profoundly affect the ability of organizational personnel to work with the information they require.

When developing a list of external databases, the database manager will probably receive employee requests in the form of trademark or service-mark names. Those names may not represent the actual type of information organizational employees need to access, nor do they necessarily reveal whether equivalent information can be obtained from another information access provider. Thus, the trademark or servicemark name should be converted into a descriptive statement of the employee's information access requirement.

For example, an employee may request access to Dow Jones Information Services, but after questioning the employee, the database manager might determine that he or she actually needs to access a very limited amount of financial information, such as the relationship between German marks and US dollars over the past five years. This should be the database manager's external database access requirement. Specifically saying what is needed helps the manager locate alternative information access providers and avoid paying for unnecessary information.

After defining the necessary content of external databases, the database manager should try to locate alternative information providers. In doing so, the manager should note the method or methods by which information can be accessed. This is the third step in developing an effective strategy for accessing external database information.

INFORMATION ACCESS METHODS

Data communications is just one of several methods for accessing external databases that the database manager should consider. Other methods include optical and magnetic media distributed as part of a subscription service, as well as conventional printed media. Even when considering the use of data communications, the database manager should look at several access methods.

Some information access providers can be reached only through a direct-dial modem call. Such providers may not have a national toll-free number, and the database manager must include the cost of long-distance telephone communications, as well as the cost of accessing information, when evaluating these providers. Other providers that support modem access may be connected to such value-added carrier X.25 based packet transmission networks as SprintNet or BT Tymnet. Using those networks to

Exhibit 33-1. Database access methods.

- Communications facilities
- Direct-dial by means of a modem
- Access through a value-added-carrier
- Access through the Internet
- Mail, subscription service
- Printed media
- Magnetic media
- Optical media

access the resources of an information access provider can involve half or less of the cost of a conventional long-distance call made over the public, switched telephone network (the only cost being local phone connection time, plus any network fees).

Within the past two years, several information access providers have established connections to the Internet, providing a third communications method for accessing external information. In addition, thousands of anonymous File Transfer Protocol sites provide free access to a wealth of information, ranging from economic data from the Federal Reserve Bank of Boston to weather data provided by NASA.

Exhibit 1 lists database access methods that the database manager should consider before selecting a database or group of databases to support organizational information requirements. The relative access cost should be considered in negotiating contracts with information access providers.

UPDATE FREQUENCY

The key advantage of communications access over subscription access to external database information is in update frequency. When users access an external database through data communications, they can obtain immediate information updates to the database they are accessing. (Of course, it is important to note the time that elapses between real world changes and a service's database updates.) Database information received from a mailed subscription service, on the other hand, can be considerably aged. For example, it may take the information provider a week or more to master a CD-ROM disk, duplicate it, and mail new disks to subscribers. If updates are furnished on a monthly basis, users can be working with information that is five weeks old when they are just about to receive their next CD-ROM disk.

For certain applications, the frequency with which information being accessed is updated can be very important. However, for other applications, a monthly, quarterly, or semi-annual update is more than acceptable.

Thus, the database manager must consider the update frequency when considering using a particular database access method.

DATABASE ACCESS COST

Determining the type of external information that must be accessed involves considering alternative information providers. The database manager should review the information provided by external database vendors, along with their access or subscription fees, to determine the cost associated with each database. The one-time cost associated with any required hardware must also be considered; for example, the cost associated with a subscription to a database provided on CD-ROM disks includes the cost of a CD-ROM reader if one is not currently available. Similarly, if an employee requires access to a dial-in information access provider and does not have a modem, the cost of the modem should be considered.

ECONOMIZING ON MULTIPLE ACCESS REQUIREMENTS

The database manager can consider several techniques when more than one employee needs access to an external database. A local area network (LAN) can provide shared access to transmission and data storage facilities. The manager can negotiate usage-based contracts that reduce the cost of database access as access increases. Because many organizations have LANs, this chapter focuses on LAN solutions.

The first method to consider is accessing an external database over the switched telephone network. The conventional method for providing this access is to install a separate telephone line and modem for each user requiring use of the switched telephone network. Doing so can result in a one-time cost of $100 to $500for a modem and appropriate communications software, as well as a monthly business line telephone charge of $50 or more, not including the cost of long-distance charges.

Companies that have LANs can handle their various uses for the switched telephone network by connecting an asynchronous communications server to a group of modems called a modem pool. Exhibit 2 illustrates an Ethernet bus-based LAN in which each network user can access a modem from a five-modem modem pool. A workstation user can use any available modem and the business line that connects it to the switched telephone network.

The cost of an asynchronous communications server, including required hardware and software, is approximately $3,000 for a Novell NetWare-based network. Assuming the cost of each modem is$300, the total hardware and software cost to establish a five-modem modem pool is approximately $400. Assuming each business telephone line costs $50 per month, the monthly cost for the modem pool illustrated in Exhibit 2 is $250. If modems cost

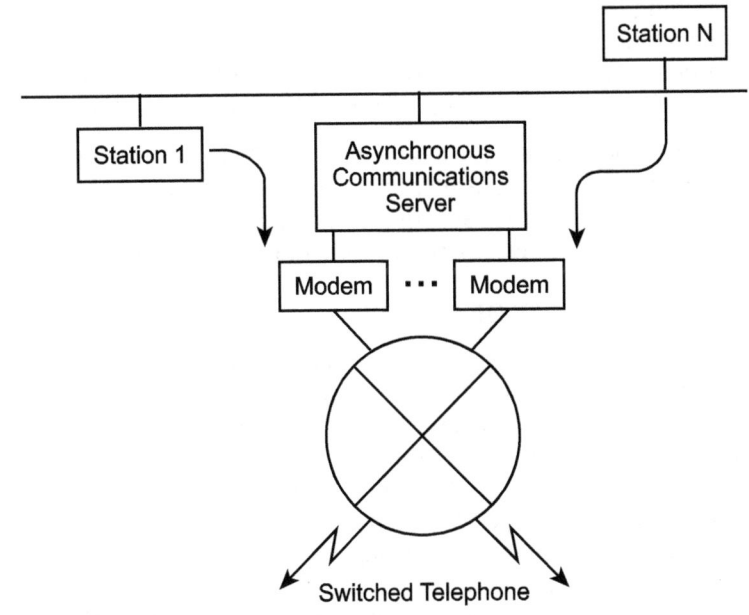

Exhibit 33-2. LAN access to a modem pool.

$300, communication software cost $100, and a business line costs $50 per month, the cost of providing ten employees individual modems, communications software, and business telephone lines is a one-time expenditure of$4,000 and a monthly recurring cost of $500. Of course, all ten employees with individual modems can simultaneously access the external database, whereas, only five could simultaneously access modems in a five-modem modem pool.

In most organizations, only a few employees usually access modems simultaneously. Thus, a 2:1 ratio of employees to modems in a modem pool is generally sufficient, and because a company saves each month on business lines by using a modem pool, the infrequent inconvenience of an employee not being able to access a modem immediately must be compared to this savings. Purchasing fax modems can provide users additional capabilities that further justify costs.

A method to reduce the cost of accessing external database information on subscription-based optical and magnetic media products involves adding a conventional or optical disk to the file server that enables multiple LAN users to access information. The following example illustrates the economics of disk access sharing. A database is available on a CD-ROM disk for $300 per year; a site license for a LAN costs $1000. If CD-ROM readers cost $400 and a Novell NetWare-compliant CD-ROM reader and software cost

$1000,providing ten employees with individual CD-ROM readers and individual subscriptions to the database runs $7000 for the first year and $3000 for subsequent years. In comparison, the use of a CD-ROM reader on a network costs $2000 for the first year and $1000 for subsequent years.

Both of these access techniques require a LAN, though neither by itself usually justifies the cost establishing a network. They can, however, be used with other organizational requirements, such as sending electronic mail and sharing files, to justify the establishment of a network.

RECOMMENDED COURSE OF ACTION

The database manager must consider many factors in developing a cost-effective strategy for providing employees access to external databases. First, the manager must determine employee requirements and alternative database providers. Using this information, the manager must consider different database access methods, matching each method against the frequency of database update that the employee requires. Once one or more access methods are identified, the manager should consider the cost associated with each access method. The database manager should conduct this study with the network administrator because the use of an existing LAN can considerably reduce the cost associated with using the switched telephone network or sharing access to a database stored on a CD-ROM disk.

Section VIII
Database Integration with the Internet and the Web

Section VIII
Database Integration with the Internet and the Web

SOLUTIONS IMPLEMENTED ON THE INTERNET OR THE WORLD WIDE WEB (WWW) GENERALLY REQUIRE CONNECTIVITY TO AN ASSORTMENT OF DISTRIBUTED DATABASES WITH AN EVER-EXPANDING SET OF BUSINESS AND TECHNICAL REQUIREMENTS. For the most part, database servers and their extensions can be viewed as encapsulated solutions that support traditional databased operations. However, significant new considerations must be evaluated to make databases operate optimally and securely on the Internet and with Internet-based development tools. This section contains the following chapters.

Chapter 34, "Developing Client/Server RDBMS Applications Using Java Servlets and JDBC," demonstrates how to develop and deploy a three-tier application using Java servlets on the Internet and the Web.

Chapter 35, "Building Database-enabled Web Applications with IDC," provides a substantial example for creating Web pages that are refreshed directly from live databases. This technique uses basic SQL statements and a minimal amount of HTML coding.

Chapter 36, "Integrating EDMSs and DBMSs," describes how to combine the strengths of a database management system and an electronic document management system to support rich and diverse information sources and datatypes, while supporting quick access and search capabilities offered by relational databases in distributed environments.

Chapter 37, "Database Management and the Internet: Developments and Challenges," examines considerations in managing databases over the Internet.

Chapter 34

Developing Client/Server RDBMS Applications Using Java Servlets and JDBC

Jonathan Held

CLIENT/SERVER COMPUTING IS BY NO MEANS A NOVEL CONCEPT; IT HAS BEEN AROUND NEARLY AS LONG AS THE COMPUTER. What is new, however, is how the rise of the World Wide Web (circa 1992) impacted this computing concept. Client/server computing, given this venue, has reached new ground and its popularity is indelibly tied to the astounding success that the Internet has seen. What makes the Web so attractive, in part, is the price — client software is free. Using Netscape's Communicator or Microsoft's Internet Explorer (or any other capable browser), one can get a multitude of information on virtually any subject. The information has to be stored somewhere, and, in most cases, it is kept in a relational database management system (RDBMS), with which the browser (translate as client) interacts.

What you'll need:

- Some prior knowledge of the Java programming language and Structured Query Language (SQL)
- Java Development Kit (JDK) 1.2
- Microsoft Access (MSACCESS)
- Sun's Servlet Software Development Kit (SDK)
- Web server software

If you think Web-based databases haven't caught on, you might want to reconsider. Consider the Web search sites (Lycos, Yahoo, Excite, Metacrawler,

Webcrawler, or Hotbot, to name a few); where do you think the "hits" come from?

If you're as much of an Internet junkie as I am, you may even go so far as to check online to see what movies are playing in your local area. Two online sites offer such information: http://www.movielink.com and http://www.moviefinder.com. I enter my zip code, click the mouse a couple of times, and I know what movies are playing at what theaters and their show times. Why pick up the phone, call the theater, and get a recording that you can barely hear? If you would rather stay at home and park yourself in front of the couch with a bag of potato chips, try http://www.tvguide.com and you can choose the television listings available by cable company. So, if you were purchasing the Sunday paper just for the *TV Week* magazine that came with it, save yourself some money and cancel your subscription.

These examples all have several things in common. The first is that the Web browser is the client application. As a developer, you can now breathe a sigh of relief knowing that you can completely concentrate your programming efforts on the server-side interface to the data repository.

So how does it all work? Well, the short (and extremely simplified) answer is that the client, you and your browser, initiate a process that somehow interacts with the back-end database. This process is also responsible for returning content back to the browser, although what it returns may vary on what action was being performed. If you are merely submitting personal information about yourself or making an entry into a guest book, the response might simply consist of a confirmation that the information was successfully entered into the database.

As you can probably well imagine, there are a number of technologies available today that would allow us to accomplish such tasks. We could opt to adopt Common Gateway Interface (CGI) scripts, but this option is replete with security risks, making it an unattractive solution to even experienced programmers. Active Server Pages (ASP), a Microsoft technology designed to operate in conjunction with that company's Internet Information Server (IIS) 4.0, is another possibility, but it locks us into an operating system and a Web server that our Internet service provider (ISP) might not be using. Of course, there are a number of other options available, but perhaps one of the better but less explored ones is made possible by Java servlets and JDBC™.

THE JAVA INCENTIVE

There are two key requirements for database programmers:

- They must have intimate knowledge of the language construct used to manipulate databases.

- They need to be cognizant of what means are available for invoking these constructs from external applications.

Of course, the syntax for performing the former task is accomplished by a data query language that is now universal across different computer systems — SQL. SQL is neither difficult to learn nor use; rather, it is the means of using SQL in programs that, until recently, presented the greater challenge.

At first, many database applications were developed by making Open Database Connectivity (ODBC) Application Programming Interface (API) calls. But despite all that Microsoft's ODBC allowed you to do, it wasn't without its own problems. Chief among these were the following:

- ODBC was written exclusively in the C programming language, so there was no concept of objects or methods. The logical organization that is intrinsic to Object Oriented Programming (OOP) was nowhere to be found, resulting in a great deal of frustration when you were trying to find the right procedure or function to call.
- The API was extremely large, hard to follow, and required a fair amount of knowledge on the part of the programmer.

These shortcomings were noted and Microsoft proceeded to create several object models that programmers could use instead. These new collections of objects and methods were ODBC wrappers; they encapsulated calls into the ODBC API and hid the implementation details from the programmer. They exist today in the form of Data Access Objects (DAO), Remote Data Objects (RDO), and the more recent ActiveX Data Objects (ADO), as illustrated in Exhibit 34-1.

Then came Sun Microsystems and the rise of Java. Java made many new promises, but what made it so attractive was that it was designed to offer

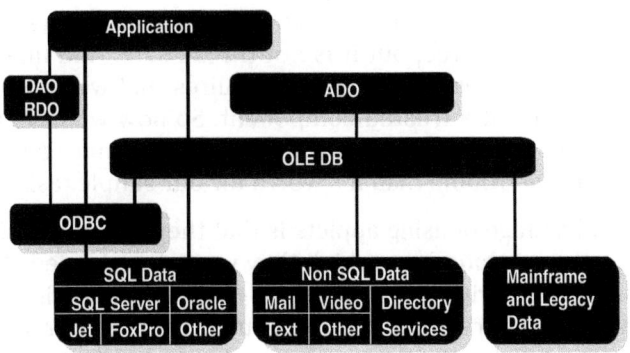

Exhibit 34-1. Comparison of ADO, DAO, and RDO.

a secure (or more secure) programming environment and could run on any platform regardless of the operating system being used. Now, if one could create a Java database application, the days of porting programs from one machine to another were all but gone. The only problem was that Java, like all new things, was extremely immature and no part of the core language had database-enabled applications. That shortcoming was noticed and fixed with the subsequent release of the *java.sql* package, which contains the JDBC object model. The JDBC API became the mechanism by which programmers bridged the gap between their applications and databases. It defines a number of Java classes that allow programmers to issue SQL statements and process the results, dynamically learn about a database's schema etc. It is by far one of the easier to understand object models, and it is nearly effortless to incorporate it into Java applications.

THE PROJECT

So what is it that we're going to set out to do? Let's suppose we wanted to create a fortune/quotation server that interacts with a Microsoft Access database and returns an entry and five lucky, random numbers back to the client's browser. We're going to create this application and support this functionality using Java and JDBC, but one more thing is needed that requires us to make some development decisions.

We could create an applet that is downloaded by the browser and provides a user interface enabling information retrieval from the database. However, this solution has some notable drawbacks. First and foremost, to use an applet and interact with a database requires a JDBC driver. There are many types of commercially available drivers, but they are prohibitively expensive and a project of this scope does not justify the expense. Another disadvantage to using these drivers is that they typically consist of a large number of class files. The more files that the browser has to download over a slow connection, the more irate clients will get at using the system, eventually abandoning it if it becomes to burdensome (i.e., time-consuming) to use. We could opt to use Sun Microsystem's JDBC-ODBC bridge, which is free, but it is not thread-safe. And unfortunately, incorporating this driver into an applet requires that we take some additional steps to make it a trusted component. So now we have to explore how we can manipulate the browser's built-in security manager so it works, and this is far more trouble than it's worth for our simple task.

A final disadvantage of using applets is that they can only make connections back to the machine from which they were downloaded. This means that if we use a JDBC driver, the database it communicates with must be co-located with the Web server. It is possible to use a proxy server to circumvent this restriction, but, short of doing this, we should see if an easier solution exists (after all, why make more work for ourselves than is necessary?)

The solution we'll use that enables us to get around all of these potential pitfalls is the Java servlet. The servlet concept was first introduced in April of 1997, in conjunction with the first all-Java Web server. Servlets are protocol and platform independent server-side components. You can think of them as an applet for a server. They are almost identical to their CGI counterparts, and they can do anything that CGI can do. But servlets differ in several ways: they are easier to write than CGI programs/scripts written in C++ or PERL, and they are noticeably faster and much safer. There are four important reasons why we'll turn our attention to the servlet solution:

- *Performance:* Servlets do not require a new process for each request (CGI does, and if a server fails to load-balance or put a limit on the number of concurrent requests, it can easily be brought to its knees). The servlet *init()* method allows programmers to perform resource-intensive operations common to all servlet invocations once at startup. For example, by having the *init()* method establish a database connection, this process can be done once. Consequently, the slowest performance occurs the very first time the servlet is executed; subsequent invocations occur much more rapidly.
- *Portability:* Because Java is platform independent, so are servlets. We can move our compiled servlet code from one machine to another without having to recompile, and we can use our code with many different types of Web servers.
- *Security:* Servlets have the Java advantage — memory access and strong typing violations are simply not possible. By default, all servlets are untrusted components and they are not allowed to perform operations such as accessing network services or local files unless they are digitally signed and accorded more freedom by manipulating Java's security manager.
- *Flexibility:* Although servlets are written in Java, their clients can be written in any programming language. Servlets can be written as clients to other services that are written in any programming language. For example, we can use them with JDBC to contact a RDBMS. They can process data submitted via an HTML form, allow collaboration between people by synchronizing requests to support systems, such as online conferencing, and pass requests to other servlets to load-balance the amount of work that a system or servlet is performing.

With all these good things going for us, we should be convinced that servlets are a viable option for our project. The only part that remains now is to put this thing together, but that is where the fun begins.

THE BACK-END DATABASE

Creating the database for this project was by no means a difficult process, but it was time-consuming to populate it with 700 fortunes/quota-

▦ Fortunes : Table			_ □ ✕
Field Name	Data Type	Description	▲
▶ Fortune_ID	AutoNumber		
Fortune	Text		
			▼

Field Properties

General	Lookup	
Field Size	Long Integer	
New Values	Increment	
Format		
Caption		
Indexed	Yes (No Duplicates)	▼

Exhibit 34-2. The *Fortunes* table schema.

tions. Fortunately, should you decide to put this project together on your own personal computer, you can just download the Microsoft Access database. To give you an appreciation of what was done and how, we'll briefly outline the database's schema, and how we used and configured the control panel ODBC applet.

The fortune database has only one table. This table has two fields:

- a *Fortune_ID*, and
- a *Fortune*.

The *Fortune_ID* is a unique, self-generated autonumber that is indexed and serves as the table's primary key. The *Fortune*, as you might expect, is a text entry of up to 200 characters that holds all the wise adages we'll be delivering to the client. Exhibit 34-2 is a screen capture of the database design view as it appears in Microsoft Access, and Exhibit 34-3 shows you the datasheet view.

We now need to decide where to place the Access database in the file system. Because we intend to use our database from the web, We might be inclined at first to move it to where all our other Web files are located. A better solution, though, is to place the *.mdb* Access file in a directory named *Internet Databases* (or whatever name you choose) that resides entirely elsewhere. This is a good practice in general, especially for security reasons (we don't want someone downloading our database, do we?).

Fortune ID	Fortune
93	It is unwise to be too sure of one's own wisdom. It is healthy to be reminded that the stron
94	In the attitude of silence the soul finds the path in a clearer light, and what is elusive and c
95	Adaptability is not imitation. It means power of resistance and assimilation.
96	It is the quality of our work which will please God and not the quantity.
97	Honest differences are often a healthy sign of progress.
98	A keen sense of humor helps us to overlook the unbecoming, understand the unconvention
99	Hot heads and cold hearts never solved anything.
100	Most of us follow our conscience as we follow a wheelbarrow. We push it in front of us in th
101	The test of a preacher is that his congregation goes away saying, not, What a lovely sermc
102	Comfort and prosperity have never enriched the world as much as adversity has.
103	Abstaining is favorable both to the head and the pocket.
104	Fame usually comes to those who are thinking of something else.
105	Common sense is very uncommon.
106	Journalism will kill you, but it will keep you alive while you're at it.
107	Fame is vapor, popularity an accident, riches take wings. Only one thing endures and that
108	If you do not expect the unexpected, you will not find it, for it is not to be reached by searcl
109	Hide our ignorance as we will, an evening of wine soon reveals it.
110	It is hard to contend against one's heart's desire, for whatever it wishes to have it buys at tt
111	The road up and the road down is one and the same.
112	Opposition brings concord. Out of discord comes the greatest harmony.
113	To be really cosmopolitan a man must be at home even in his own country.
114	Originality is simply a pair of fresh eyes.
115	When a thought takes one's breath away, a lesson in grammar seems an impertinence.

Record ◄◄ ◄ 1 ► ►◄ ►► at 700

Exhibit 34-3. The *Fortunes* table datasheet view.

To do this, create your directory. Once this is completed, open the Windows Control Panel and double click on the ODBC icon as shown in Exhibit 34-4.

This should display a tabbed dialog box appropriately titled *Data Source Administrator.* We use this program to inform the system of data source names and locations; we'll use it in our servlet programs to refer to the database we wish to manipulate with SQL statements. Once you have placed the fortune database in a directory, select the *System DSN* tab and click *Add.* You'll be prompted for the type of driver for which you want to set up a data source. Since we're using an Access database, we want the Microsoft Access driver. Click *Finish,* and you should then be directed to a new dialog titled *ODBC Microsoft Access Setup.* Here, there are two pieces of information which we have to provide:

ODBC

Exhibit 34-4. The ODBC control panel applet (also listed as ODBC Data Sources [32 bit] in Windows 98).

505

```
┌─────────────────────────────────────────────────────────────────┐
│ ODBC Microsoft Access 97 Setup                               [×] │
│                                                                   │
│ Data Source Name  [Quotation_DB|                 ]     ┌────────┐ │
│                                                        │   OK   │ │
│ Description        [                              ]    └────────┘ │
│ ┌─Database───────────────────────────────────────┐    ┌────────┐ │
│ │                                                 │    │ Cancel │ │
│ │  Database: C:\InetPub\wwwroot\fortunes.mdb      │    └────────┘ │
│ │  ┌────────┐ ┌────────┐ ┌────────┐ ┌──────────┐  │    ┌────────┐ │
│ │  │Select..│ │Create..│ │Repair..│ │ Compact..│  │    │  Help  │ │
│ │  └────────┘ └────────┘ └────────┘ └──────────┘  │    └────────┘ │
│ └─────────────────────────────────────────────────┘    ┌────────┐ │
│ ┌─System Database────────────────────────────────┐     │Advanced│ │
│ │                                                 │     └────────┘ │
│ │  ⊙ None                                         │               │
│ │                                                 │               │
│ │  ○ Database:                                    │               │
│ │                                                 │               │
│ │          ┌─────────────────┐                    │               │
│ │          │ System Database.│                    │     ┌────────┐│
│ │          └─────────────────┘                    │     │Options»││
│ └─────────────────────────────────────────────────┘     └────────┘│
└─────────────────────────────────────────────────────────────────┘
```

Exhibit 34-5. Configuring the ODBC data source.

- The name of the data source
- The location of the database

In Exhibit 34-5 above, the data source name is *Quotation_DB*, and it is located on the C drive, in the *wwwroot* subdirectory of the *InetPub* directory. You indicate this path by clicking the *Select* button and manually locating the *.mdb* file. With this step of the process successfully completed, you are one third of the way in creating the client/server application.

THE HTML FRONT END

We now need to provide a Web interface through which the client will interact with the database we have set up. The easiest and quickest way to do this is by using a form on an HTML page. Forms enable page authors, such as us, a means of requesting and then processing user input. Every form is submitted to the server via a method specified by the *ACTION* attribute. This attribute can have one of two values:

- *GET*: This operation sends name/value pairs for each form element appended to the end of the URL. Each name/value pair is encoded and separated by an ampersand before being sent to the server.
- *POST*: Data are transmitted to the server via the standard-input, i.e., via HyperText Transfer Protocol (HTTP) headers. Information can be posted only to files that are executable, such as CGI scripts.

To demonstrate how this works, we'll create two forms — one that uses the *GET* method to get a fortune/quotation and five lucky numbers, and one that uses the *POST* method to search the database for a particular keyword. The HTML source code is displayed in Exhibit 34-6, and Exhibit 34-7 illustrates what you should see in your browser.

```html
<html>
<head>
<meta http-equiv="Content-Type"
content="text/html; charset=iso-8859-1">
<title>So you want a fortune?</title>
</head>
<body bgcolor="#000080">
<CENTER><font color="#FFFFFF" size="6">700 Quotations/Fortunes as of
    10/19/98!!!</font></p></CENTER><BR>
<form action="127.0.0.1:8080/servlet/FortuneClientServlet" method="GET">
<CENTER><font color="#FF0000" size="5"><strong>So you want a
    fortune/quotation, huh? Don't we all... <br>
We got good ones and bad ones, so take a chance and grab one (or
    many)...</strong></font></CENTER><BR>
<CENTER>
<input type="submit" name="B1" value="I'm daring enough to push this
    button!">
</CENTER>
</form>

<form action="127.0.0.1:8080/servlet/QuoteSearch" method="POST">
<table border="0" width="100%">
    <tr>
        <td><CENTER><font color="#FFFF00" size="5"><strong>ADDED 10/20/98:
            SEARCH THE QUOTATION DATABASE BY KEYWORD!!!!<br>
        </strong></font><font color="#FF00FF" size="3"><strong>(Be patient,
            as the search may take some time.)</strong></font></CENTER>
        </td>
    </tr>
    <tr>
        <td><table border="0" width="100%">
            <tr>
                <td><CENTER><font color="#FF8040" size="5">Text you want to
                    search for:</font></p>
                </td></CENTER>
                <td><input type="text" size="38" name="keyword">
                </td>
            </tr>
        </table>
        </td>
    </tr>
    <tr>
        <td><CENTER><input type="submit" name="B1" value="Search!"></CENTER>
        </td>
    </tr>
</table>
</form>
</body>
</html>
```

Exhibit 34-6. Raw HTML source code.

THE MIDDLEWARE

In a two-tier client/server system, the business logic is either contained in a user interface like an applet, or it resides within the database on the server (e.g., a set of stored procedures). Alternatively, it can be in both locations. Two-tier systems are slightly more complex to manage because they are not as modular as systems which successfully separate the application and business logic from each other and the data. Our servlet project is a

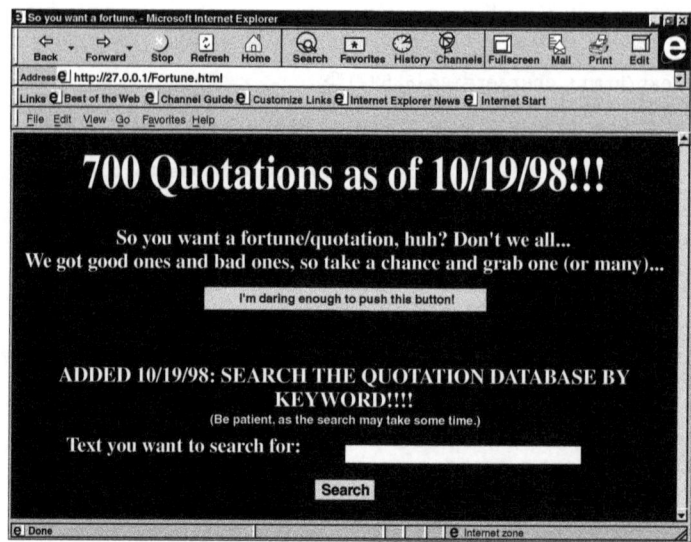

Exhibit 34-7. Visual representation of the HTML displayed in Exhibit 34-6.

three-tier example that does just this. Here, the application logic (user interface) we don't even need to worry about — Microsoft, Netscape, and others have done the work for us. The servlet is the business logic which is going to mediate access between the client and the RDBMS. The servlet can be considered middleware, a vague term that refers to all the software needed to support interactions between clients and servers.

The first thing we're going to do before we even write a servlet, however, is to concentrate on the Fortune/Quotation server. The code for this project component is shown in Exhibit 34-8.

How Does the Server Work?

Let's examine the code and get a general idea of what's going on here, and how this component can be used in conjunction with servlets to complement our project. First, notice that the *FortuneServer* class is a subclass of *Thread*. This means that it has all of the *Thread* methods and data members, and the methods will remain as written unless we explicitly override them by redefining their behavior. The server is going to be a multithreaded process so it can capably handle many concurrent requests.

The *FortuneServer* begins by executing code contained in its *main()* method. It is here that we simply create a new *FortuneServer*, and then start the thread that the application just spawned. We should briefly look at the class constructor to see what happens when we create a new *FortuneServer*

```java
import java.net.*;
import java.io.*;
import java.sql.*;
import RequestProcessor;
import WriteToFile;

/**
 * The FortuneServer object binds to port 8888 and waits for clients to
 * connect. When it receives a connection, it interprets this as a request
 * for a fortune and starts a  RequestProcessor thread to handle the
 * request.
 * Created October 15, 1998.
 * @author Jonathan S. Held
 * @version 1.0
 * @see RequestProcessor
 */
public class FortuneServer extends Thread {

    java.net.ServerSocket fortuneSocket = null;
    java.net.Socket clientSocket = null;
    java.lang.String url = "jdbc:odbc:Quotation_DB";
    java.sql.Connection con = null;
    java.sql.Statement stmt = null;
    static long numberOfRequests = 0;
    final int DB_SIZE = 700, DATA_DUMP = 50;
    static int queries[];

    /**
     * Class constructor
     * Creates a socket on port 8888 and binds to it. Attempts to load the
     * Sun bridge driver which is used to talk to the MSAccess database.
     * Enters into the log file fortune.log the date on which the log file
     * entries that follow were created.
     * @param none
     * @exception ClassNotFoundException thrown if the FortuneServer is
     * unable to load the Sun Jdbc-Odbc bridge driver
     * @exception SQLException thrown if the database url is unaccessible
     * @exception IOException thrown if unable to bind to port 8888 (e.g.,
     * the port is already in use by another process)
     */
    FortuneServer(){
        try {
            queries = new int[DB_SIZE];
            fortuneSocket = new ServerSocket(8888);
            System.runFinalizersOnExit(true);
            System.out.println("Fortune server successfully bound to port
                8888.");

            try {
                Class.forName("sun.jdbc.odbc.JdbcOdbcDriver");
                con = DriverManager.getConnection(url, "sa", "");
                stmt = con.createStatement();
                System.out.println("Established connection to database.");
                System.out.println("Awaiting client requests...");
                java.util.Calendar ts = java.util.Calendar.getInstance();
                java.lang.String info = new String("Log file created on " +
                    ts.getTime().toString());
                (new WriteToFile(info)).start();
```

Exhibit 34-8. The *FortuneServer* Java code.

```
        }
        catch (java.lang.ClassNotFoundException e1) {
            System.err.println(e1.toString());
        }
        catch (java.sql.SQLException e2){
            System.err.println(e2.toString());
        }
    }
    catch (java.io.IOException e3){
        System.err.println("Unable to bind to port 8888.");
        System.err.println(e3.toString());
        System.err.println("Hit any key to continue.");
        try {
            System.in.read();
        }
        catch (java.io.IOException e4){
            System.out.println(e4.toString());
        }
    }
}
}//end FortuneServer() constructor

/**
 * Uses the socket.accept() method to wait for an incoming request. The
 * server indicates how many requests it has processed, determines if
 * it needs to dump statistical information to the log file (currently
 * done after every 50 requests), and then starts a new
 * RequestProcessor thread to handle the request. The RequestProcessor
 * object is passed the client's socket information as well as a JDBC
 * statement object that is used to query the MSAccess database.
 * This method is run in a while(true) loop and can only be terminated
 * by system shutdown or CTRL-C.
 * @param none
 * @see RequestProcessor
 * @exception IOException thrown if unable to accept incoming client
 * requests
 * @return none
 */
private void runServer(){
    while (true){
        try {
            clientSocket = fortuneSocket.accept();
            System.out.println("Processing request number " +
                (++numberOfRequests));
            if (numberOfRequests % DATA_DUMP == 0)
                writeStatistics();
        (new RequestProcessor(clientSocket, stmt)).start();
        }
        catch (java.io.IOException e){
            System.out.println("Unable to fulfill fortune request.");
            System.out.println(e.toString());
        }
    }
}//end runServer()

/**
 * Creates a new FortuneServer object and calls the thread's start
 * method. @param args[] a series of command line arguments stored in
 * array; not used.
 * @exception none
```

Exhibit 34-8. (*continued*)

```
   * @return none
   */
  public static void main(String args[]){
     //start a new FortuneServer
     (new FortuneServer()).start();
  }//end main()

  /**
   * Called when the thread is started; calls the private utility method
   * runServer
   * @param none
   * @return void
   */
  public void run(){
     runServer();
  }//end run()

  /**
   * responsible for creating a new WriteToFile object and writing
   * information to the  logfile fortune.log.
   * @param none
   * @see WriteToFile
   * @return void
   */
  private void writeStatistics(){
     java.lang.StringBuffer statistics = new StringBuffer("Data Dump for
        " + Long.toString(numberOfRequests) + " requests: ");
     for (int ix=0; ix < DB_SIZE; ix++){
        statistics.append(Integer.toString(queries[ix]) + " ");
        if ((ix !=0) && (ix % 25 == 0))
           statistics.append(" | BREAK | ");
     }
     (new WriteToFile(statistics.toString())).start();
  }//end writeStatistics()
}//end class FortuneServer
```

Exhibit 34-8. (*continued*)

object. Here, the variable *queries*, a 700-element integer array, is created and its contents are initialized to 0. We're going to use this variable to keep track of how many times a particular fortune was displayed. In this manner, we can examine our logfile later to determine if we're really getting a random, distributed return of fortunes. Once the array has been initialized, we need to get the server to bind to a port. We do this by creating a new *ServerSocket* called *fortuneSocket* and binding it to port 8888. If all is successful, you should see the message "Fortune server successfully bound to port 8888" when you run the program.

Of course, the next important step the server needs to make is to connect to the database. We could leave this task to the servlet, and do it once and only once in its *init()* method; however, it's just as appropriate for the *FortuneServer* to do this job on its own. This is exactly what happens in the *try/catch* block that follows. We load the *sun.jdbc.odbc.JdbcOdbcDriver* and then use a JDBC *Connection* object to connect to our remote data source. Notice that we specify what data source we want to use with a string. In our example, the string is set to "jdbc:odbc:Quotation_DB", where *jdbc* is the protocol, *odbc* is the subprotocol, and *Quotation_DB* is the name of the data source. Because the server is going to run on the same machine as the data source, there is no need for a host name or Internet Protocol (IP) address to let the application know where the database is. If this were not the case, i.e., there was physical separation between the server and the database, you would need to use a different driver and syntax.

This brings us to the *run()* method, where most threads contain the specialized code they are going to perform during their lifetime. Our *run()* method is called *runServer()*, which waits for a client to connect. The *fortuneSocket accept()* method is a blocking call which keeps the program waiting here until that connection is made. Once a client binds to the port the server is listening on, another message appears that indicates what request number is being processed. A data dump of the *queries* variable into our logfile occurs every 50 requests (by making a call to *writeStatistics()*), and execution continues by turning over control to the *RequestProcessor* component. This allows the server to continue its job of waiting for requests, while some other part of the system processes the actual request and responds to the client. The *RequestProcessor* code is shown in Exhibit 34-9.

What does the RequestProcessor do? The *RequestProcessor* is itself a thread, and the server spawns a new *RequestProcessor* thread for each new client request. Notice that this class does not have a *main()* method; rather, the object's *start()* method is called and control is eventually routed to the *run()* method. When one of these objects is created, two vitally important pieces of information are needed — the client's socket and an initialized JDBC *Statement* object. We retain the information about the client because it is to this port number that we are going to transfer information. The *Statement* object is initialized from the *Connection* object, so whenever we perform SQL operations (which is why we want it), the *Statement* object inherently knows what data source it is tied to.

The SQL statement we're going to use is

"SELECT * FROM Fortunes WHERE Fortune_ID = " + random

This object's *run()* method generates a random number which corresponds to the fortune/quotation we are going to return. The SQL statement is executed by using a *ResultSet* object. The net effect of the line that reads

rs = statement.executeQuery(query)

is to execute the SQL string specified by the variable *query* and to return a reference of the results back to the *ResultSet* object that invoked the method. In this case, we expect to get only one tuple (or row) back from

```
import java.net.*;
import java.io.*;
import java.sql.*;
import FortuneServer;
import java.util.Random;


/**
 * The RequestProcessor object is used by the FortuneServer to handle
 * client requests. This thread is created when the server needs to get a
 * quotation or fortune from the MSAccess database, generate five lucky
 * numbers, and send the information back to the FortuneClientServlet.
 * Created October 15, 1998.
 * @author Jonathan S. Held
 * @version 1.0
 * @see FortuneClientServlet
 */
public class RequestProcessor extends Thread {

    java.net.Socket cs = null;
    java.sql.Statement statement = null;
    final int MAX_FORTUNES = 700;
    final int LUCKY_NUMBERS = 5;
    final int LOTTERY_NUMBER_MAX_VALUE = 50;

    /**
     * Class constructor
     * @param clientSocket the socket the client attached from
     * @exception statement a JDBC Statement object associated with a
     * database connection; these parameters are passed from the
     * FortuneServer at the time a new RequestProcessor object is created
     */
    RequestProcessor(java.net.Socket clientSocket, java.sql.Statement
        stmt){
        cs = clientSocket;
        statement = stmt;
    }

    /**
     * Called when the RequestProcessor thread is started; run generates a
     * random number, selects the quotation from the database based on this
     * number, then makes creates random numbers; this information is sent
     * back to the FortuneClientServlet, which will then process it and
     * send it back to the client's browser.
     * @param none
     * @return void
     * @exception IOException thrown if an outputstream cannot be created
     * to the client @exception SQLException thrown if an SQL error occurs
     * when trying to query the database
     */
    public void run(){

        try {
            Random generator = new Random();
            int random = Math.abs(generator.nextInt() % MAX_FORTUNES) + 1;
            int num[] = new int[LUCKY_NUMBERS];
            java.lang.String query = new String("SELECT * FROM Fortunes WHERE
                Fortune_ID = " + random);
            FortuneServer.queries[random-1] += 1;
```

Exhibit 34-9. The *RequestProcessor* Java code.

```
        java.lang.String response = null;
        java.sql.ResultSet rs = statement.executeQuery(query);
        while (rs.next()){
            rs.getInt(1);
            response = new String(rs.getString(2));
            response += "<BR><BR><font color='#004080'>Your lucky numbers
                are: </font>";

            for (int ix=0; ix<LUCKY_NUMBERS; ix++){
                int number = Math.abs(generator.nextInt() %
                    LOTTERY_NUMBER_MAX_VALUE) + 1;

                if (ix !=0){
                    boolean check = true;
                    while (check){
                        for (int jx=0; jx <= ix; jx++){
                            if (num[jx] == number)
                                number = Math.abs(generator.nextInt() %
                                    LOTTERY_NUMBER_MAX_VALUE) + 1;
                            else {
                                check = false;
                                num[ix] = number;
                            }
                        }
                    }
                }
                else num[ix] = number;
            }
            response += "<font color='#FF0000'>" + num[0] + ", " + num[1]
                + ", " + num[2] + ", " + num[3] + ", " + num[4] +
                "</font>";
            if (response != null){ break; }
        }
        java.io.BufferedWriter out = new java.io.BufferedWriter(new
        OutputStreamWriter(cs.getOutputStream()));
        out.write(response, 0, response.length());
        out.flush();
        out.close();
        cs.close();
    }
    catch (java.io.IOException e1){
        e1.printStackTrace();
    }
    catch (java.sql.SQLException e2){
        System.out.println(e2.toString());
    }
  }//end run()
}//end class RequestProcessor
```

Exhibit 34-9. (*continued*)

the database. The *getXXX()* methods of the rs object allow us to pick off the values contained in each column (or field). Without any real reason, we make a call to rs.getInt(1) to illustrate how to retrieve the *Fortune_ID* number. It is the next part that we make use of — rs.getString(2) returns the text of the fortune/quotation to the *response* string. To this, we append our five lucky numbers (which includes a little algorithm for ensuring all numbers are unique), and generate some HTML code that is sent back to a servlet via a *BufferedWriter* object.

The only part that remains is somehow to tie the browser and the server together. We do this with the *FortuneClientServlet*. This component will be invoked by the HTML form and will connect to the server on the client's behalf. Once this is done, all of the actions that were described above take place. Let's turn our attention to this project's centerpiece, the *FortuneClientServlet* code (see Exhibit 34-10), as without it we would be unable to make any of this happen.

Creating the Client Servlet

The *FortuneClientServlet* is a subclass of *HttpServlet*. It contains one and only one method -*doGet()* — that redefines the behavior the superclass provided. When we click the button "I'm daring enough to push this button," on the HTML form, a program called *servletrunner* (part of the servlet SDK) is executing on the target machine, takes the form request and any information the form contains, and acts as a proxy by directing it to the appropriate servlet. Our *FortuneClientServlet* gets called, and code execution begins in the method *doGet()* — *doPost()* if this were a *POST* action. Notice that the *FortuneClientServlet* attaches to the port the server is listening to; the server delegates the task of getting a fortune to the *RequestProcessor,* and this last component returns the fortune to the servlet. The servlet has initiated a chain of events that effectively limits its participation in this system to receiving a fortune, then forwarding it to the client that requested it. The culmination of this part of the project is shown in Exhibit 34-11.

Searching the Database

Surely one of the more popular tasks today is being able to perform searches against databases. For that reason, we've developed a *QuoteSearch* servlet. The client can enter a keyword, then exhaustively search all 700 fortunes/quotations, and, if the keyword is found, the entry is returned. This servlet is no more difficult to develop than the former; however, it does illustrate some things we haven't talked about, e.g., how do we capture form input from a servlet and how do we use the *init()* method to our benefit? Before we continue, take some time to examine the code in Exhibit 34-12.

Much of the code we see here should look familiar — the process of connecting to the database and working with SQL statements remains the same. We perform the initial resource-intensive operation of connecting to the database only once — in the *init()* method. The *servletrunner* proxy, which listens for servlet requests, ensures that each servlet's *init()* is executed just once.

After the client enters the keyword and clicks the Submit button, a *POST* operation is performed. For this reason, we override the *doPost()* method and tailor our response to the client's action with any code we place in

```java
import java.io.*;
import java.net.*;
import javax.servlet.*;
import javax.servlet.http.*;
import WriteToFile;

/**
 * FortuneClientServlet creates a new socket and attaches to the
 * FortuneServer object. The connection to the fortune server generates a
 * request for a fortune, and FortuneClientServlet waits until its request
 * has been fulfilled before returning the fortune and five lucky numbers
 * to the client that invoked it. Please note that this is not like a
 * regular object (there is no constructor). Creation of the
 * FortuneClientServlet is done by the servletrunner utility program,
 * which is part of the Servlet Software Development Kit (SDK).
 * Created October 15, 1998.
 * For more information, please see <a href="http://jserv.java.sun.com/
 * products/java-
 * server/servlets/index.html">the Servlet SDK.</a>
 * @author Jonathan S. Held
 * @version 1.0
 */

public class FortuneClientServlet extends HttpServlet
{

    /**
     * doGet() - Overridden from HttpServlet to handle GET operations.
     * @param request HttpServlet request object encapsulating
     * communication from the client
     * @param response HttpServletResponse object encapsulating means of
     * communicating from the server back to the client
     * @return void
     * @exception IOException thrown if the servlet cannot create a socket
     * to the server on port 8888
     * @exception ServletException handled by the superclass
     * This method implements a GET operation called from an HTML form's
     * ACTION URL. HTML is sent back to the client via the response object.
     */
    public void doGet (HttpServletRequest request, HttpServletResponse
        response) throws ServletException, IOException
    {
            java.lang.String fortune = new String();
            java.io.PrintWriter out;
            String title = "Your lucky fortune/quotation...";
            response.setContentType("text/html");
            out = response.getWriter();
            out.println("<HTML><HEAD><TITLE>");
            out.println(title);
            out.println("</TITLE></HEAD><BODY>");
            out.println("<body bgcolor='#FFFF00'>");
    try {
        java.net.Socket socket = new Socket("127.0.0.1", 8888);
        java.io.BufferedReader in = new BufferedReader(new
        InputStreamReader(socket.getInputStream()));

            for (int ch = in.read(); ch > 0; ch = in.read())
            fortune += (char)(ch);

            socket.close();
```

Exhibit 34-10. The *FortuneClientServlet* code.

```
    }
    catch (java.io.IOException e){}

    out.println("<CENTER><font color='#000000'><H1><B><I>" + fortune +
        "</I></B></H1></font><BR></CENTER>");
    out.println("</BODY></HTML>");
    out.close();

    java.util.Calendar ts = java.util.Calendar.getInstance();
    java.lang.String info = "On " + ts.getTime().toString() + " received
        request from " + request.getRemoteAddr();
    System.out.println(info);
    (new WriteToFile(info)).start();
  }//end doGet()
}//end class FortuneClientServlet
```

Exhibit 34-10. (*continued*)

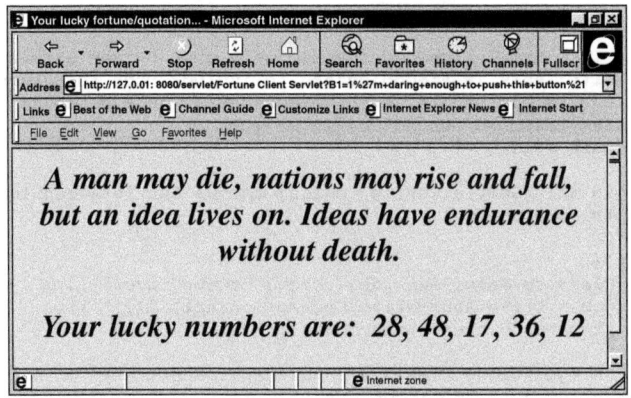

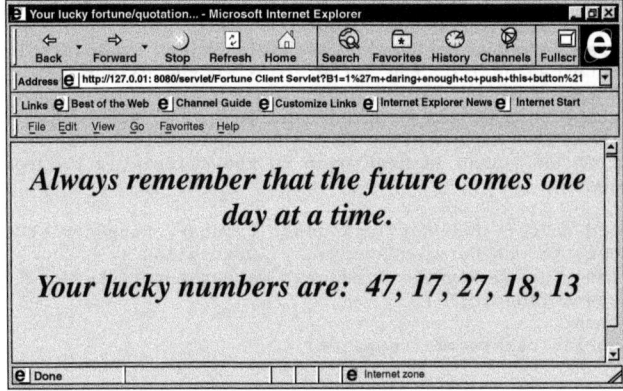

Exhibit 34-11. Random fortunes and quotations as seen by the client.

517

```
import java.io.*;
import javax.servlet.*;
import javax.servlet.http.*;
import java.sql.*;

/**
 * QuoteSearch is a Java servlet created to allow a client to search the
 * database for a keyword.
 * Created October 15, 1998.
 * For more information, please see <a href="http://jserv.java.sun.com/
 * products/java-server/servlets/index.html">the Servlet SDK.</a>
 * @author Jonathan S. Held
 * @version 1.0
 */
public class QuoteSearch extends HttpServlet
{
    static java.sql.Connection con;
    static java.sql.Statement stmt;
    static final java.lang.String url = "jdbc:odbc:Quotation_DB";
    static final int INITIAL_SIZE = 20;

    /**
     * init() - Servlet method invoked only once by the servletrunner
     * utility; this is a good method to include code for resource-
     * intensive operations, such as connecting to a database
     * @param response ServletConfig object
     * @return void
     */
    public void init(ServletConfig config) throws ServletException {
        super.init(config);

        try {
            Class.forName("sun.jdbc.odbc.JdbcOdbcDriver");
            con = DriverManager.getConnection(url, "", "");
            stmt = con.createStatement();
        }
        catch (java.lang.ClassNotFoundException e1) { }
        catch (java.sql.SQLException e2){ }
    }//end init()

    /**
     * doPost() - Overridden from HttpServlet to handle POST operations.
     * @param request HttpServlet request object encapsulating
     * communication from the client
     * @param response HttpServletResponse object encapsulating means of
     * communicating from the server back to the client
     * @return void
     * @exception ServletException handled by the superclass
     * This method implements a GET operation called from an HTML form's
     * ACTION URL. HTML is sent back to the client via the response
     * object.
     */
    public void doPost (HttpServletRequest request, HttpServletResponse
    response) throws ServletException, IOException {
        java.lang.String keyword = request.getParameter("keyword");
        if (keyword.equals(""))
            return;
        else goFindIt(keyword, response);
    }
```

Exhibit 34-12. The *QuoteSearch Servlet* code.

518

```
/**
 * goFindIt() - Searches for a keyword in a fortune/quotation.
 * Returns the fortune/quotation with the keyword highlighted to the
 * client.
 * @param response whatToFind a string representing the keyword to
 * find
 * @param response HttpServletResponse object encapsulating means of
 * communicating from the server back to the client
 * @return void
 */
private void goFindIt(java.lang.String whatToFind, HttpServletResponse
   response)
{
   java.lang.String query = "SELECT Fortune FROM Fortunes";
   int number_found = 0, total_quotes = 0;
   java.io.PrintWriter out;
   java.lang.String title = "Matches...";

   try {
      response.setContentType("text/html");
      out = response.getWriter();
      out.println("<HTML><HEAD><TITLE>");
      out.println(title);
      out.println("</TITLE></HEAD><BODY>");
      out.println("<body bgcolor='#800000'><font color='#00FF00'
         size='5'>");
      out.println("<H1><I>Searching... Matches appear
         below:</I></H1>");
      out.flush();
      java.sql.ResultSet rs = stmt.executeQuery(query);
      while (rs.next()){
         java.lang.String quote = rs.getString(1);
         total_quotes++;

         if (inQuote(whatToFind, quote)){
            number_found++;

            int index =
               quote.toLowerCase().indexOf(whatToFind.toLowerCase());

            out.print("<img src='http://127.0.0.1/images/speaking.gif'
               width='25' height='25'>");

            for (int ix=0; ix < index; ix++)
               out.print(quote.charAt(ix));
            out.print("<B><I><font color='#FFFF00'>");

            int match_length = whatToFind.length();
            for (int jx=index; jx<index+match_length; jx++)
               out.print(quote.charAt(jx));
            out.print("</font></B></I>");

            int start = index+whatToFind.length(), end =
               quote.length();
            for (int kx=start; kx < end; kx++)
               out.print(quote.charAt(kx));
            out.println("<BR><BR>");
            out.flush();
         }
      }
```

Exhibit 34-12. (*continued*)

```
        out.println("</font><font color='#FF0080' size='4'>");
        out.println("Number of quotations is " + total_quotes + "<BR>");
        if (number_found == 0)
            out.println("Sorry... Your keyword was not found in any " +
                "quotations/fortunes.");
        else
            out.println("Your query resulted in " + number_found + "
                matches.");
        rs.close();
        out.println("</font></BODY></HTML>");
        out.close();
    }
    catch (java.io.IOException e) { }
    catch (java.sql.SQLException e) { }

}

/**
    * inQuote() - Returns a boolean value indicating whether the
    * keyword being looked for is anywhere in the fortune/quotation;
    * this is a case insensitive search
    * @param lookingFor the keyword string
    * @param quote the text to be searched
    * @return boolean indicating whether lookingFor is in the quote or
    * not
    */
private boolean inQuote(java.lang.String lookingFor, java.lang.String
    quote)
{
    boolean found = false;
    if (quote.toLowerCase().indexOf(lookingFor.toLowerCase()) != -1)
        found = true;
        return found;
    }
}
```

Exhibit 34-12. (*continued*)

here. Notice that we have an *HttpServletRequest* and an *HttpServletResponse* object. These objects contain a number of methods that allow us to learn, respectively, information about the request that was generated (such as where it came from, information that was passed in the request via HTTP headers, etc.) and a means for responding to the request as we see fit.

We use the *HttpServletRequest* method *getParameter()* to retrieve values from forms. This method takes a string that represents the name we assigned to the HTML text control. If the client tries to submit the form without entering a keyword, which we explicitly check for, no action is taken (although a white screen will appear). We could later customize this servlet to return an error message, if we were so inclined. If a keyword is entered, we make a call to *goFindIt()*, which requires two parameters: the keyword being searched for and the *HttpServletResponse* object which is used to communicate back with the client.

Some HTML is immediately generated and sent back to the client, so when you run this servlet you'll get a maroon screen that informs you a search is in process. All quotations are retrieved from the database, and *inQuote()* determines if the keyword is found. If it is, the quotation is returned (with the keyword portion highlighted in yellow), and the search process goes on until the entire database is examined. Meanwhile, the client gets the perception that the page is still loading. When the servlet is done executing, some summary statistics are returned. I promise not to scrutinize the code any further (since you can examine it as well as I can). Suffice it to say that this search is slow and could be significantly improved in a couple of ways: if a keyword appears as part of word, the keyword portion is highlighted; if it appears twice in a fortune, only the first occurrence is highlighted. These are areas for improvement that I'll leave as an exercise for the reader. Exhibit 34-13 shows two screen captures of what you should expect the *QuoteSearch* servlet to return.

QUICK SETUP

Installation of the servlet SDK will create a JSDK2.0 directory and subdirectories for documentation (*doc*), executable programs (*bin*), library files (*lib*), and source code (*src*). You'll find the *servletrunner* utility in the *bin* directory. You configure this program, i.e., associate a servlet name and its compiled class file, by modifying the *servlet.properties* file in a text editor. Examples of how to use this file are illustrated in Exhibit 34-14.

Writing your own servlets requires two more things: all your programs must import the *javax.servlet* and *javax.servlet.http* packages, and you must start the *servletrunner* utility after you've edited the *servlet.properties* file. The easiest way to import the packages into your programs is by modifying your *CLASSPATH* setting as follows:

SET CLASSPATH = %CLASSPATH%;C:\jsdk2.0\lib\jsdk.jar

This will allow you to use the *javac* compiler without error, and the only thing left to do is to start the *servletrunner* utility. You can do this by simply typing the name of the program at a DOS command prompt, or you can append a number of parameters to customize its configuration. Exhibit 34-15 shows you what command-line parameters are available.

CONCLUDING REMARKS

Servlets are a useful extension to the Java programming language that have almost the identical functionality and utility of CGI programs, but unlike the latter, they are not as prone to security risks and are much easier to write. This chapter has demonstrated how you can rapidly develop and deploy a three-tier client/server RDBMS application using this technology. If you have specific questions that you cannot find answers to after consulting the resources listed below, you may contact the author via e-mail at jsheld@hotmail.com.

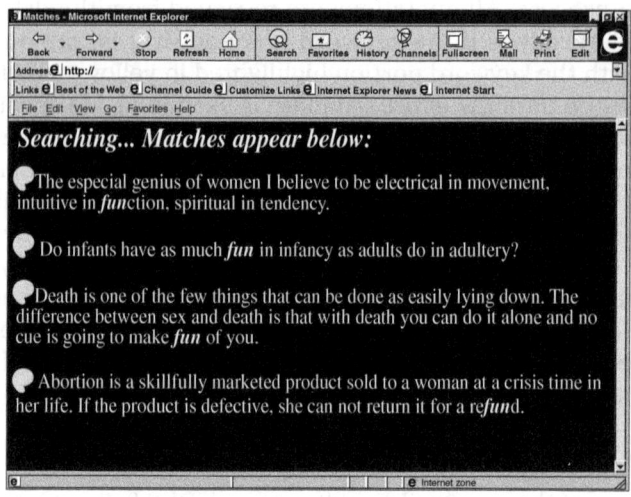

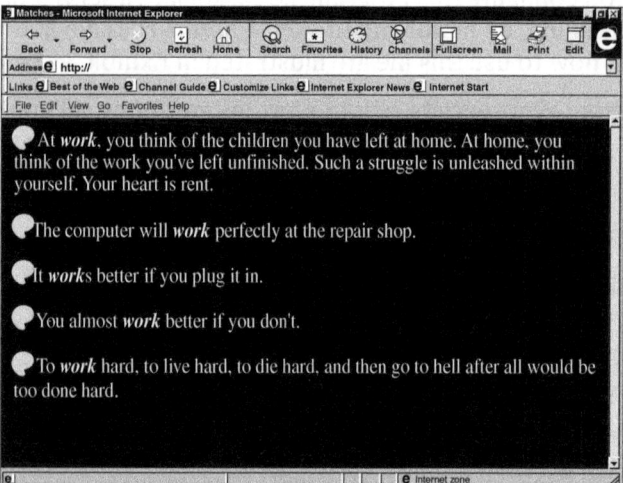

Exhibit 34-13. *QuoteSearch Servlet* **results for the keywords "fun" and "work."**

Resources

1. JDK1.2: http://www.javasoft.com/products/jdk/1.2
2. Servlet 2.1 SDK: http://www.javasoft.com/products/servlet/index.html
3. Servlet 2.1 API: http://www.javasoft.com/products/servlet/2.1/html/servletapiTOC.fm.html
4. JDBC™ 2.0 API: http://www.javasoft.com/products/jdbc/jdbcse2.html
   All Java code (source and compiled class files) and the MSAccess database for the project described in this chapter can be obtained from this magazine's Web site.

```
# @(#)servlets.properties 1.86 97/11/14
#
# Servlets Properties
#
# servlet.<name>.code=class name (foo or foo.class)
# servlet.<name>.initArgs=comma-delimited list of {name, value} pairs
#        that can be accessed by the servlet using the
#        servlet API calls
#

# simple servlet
servlet.simpleservlet.code=SimpleServlet

# survey servlet
servlet.survey.code=SurveyServlet
servlet.survey.initArgs=\
   resultsDir=/tmp

servlet.FortuneClientServlet.code = FortuneClientServlet

servlet.QuoteSearch.code = QuoteSearch
```

Exhibit 34-14. The *servlet.properties* file.

```
C:\JSDK2.0\bin>servletrunner /? >t
Usage: servletrunner [options]
Options:
    -p port       the port number to listen on
    -b backlogthe listen backlog
    -m max        maximum number of connection handlers
    -t timeout    connection timeout in milliseconds
    -d dir        servlet directory
    -s filename   servlet property file name
java.exe: No error
```

Exhibit 34-15. *Servletrunner* command-line parameters.

Chapter 35

Building Database-Enabled Web Applications With IDC

Ido Gileadi

THE WORLD WIDE WEB (THE WEB) HAS BEEN PRIMARILY CONSTRUCTED FROM STATIC HTML PAGES. These pages generally contain text, graphics, and hyperlinks that give Net users the ability to search and view information easily with the click of a mouse. The static page always displays the same information regardless of individual user selections or personal preferences. Furthermore, the static page displays the entire range of information available to it without consideration of the specific requirements of unique, busy individual users accessing the Web site.

In recent years, there has been a strong movement toward a more dynamic approach for Web page design. Web pages can now be created on the fly, customized to an individual viewer's requirements, and linked with database servers to provide accurate, up-to-the-minute data. There are many techniques for creating dynamic Web pages. Some of the technologies available involve creation of a Web page on the fly, based on selections a viewer makes in previous pages. Active pages and CGI scripting can easily achieve these tasks.

In many cases, creating dynamic Web pages that contain subsets of data based on the viewer's selection of a query is the ideal. A simple example of this type of application is a telephone directory publication on the Web. Such an application requires the ability to select and display one or more entries from the database, based on a selection (query) the user makes on the screen. Most likely, the selection will involve a last name and/or first name combination.

The traditional way of creating a database-enabled Web application, such as the telephone directory, is to use CGI scripting. The CGI script is a program that is referenced by the selection screen. It is invoked by the submission of the selection criteria (last name and first name) and receives the selections as input parameters. Once invoked, the CGI script works like any other program on the server and can access a database server to retrieve the information that is required. It then builds the dynamic Web page based on the retrieved data and presents it back to the user on the Web page.

This approach is lacking in execution speed and requires programming knowledge in Perl or some other computer language that is used to construct the CGI script. This article describes a database-enabled application using the Internet Database Connector (IDC) technology. Building this application will require no traditional programming skills and relies only on minimal coding statements.

INTERNET DATABASE CONNECTOR (IDC)

IDC is a technology developed by Microsoft to allow the execution of an SQL statement against a database and represents the results in an HTML page format. This technology works only with an Internet Information Server (IIS), which is a Microsoft Web server offering. Any browser can be used to access database information using IDC; the only requirement is that the browser be able to interpret HTML pages. Exhibit 1 depicts the way in which IDC operates.

In this example, a client machine (e.g., a PC) is running a Web browser. The browser requests an IDC page, which happens to be a text-based page. The server intercepts the request and sends the SQL statement included in the IDC file to the ODBC data source defined in the IDC file. The database returns a result set or performs the insert/update operation. The data returned is formatted, using the format specified in the HTX template, into a valid HTML stream that is then sent back to the requesting client to be displayed by the browser.

In the following sections of this article, this functionality will be demonstrated by building a simple telephone directory application.

DEVELOPING THE TELEPHONE DIRECTORY APPLICATION

Requirements

This is a small sample application designed for the sole purpose of demonstrating some principles of database access over the Web. The requirements are identified in terms of the required functionality and access. The functionality required is as follows:

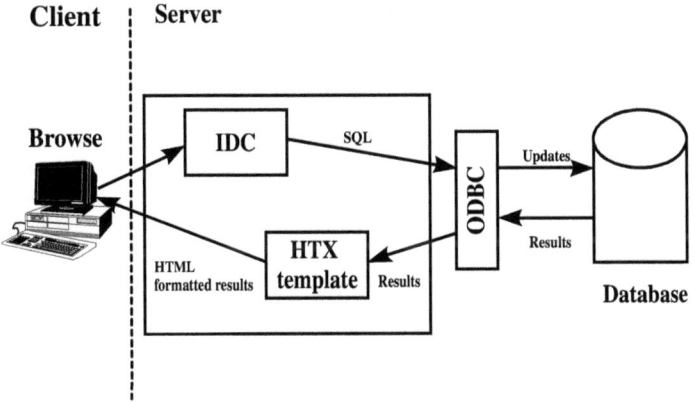

Exhibit 35-1. IDC operation.

- Store first name, last name, and telephone number of multiple individuals.
- Allow the user to search for a specific directory entry using a part or the whole of the last name and first name.
- Display a list of all matching entries as the results of a search.
- Allow the users to add a new entry to the directory.
- Allow users to access the telephone directory through a Web browser and their Internet connection.

The preceding requirements are sufficient to begin developing the application. The following sections provide a guide that can be used on a step-by-step basis to develop the application.

The Database

An access database will be used to support this sample application. Any database with an ODBC-compliant driver can be used. A new database that contains only one table will be created to contain the directory entries. The structure of the table is shown in Exhibit 2.

IDC requires an ODBC data source to communicate with the database. Here, an ODBC data source is created for the access database that has just been created using the 32-bit ODBC manager in the control panel.

Programming Tip: The datasource must be defined as a system datasource for the Web server to be able to access it.

The datasource will be named Tel_Directory and pointed to the newly created access database. Security will not be added to the database for the purpose of this example. In a real-life application, one will most likely

Exhibit 35-2. Example database structure.

Field Name	Description	Type	Comments
id	The directory entry unique id	Counter	This is an automated counter that will be incremented every time a new record is inserted into the database
LastName	Last name	Text	
FirstName	First name	Text	
tel	Telephone number	Text	

want to create a user ID and a password for the users accessing the database over the network and have them key it in at runtime. Another alternative is to create a user ID and a password with very limited permissions and include the login parameters in the IDC file to avoid the extra step of logging in.

Warning: The IDC file is a plain text file and can be easily viewed by anyone with access to the Web. When storing the login parameters in this file, one must execute great caution to restrict the user access to the very minimum required.

The Application Directory

Any directory that will be accessed by the Web server (IIS) has to be defined in the administration section of the Web server. This allows the Web server to know about the directory and allows the developer to set some parameters for each directory. The parameters of interest in this discussion include the access rights. There are two access parameters:

- **Read** access allows the server to read the files in the directory and send their contents to the requesting browser. This is sufficient for regular HTML files.
- **Execute** access allows the server to execute the program stored in the files in the directory. This is required for CGI scripts as well as IDC files.

For the application here, one directory will be created that contains all the files needed to run the application, with the exception of the database file. Both read and execute permissions will be granted to this directory.

Programming Tip: Create the directory under the Web server's home directory (typically .../wwwroot) and make sure to grant read and execute permissions to the home directory. The home directory is marked in the directory property window of the Web administration section.

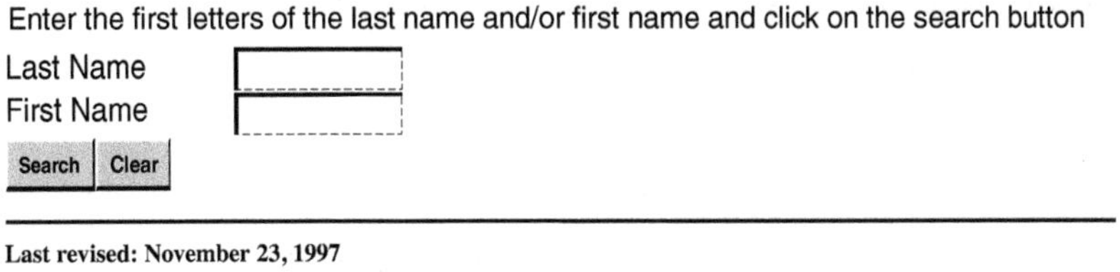

Enter the first letters of the last name and/or first name and click on the search button

Last Name [   ]
First Name [   ]

[Search | Clear]

Last revised: November 23, 1997

Exhibit 35-3. Search screen.

The Search Screen

As defined in the requirements, a search is allowed by a combination of first and last name. Defining the search screen as an HTML form will allow for passage of the user's selection as parameters to the IDC script. Exhibit 3 shows the search screen as it will display on the browser.

The HTML code for the screen in Exhibit 3 was created using Microsoft Front Page, and it consists of the following:

```
<!DOCTYPE HTML PUBLIC "-//IETF//DTD HTML//EN">

<html>


<head>

<meta http-equiv="Content-Type"

content="text/html; charset=iso-8859-1">

<meta name="GENERATOR" content="Microsoft FrontPage
2.0">

<title>Search Directory</title>

</head>


<body>


<h1>Search Directory</h1>


<hr>


<p>Enter the first letters of the last name and/or first
name and click on the search button</p>
```

```
<form action="Search.idc" method="POST">
    <table border="0">
        <tr>
            <td>Last Name</td>
            <td><input type="text" size="20"
            maxlength="20"
            name="lname"></td>
        </tr>
        <tr>
            <td>First Name</td>
            <td><input type="text" size="20"
            maxlength="20"
            name="fname"></td>
        </tr>
    </table>
    <p><input type="submit" value="Search"> <input
    type="reset"
    value="Clear"> </p>
</form>


<hr>


<h5>Last revised: November 23, 1997</h5>
</body>
</html>
```

The HTML code is a standard form with fields that are arranged into a table for cosmetic reasons. Highlighted are the names of the input fields that will be passed as parameters to the IDC script.

The Search IDC Script

The general format of an IDC script is as follows:

```
Datasource: <Name of a system ODBC datasource>
Username: <User id for accessing the database>
```

```
Password: <Password for the user>

Template: <A URL of the HTML template file *.HTX>

SQLStatement:

+<Lines of the SQL statement>

+<Lines of the SQL statement>
```

There may be more than one SQL statement in the file. This feature will be revisited in the following sections.

The IDC script used with the search screen is as follows:

```
Datasource:Tel_Directory

Username:

Password:

Template:Directory.htx

SQLStatement:

+SELECT id,FirstName,LastName,Tel from Directory

+WHERE LastName like '%lname%%' and FirstName like
'%fname%%'
```

A username or password has not been included for this sample. In a production environment, one would definitely include a user ID and password, or prompt the user for one using a login screen.

The SQL statement containing the SELECT statement will typically return a result set. The result set may be empty or contain one or more rows. The HTML template file will have to handle the display of multiple rows. The field names in the SELECT section reflect the names of the columns in the database, and the parameter names in the WHERE clause reflect the field names on the search HTML form. The parameters coming from the HTML form are enclosed in percent signs (%). In this case, the percent signs (%), are enclosed in single quotes so that the WHERE clause will contain the correct syntax for a text field. In addition, it was desirable to allow the user the flexibility of keying only the first few letters of the name. Also included is an additional percent sign (%) that acts as a wild card character, indicating that any string of characters can replace it. The final SQL statement may look like:

```
SELECT id,FirstName,LastName,Tel from Directory

WHERE LastName like 'Smi%' and FirstName like '%'
```

This will return all the entries where the last name starts with 'Smi,' regardless of the first name.

The Search Result Screen

The search results are displayed using the HTX template. The HTX file is a regular HTML file and can contain any codes included in an HTML file. In addition to the standard HTML codes, it contains the following construct:

```
<%BeginDetail%>

    Any valid HTML code <%FieldName1%><%FieldName2%>

    Any valid HTML code <%FieldName3%><%FieldName4%>

<%EndDetail%>
```

Anything contained between the <%BeginDetail%> and the <%EndDetail%> will be repeated in the constructed HTML file for each row of results coming from the database. The <%FieldName%> parameters are the fieldnames as they appear in the database, and will be substituted with the values returned from the database.

The following is the listing for the search results HTX file. The name of this file is stated in the IDC script; it is 'Directory.htx'. This template was created using Microsoft Front Page. Highlighted in the following example are the important construct elements, including begindetail, id, LastName,FirstName, Tel, enddetail, if CurrentRecord EQ 0, action="AddEntry.idc," and endif:

```
<!DOCTYPE HTML PUBLIC "-//IETF//DTD HTML//EN">

<html>


<head>

<meta http-equiv="Content-Type"

content="text/html; charset=iso-8859-1">

<meta name="GENERATOR" content="Microsoft FrontPage
2.0">

<title>Directory Listing</title>

</head>


<body bgcolor="#FFFFFF">
```

```
<p><font color="#0000FF" size="5"><em><strong>Telephone
Directory
Listing</strong></em></font></p>
<table border="2" cellpadding="2" cellspacing="3">
    <tr>
        <td><font color="#0000FF"><em><strong>Entry
        ID</strong></em></font></td>
        <td><font color="#0000FF"><em><strong>Last
        Name</strong></em></font></td>
        <td><font color="#0000FF"><em><strong>First
        Name</strong></em></font></td>
        <td><font color="#0000FF"><em><strong>Tel
        Mumber</strong></em></font></td>
    </tr>
<%begindetail%>
        <tr>
            <td><%id%></td>
            <td><%LastName%></td>
            <td><%FirstName%></td>
            <td><%Tel%></td>
        </tr>
<%enddetail%></table>

<p> </p>
<%if CurrentRecord EQ 0%>
<table border="0" cellpadding="0" cellspacing="4">
    <tr>
        <td><form action="AddEntry.idc" method="POST">
            <p><input type="submit" name="B1" value="Add
            Entry"></p>
        </form>
        </td>
    </tr>
</table>
<%endif%></body>
</html>
```

In the preceding listing, there is an additional conditional construct that looks like `<%if CurrentRecord EQ 0%>` any HTML code `<%endif%>`. This conditional construct allows for better control over the creation of the HTML code. In the example, the construct is used to add an AddEntry button that will activate the add entry screen.

Tip: The conditional construct can also contain the element <%else%>, which will allow the creation of a completely different HTML code based on the result set.

Warning: The conditional construct will not work if used before the `<%Begin-Detail%>`.

The CurrentRecord is one of the built-in variables that can be used in the template. It indicates the current record being processed. If used after, the `<%BeginDetail%>` `<%EndDetail%>` construct will hold the last record number. The record number relates to the sequential number within the result set.

The Add Entry Screen

The Add Entry button will appear on the search results screen only when there are no records in the result set. Having no records in the result set will indicate that the entry was not found and therefore may be entered into the database. The Add Entry button is a submit button within an HTML form that points to the AddEntry.idc script.

The AddEntry.idc script will fetch the total number of entries in the database and invoke the HTML template named AddEntry.htx. Following is the listing for the AddEntry.idc script:

```
Datasource:Tel_Directory
Username:
Password:
Template:AddEntry.htx
SQLStatement:
+SELECT count(id) as NumRec from Directory
```

The AddEntry.htx template is different from the search result template previously seen. The user only expects one record to be returned to this screen. That record will contain the total number of records in the database. The rest of the template is an HTML form that will allow the user to enter the details of the new directory entry and submit them to the database. Exhibit 4 shows the add entry screen.

The following example is the AddEntry.htx HTML listing supporting Exhibit 4: Add Directory Entry Screen:

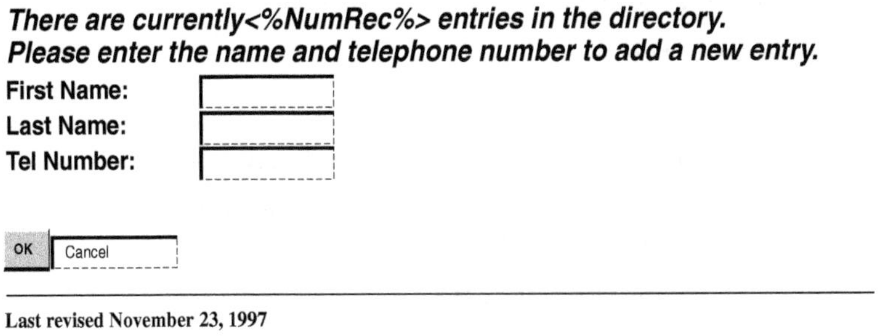

There are currently<%NumRec%> entries in the directory.
Please enter the name and telephone number to add a new entry.

First Name: [   ]
Last Name: [   ]
Tel Number: [   ]

[OK] [Cancel]

Last revised November 23, 1997

Exhibit 35-4. Add entry screen.

```
<!DOCTYPE HTML PUBLIC "-//IETF//DTD HTML//EN">

<html>

<head>

<meta http-equiv="Content-Type"

content="text/html; charset=iso-8859-1">

<meta name="GENERATOR" content="Microsoft FrontPage
2.0">

<title>Add Entry</title>

</head>


<body>

<h1>Add Directory Entry</h1>


<hr>

<%BeginDetail%>

<p><font size="4"><em><strong>There are currently

&lt;%NumRec%&gt; entries in the
directory.</strong></em></font></p>

<%EndDetail%>

<p><font size="4"><em><strong>Please enter the name and
telephone

number to add a new entry.</strong></em></font></p>
```

```html
<form action="Add2DB.idc" method="POST">
    <table border="0">
        <tr>
            <td><strong>First Name:</strong></td>
            <td><input type="text" size="20"
            maxlength="20"

            name="fname"></td>
        </tr>
        <tr>
            <td><strong>Last Name:</strong></td>
            <td><input type="text" size="20"
            maxlength="20"

            name="lname"></td>
        </tr>
        <tr>
            <td><strong>Tel Number:</strong></td>
            <td><input type="text" size="15"
            maxlength="15"

            name="tel"></td>
            </tr>
        </table>
        <blockquote>
            <p> </p>
        </blockquote>
        <p><input type="submit" value="OK"> <input
        type="button"

        value="Cancel"> </p>
</form>

<hr>

<h5>Last revised: November 23, 1997</h5>
</body>
</html>
```

In the preceding listing, note the `<%BeginDetail%>` and `<%EndDe-tail%>` around the `<%NumRec%>` variable, without which the %NumeRec% variable will not be assigned a value. Also note the form action is referencing yet another IDC script named Add2DB.idc. The Add2DB.idc script contains the SQL INSERT statement that will insert the new record into the database. The listing for the Add2DB.idc script is as follows:

```
Datasource:Tel_Directory
Username:
Password:
Template:Directory.htx
SQLStatement:
+INSERT INTO Directory (FirstName, LastName, Tel)
+VALUES ('%fname%', '%lname%', '%tel%')
SQLStatement:
+SELECT id, FirstName, LastName, Tel FROM Directory
```

Careful examination of this script reveals that it has an SQL INSERT statement that takes as parameters the values that had been entered in the HTML form. The INSERT statement is not the only statement in the script. There is a second SQL statement that selects all the records in the telephone directory. The second select statement will populate the Directory.htx template, which was seen previously. This script performs the insert action and then displays all records in the directory, including the newly inserted record.

Tip: Results returned from the database must match the template.

Each result set returned from the database will correspond with a single `<%BeginDetail%>` `<%EndDetail%>` in the template. There may be more than one `<%BeginDetail%>` `<%EndDetail%>` in the template. If one SQL statement does not return a result set it will be skipped and the next result set will be matched to the `<%BeginDetail%>` `<%EndDetail%>` in the template. In this example, the INSERT statement does not return a result set. The second SQL statement does return a result set and will therefore be used by the `<%BeginDetail%>` `<%EndDetail%>` in the template.

Organizing the Application

The application directory was created previously. All the HTML, IDC, and HTX files should now reside in the same directory. They are all built to reference each other in a cyclic fashion. Exhibit 5 depicts the relationships between the various screens and scripts.

CONCLUSION

The sample application created in this article demonstrates the principles of accessing a database through a Web server. The task is accomplished

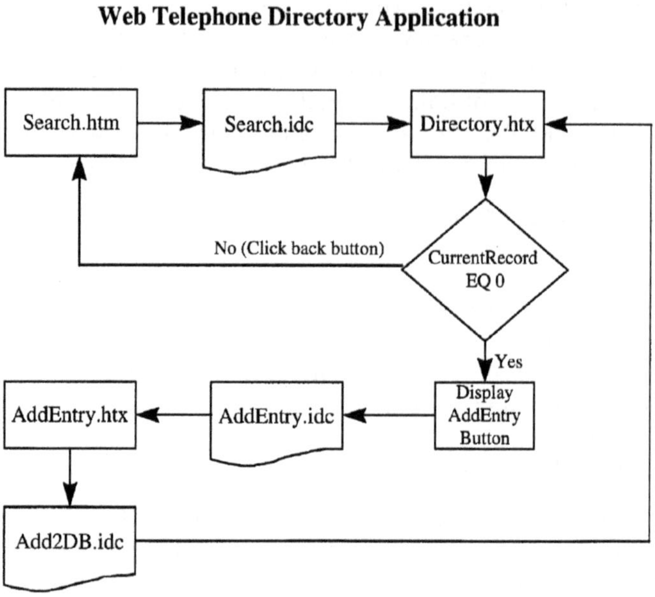

Web Telephone Directory Application

Exhibit 35-5. Web telephone directory application.

without the need for traditional programming. All the developer needs to know are basic SQL statements and some HTML coding. With this basic knowledge, an application has been created that can be useful and provide value.

The IDC technology is compatible with a Microsoft Internet Information Server. The personal Web server version was used to test this application. Users accessing the telephone directory can do so with any browser that can read and interpret HTML code (e.g., Netscape or Microsoft).

There are many ways to access data through the Web; IDC is the simplest and quickest way of doing so. If the requirements for specific applications can be met with this method, it will be a convenient and low maintenance solution.

Chapter 36
Integrating EDMSs and DBMSs

Charles Banyay

DATABASE MANAGEMENT SYSTEMS (DBMS) HAVE BEEN AN INTEGRAL PART OF INFORMATION TECHNOLOGY (IT) and the systems development life cycle since the 1960s. The database, especially the relational database, has received ever-increasing visibility during the past decade due to the mass availability of very cost-effective PC-based DBMSs. As a result, the relational database has become ingrained as the natural metaphor for an information repository with most organizations who utilize IT.

With the advent of the electronic document or, to be more precise, the electronic document management system (EDMS), as a significant new metaphor for an information repository, it is useful to juxtapose the two approaches and to explore their relative advantages. First, it is necessary to discuss the traditional process of using a DBMS in managing data. Second, it is necessary to evaluate the unique properties of documents as opposed to structured data and the challenges associated with managing information using this metaphor. Having considered these two, it is possible to discuss how the DBMS can be used cooperatively with the new metaphor for information repositories — the electronic document or EDMS.

THE DATABASE MANAGEMENT SYSTEM

The majority of IT professionals would not consider developing even the most simple of applications without employing some kind of DBMS to manage the data. The traditional approach to utilizing database technology, regardless of the application, involves some form of data analysis. Data analysis generally consists of four stages called by different names, by the various methodologies, but they all involve some form of

- Data collection and normalization
- Entity-relationship mapping
- Transaction analysis
- Data modeling

At the end of this process, once the type of database management system to be utilized is determined, one has enough information with which to begin a physical and logical database design. The data analysis activities should provide enough information to enable a design which will have a high degree of predictability in terms of data access performance and data storage size.

Data collection and normalization within any organization begins with the analysis of the data as it exists currently. Various methodologies emphasize different approaches to this analysis. Some emphasize beginning with the analysis of source documents, while others advocate analyzing the data as it is presented to the users. For this discussion it is irrelevant where one starts a project, what is important is that a "functional decomposition" process is followed in all instances. Functional decomposition attempts to distill the relevant data from some source (e.g., data collection documents or presentation documents). As recently as 1 year ago, one could have safely assumed that the documents would have been on paper; however, today that may not necessarily be so. For the purposes of this discussion, however, the medium is irrelevant.

Once this distillation process or functional decomposition is finished, one proceeds with a truly data-driven approach to analysis. The next step involves grouping the data into logical groups called entities. Using a process called normalization, one then proceeds to remove as much data redundancy as possible from these entities, sometimes producing more entities in the process. There are many good references on data normalization techniques, and for the purposes of this article there is no requirement to go into any more depth than this.

Once the entities are in third normal form one generally proceeds to associate each entity with the other entities using some entity-relationship mapping technique. Entity-relationship mapping is, in general, an attempt to reconstitute the data back into something that is meaningful to the business where the data originated. A thorough understanding of the business functions and processes that use the data is crucial for creating meaningful entity-relationship maps. During this mapping process some form of quantification of the entities also occurs.

The next step in data analysis is the transaction analysis. Transaction analysis involves listing all of the business events that could trigger access to the information within the as yet undesigned database and mapping the flow of the transaction through the entities as it satisfies its requirement for information. The transaction flow is dependent on the entity relationships. Once all the transactions are mapped in this way and the quantity of each transaction is determined, one has a good idea of how the data should be ordered and indexed.

The final step in the data analysis activity is to construct the data model. Constructing the data model involves quantitative analysis. Using the structure from the relational map and the number of accesses identified in the transactional analysis, one derives a new structure for the model. This new structure may result in new entities that may reduce the number of entities that need to be accessed for certain high-usage transactions. The first data model generally proves to be inadequate. Data analysis is therefore an iterative process. As one proceeds through the iterations, one learns more about the data. The new information may indicate that decisions made earlier in the process may not have been optimal and may need to be revisited.

The ultimate database design will not only depend on the results of the data analysis activity but also on the choice of DBMS. Good design does not just depend on knowledge of the specific data requirements of a particular application or the general information requirements of an organization. These are critical elements of the design, but almost as important is a good understanding of the particular DBMS, its architecture, and its design constraints.

The critical aspect to understand about data analysis for the purposes of this discussion is the process of functional decomposition. Functional decomposition is a process that is extremely important to data analysis. It is the process by which reality or a body of knowledge is decomposed, summarized, or reduced into its most fundamental, elementary components. This decomposition is generally from the one perspective that is important to the particular application being considered. These elementary components are the data items that then ultimately make up the database, such as those shown in Exhibit 1.

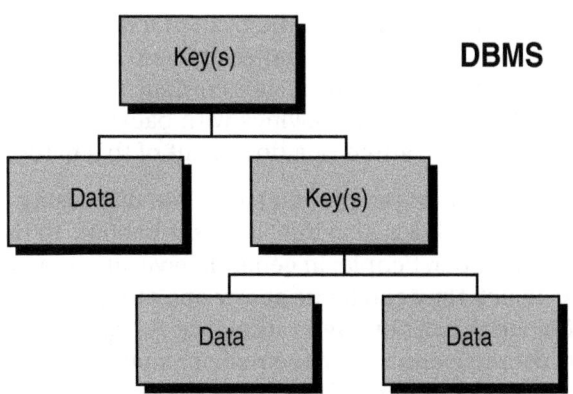

Exhibit 36-1. Elementary components.

An important consideration in Exhibit 1 is that any process of reduction or distillation results in a tremendous amount of other "stuff" that does not make it into the final version. This stuff is lost. Consequently, one advantage offered by functional decomposition is that the process reduces reality or a body of information to its elementary components that represent one or at least a very limited perspective on this body of information. This enables the construction of a database. The "bad" aspect of functional decomposition also relates to its strength, namely, that the process reduces reality or a body of information to its elementary components that represent one or at least a very limited perspective on this body of information. Much of the original body of information can be lost in the process.

THE ELECTRONIC DOCUMENT

Before comparing the DBMS with the electronic document management system as an information repository, it is useful to build a common understanding of the definition of a "document" in the context of this discussion.

The first thing that most people think of in any discussion of a document is paper. This is due to the fact that most of today's generations have grown up with paper as the most common medium on which documents have resided. A piece of paper or a collection of pieces of paper is usually referred to as a document, especially if it has a collective purpose. Paper, however, is very limiting and is just one method of representing a document. It is certainly not the only way. Even if one disregards the electronic medium for the moment, there is a myriad of ways that documents have existed and do exist. There are stone tablets, scrolls, hieroglyphics, paintings, carvings, and more recently film, just to mention a few. Even the scented letter is a document that is more than just scribbled words on a piece of paper. The scent can convey more information than the words.

If one includes the electronic medium, then a document can be much more than is allowed in the limited paper medium or in anything that has been described above. A document can contain voice-annotated video, with graphics, still images, and drawings with backup text. One can imagine the vast information content of a document of this nature.

The second feature that people think of when discussing documents is the concept of a page. This is also due, in all probability, to the association of documents with paper. People, in general, have an optimum quantum of information on which they can focus at any one moment. This is an aspect of what psychologists call bounded rationality. A page is probably an optimum quantum of information. Represented on paper, information could appear in the format that is most familiar; however, in some other form it could be quite different. The concept of a page is useful and will probably evolve as the understanding of documents evolves and as this understanding moves beyond paper as the common representation of a document. It will suffice for the purposes of this discussion to think of a page as a component of information and of a document as containing one or more pages or one or more quantums of information.

So, in summary, what is a document? The word *document* is both a verb and a noun. To document is to record (e.g., to record an event or to tell a story). It follows that anything that records an event or tells a story can be called a document. A document can and generally does contain many different types of entities. Generally there is either text or an image, but if people expand their horizon beyond paper, a document can contain voice, video, or, in the world of virtual reality, any combination of tactile stimuli. In the most general definition, a document is a representation of reality that can be reproduced and sensed by any combination of the five senses.

The preceding discussion may stretch human creative capabilities somewhat, so for the purposes of this discussion the definition of a document can be limited to a collection of images and textual information types. The information can be coded or uncoded. The essence of the definition of the document, as a representation of reality that can be reproduced and sensed, is really the crucial aspect of the definition that is most germane to this discussion. The representation of reality implies that a document captures information at a quantum level or quantum levels higher than simple data.

The best illustration of this is the well-known "A picture is worth a thousand words." A picture in one entity can represent a thousand data elements or more. An illustration may convey this idea better. Suppose one is creating a document describing an automobile accident report for a property and casualty insurance company. The document would begin with a notice of loss, which could be an electronic form, that is created initially by an agent within a call center. The agent would record all relevant information about the accident, including the name and policy number of the policyholder, the date and time of the accident, the date and time of the call, and all particulars of the loss, such as damages to the car, etc.

The agent then sends a compressed version of the document to the adjuster with some comments and instructions. The information to this point is in coded data format and could be through any traditional data system. The new capabilities of a document-based system allow the adjuster, when the document is received, to attach a few still photo shots of the automobile along with further comments and the detailed cost estimates supplied by the body shop. In addition, the adjuster can scan in the police report of the accident and attach it to the document. The claims document now contains a much more complete description of the entire event. This more complete description could produce a very different result by the end of the claims process. This more complete description is not possible through just simple coded data or traditional relational DBMS systems.

It is not necessary to describe the insurance claims process any further. What it illustrates is the wealth of information contained in a document-based approach to information processing. One needs to contrast this to an approach enabled by an application system containing only coded data in a relational format.

FUNCTIONAL DECOMPOSITION AND DATA DISTILLATION

The primary reason that traditional application systems oriented around a DBMS have sometimes failed to meet the expectations of the business community, and the reason that much of the business information today still resides on paper, is the failure of these applications to capture the entirety of the multifaceted information pertaining to an event. That is a real mouthful, but what it says is that if in capturing information electronically a business user only manages to capture the bare essentials focused on a certain perspective, and loses most of the other peripheral information which may be central to other perspectives, then the business user will, in general, not be completely satisfied. The business user is forced to keep other, non-electrical repositories of information and continue to work with information in nonelectrical media. This generally adds up to a lot of paper and a lot of traditional, inefficient, and ineffective business processes.

As discussed at the end of the data analysis activity, in any process of reduction or distillation there is a tremendous amount of other peripheral information that does not make it through the process. Reality is reduced to a very limited perspective based on what is retained. This process may leave out information of interest to other perspectives. The result is a very narrow perspective on the information, general dissatisfaction, and alternative repositories of information within the organization.

THE DBMS AND THE EDMS

So why not just discard DBMSs and why not rely totally on documents as the new metaphor for an information repository. The above discussion seems to imply that database systems are bad and documents are good — far from the truth. Documents, despite having a tremendous capability of holding a great deal of multifaceted information, have their own weaknesses. Years ago one would have begun the list of these weaknesses with the fact that documents tend to take up vast amounts of storage space, require a great deal of bandwidth for transmission, and generally require expensive equipment for good presentation, such as large, high-resolution monitors and multimedia processors. Today, these weaknesses seem to be fading in importance, although not as quickly as one had hoped and would like. Bandwidth is increasing, storage costs are plummeting, and high-resolution monitors are dropping in cost.

The real weakness of documents, and this has little to do with storage or display technology, is that they are difficult to search. Because most of the information content of a document is uncoded and because there is very little in the way of search engines for uncoded data, documents are difficult to search. Once stored, they are difficult to find unless they have been indexed with exactly the criteria for which one is searching. Unfortunately, information is of little use if it cannot be found readily when needed.

It seems, then, that there is an impasse. On the one hand, a DBMS is a tool that has tremendous capabilities to search and reproduce information to which it has access, in the combinations that users generally require. The weakness of the DBMS, however, is that it generally has access to only a limited perspective on a small body of information. On the other hand, an EDMS is a tool that can house vast amounts of content about a body of information, from a multitude of perspectives. The primary weakness of an EDMS, however, is that once the information is stored it is difficult to find.

Neither one of the tools on its own seems capable of meeting the expectations for comprehensive information management. They do however have complementary strengths. With the DBMS, information is relatively easy to find, and, with the EDMS, information content is vast and rich. If one could successfully combine these strengths, then one would have a tool that might meet the expectations of the business community better. The combination might not meet all of the expectations, but would certainly be superior to either tool in stand-alone mode. The whole promises to be greater than the sum of the parts in this case.

The logical question arises, "Why use a DBMS to store data?" Why not use the EDMS to store the information, and use the DBMS to store the data about the EDMS or metadata? This would enable one to search the DBMS for the combination of information that one requires contained in the EDMS. This is exactly the approach that many leading vendors of document management applications, such as FileNet and Documentum, have taken. Both vendors use a relational database, such as Oracle or Sybase, to store the metadata that points to various data stores, such as magnetic or optical disk, that house the documents.

The DBMS in many of these document management systems has evolved beyond simple metadata which just houses pointers to content documents. These second-generation document management systems have developed the concept of the virtual document. The virtual document illustrated in Exhibit 2 is more than a collection of pointers to content documents. The metadata in second-generation document management applications also contains far richer information, such as a comprehensive history of the virtual document. The history may contain work-in-process information or information about each member document, such as the

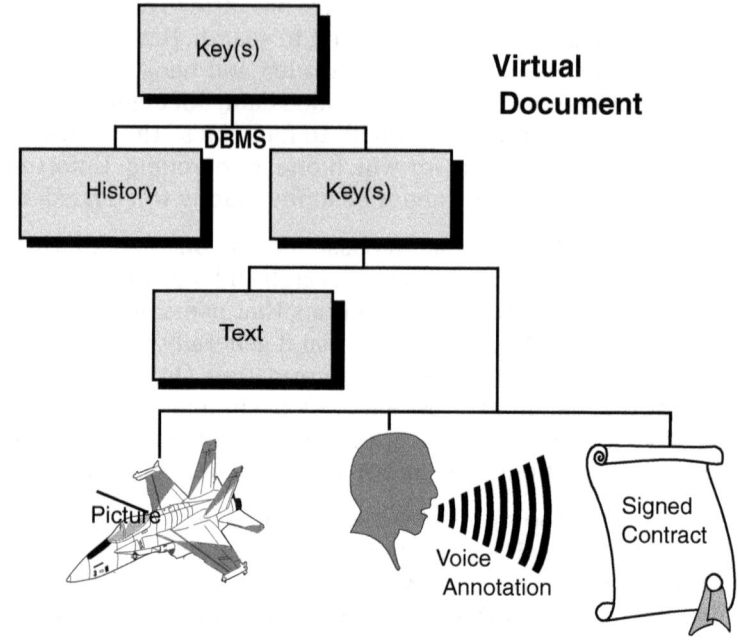

Exhibit 36-2. The virtual document.

time each was added to the document collection, who entered it, and from which application.

CONCLUSION

The combination of DBMS and EDMS certainly offers advantages over either in stand-alone mode; however, the degree of the advantage can be deceptive. The metadata in the database is just that, data about the document and not about all of the information within the document. Here is the crux of the matter. What is metadata but distillation? If the only way to find a wealth of information is through the limited perspective of its metadata, then the information is not nearly as valuable as if one could find it from the multitude of perspectives contained within the information itself.

The challenge facing most document management application vendors today is how to minimize even this more expanded data distillation. The development of new search engines may be part of the answer. Development of such technologies as pattern-recognition applications, which can scan the uncoded components of documents, may be another part.

Whatever the solution to reducing the effects of data distillation, it is not something that will be totally eliminated within the near future. Combining the strengths of a DBMS and an EDMS, however, definitely provides better access to a larger volume of information than if either one is used alone. The combination is by no means a panacea, but it is a step or a number of steps in the right direction toward solving the information-processing problems that knowledge workers face every day.

As the marriage between the DBMS and the EDMS evolves further, there may be a new dawn for IT. This new dawn will be true electronic information processing rather than electronic data processing. The real payoff in this evolution and in developments of this nature is that it may eventually solve the seeming paradox of information processing in the office environment. This paradox is that, even though there has been a tremendous investment in information technology in the office, office productivity has not risen as dramatically as expected during the past 20 to 30 years.

Chapter 37
Database Management and the Internet: Developments and Challenges

Bhavani Thuraisingham

DURING RECENT MONTHS THERE HAS BEEN AN INCREASING DEMAND TO ACCESS THE DATA STORED IN DIFFERENT DATABASES THROUGH THE INTERNET. The databases may be relational databases, object-oriented databases, or multimedia databases containing unstructured and semis-tructured data such as text, voice, video, and images. These databases are often heterogeneous in nature. Heterogeneity exists with respect to data structures, data types, semantic meanings, data models, architectures, query processing strategies, and transaction management techniques.

Many vendors of database management systems (DBMSs) are enhancing their products with capabilities for Internet access. Exhibit 1 illustrates how clients access multiple databases through the Internet. Special Internet protocols are needed for such access. The goal is to provide seamless access to the heterogeneous databases.

Although much progress has been made with respect to Internet database access, there is still room for improvement. For example, database management system (DBMS) functions such as data modeling, query processing, and transaction management are impacted by the Internet. The algorithms for query processing and transactions management may have to be modified to reflect database access through the Internet. For example, the cost models for the query algorithms may have to include the price of accessing servers on the Internet.

0-8493-0882-8/00/$0.00+$.50
© 2001 by CRC Press LLC

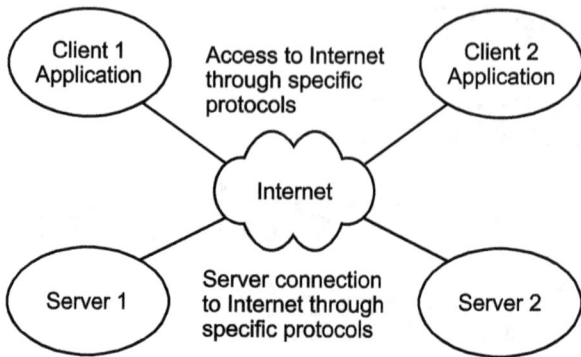

Exhibit 37-1. Internet-based client/server communication.

Furthermore, distributed object management technologies need to be examined for heterogeneous database integration through the Internet. This chapter discusses the impact of the Internet on various DBMS functions.

DBMS FUNCTIONS

Key DBMS functions include data representation, query management, transaction management, storage management, security management, integrity management, and metadata management. For an Internet database, functions such as browsing and filtering also have to be managed.

Data Representation

Various data representation schemes have been proposed for text databases, including standard generalized markup language (SGML), hypertext markup language (HTML), and office document architecture (ODA). However, a considerable amount of data will also be stored in structured (i.e., relational and object-oriented) databases. Appropriate data models for representing structured as well as unstructured databases include integrated object-oriented, relational, and hypertext-based data models for Internet database management. Currently there are no agreed-on standard data models; appropriate mappings between the standards and the heterogeneous data models used by the databases must also be developed.

Query Management

Query management involves developing language and processing techniques. The query language depends to a great extent on the data model used.

Languages based on SQL are popular for relational as well as nonrelational database systems. For example, object-oriented DBMSs use variations of SQL for database access. An appropriate SQL-based language needs to be developed for accessing structured and unstructured databases. SQL extensions are being examined to handle different data types. Once a standard language has been developed, mappings between the standard language and the languages used by the individual databases must be examined.

For efficient query processing, modifications to current algorithms for distributed and heterogeneous databases should be considered. For example, current cost models focus mainly on the amount of data transferred between the different sites. Database administrators have many issues to consider, such as:

- Are such cost models still valid for Internet databases? Are there other factors that need to be considered in query processing?
- Will the cost of accessing remote database servers over the Internet have an impact on the query algorithms?
- What are the relationships between global and local optimization strategies? What are parameters that are common to both the global and local cost models?

Because of the information explosion caused by the Internet, various technologies such as agents and mediators are being considered for locating the data sources, mediating between the different data sources, fusing the data, and giving responses to the user.

Browsing and Filtering

Although many traditional DBMSs do not support browsing, such systems on the Internet need to provide this capability. One of the main uses of the Internet is browsing through and accessing large amounts of information in a short time. Therefore, to efficiently access the database, the DBMS must be augmented by a browser. Numerous browsing tools are available for the Internet, however, they must be integrated with the DBMS.

Closely related to browsing is the filtering technique. With the Internet, the user can become overloaded with information. This means various filters have to be integrated with the browsers and the DBMSs so that unnecessary information is filtered out and users get only the information they want.

Transaction Management

Transaction management, an integral part of DBMSs, involves concurrency control and recovery. New kinds of transactions are taking place on the Internet, such as making a purchase. In some cases, multiple users may want to purchase the same item and may bid on it. In such a situation, there should be a waiting period before the item is locked. The item is then sold to the highest bidder.

The previous example illustrates the need for flexible transaction models. The ability to perform long-duration transactions and transaction models for workflow management may also be valuable. Serializability conditions may be helpful for concurrency control. Otherwise, it may not be possible to ensure that all the data items accurately reflect the real-world values.

Transaction management also requires consideration of recovery management as well as fine-grained versus coarse-grained locking issues.

Storage Management

For appropriate representation strategies for storing multimedia data, efficient access methods and index strategies are critical. A user should be able to index based on content and context. Research on extensions to various strategies such as B-trees is one possible solution. Internet database management is such a challenge because of the large amount of information and user requirements for quick access. This is why development of methods for integrating database systems with mass storage systems is so critical.

Security Management

Security is vital to Internet database management, however, the policies must be flexible. With the increasing number of databases, negotiations between the different administrators becomes important. The developers of security for Internet applications are faced with many questions, such as:

- Is there a need for one or more global Internet security administrators?That is, is there a group of one or more individuals responsible for overall database security on the Internet?
- Is it at all possible to designate a group of individuals to be in charge of global security when there may be many different systems on the Internet?
- If there are such global administrators, what are their roles?What are the security features that they enforce?
- What are the relationships between global administrators and local database administrators? That is, should the global and local administrators negotiate to determine their functions, or is there someone overseeing their actions?

If there is someone overseeing the local and global administrators' actions, then there must be a supergroup that has ultimate authority for security. If there are no global administrators, which may be the case because it would be very difficult to enforce security policies across different systems, then a type of negotiations needs to be established between the systems administrators of the individual systems on the Internet.

Other security issues include enforcing appropriate authorization and access control mechanisms. The implementation of these mechanisms depends on the standard data models and languages used. Extensions to the query language are necessary for enforcement of security constraints, including:

- Mechanisms for identifying and authenticating users.
- Laws on electronic copyright protection.
- Methods for detecting plagiarism.

There are several additional concerns if multilevel security is needed. For example, the trusted computing base must be determined, as well as how much of the Internet software should be trusted.

Integrity Management

Concurrency control and recovery techniques maintain the integrity of the data in the databases. Integrity issues revolve around data quality. With Internet database access, data could come from many different sources. Users need information concerning the accuracy of the source. Appropriate tagging techniques can be enforced and integrity constraint checking techniques used for Internet database access.

Metadata Management

Metadata describes the data in the database, including schema information. Metadata management is critical to other database functions. Metadata may include not only information about the data in the databases, but also information about the tools, resources, and policies and procedures. Metadata may be used to navigate through the Internet. In addition, information such as transactions history, access patterns, and access control may be part of the metadata. Standards and models are key, in addition to techniques for querying and updating.

Interoperability

The heterogeneous databases on the Internet must be able to interoperate. Distributed object technology can be used for interoperability.

For example, an object request broker (ORB) based on the Object Management Group's (OMG) specifications can be implemented for interoperation through the Internet (see Exhibit 2). The major challenge is to develop appropriate interfaces between the ORB and the Internet. The OMG's Internet Special Interest Group is focusing on these issues. Work is also being done on integrating OMG's CORBA, Internet, and Javasoft's Java technologies.

Java. As a programming language that can be used to develop systems as well as applications for the Internet, Java is showing a lot of promise for Internet database access. One of the major developments for data access is the standard called Java Database Connectivity (JDBC). Simply stated, database calls could be embedded in a Java application program so that databases may be accessed through these calls. JDBC may be built on other standard protocols. Many DBMS vendors are providing support for JDBC.

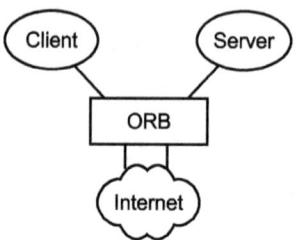

Exhibit 37-2. Internet-ORB interoperability.

CONCLUSION

This chapter has examined database management functions and discussed the possible impact of the Internet. There is a need for integrating structured and unstructured databases. Special query optimization techniques also need to be investigated and database management systems have to be integrated with browsers.

Information must be filtered so that users get only the relevant information — for this reason flexible transaction models are needed for Internet database management. Content and context-based indexing and special access methods for multimedia data should be examined. Integrating database systems with mass storage systems will become important to handling petabyte-size data stores. Support for flexible security policies and techniques for copyright protection and detecting plagiarism are also important.

Data quality issues need further investigation. There are many issues related to metadata. For example, database administrators are still trying to determine exactly what it is, who owns it, and whether it is realistic to have global managers responsible for the metadata that is not specific to any system or server.

Interoperability based on distributed object technology and Java is becoming increasingly popular. However, there is still a lot of work to be done in these areas to provide successful Internet database access. DBMS vendors are moving in the right direction, and the research community is also becoming very active. Once solutions are found to address some of the issues discussed here, users can expect efficient and secure access to the multitude of databases scattered across the various sites around the world.

Bibliography

Java White Paper, Javasoft 1996. URL: http://java.sun.com:80/doc/language_environment/

Proceedings of the First IEEE Metadata Conference (Silver Spring MD: April 1996.)

Thuraisingham, B. "Database Management and the Internet," *Object Management Group's Internet Special Interest Group Meeting Proceedings,* (Washington DC: June 1996.)

Thuraisingham, B. *Data Management Systems Evolution and Interoperation* (Boca Raton FL: CRC Press, 1997.)

Section IX
Data Migration, Conversion, and Legacy Applications

DATA MIGRATION REFERS TO THE PROCESS OF MIGRATING OR TRANSFER-
RING DATA FROM ONE SOURCE TO ANOTHER, PERHAPS REPEATEDLY OVER
THE DURATION OF A LIFECYCLE. Data conversion generally refers to a one-
way movement of data. Data conversion involves several steps, beginning
with data mapping. This involves identifying relationships between data
items in one system to the data items in another system under the context of
two sets of business rules. The quality of the data being converted must
always be determined with extensive user involvement. Data can be corrupted, out of date, or need some sort of translation in the "to be" application.
Data scrubbing is a process used to correct data after it is in the new application. Data must be validated by users after conversion through spot inspec-
tions or generated reports.

Legacy applications that are predominately operating on IBM mainframe
technology support most of the world's data in terms of sheer volume.
With the popularity of new technology architectures, a large amount of this
data must either be converted, migrated, or bridged in future applications.
This section contains the following chapters.

Chapter 38, "Relational Database Conversion: Issues and Approaches,"
examines approaches and issues that must be included in a data conversion framework that focuses on relational databases.

Chapter 39, "Data: Ever Changing and Eternally the Same," examines
common types of data changes that occur within organizations so that
project teams can focus on finding rules and information that is used to
maintain data integrity over time and through data conversion cycles.

Chapter 40, "A Practical Example of Data Conversion," looks at opportunities for categorizing data conversions in order to remove much of the
fear, apprehension, and stagnation that face many data conversion
projects. The approach defined in this chapter is iterative, with a strong
emphasis on controls.

Chapter 41, "Data Conversion: Doing It Right the First Time," describes
problems commonly encountered when converting data. This chapter also
describes steps that can be followed to perform a successful data conversion, and suggests methods for correcting errors that are detected during
the conversion process.

Chapter 42, "Migrating Data to an Integrated Database," provides an
approach for migrating a collection of files and data sources into a unified database. This chapter provides guidelines for extracting and populating a database, as well as detecting and resolving data inconsistencies after conversion.

Chapter 43, "Bridging Legacy Data and XML," discusses how dot.com start-
ups can leverage the Extensible Markup Language (XML) to access relational
database management systems (RDBMs) and other legacy data sources.

Chapter 38
Relational Database Conversion: Issues and Approaches

Chang-Yang Lin

RELATIONAL DATABASE TECHNOLOGY OFFERS MANY ADVANTAGES OVER TRADITIONAL, NONRELATIONAL FORMS OF DATABASE TECHNOLOGY. Relational databases incorporate a higher level of abstraction and therefore use logical data models that are easier to create, understand, and maintain. Relational databases allow easier, more flexible retrieval of information. Relational technology also isolates databases from the underlying systems that support database access. Therefore, relational database programs can be easier to write and maintain.

Although a growing number of organizations have already converted to relational technology, other organizations continue to use nonrelational database technology. Costs for converting to relational databases can be high, and organizations may not be able to afford abandoning their investments in existing databases. In addition, relational DBMSs may not access data as efficiently as nonrelational DBMSs.

Before converting to relational database technology, an organization must sort through the pros and cons. This chapter examines the reasons for and against converting to relational technology. It also examines the following issues involved in the conversion process:

- Relational and nonrelational database programming.
- Converting data and programs.
- The role of CASE and expert system in the conversion process.
- Strategies for making the conversion.

PROS AND CONS IN CONVERTING TO RELATIONAL TECHNOLOGY

Relational technology is receiving increased attention because it has the potential to improve application productivity and information quality.

Nevertheless, the question remains as to whether relational technology will ever be widely applied to solving business problems. Many organizations may not be convinced that it is worth the investment and risk to abandon nonrelational systems in favor of relational ones. This section provides some pros and cons on relational conversion so that organizations may decide whether or not relational systems suit their needs.

Cons

Organizations that decide to stay with nonrelational systems may argue that:

- If an existing nonrelational system is working, it should not be changed.
- Too much has been invested in the old systems under Internet Multicasting Service, Integrated Data Management System, or Virtual Storage Access Method files.
- Processing inefficiency, complexity, and extra costs are deeply inherent in relational conversion.

Although the first two arguments are general responses to any conversion project, the last one is a specific risk that organizations wish to avoid. This specific risk involves the issues discussed in the following sections.

Processing Inefficiency. Relational data access generally slows response time and adds to the hardware load, particularly when large data tables are involved. Processing inefficiency results from the enormous effort required to generate new tables based on common data elements. However, hierarchical systems are noted for their processing efficiency, making them ideal for applications in which mass transactions are required to be processed (e.g., ATM banking applications and airline reservations).

Disruption in Normal Activity. Relational conversion is a disruptive project. For instance, conventional Common Business Oriented Language programmers must be retrained in the use of fourth-generation languages (4GL) for developing new applications. IS professionals must divide their time between maintenance of older systems and the new relational systems. Certain end users must be trained to use SQL for posing ad hoc queries. Adapting to this new relational environment is so disruptive for both programmers and end users that business operations may not be conducted as usual.

Cost. Relational conversion is expensive. The relational DBMSs, CASE/AI tools, staff training and retraining, and additional programming time that are required during migration are all extra and costly. In addition, many organizations would have to scrap millions of dollars worth of investment in nonrelational software. Senior management may find all of this too expensive.

Resistance and Scarcity. A positive, cooperative attitude toward a relational working environment is important to the success of conversion, but such an attitude usually does not exist. Both end users and IS professionals are required to dramatically change their way of doing business in a relational environment. Resistance to change can always be expected. Relational conversion also requires heavy participation of knowledgeable and strategic-thinking personnel from both the IS and end-users departments. Finding such personnel, however, is never easy.

Pros

Relational systems are generally preferable to nonrelational ones because they provide the following unique features:

- A tabular data structure, which is easier to understand.
- Set operations, which have a potential for simplifying coding tasks.
- Fourth-generation languages, which facilitate prototyping.

These benefits affect new applications development, applications maintenance activities, end-user computing and decision support, and strategic competitiveness.

Faster Applications Development. Relational systems enable faster applications development. They use 4GLs that support prototyping during analysis, design, and construction phases, are less procedural and result-oriented, and therefore are easier to use. Many aspects of relational design and implementation require lower skill levels than do those of other techniques. All these factors contribute to a significant reduction in development time.

In contrast, both hierarchical and network systems require extensive record-at-a-time programming and specification of data relationships in advance. Programming in hierarchical and network environments is much more difficult than programming in relational environments.

Ad Hoc Queries and End-User Computing. Relational systems support ad hoc queries and end-user computing and therefore permit more flexible combinations of information and easier retrieval than nonrelational systems. Such capabilities are provided through the use of SQL and some 4GL facilities. SQL is more suitable for end users making ad hoc queries because it is less procedural than conventional programming languages and it allows the users to specify what results they want rather than how to achieve those results. Certain business specialists can even build their own decision support applications to generate reports or to track their personal databases by using report generators, application generators, or screen painters without assistance from systems development professionals. Thus, relational technology has created the technical platform for business specialists to play a larger role in problem solving with information systems. Improvement in personal productivity can be achieved, and applications backlogs can then be alleviated to some extent in relational systems.

Less Maintenance. Relational systems require much less maintenance activity and thus reduce the cost of maintenance. Relational databases, designed and implemented appropriately, can achieve data independence when the applications do not depend on storage structure or access strategy. Data independence, the use of 4GLs, and better relational programming allow programmers to engage in less maintenance activity. However, file processing methods may be appropriate if the solution operates as an independent application.

Competitiveness. Relational technology can enhance a competitive position for organizations. Relational data structures are becoming an increasing technological choice, and almost all of current DBMS products are relational. Other emerging information technologies (e.g., 4GLs, SQL,CASE, Decision Support System, executive information systems, and expert system) have been developed using relational databases. Some organizations even choose relational databases simply because they want to use 4GLs for applications development.

PROGRAMMING IN RELATIONAL AND NONRELATIONAL ENVIRONMENTS

During the past three decades, database software has evolved through four phases: file, hierarchical, network, and relational. From the data access perspective, programming with relational products(e.g., Oracle, SQL/DS, database 2, and INGRES) is simpler and easier than programming using nonrelational products (e.g., Integrated Data Management System, Internet Multicasting Service, and traditional file systems). This section compares programming in relational database environments with programming in file processing and nonrelational database environments.

Relational Versus File Programming

In a relational database environment, it is the DBMS, not the programmer, that deals directly with the operating system's access method. A typical DBMS provides features that shield file organization from application programs. Therefore, knowledge of how the data is actually stored is not required for relational database programming. By contrast, in a traditional file environment, knowledge of file organization (e.g., sequential file, indexed files, and relative files) and access techniques (e.g., sequential, random, and dynamic) must be built into the program logic.

In relational database programming, SQL statements are embedded in programs primarily to perform I/O tasks. A nonprocedural language, SQL requires in its programs at least two portions: definition and manipulation. The definition portion consists of declarative constructs that are needed to declare database objects. The manipulation portion consists mainly of instructions for the transfer of those objects to and from the database, though other operations are also possible. Because SQL is capable of processing a set of records rather than just one record at a time, the program logic for the I/O tasks is simplified. The program indicates only what data is required; the relational DBMS can then choose the most effective way to access that data. Therefore, specification of the access mode and associated programming logic to access the database are not required.

In traditional file systems, data depends on the programs that use it, and therefore traditional programming of I/O tasks requires more procedural treatment. I/O procedures to access data, which can be done only one record at a time, must be logically arranged. Programmers must know the file organization and access techniques and be able to express them explicitly in the program logic. This complicates coding tasks.

Relational versus Hierarchical or Network Programming

In a relational database environment, all requests from programs to access data are handled by the relational DBMS. Therefore, application programmers and end users can concentrate primarily on logical features rather than physical features. Two such logical features are that relational databases are collections of tables and that links between the tables are implied by the values of related fields in relational databases.

Hierarchical or network systems operate at a lower level of abstraction than relational systems. From a logical view, a hierarchical or a network database is composed of a set of tables and links; the links are used to connect related tables in a nonrelational database. Although the DBMS interfaces directly with the operating system's method for accessing a hierarchical or network database, application programmers must be aware of the links before they can write code for accessing nonrelational data. In addition, like traditional files, hierarchical or network databases as a rule access one record at a time. As a result of this access method, nonrelational systems require programmers to navigate manually through the database. Nonrelational programming in a hierarchical or a network environment is therefore more difficult than in a relational programming environment.

CONVERSION APPROACHES

The process of converting a nonrelational system to a relational one involves two interrelated processes: converting the databases and converting the programs. Each is described in the following sections.

Converting Databases

In general, files and hierarchical or network databases must first be reverse engineered into a logical data model. This model is in turn reengineered into a relational model, which must then be transformed into a physical database. During this conversion process, the data used in applications programs can also be analyzed to derive a logical data model.

The conversion of a file structure to a relational structure is straightforward, particularly if the old files are well designed. Programs can be written to automatically convert files from the old to the new structure. However, the database conversion effort cannot be performed automatically if:

- Old files are not in normal forms.
- Fields for linking records are not present.
- Formats of old files are significantly different from the new structure.

In these cases, some manual conversion is necessary.

The conversion of hierarchical or network databases is more difficult because records are related by embedded pointer rather than by common fields. Both reverse engineering and reengineering techniques are required to transform nonrelational databases into relational databases.

Tools are available for converting relational databases. For example, CASE tools for reverse engineering can be used to analyze existing code in data declaration sections and to translate the code to data requirements so that a logical model can be derived. CASE database generators are then used to generate SQL code from logical data specifications. An expert system is needed to analyze the applications programs when a large amount of intelligence about the data is built into the applications.

Converting Programs

Converting programs to a relational structure is not as straightforward as converting data, because programs written in a nonrelational environment typically use logic that is record oriented. These programs usually must be reverse engineered and rewritten to operate in a relational environment. There are three approaches to converting programs:

- Linking nonrelational programs with relational databases.
- Redesigning or rewriting the access to data.
- Rewriting the entire program.

The first approach to converting programs is to establish a bridge linking nonrelational programs with relational databases. A tremendous effort must be devoted to the development of a translator or a driver that can precompile existing nonrelational programs to access relational databases. Such a translator could be used in conjunction with an expert systems or

CASE tools (e.g., reverse-engineering, reengineering, and code-generating tools) during the conversion process.

The second approach is to redesign and rewrite the access of data for the existing nonrelational programs. The SQL statements are developed to replace the record-at-a-time I/O code. To identify such I/O code, an analyst must isolate data access logic from the rest of the program logic into which the SQL statements will be placed. Because data access for some nonrelational applications has similar logic, programs can be written to automatically convert data access for such applications. Finally, some old programs may have to be completely rewritten from scratch. A comprehensive approach can be used to redesign and rewrite such nonrelational programs.

STRATEGIC ISSUES

Several strategic issues must be resolved for successful conversion to a relational environment. The following sections describe these issues.

Applications Development Responsibility. First, the organization's vision of applications development responsibilities must be defined to serve as a basis for selecting an appropriate relational DBMS. For example, if systems development is primarily the responsibility of an IS department, the relational DBMS must not only support complete tasks for applications development but must perform acceptably.

If end-user computing is involved in decision support applications, relational DBMS products that are equipped with high-level visual software components (i.e., 4GL components) should be considered. These 4GL components can also be used to convert such user-developed applications as simple reports and online information inquiry. Choosing the appropriate relational DBMS is not easy. Many DBMS products that are claimed to be relational may not really meet relational criteria and should therefore not be used.

Applications Development Standards. IS management should follow applications development standards to select the proper CASE tools and expert system. As discussed in a previous section, CASE tools and expert systems, which facilitate the migration of nonrelational systems to relational systems, perform highly automated reverse engineering and reengineering functions. To be in a more competitive position, organizations should use CASE products supported by industry standards.

Policies and Guidelines. Systems development management must develop relational-specific policies, procedures, methodologies, standards, and guidelines to support the new functions introduced by the relational structure. For example, techniques for the program design and construction phase should be updated so that developers may take advantage of the set-at-a-time processing enabled by SQL. In addition, the use of a specific CASE-supported development methodology must be enforced.

The Use of Multiple DBMSs. The simultaneous use of multiple DBMSs must be planned for when a parallel installation is to be adopted during the conversion process. Policies and procedures necessary for the effective coordination of two DBMSs must be established so that the integrity of the databases is maintained and business is conducted as usual. This enhances the success of the migration to a relational structure.

Training. Systems development professionals and end users must prepare for relational technology by welcoming additional training. Systems professionals should receive comprehensive training with an emphasis on data concepts, CASE-driven systems development, and set-at-a-time programming techniques. End users should learn the use of 4GL facilities for generating reports and for retrieving information from a relational database.

FOUR STEPS OF RELATIONAL CONVERSION

To ensure better preparation for the conversion and to facilitate a smooth transition, the conversion must be carefully planned. The relational conversion process can be simplified into four important steps:

- Converting databases.
- Converting programs.
- Training IS professionals and end users.
- Documenting procedures, operations, policies, methodologies, standards, and guidelines.

In general, the conversion process is not strictly sequential. Tasks performed in each step can overlap. A nonsequential view of the conversion process is shown in Exhibit 1.

The first step is to convert databases. A set of programs must be written to read the old master file to the new relational tables. Tables that are designed to store data about events or transactions are also created. The objective is to establish relational databases that meet third normal form. In this step, relational databases and old files (or nonrelated databases) are maintained in parallel during the conversion steps.

The next step is to convert programs. Experienced programmers must be assigned to develop a translator to enable existing nonrelational programs to access relational databases. Other programmers must be responsible for the development of routines that enable the existing nonrelational programs to access relational databases. For applications that are not convertible using these methods, a total approach that redesigns and rewrites entire programs to fit into a relational structure is required.

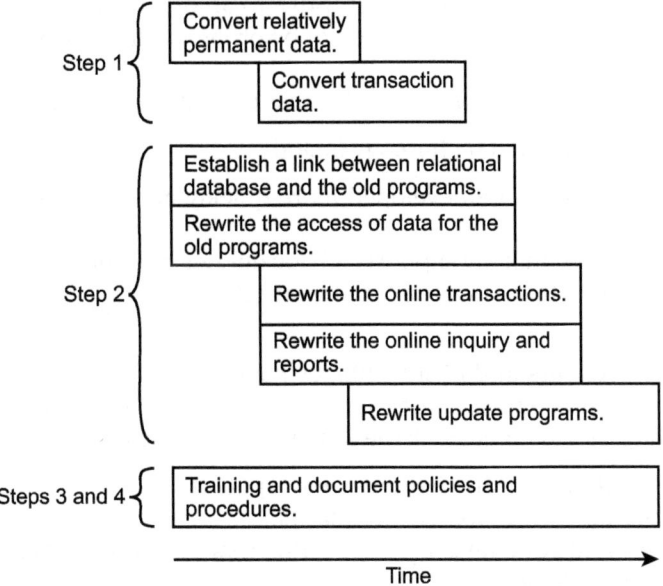

Exhibit 38-1. The four steps in relational conversion.

Nevertheless, entire applications programs must be gradually rewritten using relational database programming. Online transaction programs using 4GLs can be easily developed to collect data about events or transactions. A new relational database that uses visual4GL components to retrieve information or generate reports should also be opened for end-user computing. The conversion of the update programs then progresses to the final phase. CASE tools can be used to isolate update logic from other modules during the conversion process.

Finally, documentation of relational-specific policies and procedures is finalized. The documentation is actually a by-product of the conversion process. Among the most important components are careful planning, the resolution of strategic issues, and the adequate training of systems development professionals in the use of CASE tools.

RECOMMENDED COURSE OF ACTION

As in making any decisions that can have a large impact on an organization's operations and culture, systems development managers must weigh the pros and cons of relational and nonrelational database technology. To review, factors against converting to relational databases include:

- Relational database access can be slower.
- Relational database processing can be inefficient.

- The conversion process is disruptive to an organization's operations.
- Staff may resist the change and not be proficient in relational programming.
- Senior management may find the cost of conversion too high.

Benefits of relational technology include:

- Applications can be developed more quickly and require less maintenance.
- Relational technology supports ad hoc queries and end user computing.
- Relational databases use a tabular structure, which is easier to understand.

After the benefits and disadvantages have been weighed and the decision has been made to convert to relational technology, systems development managers must consider the following strategic issues:

- Responsibility for applications development.
- Applications development standards.
- Policies and guidelines for supporting new functions enabled by relational technology.
- The use of multiple DBMSs.
- Training development personnel and end users in the new technology.

The actual conversion process involves the following four steps:

- Converting databases.
- Converting programs.
- Training systems developers and end users.
- Documenting procedures, operations, policies, methodologies, standards, and guidelines.

Chapter 39
Data: Everchanging and Eternally the Same

Bruce Anderson

ONE OF THE CONSTANTS IN DATA PROCESSING IS THAT DATA CHANGES — vales, obviously, but also the attributes and relationships. Over time, the nature of the business changes, so data attributes follow: new systems are installed, and data must be converted; companies merge and data from disparate sources must be integrated; branch offices can often make creative interpretations of data rules. An initiative is started to create an Enterprise Data Warehouse. All of these events constitute data *changes* in the sense of this article.

All data stores have *views*. (Note: this term is being used here in a much more generic and intuitive way then a data management language *view*). Some views are embedded in a database management system. Some views are embedded in complex SQL under some sort of centralized control. Some views are embedded in programs or suites of programs under centralized control; e.g., standardized inventory reports from IT. Some views are embedded in programs, SQL or (worst of all) spreadsheets which are user built and maintained. Some DBMSs attempt to capture the business rules (i.e., the semantics) of the data in ways such as cardinality rules, foreign keys, referential integrity. Data warehouses and repositories allow for metadata with more sophisticated descriptors of what the underlying data mean. *The core problem is that, ultimately, data means whatever the end user/ decision-makers choose to make them mean or assume they mean.* There are many business rules embedded in those SQL queries; those suites of programs running against a sequence of 76 flat files; those user maintained programs and queries; and those innumerable spreadsheets that finance keeps separate from centralized data stores.

In other words, the business rules/semantics/"what the data means" are never really stored in a fully reusable manner. Many of those rules are

0-8493-0882-8/00/$0.00+$.50
© 2001 by CRC Press LLC

hidden away. The repository people are trying hard to migrate as much of the semantics as possible into a repository. We are not there yet, and (so far) there is no obvious "light at the end of the tunnel" suggesting that all of the semantics of a data store can ever be captured in a broadly re-usable way. The object-oriented people are trying hard to get us to migrate the business rule into a hierarchy of objects (Model-View-Controller). Again, we are not there yet, and again, there is no light at the end of the tunnel. Yet another way of expressing this is to say that **much of the meaning of the data is hidden in the programs**.

One way of appreciating this reality is to explore what it means to say that a program or system is "old," "obsolete" or "legacy." A critical piece of why this can happen, even in the face of all good intentions, good people and good management is that the business rules are hidden away amongst millions of lines of PL/1 or COBOL or C code, and no one remembers what they are. One of the prime motivations to senior management for funding the replacement of systems is to force staff to re-derive the enterprise's business rules. With any luck, this time around, a larger proportion of the business rules will be captured in a more explicit form than the last attempt — making business change quicker, easier, and less costly. A key reason why table driven systems such as SAP are achieving such market penetration is that they promise to capture a large fraction of the business rules in tables rather than code.

THE WINDS OF CHANGE — WHAT KINDS OF CHANGE/MISMATCH CAN HAPPEN?

We will explore three categories of change to underlying data in this chapter: (1) two data sources are merging — one has information about 'X' and the other does not; (2) one data source groups data codes data values one way, and another groups them differently; and (3) there are business rule differences between the data sources. In all cases, by understanding the kinds of change, it is easier to describe the existing options for dealing with them. In many cases, some forethought can prevent or mitigate problems.

The Case of the Missing Attribute

The simplest sort of difference is a missing attribute. For example, an insurance company decides to start tracking education level of insureds; while building the data staging process for a data warehouse, you discover that one division tracks the customers zip code while another does not. In each case, you are faced with a decision to make or delegate upwards. The data is missing from part or all of the available information over a period of time. The problem arises when someone wants to see continuity of data over time.

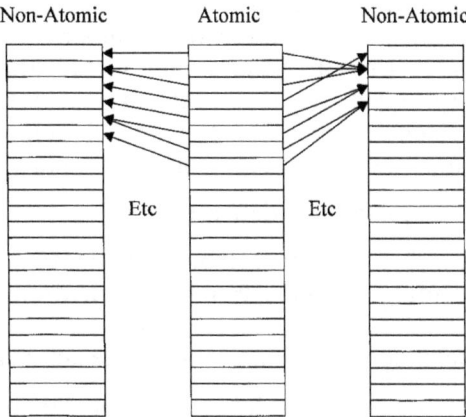

Exhibit 39-1. Atomic data.

The only appropriate systems response here is sensible expectation management. There are not many options for this one, and most managers inherently appreciate that if they did not collect the information in the first place, you cannot subsequently show it to them.

THE SHELL GAME — LOSING DATA BETWEEN THE SUMMARIES

The second sort of change or mismatch stems from what I call "non-atomic" data. For example, take age (see Exhibit 39-1). There are several ways to represent age:

- *By capturing the birth date/start date* — an "atomic" representation of age. It allows the age of the person or thing to be calculated not only as of the capture date, but for any other date as well. Atomic data presents no problems for change over time, conversion or integration since the data is at a fine a level as it can be represented. Note that it is possible to quibble with even this definition: for items that are very short-lived, the exact time of start may be critically important — e.g., the exact time that a long distance phone call began.
- *By capturing the explicit age in whatever units are appropriate (e.g., years, months, days, hours)* — this could be atomic under one set of business rules and not under another. If, for example, the age were captured in years in one system, but new rules required age in months, we have a conversion/integration problem. Also, unless the date at which the age was captured is known, ages may not be comparable.
- *By capturing a code for the age range (e.g., under 25, 26 to 35, 35 to 50, over 50)* — definitely not atomic. This concept becomes important whenever certain types of change rear their ugly head. For example,

one insurance company categorized motorcycles as "up to 250cc's" and "greater than 250cc's." The second company categorized them as "up to 100cc's," "100cc's to 450cc's" and "greater than 450cc's." When the companies merged, they had a difficult time sorting out records to develop combined actuarial results (critically important to business planning as larger sample size gives greater validity).

Other examples of non-atomic data are:

- Total sales by region (regions can be re-shuffled)
- Codes representing distance from a fire hydrant (ranges can be changed)
- Average annual income (without keeping the actual amounts)

For the mathematically inclined, the situation we are describing here arises when two different homorphic mappings are applied to the two sets of data and the underlying (atomic) data is deleted. In other words, the mappings should be views of the underlying data but the views have been kept and the underlying data discarded. As long as you have the underlying data, new views can easily be generated. Without it, life is not so simple.

Lesson 1: If you are at the planning stages, **always keep the underlying atomic data — even if management is adamant about not wanting it**. (You can always present codes as views of the atomic data). If it is too late for that, you may still have some options.

- If the atomic data is still available in electronic form, and it has appropriate identifying keys, then it should be possible to simply restore it. This is likely to be feasible and cost effective unless there is an issue of sheer magnitude. I have personally been on both sides of the decision for this category. In all cases, management made the call based on weighing the cost of restoring the data vs. the short-term benefit. Lesson: once you get into this problem, it is very difficult to sell the long-term benefits of correcting the problem.
- If the atomic data is still available but not in electronic form, if the appropriate identifying keys are available, then it should be possible to manually restore it. This may or may not be feasible, depending on the volume and complexity of the data and the business value of restoring it. Conversions of reasonable magnitude are often done manually — but that is the **whole** conversion, not the work to add a missing attribute. If there is any significant volume of data involved, it is likely to be very difficult to justify this sort of effort.
- If the atomic data is still available in any form, but the identifying keys are either missing or suspect, then this boils down to two options:
  — "Guess:" This includes any mechanism for allocating the data in the term "guess" including using suspect keys.

— "Give up:" Admit to the stakeholder that there is either no way to re-construct the data or no way to justify the cost of reconstructing it with any degree of accuracy.

- If the atomic data is not available, but the views are close, then in some special circumstances, it may be feasible to do some form of statistical reconstruction. This is not a rare thing — various categories of over-head expense are frequently allocated down to more detailed levels based on a variety of business rules — e.g., headcount, square footage, and gross sales. Warning: make sure that this option is clearly under-stood at the highest management level that will be depending on the data, as it will not be real.
- If the atomic data is not available and the views are not close to the original, then accept reality and promise to keep atomic data in your next design.

In summary, there are four ways of dealing with the situation:

- Load the atomic data in the first place.
- Restore the missing data, either electronically or manually.
- Approximate the missing data (and make sure to document very care-fully the accuracy of the approximations and the circumstances in which they may be misleading).
- Accept the fact that you are not going to be able to deliver the missing data.

Keep in mind that someone will be disappointed or misled if you end up with options 3 or 4. Further, someone may make expensive business deci-sions based on the data that they see — not realizing that it is incomplete or misleading. Make sure that you go to significant lengths to communicate to that person or persons that the data differs from reality in important ways.

A large insurance company once decided to reorganize itself into clean-er product lines. Independent insurance brokers typically come close to breaking even on the straight commissions they are paid, and make their profit on the profit sharing bonuses that most insurers pay annually. The fee paid is based on the profitability of the brokers business. It is calculated based on a complex formula that uses results in several categories over multiple years. The problem arose when the company decided to re-state each broker's historical results based on the new and cleaner definition of product lines, without having first re-stated all the basic data. There were many situations where it was not clear from historical data which of the new, cleaner product lines a piece of business belonged.

Using the analysis I've presented above, this project faced not one, but two of the core data problems: The underlying data was missing an at-tribute (the one that identified which of the new product lines any give his-torical transaction belonged to). In turn, the broker historical profitability data — a summarized view of the company transaction data — was a non-atomic summary whose definition needed to be changed. Had anyone on the project team clearly understood this situation at the time, the results might have been more pleasant. The actual results were that a massive overtime effort was undertaken to (1) re-stating the current transaction data and (2) approximate the historical data. There were two major gaps: (1) the historical data was actually re-stated a year later, so the "badness" of the approximation was then easily measured; and (2) since no one at the time clearly understood the impact of the approximations, no one could clearly communicate to the executive how good or bad the approximation was. Common sense caught a lot of bad approximations as checks were about to go out the door, but the cost was still considerable.

This anecdote points out two realities: (1) even though the categorization of data mismatches seems simple on first reading, it can be quite complex when applied to a real world situation; and (2) no matter how clever one is, it is easy to lose sight of the swamp when the alligators are closing in.

BUSINESS RULE MISMATCHES

The bigger the organization, the more energy it will take to get these sorted out. The more history an organization has, the worse the business rule matches are likely to be.

To read the marketing brochures of information warehouse providers is to wax rhapsodic in a reverie of total information availability — every fact and facet of the business instantly available at executive fingertips, all relationships neatly sorted, and all data readily comparable with other data. So if the technology is here, why isn't the dream a reality?

My answer: **business rule mismatches**. Remember that there are fairly explicit directly data related business rules like cardinality and referential integrity. There are also all those "other" nuances of data interpretation that are imbedded in all those queries, spreadsheets and programs that are lurking out there (see Exhibit 39-2).

Here is a good example that will cause lots of telco problems in the next few years. There is a historical association between NPA-NXX (known to most people as "area code" and "exchange") and a geographic location. The NXX normally corresponded with a physical structure called a frame. In fact, in the past, if you knew someone's NXX (exchange) in an urban area you could tell the general neighborhood they lived in. In the thousands upon thousands of programs that have been written to handle Telco billing and provisioning, the assumption about that connection has been so deeply embedded as to be hardly detectable. The same assumptions have been embedded in hundreds of file and database designs. This is still important

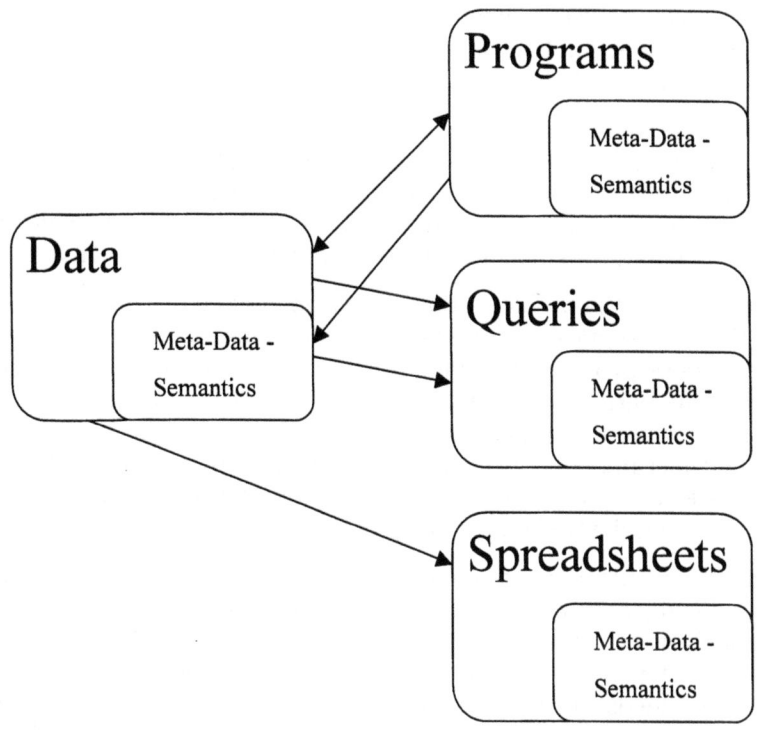

Exhibit 39-2. Data and semantics.

for two reasons: (1) someone has to know where the "end of the wire" is; and (2) someone has management responsibility for managing the frame at the "end of the wire."

Yet, technology has advanced. There are remote switches which allow large businesses, governments and universities to maintain the same NXX across what used to be NXX boundaries. With competition came Equal Ease of Access rules, local number portability, and in some areas, overlay — which means that two NPAs (area codes) can co-exist and overlap in the same geographic area.

The most obvious data mismatch here will be a missing attribute — the identity of the physical frame or frame location that represents the "end of the wire."

There are also more subtle impacts. Consider the situation where a planner depends on a query that measures working lines, and makes a prediction when the next major investment will be required on communication feeder routes. The planner enters the code number of the "Frame," but the calculations done by the query have a hidden anomaly that still assumes the old NXX to frame relationship. As a result, the planner is presented with a distorted projection that has the appearance of correct data, but the resulting decision could be tragic!

Other data "land mines" arise as a result of changing data relationships that have not been anticipated in the data manipulation/transformation code. Even the simple addition of a new product can produce unexpected results if the existing transformation code was not designed to dynamically adjust to new codes (or someone forgets to update a product–matching list).

In addition to the problems that stem from hidden or invisible business rules, there are subtle (and not-so-subtle) problems that crop up all the time when users or programmers violate an existing, but hidden rule. Senior managers are particularly adept at this as they will tend to ignore all of the subtle exceptions to normal business flow and relationships as they search for the big picture. This results in views which portray conflicting information. This leads senior management to no end of headaches, and leaves a bad taste about the "reliability" of systems. IT usually gets the blame.

Query "land mines" are not limited to incorrect data relationships. Problems frequently arise from assumptions made in the query code. Clients often wrongly assume that all attributes are data-filled, and then make wrong decisions on what they believe to be a complete answer. For example, when the planner needs to know how many customers are eligible for a new location-sensitive service, they must not rely entirely on postal codes that may or may not be data-filled. Often, this problem can be mitigated by weighing factors computed from the percent of populated data.

In another example, a client assumed that a join between the Circuit table and the Customer table would give them a list of all customers affected by the rearrangement of a high-capacity fiber optics cable. Unfortunately, the query was coded as a conventional (inside) join, resulting in the omission of switched circuits from the planning (i.e., circuits without a dedicated customer).

CONCLUSION

Data may just be strings of 1s and 0s, but the value of that data is the combination of the data and the meaning hidden in the data, data relationships, queries, interpretive programs, and the hidden assumptions of the people who use the data. Changes and mismatches occur over time as rules change, as the business rules change, as entities merge and separate and as regulations and generally accepted principles change. This article has identified the places where the **meaning** of the data is hidden, and the structure of how changes and mismatches come into being.

There are three types of mismatch: missing attributes, non-atomic data, and business rule changes. Data practitioners need to work aggressively towards gaining control of these mismatches — through central control and through making business rules explicit.

- *Lesson 1:* if you are at the planning stages, always keep the underlying atomic data — even if management is adamant about not wanting it.
- *Lesson 2:* You cannot provide an enterprise view without (central) enterprise control.
- *Lesson 3:* The more explicit you make the business rules the easier it will be for business consumers of data to validate them on an on-going basis — and thus make your life easier.
- *Lesson 4:* No matter how explicit you make the business rules, you'll have to rewrite the systems every 10 years or so to force staff (both business and IT) to rethink them all.

Chapter 40
A Practical Example of Data Conversion

Charles Banyay

CONVERSION, THE WORD IS ENOUGH TO DIM THE ENTHUSIASM of most systems developers. The word instills fear in some, trepidation and loathing in others. Regardless of the nature of the project with which she/he is involved, if there is any conversion effort involved, the reaction is the same. Exclude it from project scope! Let someone else do it! Although some might suspect that there may be some religious connotation here, and rightly so, the topic of this chapter is not converting from one religion to another. Nor is the topic software conversion, although this would be closer to the mark. This chapter deals with the various forms of the conversion of data.

Even if the project promises to be primarily development and/or implementation, which is usually the dream of most developers. Even if it involves some of the latest state-of-the-art technology, the word conversion immediately throws a pall over all the luster and glitter, and hopes of an interesting endeavor. Most systems implementations involve some form of conversion. When the software changes, the data model or the data itself often changes with it.

For some reason, conversions have come to be associated with the mundane, boring, and tiresome aspects of systems implementation. Most developers would consider conversion efforts as boring, tiresome, and devoid of interesting challenges, when compared to the implementation of state-of-the-art technology.

This is a misconception in many instances. Conversion efforts can be as challenging as any state-of-the-art technology. They can exercise the most creative abilities of technology professionals. An entire chapter probably could be devoted to discussing the possible reasons behind the general lack of enthusiasm for the conversion effort. This chapter, however, will focus on examining the following:

- Different types of conversion efforts that one encounters during systems implementation projects.
- The taxonomy of the conversion effort.
- Common pitfalls that can have rather detrimental effects on the overall effort if one is not aware of them and does not take the necessary precautions before hand.

CLASSIFYING DATA CONVERSIONS

There are a number of different ways to classify a data conversion. One of the most common ways is to classify it by what is involved in the conversion effort. This could be one or more of the following:

- Converting from one hardware platform to another, e.g., a host system upgrade (on PCs this is done on a matter-of-fact basis almost daily).
- Converting from one operating system to another, e.g., UNIX to NT.
- Converting from one file access method to another, e.g., converting from an indexed or flat file structure into a DBMS.
- Converting from one coding structure or format to another, e.g., from EBCDIC to ASCII.
- Converting application software such as upgrading versions of an application or replacing one application with another as in replacing an outmoded payroll application with a state-of-the-art pay benefits system.

One of the most common pitfalls of conversions is to combine into one conversion effort a change of too many variables, e.g., changing hardware, operating system(s), file access method(s), and application software all at once. Sometimes this cannot be avoided. Ideally, however, as few as possible of the variables should be changed at once. With only one variable changing, error detection and correction is the simplest. Any problem can be attributed to the change of the single variable and, thus, can be rectified by analyzing the single variable. With combinations and permutations, the effort increases exponentially.

Unfortunately, as often happens in life, the ideal state is the exception. In general, it is a rare conversion that does not have some combination of the above variables changing at once. The taxonomy of each, however, can be explored individually, as can most of the pitfalls. Some combinations will have unique pitfalls simply due to the combination of changes in variables.

CHANGE IN HARDWARE

In general, the simplest conversion is upgrading hardware, assuming that all of the other variables remain constant, i.e., operating systems, file access method, coding structure and format, and application software. This can be illustrated best in the PC world. PCs have been upgraded with relative ease continuously from one configuration to another for the past

10 years. As long as the operating system does not change the upgrade in hardware usually involves nothing more than copying the files from one hard disk to another. This migration of files usually is accomplished with the assistance of some standard utilities. Using utilities rather than custom-developed software lowers the amount of effort involved in ensuring that the files have migrated successfully. Most utilities provide fairly good audit trails for this purpose. Even files on the same floppies can be used in a 286, 386, 486, or Pentium machine. Data on floppies does not require any conversion.

In environments other than personal computers, the same simplicity of conversion generally holds true. Upgrading from one configuration of mainframe to another is relatively easy. Changing configurations of a minicomputer, such as from one AS/400 to a more powerful configuration of the same or from one HP/3000 to a more powerful HP/3000, generally does not require significant effort. These kinds of conversions generally are imperceptible to the users and are done without much involvement from the user community. There usually is no requirement for any user testing or programmer testing. This cannot be said for the more complex conversions such as changes in the operating system.

MIGRATING FROM ONE OPERATING SYSTEM TO ANOTHER

Changes to the operating system are generally more complicated from a conversion perspective, than changes to hardware. The complexity, however, is usually more pronounced at the application software rather than the data level. There is considerable insulation by the operating system of the application software and associated data from the hardware. In general, there is little to insulate the application software from the operating system. Object-oriented approaches are slowly changing this fact, but for now it is safe to say that a change in operating system requires a more complex conversion effort than a change in hardware.

For individuals who primarily have limited their involvement with technology to the WINTEL world, conversion complexity due to changes in operating system may come as a surprise. In the WINTEL world one generally can change from DOS to Windows 3.x to Windows 95 (or higher) with little or limited problems. In fact, most users do this on a regular basis. This may imply that changes in operating system are as simple as changes in hardware. This is a misconception. The people at Microsoft® and to a limited extent at Intel have spent innumerable hours to ensure that there exists a degree of compatibility between these operating systems that does not exist in any other environment.

Even in the WINTEL world this compatibility is breaking down. As the move to NT accelerates this is becoming evident. Users moving to NT have discovered that many of their favorite software programs are not functioning as they would like them to, or the programs are not functioning at all.

Although some form of conversion effort usually is involved when operating systems are changed, the changes in operating system more definitely impact the application software than the data. The impact on any of the data is usually from indirect sources such as from a change in one of the other variables such as data format or file access method. Different operating systems may support only different data coding structures and/or different file access methods.

CHANGES IN FILE ACCESS METHOD

It is not often that one changes a file access method while leaving the operating system and the application system the same. The general reasons for doing this would be suspect unless the current file access method was being abandoned by whomever was providing support. Another valid reason for changing file access method may be if a packaged application system vendor released a new version of their application. This new version may offer a new data architecture such as an RDBMS. There may be valid reasons, such as better-reporting capability using third-party tools, for upgrading to this new version with the RDBMS. For whatever the reason, a change in file access method usually requires some form of change in data architecture.

A simple illustration of this change in the underlying data architecture would be in converting a flat file sequential access method to an indexed file access method. Some form of indexing would have to be designed into the file structure resulting in a change in the underlying data architecture. A more complex example would be in changing from a sequential access method to a database management system.

This change at the minimum would involve some degree of data normalization and a break up of the single segment or record structure of the file. The resultant change in data architecture would be quite substantive. This type of conversion generally is not simple and requires a comprehensive conversion utility. In the case where it is a packaged application being upgraded, the vendor probably would provide the conversion utility. In the case where a custom-developed application is being converted, the conversion utility probably would have to be custom-developed as well.

In either case, the tasks are straightforward. All of the data must be converted. Every record must have a corresponding entry or entries in some table or tables. Each field in the source file needs to be transferred to the target database. Field conversion is not required. There is only a limited degree of selection involved. The conversion utility is run against the source data to create the target data store. Often there are a number of intermediate steps.

Different tables or segments of the database may be created in different steps. The resultant data is verified at each step. Taking a step-by- step approach, one can minimize the number and extent of the reruns of the conversion. This is another example of minimizing the number of variables that can change at once.

There are a number of approaches to ensuring that the resultant data store has the required integrity. These approaches are identical to the ones used to ensure the integrity of data that is converted due to a change in the application software.

The extent of the effort depends on the degree of reliability that is required. The effort has an obvious cost. The lack of data integrity also has a cost. A financial system requires a high degree of data integrity. It can be argued that the data controlling the operation of a nuclear power station requires even a higher degree of integrity.

MIGRATING FROM ONE APPLICATION SYSTEM TO ANOTHER

Changing or upgrading applications always requires converting data from the old to the new application. These conversions are generally the most complex and require the most effort.

One of the first steps in the conversion process is to decide which is the driving application. What is most important in the conversion process? Being exhaustive in converting the data in the old application or ensuring that the new application has the required fields that it needs to operate effectively. This may not be intuitively obvious. This is not to imply that the decision as to which data to convert is at the whim of the person designing the conversion programs.

There is always a base amount of data that must be converted. Many old applications, however, accumulate various codes and indicators over the years that either lose meaning over time or are particular to that application and are not required in a new application. This situation is more particular to operational applications such as payroll, materials management, etc. When converting data in an operational application, the emphasis is on converting the minimum amount of current data for the new application to fulfill its role and be able to operate. The data requirements of the new application drive the conversion design.

Record-keeping applications on the other hand, such as document management systems and pension administration systems need to retain almost all of the information within the current database. These applications generally hold a tremendous amount of history that needs to be retained. Recordkeeping applications as a rule require that the emphasis be on being exhaustive in converting all of the information within the current database. The data requirements of the old application drive the conversion design.

Generally speaking converting operational applications is considerably easier than converting recordkeeping applications. Populating fields necessary for the operation of a particular piece of software can be done in various ways. New information required for the effective operation of the new application, which is not available from the old application, can be collected from other repositories. This is generally the most time-consuming and complex way of meeting the data requirements of the new application. On the one extreme of the conversion continuum is the possibility of disregarding the old application completely and satisfying the data requirements of the new application by collecting the data from original sources. This approach is particularly useful when the data integrity of the old application is very suspect.

New information also can be provided as defaults based on other data, which are available from the old application. For example, in classifying employees for payroll purposes, give each employee the same classification based on the department where they work. In some instances new information can be fudged if the new data are not critical to the output required. For example, if source medium for an invoice is a required field in a new accounts payable application and it is not a current business requirement to keep source medium, then it could be assumed that all invoices are on paper and the information fudged with that indicator.

Being exhaustive and ensuring that all of the data in an old application are converted to a new application, as a rule, is more complex than meeting the data requirements of a new application. The complexity is not just in the conversion. The old application must be analyzed much more thoroughly to ensure that all of the data are understood and put into proper context. The converted data must be screened much more thoroughly to ensure that everything has been converted appropriately and is in the proper context within the new application. In addition there are still the data requirements of the new application to consider.

Converting historical information often requires shoehorning existing data into fields that were not designed for that data. Very often field conversions are required. For various reasons there may be an array of information in the old application, for which there is only one field in the new application. Pension administration systems are notorious for this. For example, it is not uncommon to have numerous pension enrollment dates depending on the prior plans of which an individual was a member. The new application, especially if it is not sophisticated, may provide only one pension enrollment date.

Acquisitions, mergers, and changes in union agreements and government legislation can cause havoc with historical recordkeeping systems. These then result in a nightmare of a conversion when one of these applications needs to be converted to a new application system. A very common experience is that the conversion routines often approach the complexity of artificial intelligence applications. These are the conversions that tax the abilities of even the most experienced developers. These conversions are also the ones that are potentially the most interesting and challenging to complete.

Once the driving application is determined, the next decision, which is basic to any conversion, is whether an automated conversion is the most effective way of transferring the data to the new application. In certain instances an automated conversion may not be possible. For example, if the source data architecture or the data format is not known and cannot be determined, and there is no export utility provided by the application, then it would be very difficult to develop an automated conversion utility. In certain instances it is simply not cost-effective to develop an automated conversion utility. If the volume of source data is relatively low and the complexity of the data requires conversion routines approaching the complexity of artificial intelligence routines, then a manual conversion effort may be more cost-effective.

The next conversion decision that must be made is how to get the data into the new application. For some reason many application system designers never think of the initial population of their application with the relevant data. It is as if this was supposed to occur by magic. There are four basic ways of populating the new application. In order of relative complexity these are

1. Using a bulk load facility if one is provided by the target application.
2. Generating input transactions into the new application if the application is transaction-based and the format of the transactions is known.
3. Real-time data entry through key stroke emulation.
4. Creating the target database so that it is external to the application.

Bulk load facilities often are provided by most packaged application system vendors. If a bulk load facility is not provided, then the vendor often provides the necessary APIs in order that a bulk load facility can be developed. Bulk load facilities are the most effective tools with which to populate a new application. The bulk load facility generally provides the necessary native edit and validation routines required by the application, while providing the necessary audit capabilities with which to determine the degree of success of the conversion.

If a bulk load facility is not provided and cannot be developed from vendor-provided APIs, then the next best thing is to generate the transactions which ordinarily would be used to enter data into the system. In this way the data is cleansed by the application-provided routines, and one is ensured that the resultant data has the required integrity from the application perspective and is appropriately converted. This approach generally requires multiple conversion routines, possibly one per transaction type and multiple iterations of the conversion as the transactions are loaded.

If neither of the previous methods for converting the data is available, then one can explore using key stroke emulation as a method of entering the data. There are numerous key stroke emulation or screen scraping utilities available that can assist in this endeavor. The trick here is to generate flat files from the source application and then to assemble screens of information that ordinarily are used by the application for data entry. The application is in essence fooled into behaving as if a client was communicating with it for data entry.

There are some technical limitations or challenges with this approach. With large volumes of information, multiple clients with multiple client sessions may have to be established. This is dependent on the efficiency of the client application. The slower the client application and the higher the volume of data, the greater the number of clients who need to operate simultaneously. The more client sessions the higher the risk of malfunction. Auditing this type of conversion effort is usually quite challenging. The audit process needs to be very thorough to ensure that all of the data is converted. As with the previous approaches to conversion, by using this process one is still assured that the data that does make it to the new application have been validated and edited by the application-provided routines.

As a last resort, if it is determined that none of the above alternatives are feasible or available, then one can attempt to use the following approach. The tool of last resort is to convert the data from the source application by constructing the target database from outside the application. In the past, when applications and application data architectures were relatively simple, i.e., a flat file structure, this approach was used quite frequently. The trick here is that the conversion designer must have an intimate knowledge of the application design and underlying data architecture and the context of the data. With a simple application and a simple data architecture, this is not a daunting requirement. With today's complex application packages, however, this approach is almost not supportable. For example, creating the application database for an SAP implementation outside of the application would be out of the question.

Once the decision is made as to which approach to use for the conversion, the actual conversion routines need to be written and tested just like any piece of application code. There usually is no user testing required at this point. When the routines are ready and thoroughly tested the time comes for the actual conversion. This is the trickiest part of the entire effort. It is rare to have the luxury of ample time between running the conversion and certifying the resultant database for live operation. The planning of the actual conversion, checking the resultant database, and certifying the data must be planned with military precision.

586

Checking the data usually is done using multiple independent audit trails at least providing the count of data records converted and some hash totals on certain fields. The amount of effort expended is usually commensurate with the cost and impact of an error. The users of the data must be involved and have the final sign-off. Whatever audit trails are used, the results and associated statistics must be kept in archives at least for the first few years of operation of the new application. A copy of the source database used for the conversion also should be archived together with some application code that can access the data for reporting purposes. If questions with regard to the conversion process arise at a later date, then one has something to go back to for verification.

After a successful conversion, the last step involves decommissioning the old application. This sounds much simpler than it actually is. It is not unusual; in fact, it is often absolutely mandatory that the old and the new applications be run in parallel for some specified time period. Weaning users from the old application can sometimes be a major challenge. That, however, is not a subject for a chapter on conversions, but is more in the realm of change management.

CONCLUSION

As the preceding discussion illustrates, conversions are not as boring and lacking in challenges as most professionals assume. Neither are conversions as frightening as they are made out to be. Most systems implementations involve some form of data conversion. When the software changes, the data model or the data itself often changes with it. Conversion software design and development can challenge the most creative juices of the most skilled developers. Conversions can be interesting and fun. Keep this in mind the next time you hear the word "conversion."

Chapter 41
Data Conversion: Doing it Right the First Time

Michael Zimmer

WHEN SYSTEMS DEVELOPERS BUILD INFORMATION SYSTEMS, they usually do not start with a clean slate. Often, they are replacing an existing application. They must always determine if the existing information should be preserved. Usually the older information is transferred to the new system — a process known as data conversion.

Data conversion can involve moving data from flat file systems to relational database management systems (RDBMS). It also can involve changing from systems with loose constraints to new systems with tight constraints.

This chapter focuses on laying the groundwork for successfully executing a data conversion effort the first time around. It is assumed in this chapter that data modeling is being done and that relational database technology is employed. At the logical level, the terms *entity set, entity,* and *attribute* are used in place of the terms *file, record,* and *field.* At the physical level, the terms *table, row,* and *column* are used instead of *file, record,* and *field.* The members of IS engaged in the data conversion effort are referred to as the data conversion team (DCT).

COMMON PROBLEMS WITH DATA

The difficulties of a data conversion effort almost always are underestimated. Usually the conversion costs many times more than originally anticipated. This is invariably the result of an inadequate understanding of the cost and effort required to correct errors in the data. Usually the quality of the existing data is much worse than the users and development team anticipate.

Problems with data can result from missing information and mismatches between the old model (often only implicit) and the new model (usually explicitly documented). Problems also result if the conversion effort is started too late in the project and is under-resourced. The most common sources of problems are data quality and incomplete data.

Costs and Benefits of Data Conversion

Before embarking on data conversion, the data conversion team should decide whether data really needs to be converted and if it is feasible to abandon the noncurrent data. Starting fresh is an option.

The customers may decide that the cost to preserve and correct old information exceeds the benefit expected. Often, they will want to preserve old information, but may not have the resources to correct historical errors. With a data warehouse project, it is given that the data will be converted. Preservation of old information is critical.

The Cost of Not Converting

The DCT first should demonstrate the cost of permitting erroneous information into the new database. It is a decision to be made by user management.

In the long run, permitting erroneous data into the new application usually will be costly. The data conversion team should explain what the risks are to justify the costs for robust programming and data error correction.

Costs of Converting

It is no easier to estimate the cost of a conversion effort than to estimate the cost of any other development effort. The special considerations are that there may be a great deal of manual intervention, and subsequently extra programming, to remedy data errors. A simple copy procedure usually does not serve the organization's needs. If the early exploration of data quality and robust design and programming for the conversion routines is skimped on, IS generally will pay for it.

STEPS IN THE DATA CONVERSION PROCESS

In even the simplest IT systems development projects, the efforts of many players must come together. At the managerial and employee levels, certain users should be involved, in addition to the applications development group, data administration, database administration, computer operations, and quality assurance. The responsibilities of the various groups must be defined clearly.

In the simplest terms, data conversion involves the following steps:

- Determining if conversion is required
- Planning the conversion
- Determining the conversion rules
- Identifying problems
- Writing up the requirements
- Correcting the data
- Programming the conversion
- Running the conversion
- Checking audit reports
- Institutionalizing

Determining If Conversion Is Required

In some cases, data does not need to be converted. IS may find that there is no real need to retain old information. The data could be available elsewhere, such as on microfiche. Another possibility is that the current data is so erroneous, incomplete, or inadequate that there is no reason to keep it. The options must be presented for the clients so that they can decide.

Planning the Conversion and Determining the Conversion Rules

Once the DCT and the client have accepted the need for a conversion, the work can be planned in detail. The planning activities for conversion are standard in most respects and are typical of development projects.

Beyond sound project management, it is helpful for the DCT to keep in mind that error correction activities may be particularly time-consuming. Determination of the conversion rules consists of these steps, usually done in sequence:

- Analyzing the old physical data model
- Conducting a preliminary investigation on data quality
- Analyzing the old logical data model
- Analyzing the new logical data model
- Analyzing the new physical data model
- Determining the data mapping
- Determining how to treat missing information

Analyzing the Old Physical Data Model

Some published development methods imply that development starts with a blank slate. As a result, analysis of the existing system is neglected.

The reverse engineering paradigm asserts that the DCT should start with the existing computer application to discern the business rules. Data conversion requires this approach for data analysis. The DCT can look at old documentation, database definitions, file descriptions, and record layouts to understand the current physical data model.

Conducting a Preliminary Investigation of Data Quality

Without some understanding of data structures for the current application, it is not possible to look at the quality of the data. To examine the quality of the data, the DCT can run existing reports, do online queries and, if
possible, quickly write some fourth-generation language programs to examine issues such as referential, primary key, and domain integrity violations that the users might never notice. When the investigation is done, the
findings can be documented formally.

Analyzing the Old Logical Data Model

When the physical structure of the data is understood, it can be represented in its normalized logical structure. This step, although seemingly
unnecessary, allows the DCT to specify the mapping in a much more reliable fashion. The results should be documented with the aid of an entity-
relationship diagram accompanied by dictionary descriptions.

Analyzing the New Physical Data Model

The new logical model should be transformed into a physical representation. If a relational database is being used, this may be a simple step.
Once this model is done, the mapping can be specified.

Determining the Data Mapping

This step is often more difficult than it might seem initially. Usually, the
exceptions are one old file-to-one new file, and one old field-to-one new
field.

Often there are cases where the old domain must be transformed into a
new one; an old field is split into two new ones; two old fields become one
new one; or multiple records are looked at to derive a new one. There are
many ways of reworking the data, and an unlimited number of special cases
may exist. Not only are the possibilities for mapping numerous and complex, in some cases it is not possible at all to map to the new model because
key information was not collected in the old system.

Determining How to Treat Missing Information

It is common when doing conversion to discover that some of the data
to populate the new application is not available, and there is no provision
for it in the old database. It may be available elsewhere as manual records,
or it may never have been recorded at all.

Sometimes, this is only an inconvenience — dummy values can be put in
certain fields to indicate that the value is not known. In the more serious
case, the missing information would be required to create a primary key or
a foreign key. This can occur when the new model is significantly different

from the old. In this case, the dummy value strategy may be appropriate, but it must be explained fully to the client.

Identifying Problems

Data problems only can be detected after the old data structure is fully understood. Once it is determined what the new model will look like, a deeper analysis of the issue can be done.

A full analysis of the issue includes looking for erroneous information, missing information, redundancies, inconsistencies, missing keys, and any other problem that will make the conversion difficult or impossible without a lot of manual intervention. Any findings should be documented and brought to the attention of the client. Information must be documented in a fashion that makes sense to the client.

Once the problems have been identified, the DCT can help the client identify a corrective strategy. The client must understand why errors have been creeping into the systems. The cause is usually a mixture of problems with the old data structure, problems with the existing input system, and data entry problems that have been ongoing. It may be that the existing system does not reflect the business properly. The users may have been working around the system's deficiencies for years in ways that violated its integrity. In any case, the new system should be tighter than the old one at the programming and database level, should reflect the business properly, and the new procedures should not result in problems with usability or data quality.

Documenting the Requirements

After the initial study of the conversion is done, the findings should be documented. Some of this work will have been done as part of the regular system design. There must also be a design for the conversion programs, whether it is a one-time or an ongoing activity. First-time as well as ongoing load requirements must be examined.

Estimates should include the time necessary to extract, edit, correct, and upload data. Costs for disk storage and CPUs also should be projected. In addition, the sizing requirements should be estimated well in advance of hardware purchases.

Correcting the Data

The client may want to correct the data before the conversion effort begins or may be willing to convert the data over time. It is best to make sure that the data that is converted is error-free, at least with respect to the formal integrity constraints defined for the new model.

If erroneous information is permitted into the new system, it probably will be problematic later. The correction process may involve using the existing system to make changes. Often, the types of errors that are encountered may require some extra programming facilities. Not all systems provide all of the data modification capabilities that might be necessary. In any case, this step sometimes can take months of effort and requires a mechanism for evaluating the success of the correction effort.

Programming the Conversion

The conversion programs should be designed, constructed, and tested with the same discipline used for any other software development. Although the number of workable designs is unlimited, there are a few helpful rules of thumb:

- The conversion program should edit for all business rule violations and reject nonconforming information. The erroneous transactions should go to an error file, and a log of the problem should be written. The soundest course is to avoid putting incorrect data into the new system.
- The conversion programs must produce an audit trail of the transactions processes. This includes control totals, checksums, and date and time stamps. This provides a record of how the data was converted after the job is done.
- Tests should be as rigorous as possible. All design documents and code should be tested in a structured fashion. This is less costly than patching up problems caused by a data corruption in a million record file.
- Provisions should be made for restart in case of interruption in the run.
- It should be possible to roll back to some known point if there are errors.
- Special audit reports should be prepared to run against the old and new data to demonstrate that the procedures worked. This reporting can be done in addition to the standard control totals from the programs.

Running the Conversion

It may be desirable to run a test conversion to populate a test database. Once the programs are ready and volume testing has been done, it is time for the first conversion, which may be only one of many.

If this is a data warehouse application, the conversion could be an ongoing effort. It is important to know how long the initial loads will take so that scheduling can be done appropriately. The conversion then can be scheduled for an opportune cutover time. The conversion will go smoothly if contingencies are built-in and sound risk management procedures are followed. There may be a number of static tables, perhaps used for code lookup that can be converted without as much fanfare, but the main conversion will take time.

At the time planned for cutover, the old production system can be frozen from update or run in parallel. The production database then can be initialized and test records removed (if any have been created). The conversion and any verification and validation routines can be run at this point.

Checking Audit Reports

Once the conversion is finished, special audit reports should be run to prove that it worked, to check control totals, and to deal with any problems. It may be necessary to roll back to the old system if problems are excessive. The new application should not be used until it is verified that the conversion was correct, or a lot of work could be lost.

Institutionalizing

In many cases, as in data warehousing, conversion will be a continuous process and must be institutionalized. Procedural controls are necessary to make sure that the conversion runs on schedule, results are checked rigorously, rejected data is dealt with appropriately, and failed runs are handled correctly.

DATA QUALITY

A strategy to identify data problems early in the project should be in place, though details will change according to the project. A preliminary investigation can be done as soon as the old physical data model has been determined. It is important to document the quality of the current data, but this step may require programming resources. Customers at all levels should be notified if there are data-quality issues to be resolved. Knowledge of the extent of data-quality problems may influence the user's decision to convert or abandon the data.

Keeping the Data Clean

If the data is corrected on a one-time basis, it is important to ensure that more erroneous data is not being generated by some faulty process or programming. There may be a considerable time interval between data correction and conversion to the new system.

Types of Data Abnormalities

There may be integrity problems in the old system. For example, there may be no unique primary key for some of the old files, which almost guarantees redundancy in the data. This violation of entity integrity can be quite serious.

To ensure entity integrity in the new system, the DCT will have to choose which of the old records is to be accepted as the correct one to move into the new system. It is helpful for audit routines to report on this fact. In addition, in the new system it will be necessary to devise a primary key, which may not be available in the old data.

Uniqueness

In many cases, there are other fields that also should be unique and serve as an alternate primary key. In some cases, even if there is primary key integrity, there are redundancies in other alternative keys, which again creates a problem for integrity in the new system.

Referential Integrity

The DCT should determine whether the data correctly reflects referential integrity constraints. In a relational system, tables are joined together by primary key/foreign key links. The information to create this link may not be available in the old data. If records from different files are to be matched and joined, it should be determined whether the information exists to do the join correctly (i.e., a unique primary key and a foreign key). Again, this problem needs to be addressed prior to conversion.

Domain Integrity

The domain for a field imposes constraints on the values that should be found there. IS should determine if there are data domains that have been coded into character or numeric fields in an undisciplined and inconsistent fashion. It should further be determined whether there are numeric domains that have been coded into character fields, perhaps with some non-numeric values. There may be date fields that are just text strings, and the dates may be in any order. A common problem is that date or numeric fields stored as text may contain absurd values with the wrong data type entirely.

Another determination that should be made is whether the domain-coding rules have changed over time and whether they have been recoded. It is common for coded fields to contain codes that are no longer in use and often codes that never were in use. Also, numeric fields may contain out-of-range values. Composite domains could cause problems when trying to separate them for storage in multiple fields. The boundaries for each sub-item may not be in fixed columns.

There may be domains that incorrectly model internal hierarchy. This is common in old-style systems and makes data modeling difficult. There could be attributes based on more than one domain. Not all domain problems will create conversion difficulties, but they may be problematic later if it cannot be proven that these were preexisting anomalies and not a result of the conversion efforts.

Wrong Cardinality

The old data could contain cardinality violations. For example, the structure may say that each employee has only one job record, but in fact some may have five or six. These sorts of problems make database design difficult.

Wrong Optionality

Another common problem is the absence of a record when one should be there. It may be a rule that every employee has at least one record of appointment, but for some reason 1% of old records show no job for an employee. This inconsistency must be resolved by the client.

Orphaned Records

In many cases, a record is supposed to refer back to some other record by making reference to the key value for that other record. In many badly designed system, there is no key to refer back to, at least not one that uniquely identifies the record. Technically, there is no primary key. In some cases, there is no field available to make this reference, which means that there is no foreign key. In other cases, the key structure is fine, but the actual record referred back to does not exist. This is a problem with referential integrity. This record without a parent is called an orphan.

Inconsistent Redundancy

If each data item is determined fully by its key, there will be no undesirable redundancy, and the new database will be normalized. If attempts at normalization are made where there is redundant information, the DCT will be unable to make consistent automated choices about which of the redundant values to select for the conversion.

On badly designed systems, there will be a great deal of undesirable redundancy. For example, a given fact may be stored in multiple places. This type of redundancy wastes disk storage, but in some cases may permit faster queries.

The problem is that without concerted programming efforts, this redundant information almost certainly is going to become inconsistent. If the old data has confusing redundancies, it is important to determine whether they are due to historical changes in the business rules or historical changes in the values of fields and records.

The DCT also should determine whether the redundancies are found across files or within individual files across records. There may be no way to determine which data is current, and an arbitrary choice will have to be made. If the DCT chooses to keep all of the information to reflect the changes over time, it cannot be stored correctly because the date information will not be in the system. This is an extremely common problem.

Missing Information

When dealing with missing information, it is helpful to determine whether:

- The old data is complete.
- Mandatory fields are filled in.
- All necessary fields are available in the files.
- All records are present.
- Default or dummy values can be inserted where there is missing information.

Date Inconsistencies

When examining the conversion process, it is helpful to determine whether:

- The time dimension is represented correctly.
- The data spans a long enough time period.
- The data correctly reflects the state of the business for the time at which it was captured.
- All necessary date fields are available to model the time dimension properly.
- Dates are stored with century information.
- Date ranges are in the correct sequence within a given record.
- Dates are correct from record to record.

Miscellaneous Inconsistencies

In some fields, there will be values derived from other fields. A derived field might be computed from other fields in the same record or may be a function of multiple records. The derived fields may be stored in an entirely different file. In any case, the derived values may be incorrect for the existing data. Given this sort of inconsistency, it should be determined which is correct — the detail or the summary information.

Intelligent Keys

An intelligent key results from a fairly subtle data-modeling problem. For example, there are two different independent items from the real world, such as employee and department, where the employee is given a key that consists in part of the department key. The implication is that if a department is deleted, the employee record will be orphaned, and if an employee changes departments, the employee key will have to change. When doing a conversion, it would be desirable to remove the intelligent key structure.

Other Problems

Often other problems with the old data cannot be classified easily. These problems involve errors in the data that cannot be detected except by going back to the source, or violations of various arcane constraints that have not been programmed as edit checks in the existing system. There may be special rules that tie field values to multiple records, multiple fields, or multiple files. Although they may not have a practical implication for the conversion effort, if these problems become obvious, they might falsely be attributed to the conversion routines.

THE ERROR CORRECTION PROCESS

The data correction effort should be run as part of a separate subproject. The DCT should determine whether the resources to correct the data can be made available. A wholesale commitment from the owners of the data will be required, and probably a commitment of programming resources as well. Error correction cannot be done within the context of rapid applications development (RAD).

Resources for the Correction Effort

Concerning resources for the correction effort, the best-case scenario would ensure that:

- Resources are obtained from the client if a major correction effort is required.
- Management pays adequate attention to the issue if a data-quality problem is identified.
- The sources of the problem will be identified in a fair and nonjudgmental manner if a data-quality problem is identified.

Choices for Correction

The effort required to write an edit program to look for errors is considerable, and chances are good that this will be part of the conversion code and not an independent set of audit programs. Some of the errors may be detected before conversion begins, but it is likely that many of the problems will be found during the conversion run.

Once data errors are discovered, data can be copied as is, corrected, or abandoned. The conversion programs should reject erroneous transactions and provide reports that explain why data was rejected. If the decision is made to correct the data, it probably will have to be reentered. Again, in some cases, additional programming can help remedy the problems.

Programming for Data Correction

Some simple automated routines can make the job of data correction much easier. If they require no manual intervention, it could be advantageous to simply put them into the main conversion program. However, the program may require that a user make the decision.

If the existing data entry programs are not adequate for large-scale data correction efforts, some additional programs might have to be written for error repair. For example, the existing system may not allow the display of records with a referential integrity problem, which are probably the very records that need correction. Custom programming will be required to make the change.

SPECIFYING THE MAPPING

Often, crucial information needed for the conversion will be missing. If the old system can accommodate the missing information, it may be a matter of keying it in from original paper records. However, the original information may not be available anymore, or it may never have been collected. In that case, it may be necessary to put in special markers to show that the information is not available.

Model Mismatches

It can be difficult to go from an non-normalized structure to a normalized structure because of the potential for problems in mapping from old to new. Many problems are the result of inconsistent and redundant data, a poor key structure, or missing information. If there is a normalized structure in the old system, there probably will not be as many difficulties. Other problems result from changed assumptions about the cardinality of relationships or actual changes in the business rules.

Discovered Requirements

The requirements of a system almost never are understood fully by the user or the developer prior to construction of the system. Some of the data requirements do not become clear until the test conversions are being run. At that point, it may be necessary to go back and revisit the whole development effort. Standard change and scope control techniques apply.

Existing Documentation

Data requirements are rarely right the first time because the initial documentation is seldom correct. There may be abandoned fields, mystery fields, obscure coding schemes, or undocumented relationships. If the documentation is thorough, many data conversion pitfalls can be avoided.

Possible Mapping Patterns

The mapping of old to new is usually very complex. There seems to be no useful canonical scheme for dealing with this set of problems. Each new conversion seems to consist of myriad special cases. In the general case, a given new field may depend on the values found in multiple fields contained in multiple records of a number of files. This works the other way as well — one field in an old record may be assigned to different fields or even to different tables, depending on the values encountered.

If the conversion also requires intelligent handling of updates and deletes to the old system, the problem is complicated even further. This is true when one source file is split into several destination files and, at the same time, one destination file receives data from several source files. Then, if just one record is deleted in a source file, some fields will have to be set to null in the destination file, but only those coming from the deleted source record. This method, however, may violate some of the integrity rules in the new database.

It may be best to specify the mapping in simple tabular and textual fashion. Each new field will have the corresponding old fields listed, along with any special translation rules required. These rules could be documented as decision tables, decision trees, pseudo code, or action diagrams.

Relational Mathematics

In database theory, it is possible to join together all fields in a database in a systematic manner and to create what is called the "universal relation." Although this technique has little merit as a scheme for designing or implementing a database, it may be a useful device for thinking about the mapping of old to new. It should be possible to specify any complex mapping as a view based on the universal relation. The relational algebra or the relational calculus could be used as the specification medium for detailing the rules of the mapping in a declarative fashion.

DESIGNING THE CONVERSION

Before starting to design a computer program, reentering the data manually from source records should be considered as a possibility.

Special Requirements for Data Warehousing

Data warehousing assumes that the conversion issue arises on a routine, periodic basis. All of the problems that arise in a one-time conversion must be dealt with for an initial load, and then must be dealt with again for the periodic update.

In a data warehouse situation, there most likely will be changes to source records that must be reflected into the data warehouse files. As discussed previously, there may be some complex mapping from old to new, and updates and deletes will increase the complexity greatly. There will have to be a provision for add, change, and delete transactions. A change transaction often can be handled as a paired delete and add, in some cases simplifying the programming.

Extra Space Requirements

In a conversion, it will be necessary to have large temporary files available. These could double the amount of disk space required for the job. If it is not possible to provide this extra storage, it will be necessary to ensure that the design does not demand extra space.

Choice of Language

The criteria for programming languages is not going to be too different from that used in any other application area. The programming language should be chosen according to the skills of the IS team and what will run on the organization's hardware. The most appropriate language will allow error recovery, exception handling, control totals reporting, checkpoint and restart capabilities, full procedural capability, and adequate throughput.

Most third-generation languages are sufficient, if an interface to the source and target databases or file systems is available. Various classes of programs could be used, with different languages for each. For example, the records may be extracted from the old database with one proprietary product, verified and converted to the new layout with C, and input into the new database with a proprietary loader.

SQL as a Design Medium

The SQL language should be powerful enough to handle any data conversion job. The problem with SQL is that it has no error-handling capabilities and cannot produce a satisfactory control totals report as part of the update without going back and requerying the database in various ways.

Despite the deficiencies of SQL as a robust data conversion language, it may be ideal for specifying the conversion rules. Each destination field could have a corresponding SQL fragment that gave the rules for the mapping in a declarative fashion. The use of SQL as a design medium should lead to a very tight specification. The added advantage is that it translates to an SQL program very readily.

Processing Time

IS must have a good estimate for the amount of elapsed time and CPU time required to do the conversion. If there are excessive volumes of data, special efforts will be required to ensure adequate throughput. These efforts could involve making parallel runs, converting overnight and over weekends, buying extra-fast hardware, or fine-tuning programs.

These issues are not unique to conversions, but they must not be neglected to avoid surprises on the day of cutover to the new system. These issues are especially significant when there are large volumes of historical data for an initial conversion, even if ongoing runs will be much smaller.

Interoperability

There is a strong possibility that the old system and the new system will be on different platforms. There should be a mechanism for transferring the data from one to the other. Tape, disk, or a network connection could be used. It is essential to provide some mechanism for interoperability. In addition, it is important to make sure that the media chosen can support the volumes of data and provide the necessary throughput.

Routine Error Handling

The conversion routine must support sufficient edit code to enforce all business rules. When erroneous data is encountered, there might be a policy of setting the field to a default value. At other times, the record may be rejected entirely.

In either case, a meaningful report of the error encountered and the resultant action should be generated. It will be best if the record in error is sent off to an error file. There may be some larger logical unit of work than the record. If so, that larger unit should be sent to the error file and that transaction rolled back.

Control Totals

Every run of the conversion programs should produce control totals. At a minimum, there should be counts for every input record, every rejected record, every accepted record, and every record inserted into each output file or table. Finer breakdowns are desirable for each of these types of inputs and outputs. Every conversion run should be date- and time-stamped with start and end times, and the control report should be filed after inspection.

RECOVERY FROM ERROR

Certain types of errors, such as a power failure, will interrupt the processing. If the system goes out in the middle of a 20-hour run, there will have to be some facility for restarting appropriately. Checkpoint and restart mechanisms are desirable. The operating system may be able to provide these facilities. If not, there should be an explicit provision in the design and procedures for dealing with this possibility. In some cases, it may be necessary to ensure that files are backed up prior to conversion.

Audit Records

After the data has been converted, there must be an auditable record of the conversion. This is also true if the conversion is an ongoing effort. In general, the audit record depends on the conversion strategy. There may be counts, checksums (i.e., row and column), or even old vs. new comparisons done with an automated set of routines. These audit procedures are not the same as the test cases run to verify that the conversion programs worked. They are records produced when the conversions are run.

CONCLUSION

Almost all IS development work involves conversion of data from an old system to a new application. This is seldom a trivial exercise, and in many projects it is the biggest single source of customer dissatisfaction. The conversion needs to be given serious attention, and the conversion process needs to be planned as carefully as any other part of the project. Old applications are fraught with problems, and errors in the data will be common. The more tightly programmed the new application, the more problematic the conversion.

It is increasingly common to make the conversion part of an ongoing process, especially when the operational data is in one system, and the management information in another. Any data changes are made on the operational system and then, at periodic intervals, copied to the other application. This is a key feature of the data warehouse approach. All of the same considerations apply.

In addition, it will be important to institutionalize the procedures for dealing with conversion. The conversion programs must be able to deal with changes to the operational system by reflecting them in the data warehouse. Special care will be required to design the programs accordingly.

Chapter 42
Migrating Data to an Integrated Database
James A. Larson and Carol L. Larson

RDBMS ARE A GREAT BOON TO DATA ACCESS. However, migrating data into a unified relational database can be quite challenging. To perform a successful migration, database administrators need to know how to:

- Detect and resolve structural inconsistencies.
- Detect and resolve value inconsistencies.
- Balance the tradeoff between the cost of maintaining an accurate database with the cost of mistakes due to inaccurate data.

STRUCTURAL INCONSISTENCIES

Inconsistencies among data files can be classified as either structural or value. Structural inconsistencies are incompatibilities among the schemas or file descriptions and should be identified and resolved before migrating data between the source and target files. Value inconsistencies are differences in values of corresponding schema items and can be identified only as data is moved and integrated from multiple sources into a single target file. Database administrators deal with each of these two inconsistencies in very different ways.

Structural inconsistency is the situation where the organization and formats of the target schema are different from the organization and formats of the source schema. Types of structural inconsistencies include naming issues, different abstraction levels, inconsistent coding structures, inconsistent data formats, and unneeded or missing data.

Naming Issues

The first task facing database administrators in determining how the data items of a source file relate to the data items of a target file is the identification of corresponding data elements. Database administrators often use data element names as clues to map data elements of a source file into the data elements of a target file. Exhibit 1 illustrates the notation used to

0-8493-0882-8/00/$0.00+$.50
© 2001 by CRC Press LLC

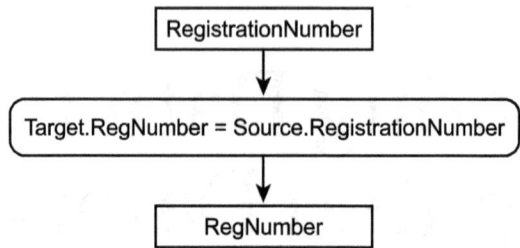

Exhibit 42-1. Indicating the correspondence between a source data element and a target data element.

indicate how a data element (i.e., RegistrationNumber) in the source file maps to a data element (i.e., RegNumber) in the target file.

Frequently, the names of two corresponding data items in the source and target files are similar, so the database administrator has no trouble identifying the correspondence. However, at times, data elements with the same name or nearly the same name may have very different meanings. For example, "date" may have several different meanings, including start date, end date, date the data was entered, publication date, date of issue, or date something becomes active. Database administrators must understand how the data will be used to determine precisely if two data elements really mean the same thing.

Sometimes, data elements with different names mean the same thing, as in title and job, level and class, rank and position, and location and address. Again, database administrators must understand how data will be used to determine whether data items with different names are equivalent.

Different Abstraction Levels

Two similar data items may represent similar information at different levels of abstraction. For example, the data item BirthDate is more specific than BirthYear because BirthDate includes the month and day of birth. In another example, the data element Author is binary and indicates only whether a person has authored one or more books. However, the element NumberBooksAuthored is much more specific; it indicates that a person is an author and the number of books authored.

It is always possible to define a mapping from the specific to the more general data element. Exhibit 2 illustrates the mappings from BirthDate to Birth-Year and from NumberBooksAuthored to Author. However, additional information is required to map a general data item to a more specific data item. Retaining as much specificity as possible is recommended, so information from the source database is not lost as it is migrated to the target database.

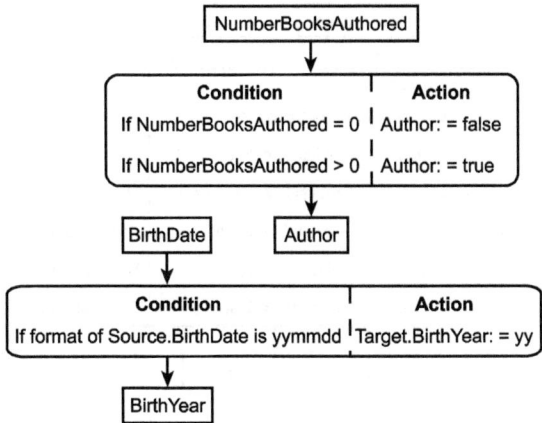

Exhibit 42-2. Mapping specific data elements to general data elements.

Inconsistent Coding Structures

The values used to represent information may differ between two data items. As illustrated in Exhibit 3, the source data element may use "S" for single and "M" for married, and the target data element may use "1" for single and "2" for married. In this case, mapping between the two coding structures is straightforward.

In some cases, one coding structure is more specific than another. For example, the source data element uses "U" for undergraduate and "G" for graduate and the target data element uses four different codes ("F" for Freshman, "S" for Sophomore, "J" for Junior, and "R" for Senior) for undergraduates, and two codes ("M" for Masters and "P" for PhD) for graduate students. Retaining the more specific coding structures is recommended. As the mappings in Exhibit 4 illustrate, additional information is necessary to map the general codes — G and U — to the specific codes — F, S, J, R, M, and P.

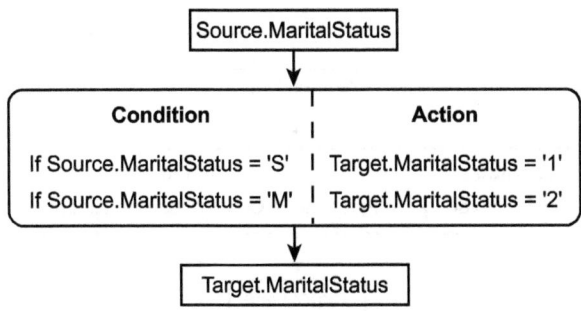

Exhibit 42-3. Mapping between different codes.

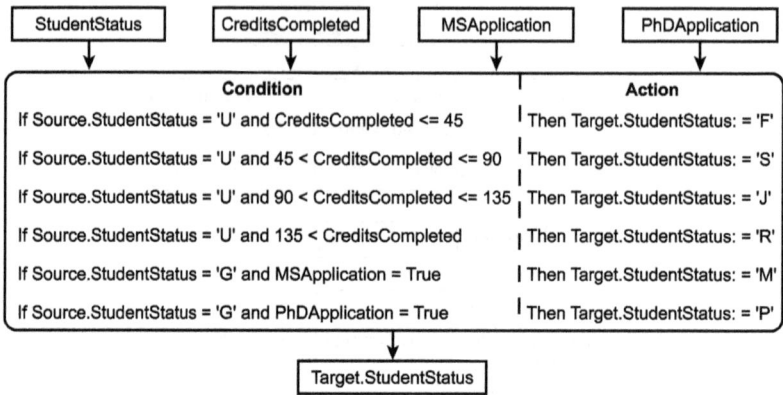

Exhibit 42-4. Deriving values for a more specific data element.

Inconsistent Data Formats

Data elements from different databases frequently use different data formats. For example, a date may be represented as mm/dd/yy, yy/mm/dd, or in Julian formats. Most database management systems (DBMSs) have utility conversion routines for automatic data format translation, as shown in Exhibit 5.

Occasionally, multiple data items from one file map to a single data item in another file. For example, BirthMonth, BirthDay, and BirthYear map to BirthDate, and, as illustrated in Exhibit 6, LastName and FirstName map to CompleteName.

Unneeded or Missing Data

Database administrators should pay special attention to data that is contained in the source file but missing from the target file. Missing data may indicate that an application using the target file may have been overlooked during the analysis. Because the required data is missing from the

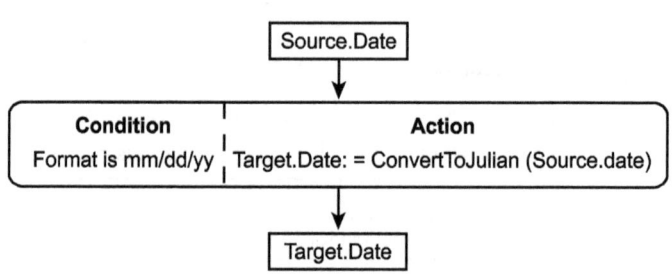

Exhibit 42-5. Using a utility to define mappings.

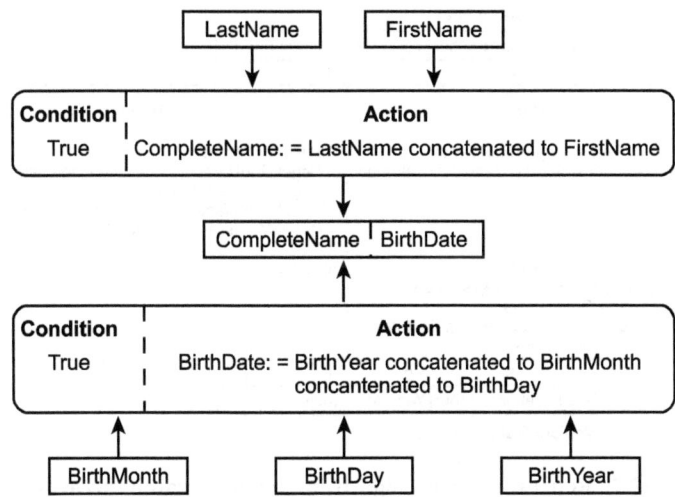

Exhibit 42-6. Combining two source data elements to create a single target.

integrated database, these applications cannot be executed. Database administrators should validate that the data in the source file is not needed in the target file.

Database administrators should also pay special attention to data in the target file that is not present in the source file. This data represents new database requirements and may indicate that an expensive data collection effort may be necessary to populate the new data item, so applications accessing the new data can be executed.

VALUE INCONSISTENCIES

Whenever there are two independent sources of values for a data item, it is possible that the values may be inconsistent. Exhibit 7 includes an algorithm for detecting such inconsistencies. It is assumed that the first source of values has already been migrated to the target Vehicle file. Exhibit 7 also illustrates the pseudocode for detecting inconsistencies between records of the source Truck file and the target Vehicle file. If there is no matching Vehicle record for the Truck record, then a new Vehicle record should be created and values should be moved into the corresponding data elements of the Vehicle record. However, if there is a matching Vehicle record for the Truck record, then the values of the corresponding elements should be compared. If an inconsistency is detected, the error should be reported right away so that the inconsistency can be corrected manually.

When inconsistencies occur, some database administrators calculate the maximum of the values, the minimum of the values, the average of the

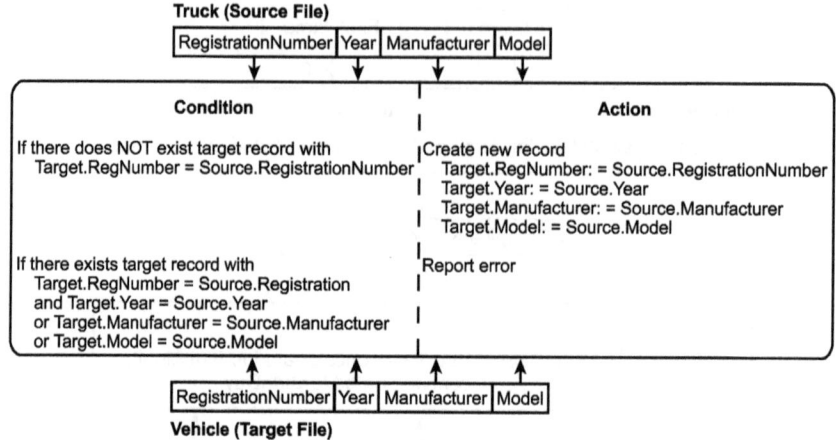

Exhibit 42-7. Representing an algorithm to detect value inconsistencies.

values, or some other automatic calculation to derive a single target value. These approaches are not recommended because they do not improve the accuracy of the data.

On the other hand, some database administrators retain both values in the database to let the end user choose which value to use. This method is not recommended either because it puts the burden on the individual using the data, instead of the individual entering the data.

It is recommended that the owner of the data refer back to the original source to determine the accurate value of the data. However, this can be an expensive and time-consuming activity. The database administrator should consider how to balance the cost of obtaining accurate data with the cost of mistakes due to inaccurate data to determine how much effort should be expended to correct known database errors.

A completely accurate database may be very expensive to maintain because of the cost of validating each data item. However, this may be necessary for databases that may have serious implications when their users take inappropriate actions based on inaccurate or out-of-date data. For example, errors in a police warrant database or a pharmacy's drug interaction database may result in loss of life, but errors in a holiday card mailing list or a television broadcast schedule are not life-threatening.

DATA MIGRATION TOOLS AND SERVICES

Many tools are available for migrating data from a source database to a target database. Generally, data migration tools assist the database administrator in constructing scripts that:

- Extract data from the source database files.
- Convert data to the format required by the target database.
- Detect inconsistencies between similar data from two sources.
- Insert the extracted data into the target database.

Some data migration tools contain a scripting language used to specify the four migration operations (i.e., extracting the data, converting the data, detecting inconsistencies, and inserting the extracted data). The scripting language can also be used to execute the scripts. After executing the scripts, the database administrator examines reports generated by the scripts and resolves any detected errors and data inconsistencies.

Some tools use a GUI to display the data elements from the source schema and the proposed data elements in the target schema. Using drag-and-drop operations, the database administrator identifies and specifies each of the migration operations. The GUI interface then generates the scripts. The database administrator may then edit the scripts to include additional functions and operations.

Despite the variety of data migration tools available, most tools only work with specific DBMSs. Vendors often provide tools for migrating data from files or from other DBMSs to their products, but rarely provide tools for migrating data from their products. The migrating tool marketplace is dynamic — new tools are announced frequently, and existing tools become outdated quickly.

Users can contact DBMS vendors for an up-to-date list of migration tools that work with particular DBMSs and solicit the vendor's recommendation about the usefulness of each tool. Costs for the tools vary. Some tools may be available at no cost from the vendor.

Because database administrators are familiar with the meaning and use of each data item, it is recommended that they perform their own data migration. However, if it is difficult to obtain and learn to use migration tools, hiring a service organization to migrate the data may be cost-effective. Database administrators should work closely with the service organization to develop the appropriate mappings between the source and target data and to resolve the data inconsistencies when detected.

RECOMMENDED COURSE OF ACTION

Database administrators should identify structural relationships between the source and target data elements. If the corresponding data elements are structured differently, pseudocode should be written for mapping the source data elements to the target data elements. From this pseudocode, code can be written or generated to migrate the source table to the target table. When migrating data to a data element already containing values, values should be checked and corrected according to the enterprise's general policy for tolerating and correcting erroneous data.

Bibliography

1. Brodie, M. L., and Stonebraker, M. Migrating Legacy Systems: Gateways, Interfaces and the Incremental Approach. San Francisco: Morgan-Kaufman, 1995.

Chapter 43
Bridging Legacy Data with XML

Frank Cullen

EXTENSIVE MARKUP LANGUAGE (XML) IS CURRENTLY BEING CHAMPIONED AS THE LANGUAGE OF THE FUTURE FOR GREASING THE WHEELS OF THE DRIVE TOWARD E-COMMERCE OVER THE "NET." Already, thousands of new "dot.coms" have started from scratch to specifically take advantage of the booming web-based business world. Light on their feet and already relying on modern relational database management systems (RDBMS), they are readily equipped to switch over to XML.

However, what about the long-established businesses whose database systems harken back to the days of "big iron?" These behemoths also recognize the need to migrate toward a web-based commerce, and their long track records often endow them with the financial means to make the leap past HTML-prepared data, directly to XML. However, this feat is much easier said than done.

The necessary tagging — or assigning of a Data Type Definition (DTD) — to pre-relational legacy database systems is fraught with unexpected pitfalls for the unwary. Quick solutions are hard to come by. Yet, understanding how to use data-cleansing tools to first untangle, and the migrate, data from older data structures can help immeasurably.

But first, a review of some of the common structures found in legacy databases will help uncover some of the problems often encountered in "untangling" or pointing this data to more modern XML.

DIFFICULTIES ENCOUNTERED WITH LEGACY DATA

The major areas of problems/challenges in legacy data management stem from five main categories:

1. Character sets and translations.
2. Poor data typing.
3. Hierarchical structures — header/trailer record systems.
4. Embedded sub table structures.
5. Departed "Legacy Programmers"

We will take a brief look of each of these areas and examine the problems, challenges and solutions that arise as the migration to XML is performed.

Character Sets and Translations. The translation and movement of data between IBM midrange and mainframe systems, for example, introduces a huge potential for faulty translation and data corruption. That's because data stored on computer systems has two main forms: Full character (display) form; and packed form (including signed numeric, packed-decimal, computational, and binary).

Full-character forms are used extensively whenever alphanumeric data is present — in descriptions, names, etc. Conversion here is almost never a problem. However, packed data forms are an entirely different matter. These are reliant not on the 8-bit character as a whole, but rather on the parts (sometime even the bit configuration) of each character. Translating computational and binary items almost never works and provides a host of examples why character-for-character translations corrupt data irretrievably.

Poor Data Typing. One of the principal contributors to data migration problems in mainframe applications is the lack of strong data typing (and enforcement). Calendar dates are an excellent example of items which are hybrids of data types, but there are countless others.

Fortunately, the development and popularization RDBMSs, such as SQL, has had the wonderful effect of formalizing the idea of rich data types and strict enforcement of data domain rules.

Hierarchical Data Structures. A hierarchical data structure has more than one record type. When a record can belong to at most one other record type, the relationship is said to be a "proper hierarchy." Data hierarchies play a crucial role in the philosophy and implementation of XML.

Adding records to the end of a hierarchical data file will usually not cause problems. But when records are added to the middle of the file, all the relative record numbers of the records beyond the point of insertion are bumped down. The idea of using relative record position as an ID generator is only valid for a "one time" or "cut-and-run" conversion.

Embedded Sub-Table Structures. The popularization of variable length record techniques brought with it a tremendous savings in mass storage space at reasonable small price. However, a maximum allowable number of additional fields must be set. Unfortunately, overestimating the number wastes valuable space, while underestimating causes program failure.

Departed "Legacy Programmers." Most companies have a "Super Programmer," who in times of trouble can be your only hope. But Super Programmers can define hideously complex records with bizarre relationships collapsed into variable length and self-describing attributes. When they leave the organization, their work can be your worst nightmare. It becomes extremely difficult to clean up after their "legacy."

THE DATA MIGRATION/TRANSFORMATION PROCESS

Preparing flat-plane databases for XML tagging requires a three step process. Not a single step can be omitted, or the conversion is destined to create more problems that it solves.

1. Analyze current data
2. Clean up current data
3. Transform the data

Analyze Current Data

Once you've decided to migrate your data form one structure to another, the first step is to thoroughly analyze your existing data. This process should especially focus on domain analysis, since it will help set the stage for data type identification.

If you've already analyzed your data during the Y2K compliance effort, the results of your analysis can be used again for the data transformation effort. This process should have already included the thorough testing of the output.

Clean Up Current Data

The next step is to clean up any bad data revealed during analysis and testing. In many cases, this involves straightforward corrections to field values. What may sound easy at first, is complicated by values that intentionally don't fit the format. Some of these exceptional values carry specific meaning and are commonly referred to as embedded rules. An example might be XXXX or 9999 to indicate "date unknown" in a field using YYMM format. You may wish to preserve these special rules or replace them with new ones. This can be done with such tools as Data Commander, which analyzes, cleanses, and transforms pre-relational legacy mainframe data and is available from Blackstone & Cullen of Atlanta, Georgia. Its EXCEPTION statements allows you to exempt specified fields from the general conversion (or migration or transformation) process or to convert them in a manner different from the rest of the data fields. Exhibit 1 illustrates some of the processes that are a part of the entire migration effort.

The actual preparation and migration of legacy data from a pre-relational mainframe environment to a clean, consistent relational data store happens in two major places: The host (or mainframe) location, where the main "untangling" takes place and the data is cleaned, reformatted, and scripted; and the server, where the web client resides. The data untangling is best done on the host, as moving the data en masse to a server fight must

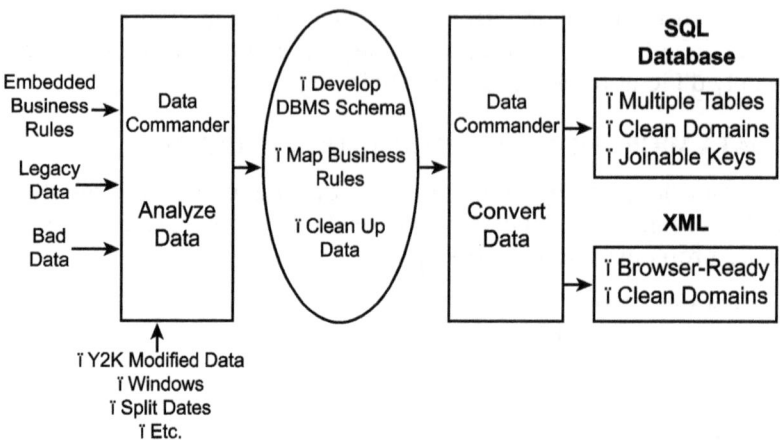

Exhibit 43-1. Pre-relational data analysis and migration process.

corrupt the packed, binary and signed data during the conversion of the characters from the host to the server.

Denormalizing Data for XML Output. One of the most important steps of the cleansing process is the denormalization (to 1st Normal Form) of the data. There are two main reasons for this: To avoid making multiple passes through the source data; and to provide data in a single-level hierarchy for an XML table for easier manipulation/access.

This process is also called "flattening" or "spreading" the hierarchy of the data. Exhibit 2 illustrates the general scheme used to both flatten and spread a hierarchy and generate XML output.

Transform the Data

Once the cleansing processes is complete, the output data can then be converted directly as XML 1.0 tagged; or even as field-sensitive formats and SQL INSERT syntax (for RDBMS population).

The main benefit of direct output to XML rather than the movement to an intermediate data store (such as a SQL-based Transformation Data Store) is that there is no requirement on having a SQL engine or other RDBMS processor to receive the data and pass it on — the transfer is direct. The number of characters it takes to represent (and transmit) data originally in packed and/or binary form on a mainframe may blow up to 10-20 times that amount when all the unpacking and XML field tag insertion is done.

Nevertheless, there are an increasing number of options for receiving and processing XML-encoded data currently available. The ability to publish the legacy as XML data (either spread or not) directly to a Web Browser using Data Commander is illustrated in Exhibit 3.

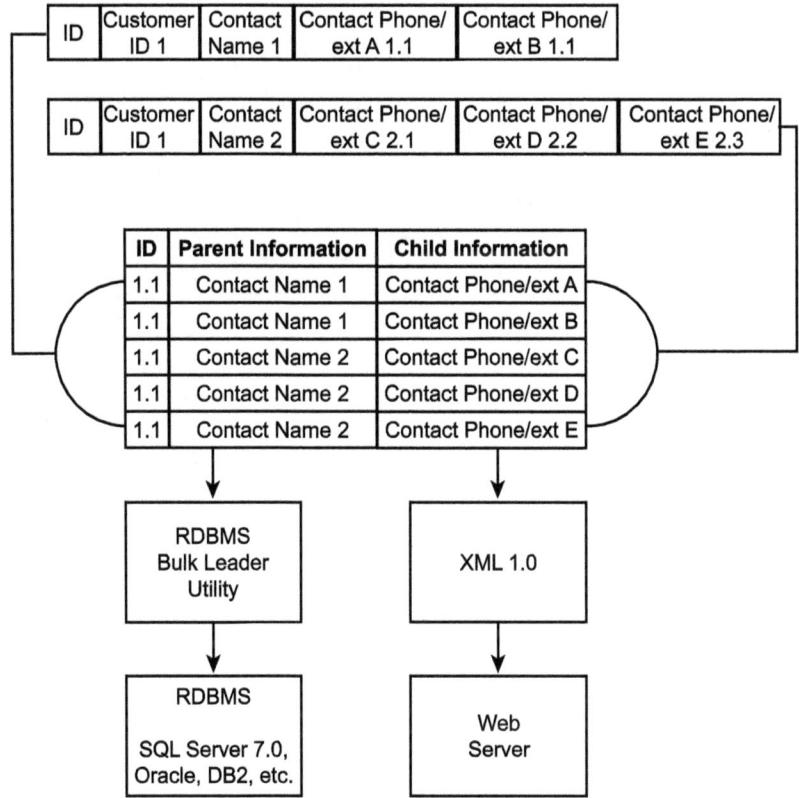

Exhibit 43-2. Flattening and spreading hierarchy denormalizing for data warehouse bulk loading and XML generation.

Instead of SQL output, Data Commander can generate XML DTD (Data Type Definition) syntax. This generation is turned on or off in an OPTION statement, so Data Commander can be used to construct DTD-less XML data islands. The combination of the flattening/spreading with the suppression of header record XML syntax and DTD generation provide an easy method to generate XML strings immediately usable for IE5 data islands in live web pages.

SUMMARY

Legacy data may represent a "Fort Knox" of wealth, but often this data is abandoned solely because it is difficult to access and get into a usable form. But cross-platform tools can extract valuable data from these complex structures, clean it, and generate XML syntax. Established organizations of any size can then take advantage of the golden opportunities afforded by web commerce.

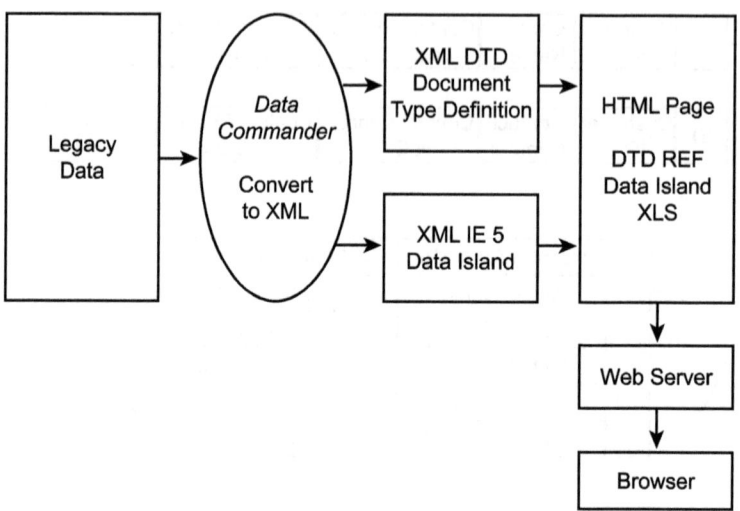

Exhibit 43-3. Legacy data to XML with Data Commander.

Section X
Performance Tuning

THIS SECTION DESCRIBES ANOTHER LEVEL OF PERFORMANCE TUNING FOR DATABASES AND APPLICATIONS TO IMPROVE APPLICATION RESPONSE TIME. Overall application performance is the result of the sum of the individual performances of each component involved in a transaction, plus some overheads. Performance tuning is an iterative process that requires extensive testing to locate bottlenecks and other exposures anywhere in a solution. A well-respected performance tuning approach involves tuning components that give the biggest impact on the bottom line, and then continuing the process until application performance is within an acceptable range.

Performance tuning in Web-based applications requires traditional techniques, such as database tuning, indexing, locking, and efficient algorithms. However, the Web-based components require additional approaches, techniques, and tools to optimize application performance. This section provides a cross-section of chapters that examine approaches for improving various components in an overall architecture to maximize application performance.

Chapter 44, "Improving User Experience Through Improved Web Design and Database Performance," examines considerations to improve overall application performance and Web site design. This chapter offers suggestions for improving the overall user experience by improving application performance and the appeal of the user interface layout and user interaction.

Chapter 45, "Web-based Testing and Capacity Planning," examines some of the key differences in testing a Web site compared to other technical architectures. The chapter also examines some of the specific capacity-planning issues facing Web design. Transaction volumes against Web sites are unpredictable, as the potential user base consists of anyone with a computer and a password. Because many Web sites allow users to get an account with relative ease, the number and complexity of operations require a more sophisticated approach and testing harness than do other non-Web architectures.

Chapter 46, "The Advanced Art of Indexing," describes the developments and challenges of indexing database tables to improve the performance of operations against the tables. Some operations, such as joins, updates, and subqueries, can be greatly improved by traversing indexes during parts of the transaction execution. Optimizing index utilization requires significant trial and error, and a highly iterative approach. Various indexing techniques such as B-Trees, bitmaps, and inverted files are examined in this chapter.

Chapter 47, "Parallel Databases," examines opportunities to improve application perfomance by leveraging multiprocessing and multithreading via parallel architecture to distribute workload over a wider base of tools.

Chapter 48, "Leveraging Checkpoint Processing," shows how to build checkpoints into batch processes to allow jobs to be restarted in the event that processing problems are encountered. This is needed to allow batch jobs to complete in scheduled batch windows, thereby allowing systems to become active and available to users at the normally scheduled time. Although Web solutions, almost by definition, rely on real-time data management, there is still a need for batch processing (e.g., for some reports or mass updates).

Chapter 49, "The Denormalization Decision in Database System Design," examines opportunities to improve database performance by denormalizing a physical data model or database based on transaction peaks. Denormalization is an accepted technique for modifying the physical structure and layout of database tables to support commonly executed transactions — although some normal forms are violated (i.e., the introduction of data redundancy).

Chapter 44

Improving User Experience through Improved Web Design and Database Performance

Srinivas Padmanabharao

THE LAST FEW YEARS HAVE SEEN AN EXPLOSION IN THE NUMBER OF WEB-SITES THAT CAN BE SURFED BY USERS, AS WELL, AS A CORRESPONDINGLY LARGE INCREASE IN THE BUSINESS VOLUMES THAT ARE CONDUCTED OVER THE INTERNET. Many factors affect the end-user experience including the speed of the connection, the nature of the transaction, the appearance of the screen, and content that stretch beyond the type of business conducted on a web site. Out of this list of factors, web site performance is increasingly proving to be a key competitive advantage (or disadvantage) that firms can use to win in the marketplace.

Most web sites can usually be looked upon as consisting of two main components, which are: (i) the front end that the user interacts with (e.g. web pages); and (ii) everything else that includes business components and data repositories that power the web-site. It is vital that businesses pay due attention to both components in order to improve the end-user experience and the performance of the application.

This work examines some of the issues that go into determining the full end user experience. It also explores some of the strategies that businesses can employ to improve web site design and database performance. It then reviews some tools that are available in the market to evaluate the performance of web sites.

FACTORS INFLUENCING THE END USER EXPERIENCE

This section outlines some factors that go into determining the full, integrated end-user experience.

Content

Content is undoubtedly one of the most important factors influencing end user satisfaction with a web site. For example, it can be an extremely frustrating experience for an end user to discover erroneous information shown on a web page. There are three web content qualities that must be met, namely: accuracy, appropriateness and scope.

Accuracy involves the presentation of error free information that is current and updated as frequently as it is needed. While it may serve as a medium of advertising for the company's products and services it must try and present a balanced and objective view, especially at web sites that are supposed to act as sources of information.

Appropriateness of a web site involves the use of concepts and information that is relevant to the target group of users. Use of appropriate language and content is especially important given that children are increasing becoming consumers of the web. Only information relevant to the business objective of the organization and supporting information must be presented on a web site.

Scope involves the presentment of information that is sufficient in scope to adequately cover the topic or message for the intended audience. This could be for the purchasing of goods & services or for the dissemination of information. Companies can enhance the value of their web sites by presenting information that is not easily attainable from other sources.

Technical Competence

The technical competence of a web site directly impacts the end-user experience. This involves navigational and presentation approaches.

A web site must be intuitive and easy to navigate. It must not be overloaded with graphics and must have reasonable download times. It must be complete with no broken links and must adhere to standard formats. It must provide logical options for printing and downloading selected components such as white papers and product information.

Presentation involves leveraging good graphic design principles where the use of images and multimedia is functional and not merely decorative. Appropriate text size, uncluttered screen displays and captions, labels or legends for all visuals must be used. Information must be presented in a manner to stimulate imagination and curiosity. At the same time product advertising must not be intrusive to users.

Trust

A web site must be able to gain the confidence of the consumer and establish trust as a basis for all transactions. Hackers that hit web sites with too many messages or erroneous data heighten security concerns for all users of the web. Hence for companies that intend to do business on the web this issue is of key concern. Companies must publish and adhere to their privacy policy on the web. They must not solicit any information from the user that is not directly relevant to complete the business transaction. This information must not be used to support email or other web marketing campaigns without the permission of the users. Web sites must also employ adequate technology to prevent the misuse of information collected from users.

WEB SITE DESIGN CONSIDERATIONS

A web site is not just a company's address on the web. It is a home. It is the only "face" of the company that an online consumer may ever see. Hence the importance of good design in putting up a web site cannot be underestimated. This section reviews some of the key points that companies should consider while designing their "homes' on the web".

The Business Objective

The web site must be a part of an overall corporate strategy to acquire and retain customers. In this respect it is important to clearly establish the business objective for building a web site before one goes about designing it. This has a direct and immediate impact on the content of a web site. However it also impacts factors such as technology used, investment made, and the time to completion.

Companies could choose to make their web-site a primary mode of information dissemination e.g. Autobytel acts as a single source of information on all models of cars. Other companies could make them the primary mode of transacting business and generating revenue, e.g. Amazon wants the customer to complete the purchase of the books online. Companies could use the web site as a launch pad to generate excitement about a new product or service they are planning to introduce and use it to gauge the market potential of the service or product.

Ergonomics

The issue of ergonomics in web site design is becoming increasingly important. This involves a company paying due attention to factors such as the visual appearance of the web pages, the presentation of content in the web pages through the use of text/images/video & audio, the ease with which a user can navigate around the web site and how intuitively the web site is organized. Companies will also have to pay attention to the task of developing and deploying a whole variety of web site aids. The most basic of these aid tools includes the "Site Map" and "Search" functions. However companies need to go beyond this and use this as an opportunity to build a more interactive experience with the user through more web tools. Examples of such tools include – Banks providing mortgage calculators online and Amazon automatically providing you with a list of books that users who bought the book you are interested in also bought themselves.

Size of the Site

The size of a web site must be determined by various factors and issues such as the business objective, the expected number of customers/the volume of traffic the web site is expected to generate, and the number of transactions expected (if so designed). While deciding on the size of the web site it is also important to evaluate the content of your web site and appropriately size the servers and other hardware that is required to run the web site. The overall systems infrastructure is crucial to the overall performance of the web site. Due attention must also be paid to the bandwidth needs of the web site and that an appropriate hosting solution chosen (e.g. either in-house or through a specialized vendor).

Investment in Building the Site

Gone are the days when companies could quickly put up a couple of web pages and claim to have become an e-business. The whole act of putting up a quality web site requires a significant investment of time and money. Companies are increasingly putting senior management in direct charge of such activities in order to demonstrate their commitment to a strong product. Companies also have to evaluate whether they already have the content required to build the web site or if it needs to be developed from scratch. These are separate from the obvious costs involved in hiring programmers, building the infrastructure to host the site (or an agreement with a web hosting service), software tools needed to build and power the web site like web servers, security mechanisms (firewalls), and billing systems. In addition, companies will also need to invest in integrating the web site with their existing back office systems to achieve true seamless business integration.

Investment in Maintaining the Site

A static web site is a sign of a dead or stagnant business. Web sites need to be constantly monitored, reviewed and updated with fresh content on a regular basis. While the frequency of this varies based on the nature of the site (ESPN may need to update it many times a day while FORD may only revise it once a month) the need to plan for this and incorporate this into the business process, as determined by the business objective, cannot be over emphasized. Ongoing maintenance can also include training requirements for the staff maintaining the web sites, cost of upgrading and maintaining the infrastructure including the hardware and software, and the cost of communications. Such recurring expenditures must be included in the budgeted.

DATABASE REQUIREMENTS IN E-BUSINESS

A well-designed web site offers a good start for attracting potential customers to your business. Most commercial sites handle volumes of information that need the use of a database at the back end to both hold corporate information and to track customer related information. This places enormous demands on the database servers to support applications that have an unpredictable number of transactions, potentially large data flow, and high performance requirements. All these factors taken together are unprecedented.

Availability

While availability of the database server and its "up-time" has always been a key concern for IS managers at corporations, the 365x24x7 nature of the web places unprecedented demands. There cannot be any *"scheduled maintenance downtimes"* let alone any unplanned outages. Competitors are only a click away and a customer who cannot use your web-site is a lost customer.

Security

Web sites are open around the clock and are also open to users from all over the world. All information needed by customers must be accessible via the web site. This presents a security nightmare from the IS managers viewpoint. These requirements can be an open invitation to hackers and people with malicious intent to come in and create havoc at your web site. Databases, containing the core value of your business, must be protected from such elements. Adequate security architecture must be build across the key elements of the database server. If the data is spread across multiple instances of the database then critical customer and business information, like credit cards and financial details, need extra security when compared to data that is not quite so strategic (e.g. product catalogs).

Scalability

In the earlier days of databases corporate IS managers had a pretty good handle on issues like number of users, number and type of transactions/queries and rate of data growth. However in the world of e-business these are all variables which are difficult to predict with accuracy. There could be millions of concurrent users on the Internet. In addition the IS

627

manager does not have the option of balancing the load across over the day and the night. Hence the scalability of the database and its ability to manage the varying load patterns across time is crucial to ensuring acceptable performance levels from an end user perspective.

Integration

The use of the Internet for commercial transactions requires that databases be able to talk to other databases to exchange information. This means that databases may soon be required to send, receive and store a messaging mechanism that is standardized across the web. The Extensible Markup Language (XML) is becoming the communication language of the web. Hence databases may soon be required to process XML statements.

Huge Amounts of Data Processed in Real Time

There is an increasing trend towards storing all the user actions occurring in a web site in a data warehouse where it is then analyzed and mined to better understand customer behavior, customer and product profitability, and other e-business issues. Such data can grow exponentially and the overall size of the data warehouses soon becomes a difficult issue to deal with. E-business is also focused on a faster moving world. The information flowing into the data warehouse, both continuously and in large volumes, must be exploited more or less immediately, and then be relayed to operational systems for further processing.

STRATEGIES TO IMPROVE DATABASE PERFORMANCE

E-business poses significant new challenges to IS managers. This section examines some options that can be used to improve database performance.

Architecture

In order to improve the database performance from the end user perspective the first issue that IS managers may need to address is the overall IT application architecture. In order to achieve and address the twin challenges of scalability and performance, it's a good idea to explore the use of a three-tier architecture involving the use of a middleware product.

From a database perspective e-businesses tend to drive the centralization of data. However the use of multiple, distributed databases should be explored. The best approach may turn out to be to distribute the data across multiple databases based on an analysis of the nature of transactions being carried out against the entire spectrum of data. If most visitors to the web site just want details on products and services offered by the business then it may be appropriate to dedicate a database to this and hold customer demographic information in a separate database.

Sizing

The size of databases is constantly increasing. These days e-business databases will routinely begin to approach the terabyte range and enter into the realm of what are commonly called "Very Large Databases". This poses two challenges. The first is to be able to estimate the rate of growth and ensure that appropriate processes to manage this volume of data are put in place. This may involve regular archiving of information into a backup data warehouse while keeping the "live" database within manageable limits. The second challenge is to determine and obtain the appropriate hardware for the size of the database expected. Significant investments in hardware to help improve performance must not be ruled out and all limits from a hardware perspective, such as increasing the RAM or number of processors, must be explored.

Data Organization

The organization of the data within the database is the most important factor influencing the performance of the database. This involves building a list of data requirements, translating the same into a data model, normalizing the data model and implementing the normalized structure in the database. However it must be cautioned that non-normalized databases are found in commercial applications and this may actually enhance performance as per the application requirements. Another key factor that may need to be considered is the skew in the data that one expects to store. In a relational database, data is "skewed" when the distinct values in a column are not uniformly distributed over the table's rows. Expected instances of skew in data must be duly considered while designing SQL queries and creating indexes.

Database Design

Finally the traditional issues that must be considered during database design must not be ignored. These include but are not limited to the following:

- *Simplicity.* An attempt must be made to keep the queries focused and simple. Many tasks may be better accomplished at the client end rather than at the server side.
- *Get rid of useless indexes.* While having appropriate indexes has always been emphasized, lately more emphasis has been placed on removing (or concatenating the other way round) indexes which may not be used.
- *Pay attention to nested scans.* On an enormous table, indexes are rarely lightweight themselves, even if they seem small by comparison. A full index scan, and even a range scan can significant performance implications.

EVALUATING WEB SITE PERFORMANCE

It is becoming increasingly clear that companies will need to be able to constantly monitor the performance of their web sites and fine tune all aspects of the web site to ensure a better end user experience. This section reviews a couple of such tools, but does not provide a recommendation on which tool to actually use. This is an assessment that you must do for your own unique situation.

FireHunter

This is a product from Agilent technologies a subsidiary of Hewlett Packard corporation. The Firehunter family of products provides e-businesses with critical capabilities for proactive management of the performance and availability of business-critical services. It supports the monitoring of service-levels and can be used to maintain a strict control over the end user experience. These powerful capabilities can help a business gain immediate revenue increases due to increased control over the business. It can be used to monitor, manage and report on your basic Internet services, such as mail, news and Web, as well as your value-added services, such as Web-hosting and e-commerce.

Jyra

Jyra provides companies with an e-commerce performance assessment solution that can access, browse and log onto sites on the Internet in the same way as any live user or eCommerce customer, thus simulating an end user experience. Jyra can provide a graphical representation of customer's experience when purchasing from a site displaying what the customer experience is and management reports pointing out real peaks and lost business due to poor performance. Jyra can also be used to gather information the most immediate cause of poor performance, be it network, load balancing systems, firewalls, persistent connection failures, server capacity or bandwidth capacity.

CONCLUSION

The rapid growth of e-business is posing significant challenges to IS managers in providing acceptable levels of performance from their web applications. Adopting a holistic approach that involves examining both the front and back ends (and everything in between) of a web-based application will help IS managers achieve their objectives. Businesses will need to adapt their infrastructure to successfully compete in this environment. Firms that can provide their customers with superior performance will succeed in the next millennium.

Chapter 45
Web-Based Testing and Capacity Planning

Trevor Clarke

EVERYDAY, MORE AND MORE COMPANIES ARE ENTERING THE E-MARKET-PLACE BY OFFERING THEIR PRODUCTS AND SERVICES THROUGH THE INTERNET. This shift has led to fundamental changes in the product-development life-cycle. The challenges facing CIOs and IT managers have increased accordingly as they are expected to deliver complex applications and application environments in less time than traditional client-server applications in order to meet the more sophisticated demands of their customers and to remain competitive. Consequently, a much more rigorous testing process, completed in a shorter time frame, is required.

Coupled with this new medium of transacting business is a much larger marketplace, which makes it increasingly difficult for IT managers to predict loads and appropriately provision infrastructure. Failure to sufficiently provision the infrastructure will result in performance degradations and ultimately, the loss of customers. This article addresses two key challenges facing CIOs and IT managers including web-based testing and capacity planning in a rapidly changing Internet environment.

THE ADDED COMPLEXITIES

Web-based systems introduce many additional and different complexities over traditional client-server systems and the earlier mainframe environments. As businesses go on-line, there are many unknowns that could adversely affect the success of their e-business venture. The following list identifies some of the major complexities and unknowns that your testing organization will have to consider to ensure a quality service:

- *Speed:* The increased competition faced by companies doing business on the Internet has resulted in shorter development life cycles. To meet customer expectations, companies have to respond quickly to market demands and continuously improve their site to keep existing customers and attract new customers. Testing must also be completed in much shorter time frames than experienced with client-server solutions.

- *Scenario Development:* A key challenge with web-based systems is the development and testing of all possible scenarios of user interaction with the system. For transaction based-systems, rigorous testing needs to occur to ensure the integrity of transactions as users may willingly or unwillingly be disconnected from the system. Also, transaction integrity needs to be ensured during peak-activity when performance degradations and system time-outs are more likely. Finally, the testing organization also needs to consider that users may freely navigate forward or backwards within a web site and may cause unwanted duplication of transactions.

- *Performance Testing:* Ensuring the performance of your web-based system is another key challenge as some components are not under direct control of your enterprise. The system or the network could cause performance issues in a web-based environment. Keynote, The Internet Performance Authority, indicates that Internet performance problems are generally not server problems.[1] They demonstrated that most performance problems occur out in the Internet infrastructure between the users and web-servers at network access points (NAPs), routers, or in a Domain Name Server (DNS). Assuring performance could equate to your companies ability to attract and keep customers loyal to your web site.

- *Capacity Planning:* Effectively planning the capacity of your systems and networks becomes difficult as your business becomes global when on-line. Ineffective planning could lead to excessive performance issues that result in loss of customers.

- *Security:* Additional security risks are associated with web-based systems as they operate in a relatively "open" environment and could provide access to your company's confidential systems and data by unauthorized users. Simple bugs in the web-server could enable users to corrupt or steal data from the system or even render your systems unavailable.

- *Multiple Technologies:* A complete testing cycle would include all possible software configurations that users leverage to access with your site (primarily Netscape or Microsoft's Explorer). Configurations may include various browser versions and Service Packs.

THE TESTING CYCLE

Utilizing typical client-server testing approaches will not address the many added complexities resulting from a web-based system. Additionally, the more aggressive time schedules involved in web-site development projects result in a need for your organization to develop a different and effective approach.

Defining Testing Scope

Determining the testing scope is critical to the success of a web-based testing project. Due to the short time-frame associated with web-site testing, it can become difficult to test all components of the application and network. When possible, testing the complete web-based environment is ideal. However, when time constraints and/or budget constraints are incorporated, your organization may need to determine critical requirements and potential high-risk areas and focus testing effort on these areas.

Critical requirements and high-risk areas can be determined by analyzing the requirements to determine the functionality that is most important to the success of the web site, the areas within the web site that will draw most customer focus (both positive and negative), and areas of the web site that pose security threats.

Testing scope may include the complete system environment, including network performance testing. Alternatively, testing scope may be isolated to a particular module of the web site or system environment (e.g. web server, application server, database, etc.). Although not every component of the web-based application or infrastructure may be tested before production, it is recommended that testing continue post-production for components not initially tested.

Test Planning

Based on the testing scope, the testing organization needs to plan the testing phase, including the types and timing of tests to be performed in both the pre- and post-release stages. The following testing types would be executed in a complete testing cycle:

- *Unit Testing:* Unit testing is the process of testing individual application objects or functions in an isolated environment before testing the integration with other tested units. Unit testing is the most efficient and effective phase in terms of defect detection.
- *Integration Testing:* The purpose of integration testing is to verify proper integrated functioning of the modules (objects, functions) that make up a sub-system. The focus of integration testing is on cross-functional tests rather than on unit tests within one module.
- *End-to-End Testing:* End-to-end testing is a comprehensive test of the integration of subsystems and interfaces that make up the web site. Typically, end-to-end testing models all scenarios of user or business activity possible on your web site. Included within this testing phase is the verification of all links to other web sites, whether internal or external (referred to as link testing). Link testing is a key activity that

should be completed on a recurring basis as web sites tend to change URLs or are discontinued.

- *Security Testing:* Although implemented security measures are considered as part of the end-to-end solution, this testing type is kept separate due to its importance. Security testing involves two key processes. The first is the assurance that unauthorized users are blocked from accessing data and systems not intended for the user population. The second involves the testing of the data encryption techniques employed by your organization.
- *Regression Testing:* Regression testing ensures that code changes made during application testing or post-production have not introduced any additional defects into previously tested code.
- *Usability Testing:* Usability testing ensures the presentation, flow, and general ergonomics of your web site is accepted by the intended user community. This testing phase is critical as it enables your organization to measure the effectiveness of the content and design of your web site, which ultimately leads to the ability to attract and keep customers.
- *Stress Testing:* Stress testing observes the capabilities of production hardware and software to continue to function properly under a predetermined set and volume of test scenarios. The purpose of stress testing is to ensure that the system can maintain throughput and efficient operation under different load conditions.

    Stress testing enables your organization to determine what conditions are likely to cause system (hardware or software) failures. This testing phase needs to consider the possible hardware platforms, operating systems and browsers used by customers. Results from stress testing are also a key component used for capacity planning (capacity planning is discussed later in this article).
- *Performance Testing:* Performance testing observes the response times of your systems (i.e. web-server, database, etc.) and capabilities of your network to efficiently transmit data under varied load conditions. Performance testing should enable your organization to determine and resolve bottlenecks within the application and infrastructure. Performance testing should also consider the possible hardware platforms, operating systems and browsers used by customers.

If testing scope has been limited to a certain aspect of the system and/or network environment, only a limited set of tests will be completed in the pre-production phase. Based on the priorities set in the scoping phase, the test manager needs to determine the set of test types and resources required in the pre-production testing phase and those that will be completed in the post-production phase. The minimum testing that needs to occur for code changes is unit and integration testing for the modules affected by the code change.

The requirement for much quicker development and testing cycles has led to the creation of sophisticated software quality tools that automate many of the test types described above. Key competitors in this marketplace include Segue Software, Mercury Interactive, RadView Software and RSW Software. The following paragraphs describe the solutions offered by each company:

Segue Software. Segue Software's Silk family of e-business testing products automates several threads of the testing process including functional (unit) and regression testing (SilkTest), load and performance testing (SilkPerformer) and scenario testing (SilkRealizer). Seque also provides professional services to help install and configure the Silk products to test your company's products.

Additional value-add products in the Silk line include SilkMonitor (24x7 monitoring and reporting of Web, application and database servers), SilkObserver (end-to-end transaction management and monitoring of CORBA applications, SilkMeter (access control and usage metering), and SilkRadar (automated defect tracking).

For more information, visit Seque Software's web site at www.segue.com.

Mercury Interactive. Mercury Interactive provides the Astra suite of web-based testing products. Specific modules include Astra LoadTest to test scalability and performance, and Astra QuickTest for functional and regression testing. Additional value-add tools include Astra SiteManager to manage the web site and identify problems and user "hotspots".

For more information, visit Mercury Interactive's web site at www.mercury-interactive.com.

Radview Software. Radview's WebLoad product line provides tools for verifying application scalability and integrity. Scalability and integrity refers to load and functional testing. Additional products include WebLoad Resource Manager to facilitate and coordinate testing and resources in the development lifecycle.

For more information, visit Radview Software's web site at www.radview.com.

RSW Software. RSW's e-Test suite of products provides solutions to test the functionality, scalability and availability of web-based applications. e-Load is used for load and scalability testing while e-Tester is used for functional and regression testing. Additional value-add modules include e-Monitor, which provides 7x24 monitoring of deployed applications.

For more information, visit RSW Software's web site at www.rswoftware.com.

To significantly decrease the time required to perform testing, it is recommended to assess your organizations testing requirements and choose an automated software quality tool to expedite repetitive testing tasks. Additionally, these test tools will enable your organization to perform stress testing, which is key to ensuring sufficient network and server resource levels for the production environment.

Capacity Planning

Effective performance testing is difficult without an accurate depiction of future loads. Many companies simply over-engineer hardware and networks at high costs to minimize potential performance issues leading to service degradations or deal with performance issues on a reactive basis. Reacting to performance issues in today's highly competitive marketplace could ultimately lead to the loss of customers during system downtime or periods of poor performance. Planning capacity is a critical step required to ensure the future performance of your web-based environment. The key components involved are network, server (e.g. memory, CPU, I/O) and storage capacity.

Establishing performance benchmarks and subsequently estimating future growth is critical to planning the capacity of the network and servers. Although benchmarks are published by the Standard Performance Evaluation Corporation for web servers (www.specbench.org), there uses are limited and do not accurately represent a real-world integrated web environment. Alternatively, benchmarks can be determined through stress testing and mapping of performance (e.g. response times) to specific network or hardware configurations under varying loads. Modeling tools and techniques can also be used to determine performance characteristics under varying loads.

Once initial benchmarks are established, future production loads can be estimated using historical growth statistics and/or growth predictions estimated by various Internet-analyst groups (e.g. IDC, GartnerGroup, and Forrester Research). Subsequently, the growth forecasts can be put to test to determine the resource and scalability requirements of the network and hardware in the future. Note that peak loads of 3-4 times average loads should be tested during the stress test phase. Additional stress testing considerations is to model higher-volume loads for cyclical periods. For example, online retailers may have much higher loads during the Christmas period than during the rest of the year. Ensuring performance, especially during these peak periods, will have an impact on web-site success. For this reason, over-provisioning hardware or network components to a certain level is justified.

Although effective capacity planning should enable your systems to handle future growth, monitoring of your networks and server resources should continue to ensure capacity is within acceptable limits.

CONCLUSIONS

Web-based applications have resulted in many challenges for the testing community. The ability of an organization to effectively prioritize the components requiring testing and to rapidly execute the tests is a requirement in a competitive e-marketplace. Leveraging the tools designed specifically for web-based testing will enhance the organization's ability to get a quality product to market faster. Finally, proactive capacity planning rather than reactive performance issue resolution will result in greater customer satisfaction and ultimately in greater revenue.

Note

1. "Top 10 Discoveries About the Internet", Keynote Systems, Inc., 1998.

Chapter 46
The Advancing Art of Indexing

Lois Richards

DESPITE THE ENORMOUS SUMS OF MONEY SPENT on client/server, data warehousing, LAN technology, UNIX systems, and PC access tools, the job of delivering information to end-users in an efficient manner remains difficult. With all the new technology and computing power now available, why are IS departments still struggling to answer this fundamental need? More important, is a solution at hand?

IN THE BEGINNING, THERE WAS DATA

In retrospect, it seemed so simple. Of course, data was there to be used. The problem was that traditional systems were designed for record keeping. Data gathering was the priority, not data dissemination. The end-user, however, was unaware of this barrier.

Finance departments were the first to see the benefit of the summary reports and analyses. Marketing departments were not far behind in asking for reports on their customers and prospects. Inventory management, manufacturing, engineering, personnel ... soon all departments could see the need for access to the data in these computerized corporate storehouses.

THEN THERE WERE USERS: THE REIGN OF THE 4GL

What evolved was the decision support system (DSS). DSS applications may access just the back-end or legacy systems, may include data warehousing, or may encompass an enterprisewide client/server information system. Decision support applications all require extensive access to corporate data stowed in the coffers of the computer system. Whether the data base is a relational or other file structure, these decision support inquiries contribute to analyses of the selected data or display of the selected data in reports. In addition, the users submitting these inquiries insist on consistent, immediate response. IS must respond to these demands.

Whenever tackling any daunting task, most practitioners undertake the most obvious issues first. Thus, when it came to providing enterprisewide data access, the most prominent roadblock was getting users onto the system with the appropriate levels of security and programs to access the data they needed.

In the 1980s, such companies as Information Builders, Cognos, and Uniface launched the first revolution in end-user access by selling fourth-generation language (4GL) development tools. Fourth-generation languages made it possible to develop new applications in a fraction of the time required by conventional programming techniques. Meanwhile, PCS were gaining favor in the corporate world. Terminal emulation software sold by the thousands — then millions — as the proliferation of PCS became the new way to get access to the corporate system.

These new applications and terminal emulation techniques allowed a multitude of users to directly access data in corporate systems. The decision support system for the organization's knowledge worker was on its way. Granted, the access was usually reserved for either the data-entry level technician who used the system to enter, update, and delete information, or the hearty few who were confident enough to manipulate the applications. But the revolutionary step of allowing users directly on the system had taken place. The idea of interactive data access had become the norm. Users requested access to data immediately — online!

LET THERE BE UNIVERSAL ACCESS: CLIENT/SERVER AND NETWORKS

Throughout the 1980s and early 1990s, millions of users were brought online. Data bases grew larger while the number of users who accessed them and the frequency of their access continued to expand. Even as users were clamoring for more, organizations were failing to see the return they had expected from their investments in technology.

Even though these new applications allowed access to corporate data, it was in a rigid, predefined manner that protected system resources. Users who were not comfortable with a character environment, or who did not take the time to learn the cryptic commands and data layouts, still needed to depend on the IS department for their data needs. Information could still take weeks to get if it differed from the preestablished reports. Individual access was limited to one system at a time. Access to multiple data sources on various hosts from the same terminal was virtually impossible.

The next step was inevitable. The obvious choice to many was to marry the now-pervasive PC and its user-friendliness with the power of the corporate system. By the early 1990s, most corporations began developing some form of client/server system to increase efficiency and end-user access.

Client/server systems answered, at least temporarily, the next level of end-user access issues. The point-and-click interfaces of Windows and Macintosh systems made interacting with the data far easier. Users no longer had to memorize command sequences to get in and out of applications and data bases. They could perform queries and create reports on the fly, and download data directly into the PC. Advances in network technology made it possible to have access to any number of corporate systems from the same PC or workstation.

With client/server connections, middleware connectivity tools, and networking, IS has solved the second hurdle of providing universal access: users are online and can request information through a relatively intuitive graphical environment. Fast access to information through online inquiry, analysis, and reporting remains a crucial factor if today's knowledge workers are to get their questions answered and work completed. But, as with most elements of progress, this new access has brought with it another dilemma — performance.

THE PERFORMANCE DILEMMA

Unfortunately, there appears to be one indisputable constant: fast is never fast enough.

As users point-and-click their way to the data they need, both users and IS now dread the infamous QFH ("query from hell"). Perfectly reasonable business questions such as "How many customers in the northeast region bought our product last quarter at the promotional price?" can bring even the most powerful server with millions of records to its knees — and all other users along with it. Because of this slow response time, interacting with the data is clumsy at best and impossible at worst.

Without question, CPU-intensive tasks, such as engineering and scientific applications, have seen dramatic increases in speed. In addition, the CPU-intensive tasks required in data base applications, such as sorting, are considerably faster. With CPU speeds increasing and the cost per millions of instructions per second (MIPS) dropping, it might appear that the solution to transaction and analysis bottlenecks experienced in most data base applications has been met. Unfortunately, this is not true.

The reason is that most data base applications benefit only modestly from higher-speed CPUs. Typically, the inability to resolve user queries comes from the application being disk I/O-bound rather than CPU-bound. The CPU is busy reading the data from disk in order to answer, or process, the request. Two basic strategies have emerged in an attempt to solve the performance dilemma:

- Limit the number, type, or timing of the queries that can be done through the client/server system.

- Pull the analytical/historical data into a data warehouse, so that the queries do not affect online production performance.

DSS inquiries and reports require access to large amounts of data, even when only a small subset of records is of interest. Consequently, placing limits on queries is generally unsatisfactory for all involved. The time required to accomplish the DSS request depends on disk throughput rather than CPU speed. While CPU speeds continue to increase and disk capacities see great gains, the transfer speeds (disk I/O) have only made incremental gains. So, users continue to be frustrated about the limits that are set, and IS is again put in the position of "policing" access to data.

Offloading data into a data warehouse only shifts the problem from one data structure to another. The assumption made with moving the data into a query-focused data base is that the data warehouse, unlike a production system, does not require the same response times. Knowledge workers must wait hours, and sometimes days, for information they need.

The solution is to reduce the amount of disk I/O required to get the job done. In data base applications, this means minimizing the amount of I/O needed to select and retrieve a desired subset of records for display or reporting. With this in mind, indexing becomes one of the most important aspects of any decision support system.

INDEXING — THE FUTURE IS NOW

Decision support applications require users to query, analyze, and report data. As data structures increase in size (millions and billions of records of data), the ability to meet the need to query, analyze, and report on data becomes burdensome — even for a super-powered computer. Whether a DSS application is in the conceptual stage or already developed, the issue of making data easily and immediately accessible to users will always be a challenge. Indexing provides a way to realize optimal benefits with minimal investment in new technologies or equipment.

Sophisticated indexing is the most effective way to reduce the disk I/O required to retrieve a subset of data. With advanced indexing techniques, record selections by any criteria are accomplished using few disk reads. As a result, complex selections from large data bases execute in seconds.

Not the New Kid on the Block, But Effective

Data file structures offer several ways to access data. Foremost among them, sequential searches, or table scans, match data to the user's criteria. This technique requires access to every record and, consequently, large disk I/O. If available, an index can expedite this process by decreasing the number of reads.

B-Tree Indexing. The native indexes in relational data bases such as Oracle, Informix, Sybase, and other relational data base management systems (RDBMSs) use a B-tree structure that allows partial key retrievals, sorted retrievals, and concatenation of columns. B-tree indexing has been effectively used for years but has several drawbacks, including:

- *Limited to single attribute.* There is no efficient way to combine multiple criteria to narrow a search through thousands and millions of records.
- *Limited to support of full key values in left-to-right sequence.* Users must enter the search criteria in the same order the data was entered, in order to attain the most efficient search.
- *Limited to exact match of criteria to data stored.* Again, users must be aware of how the data was entered.

Several RDBMSs also have a "hashed" key capability, which is fast but not flexible. Hashed indexes require a full key lookup and a perfect match, including upper or lower case letters, spaces, and punctuation.

Though indexing has been around for as long as the computer file, there have been great advances in indexing technology. Specialized indexes provide new and improved solutions to the high-performance needs of decision support data access. Advanced indexing can deliver true interactive DSS query capabilities to the knowledge worker.

Bit-Map Indexing. One advanced indexing technology is bit-map indexing. Bit-map indexing represents each unique value in the underlying file structure as an array of bits, setting the bits ON or OFF. This indexing structure can provide high-speed index-only processing.

Bit-map indexing has been targeted to be most effective for low cardinality data (i.e., data with few unique values, such as male/female, yes/no, or coded data). Its weakness, however, is in its limitation to high cardinality data (i.e., data with many varying values, such as text data, name fields, and descriptive fields). The more varying the data, the more bit-maps that must be created and maintained.

There is a focus on positioning bit-map indexing as the indexing solution for the data warehouse. This approach often assumes that the data is static (i.e., lower index maintenance) and that the underlying data can be off-loaded (i.e., lower online disk utilization).

Inverted File Indexing. Another advanced indexing technology is inverted indexing. Inverted indexes store pointers to the data base as data, and the data from the data base as keys. Inverted file indexing maintains indexes to all values contained in an indexed field.

Inverted indexing delivers the broadest range of function and flexibility for ad hoc data access and analysis. Users can obtain truly interactive access to data across the enterprise.

Inverted indexes expedite fast, ad hoc searches of previously undefined queries. Inverted file indexing allows users to find information based on any combination of qualifying criteria. Regardless of where the criteria occur in a field, query results process in seconds — without serial reads or sequential index.

An Example. For example, a user wants to know, "How many customers in the northeast (NE) region bought a product last quarter at the promotional price?" The traditional index, or B-tree, could quickly identify all the NE region customers, but would be of no use to also select those that bought in the last quarter at a particular price. To find those records, the processor must retrieve the NE region customer records from disk and evaluate each one for the remaining criteria. If the initial selection yields a large result — say, several hundred thousand records — the processor must physically retrieve every record. Next, it must evaluate the transaction date and amount fields for a match to the query criteria. Furthermore, B-tree indexes are required to scan records byte-by-byte. They can be of no use when searching for records where the selection criteria is buried within the record, such as an appended product code or first name in a name field listing lastname-firstname.

In contrast, inverted file indexes sort and store all values in indexed fields. If a table contains sales data with records 1, 5, 13, 22, and 70 representing the NE region, an inverted index would contain NE with pointers to records 1, 5, 13, 22, and 70. They select records almost instantly by simply scanning the index files for the appropriate values and comparing the record IDs for the shared values — the kind of computation a computer excels at doing. This process takes place at the index level. Inverted indexes augment the relational data base to provide the high-performance data access that native B-trees cannot.

RELATIONAL INDEXES VERSUS INVERTED INDEXES

Relational data bases offer great retrieval capabilities and flexibility, allowing users to access the data in whatever way they need — unfortunately, it is often at the cost of performance. Though structured query language (SQL) contains syntax for the addition and deletion of indexes, no syntax is included to refer to an index in a query. Therefore, indexed searches are controlled by the RDBMS and, if available, an optimizer.

When a user submits a query, the RDBMS determines how to resolve the query, choosing an index, if defined, to improve performance. Without an index, a sequential search or table scan will be used. The more complex the query, the greater the likelihood of a table scan, because of the limitation that B-tree indexes provide a single key access. If a query encompasses more than one column, only one B-tree can be used, even if every column in the query is indexed. The optimizer then "weighs" which column of a multicolumn query will generate the smallest result. All other columns in the query are evaluated through a table scan.

Inverted file indexing offers a far more efficient method to access data in an ad hoc decision support environment. Inverted file indexes, in contrast to native B-tree indexes, sort and store all values contained in an indexed field. Since most of the work is being done at the index level, the inverted index will prequalify records before they are actually read. Queries are resolved instantaneously by simply scanning the index files for the appropriate values that meet the selection criteria. In addition, inverted file indexes provide a count of the records that qualify before records are retrieved.

An inverted file structure also provides greater capabilities and flexibility than B-tree indexes. Users can enter queries in any combination to identify records that contain them, without concern for query performance. In multicolumn queries, the index of one column is compared to the index of another column. No data base records are being accessed. The result of a multicolumn query is a list (or address) of the records that qualify — fast and efficiently.

Exhibit 1 compares the functionality of relational access methods and inverted indexing. A subsequent section discusses in more detail the advanced features of inverted indexing.

USING INVERTED FILE INDEXES WITH APPLICATIONS

Only a handful of vendors offer advanced indexing that works on various standard data bases and file structures. A wide variety of applications — online production systems, decision support, data warehousing — can use these indexes to support a variety of data base structures.

Inverted indexes do not change the existing structure in any way, nor do they involve installing some other proprietary database. Consequently, an IS organization can implement one indexing strategy across multiple hardware and data base platforms. As a data base changes, so do the indexes. Therefore, it is possible to synchronize indexes in real time or on a regular schedule (e.g., nightly or weekly).

Inverted file indexing can be integrated into applications in a variety of ways. Application programming interfaces (APIs), Open DataBase Connectivity (ODBC), and callable objects are just a few methods for transparently delivering advanced indexing to business applications.

Access Methods / Search Techniques	Sequential Scan	Relational Key	Inverted Index
Keyword Searches	Yes	-	Yes
Partial Key Searches	Yes	Yes[1]	Yes
Progressive Searches (drill-throughs)	-	-	Yes
Multiple Key Combinations	-[3]	Yes[2]	Yes
Automatic Qualifying Count	-	-	Yes
Case Insensitivity	-	-	Yes
Position Insensitivity	-	-	Yes
Pre-Joined Indexes	-	-	Yes
Relational Logic (equal to/greater/less than)	Yes	Yes	Yes
Boolean Logic (and/or/not)	Yes	Yes	Yes
Soundex	-	-	Yes
Excluded Words	-	-	Yes
Concatenated Keys	-[3]	Yes	Yes
Composite Keys	-	-	Yes
Grouping of Columns	-	-	Yes
Batch Indexing	-	-	Yes

[1]Inverted indexing provides partial keyword lookups, whereas partial lookups with a relational index must start with the leftmost byte of the column.
[2]Inverted indexing performs a lookup on each indexed column in combination, whereas only one relational index can be read then the records are scanned for matches on the others.
[3]Inverted indexing and relational indexes can perform lookups on a combination of columns. A sequential scan can obtain the same net effect, with time.

Note: Hashed keys were omitted because of their limited functional capabilities, although they are the optimal when users have a full-key exact match.

Exhibit 46-1. Access method comparison.

INVERTED INDEXING

What do users and IS practitioners achieve through inverted indexing? Inverted indexing provides information retrieval capabilities superior to relational indexes. Both users and IS benefit from the added functionality and enhanced performance gained. Users can freely inquire into the corporate data stores while IS need not worry about problematic queries.

Flexible Retrievals

In addition to the tremendous speed advantages that inverted indexing provides, it delivers great flexibility to users in the ways they can search and query data. Users can intuitively search through data, finding records in a way that is obvious and logical. Users are not limited by computer query languages and constructs. Some of these intuitive search capabilities include keyword searches, multiple criteria iterative searches, and qualifying counts.

Keyword Searches. A keyword is any word or value surrounded by spaces or punctuation. Each word or value (keyword) in a column is indexed separately, so that keyword searches perform a fast, efficient lookup on a value that occurs anywhere in a column. Keyword searches are ideal for descriptive data, free-form text, dates, and numeric data, allowing users to find records using words (or strings) that appear anywhere in the indexed column.

In contrast, native relational indexes, B-trees, support searches on full key values in left-to-right sequence. A name field, for example, may contain the last name, followed by the first name (SMITH, JOHN). To efficiently find customer JOHN SMITH, a user must know that SMITH precedes JOHN. A B-tree index on this name field would be useless if users only knew the first name (JOHN) in the record they were searching for. The only alternative is a sequential scan of all the data rows to find an embedded value and do a pattern match.

Progressive Searches and Multiple Key Combinations. Keyword searches can combine multiple keywords against one or more columns. This capability allows users to progressively search, or iteratively "drill through," and refine their queries to contain only that subset of data needed. Users can select and analyze the data in many different ways without incurring the overhead of retrieving the rows.

Relational data bases using SQL do not inherently provide a progressive search capability. Since B-trees are limited to a single attribute, there is no efficient way to combine multiple criteria to narrow your search through thousands or millions of rows of data. The user must enter all the selection criteria up front in one SELECT statement. If the user wants to modify just one component of the selection criteria, or just continue to narrow the search, the user must resubmit the query.

For example, a user submits a query to retrieve on SMITH. If this query qualifies a million records, this may not exactly be the data needed. If the user then needs to either narrow or widen the search, he must submit another retrieval, such as JOHN OR JIM SMITH.

Qualifying Counts. Another feature of keyword searches is the automatic return of qualifying counts. These counts tell users how many rows qualified for the current search criteria. Instant qualification counts provide feedback to the user on how many records fit a given query, before accessing the underlying database. The search can be further qualified, expanded, or discarded if the results are unsatisfactory, without touching the data base itself.

The qualifying count eliminates wasteful sequential reads of massive tables that select no records, or searches that accidentally select almost the whole table. This type of search capability is extremely valuable for applications where minimizing the CPU overhead is important. In a client/server environment, the qualifying count is especially critical in managing network traffic loads. Imagine the impact of an SQL query that inadvertently selects most of a 1-million row table.

B-trees incur additional overhead in order to return a count of qualified records. A qualifying count requires retrieval and tabulation of the underlying data.

Case and Position Insensitivity. Inverted index keyword searches are both case and position insensitive. Users can quickly find the rows that meet their selection criteria wherever the keyword appears and regardless of whether the value is in upper case, lower case, or a combination of both.

B-trees typically require an exact match to the stored data. If a name was entered as SMITH, JOHN, but users searched for Smith, John, they would not find the record. To perform the most efficient index search, the retrieval criteria must exactly match the value in the data base, including upper or lower case letters, spaces and punctuation, and the order entered.

An inverted index lets users index and find records regardless of the data's format. Users can easily find "SMITH," whether it was entered as "Smith," "SMITH," or even "sMith." In addition, because inverted indexing is nonpositional, a retrieval using "JOHN OR JIM AND SMITH" will find any of the following names:

JOHN SMITH   John jim smith   SMITH, JOHN   Smith, Jim JOhn

Multidimensional Capabilities. With inverted indexing, users can enter a combination of keys to invoke a multiple index query. This capability allows users to easily and quickly query any number of criteria across one or more columns, across one or more tables. Thus, true multidimensional function is delivered without the added maintenance and limitations of multidimensional data bases.

For example, consider a SALES-HISTORY data base whose PRODUCT and CUSTOMER tables have inverted indexes on STATE, PRODUCT, DATE, and STATUS. Users can enter any combination of values for a retrieval. A sample retrieval could be: PRODUCT = "ABC OR XYZ," DATE = "95*," STATUS = "Shipped," and STATE = "CA." The inverted indexes on STATE, PRODUCT, DATE, and STATUS invoke a search across multiple indexes, without retrieving the individual data records.

Most RDBMSs can use only one index per SELECT statement. Even if there are indexes on more than one column, the RDBMS uses only index. An option in relational data bases is to concatenate the columns into one index to provide a keyed retrieval.

Moreover, RDBMSs require a different index definition for each component combination. To retrieve any combination of five columns in a table, a large number of relational indexes (5 factorial, or 120) would be needed.

Inverted indexing can provide greater functionality with just five indexes defined. Multidimensional data bases attempt to address multiple column, high-performance querying, but they have met maximum dimension constraints (up to 10 dimensions) and require additional maintenance (both design and star-schema management).

Prejoined Indexes. Inverted indexing allows the indexing of columns from more than one table or file to be combined into a single index. This "prejoining" of the indexes yields fast, optimized cross-table joins for searches that span more than one table.

For example, users could search for all the customers in a particular city and state (from CUSTOMERS table) who ordered a particular product (from PRODUCT table) within a date range (from ORDERS table). The intersection is performed at the index level, rather than incurring the overhead of large table joins and excessive data I/O.

Because each index in an RDBMS is separate and cannot be prejoined, cross-table joins are notoriously slow, especially on large tables. The best the user can do is key the desired columns in both tables and the common column. Even then, the data is intersected by doing a keyed read on one table, joining to the second table, reading all the related rows, and selecting the rows that meet the second criteria. The alternative is to do a parallel sort and merge. The method the optimizer chooses, however, may not be the most efficient.

Some relational data bases try to make retrievals faster by allowing clustered indexes or data clusters, which refers to the physical placement of related rows contiguously on disk. This approach reduces the amount of I/O to read the rows, but the fact remains that more rows are read than meet all the selection criteria. Inverted index retrievals remain the more efficient and flexible option.

Various Search Operations. With inverted file indexing, users can combine various operations to define their search criteria. These operations include relational logic (equal to, less than, greater than), Boolean logic (AND, NOT, OR), and ranges (TO). In addition, a "sounds-like" feature (also known as Soundex) allows phonetic searches on data. Commonly used for name searches, a phonetic search allows users to find, for example, "SMITH" even when spelled "SMYTHE."

Users can easily carry these operations across keyword indexes, in one or more tables, to access data across the enterprise without concern of data navigation or performance constraints.

RDBMSs support most of these operations, except a sounds-like functionality. Still, the more complex the users' criteria, the greater the exposure to poor performance.

Excluded Words. Inverted indexing allows users to designate noise words — words such as "the" or "an" that are typically useless for retrieval — to be excluded from indexing. This feature reduces the amount of time it takes to load indexes and reduces the amount of storage space that indexes require.

RDBMSs are unable to exclude values from indexing.

Composite Keys. A composite key is a virtual key that allows the redefinition of one or more existing columns. Users can easily create indexes from entire fields or parts of fields. For example, a user can break an ACCOUNT-NUMBER column into its components — DIVISION, DEPARTMENT, NATURAL ACCOUNT — without duplicating the data. In addition, composite keys can reorganize the bytes of a column into a new key. An example would be rearranging a MMDDYY date column to YYMMDD.

RDBMSs do not allow composite keys. They require an index to be comprised of an entire column, in its existing order, or a combination of columns.

Grouping of Columns. Grouping is a powerful feature that lets users index several keyword indexes in one index, thus providing the flexibility to query several similar columns at one time. Say, for example, ADDRESS1, ADDRESS2, and ADDRESS3 contained various address information, including city, state, and country. By grouping these three columns, the index treats them as one logical key or retrieval unit. Users can easily retrieve on city, state, or address information, regardless of which column the data was entered into.

RDBMSs do not have a grouping capability.

PERFORMANCE BENCHMARKS

In summary, inverted file indexes allow a variety of sophisticated search techniques: full keyword searches (e.g., find all customers with the word "Mark" somewhere in the company name), multidimensional searches (e.g., find all customers with the word "Mark" somewhere in the company name that has done business with the company in the last 6 months), range searches (e.g., find all records with transactions between June and December), Soundex (e.g., find all records with any word that sounds like Mark [Marc] in the company name), plurality, synonym searches, and searches that ignore differences in capitalization. In addition, inverted file indexes can deliver performance improvements of as much as 1000% on multiple selection searches, allowing retrievals that might otherwise take minutes or even hours to be completed in seconds.

Query Performance Data File Structure	Without Inverted Indexes	With Inverted Indexes
Oracle	33 minutes	1.6 seconds
Sybase	35 minutes	1.9 seconds
Informix	34 minutes	1.8 seconds
Rdb	36 minutes	1.7 seconds
Digital RM	42 minutes	2.5 seconds

Exhibit 46-2. Performance comparison of a query with and without inverted indexes.

Benchmarks were performed against various data file structures, including relational and flat file. In this case, a query performed on a 1-million record data base needed to find all customers in Texas who ordered in the previous month. This query required a cross-table join, based on a free-format address field in the CUSTOMER file and a date range in the ORDER file. The results are shown in Exhibit 2 and demonstrate that inverted indexing can guarantee consistent performance enhancements for an organization's data access requirements.

SUMMARY

In the rush to serve the constantly expanding demands of knowledge workers, businesses have created a complex environment for IS to develop and maintain enterprisewide data access services. Parallel processing, multidimensional servers, and partitioning are all brute-force methods proposed to address data access performance and query flexibility. Alternatives that minimize I/O and maximize memory processing may deliver the best performance for the price. Inverted file indexing may be a relatively simpler and cost-effective solution for many businesses. These multiple keyword indexes allow users to perform ad hoc queries with minimal impact to online systems. Users are also able to construct complex queries quickly. In addition, by providing feedback to the user on the size of their request before data is retrieved, client/server network traffic is minimized.

Inverted indexing leverages investments in existing hardware and software, allowing for the integration of new technologies while protecting much of the application developed. Inverted indexes provide the broadest range of flexibility for providing true data access across the enterprise. Sometimes, simple is better.

Chapter 47
Parallel Databases
Stewart S. Miller

PARALLEL PROCESSORS CAN EFFICIENTLY SEARCH VERY LARGE DATA-BASES (VLDBs) OR HIGH-TRANSACTION-VOLUME APPLICATIONS THAT INCLUDE GIGABYTES OF INFORMATION. Instead of scanning the databases sequentially, a database management system (DBMS) constructed for parallel processing performs several concurrent searches. Instead of forcing transactions into a queue waiting for a single Central Processing Unit, these transactions and other DBMS tasks can be processed simultaneously, which increases system throughput. Parallel processing offers improved speed and performance, which translates into a lower cost per workstation. Because of its expanded performance and greater capacity, companies find this technology especially useful when examining their large transaction data volumes for purchasing, inventory, and budget analysis.

BUSINESS BENEFITS OF PARALLEL PROCESSING

A parallel architecture permits enormous data collections to be mined. Companies using this technology can access strategically useful information originally hidden or lost in the data masses. Businesses find they can make more accurate predictions regarding shipments, volumes, and identification of sales territories if they mine large databases rather than randomly scanning samples. Geographical patterns emerge from the data, which gives executives better foresight for moving products to regions where they will sell more quickly. Customer buying patterns become evident as retailers examine transaction data on an individual customer basis. Analyzing buying patterns also helps retailers conduct more effective promotions and pinpoint cross-selling opportunities. Inventory flow is also improved when retailers are able to analyze sales data on a daily basis.

SERIAL DATABASES AND PARALLEL PROCESSING PERFORMANCE

Relational database management systems (RDBMSs), such as IBM's database 2 Parallel Edition (DB2 PE), are powerful time-saving tools — and in the business mind-set, time is money. However, parallelism is not particularly useful for serial databases. Intensive serial work queries do not reflect linear speed or scalability. When the coordinator activity is high

0-8493-0882-8/00/$0.00+$.50
© 2001 by CRC Press LLC

with respect to total activity, systems performance decreases. Performance improvements are only negligible for queries executed in extremely short times on a serial database. Serial database execution strategy is efficient and would not benefit much from parallelism. Parallelism is only relevant when an index is extremely large.

Databases such as IBM's DB2 PE have an optimizer that performs sorts, unions, aggregations, and joins on each node in the massively parallel processing (MPP) configuration. In addition, some DBMSs provide a rebalance utility for redistributing data over existing nodes to maximize throughput when processing queries. This type of parallel architecture lets the user create a network of several hundred nodes that can process operations within a given query simultaneously. Excellent response times are maintained, even when handling terabytes of data.

PROCESSOR INDEPENDENCE

There are two primary approaches to parallel processor independence: a shared-nothing environment and function shipping.

Shared-Nothing Parallel Architecture. An example of a shared-nothing environment is IBM's database 2 PE (see Exhibit 1). Each processor has its own independent operating system, memory, and disk. Performance improves as the number of processors increases. Query speed is nearly linear, so doubling the number of processors results in queries that execute in approximately half the time.

Function Shipping. In contrast, function shipping, which is possible when resources are not shared, allows database operations to be performed where the data resides. Effective parallelism is achieved by eliminating unimportant data, which reduces network traffic. The query compiler deter-

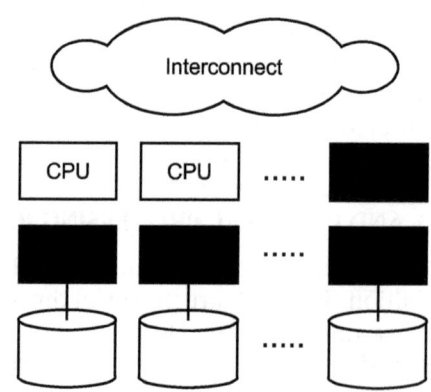

Exhibit 47-1. The shared-nothing architecture.

mines the function to be performed by each task at run-time when dealing with task structure for simple queries. Coordinator tasks are specifically determined on the application node; slave tasks (i.e., subordinate tasks) are determined on the nodes where the accessed data resides. Function shipping minimizes communication between processors; relational operators are executed on the processor containing the data when possible.

Function shipping is not limited to queries. Examples of function shipping, as applied in DB2 PE, include the following: The hashing algorithm, used for table partitioning, inputs a row into a table and outputs it to the node to be inserted. As index maintenance, locking, and logging are distributed across processors, index entries are updated and row information is logged at the same node. DB2 PE enables each processor to access only the database portion that it owns locally. A processor does not require access permission from remote processors before it accesses its local data, thereby eliminating the requirements for a global lock table.

HOW PARALLEL PERFORMANCE IS ACHIEVED

Structured query language (SQL) statements are executed using a parallel processing relational database optimizer. Many different execution strategies are considered for each SQL statement and then divided into several separate tasks. The coordinator task runs on the node at which the application resides. It retrieves the input data from the application and sends the answer set to it. Slave tasks accept the majority of activity needed by the query. However, the tasks cooperate with each other only when necessary. Although slave tasks can appear several times, coordinator tasks can appear only one time for each application. Data manipulation queries neither have any new restrictions nor requirements in the parallel edition, thereby protecting user investments in developing applications. Many DBMS applications do not need to be recompiled to take advantage of parallel execution. SQL statements are optimized in the parallel environment through both the specific distribution of data across nodes as well as the cost of functions associated with different operations.

Principles of Parallel Execution

Parallel execution, usually generated by the compiler component of the RDBM, is implemented on the following principles:

- *Cost-based optimization.* The compiler generates different parallel execution plans in optimization mode while determining the lowest-cost optimization plan. The optimizer is responsible for the parallelism of several operations.
- *Data distribution.* The optimizer comprehensively distributes data and partitions information from the base and intermediate table in each query while determining parallel execution strategies.

- *Transparent parallelism.* In leading RDBMs, applications employing data manipulation statements do not need to change much to execute in the parallel database. For example, application products for DB2/6000 need not be totally recompiled. Applications only require a rebind to the parallel database, thereby generating the least cost-parallel plan for several SQL statements as well as storing them.

Query Execution

Query execution may require several logical tasks, where each task may be accomplished across multiple nodes. Coordinator task operators can control the run-time of slave tasks. database 2 PE requires interprocess communication operators resulting from multiple processors. Query execution is analogous to data flowing on trees of operators divided by tasks, with sends and receives being used for intertask communication. The query optimizer picks the optimal join order, the best manner to access base tables and to compute each join, and the repartitioning strategy to determine the nodes on which operations need to be completed. (The inner and outer tables may not be on the same set of nodes.)

Query Optimization

The query optimizer determines the cost of a plan by choosing between system resources and response time. Query optimization problems are kept manageable because database 2 PE maintains total system resources accumulated during the bottom-up generation of a query plan on a per-node basis. Response time is a measure of the maximum resources used across all of the nodes and network. Some subsets used to execute a join include all the nodes on which the inner table is partitioned and the nodes on which the outer table is partitioned. DB2/6000 query optimization uses a heuristic to differentiate between parallel join execution strategies. In complicated queries, the coordinator both returns the answer to the application and binds any information needed to compute the answer. DB2 PE also performs aggregation, including the count function in two steps: The slave tasks compute local counts and the coordinator sums the counts and sends the answer to the application.

Interprocess Communication

Query plans or Data Definition Language statements are executed in parallel. Run-time software accomplishes this task. Interprocess communication is provided through:

- Control services, which manage interprocess control message flow.
- Table queue services, which manage exchange of rows between agents of the parallel edition across or within a node. They are responsible for proper execution of data flow operators connecting different slave tasks.

- The communications manager, which directs the messages using the communications protocol in place.

A coordinating agent deals with requests to use the database manager, create or drop a database, or monitor an application. The coordinating agent is responsible for requests from one application and is active only at the same time as the application. A parallel agent segments each request into subrequests for the application. In addition, it coordinates the activities of other parallel agents operating on the same application, thereby permitting several agents to work for one application across several nodes or within one node.

Single nodes have their own pool of agents from which the parallel agents are absorbed. Agents are neither created nor destroyed each time one is needed or is finished with its work with the pool. This is beneficial because a parallel agent may only be required for a short time to process a request. The database manager saves time on application and database initialization by trying to have parallel agents process several requests from the same application.

The coordinator executes a query subtask (i.e., subsection), which distributes the other subsections to be executed at the appropriate nodes. It sends connection information along with every request for the table queues and any host variable information that may be required. Based on the query structure, the parallel database is capable of choosing nodes at run-time. In long-running queries, the process creation is amortized over several million instructions. However, considerable overhead is apparent for shorter queries and several optimizations are needed to decrease it. A pool of processes is instituted on each node. Process creation for short queries is reduced through retrieving processes from the pool instead of creating them.

Table queues are interprocess data flow constructs. They can be thought of as a temporary table, though they need not be completely built before rows can be retrieved from them. Table queues let the SQL compiler and optimizer produce the most efficient parallel plan, yet each subsection is executed on more than one node. Each sending process can send a row to all or one receiver process depending on the table queues' associated partitioning information.

The communications subsystem permits parallel communication that accepts messages and performs multiplexing and demultiplexing of messages between nodes. Its delivery uses the Transmission Control Protocol/Internet Protocol (TCP/IP) interface.

In serial databases, the application or the database system may be busy handling just one request per application. Parallel processing maintains the database system concurrently with the application and can process more than one query for the same application. Although a row is ready to be retrieved, error handling of a node is defined where the error indication is returned to the application at the earliest possible time.

Data Placement and Storage

Data definition language extensions allow users to control the placement of database tables throughout the nodes in a parallel system. Data placement in a parallel system, or the best storage strategy for database tables, is difficult. Three techniques — declustering, assignment, and partitioning — solve this problem.

Declustering distributes individual table rows across multiple nodes. Tables are completely declustered when rows are stored throughout all the nodes of the parallel database system. Partial declustering denotes that rows are distributed across a subset of nodes. The amount of declustering is the same as the number of table partitions, which are sets of rows for a given table that are all stored at one node of a share-nothing system.

It is also necessary to determine the specific set of nodes where table partitions are stored. Overlapped assignments indicate that two tables share one node; conversely, a non-overlapped assignment indicates that no common nodes are shared between tables. If both tables share the same set of nodes, they are fully overlapped. Assignment is restricted to full overlapping upon full declustering; partial declustering allows for full freedom in table partition assignments.

Parallel Database Management

Parallel processing can load large volumes of data into the database for applications that require hundreds of gigabytes. Load utilities that contain a table partition for a given table permit data to be loaded in parallel into a single table. Input files can be segmented into multiple files and loaded in parallel (i.e., one per table partition) by using a data partitioning utility in addition to an application programming interface.

Reorganization and Redistribution of Data

Data reorganization is necessary when disk space cannot be used effectively. The physical layout of database tables changes because of insert, delete, and update activities. overflow data blocks can be created to compensate for gaps from deletions. Data belonging to the table may no longer be stored contiguously for disk pages. Insert and delete activity results in table partitions that have more data at some nodes than others. When a table is partitioned across a set of nodes, it creates a skew in the data distribution. When additional data accumulates in the database over time, it is often necessary to increase the degree of table declustering to permit additional data.

Some partitioning strategies cause skewed distribution either because they include the distribution of attribute values in a relation or because of the constitution of the partitioning strategy. If data is analyzed at initial placement, it is possible to determine the distribution of input attribute values and obtain minimized data skew.

A data redistribution utility minimizes skew on data in a table. Data redistribution operations determine the set of partitions of the partitioning map that need to be moved to obtain even distribution of data across the nodes of a nodegroup. Redistributing one table and ignoring the others results in loss of collocation for a nodegroup that contains several tables. The redistribution operation must operate on all tables in the nodegroup while each table is redistributed in turn to preserve table collocation. Data distribution across partitions and nodes is determined through two new SQL scalar functions, partition and node, which return the partition number and node number to the row where the table is mapped.

CONCLUSION

All major RDBMs vendors are pursuing a parallel architecture option. In summary, parallel processing provides a number of performance advantages in specific high-transaction-volume systems. There are several approaches to implementation of the parallel architecture, each with different performance and cost issues. Organizations considering parallel architecture solutions should first review their transaction requirements. Only then can an appropriate technical solution be pursued cost-effectively.

The parallel database implementation discussed in this chapter is beneficial for complex query environments. The serial database system can be extended with software that ties nodes together, yielding the appearance of a single-system for the user. This approach illustrates a scalable, shared-nothing database system. Necessary software components include query optimization and processing, run-time system, and database utilities.

The shared-nothing parallel architecture has been criticized because of its static data partitioning. However, proper rebalancing tools can prevent database operations from slowing. Decision support data is not operated on until it is correctly in place. Most parallel DBMSs allow data to be loaded correctly, balanced, and indexed, which improves query response. Speeds are consistent for hundreds or thousands of gigabytes extending beyond the capability of shared-memory architectures.

Chapter 48
Leveraging Checkpoint Processing

William Pearson

ON THE ROAD TO THE ENTERPRISE SERVER, following are a few reflections on lessons learned in the "glass house." I will introduce the concept of checkpoint restartability. Then, I will go on to explain how this can shave hours off of your batch window, just when you need it the most. Finally, I will show how you can apply checkpoint restart to any database management system (DBMS) such as DB2, ORACLE, SYSBASE or SQL server.

Murphy's Law proposes that anything that can go wrong, will, and usually at the worst possible time. For the manager of a support application, this usually means that the day begins sitting down to talk with a disheveled programmer. Now, given the 1990s dress code, your first clue that something went wrong during the night is not the faded T-shirt and blue jeans; nor is it the bags under the eyes, the five o'clock shadow, or even the extra large coffee mug clutched between white knuckles, has started weaving intricate patterns over your special report. No, it's the socks! They don't match — one of them is definitely black while the other is quite red.

The story is the old classic of heroic recovery where once again good triumphs over evil. It starts with a beep in the middle of the night and a 2:30 a.m. call to operations. Next comes the 45-minute drive to work, where, upon arrival, it only takes 15 minutes to analyze and resolve the problem (note the 'genius at work' logo on T-shirt). Then, 30 minutes to recover files to a prior run state. Finally, a long 1 1/2 hour wait to reprocess transaction records to get back to where the original ABEND occurred...only to discover a minor typo in the 'fix'; completely, understandable, under the circumstances. Fast forward 2 hours and 15 minutes to when the run finishes and your story's main character has just the time to buy a coffee and appear at your desk by 8:00 a.m.

0-8493-0882-8/00/$0.00+$.50
© 2001 by CRC Press LLC

Global competition has ushered in a 7/24 world — your new Internet application is expected to run 24 hours a day, 7 days a week. Customers could be making online updates anytime from anywhere. Your nightly batch window has shrunk to zero. You do not have time for a 4-hour heroic delay to your 'daily' cycle. You do not have time to relive last night's adventure tale. If only the problem had been resolved quickly. If only there wasn't always a 30-minute recovery and a 1 1/2-hour reprocessing delay. Just imagine... you could be reading a short update via internal mail instead of listening to a blow-by-blow account of last night's epic drama, all the time wishing that the blinking red light on your phone, indicating a voice mail from your boss's boss, would go away!

Instigating a new closed-door policy will not solve this problem. Rather, I suggest that you start looking into making your programs Checkpoint Restartable. First, I will review some general principles. Next, using existing IMS Checkpoint/Restart functions as a starting base, I will go over the fundamental parts of taking checkpoints, using Save-Areas and performing a Restart. Then, I will review some basic principles to help you design with Restart in mind. Lastly, I will show you how to apply the above principles to any SQL Database Management System to bring Checkpoint Restartability to a programmer near you!

GENERAL PRINCIPLES

All programs should be transaction based. Simply put, this means that while a program's logic may read many tables, take locks, and update data, the complete process must be contained in a single 'unit of work.' A transaction manager then makes sure that all database updates processed in this unit of work are committed or rolled back together. This all or nothing approach is required to maintain data integrity.

An on-line program processes one transaction at a time and makes a commit decision at the end of each unit of work. We can say that it has a default checkpoint frequency of one. Batch programs should also be transaction based. Each input transaction represents a discrete unit of work. All processing for each input 'transaction' should be completed before continuing to the next one. The difference is that you can give batch programs a checkpoint frequency of 5, 50, or 50,000. For example, one of your 'nightly' batch programs takes 2 hours to process 500,000 input transactions. Your DBA recommends a checkpoint frequency of 50,000. If the program were to ABEND after 90 minutes, it would have successfully taken 7 checkpoints, one approximately every 12 minutes. The last one would have occurred after 84 minutes. Up to this point, 350,000 units of work would have been successfully committed. The last 6 minutes of work, approximately 25,000 transactions, would be rolled back. Under this scenario, let us pick up our story just after the original ABEND occurred.

It still takes the programmer 45 minutes to arrive and 15 minutes to fix the problem. This time, however, zero time is spent on database recovery because all updates are valid. Moreover, the second ABEND, due to that typo in the programming fix, occurs after only about 6 minutes. Again, potential updates are rolled back. Thus, 22 minutes later, the program is past the problem. By the time the hero has mailed you a short problem report, the batch cycle has completed. It is still night, so your tired programmer returns home.

IMS CHECKPOINT/RESTART FUNCTIONS

In the above story, there is a conspicuous usage of a black box labeled, "a miracle happens here." In the following paragraphs, I will attempt to demystify this box by reviewing the basic functions that allow checkpoint restart to work.

Checkpoint Frequency

Usually, a simple Control Card interface serves to supply this value to your program. It allows you to control the number of input transactions that a program processes between commit points. The value should be easy to change as estimating the frequency is not an exact science. For example, 50,000 is too high if your program only processes an average of 40,000 transactions each run. On the other hand, 1 is too small.

Recommendation: Talk to your DBA about checkpoint frequency. As a rule of thumb, I suggest a minimum of 10 checkpoints per run and/or an average elapse time between checkpoints of less than 15 minutes.

Checkpoint Call

This is where your program commits all IMS database, DB2 table and sequential file (GSAM) updates. All locks held by your DBMS are released. All data is written to disk or tape. Save areas are copied to the log. Conversely, in the case of a program ABEND, a roll back call should be performed to undo all updates, release all locks and make sure that no data is written to disk.

At the end of the 'unit of work' for each input transaction, your program should update a transaction counter and compare the current value to the checkpoint frequency number. Upon reaching the checkpoint frequency, your program may make a checkpoint call and reset the transaction counter to zero.

Recommendation: Do not take a checkpoint, unless your program can restart from there. For example, if your input transactions are driven by an SQL FETCH then make sure that your program has just crossed a break point from which the process can be restarted. After all, the program must be able to reopen this CURSOR exactly where it left off.

Save-Areas

Under IMS, a checkpoint call may contain up to seven Save-Areas. Each one may represent a 01 level in Working Storage several thousand bytes long. It allows you to save several fields or several blocks of data by writing the information to the IMS log dataset. Upon restart, the system retrieves the data from the log and places it back into these specified data areas. Thus, your program can save more data than you should ever need.

Recommendation: Only save the minimum amount of data. I have known some misguided individuals who liked to save their program's entire working storage. Please use some common sense. After all, you designed the program to completely finish processing one transaction before proceeding to the next one, so what data needs to be kept?

Here are four suggestions:

- Always keep the Checkpoint ID and counter. This permits your program to write out checkpoints sequentially. While IMS expects this, it is also reassuring to anyone double checking last night's batch run report. It is also useful during testing to show that save-areas work.
- Keep the Run date that your program displays on any reports. After all, if the date suddenly changes on page 21 of a report, users will assume that the entire results must be wrong! (You may skip this one, if your program obtains this value from a control card.)
- Do not save the Checkpoint frequency. Upon restart, your program should always re-input this value from the control card. This is just in case you decide to change it during the run.
- The transaction records driving the batch process, frequently, come from a sequential file. In this case, the IMS RESTART command automatically repositions the sequential (GSAM) file upon restart. However, if the process driving your program is either IMS GN calls or DB2 FETCHs then this reposition is not done. You must add code to your program to save the key field data needed to reposition itself. For IMS, I also recommend adding a qualified GU call in the Restart paragraph to actually reposition the IMS database. For DB2, your existing OPEN CURSOR statement should work. However, this assumes that the WHERE clause in the FETCH's DECLARE statement contains greater than and/or less than logic to use the saved key field data in order to effectively reposition the CURSOR.

That is it...unless the program is maintaining a list of summary totals by branch, by region, by division. In this case, you must save the summary field area(s) so that, upon restart, your program may continue to add more data to these values.

Restart Call

This should be the first IMS call in your program. It serves to determine whether to continue processing as a normal (cold start) or to restart the program from a post ABEND state (warm start). Following the call, your program should test for SPACES in the Checkpoint ID field. If found then a normal start is performed. If not, then a restart is done. Regardless of which logic path is chosen, the majority of your program's initialize logic should be always followed. For example, control card files for Checkpoint frequency should be opened and read. Initialization of working storage area done. Transaction control flags set. There are, however, a few items that require your consideration.

Normal Start Paragraph

1. Initialize the Checkpoint Id field, for example **PCIP0000**. IMS expects your program to take unique checkpoints. Follow your company standards. For example, we use an 8-byte field, made up of a 4-byte character name and a 4-byte counter field. Your program updates the counter field by one before it takes each checkpoint. Thus, it is possible to restart the program back at any of the checkpoints that have been taken. Of course, you would normally want to restart at the last checkpoint.

2. Initialize any Save-Area fields. This is where you get the date field, set any summary fields to zero. If the transaction records driving your batch process come from a DB2 Fetch, make sure that any host fields used in the SQL DECLARE's WHERE clause to guarantee repositioning during a restart are set to appropriate low-values.

3. If the transaction records driving the batch process come from a sequential file then you must access this file as an IMS GSAM databases. You want to use IMS because the RESTART call automatically repositions GSAM databases.

   In COBOL, this means replacing the usual READ and WRITE commands with IMS GN and ISRT calls. The file should also be deleted from the FD section, etc. Please note that GSAM databases do not need to be explicitly opened. However, if you wish to insert this code, do so here.

4. Sequential output files, such as report files, must also be accesses as IMS GSAM databases. This is because IMS automatically repositions GSAM databases during a restart. Again, GSAM databases do not need to be explicitly opened.

Restart Paragraph

1. The IMS Restart call returns the Checkpoint Id value used to restart, for example: PCIP0007. Before the program takes the next checkpoint, it updates the counter field by one. During each Checkpoint call, IMS automatically displays the Checkpoint ID as well as the system date and time. This is a simple way to confirm that restart logic is processing as expected.
2. Do not initialize any Save-Area fields. The restart call automatically retrieves the data from the log and updates these fields. You may need to make sure that the program properly sets up any SQL Fetch criteria used to guarantee repositioning during a restart from data previously stored in saved fields.
3. The system automatically opens and repositions both input and output sequential files (GSAMs only) to the correct relative byte address as of the checkpoint.
4. Your program is responsible for reopening DB2 cursors and repositioning any IMS databases. Once again, since the processing path of secondary database calls should be dictated by data in the transaction record, no special coding considerations should be required.

Sample Program Flow

See Exhibit 20.1 for a sample program flow.

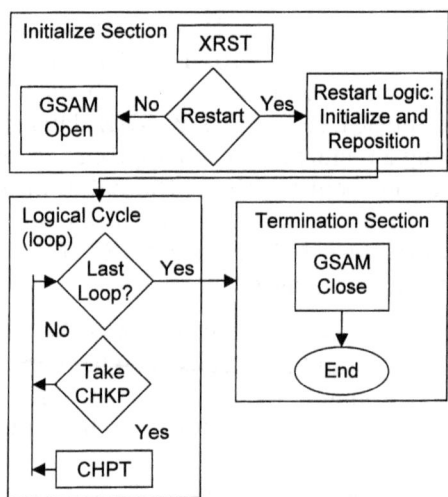

Exhibit 48-1. Sample program flow.

DESIGN CONSIDERATIONS

We covered all the main points. You have added restart and checkpoint logic to your program and converted the sequential input and two report files to use GSAM calls. Well, you are not quite done! There is one final design consideration. Your program's main processing loop has shifted from inside the program to that of submitting the entire job. That's correct. You must include the job's JCL in your design and make sure that your checkpoint/restart scenario is bullet proof. I recommend that you walk through the job's JCL and make sure that is restartable. For instance, upon restart, would your output report file be deleted and reallocated? Thereby, losing all the data written during processing of the first 350,000 records as per our previous example. Would generation dataset file indicators need to be changed? Does the JOB run two separate programs? If so, how would you restart if the second one abends?

Secondly, I recommend that you actually test the restart logic, as follows:

1. Perform a sample test run to a successful completion. Then, back up the output report files.
2. Refresh the test environment and begin the sample test run. This time force an ABEND by canceling the program.
   N.B. — you may need to reduce the Checkpoint frequency to an arbitrary low value such as 2 in order to produce sufficient checkpoints.
3. Restart your program and let it run to a successful completion. Check to see if the Checkpoints correctly picked up where they finished. Compare the output files to those of the first sample run; they should be exactly the same!

Do's and Don'ts

- Test an ABEND — most programmers assume that their program works. Make sure that they have forced an ABEND and done a successful restart. You would be surprised at the number of typos that can be caught.
- Remember to test restarting the JOB from the top; 3:00 a.m. is not the time to expect people to restructure JCL to restart in the proper sequence.
- Set a single consistent Restart policy. I know of a case where two checkpoint/restart programs run in a single JOB. The second program failed. Upon restart, the first program ran successfully again. (Alas, it was not the payroll system.)

Recommendation: All jobs should be restartable by just submitting them again. (Of course, you may have to change the JCL to provide the system with the checkpoint id indicating the correct restart point.)

- File Allocation: Make sure that all output files have DISP=OLD. This means that they are exclusively reserved for use by your program. It also means that you will not attempt to reallocate them during a restart. Allocate report files in a different job. The last thing that you need is to have an important report file deleted and reallocated during a restart.
- Do not write directly to a +1 version of a Generation Dataset. Once again, upon restart, a +1 G.D.G. would refer to a different dataset. Instead of changing all +1 to +0 just before a restart, I recommend that you write to a simple sequential file. You can use IEBGENER utility to back it up to a +1 G.D.G. in a following step after the program has successfully completed. There are other approaches that would work just as well.

APPLYING CHECKPOINT RESTART TO ANY SQL BASED DBMS

You want to use Checkpoint/Restart in all your batch programs. But, you don't have IMS. Nor do you have a vendor tool. However, you do have an SQL database management system (DBMS) such as DB2, ORACLE, SYSBASE or SQL SERVER. In this case, I propose the following "magic-box" solution. It requires the use of 2 new tables; one to record Save-area data and a second table to record output file records.

```
CREATE SAVE_AREA_DATA TABLE

PROGRAM_NAME                 8 CHARACTER,

CHECKPOINT_ID                8 CHARACTER,

DATE_CHPT_TAKEN              DATE,

TIME_CHPT_TAKEN              TIME,

SAVE_FIELD_AREA_ID           SMALL INT,

SAVE_FIELD_DATA              VARCHAR;

CREATE OUTPUT_FILE_DATA TABLE

PROGRAM_NAME                 8 CHARACTER,

FILE_DDNAME                  8 CHARACTER,

RECORD_COUNTER               INTEGER,

RECORD_DATA                  133 CHARACTER;
```

Generic Restart

1. IMS accepts the Checkpoint ID via an existing input parameter string. In a generic solution, you may simply supply this value via a new control card. A DUMMY entry or SPACES would indicate a normal start while an actual Checkpoint Id would mean a restart.
2. In the program's Restart section, add logic to FETCH save-areas and move the data retrieved into the correct working storage areas using the SAVE_FIELD_AREA_ID as a key.
3. Input file repositioning — add logic to open sequential file and perform a read loop until you reached the last input record as indicated by a count field in the save-area.

   Add counter field updates to input I/O logic and store value(s) in save-areas.
4. Output file repositioning. I propose avoiding repositioning by replacing sequential file WRITE statement with SQL INSERTs to the OUTPUT_FILE_DATA table. Upon restart, your program may be continuing to INSERT output records as rows in the OUTPUT_FILE_DATA table. Upon completion of all transactions, your program may retrieve the data from the table and write the records out to a flat file.

   A generic program could be written to FETCH the output file records, write them to a sequential file and then delete them. This program would run as a following step after the successful completion of the main program.

Generic Checkpoints

1. Change the CHKP call to an SQL COMMIT. This will release all locks and write data to disk.
2. Add logic to INSERT records into the SAVE_AREA_DATA table, making sure that each save-area has a different SAVE_FIELD_AREA_ID.
3. If required, add logic to make sure that the value of the input record counter field is placed into a save area.

CONCLUSION

Getting your super programmers to adopt checkpoint restart may turn out to be your biggest challenge. Have them try it at least once. Then, if they still enjoy fumbling for socks in the middle of the night, you could indicate that you appreciate a quick recovery much more than a time-consuming effort of epic proportions.

Now that your team has successfully adopted Checkpoint/Restart, you can spend the morning concentrating on reducing the next major bottleneck — the 45 minutes wasted in travel time. Clearly, on call staff should bunk in at their desk!

Chapter 49
The Denormalization Decision in Relational Database Systems Design

Bonn-Oh Kim

DURING THE DESIGN OF A RELATIONAL DATABASE SYSTEM, NORMALIZATION HELPS TO IMPROVE THE RELATIONAL SCHEMA BY REDUCING POTENTIAL UPDATE ANOMALIES. However, normalization necessitates the use of additional computing time and memory space, primarily when join operations are applied to more than one relation produced by the normalization process. Quite often, therefore, database designers must choose between minimizing update anomalies (i.e., normalization of relations) and reducing computing costs (i.e., denormalization of relations).

Denormalization is often considered just a performance issue, whereas normalization is regarded as a conceptual design problem. However, given a conceptual framework for denormalization, denormalization can be discussed as a conceptual design issue. Although normalization is based on the existence of functional dependencies, this existence does not indicate a dependency's significance in terms of usage. If an identified functional dependency is rarely used in actual applications, there is little reason to normalize the relation based on that functional dependency. This chapter proposes the idea of usage of functional dependency as a criterion that database designers and administrators can use to decide whether to normalize transitive functional dependencies.

BACKGROUND

E Codd's relational model has become the standard for designing database systems, and most commercial database management systems have been built on the relational model. It uses a combination of relations to represent the data of an enterprise. Each relation represents a portion of the semantics of the data required: specifically, a relation is an aggregation of attributes of an entity type. Thus, an important question in designing a relational database is how data attributes can be aggregated in each relation. Each relation can contain a huge amount of semantically unrelated attributes, or it can be designed to contain only semantically cohesive attributes. Depending on how attributes are aggregated among the relations, a relational schema can involve duplication and inconsistency among data (i.e., update anomalies).

Normalization theory was developed to reduce potential update anomalies by providing a systematic way of aggregating or disaggregating attributes. In database systems design, normalization is viewed as a conceptual or semantic aspect of the design process because it is independent of any performance-related physical implementations. However, normalization can incur extra computing costs because of the multiple joins of database tables that are often required to respond to queries. Thus, denormalization of relations is occasionally applied to improve a system's performance.

Although normalization is based on a sound theory of functional dependency, denormalization has no underlying theory to support it. Denormalization is conducted haphazardly by database administrators inspecting the performance of database systems. This chapter proposes a theoretical framework and method of denormalization to provide a rigorous tool for deciding whether to normalize or denormalize relations. Specifically, the normalization process based on a transitive functional dependency is discussed in terms of update anomalies and computing costs. A notion of *usage* of functional dependencies is proposed to characterize two types of transitive functional dependencies. Finally, a method is explained for making a denormalization decision.

FUNCTIONAL DEPENDENCY

When a data model is normalized to reduce update anomalies, Boyce-Codd Normal Form (BCNF) is often the highest normal form actually being used. (If there is a multivalued attribute, fourth normal form can be used as a higher normal form. Fifth or higher normal forms are rarely used.) When a relation is upgraded to BCNF, all determinants of a functional dependency in the relation become a candidate key so that BCNF is free of partial functional dependencies and transitive functional dependencies. BCNF is stricter than second normal form (2NF) because transitive functional dependencies are removed. BCNF is also stricter than third normal form (3NF) because nonprime attributes (an attribute of a relation is a prime attribute if it is a member of a candidate key) as well as prime attributes are free of transitive functional dependencies. Various update anomalies (i.e., insertion, modification, and deletion anomalies) can be eliminated by converting a relation to BCNF.

WAREHOUSE_INFO

PK

WH#	WHAddress	WHCapacity	MgrSS#	MgrName	MgrSalary

FD1: WH#   > WHAddress|WHCapacity|MgrSS#|
FD2: MgrSS# > MgrName|MgrSalary
TFD: WH#   > MgrName|MgrSalary

PERSON_INFO

PK

SS#	Name	Street	City	State	ZIP

FD1: SS#   > Name|Street|City|State|ZIP
FD2: ZIP   > City|State
TFD: SS#   > City|State

Exhibit 49-1. Transitive functional dependencies for WAREHOUSE_INFO.

When a relation is converted to BCNF from the lower normal forms, it is broken into multiple relations in such a way that all nonprime attributes of each relation depend on a primary key. Exhibit 1 displays the transitive functional dependencies among warehouse number (WH#) and manager's name (MgrName) and manager's salary (MgrSalary) by means of the manager's social security number (MgrSS#). These transitive functional dependencies can cause update anomalies when the data in the relation WAREHOUSE_INFO is modified, inserted, or deleted. To remove the redundancies from the potential update anomalies, the WAREHOUSE_INFO relation can be divided, or normalized, into two relations(WAREHOUSE_INFO and EMPLOYEE as shown in Exhibit 2). The relations of WAREHOUSE and EMPLOYEE possess no transitive functional dependencies, and the potential update anomalies are removed.

Cost of Normalization

Because normalization of data usually improves data integrity, it also increases the effectiveness of a database system's long-term maintenance. In addition, a normalized data model can reflect business rules and become a useful vehicle for their refinement. However, this organization of data involves computational costs.

Normalization can be viewed as the decomposition of a large relation into smaller relations. The JOIN operation is needed to retrieve the same kind of information from the decomposed relations, whereas the operation is not necessary for the relation before decomposition.

For example, to retrieve information on the social security number, name, street, city, state, and zip code of an employee, programmers can write SQL queries by using PERSON_INFO (as shown in Exhibit 1), or PERSON and CODE (as shown in Exhibit 2) as follows:

WAREHOUSE

PK

WH#	WHAddress	WHCapacity	MgrSS#	MgrName	MgrSalary

FD1: WH#　　　> WHAddress|WHCapacity|MgrSS#|

EMPLOYEE

PK

MgrSS#	MgrName	MgrSalary

FD2: MgrSS# > MgrName|MgrSalary

PERSON

PK

SS#	Name	Street	City	State	ZIP

FD1: SS#　　　> Name|Street|ZIP

CODE

PK

ZIP	City	State

FD2: ZIP#　　> City|State

Exhibit 49-2. Normalized relations to BCNF for WAREHOUSE_INFO.

- SQL query without using JOIN operation:
  - SELECT social number, name, street, city, state, zip FROM PERSON_INFO
- SQL query using JOIN operation:
  - SELECT social number, name, street, city, state, zip FROM PERSON, CODE WHERE PERSON. ZIP-CODE-ZIP

Normalizing the PERSON_INFO relation results in the PERSON and CODE relations.

The JOIN operation is expensive. Relational operations on one relation are intrinsically more efficient than the same operations on more than one relation, even though the JOIN operation can be implemented efficiently (e.g., the clustering of two files). Thus, normalization should be conducted carefully, with consideration of costs involved.

A METHOD FOR MAKING A DENORMALIZATION DECISION FOR TRANSITIVE FUNCTIONAL DEPENDENCY

In current practice of database systems design, a relational model is designed and normalized up to a certain normal form (e.g., usually, Boyce-Codd Normal Form or 4NF), and a normalized relation is subsequently denormalized ad hoc, as necessary to improve performance. Unfortunately, there are few guidelines for this denormalization.

674

Usage of Functional Dependency

As a criterion for denormalization, functional dependency theory does not address the issue of usage; instead it just specifies the existence of semantic constraints. If a certain functional dependency is rarely used, it may not be used as a criterion for normalization. Thus, the usage as well as existence of specified functional dependencies should contribute to making a normalization or denormalization decision. Although the existence of functional dependency determines the need for normalization, the usage of functional dependency determines the need for denormalization.

It is necessary to analyze the operations applied on a database to measure the usage of functional dependencies. Database operations can be classified in various ways, depending on domain-specific applications. However, each database operation, regardless of its application-dependent context, belongs to one of the following four generic categories: create, read, update, and delete (CRUD). In the proposed denormalization method, the usage of functional dependency is measured for each database operation.

The first column of Exhibit 3 shows these four generic database operations. For each, a weight, wi, is given for measuring the significance of processing speed. When a database operation needs real-time processing, wi should receive a high value. When batch processing is allowed or time is not significant, wi should be low. A value of 10 indicates the most pressing time constraint. The lowest value for wi is 1.

In Exhibit 3, the third and fourth columns show the frequency of each database operation for the identified functional dependency. The frequency

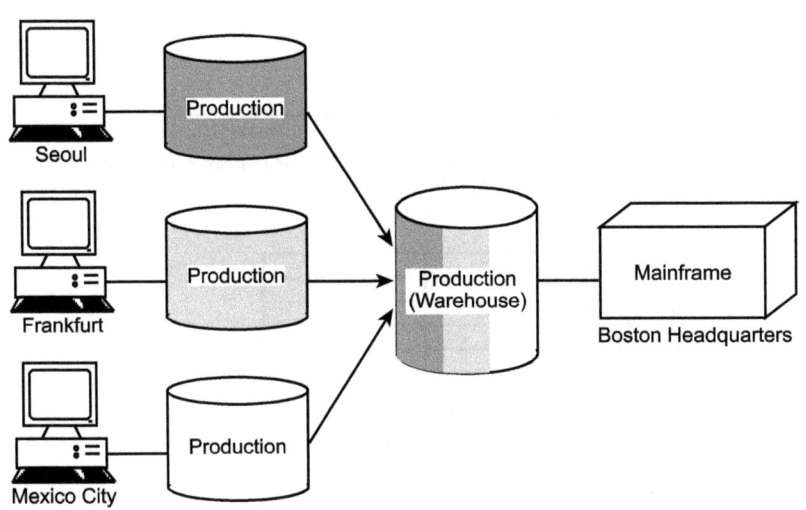

Exhibit 49-3. FD usage table.

can be measured in many ways, depending on application domains (e.g., a number of operations conducted in a minute, hour, or day). Given a certain time interval, the frequency value (vij) is measured on a scale of ten for the highest frequency to one for the lowest.

The usage value of each functional dependency can be computed by summing the frequency values adjusted by the weight of each database operation. In Exhibit 3, the usage value ($UValue_{fd1}$) of functional dependency 1 is computed by summing vc1 * wc, vr1 * wr, vu1*wu, and vd1 * wd (i.e.,$UValue_{fd1} = \Sigma wi * vi1$ where i = (c, r, u, d)).

The ratio of the usage values for functional dependencies is calculated by dividing the usage value of the functional dependency by that of the transitive functional dependency. As shown in Exhibit 3, this ratio is calculated as follows: U-Ratio = $UValue_{fd2}/UValue_{fd1}$, where fd1 includes fd2 as a transitive functional dependency. Because fd2 is part of fd1, whenever fd2 is used, fd1 is automatically used. Thus, the range of U-Ratio is between zero and one. If the U-Ratio is zero, functional dependency fd2 alone is never used by an application.

If the U-Ratio value is high (i.e., close to one), the transitive functional dependency should be normalized. If the U-Ratio is low (i.e., close to zero), a relation including the transitive functional dependency may well not be normalized.

Examples

Exhibit 4 shows a relation, WAREHOUSE_INFO, and identifies functional dependencies fd1 and fd2. Attributes of MgrName and MgrSalary are functionally dependent on MgrSS# and transitively functionally dependent on

---

WAREHOUSE_INFO

PK

| WH# | WHAddress | WHCapacity | MgrSS# | MgrName | MgrSalary |

FD1: WH# > WHAddress|WHCapacity|MgrSS#|MgrName|MgrSalary
FD2: MgrSS# > MgrName|MgrSalary
TFD: WH# > MgrName|MgrSalary

	Wt	FD1	FD2
C	5	5	4
R	7	8	7
U	7	8	8
D	3	6	6

$UValue_{fd1}$ = (5 * 5 + 7 * 8 + 7 * 8 + 3 * 6) = 155
$UValue_{fd2}$ = (5 * 4 + 7 * 7 + 7 * 8 + 3 * 6) = 143

U-Ration = 143/155 = .92

Exhibit 49-4. An example of high FD usage.

PERSON_INFO

PK

| SS# | Name | Street | City | State | ZIP |

FD1: SS#   > Name|Street|City|State|ZIP
FD2: ZIP#   > City|State
TFD: SS#   > City|State

	Wt	FD1	FD2
C	5	8	3
R	7	9	2
U	7	9	1
D	3	6	1

$UValue_{fd1} = (5 * 8 + 7 * 9 + 7 * 9 + 3 * 6) = 184$
$UValue_{fd2} = (5 * 3 + 7 * 2 + 7 * 1 + 3 * 1) = 39$

U-Ration = 39/184 = .21

Exhibit 49-5. An example of low FD usage.

WH#. fd1 in Exhibit 4 includes fd2 as a transitive functional dependency. After being normalized to BCNF, WAREHOUSE_INFO is decomposed into two relations, as shown in Exhibit 2 (i.e., WAREHOUSE and EMPLOYEE). According to the previously explained method, the U-Ratio of the functional dependencies is calculated as .92. This high U-Ratio implies that fd2 is used quite frequently independently of fd1. Thus, WAREHOUSE_INFO should be normalized into two relations (i.e., WAREHOUSE and EMPLOYEE).

Exhibit 5 demonstrates a different case. Even though attributes of state and zip code in the relation PERSON_INFO are transitively functionally dependent on SS#, the low U-Ratio of.21 shows that fd2 alone is not very often used independently of fd1and thus that fd2 is not frequently used in application programs. Consequently, there will be minimal update anomalies even though the PERSON_INFO relation is not normalized into two relations (i.e., PERSON and CODE as shown in Exhibit 2b). Thus, PERSON_INFO may not be decomposed into the relations, PERSON and CODE.

RECOMMENDED COURSE OF ACTION

Although normalization is based on functional dependency theory, denormalization is often conducted without any consistent theory. Normalization theory is based on functional dependencies in a relation. A properly normalized model removes the potential update anomalies. However, an existing functional dependency may rarely be used in application programs. Thus, the use of functional dependency should be addressed when the denormalization decision is made. This chapter proposes a method for making this denormalization decision, based on the idea of functional dependencies.

Section XI
Data Administration and Operations

AFTER A DATA ARCHITECTURE AND ENVIRONMENT IS IMPLEMENTED, IT BECOMES NECESSARY TO ADMINISTER IT ON AN OPERATIONAL BASIS. In a Web-enabled environment, the application may need to be online 7/24 and support many time zones simultaneously. The data administration and operations activities include system management, configuration management, asset management, and ongoing operations and tuning. These activities can be automated or manually applied in the application environment. Application data must also be secured against viruses, unauthorized access, and data corruption. Ongoing operations include processes and procedures for maintaining data stores, regular backups, and data recovery procedures.

As organizations and individuals continue to leverage the Web for a larger portion of their transactions and activities, the need to apply traditional mainframe operational standards becomes more imperative in n-tier/Web-based Internet environments. This section contains the following chapters.

Chapter 50, "Assessing a Data Administrative Program," examines considerations in selecting a suitable data administrative approach for an organization based on techniques and tools.

Chapter 51, "Managing Database Backup and Recovery," discusses how to invest in a sound database backup and recovery process to protect corporate data. This involves examining the degrees of recoverability required by the business, fault tolerance alternatives, virus infiltration, and unauthorized tampering through the Internet.

Chapter 52, "Advanced Database Compression," examines techniques for reducing data storage requirements by reducing the physical footprint of stored data.

Chapter 53, "How to Handle Data Loss and Backup," examines the operation of backup and recovery plans as part of a wider contingency or disaster recovery plan.

Chapter 50
Assessing a Data Administrative Program

Jennifer Little

DATA ADMINISTRATION PROGRAM ASSESSMENTS ARE PERFORMED FOR MANY REASONS, WHICH DETERMINE THE ASSESSMENT'S PERSPECTIVE (I.E., INTERNAL OR EXTERNAL). Some of the more common reasons include the following:

- To help keep the data administration program on track.
- To quantify and publicize the benefits of data administration.
- To help justify the existence of the data administration function during tight financial times.
- To expand data administration in terms of its responsibilities, the scope of the data that is managed, or its level of authority.

The goals originally established for any particular data administration program usually take years to accomplish. In addition, it is not feasible to try to list every day-to-day data administration task that must be performed to reach those goals. Broad objectives are specified for the program, and the subsequent day-to-day activities are expected to fall under those objectives. It would be easy to stray from the course initially established if several mid-course corrections were not made. A program assessment provides the information required to determine where the program is and where it is headed to make the course corrections.

Making a mid-course adjustment does not signify that judgment errors have been made. Data administration programs are often affected by many different organizational factors (e.g., budget constraints, customer demands, organizational mission changes, and technological advances). Data administrators must take advantage of the positive factors and cope with the others as best they can. Some activities that an organization is involved in may not be seen as traditional data administration functions. If these activities are not characterized by high visibility and strong resources (e.g., funding and people), however, important benefits can be achieved.

When data administrators participate in nontraditional data administration activities, it is like a captain taking the furthest-reaching tack to reach a buoy in a boat race. Speed may increase, but this tack is further from the straight line to the target. The environmental factors are the current, the wind, and the other boats. These factors prevent a straight course to the target. Nontraditional data administration activities differ among organizations.

At other times, data administrators perform their core data administration activities so that they may be on the tighter tack. Speed on this tack is slower, but it is closer to the straight line to the target. Speed may be slowed because of lack of adequate staff to provide all the necessary training or to write all the necessary policies. Progress toward the long-range data administration goals is likely to be a combination of activities that are considered to be on both the faster but not as direct tack and the more direct but slower tack. Data administrators must assess and adjust the variables over which they have control to reach their targets.

The more experienced data administrators, like the more experienced sailing crew, see more opportunities and know how to take advantage of them. The maturity level of the data administration program affects an assessment in several ways. It influences the reasons for conducting an assessment, the format of the assessment, and the results of the assessment. As data administration programs mature, assessments are more likely to expand the data that is managed, or its level of authority. This is part of institutionalizing the data administration function. For data administration programs to mature successfully, the data administration functions must be institutionalized within the context of the other organization activities.

INSTITUTIONALIZING DATA ADMINISTRATION

Like many disciplines, data administration benefited from separating itself somewhat from mainstream IS management functions to develop its own techniques, methods, tools, principles, rules, policies, and goals. A mature data administration organization, however, must be able to work with the broader Information Resource Management environment to produce data administration benefits. Data administration cannot remain isolated any longer. Data administration activities must be well integrated into the entire information systems planning, development, and maintenance activities as well as with other non-automated information management functions (e.g., forms and document management).

Institutionalizing data administration activities throughout the organization is similar to the way in which personnel management functions are integrated with other organizational functions. It is understood that human resource divisions are responsible for establishing personnel policies, coordinating personnel actions and training, and monitoring the organization's compliance with personnel laws and rules. Many personnel actions are performed by everyone in the organization, however, and the personnel specialists in HR divisions provide training and assistance to the rest of the organization so they can perform those functions. For example, the HR division does not unilaterally:

- Decide what skills are needed.
- Advertise for certain kinds of professionals.
- Interview and hire the candidates.
- Conduct performance evaluations.
- Layoff or retire people.

The way in which personnel management is accepted and integrated into the everyday workings of the entire organization is the situation that data administration should be evolving toward. For that to happen, data administration organizations must determine exactly where they are along their evolutionary path now. A program assessment can help do that.

Part of institutionalizing data administration is ensuring that data administration does not become a bottleneck to the rest of the development activities. When a data administration department consists solely of inspectors who review products after the fact, it is not an integral part of the process. this is not to say that the policing aspect of data administration should go away. But there are different ways of providing review services, and customers react to them differently.

A data administration function can be performed in a way that appears to be either helpful or controlling. Current functions that are viewed as controlling can be changed so they are viewed as helpful. For example, a data administration department may be responsible for ensuring that systems development and maintenance teams develop data elements that comply with standards. Data administrators may currently require the development team to construct the data elements on their own. The data administration department may check the data elements after the software version has been released to tell the development team which data elements were not constructed properly. The same function could be carried out in a helpful way if the data administration department helps the development team create standard data elements during the analysis and design phases so when the software version is ready to be released, the data elements are already in compliance with the standards. Data administration departments that provide helpful services are going to be more successful institutionalizing data administration in their organizations.

THE DATA ADMINISTRATION CUSTOMER

This brings up the question, who are the recipients of data administration services? What they want? Do data administration departments listen to their customers and understand what they need? A program assessment will help document a baseline of customer opinions of the services they receive that can be used to identify potential changes to the data administration program.

Organizations have applied Total Quality Management principles to their business functions and have determined what their value chains are in part to get each employee to understand how what they do affects the customer. Some municipal motor vehicle offices have instituted customer service representatives that are trained to take a customer's problem, issue, or request and complete all the steps necessary to resolve it; the customer is not sent from window to window or from department to department.

Who is the data administration customer? Is there one customer or more than one customer? Is the data administration customer the immediate, next-in-line customer (e.g., a database administrator or systems project manager)? Is it the end-of-the-line customer (e.g., the information requestor or systems users)? Is it the end of the end-of-the-line customer of the information system (e.g., a consumer of employee)? Where is the data administration program money coming from? Is that the customer? Should it be the customer? If it is not the next-in-line or end-of-the-line customer, should the money come from one of them instead?

The interconnection of customers is complex, and most data administration departments will find that they have several different kinds of customers. There are advantages and disadvantages for specifying any combination of these as the primary customer. For purposes of conducting a data administration program assessment, it would be better to keep the number of types of customers small, but significant. The groups included should have awareness of the data administration program well before the assessment is going to be conducted. they should have been participating in some data administration-sponsored activities for some time. They should be positioned within the organization in such a way that their opinions will carry weight with the main audience for the assessment results.

While identifying the customers, data administrators should ask themselves are we listening to our customers? These are some examples of customer complaints that the data administration organization may hear:

- My system does not work!
- Someone changed MY data!
- These reports are wrong!
- How can I figure out how many employees are eligible for this?
- Why does it take so long to make changes to the system?

Some may think that these customers do not care about data administration when they make these kinds of complaints. It may be that the data administrators are not listening to them correctly. Most customers will not be able to explain their requirements in data administration terms. So data administrators must translate what the customers are saying into the implications for data administration. That is not to say that the entire customer requirement is a data administration issue, or even that all customer requirements have a data administration aspect to them. However, data administrators must pay more attention to the customers' complaints and figure out how to address them from a data administration point of view.

Data administration is a service function. Its general goals are to improve quality and accessibility of data. At the same time that data administrators need to listen to customers' complaints correctly, the customers must be able to see data administration listening to them and taking appropriate actions. A program assessment is one way of bridging the gap between the two groups.

ASSESSMENT FORMATION

Once the customers have been identified, the assessment format must be chosen. There are several ways of structuring the assessment: measuring the progress toward the original goals, comparing the program to what the data administration experts prescribe, or comparing the program to other similar programs. If the program goals and objectives were not originally established with measuring them in mind, it will be more challenging, but not impossible, to find adequate measurement techniques.

Most data administration programs have evolved over the years to look different from the way they were originally intended. A program assessment can compare the current program to the original plan and measure the degree to which the original planned activities have been accomplished. That would not take into account the accomplishments that were not in the original plan, however, nor would it address advances in data administration tools and techniques. Another alternative is to compare the current program to what some of the data administration experts recommend. These could be such experts as Ron Ross, Bill Durell, Arnold Barnett, or Clive Finkelstein. Their recommendations, however, may include activities that are not practical to implement in all organizations. A third alternative is to compare the current program to data administration programs in other similar organizations. To some extent, this type of comparison is happening constantly as data administrators meet in such forums as the Data Administration Management Association (DAMA) and Data Administration Users Group (DAUG). These forums provide a feel for how one data administration department stacks up against another, but a structured comparison would be more valuable to include an official data administration program assessment. It would be time-consuming and costly to visit several data administration departments in other companies or agencies and collect the detailed information necessary for a thorough comparison. A different way to compare programs is to use the results from assessments or surveys of data administration programs that have already been completed. This approach and some sample surveys are discussed later in this chapter. A combination of the three approaches will probably serve most data administration departments best.

STEPS TO CONDUCTING AN ASSESSMENT

If a data administration program has been created with program assessment in mind (i.e., designed with program assessment and feedback into program planning included in its functions), each of these steps should be much easier. These steps will also be easier for data administration programs that have reached higher maturity levels. To get there, they have had to struggle through many of these issues (e.g., operationally defining their goals to achieve them). Unfortunately, many data administration functions are not even recognized as programs. They may have evolved over time from some other function so they do not have the underlying structure that a program charter and roles and responsibilities would provide. For those data administration programs these steps will take longer. They will be building part of that structure they lack, however, so at the end of the assessment they will have more than just a report card. The following sections detail what is involved in each of the six steps.

Step 1: Deciding what to assess. The first question to ask here is, what is going to be measured? If initial goals were set for the program, the program's progress toward those goals can be measured. For example, if no formal goals were originally established for the data administration program, some general goals should be inferred from the original purpose and intent of the data administration program. Measurements can then be made against the inferred goals.

Step 2: Deciding how to assess. If progress toward program goals has been selected as the what, there are many possible hows. They depend on the operational definition of the goal. The goals of most data administration programs are general and broad, but they must be more specific to make actual measurements. Operational definitions provide the specifics required to make measurements; they link the abstract concepts included in the goal to real-world observable facts. For example, improving data quality may be a program goal. To measure data quality, a data administration program may have developed metadata to capture data quality requirements and implemented a data quality measurement process. The metadata may be timeliness, accuracy, and completeness. For this data administration program, the operational definition of data quality is the metadata they developed. Although data administration programs that have not already operationally defined their goals will not be able to develop elaborate arrangements like metadata to capture their data quality requirements, they could still measure their progress toward their goal to improve data quality. They could select specific problem data that existed before the data administration program went into effect and collect opinions about the quality of the current data from the users. This will not produce a result as scientific as the data administration program that has the metadata to measure the data quality for all its data, but it is a workable operational definition.

Step 3: Developing measuring instruments. Surveys are frequently used as measuring instruments to collect information from a wide group of participants. Surveys can collect opinions and facts (e.g., dates, numbers of data elements, and models). Many professional services are available to create and conduct surveys. if these services are not feasible, and the data administration staff decides to create the survey themselves, they should at least consult with some survey reference materials for assistance. Survey validity, clarity, structure, and format ate likely to suffer from the lack of professional involvement. Software is also available to help develop the survey, collect measurements, and calculate results. The survey should be designed to collect the measurements that have been decided upon in the what and how steps. Data administration staff members should be warned against only including opinion-type questions in the survey. They should resort to collecting opinions only when there is no reasonable method to collect facts. Opinion-only survey results contain the biases of the participants and may not portray a realistic view of the situation. If the goal is to collect customers' opinions of the data administration program, customer comment cards can provide the opportunity for them to comment on every interaction with the data administration program. This way, collecting customers' opinion would be a part of the data administration function instead of an added function that is only done once every four or five years.

Step 4: Collecting measurements. One-on-one interview meetings can be used to administer the survey to executive-level or functional area project-system sponsors. These are often the assigned data stewards or custodians, and that may be a new role for them that they are just learning about. A data administration staff member or a survey expert can perform the interviewer role. The data administrator should attend this meeting too, so the interviewer can concentrate on collecting the information and the data administrator can answer questions about the program. A notification letter should be sent to the interviewees beforehand to prepare them. The notification should include the purpose of the assessment, provide a copy of the assessment schedule with the high-level assessment activities, and indicate when and in what form the final results of the survey will be made available.

A wide variety of ways to collect measurements are not included on the survey. For example, the program that has the goal of improving data quality and the data quality metadata will simply collect the measurements that already exist. Data administration programs that have operationally defined all their goals in this way would be able to conduct assessment of their program at any time.

Step 5: Collating information and calculating results. Storing the raw data collected in a database allows the data administration department to use it in the future (e.g., for comparison with future assessments or for other program uses). A program assessment is likely to be a large investment — one that must be protected. If a survey software package is used, it will likely support the long-term storage of the survey itself, the raw measurements, and the compiled results. Several statistical analyses can be performed on the results. If unfavorable results occur from running the statistical analyses, they should not be ignored. If they are accurate, no matter how unpleasant, they are revealing something significant about the program. Data administrators should take this opportunity to address them with assertive solutions.

Step 6: Reporting results. This step is imperative. It is worse to conduct an assessment and not report the results than to not perform an assessment. If the results are not flattering, it should be used as an opportunity to focus on how to improve things. if the results are flattering, data administrators should shout them from the rooftops and send a copy of the results to everyone. One of the final products of the assessment should be an updated data administration program plan. It should document the data administration program accomplishment, provide the rationale for dropping any tasks from the original plan, and forecast the strategies and tasks for the out years.

USING RESULTS FROM OTHER SURVEYS

The ideal situation would be to conduct periodic surveys and keep the results to compare year after year. Few data administration programs are old enough to have had this luxury. They can simulate that situation by using the results of other surveys. Some example surveys include:

- DAUG, "Data Administration Survey Report."
- GUIDE "Selling Data Administration for the 80s and Beyond."
- Center for Information System Research, MIT, Sloan School of Management, "Managing the Data Resource: A contingency perspective." This paper presents case studies of 31 data management efforts in 20 different firms.
- Database Newsletter, "Results of the 1991 Advanced Information Resource Management Survey Part I." The survey collected information from US and Canadian firms.

When using the results of a previously conducted survey, it is important to determine the similarity of the responding organizations. The surveys mentioned here reported background statistics on the responding organizations that show a wide variety of type and size organizations participated. Unfortunately, none of these surveys reported correlations between those background statistics and the respondents answers to any of the other questions. Another difficulty in working with results like these is that the same category of information may have been collected, but the specific operational definitions are often not compatible. Even with these drawbacks, results of other surveys can be very useful in performing an assessment.

Some similarities exist among the lists of the important data administration functions constructed from the responses to these surveys. It would be valuable to correlate the organizational characteristics of the data administration programs to this information. For example, are the data administration offices that have only been in place for a short time the ones that see data modeling as the most important function and the more mature data administration offices are focusing on supporting systems development? Unfortunately, this cannot be determined from the information as presented.

The results from other assessments or surveys can be used to assess a data administration program's maturity level. Its relative level of maturity can be estimated before the assessment to compare it with other data administration programs, or its level of maturity could be judged after the assessment using the measurements collected to show comparisons when reporting the results. There are different sources of information that can be used to calculate the maturity level. One specific maturity model that could be used is a six-stage maturity model. This may be useful because it looks at the evolution within the data processing environment and recognizes that even with advanced technological tools, data processing shops can be in any of these stages.

CONCLUSION

An assessment can assist an organization in identifying and capitalizing on the benefits it has gained from its data administration program. It can also help target problem areas and specify the resources necessary to rectify them. Like any important undertaking, an assessment must be well-planned and it needs management's support and commitment. Whatever the results, it will also help anchor the data administration department in the organizational structure. Therefore, proper preparation and planning for different outcomes before the assessment is conducted is crucial.

Chapter 51
Managing Database Backup and Recovery

Michael Simonyi

INTRODUCTION

Management of the corporate database is arguably one of the most mismanaged areas in information technology today. Database technology has evolved from historical glass-house foundations of the past into the point-and-click implementations that come right out of the box today. Where databases and systems were once carefully designed, implemented, and deployed, they are now installed, loaded, and deployed without regard to basic effective design. This article addresses the concepts necessary to formulate a method to protect, back up, and, in the event of failure, recover perhaps the most important aspect of a business — its database. Without proper preparation, planning, and testing, an entire database infrastructure can become the target of lost devices, indexes, degraded backup mechanisms, and corrupted data.

HIGH AVAILABILITY VS. RECOVERABILITY

There are important differences between database availability and recoverability. Database availability can be a driving factor to recoverability, but it does not guarantee recoverability. Database availability is the measurement of production uptime and physical access to production data in a networked environment. In contrast, database recoverability refers to the ability to recover a database successfully in its entirety. Recoverability is a measurement of how accurate and lengthy the process of recovering from partial or total failure can be. The difference lies in the application of backup tools used in conjunction with high-availability tools. The redundancy of high-availability systems in an environment can directly relate to a higher grade of successful backups for the database environment as well as the supporting systems. In this article, a database environment is defined as the database, connecting middleware, and application front-end screens. These technologies are used to complement each other to offer accuracy, reliability, and stability.

METHODS OF DATA PROTECTION

The common methods of data production include the following: (1) tape; (2) mirroring (RAID 0); (3) data guarding (RAID 5); (4) duplexing; (5) partitioning; (6) replication; and (7) clustering. Each of these are explained further in this section.

Before investigating these different methods available for protecting a database environment, this article discusses the business requirements for data recoverability and availability. For example, if a database, in the event of failure, would place individuals in a life-threatening situation or would place the organization into financial chaos and eventual closure, then it is necessary to implement all available methods to become 100% fault tolerant. However, if a failure would be merely an inconvenience, then a simple tape backup procedure may suffice. Most organizations seek the middle ground.

Tape Backup

Tape backup should form the foundation of a corporate backup strategy because of its ease of use and low cost. In order for the tape backup mechanism to be useful it must be well designed and tested regularly. At a minimum, backups should be performed on a daily basis and not less than weekly. If possible, the entire database(s) should be backed up on a daily basis. The database transaction logs should be backed up during and after business hours, or whenever feasible to minimize the risk of lost data.

Mirroring

Mirroring or RAID 0 provides for duplicate sets of data on two separate hard disk drives, a primary and a secondary. This is also known as a master–slave configuration. For each logical write operation there are two physical write operations to the hard disks. This scenario protects against failure of an individual or set of drives. If either the primary or secondary drive fails, the data on the surviving drive allows for system recovery. In most situations, this option is ideal for protection of the database transaction logs. However, it does not offer protection against multiple simultaneous failures.

Data Guarding

Data guarding or RAID 5 has the ability to stripe redundant data across multiple drives (minimum three) in an array. The striping of data protects against a single drive failure in the array. When an array loses a drive, the system still functions by using the redundant data found on the surviving drives. There are two types of RAID 5 available today, namely, software- and hardware-based RAID 5. Hardware RAID is the more desirable implementation method because it was designed with drive failures in mind. Extending the tolerance level of a RAID 5 system can then be achieved by mirroring or duplexing drive arrays. This type of extension allows for whole drive arrays to fail without impacting the system

Duplexing

Duplexing is similar to mirroring except that in a duplexed configuration separate controller cards manage each drive or sets of drives. In essence, duplexing is Raid 0 with an additional layer or redundancy. The second disk controller cards remove a single point of failure that is exhibited in a standard mirroring (Raid 0) configuration.

Partitioning

Partitioning is the ability to deploy a database system across multiple servers where each server houses a different portion of the overall database. Should a server go down, only the component running on that server becomes unavailable. In this scenario the database can continue to function normally, provided applications are written to handle these types of situations. Additional protection can be achieved by employing RAID 0, RAID 5, or duplexing to minimize system downtime further.

Replication

Replication offers the ability to publish the contents (complete or portions thereof) of a database to another or multiple servers in an environment. The technique is similar to partitioning; however, to employ replication requires sophisticated application transaction logic to be used effectively. Replication allows for the mirroring of database transactions to be replicated in a secondary database at the central site or in a distributed location. Ideally, all transactions should be processed at a central database and the transactions should be replaced to the other subscribing sites. This eliminates the difficulty that becomes inherent with transaction logic of the traditional two-phase commit that fails as a result of hardware failures.

Clustering

Clustering is the ability of a group of *n* servers to share or cooperate with each other in utilizing common resources. Clustering allows systems to monitor each other and, in the advent of failure, transfer processing to their counterpart. Clustering is a very reliable method for maintaining a fault tolerant and highly available systems environment; however, vendors approach clustering differently. It is recommended that organizations examine their application architecture and processing requirements prior to selecting a clustering strategy and infrastructure.

Each of these individual methods can be used in tandem with each other to build a graded level of fault tolerance and high availability. Again, as with any other technology, the system requirements dictate the configuration and detail that is ultimately required. In most cases the higher the required tolerance, the more methods that are included in the solution.

Batch Cycles

The size and complexity of the database environment determines the most suitable backup cycle. A small site can afford the luxury of daily full database and transaction log backups. A medium-sized site must perform a mix of backups of full database and transaction log backups on daily and weekly cycles. A large site requires multiple staggered sets of backups and transaction logs on a daily basis with weekly and even monthly cycles backing up segments of the database to achieve a full database backup.

Transaction logs should be backed up at least once during the day. However, this depends on the transaction flow of the database. A low-volume online transaction processing (OLTP) database may only require a single transaction log backup at the end of a business day, before or after any additional processing is enacted on the data. In the case of high-volume OLTP processing environments, the backup of the transaction log may require hourly backups. It will be necessary to gauge the transaction flow of the environment to determine the backup schedule of the transaction logs.

Sample backup schedules for small, medium, and large sites are shown in the tables given in Exhibit 1. With each scenario outlined above, the robustness of the hardware also impacts the backup schedule of an organization. Since most organizations cannot afford to replace hardware on an as-needed basis, different backup schedules may need to be adopted over time, for different pieces of hardware.

ACCURACY OF BACKUPS

Although data backups are important, equally important is the need to determine the accuracy of the data prior to backup and the ability to guarantee the restoration of the contents of the backup into the original database or backup database system. The accuracy or consistency of the backup is paramount for recoverability. Should inconsistent data or data structures be stored onto the backup media, any attempt to restore them will most likely render the database inoperable or, worse, introduce inconsistent data into the production environment that may unknowingly place the organization at risk.

Exhibit 51-1. Sample backup schedules for small, medium, and large sites.

Time	Mon	Tues	Wed	Thurs	Fri	Sat	Sun
Schedule for a Small Site for Database Less Than 10GB							
12am	DB Check	DB Check	DB Check	DB Check	DB Check	DB Check	DB Check
1am		Full DB	Full DB	Full DB	Full DB		
5pm	Tlog	TLog	Tlog	TLog	TLog		
9pm	Purge Log	Purge Log	Purge Log	Purge Log	Purge Log		
Schedule for a Medium Site for Databases Greater Than 10GB but Less Than 100GB							
12am	DB Check	DB Check	DB Check	DB Check	DB Check	DB Check	DB Check
1am						Full DB	
5pm	Tlog	TLog	Tlog	TLog	TLog		
9pm	Purge Log	Purge Log	Purge Log	Purge Log	Purge Log		
Schedule for a Large Site for Databases Greater Than 100 GB							
12am	DB Check	DB Check	DB Check	DB Check	DB Check	DB Check	DB Check
1am	DB Seg 1	DB Seg 2	DB Seg 3	DB Seg 4	DB Seg 5	DB Seg 6	DB Seg 7
5pm	Tlog	TLog	Tlog	TLog	TLog	TLog	TLog
9pm	Purge Log	Purge Log	Purge Log	Purge Log	Purge Log	Purge Log	Purge Log

Times noted are for clarity only.

DB Seg refers to a portion or segment of the database to be backed up. Each segment or portion of the database in conjunction with the transaction logs will provide for a full database backup at any point in time.

Most databases on the market today provide built-in tools that provide some level of data integrity checking that verifies that internal data structures are intact and tables, indexes, and page linkage is consistent. Any warnings or errors reported for these utilities should be acted upon at once. Failure to act on these messages can render a database inoperable and, depending on when the problem surfaced, can cause a loss of data. The following pseudoimplementation provides an approach to handling a database backup.

Generic Backup Stream

Perform a data integrity check on the contents of the database.

1.1. Have inconsistencies been found in the database?
   1.1.1. Send alert to DBA and Operations staff, write events to log file.
   1.1.2. Halt backup stream. (Problem resolution takes place at this point.)
   1.1.3. Reestablish backup stream after problem has been resolved.

1.2. Database is free of defects.
   Begin backup stream.
   Verify completion status.
   Notify operations and DBA of backup completion.

Incremental Backups

Incremental backups are something that should only be performed if it is not possible to complete a full backup during the allotted time frame or backup window. Incremental backups extend the time required for restoring the contents of a database in the event of a failure. Although unavoidable in huge database environments where incremental backups are the mainstay, they should still be staggered in such environments.

Backing Up in a Distributed LAN/WAN Environment

Backing up a distributed database in the LAN/WAN environment can be a nightmarish challenge. Time zones and production uptime in differing geographical areas can affect a reliable and accurate backup. If the data volumes are small and maintainable, it will be possible to coordinate backups and replication over the WAN. Some thought should be given to using redundant WAN links so as not to affect other communications over primary WAN links. If data volumes are extremely high or if the network spans the globe, it may become practical to build a hot site for this type of environment. Whether the site is built and maintained internally or through third-party vendors is purely academic. The rationale is to provide a site for conducting business transactions should the primary production facilities fail. The site should mirror the current production facilities at all times. It can be updated by replication or by use of tape media. Such a site should also be tested on a regular basis to ensure accuracy and guarantee the ability to continue business if failure encroaches upon the production systems (see Exhibit 2).

Administration Tools

As mentioned previously, most products on the market ship together with some sort of administration tool sets to maintain and administer database environments. These tools can be either GUI based or Command line based, and, at a minimum, the following tasks should be included in the process: user management, DDL scripting, data import and export, database consistency, device management, data recovery, and security utilities. Some database vendors also provide additional utilities in the areas of hierarchical storage management (HSM), database cluster management, and online statistics monitoring tools. If a database does not provide for a specific level of administration, there are many third-party products available on the market that can complement most database environments.

Areas to Protect

There are three basic areas of a database that must be protected: the data, of course, being the blood of the system; the catalogs, which are the skeleton of the system; and the transaction logs, which are the heart of a database because they detail all the events that have transpired against the data since the last full backup.

The transaction logs are considered paramount for any database system, especially after a database failure. Without the ability to maintain a readable copy of the transaction logs, any failure in the database places the data at extreme risk. For example, suppose a database is backed up fully once a week on Friday nights. During the week, the transaction logs are written onto the hard disk. If the hard disk that holds the transaction log fails on a Thursday, and no prior backup of the transactions logs has taken place, the database will only be recoverable to the last point of full backup — the preceding Friday.

The database catalogs, as described above, act as the skeleton for the database. They detail the structure of the physical database. The catalogs must be rigorously maintained. Each and every change to the database modifies the catalog. The catalog has two facets to it: the system catalog and the user database catalog. Each has it own specialized backup requirements.

The system catalog defines the database environment, including the disk drives, database devices, configuration, log-on privileges, tuning parameters, and device load points. This catalog must be backed up after every change because it affects the entire database environment. Any changes to the system catalog that are lost will seriously impair the ability

699

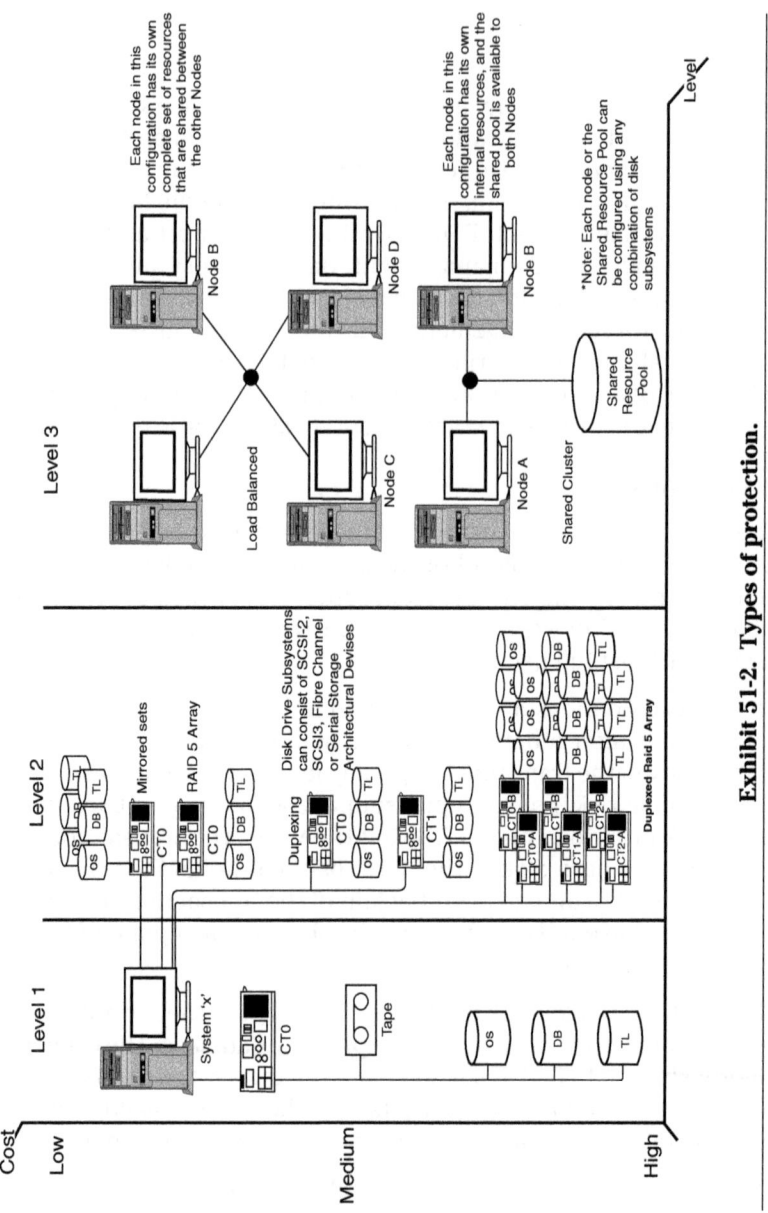

Exhibit 51-2. Types of protection.

to recover a database. In addition to having a backed-up system catalog, a paper-based reproduction of the system catalog can be beneficial for audit purposes or if the need ever arises to restore an older database backup on a system prior to the installation of a new RAID array. As hardware is added to the system, database load points will vary. This can have undesirable effects when loading an older version of a database back onto the server.

The user database catalog, on the other hand, is the definition of the user database. It contains all the details regarding the tables and indexes used in the physical implementation of the database and must be kept under strict observance. It should follow a strict change control process and must be backed up after each and every change to the database using a version control system. A failure to backup the database catalogs will result in loss of data if the database must ever be reloaded from flat files. The database catalog, sometimes referred to as a schema, is the blueprint of the database, the foundation of the database. It must be kept up to date, and its path of evolution must be able to be retraced.

The data, of course, as the lifeblood of the database and the reason for its existence, must also be safeguarded. The data should be backed up on a daily basis, if time permits, but no less than once a week. Backups should be restored from time to time to verify the validity of the backup and its state. There is no point in performing a backup if it is not tested periodically. What may have been restorable last year may not be restorable now. Also, recoverability from tape backups must be carefully tested.

Levels of Protection

Each of the individual methods provides a level of afforded protection. The base level of protection and last line of defense for a system failure should be a tape backup. This is deemed the last line of defense, as it is the slowest of all methods to get the system back into operation when disaster strikes. The highest level is a hybrid system. Exhibit 3 demonstrates the varying levels of recovery and associated costs.

Exhibit 51-3. The varying levels of database recovery and associated costs.

Method	Level	Cost	Downtime
Tape (mandatory)	Low	Low	Hours
Mirroring	Medium	Low	Minutes to hours
Duplexing	Medium	Low	Minutes to hours
Data Guarding	High	Medium	Minutes
Partitioning	Medium	High	Minutes to hours
Replication	High	High	Minutes
Clustering	Very High	Very High	Seconds to minutes
Hybrid Combinations	Extremely High	Extremely High	Seconds

The application of each method will dictate the level of availability in the system and the degree of time required in recovering from a failure. For example, in a partitioned system the database is distributed between many separate servers. Should one of the servers go down, only a portion of the database becomes unavailable. Its cost is relatively high as there are many servers deployed and it is set up in a modular fashion. Each server then employs its own recovery mechanism.

In defining the level of protection needed to meet particular needs these questions should be asked:

- Can the company run without the database for an extended period of time?
- Are customer relationships risked if the database is unavailable?
- If the system becomes unavailable, is human life at risk?

If the answer is yes to any one of the above questions, some form of high availability solution will be needed to meet the needs. As mentioned previously, a tape backup should form the foundation of any backup strategy. Use the decision tree in Exhibit 4 to help guide the requirements for the backup strategy.

Virus Protection

Although a database system is usually well protected against direct virus attacks, the database should be well secured from the rest of the computing environment. This usually means protecting the database by placing it on a dedicated system, making sure that the only way of reaching the system is via administrative tools, the deployed middleware, or operating system-related administrative tools.

Even with a well-secured database, similar precautions will need to be taken on the front-end systems, as well. Virus-checking utilities should be deployed at the end user client workstations, and at any point in the environment where data will be fed into the database. Of course, this depends on the types of data being stored in the database. If binary large objects (BLOBs) are allowed to be inserted into documents, applications, or images that a virus can attach to, it may be necessary to implement additional levels of virus protection.

Internet and Intranet Firewalls

Database vendors are pursuing the ability to allow corporate data to become extensible to the Web if it is not already there. Most databases provide for this by using extensions to the middleware or database interface, providing extended data types in the database or providing plug-ins to the database. This presents the problem of how to ensure that no one can gain direct access to a corporate database. By implementing hardware/software

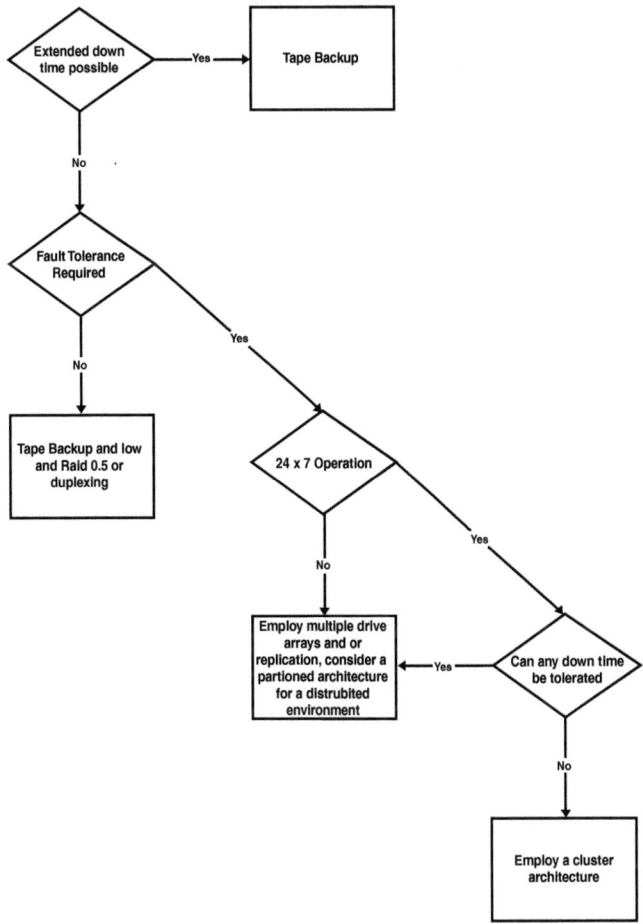

Exhibit 51-4. Decision tree for selecting desired level of protection.

firewall combinations and proxies, it is possible to segregate the database carefully from the publicly exposed portion of a network. This allows construction of unidirectional paths into and out of the database that cannot be easily compromised.

CONCLUSION

In the author's experience, there is never too much protection, only too little. Having a well-thought-out backup-and-recovery procedure in place will save time, money, and embarrassment when things go wrong. All of the topics examined within the body of this article detail methods that can be used to safeguard corporate databases or any other system, for that matter. Readers should pick and choose the pieces that best suit their needs when building a fail-safe environment.

Chapter 52
Database Compression Technologies

Nathan J. Muller

TRYING TO PUT TOO MUCH INFORMATION INTO A LIMITED SPACE — WHETHER HARD DISK OR NETWORK BANDWIDTH — BOGS DOWN PERFORMANCE. This not only wastes time and money, it frustrates users whose productivity can be greatly diminished. Rather than adding expensive disk packs and communications lines, the remedy of choice is often data compression.

Although compression, along with error correction, has long been a part of modem communications and tape backup systems on PCs and servers, it is now being used for many other purposes as well, especially large databases in direct-access storage device (DASD) and UNIX environments.

Case Study

Compressing large databases, such as the IBM DB2 family of relational database products, can yield multiple benefits, as the following case study reveals.

At the data center of one bank in Columbus, OH, a relatively insignificant DB2 table was experiencing such heavy update activity that it threatened to consume an IBM 3480 tape cartridge every 10 minutes. Even without the floor space problems typical in most corporate data centers, buying and storing such an extraordinary number of tape cartridges was clearly out of the question.

The troublesome DB2 table was a temporary storage or "scratchpad," table used by the bank to build a customer information system and a banking office and backroom operations support system. This scratchpad table is used to transfer data between transactions and to restart transactions and transaction flows.

The net result is a very active DB2 table with extremely high log rates. Using the IBM guideline that DB2 logs should be sized at 90% of a 3480 cartridge, the bank found that, if it adhered to this rule of thumb without doing something about the amount of log data that it was creating, log files would have to be changed about every 10 minutes. In other words, the bank would be trying to spin off a 3480 cartridge every 10 minutes — not a very tenable situation.

Based on the recommendation of a consulting firm that was designing the bank's DB2 environment, the bank installed SAMS:Compress for DB2, the Sterling Software data compression system for DB2 tables. The result of compressing that single DB2 table was a 75% reduction in DB2 log volume and a fivefold decrease in tape consumption for archiving. More important, the bank achieved significant improvements in performance and operational throughput, in addition to DASD savings.

SAMS:Compress for DB2 automatically compresses and restores data being written to or read from a DB2 table to conserve DASD space. The product allows users to select both the DB2 tables for compression and the compression technique, balancing the benefits of substantial storage space savings against CPU overhead requirements. An integral compression analysis utility helps users select the optimal compression technique for their DB2 tables.

DASD COMPRESSION

The storage facility commonly found in the IBM mainframe and midrange environments is DASD. Although originated by IBM, there are several third-party suppliers as well. In essence, DASD provides consistently fast access to data, regardless of its specific location in massive databases. Typically, the available storage space is allocated to specific applications so that frequently used information is made immediately available. Less frequently used information is stored on less-expensive archival media. In a document-imaging application, for example, active documents in electronic file folders would be stored on DASD for quick retrieval, while inactive files or folders may be stored on magnetic tape. Those that are considered closed would be permanently archived to tape or optical media.

Organizations using DASD also most likely use the popular IBM DB2, a family of relational database products that is used for decision support, transaction processing, and an extensive range of business applications. The DB2 family spans AS/400 systems, RISC System/6000 hardware, IBM mainframes, non-IBM machines from Hewlett-Packard and Sun Microsystems, and operating systems such as OS/2, Windows (95 and NT), AIX, HP-UX, SINIX, SCO OpenServer, and the Solaris Operating Environment. In fact, DB2 is the backbone database server in many of the largest corporation in the world, handling over 7.7 billion transactions worldwide every day.

The problem with DB2 is that it has a large appetite for DASD space. Any needless use of DASD space can greatly inflate the cost of the applications. According to a survey by Candle Corp., DB2 wastes large amounts of DASD space at an annual cost of between $40,000 and 100,000 per organization. On very large enterprise systems, the annual cost of such wasted space can run into millions of dollars.

Available DASD space is typically allocated among the most often used applications, including DB2. In addition to using compression to conserve scarce DASD space, several advantages can be accrued by compressing large DB2 tables. Aside from freeing up scarce DASD space for other applications and saving on the cost of more space, structured query language (SQL) query-and-response time can be improved. Compression also speeds batch processing and DB2 utility processing, and improves I/O operations by squeezing more data into the same number of pages.

Third-Party Solutions

Among the third-party products that can be used to compress DASD is SAMS:Compress for DB2 from Sterling Software and Data Packer from BMC Software. Of course, IBM offers DB2 compression solutions as well.

The Sterling Software SAMS:Compress for DB2 provides automatic compression and expansion of IBM DB2 relational database tables. Users can achieve 20 to 80% compression, depending on the type of DB2 data and the compression technique employed, which quickly and easily reclaims significant amounts of DASD space.

Compression can be applied at either the row or column level. Because DB2 reads and writes using pages containing rows of data, compressing rows creates room for more rows per page. System performance improvements can be realized because fewer pages are required, resulting in improved I/O, memory management, and paging.

A choice of compression routines is offered that are specifically designed for the DB2 environment, enabling users to select the best balance between compression levels and CPU overhead. Additionally, SAMS:Compress provides users with the flexibility to implement compression without having to drop and re-create the table. This flexibility also provides the ability to add new columns into a compressed table.

A simulation tool is used to forecast the effectiveness of data compression without actually compressing the data. The tool identifies the best compression routines and displays the amount of compression and relative CPU performance that would result from their use. The routines are listed in order of the amount of compression delivered, enabling the user to determine easily which data to compress and with which routine, while assessing CPU overhead. The results of compression analysis can be stored in a repository for future reference. This eliminates the need to rerun compression analysis by allowing the user to call up and display the results of a previous analysis. These results can then be compared with a current analysis in order to select the optimum compression method.

Another product, Data Packer from BMC Software, can reduce DASD requirements for DB2 tables an average of 30 to 80%. Additional hardware compression techniques can result in another 10% reduction.

Data Packer offers a choice of compression techniques to choose from, including

- Hardware compression, which exploits the hardware compression facility of IBM products or, when hardware is not available, provides software emulation;
- Custom dictionary for hardware, which builds a dictionary based on the unique characteristics of the actual data, resulting in higher compression — up to 90% — while reducing overhead;
- Dynamic adaptive, which analyzes data and chooses either the Static Huffman or Extended Character technique for compression;
- Extended character, which recognizes repeating strings of characters and reduces them to a smaller symbolic character;
- Static Huffman, which utilizes static compression tables that are built using representative samples of typical business data;
- Custom Huffman, which builds custom compression tables using representative samples of actual data;
- Repeating character, which identifies and eliminates repeating characters to achieve higher compression.

With Data Packer, there is no need to drop tables to add or change compression. This eliminates the downtime associated with DB2 compression. Data that has already been compressed is never recompressed, and there is no attempt to expand uncompressed data.

BMC Software also offers an analysis tool that lets the user determine the most effective compression technique by trying multiple techniques for one table in one pass. It can perform trial compression on an uncompressed table, verify compression results by confirming the actual amount of compression, and generate customized EDITPROCs that create optimal compression for different types of data.

IBM Solutions

IBM has been offering DASD/DB2 compression since the early 1990s. The company even offers a data compression program for VM/ESA, enabling VM users to compress and expand CMS minidisk file data automatically and transparently. This capability can help reduce DASD utilization, load on the I/O subsystem, and staff time spent managing minidisk space and monitoring "disk-full" conditions.

The product, VM Data Compression, performs compression and expansion dynamically as files are being created and updated or read by application programs. Because data compression is automatic and transparent, no modifications are required to existing application programs. Data compression is controlled through the use of compression rules stored in a rules database managed by a rules server virtual machine.

Five compression techniques are offered, including a dynamic data analyzer that selects the compression technique that yields the best compression performance with the least consumption of system resources. A trial utility and compression simulator allows system administrators to evaluate the benefits of data compression without actually writing compressed data in CMS files. Compression activity is reported in compression statistics records, which are stored in a statistics database managed by a statistics server virtual machine.

For IMS/ESA users, IBM offers IMS Compression-Extended to help reduce DASD storage requirements for databases, reduce database I/O, and improve performance. The most efficient compression is accomplished by exploiting select ES/9000 hardware. However, if there is no compression hardware installed, MVS compression services simulate the hardware instructions with software.

To use the hardware data compression capabilities, MVS requires that compression dictionaries be provided in a specific format. IMS Compression-Extended provides both a generic dictionary and the capabilities to create enterprise and custom dictionaries. The generic dictionary immediately provides the means for good compression, with minimal effort. The enterprise dictionary maximizes compression for similar enterprise databases. The custom dictionary maximizes compression for a specific database. IMS Compression-Extended links these dictionaries with MVS services to create IMS Segment Edit/Compression exit routines.

IMS Compression-Extended is designed around the activities needed to implement compression:

The Analyze function reads sample data from a specific database, simulates a dictionary, and reports potential compression statistics.

The Build function uses the same input sources as the Analyze function to build, verify, and archive a compression dictionary. By linking this dictionary to the Base Exit Routine, it creates the Edit/Compression exit routine necessary for compression.

The Compress function provides JCL (job control language) to assist with the implementation of compression. This function uses the Edit/Compression routine defined in the DBDGEN to reload and compress a database after building the Reload JCL.

709

The Examine function evaluates various combinations of dictionaries and databases, and monitors installed dictionary performance. It examines the effectiveness of hardware data compression routines as the content of the database changes, and evaluates the effectiveness of the generic dictionary or an enterprise dictionary when used on a database other than the one used to create the dictionary.

There are more than a dozen compression products for the DASD environment. The most compelling features of these products include the ability to choose from a variety of compression algorithms, the ability to test the compression method on real databases before actually applying it, and the ability to apply the selected method of compression to the database without taking the database offline.

UNIX DATABASE COMPRESSION

Since its creation in 1965, the UNIX operating system has been used primarily within academic and research institutions. It took much longer to become accepted for business use, largely because there were few mainstream applications that could take advantage of its powerful features. This situation began to change in the late 1980s. The UNIX operating system contains a rich set of features, including integral TCP/IP networking. The widespread acceptance of UNIX today is directly related to the growing popularity of the TCP/IP-based Internet. Now, with a wide selection of applications, including graphical user interfaces and management tools, the operating system has migrated into the corporate environment with such success that in 1994 Microsoft Corporation entered the market with a UNIX alternative — Windows NT Server and, later, Windows NT Workstation.

Today, huge databases reside on such UNIX platforms as Sun SPARC running Solaris, Hewlett-Packard HP/9000 Series 800 running HP/UX, and IBM RS/6000 running AIX. In fact, it is not uncommon among large firms to see production databases grow by 40 to 60% annually. Even if IS staff are confident that storage technology will catch up and that prices will come down, there are the problems of how to manage all of that storage and how to find the time to tune the database load across those devices.

A handful of vendors have developed effective solutions for these problems. One company, DataTools, Inc., offers a solution called Data Optimizer, which reduces the costs of database growth by dynamically compressing data and balancing database I/O loads across available disk devices. The company's Predict program allows users to determine exactly how much storage they will save before actually implementing compression.

Unlike file-based compression products — such as the UNIX tar program, which is limited to writing data in 5K blocks — Data Optimizer is designed to compress groups of blocks transparently. This means that it can support databases or other data stored in raw partitions or UNIX file systems. For optimal performance, data is written uncompressed, then compressed during a low-usage, user-definable maintenance period, or when available disk space reaches a user-definable threshold. On database reads, data is dynamically decompressed transparently to the database application. Existing data is never overwritten until the data has been successfully compressed and written.

Compression ratios of 4 to 1 or better can be achieved for most databases. A 20-gigabyte database, for example, can grow to 80 gigabytes without adding more storage devices. With this kind of storage savings, the IS department can use existing disks to implement disk mirroring, or can buy RAID devices to achieve higher levels of data protection.

One key to improving database performance is spreading database I/O among multiple physical disk devices. By accessing multiple devices simultaneously, the overall throughput of the database application can be greatly improved. A popular method for distributing database load is striping data across multiple disks. Unfortunately, this is a rigid method for a growing database, since more devices cannot be added later without rewriting the data. Data Optimizer not only distributes the load across devices, it allows new devices to be added at any time. IS staff simply define one or more logical volumes, which look like UNIX disk devices to the applications. These volumes consist of multiple physical devices, which may include RAID devices or other mirrored disks. Data Optimizer keeps track of what data resides in each physical location.

Through a centralized control and reporting facility, IS staff can monitor disk usage, available space, and data access patterns. When there is a need to add disk space, IS staff just add another physical device to the Data Optimizer pool, associated with one or more logical volumes. Alternatively, the process can be automated by setting up a pool of spare devices. When Data Optimizer needs more storage, it automatically adds a device from the spare pool.

WEB DATABASES

With the increasing popularity of the public Internet and corporate intranets, organizations of all types and sizes are faced with publishing information and developing electronic commerce and other applications for the World Wide Web (WWW). Many of these efforts make generous use of image files to enhance the visual appeal of the Web site in order to capture and retain visitors. Some companies are using streaming video to deliver training and other internal programming to remote sites. Unfortunately, these types of files usually are quite large and take a long time to download from Web servers to browser-equipped clients all over the world. The problem is exacerbated by the inherent delay of these networks, which is caused by such things as resource contention, congestion avoidance, and node failures. This means individual packets almost always end up taking different routes to their destination.

Bit-intensive image files and video streams must therefore be compressed and otherwise manipulated to minimize the download time, or risk having users avoid the Web site entirely. Although some compression tools will compress an entire database of images and decompress them dynamically for access over the Web, this does not solve the fundamental problem of transferring large images over the Internet. The best way to compress a large image database on a Web server is to ensure that the right file type is used in the first place.

Several compression standards have been issued to meet varying applications needs. For image files, a compression standard has been issued by the Joint Photographic Experts Group (JPEG). For video streams, a compression standard has been issued by the Motion Picture Experts Group (MPEG). For other image databases used in the advertising and publishing businesses, for example, there is fractal compression. There are many standards for compressing audio files, including GSM, which is the same compression algorithm used in conjunction with digital cellular telephone service.

JPEG

Most Web browsers support two image formats: GIF and JPEG. In general, line drawings and flat-color illustrations are better stored in GIF format, whereas photographs and complex images are more suitable for JPEG format. Of the two types of image files, only the latter offers user-selectable compression. There is no compression selection with GIF files, but most graphics programs allow users to specify high, medium, or low compression for JPEG files. Other image formats can be used on the Web, but they require the use of an external viewer, which the browser must call up and open. The time it takes for this process to work can disrupt the smooth flow of information presentation. Most consumers have only low-speed dial-up connections to the Internet and have little patience for long file downloads.

JPEG was designed for compressing continuous-tone (photographic-quality), monochrome and color still images. It is based on a discrete cosine transform (DCT)-based algorithm, which eliminates redundant image information by dividing the image into small blocks. The higher the compression ratio, the more information that is deleted and, therefore, the more image detail that is lost.

JPEG can be used to compress images at ratios as high as 25 to 1 without a noticeable loss of image quality. This is because the human eye has the capacity to fill in missing detail, making the image intelligible to the viewer. Therefore, a 25M-byte image file can be cut to less than 1M byte. Higher compression rates are possible with JPEG — as much as 100 to 1 — but, beyond 25 to 1, the loss of image quality starts to become noticeable.

For Web use, the palette of the image can be modified so that no more colors are used than is necessary. This ensures that the JPEG compression algorithm will have a smaller range of colors to work with and therefore will be able to find more and longer sequences to encode. Thus, by minimizing the number of colors in an image to only those that are essential, the compression factor can be increased substantially.

JPEG is symmetrical, meaning that, with all being equal, the same amount of computing power is used to compress an image as is used to decompress it. Compression and decompression times are about the same when it is done in software. With hardware-assisted compression, however, a significant performance boost occurs on the compression side.

JPEG also can be used to compress video in multimedia databases. It treats each frame as a separate image and compresses each frame individually through a process called intraframe coding. An added benefit of this technique is that it permits the user to access randomly any individual frame within the compressed video. Even with compression ratios of 25 to 1, however, a few seconds of compressed 24-bit-color video with a resolution of 640 by 480 pixels requires a large hard disk for storage.

MPEG

For streaming video, there is a compression standard offered by the MPEG. This compression standard goes beyond that offered by JPEG, making it better suited for video.

The MPEG standard was designed specifically for video. Along with intraframe coding for removing redundancies within a frame, MPEG employs interframe coding, which eliminates redundant information between frames. In a video sequence, for instance, an actor might only turn his head; the background stays the same. MPEG recognizes that the background is redundant and does not need to be stored for each frame. This scheme prevents easy access to individual frames within a compressed MPEG video sequence.

With MPEG, there is an interframe about every 15 frames (i.e., every half second). If a multimedia application required access to an individual frame, it would have to reconstruct or interpolate the data using several frames. This means that there can be no really random access to individual frames. This sacrifice, however, allows for compression rates with lower loss rate than JPEG-compressed video.

MPEG can compress video at rates as high as 50 to 1. It has the added advantage of allowing random access to video data and the synchronization of video and audio tracks by multimedia workstations. Unlike JPEG, MPEG takes an asymmetrical approach to compression (i.e., more computing power is required to compress full-motion video and audio than to decompress it). Multimedia applications that require video to be compressed only once and decompressed over and over again include training, publishing, and reference databases, which are readily available on CD-ROM disks.

There are some proprietary implementations of MPEG that improve upon the performance of the industry standard, but which are not compatible with it. For example, Cubic VideoComm, Inc., offers CVideoNow, which it claims delivers a video stream comparable in quality to MPEG video at 1.5M bps over a connection of only 384K bps. CVideoNow Producer, the utility for preparing video for streaming, uses proprietary compression technology to achieve ratios of 500 to 1. Developers can exert fine control over image quality during the encoding process. The video stream is eight-bit color. Over a T1 or Ethernet connection, CVideoNow can deliver an image of 320 by 240 pixels at around 15 to 30 frames per second.

Fractals

For databases that contain large image and graphics files that are not intended for public access over the Web, there is a method of compression known as fractal compression. This type of compression is used for amassing large archives of image files used in the advertising and magazine publishing businesses, for example. It is also useful in engineering and design applications. Its properties make it an effective format for certain types of multimedia content intended for distribution over a corporate LAN.

With this type of compression, repetitive patterns on an image or graphic file are identified and matched. Two patterns are considered the same as long as one can be stretched, squeezed, or rotated into looking like the other. The process continues until the image is the size specified by the user. This process is computationally intensive, with compression generally taking longer than decompression (asymmetrical). Compression rates of 100 to 1 are achievable with no loss of image quality. At 100 to 1 compression, 5M bytes of image information can be taken down to only 50K bytes.

Although JPEG products compress files quickly, their decompression rate may be unacceptably slow for some applications (e.g., multimedia training). With fractal compression, the reverse is true, making it suitable for compressed databases that rely heavily on repeated decompressions to server users.

Another advantage of the fractal method is scalability. Because patterns — rather than pixels — are viewed as the fundamental blocks of image construction, the fractal algorithm can fill in missing detail during decompression by mathematically scaling the pattern instead of just inserting extra pixels. This results in a higher degree of accuracy for decompressed images, which may be very important in multimedia, engineering, and design applications.

Audio Compression

Audio files are used over the Internet in a variety of ways. Radio stations have set up Web sites to allow access to program archives. Music companies publish selections from new CDs to encourage sales. Many instructors tape their lessons and post the audio files on the Web as part of the learning at a distance program at their college. Corporations are starting to put the contents of executive speeches and annual meetings on their Web sites. In addition, audio files can be created by sound recorders on PCs for transmission over the Internet as voice mail messages.

There are several algorithms in use that compress audio files and employ optimization techniques to ensure efficient delivery over the Internet. Among the noteworthy voice compression algorithms in popular use today are GSM and TrueSpeech.

GSM is the global system for mobile telecommunication and is a worldwide standard for digital cellular communications. It provides close to a 5 to 1 compression of raw audio with an acceptable loss of audio quality upon decompression. Although the GSM codec was originally developed for real-time conversations by cell phone, it has been adapted for several other uses, including Internet telephony, audio file distribution, and voice mail.

TrueSpeech is a product of The DSP Group, Inc. It can provide upward of 18 to 1 compression of raw audio with an imperceptible loss of audio quality on decompression. Offering a high compression ratio, TrueSpeech is more CPU-intensive than GSM, so it requires a faster processor to compress the same amount of audio in real time. Like GSM, TrueSpeech is used for Internet telephony, audio file distribution, and voice mail.

The G.723.1 voice codec is based in large part on The DSP Group's TrueSpeech. G.723.1, which combines low bit-rate compression with toll-quality communications at highly compressed rates of 6.3 and 5.3K bps, was developed for videophone and videoconferencing applications over public switched telephone networks, and adopted by the International Telecommunications Union (ITU) in 1995. By way of G.723.1, TrueSpeech is also found in the ITU H.324 standard for video telephony over ordinary telephone networks as well as the ITU H.323 standard for videoconferencing.

CONCLUSION

Compression products have permeated every nook and cranny of the data-processing, applications development, and Internet environments. Despite the higher capacities and lower costs of magnetic disks, there appears to be no letup in the demand for data compression. One explanation for these seemingly divergent trends is that there continues to be great interest in reducing costs, regardless of how good or bad the economy is doing, or how good or bad a particular market segment is doing. Another explanation is that the amount of data that companies generate is increasing by leaps and bounds, making data compression a vital necessity. Not only does database compression help achieve cost savings, it can result in improvements in applications performance. With so many data compression technologies and management tools available, the task becomes one of choosing the right product for the job. This determines to what extent the need for extra disk space and other hardware can be eliminated.

Chapter 53
How to Handle Data Loss and Backup
William Krouslis

DATA LOSS OCCURS FOR MANY REASONS. In the order of the frequency of their occurrence, the 12 most common causes of data loss are:

- The unintentional overwriting of a data file.
- The failure to back up microcomputer or workstation records on a diskette or magnetic tape because of time pressures or other tasks that appear to take precedence.
- The crash of a hard disk on a workstation or a network file server, causing not only the loss of information but also the damage to or loss of both the operating systems and the bindery of affected network management systems.
- The malfunction of diskettes or magnetic tapes that prevents them from recording data properly. This is a significant problem with tapes because they can write errors during a backup or read errors when trying to read data back. These problems are exacerbated when the read heads are not cleaned regularly.
- The inability to locate the diskettes or tapes on which desired data is stored. This usually occurs when material is stored in inappropriately or unmarked boxes or, equally likely, in boxes that were indexed in a fashion that nobody in the organization now understands.
- The loss of data because of an unexpected electrical power supply failure.
- Damage to diskettes or tapes in transit or at a secondary storage site.
- A computer virus that damages or destroys data files and operating systems.
- The theft or misuse of data, including its removal or use by unauthorized persons.
- The degradation over time of the magnetic signal — perhaps by just one byte or even a bit — on a diskette or tape. Such changes can make the content of a disk or tape unreadable without the performance of some sophisticated, costly, and time-consuming retrieval activities.
- The changing of one or more versions of an operating system or application previously used to create and record data so this data cannot

be read without reloading the original software (if it can be found at all) or running routines of varying complexities to convert the data into compatible formats.

• The destruction of a building or a work area within it by fire, earthquakes, temperature extremes, flood, or other such catastrophes that render diskettes or tapes unreadable or unavailable.

Once lost, data cannot be replaced. Accepting this fact, the prudent user routinely backs up data to a medium and location that together guarantee that no single disaster can destroy both the primary electronic source record and the backup copy simultaneously. Choosing a procedure that protects an organization from anything from accidental data erasure to data destruction in a building fire is the first step in creating a workable backup routine.

SIX BACKUP OPTIONS

There are six principal backup options. They are discussed in the following sections.

Do Nothing

Many now follow this course. They risk the complete loss of their data files.

Use Magnetic Tapes and Diskettes and Carry Them Off-Site

This method is the cheapest and the most commonly used. However, it involves many potential problems in cataloging, maintaining, and recovering data.

The traditional method of assigning data owners the responsibility of regularly backing up data and storing it on a diskette does not work for two main reasons. First, users take diskettes containing their backup copies home at the end of the work day, compromising the security of these backups. Second, users stop backing up data regularly when their files grow to require multiple diskettes. When the backup process annoys the data owner, the manual backup procedure is dead.

Centralizing all backup activities and having them performed by specific individuals does not work either. The backup records become sloppy, and labeling them becomes an administrative nightmare. The people responsible for making backups leave the organization, or they have new responsibilities that interfere with the backup process. As a result, the backups are made less frequently, and eventually the backup process stops altogether.

Tape backups can be made automatically. But tape drives can be expensive, and the time necessary to write to tape can be long, especially if the backup is done in the verify mode. Tape drive heads also become dirty, diminishing the quality of backup information.

Using a typical tape rotation schedule results in a reasonable backup, as long as the tape containing the backup is moved to a secure off-site location. Unfortunately, most backup tapes never make their final journey. Left unprotected in the same area where servers are, they are subject to the same event that might cause the primary data source to be lost. A vigorous off-site storage transfer and management procedure is therefore necessary.

Employ a System That Can Be Connected to Multiple Disks

These disks must be adapted to provide limited random access. Organizations using this arrangement must have sophisticated on-site management, and even with it, they face many of the problems common to tape systems. This arrangement also does not aid in disaster recovery.

When data is written to disks simultaneously over the same channel, a fault-tolerant mechanism protects the information. Although this approach is better than nothing, a failure encompassing more than just the storage device would render both sources of data unavailable. Adding channel extension and disk duplexing to this arrangement provides added redundancy. However, if both disks are in the same server, a single event could still compromise both sources of data.

Another option may be the use of a Redundant Arrays of Inexpensive Disks (redundant array of inexpensive disks). Spreading data across multiple drives obviously reduces the risk associated with the failure of a single drive. However, the use of Redundant Arrays of Inexpensive Disks does not eliminate the need to backup.

Use an Off-Site, Electronic Vaulting Service

Using these services eliminates the maintenance and recovery problems associated with backing up data files. Although this type of service has been available for many years for mainframes, it is just becoming available for local area networks and microcomputers. For example, Surefind, using technology developed by AT&T Commvault Systems, can back up UNIX, Digital Equipment Corporation-VMS, Novell Netware, and MS-DOS and can transmit data over ordinary telephone lines to a secure location containing optical storage devices.[1]

These services usually incorporate optical media with either Write-Once Read Many (WORM) or erasable optical disks. Because the optical disk is a random-access unit (as opposed to sequential tape), lost files are available directly, and because the storage mechanism is located at a distance from the primary place where data is stored, this type of service offers real data processing disaster recovery capabilities. Outsourcing the backup mechanism to a third-party source may therefore be the most reasonable solution for the small and medium user.

Purchase Mass Storage Equipment and Install it In-House

This arrangement is useful in organizations with several local area networks that generate sufficient amounts of data. Off-site disaster recovery is provided by placing the storage devices in a location different than the one that houses network hubs and servers. This solution is reasonable for large users with large amounts of data. The basic technology employed in Surefind was developed initially in this type of setting.

Funnel Data through an In-House Network for Storage by a Mainframe and Peripherals

This approach provides reliable data storage and retrieval and, often, prompt data access. However, unless an organization has excess storage capability in the data center housing the mainframe, using this mainframe and its peripherals to store and retrieve microcomputer data is relatively costly. Organizations using this approach must also put their network administrators under the control of the their information services departments with respect to matters of scheduling and systems development.

BACKUP SYSTEM EVALUATION

When evaluating a backup system, the EUC manager should ask these questions:

- Does the system daily and automatically back up all necessary data that the organization produces?
- Does it maintain duplicate, verified, and separately stored data and applications that cannot be erased or destroyed by such catastrophes as fire, theft, or computer viruses? Can the content of data files be changed or manipulated once recorded?
- Does the backup system limit access to files to only authorized persons, and does it routinely encrypt all data flowing to and from the storage array?
- Does the backup system permit round-the-clock access to files, according to various search criteria, and can files be restored, if necessary, within minutes?
- Does the system restore files and support software, including binderies, after computer equipment malfunctions, is destroyed, or becomes inaccessible to users? Can the system return lost files and software to the repaired equipment or send them to another authorized location?
- Can the system write all versions of all files as they are received from each local area network so that other files and software already stored remain separate and isolated, thus eliminating the spread of any computer viruses? Does the system permit these files to be restored to their original state before a virus occurred?

- Does the system bar manipulation of stored data? Is an electronic audit trail of what happens to this data available to the organization s internal and external auditors?
- Does the system automatically retain specified data elements online, while providing quick access to off-line items over any period of time (but generally for a minimum of seven years)?
- Is the system cost-effective? Does it eliminate both the obvious and hidden costs of conventional backup procedures, including the cost of on-site storage equipment, off-site storage packaging, as well as the personnel required to back up, catalog, transport, store, and retrieve data?

A key point to consider in evaluating any backup routine is whether the procedure facilitates disaster recovery. To ensure recovery, many small and medium users consider outsourcing.

BACKUP METHOD COST COMPARISON

The costs associated with any backup mechanism cannot be overlooked. Those organizations that back up data consistently incur measurable costs to maintain their backup procedures. These costs include not only the time and cost of the people, equipment, and storage space needed for a backup facility but, more critically, expenses associated with the time to retrieve stored data. Retrieval, the reason organizations back up data, is always labor intensive — an administrator must load and unload tapes, label and store them, and retrieve them as necessary to restore data requested by a user.

Organizations should compare the costs of outsourcing backup to that of an in-house solution. In doing so, they should examine the following factors:

- Maintenance of data integrity (over any length of time).
- Safety of the storage facilities.
- Desired levels of control.
- Convenience of data access.

In addition, consideration must be given to the fact that an organization cannot replace lost data, even if it receives significant insurance payments, and the untimely delivery of data can be useless, if not disastrous, to an organization if crucial information is unavailable when required for critical decision making.

CONCLUSION

Information is the heart and soul of an organization. Accepting the importance of data backup is the crucial first step in allocating the resources necessary to ensure that data remains accessible, readable, and retrievable.

DATA ADMINISTRATION AND OPERATIONS

Note

1. For more information about Surefind, contact Romax, Inc., 14 Holland Rd., Middletown, NJ 07748, telephone: (908) 615-0900.

Section XII
Database Security

WEB-BASED APPLICATIONS SUFFER FROM MANY SECURITY EXPOSURES. This includes all the traditional issues facing databases and applications, as well as the threat of constant access from many unknown users at any time of the day from virtually any position on the planet. With so many potential security risks and points of failure, it is a necessity for the data architecture of a Web-based solution to incorporate security mechanisms from the start of the development cycle, with regular reviews to ensure its effectiveness on an ongoing basis. This section contains the following chapters.

Chapter 54, "Security Management for the World Wide Web," provides a solution set to leverage an organization's existing skills, resources, and security implementations in building an underlying baseline security framework for transacting corporate business over the Internet and the World Wide Web.

Chapter 55, "Establishing Security Controls in a Distributed Database," provides a detailed analysis of information security issues in the distributed database environment. Recommendations for establishing and implementing effective security controls are also provided.

Chapter 56, "Understanding Relational Databases and Assessing Their Security," is a primer to evaluate discretionary controls and sophisticated multilevel secure databases.

Chapter 57, "Virus Protection in a Web Environment," examines techniques for protecting Web-based applications against virus infiltration from a variety of sources.

Chapter 54
Security Management for the World Wide Web

Lynda L. McGhie and Phillip Q. Maier

COMPANIES CONTINUE TO FLOCK TO THE INTERNET in ever-increasing numbers, despite the fact that the overall and underlying environment is not secure. To further complicate the matter, vendors, standards bodies, security organizations, and practitioners cannot agree on a standard, compliant, and technically available approach. As a group of investors concerned with the success of the Internet for business purposes, it is critical that we pull our collective resources and work together to quickly establish and support interoperable security standards; open security interfaces to existing security products and security control mechanisms within other program products; and hardware and software solutions within heterogeneous operating systems which will facilitate smooth transitions.

Interfaces and teaming relationships to further this goal include computer and network security and information security professional associations (CSI, ISSA, NCSA), professional technical and engineering organizations (I/EEE, IETF), vendor and product user groups, government and standards bodies, seminars and conferences, training companies/institutes (MIS), and informal networking among practitioners.

Having the tools and solutions available within the marketplace is a beginning, but we also need strategies and migration paths to accommodate and integrate Internet, intranet, and World Wide Web (WWW) technologies into our existing IT infrastructure. While there are always emerging challenges, introduction of newer technologies, and customers with challenging and perplexing problems to solve, this approach should enable us to maximize the effectiveness of our existing security investments, while bridging the gap to the long awaited and always sought after perfect solution!

Security solutions are slowly emerging, but interoperability, universally accepted security standards, application programming interfaces (APIs) for security, vendor support and cooperation, and multiplatform security products are still problematic. Where there are products and solutions, they tend to have niche applicability, be vendor-centric or only address one of a larger set of security problems and requirements. For the most part, no single vendor or even software/vendor consortium has addressed the overall security problem within open systems and public networks. This indicates that the problem is very large, and that we are years away from solving todays problem, not to mention tomorrows.

By acknowledging todays challenges, bench-marking todays requirements, and understanding our "as is condition" accordingly, we as security practitioners can best plan for security in the twenty-first century. Added benefits adjacent to this strategy will hopefully include a more cost-effective and seamless integration of security policies, security architectures, security control mechanisms, and security management processes to support this environment.

For most companies, the transition to "open" systems technologies is still in progress and most of us are somewhere in the process of converting mainframe applications and systems to distributed network-centric client-server infrastructures. Nevertheless, we are continually challenged to provide a secure environment today, tomorrow, and in the future, including smooth transitions from one generation to another. This article considers a phased integration methodology that initially focuses on the update of corporate policies and procedures, including most security policies and procedures; secondly, enhances existing distributed security architectures to accommodate the use of the Internet, intranet, and WWW technologies; thirdly, devises a security implementation plan that incorporates the use of new and emerging security products and techniques; and finally, addresses security management and infrastructure support requirements to tie it all together.

It is important to keep in mind, as with any new and emerging technology, Internet, intranet, and WWW technologies do not necessarily bring new and unique security concerns, risks, and vulnerabilities, but rather introduce new problems, challenges and approaches within our existing security infrastructure.

Security requirements, goals, and objectives remain the same, while the application of security, control mechanisms, and solution sets are different and require the involvement and cooperation of multidisciplined technical and functional area teams. As in any distributed environment, there are more players, and it is more difficult to find or interpret the overall requirements or even talk to anyone who sees or understands the big picture. More people are involved than ever before, emphasizing the need to communicate both strategic and tactical security plans broadly and effectively throughout the entire enterprise. The security challenges and the resultant problems become larger and more complex in this environment. Management must be kept up-to-date and thoroughly understand overall risk to the corporations information assets with the implementation or decisions to implement new technologies. They must also understand, fund, and support the influx of resources required to manage the security environment.

As with any new and emerging technology, security should be addressed early in terms of understanding the requirements, participating in the evaluation of products and related technologies, and finally in the engineering, design, and implementation of new applications and systems. Security should also be considered during all phases of the systems development life cycle. This is nothing new, and many of us have learned this lesson painfully over the years as we have tried to retrofit security solutions as an adjunct to the implementation of some large and complex system. Another important point to consider throughout the integration of new technologies, is "technology does not drive or dictate security policies, but the existing and established security policies drive the application of new technologies." This point must be made to management, customers, and supporting IT personnel.

For most of us, the WWW will be one of the most universal and influential trends impacting our internal enterprise and its computing and networking support structure. It will widely influence our decisions to extend our internal business processes out to the Internet and beyond. It will enable us to use the same user interface, the same critical systems and applications, work towards one single original source of data, and continue to address the age-old problem: how can I reach the largest number of users at the lowest cost possible?

THE PATH TO INTERNET/BROWSER TECHNOLOGIES

Everyone is aware of the staggering statistics relative to the burgeoning growth of the Internet over the last decade. The use of the WWW can even top that growth, causing the traffic on the Internet to double every six months. With five internal Web servers being deployed for every one external Web server, the rise of the intranet is also more than just hype. Companies are predominately using the web technologies on the intranet to share information and documents. Future application possibilities are basically any enterprise-wide application such as education and training; corporate policies and procedures; human resources applications such as a resume, job posting, etc.; and company information. External Web applications include marketing and sales.

For the purpose of this discussion, we can generally think of the Internet in three evolutionary phases. While each succeeding phase has brought with it more utility and the availability of a wealth of electronic and automated resources, each phase has also exponentially increased the risk to our internal networks and computing environments.

Phase I, the early days, is characterized by a limited use of the Internet, due in the most part to its complexity and universal accessibility. The user interface was anything but user friendly, typically limited to the use of complex UNIX-based commands via line mode. Security by obscurity was definitely a popular and acceptable way of addressing security in those early days, as security organizations and MIS management convinced themselves that the potential risks were confined to small user populations centered around homogeneous computing and networking environments. Most companies were not externally connected in those days, and certainly not to the Internet.

Phase II is characterized by the introduction of the first versions of database search engines, including Gopher and Wide Area Information System (WAIS). These tools were mostly used in the government and university environments and were not well known nor generally proliferated in the commercial sector.

Phase III brings us up to todays environment, where Internet browsers are relatively inexpensive, readily available, easy to install, easy to use through GUI frontends and interfaces, interoperable across heterogeneous platforms, and ubiquitous in terms of information access.

The growing popularity of the Internet and the introduction of the Internet should not come as a surprise to corporate executives who are generally well read on such issues and tied into major information technology (IT) vendors and consultants. However, quite frequently companies continue to select one of two choices when considering the implementation of WWW and Internet technologies. Some companies, who are more technically astute and competitive, have jumped in totally and are exploiting Internet technologies, electronic commerce, and the use of the Web. Others, of a more conservative nature and more technically inexperienced, continue to maintain a hard-line policy on external connectivity, which basically continues to say "NO."

Internet technologies offer great potential for cost savings over existing technologies, representing huge investments over the years in terms of revenue and resources now supporting corporate information infrastructures and contributing to the business imperatives of those enterprises. Internet-based applications provide a standard communications interface and protocol suite ensuring interoperability and access to the organization's heterogeneous data and information resources. Most WWW browsers run on all systems and provide a common user interface and ease of use to a wide range of corporate employees.

Benefits derived from the development of WWW-based applications for internal and external use can be categorized by the cost savings related to deployment, generally requiring very little support or end-user training. The browser software is typically free, bundled in vendor product suites, or very affordable. Access to information, as previously stated, is ubiquitous and fairly straightforward.

Use of internal WWW applications can change the very way organizations interact and share information. When established and maintained properly, an internal WWW application can enable everyone on the internal network to share information resources, update common use applications, receive education and training, and keep in touch with colleagues at their home base, from remote locations, or on the road.

INTERNET/WWW SECURITY OBJECTIVES

As mentioned earlier, security requirements do not change with the introduction and use of these technologies, but the emphasis on where security is placed and how it is implemented does change. The company's Internet, intranet, and WWW security strategies should address the following objectives, in combination or in prioritized sequence, depending on security and access requirements, company philosophy, the relative sensitivity of the companys information resources, and the business imperative for using these technologies.

- Ensure that Internet- and WWW-based application and the resultant access to information resources are protected and that there is a cost-effective and user-friendly way to maintain and manage the underlying security components, over time as new technology evolves and security solutions mature in response.
- Information assets should be protected against unauthorized usage and destruction. Communication paths should be encrypted as well as transmitted information that is broadcast over public networks.
- Receipt of information from external sources should be decrypted and authenticated. Internet- and WWW-based applications, WWW pages, directories, discussion groups, and databases should all be secured using access control mechanisms.
- Security administration and overall support should accommodate a combination of centralized and decentralized management.
- User privileges should be linked to resources, with privileges to those resources managed and distributed through directory services.
- Mail and real-time communications should also be consistently protected. Encryption key management systems should be easy to administer, compliant with existing security architectures, compatible with existing security strategies and tactical plans, and secure to manage and administer.

- New security policies, security architectures, and control mechanisms should evolve to accommodate this new technology; not change in principle or design.

Continue to use risk management methodologies as a baseline for deciding how many of the new Internet, intranet, and WWW technologies to use and how to integrate them into the existing Information Security Distributed Architecture. As always, ensure that the optimum balance between access to information and protection of information is achieved during all phases of the development, integration, implementation, and operational support life cycle.

INTERNET AND WWW SECURITY POLICIES AND PROCEDURES

Having said all of this, it is clear that we need new and different policies, or minimally, an enhancement or refreshing of current policies supporting more traditional means of sharing, accessing, storing, and transmitting information. In general, high-level security philosophies, policies, and procedures should not change. In other words, who is responsible for what (the fundamental purpose of most high-level security policies) does not change. These policies are fundamentally directed at corporate management, process, application and system owners, functional area management, and those tasked with the implementation and support of the overall IT environment. There should be minimal changes to these policies, perhaps only adding the Internet and WWW terminology.

Other high level corporate policies must also be modified, such as the use of corporate assets, responsibility for sharing and protecting corporate information, etc. The second-level corporate policies, usually more procedure oriented typically addressing more of the "how," should be more closely scrutinized and may change the most when addressing the use of the Internet, intranet, and Web technologies for corporate business purposes. New classifications and categories of information may need to be established and new labeling mechanisms denoting a category of information that cannot be displayed on the Internet or new meanings to "all allow" or "public" data. The term "public," for instance, when used internally, usually means anyone authorized to use internal systems. In most companies, access to internal networks, computing systems, and information is severely restricted and "public" would not mean unauthorized users, and certainly not any user on the Internet.

Candidate lower-level policies and procedures for update to accommodate the Internet and WWW include external connectivity, network security, transmission of data, use of electronic commerce, sourcing and procurement, electronic mail, nonemployee use of corporate information and electronic systems, access to information, appropriate use of electronic systems, use of corporate assets, etc.

New policies and procedures (most likely enhancements to existing policies) highlight the new environment and present an opportunity to dust off and update old policies. Involve a broad group of customers and functional support areas in the update to these policies. The benefits are many. It exposes everyone to the issues surrounding the new technologies, the new security issues and challenges, and gains buy-in through the development and approval process from those who will have to comply when the policies are approved. It is also an excellent way to raise the awareness level and get attention to security up front.

The most successful corporate security policies and procedures address security at three levels, at the management level through high-level policies, at the functional level through security procedures and technical guidelines, and at the end-user level through user awareness and training guidelines. Consider the opportunity to create or update all three when implementing Internet, intranet, and WWW technologies.

Since these new technologies increase the level of risk and vulnerability to your corporate computing and network environment, security policies should probably be beefed up in the areas of audit and monitoring. This is particularly important because security and technical control mechanisms are not mature for the Internet and WWW and therefore more manual processes need to be put in place and mandated to ensure the protection of information.

The distributed nature of Internet, intranet, and WWW and their inherent security issues can be addressed at a more detailed level through an integrated set of policies, procedures, and technical guidelines. Because these policies and processes will be implemented by various functional support areas, there is a great need to obtain buy-in from these groups and ensure coordination and integration through all phases of the systems' life cycle. Individual and collective roles and responsibilities should be clearly delineated to include monitoring and enforcement.

Other areas to consider in the policy update include legal liabilities, risk to competition-sensitive information, employees' use of company time while "surfing" the Internet, use of company logos and trade names by employees using the Internet, defamation of character involving company employees, loss of trade secrets, loss of the competitive edge, ethical use of the Internet, etc.

DATA CLASSIFICATION SCHEME

A data classification scheme is important to both reflect existing categories of data and introduce any new categories of data needed to support the business use of the Internet, electronic commerce, and information sharing through new intranet and WWW technologies. The whole area of

Exhibit 54-1.   Sample data protection classification hierarchy.

	Auth.	Trans. Controls	Encryption	Audit	Ownership
External Public Data				(X)	X
Internal Public Data				(X)	X
Internal Cntl. Data	X	X	(X)	X	X
External Cntl. Data	X	X	X	X	X
Update Applications	X	X		X	X

nonemployee access to information changes the approach to categorizing and protecting company information.

The sample chart in Exhibit 1 is an example of how general to specific categories of company information can be listed, with their corresponding security and protection requirements to be used as a checklist by application, process, and data owners to ensure the appropriate level of protection, and also as a communication tool to functional area support personnel tasked with resource and information protection. A supplemental chart could include application and system names familiar to corporate employees, or types of general applications and information such as payroll, HR, marketing, manufacturing, etc.

Note that encryption may not be required for the same level of data classification in the mainframe and proprietary networking environment, but in "open" systems and distributed and global networks transmitted data are much more easily compromised. Security should be applied based on a thorough risk assessment considering the value of the information, the risk introduced by the computing and network environment, the technical control mechanisms feasible or available for implementation, and the ease of administration and management support. Be careful to apply the right "balance" of security. Too much is just as costly and ineffective as too little in most cases.

APPROPRIATE USE POLICY

It is important to communicate management's expectation for employee's use of these new technologies. An effective way to do that is to supplement the corporate policies and procedures with a more user-friendly bulletined list of requirements. The list should be specific, highlight employee expectations and outline what employees can and cannot do on the Internet, intranet, and WWW. The goal is to communicate with each and every employee, leaving little room for doubt or confusion. An Appropriate Use Policy (Exhibit 2) could achieve these goals and reinforce the higher level. Areas to address include the proper use of employee time, corporate computing and networking resources, and acceptable material to be viewed or downloaded to company resources.

Exhibit 54-2. Appropriate use policy.

Examples of unacceptable use include but not limited to the following:

1.) Using Co. equipment, functions or services for non-business related activities while on company time; which in effect is mischarging;
2.) Using the equipment or services for financial or commercial gain;
3.) Using the equipment or services for any illegal activity;
4.) Dial-in usage from home for Internet services for personal gain;
5.) Accessing non-business related news groups or BBS;
6.) Willful intent to degrade or disrupt equipment, software or system performance;
7.) Vandalizing the data or information of another user;
8.) Gaining unauthorized access to resources or information;
9.) Invading the privacy of individuals;
10.) Masquerading as or using an account owned by another user;
11.) Posting anonymous messages or mail for malicious intent;
12.) Posting another employee's personal communication or mail without the original author's consent; this excludes normal business E-mail forwarding;
13.) Downloading, storing, printing or displaying files or messages that are profane, obscene, or that use language or graphics which offends or tends to degrade others;
14.) Transmitting company data over the network to non-company employees without following proper release procedures;
15.) Loading software obtained from outside the Corporation's standard company's procurement channels onto a company system without proper testing and approval;
16.) Initiating or forwarding electronic chain mail.

Examples of acceptable use includes but is not limited to the following:

1.) Accessing the Internet, computer resources, fax machines and phones for information directly related to your work assignment;
2.) Off-hour usage of computer systems for degree related school work where allowed by local site practices;
3.) Job related On-Job Training (OJT).

Most companies are concerned with the Telecommunications Act and their liabilities in terms of allowing employees to use the Internet on company time and with company resources. Most find that the trade-off is highly skewed to the benefit of the corporation in support of the utility of the Internet. Guidelines must be carefully spelled out and coordinated with the legal department to ensure that company liabilities are addressed through clear specification of roles and responsibilities. Most companies do not monitor their employee's use of the Internet or the intranet, but find that audit trail information is critical to prosecution and defense for computer crime.

Overall computer security policies and procedures are the baseline for any security architecture and the first thing to do when implementing any new technology. However, you are never really finished as the development and support of security policies is an iterative process and should be revisited on an ongoing basis to ensure that they are up-to-date, accommodate new technologies, address current risk levels, and reflect the company's use of information and network and computing resources.

There are four basic threats to consider when you begin to use Internet, intranet, and Web technologies:

- Unauthorized alteration of data
- Unauthorized access to the underlying operating system
- Eavesdropping on messages passed between a server and a browser
- Impersonation

Your security strategies should address all four. These threats are common to any technology in terms of protecting information. In the remainder of this chapter, we will build upon the "general good security practices and traditional security management" discussed in the first section and apply these lessons to the technical implementation of security and control mechanisms in the Internet, intranet, and Web environments.

The profile of a computer hacker is changing with the exploitation of Internet and Web technologies. Computerized bulletin board services and network chat groups link computer hackers (formerly characterized as loners and misfits) together. Hacker techniques, programs and utilities, and easy-to-follow instructions are readily available on the net. This enables hackers to more quickly assemble the tools to steal information and break into computers and networks, and it also provides the "would-be" hacker a readily available arsenal of tools.

INTERNAL/EXTERNAL APPLICATIONS

Most companies segment their networks and use firewalls to separate the internal and external networks. Most have also chosen to push their marketing, publications, and services to the public side of the firewall using file servers and web servers. There are benefits and challenges to each of these approaches. It is difficult to keep data synchronized when duplicating applications outside the network. It is also difficult to ensure the security of those applications and the integrity of the information. Outside the firewall is simply *outside*, and therefore also outside the protections of the internal security environment. It is possible to protect that information and the underlying system through the use of new security technologies for authentication and authorization. These techniques are not without trade-offs in terms of cost and ongoing administration, management, and support.

Security goals for external applications that bridge the gap between internal and external, and for internal applications using the Internet, intranet, and WWW technologies should all address these traditional security controls:

- Authentication
- Authorization
- Access control
- Audit
- Security administration

Some of what you already used can be ported to the new environment, and some of the techniques and supporting infrastructure already in place supporting mainframe-based applications can be applied to securing the new technologies.

Using the Internet and other public networks is an attractive option, not only for conducting business-related transactions and electronic commerce, but also for providing remote access for employees, sharing information with business partners and customers, and supplying products and services. However, public networks create added security challenges for IS management and security practitioners, who must devise security systems and solutions to protect company computing, networking, and information resources. Security is a CRITICAL component.

Two watchdog groups are trying to protect on-line businesses and consumers from hackers and fraud. The council of Better Business Bureaus has launched BBBOnline, a service that provides a way to evaluate the legitimacy of on-line businesses. In addition, the national computer security association, NCSA, launched a certification program for secure WWW sites. Among the qualities that NCSA looks for in its certification process are extensive logging, the use of encryption including those addressed in this chapter, and authentication services.

There are a variety of protection measures that can be implemented to reduce the threats in the Web/server environment, making it more acceptable for business use. Direct server protection measures include secure Web server products which use differing designs to enhance the security over user access and data transmittal. In addition to enhanced secure Web server products, the Web server network architecture can also be addressed to protect the server and the corporate enterprise which could be placed in a vulnerable position due to served enabled connectivity. Both secure server and secure web server designs will be addressed, including the application and benefits to using each.

WHERE ARE YOUR USERS?

Discuss how the access point where your users reside contributes to the risk and the security solutions set. Discuss the challenge when users are all over the place and you have to rely on remote security services that are only as good as the users' correct usage. Issues of evolving technologies

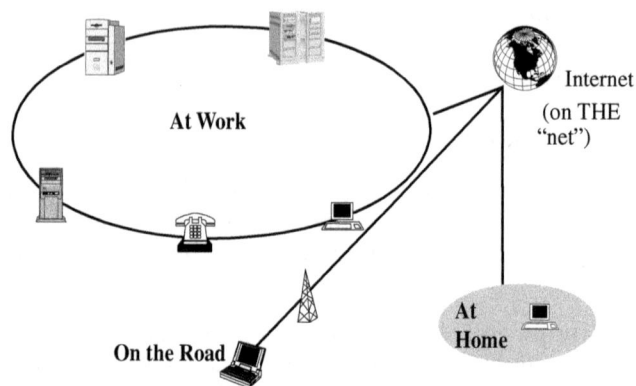

Exhibit 54-3. Where are your users?

can also be addressed. Concerns for multiple layering of controls and dissatisfied users with layers of security controls, passwords, hoops, etc. can also be addressed (Exhibit 3).

WEB BROWSER SECURITY STRATEGIES

Ideally, Web browser security strategies should use a network-based security architecture that integrates your company's external Internet and the internal intranet security policies. Ensure that users on any platform, with any browser, can access any system from any location if they are authorized and have a "need-to-know." Be careful not to adopt the latest evolving security product from a new vendor or an old vendor capitalizing on a hot marketplace.

Recognizing that the security environment is changing rapidly, and knowing that we don't want to change our security strategy, architecture, and control mechanisms every time a new product or solution emerges, we need to take time and use precautions when devising browser security solutions. It is sometimes a better strategy to stick with the vendors that you have already invested in and negotiate with them to enhance their existing products, or even contract with them to make product changes specific or tailored to accommodate your individual company requirements. Be careful in these negotiations as it is extremely likely that other companies have the very same requirements. User groups can also form a common position and interface to vendors for added clout and pressure.

You can basically secure your web server as much as or as little as you wish with the current available security products and technologies. The tradeoffs are obvious: cost, management, administrative requirements, and time. Solutions can be hardware, software and personnel intensive.

Enhancing the security of the web server itself has been a paramount concern since the first Web server initially emerged, but progress has been slow in deployment and implementation. As the market has mushroomed for server use, and the diversity of data types that are being placed on the server has grown, the demand has increased for enhanced Web server security. Various approaches have emerged, with no single *de facto* standard yet emerging (though there are some early leaders — among them Secure Sockets Layer [SSL] and Secure Hypertext Transfer Protocol [S-HTTP]). These are two significantly different approaches, but both widely seen in the marketplace.

Secure Socket Layer (SSL) Trust Model

One of the early entrants into the secure Web server and client arena is Netscape's Commerce Server, which utilizes the Secure Sockets Layer (SSL) trust model. This model is built around the RSA Public Key/Private Key architecture. Under this model, the SSL-enabled server is authenticated to SSL-aware clients, proving its identity at each SSL connection. This proof of identity is conducted through the use of a public/private key pair issued to the server validated with x.509 digital certificates. Under the SSL architecture, web server validation can be the only validation performed, which may be all that is needed in some circumstances. This would be applicable for those applications where it is important to the user to be assured of the identity of the target server, such as when placing company orders, or other information submittal where the client is expecting some important action to take place. Exhibit 4 diagrams this process.

Optionally, SSL sessions can be established that also authenticate the client and encrypt the data transmission between the client and the server for multiple I/P services (HTTP, Telnet, FTP). The multiservice encryption capability is available because SSL operates below the application layer and above the TCP/IP connection layer in the protocol stack, and thus other TCP/IP services can operate on top of a SSL-secured session.

Optionally, authentication of a SSL client is available when the client is registered with the SSL server, and occurs after the SSL-aware client connects and authenticates the SSL server. The SSL client then submits its digital certificate to the SSL server, where the SSL server validates the clients certificate and proceeds to exchange a session key to provide encrypted transmissions between the client and the server. Exhibit 5 provides a graphical representation of this process for mutual client and server authentication under the SSL architecture. This type of mutual client/server authentication process should be considered when the data being submitted by the client are sensitive enough to warrant encryption prior to being submitted over a network transmission path.

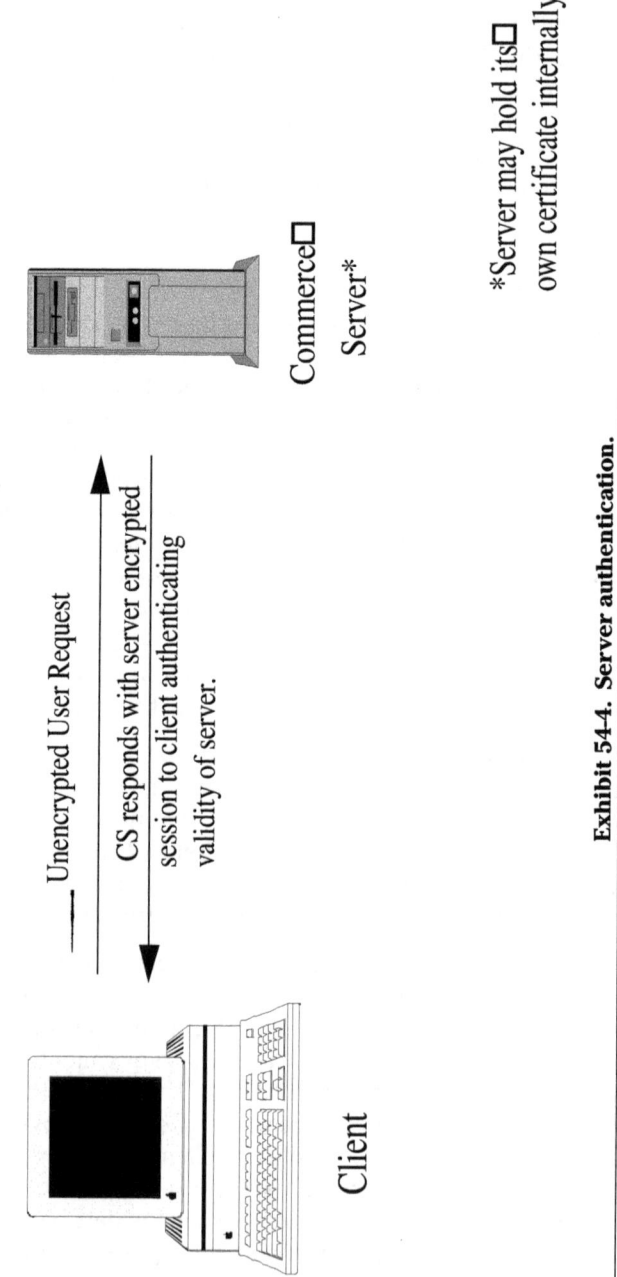

Exhibit 54-4. Server authentication.

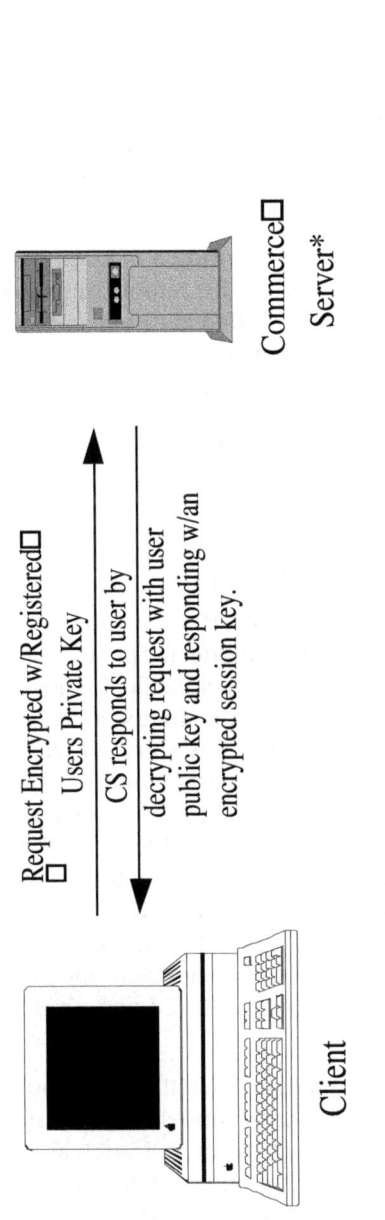

Commerce□
Server*

Request Encrypted w/Registered□
□ Users Private Key

CS responds to user by
decrypting request with user
public key and responding w/an
encrypted session key.

Client

*Assumes CS has access to a key directory\
server, most likely LDAP compliant.

Exhibit 54-5. Client and server authentication.

Though there are some "costs" with implementing this architecture, these cost variables must be considered when proposing a SSL server implementation to enhance your web server security. First of all, the design needs to consider whether to only provide server authentication, or both server and client authentication. The issue when expanding the authentication to include client authentication includes the administrative overhead of managing the user keys, including a key revocation function. This consideration, of course, has to assess the size of the user base, potential for growth of your user base, and stability of your proposed user community. All of these factors will impact the administrative burden of key management, especially if there is the potential for a highly unstable or transient user community.

The positive considerations for implementing a SSL-secured server is the added ability to secure other I/P services for remote or external SSL clients. SSL-registered clients now have the added ability to communicate securely by utilizing Tenet and FTP (or other I/P services) after passing SSL client authentication and receiving their session encryption key. In general the SSL approach has very broad benefits, but these benefits come with the potential added burden of higher administration costs, though if the value of potential data loss is great, then it is easily offset by the administration cost identified above.

Secure Hypertext Transfer Protocol (S-HTTP)

Secure Hypertext Transfer Protocol, (S-HTTP) is emerging as another security tool and incorporates a flexible trust model for providing secure web server and client HTTP communications. It is specifically designed for direct integration into HTTP transactions, with its focus on flexibility for establishing secure communications in a HTTP environment while providing transaction confidentiality, authenticity/integrity, and nonrepudiation. S-HTTP incorporates a great deal of flexibility in its trust model by leaving defined variable fields in the header definition which identifies the trust model or security algorithm to be used to enable a secure transaction. S-HTTP can support symmetric or asymmetric keys, and even a Kerberos-based trust model. The intention of the authors was to build a flexible protocol that supports multiple trusted modes, key management mechanisms, and cryptographic algorithms through clearly defined negotiation between parties for specific transactions.

At a high level the transactions can begin in a untrusted mode (standard HTTP communication), and "setup" of a trust model can be initiated so that the client and the server can negotiate a trust model, such as a symmetric key-based model on a previously agreed-upon symmetric key, to begin encrypted authentication and communication. The advantage of a S-HTTP-enabled server is the high degree of flexibility in securely communicating with web clients. A single server, if appropriately configured and network enabled, can support multiple trust models under the S-HTTP architecture and serve multiple client types. In addition to being able to serve a flexible user base, it can also be used to address multiple data classifications on a single server where some data types require higher-level encryption or protection than other data types on the same server and therefore varying trust models could be utilized.

The S-HTTP model provides flexibility in its secure transaction architecture, but focuses on HTTP transaction vs. SSL which mandates the trust model of a public/private key security model, which can be used to address multiple I/P services. But the S-HTTP mode is limited to only HTTP communications.

INTERNET, INTRANET, AND WORLD WIDE WEB SECURITY ARCHITECTURES

Implementing a secure server architecture, where appropriate, should also take into consideration the existing enterprise network security architecture and incorporate the secure server as part of this overall architecture. In order to discuss this level of integration, we will make an assumption that the secure web server is to provide secure data dissemination for external (outside the enterprise) distribution and/or access. A discussion of such a network security architecture would not be complete without addressing the placement of the Web server in relation to the enterprise firewall (the firewall being the dividing line between the protected internal enterprise environment and the external "public" environment).

Setting the stage for this discussion calls for some identification of the requirements, so the following list outlines some sample requirements for this architectural discussion on integrating a secure HTTP server with an enterprise firewall.

- Remote client is on public network accessing sensitive company data.
- Remote client is required to authenticate prior to receiving data.
- Remote client only accesses data via HTTP.
- Data is only updated periodically.
- Host site maintains firewall.
- Sensitive company data must be encrypted on public networks.
- Company support personnel can load HTTP server from inside the enterprise.

Based on these high-level requirements, an architecture could be set up that would place a S-HTTP server external to the firewall, with one-way communications from inside the enterprise "to" the external server to perform routine administration, and periodic data updates. Remote users would access the S-HTTP server utilizing specified S-HTTP secure transaction

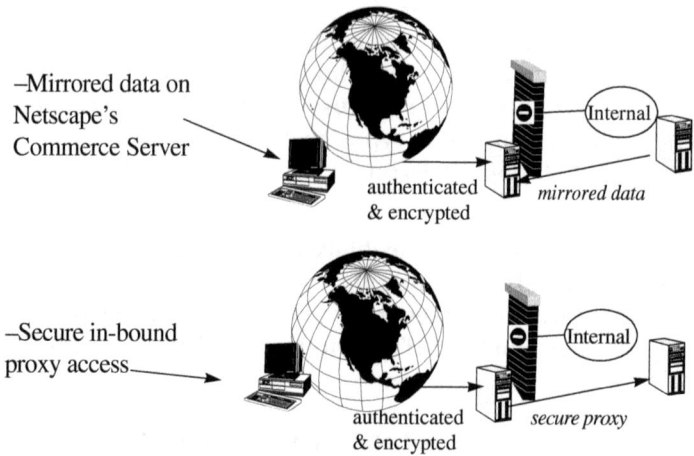

-Mirrored data on
Netscape's
Commerce Server

authenticated
& encrypted

mirrored data

-Secure in-bound
proxy access

authenticated
& encrypted

secure proxy

Exhibit 54-6. Externally placed server.

modes, and be required to identify themselves to the server prior to being granted access to secure data residing on the server. Exhibit 6 depicts this architecture at a high level. This architecture would support a secure HTTP distribution of sensitive company data, but doesn't provide absolute protection due to the placement of the S-HTTP server entirely external to the protected enterprise. There are some schools of thought that since this server is unprotected by the company-controlled firewall, the S-HTTP server itself is vulnerable, thus risking the very control mechanism itself and the data residing on it. The opposing view on this is that the risk to the overall enterprise is minimized, as only this server is placed at risk and its own protection is the S-HTTP process itself. This process has been a leading method to secure the data, without placing the rest of the enterprise at risk, by placing the S-HTTP server logically and physically outside the enterprise security firewall.

A slightly different architecture has been advertised that would position the S-HTTP server inside the protected domain, as Exhibit 7 indicates. The philosophy behind this architecture is that the controls of the firewall (and inherent audits) are strong enough to control the authorized access to the S-HTTP server, and also thwart any attacks against the server itself. Additionally, the firewall can control external users so that they only have S-HTTP access via a logically dedicated path, and only to the designated S-HTTP server itself, without placing the rest of the internal enterprise at risk. This architecture relies on the absolute ability of the firewall and S-HTTP of always performing their designated security function as defined; otherwise, the enterprise has been opened for attack through the allowed path from external users to the internal S-HTTP server. Because these conditions are always required to be true and intact,

authenticated□
& encrypted

Exhibit 54-7. Internally placed server.

the model with the server external to the firewall has been more readily accepted and implemented.

Both of these architectures can offer a degree of data protection in a S-HTTP architecture when integrated with the existing enterprise firewall architecture. As an aid in determining which architectural approach is right for a given enterprise, a risk assessment can provide great input to the decision. This risk assessment may include decision points such as:

- Available resources to maintain a high degree of firewall audit and S-HTTP server audit.
- Experience in firewall and server administration.
- Strength of their existing firewall architecture.

SECURE WWW CLIENT CONFIGURATION

There is much more reliance on the knowledge and cooperation of the end user and the use of a combination of desktop and workstation software, security control parameters within client software, and security products all working together to mimic the security of the mainframe and distributed application's environments. Consider the areas below during the risk assessment process and the design of WWW security solution sets.

- Ensure that all internal and external company-used workstations have resident and active antivirus software products installed. Preferably use a minimum number of vendor products to reduce security support and vulnerabilities as there are varying vendor schedules for providing virus signature updates.
- Ensure that all workstation and browser client software is preconfigured to return all WWW and other external file transfers to temporary files on the desktop. Under no circumstances should client server applications or process-to-process automated routines download files to system files, preference files, bat files, start-up files, etc.
- Ensure that Java script is turned off in the browser client software desktop configuration.

745

- Configure browser client software to automatically flush the cache, either upon closing the browser or disconnecting from each Web site.
- When possible or available, implement one of the new security products that scans WWW downloads for viruses.
- Provide user awareness and education to all desktop WWW and Internet users to alert them to the inherent dangers involved in using the Internet and WWW. Include information on detecting problems, their roles and responsibilities, your expectations, security products available, how to set and configure their workstations and program products, etc.
- Suggest or mandate the use of screen savers, security software programs, etc., in conjunction with your security policies and distributed security architectures.

This is a list of current areas of concern from a security perspective. There are options that when combined can tailor the browser to the specifications of individual workgroups or individuals. These options will evolve with the browser technology. The list should continue to be modified as security problems are corrected or as new problems occur.

AUDIT TOOLS AND CAPABILITIES

As we move further and further from the "good old days" when we were readily able to secure the "glass house," we rely more on good and sound auditing practices. As acknowledged throughout this chapter, security control mechanisms are mediocre at best in today's distributed networking and computing environments. Today's auditing strategies must be robust, available across multiple heterogeneous platforms, computing and network based, real-time and automated, and integrated across the enterprise.

Today, information assets are distributed all over the enterprise, and therefore auditing strategies must acknowledge and accept this challenge and accommodate more robust and dicey requirements. As is the case when implementating distributed security control mechanisms, in the audit environment there are also many players and functional support areas involved in collecting, integrating, synthesizing, reporting, and reconciling audit trails and audit information. The list includes applications and applications developers and programs, database management systems and database administrators, operating systems and systems administrators, local area network (LAN) administrators and network operating systems (NOS), security administrators and security software products, problem reporting and tracking systems and helpline administrators, and others unique to the company's environment.

As well as real-time, the audit system should provide for tracking and alarming, both to the systems and network management systems, and via pagers to support personnel. Policies and procedures should be developed for handling alarms and problems, i.e., isolate and monitor, disconnect, etc.

There are many audit facilities available today, including special audit software products for the Internet, distributed client server environments, WWW clients and servers, Internet firewalls, E-mail, News Groups, etc. The application of one or more of these must be consistent with your risk assessment, security requirements, technology availability, etc. The most important point to make here is the fundamental need to centralize distributed systems auditing (not an oxymoron). Centrally collect, sort, delete, process, report, take action and store critical audit information. Automate any and all steps and processes. It is a well-established fact that human beings cannot review large numbers of audit records and logs and reports without error. Today's audit function is an adjunct to the security function, and as such is more important and critical than ever before. It should be part of the overall security strategy and implementation plan.

The overall audit solutions set should incorporate the use of browser access logs, enterprise security server audit logs, network and firewall system authentication server audit logs, application and middle-ware audit logs, URL filters and access information, mainframe system audit information, distributed systems operating system audit logs, database management system audit logs, and other utilities that provide audit trail information such as accounting programs, network management products, etc.

The establishment of auditing capabilities over WWW environments follows closely with the integration of all external WWW servers with the firewall, as previously mentioned. This is important when looking at the various options available to address a comprehensive audit approach.

WWW servers can offer a degree of auditability based on the operating system of the server on which they reside. The more time-tested environments such as UNIX are perceived to be difficult to secure, whereas the emerging NT platform with its enhanced security features supposedly make it a more secure and trusted platform with a wide degree of audit tools and capabilities (though the vote is still out on NT, as some feel it hasn't had the time and exposure to discover all the potential security holes, perceived or real). The point, though, is that in order to provide some auditing the first place to potentially implement the first audit is on the platform where the WWW server resides. Issues here are the use of privileged accounts and file logs and access logs for log-ins to the operating system, which could indicate a backdoor attack on the WWW server itself. If server-based log are utilized, they of course must be file protected and should be off-loaded to a nonserver-based machine to protect against after-the-fact corruption.

Though the server logs aren't the only defensive logs that should be relied upon in a public WWW server environment, the other components in the access architecture should be considered for use as audit log tools. As previously mentioned, the WWW server should be placed in respect to its required controls in relation to the network security firewall. If it is a S-HTTP server that is placed behind (Exhibit 4) the firewall then the firewall of course has the ability to log all access to the S-HTTP server and provide a log separate from the WWW server-based logs, and is potentially more secure should the WWW server somehow become compromised.

The prevalent security architecture places externally accessible WWW servers wholly outside the firewall, thus virtually eliminating the capability of auditing access to the WWW server except from users internal to the enterprise. In this case, the network security audit in the form of the network management tool, which monitors the "health" of enterprise components can be called upon to provide a minimal degree of audit over the status of your external WWW server. This type of audit can be important when protecting data which resides on your external server from being subject to "denial of service" attacks, which are not uncommon for external devices. But by utilizing your network management tool to guard against such attacks, and monitoring log alerts on the status or health of this external server, you can reduce the exposure to this type of attack.

Other outside devices that can be utilized to provide audit include the network router between the external WWW server and the true external environment, though these devices are not normally readily set up for comprehensive audit logs, but in some critical cases they could be reconfigured with added hardware and minimal customized programming. One such example would be the "I/P Accounting" function on a popular router product line, which allows off-loading of addresses and protocols through its external interface. This could be beneficial to analyze traffic, and if an attack alert was generated from one of the other logs mentioned, then these router logs could assist in possibly identifying the origin of the attack.

Another possible source of audit logging could come from "back end" systems that the WWW server is programmed to "mine" data from. Many WWW environments are being established to serve as "front ends" for much larger data repositories, such as Oracle databases, where the WWW server receives user requests for data over HTTP, and the WWW server launches SQL_Net queries to a back end Oracle database. In this type of architecture the more developed logging inherent to the Oracle environment can be called upon to provide audits over the WWW queries. The detailed Oracle logs can specify the quantity, data type, and other activity over all the queries that the WWW server has made, thus providing a comprehensive activity log that can be consolidated and reviewed should any type of

WWW server compromise be suspected. A site could potentially discover the degree of data exposure though these logs.

These are some of the major areas where auditing can be put in place to monitor the WWW environment while enhancing its overall security. It is important to note that the potential placement of audits encompasses the entire distributed computing infrastructure environment, not just the new WWW server itself. In fact, there are some schools of thought that consider the more reliable audits to be those that are somewhat distanced from the target server, thus reducing the potential threat of compromise to the audit logs themselves. In general, the important point is to look at the big picture when designing the security controls and a supporting audit solution.

WWW/Internet Audit Considerations

After your distributed Internet, intranet, and WWW security policies are firmly established, distributed security architectures are updated to accommodate this new environment. When planning for audit, and security control mechanisms are designed and implemented, you should plan how you will implement the audit environment — not only which audit facilities to use to collect and centralize the audit function, but how much and what type of information to capture, how to filter and review the audit data and logs, and what actions to take on the violations or anomalies identified. Additional consideration should be given to secure storage and access to the audit data. Other considerations include:

- Timely resolution of violations.
- Disk space storage availability.
- Increased staffing and administration.
- In-house developed programming.
- Ability to alarm and monitor in real time.

WWW SECURITY FLAWS

As with all new and emerging technology, many initial releases come with some deficiency. But this has been of critical importance when that deficiency can impact the access or corruption of a whole corporation or enterprise's display to the world. This can be the case with Web implementations utilizing the most current releases which have been found to contain some impacting code deficiencies, though up to this point most of these deficiencies have been identified before any major damage has been done. This underlines the need to maintain a strong link or connection with industry organizations that announce code shortcomings that impact a sites Web implementation. A couple of the leading organizations are CERT, the Computer Emergency Response Team, and CIAC, Computer Incident Advisory Capability.

Just a few of these types of code or design issues that could impact a sites web security include initial issues with the Sun JAVA language and Netscapes JavaScript (which is an extension library of their HyperText Markup Language, HTML).

The Sun Java language was actually designed with some aspects of security in mind, though upon its initial release there were several functions that were found to be a security risk. One of the most impacting bugs in an early release was the ability to execute arbitrary machine instructions by loading a malicious Java applet. By utilizing Netscape's caching mechanism a malicious machine instruction can be downloaded into a user's machine and Java can be tricked into executing it. This doesn't present a risk to the enterprise server, but the user community within one's enterprise is of course at risk.

Other Sun Java language bugs include the ability to make network connections with arbitrary hosts (though this has since been patched with the following release) and Java's ability to launch denial of service attacks through the use of corrupt applets.

These types of security holes are more prevalent than the security profession would like to believe, as the JavaScript environment also was found to contain capabilities that allowed malicious functions to take place. The following three are among the most current and prevalent risks:

- JavaScripts ability to trick the user into uploading a file on his local hard disk to an arbitrary machine on the Internet.
- The ability to hand out the user's directory listing from the internal hard disk.
- The ability to monitor all pages the user visits during a session.

The following are among the possible protection mechanisms:

- Maintain monitoring through CERT or CIAC, or other industry organizations that highlight such security risks.
- Utilize a strong software distribution and control capability, so that early releases aren't immediately distributed, and that new patched code known to fix a previous bug is released when deemed safe.
- In sensitive environments it may become necessary to disable the browsers capability to even utilize or execute Java or JavaScript — a selectable function now available in many browsers.

In the last point, it can be disturbing to some in the user community to disallow the use of such powerful tools, because they can be utilized against trusted Web pages, or those that require authentication through the use of SSL or S-HTTP. This approach can be coupled with the connection to S-HTTP pages where the target page has to prove its identity to the client user. In this case, enabling Java or JavaScripts to execute on the browser (a user-selectable option) could be done with a degree of confidence.

Other perceived security risks exist in a browser feature referred to as HTTP "Cookies." This is a feature that allows servers to store information on the client machine in order to reduce the store and retrieve requirements of the server. The cookies file can be written to by the server, and that server, in theory, is the only one that can read back their cookies entry. Uses of the cookie file include storing user's preferences or browser history on a particular server or page, which can assist in guiding the user on their next visit to that same page. The entry in the cookies file identifies the information to be stored and the uniform resource locator (URL) or server page that can read back that information, though this address can be masked to some degree so multiple pages can read back the information.

The perceived security concern is that pages impersonating cookies-readable pages could read back a users cookies information without the user knowing it, or discover what information is stored in their cookie file. The threat depends on the nature of the data stored in the cookie file, which is dependent on what the server chooses to write into a user's cookie file. This issue is currently under review, with the intention of adding additional security controls to the cookie file and its function. At this point it is important that users are aware of the existence of this file, which is viewable in the Macintosh environment as a Netscape file and in the Win environment as a cookies.txt file. There are already some inherent protections in the cookie file: one is the fact that the cookie file currently has a maximum of 20 entries, which potentially limits the exposure. Also, these entries can be set up with expiration dates to they don't have an unlimited lifetime.

WWW SECURITY MANAGEMENT

Consider the overall management of the Internet, intranet, and WWW environment. As previously mentioned, there are many players in the support role and for many of them this is not their primary job or priority. Regardless of where the following items fall in the support infrastructure, also consider these points when implementing ongoing operational support:

- Implement WWW browser and server standards.
- Control release and version distribution.
- Implement secure server administration including the use of products and utilities to erase sensitive data cache (NSClean).
- Ensure prompt problem resolution, management, and notification.
- Follow industry and vendor discourse on WWW security flaws and bugs including CERT distribution.
- Stay current on new Internet and WWW security problems, Netscape encryption, JAVA, Cookies, etc.

WWW SUPPORT INFRASTRUCTURE

- WWW servers accessible from external networks should reside outside the firewall and be managed centrally.
- By special approval, decentralized programs can manage external servers, but must do so in accordance with corporate policy and be subjected to rigorous audits.
- Externally published company information must be cleared through legal and public relations departments (i.e., follow company procedures).
- External outbound http access should utilize proxy services for additional controls and audit.
- WWW application updates must be authenticated utilizing standard company security systems (as required).
- Filtering and monitoring software must be incorporated into the firewall.
- The use of discovery crawler programs must be monitored and controlled.
- Virus software must be active on all desktop systems utilizing WWW.
- Externally published information should be routinely updated or verified through integrity checks.

In conclusion, as information security practitioners embracing the technical challenges of the twenty-first century, we are continually challenged to integrate new technology smoothly into our existing and underlying security architectures. Having a firm foundation or set of security principles, frameworks, philosophies and supporting policies, procedures, technical architectures, etc. will assist in the transition and our success.

Approach new technologies by developing processes to manage the integration and update the security framework and supporting infrastructure, as opposed to changing it. The Internet, intranet, and the World Wide Web is exploding around us — what is new today is old technology tomorrow. We should continue to acknowledge this fact while working aggressively with other MIS and customer functional areas to slow down the train to progress, be realistic, disciplined, and plan for new technology deployment.

Chapter 55
Establishing Security Controls in a Distributed Database

Sooun Lee, Mohamed Nour, and Soong H. Chung

IN RECENT YEARS, THE COMPUTING ENVIRONMENT HAS SHIFTED FROM THE CENTRALIZED MODEL TO A MORE DECENTRALIZED ONE. This shift has been motivated primarily by the increased decentralization of most business operations as well as the perceived advantages of decentralized computing environments.

Distributed database systems (DDBSs) are an important element in distributed processing systems. The concept of DDBS has been evolving during the past few years and a great deal of uncertainty still exists about what the concept means and what these systems do. A particular challenge associated with distributed databases concerns information security. Although DDBSs share some of the same security problems as centralized databases, their unique characteristics add other security concerns not found in the centralized environment.

This chapter describes the features and benefits of the distributed environment and how the proliferation of this recently introduced technology has led to a greater need to establish an information security plan. The chapter presents a model for securing data, taking into consideration the special needs of this environment.

THE BENEFITS AND FEATURES OF DDBSS

There are perhaps as many definitions of DDBS as there are authors who write about them; this is partly due to the relatively recent development of the technology and the confusion surrounding its definition. A distributed database environment has been described as a communications network comprising individual sites with their own standalone databases and with local operation. The database may be distributed because of geographical, performance or effectiveness, and efficiency reasons.

The objectives and benefits of DDBSs include:

- Increased system availability and better performance.
- Higher system throughput.
- Improved disaster recovery.
- System reliability.
- Reduced communications costs.
- Information-sharing capabilities.
- Distribution of certain applications.
- Flexibility and extensibility.
- Local control.
- Incremental database growth.

These benefits do not come without a price, however, and the distributed nature of the database is the source of most of the problems of DDBSs. These problems include higher operating costs, communications delays, consistency (i.e., update) problems, concurrency control, and data security problems. Compared to a centralized database, a distributed database is much more vulnerable to possible security threats — for example, theft, invasion of privacy, updating, and unauthorized access — because of the dispersed structure of its data.

Data can be distributed over multiple computer systems in three ways: through replication, partitioning, or allocation. Replication implies that the same copy of the database is stored in each of the sites or nodes in the computer network. Partitioning, however, means that data is stored in the site where it is most needed. Partitioning is sometimes known as data fragmentation, whereby logically related sets of data are stored in the same site. Allocation is a hybrid of partitioning and replication. Each method has its own implications for data recovery, updating and concurrency control, system reliability and availability, data security and integrity, and transmission costs.

SECURITY THREATS IN A DISTRIBUTED DATABASE

The basic threats to the security of data in a distributed database environment are not very different from those affecting centralized computer systems. They include crime, employee negligence, accidents, technical faults, viruses and worms, environmental factors, and natural disasters. However, certain characteristics of distributed databases (e.g., increases in the points of entry to the system, in user autonomy, and in the number of users) create additional security concerns.

The consequences of security violations can be classified into the following:

- Loss or destruction of data.
- Theft of data.
- Corruption or modification of data.

754

- Disclosure of data.
- Delay or denial of use of data.
- Misinterpretation of data.

Each of these data security violations could have a dramatic effect on an organization's operations or even its survival. Therefore, the need for effective management and control of data security in a DDBS is compelling. The conceptual security policy model, described in the following section of the chapter, is suggested to provide practitioners with guidelines for managing security in a distributed database environment.

THE CONCEPTUAL SECURITY POLICY MODEL

The information security model described in this chapter involves a three-step process:

1. Classifying the data.
2. Determining the organization's security needs.
3. Selecting the appropriate security techniques.

Each step is described in detail in the following sections.

Step 1: Classifying the Data

The first step in the development of an effective security model in a distributed database environment is to classify the distributed data into three dimensions: location, sensitivity, and vulnerability. These three dimensions serve as the basis for the security plan.

First, data must be classified from its current processing status as either data in place or data en route. This dichotomy reflects the two states of data in a distributed database environment at any particular time. The category *data in place* refers to data currently residing in a distributed database environment. *Data en route* refers to data in transmission. If the data is replicated, more attention should be given to data in place than to data en route, because most processing in this case is local. If, however, the database is partitioned or allocated, more data is en route (i.e., transmitted), and consequently, more concern should be shown for protecting this transmitted data. Tolerance techniques can be used to protect data classified in this category. (These techniques are discussed in more detail in a subsequent section of the chapter.)

Second, the possible vulnerabilities or weaknesses in the distributed database environment must be recognized and assessed. This assessment of potential sources of data security threats can contribute to finding the needs for the avoidance techniques discussed in a subsequent section. This assessment can also help managers establish the following managerial guidelines:

- Determining the types of security control required.
- Assessing the efficacy of existing safeguards.
- Identifying necessary additions and improvements in security measures.
- Determining the availability of resources.
- Determining the level of security coverage needed.

Managers should understand that at this point, probably the most serious threats are from the employees within the organization.

Finally, data must be classified according to its sensitivity and importance. For example, the data can be classified as routine, private, confidential, or strictly confidential. Depending on the sensitivity level, different types of security mechanisms may be needed. This classification can also be used as a significant determinant in measuring the resource requirements for the security model. Data must be examined and evaluated according to the three classifications — location, sensitivity, and vulnerability — to determine the organization's basic security needs.

Step 2: Determining Security Needs

After the data has been classified, the next step in the model is to determine and formalize the organization's general security needs. At this stage, general decisions regarding such issues as the security level of preventive and detective controls. Total security is hardly attainable or economical. It would be meaningless to spend, for example, $1 million to protect information that is worth only half that amount. An organization needs protection that is reasonable in view of the importance and value of the object of protection (i.e., data). As a general rule, data security should be acquired as long as benefits exceed costs.

The nature and types of security needs of an organization depend on such factors as the characteristics of the organization and its employees or users, and the sensitivity of its data to security violations. An organization that is not significantly affected by the disclosure of its information resource to competitors and adversaries would not be inclined to spend a significant amount of money on security. As this information becomes critical to the business and survival of the organization, the organization becomes more willing to spend for the sake of protecting its data.

Another important decision is to determine the security methods an organization needs (e.g., tolerance, avoidance, or a combination of both). This decision depends on the types and nature of the distributed databases and available resources. These two methods involve different sets of protection tools with different costs, which is discussed in more detail in the following section of the chapter. The suggested model serves only as a guidepost and does not propose to define exactly how to select from among the two methods.

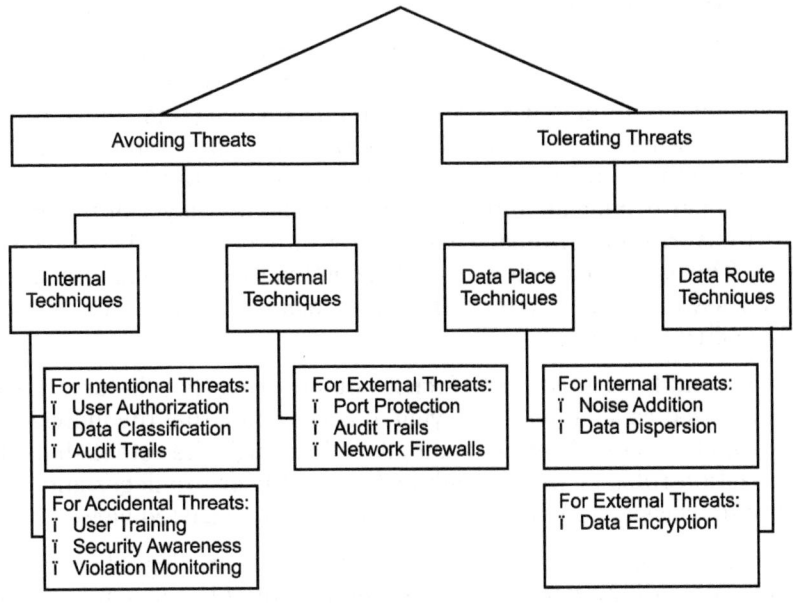

Exhibit 55-1. Selection model.

Step 3: Selecting the Appropriate Technique

Exhibit 1 illustrates the relationships between the various mechanisms of the protection methods and techniques. The basic concepts in the model are avoidance and tolerance.

Avoidance techniques pertain to internal as well as external threats to distributed database security. Internal threats in turn are generally from employees and legitimate users. These threats may be intentional (i.e., caused by dishonesty) or accidental (i.e., caused by negligence and errors).

Tolerance, however, pertains to threats to the two types of data in a distributed database environment: data in place and data en route, as discussed previously. The concept of risk or threat tolerance focuses on the idea that rather than denying a potential intruder access to data, the data should be made useless to the intruder.

This step involves specific security techniques using parameters described in the second step. The following section explores these techniques in detail.

AVOIDANCE TECHNIQUES

Avoidance techniques pertain to internal threats, both intentional and accidental, and external threats. These types of threats and techniques for avoiding them are explained in the following paragraphs.

Internal, Intentional Threats

Internal, intentional threats come from employees who, for professional or personal reasons, try to defraud the organization by stealing, disclosing, or destroying data in DDBS. Preventive measures against these threats focus on ensuring that the potential user in a distributed database environment is a legitimate user, who is trying to access an authorized data object or file and performing an authorized action. The first layer of this type of security ensures the legitimacy of a user by authenticating the individual's identity. The user is identified through a combination of some form of user ID and password. Other methods include the use of smart cards or tokens and biometrics systems.

The second layer of security focuses on ensuring that the user, having been identified as legitimate, is trying to access data that the individual is authorized to access. This is accomplished through the establishment of authorization rules involving such methods as user privileges and clearances, data classification and fragmentation, and restricted views.

Users are assigned clearances according to their privileges in using specific segments of the database. Given the nature of the distributed database environment, the assignment and tracking of clearances can be a difficult task because the population of potential users includes all those in the multiple nodes of the DDBSs. This procedure, however, helps determine who is authorized to access which object or segment of the database. Data classification assigns sensitivity levels to different segments of the database. Together, with the user classification, data sensitivity levels help determine the domain of each user.

The third layer of security is accomplished by the implementation of embedded controls in the DDBSs (the software that runs the distributed database) and audit trails. Although access and authorization controls through audit trails are retrospective in nature, high-quality audit trails can provide a complete record of every activity that an individual performs.

Internal, Accidental Threats

Accidental threats from DDBSs users may be considered less serious than intentional employee threats because, unlike intentional threats, there is no malicious intent behind them. Nevertheless, the effects could still theoretically ruin an organization, especially if very sensitive, private data is involved. Measures to handle these threats include the implementation of extensive training programs, the heightening of user security awareness, and constant monitoring and assessment of security violations resulting from user negligence, ignorance, or omission of automatic error-checking methods.

External Threats

Protection against outsiders includes port protection measures, network firewalls, and audit trails. The purpose of installing port protection measures is to limit or prevent access to the system from outside. This could be implemented through a dial-back mechanism that checks the validity of the caller. Network firewalls can be established to automatically screen out external intruders.

The other method for protecting against would-be security violators is audit trails. The mere fact that the system traces intruders' paths limits the possibility of getting away without being detected and may prevent the intruders from even attempting to enter the system.

TOLERANCE TECHNIQUES

The storage and transmission of data in a distributed database produces significant security risks. The tolerance approach allows potential violators to access data, but the data is made unmanipulable or unintelligible, thus preventing the likelihood of data abuse. Data in a distributed database lies in one of its two states, in place or en route.

Techniques for Protecting Data In Place

For data in place, some methods have been developed to protect data by modifying the data in some fashion. Two of these techniques are noise addition and data dispersal. Noise addition involves adding noise to the database objects, which are designated as Os. If noise were represented by the variable es, the equation would read as follows:

$$Os^* = Os + (es)$$

For example, an organization might wish to protect the confidentiality of such data as employee salaries, ages, or sales per product or territory. To make these data elements not directly useful to an intruder, management could disguise these figures by adding fictitious data elements (possibly of the same data type) to these figures. Thus, age a can be replaced with a disguised age ($a1^*$). This is accomplished by subtracting a random number from the age as in the following equation:

$$a(1)^* = a(1) + (-100) = a(1) - 100$$

The negative nature of the resulting age figure would make it virtually useless for almost any purpose. Likewise, for example, sales by product can be disguised from possible competitor intelligence by adding a false component to it. Thus, if the sales of product i is denoted by $S1$, then the disguised sales figure ($S1$) would be:

$$S(1)^* = S(1) + e(1)$$

where $e1$ could be a function (e.g., 75%) of $S1$ or an independent and probably constant component, as in the age example previously stated. For example, if $S1$ is \$982,000, the figure can be disguised as follows:

$$S(1)^* = 982,000 - 75\% \ (982,000) = \$245,500$$

To reconstruct the true figure, in the knowledge that 245,500 is 25% of $S1$, $S1^*$ can be divided by 25 and multiplied by 100 as follows:

$$S(1) = S(1)^* \times 100/25 = 245,500 \times 100/25 = 982,000$$

The important point to remember is that it must be preestablished whether a constant value or a function of the value is used. Therefore, the previous example would read as follows:

$$S(1)^* = S(1) = f(S(1)) = S(1) - aS(1) = S(1)(1 - a)$$

where a happens to be .75. To reconstruct $S1$, $S1^*$ is divided by $1\text{-}a$.

Like noise addition, data dispersal, or scattering, is used to protect individual data objects in a distributed database environment. An Information Dispersal Algorithm has been proposed that disperses a data object (e.g., an employee record) into various storage areas (e.g., the address, salary, and employee identification number would be stored in different databases). The data object, represented by o, would be divided into n pieces. The series of subvalues would be represented as oi, where i is greater than or equal to l but is less than n (i.e., the number of pieces). The number of pieces must suffice for reconstructing the data object o. Each one of these pieces, or a reasonable combination of them, is stored in a different node in the distributed system. This technique makes it virtually impossible for a would-be intruder to access all the pieces to reconstruct the original data object for several reasons. First, the intruder might not be aware of the existence of all the nodes. Second, even if the nodes are known, accessing all of them might be too difficult or time-consuming. Finally, even if all nodes are accessed and the data objects are collected, a considerable amount of effort might be needed to combine them into a whole that makes reasonable sense.

The value of this technique is even greater when placed in a real-world context. For example, assuming that a record includes n data elements (i.e., fields), these data elements could be distributed over the m nodes of the distributed database. If $n > m$, the remaining $n\text{-}m$ elements could be distributed again over the nodes so that each node has one or more elements but less than n. Therefore, by accessing only one node, an intruder will not be able to access the full record, assuming that only a complete record can be useful. All the records of a sensitive file can be distributed in this fashion.

A way is needed to reconstruct the records, and therefore, the file, when desired. This is accomplished by having a control file within the operating system or an application program, where the locations, and probably the addresses of each distributed data item are stored. It should be relatively easy to implement these two approaches by means of systems software or applications programs.

Techniques for Protecting Data En Route

For transmitted data, or data en route, data encryption can be used to protect data transmitted in a communications network.

LIMITATIONS OF THE MODEL

The model suggested in this chapter has at least three limitations. First, the model does not identify all possible data protection techniques; the lists are therefore not meant to be all-inclusive. Second, the model does not compare the various techniques in terms of effectiveness and efficiency. Finally, some of the techniques or devices may not have been fully developed and made operational.

Despite these apparent deficiencies, the model provides a framework for analyzing security problems in a distributed database environment and perhaps implementing a policy model that reflects the security needs and characteristics of a business entity in a distributed database environment.

CONCLUSION

The problems of a distributed database can be mitigated if proper administrative and technical procedures are devised and rigorously implemented. The security problem, in particular, needs special consideration. The model used in this chapter can guide practitioners to design proper security strategies in a distributed database environment.

Chapter 56
Understanding Relational Databases and Assessing Their Security

Sean D. Doyle

THE EARLY DEVELOPMENT OF RELATIONAL DATABASE MANAGEMENT SYSTEMS (RDBMSS) FOCUSED PRIMARILY ON BASIC SYSTEM FUNCTIONS AND PERFORMANCE; SECURITY WAS NOT A HIGH PRIORITY. In recent years, however, several factors have led to the development of improved security controls. As organizations began to use relational technologies to build mission-critical applications, they became increasingly concerned about the potential legal and financial consequences of poorly managed systems. As a result, the market demanded that software developers provide effective protection mechanisms. As the relational database industry matured, it became better positioned to provide the needed solutions.

This chapter describes contemporary challenges in managing data and describes how new relational database technologies help meet those challenges. Discretionary access controls and related security and audit capabilities of new relational database products are discussed. The chapter also addresses such emerging technologies as multilevel secure (MLS) database systems. Practical tips on how to evaluate these technologies are provided. Although the issues discussed are applicable to most relational database products, specific security capabilities are illustrated using the Oracle Relational Database Management System, Version 7.0 and the Multi-Level Secure Oracle Relational Database Management System, Version 1.0.

CHALLENGES IN RELATIONAL DATABASE SECURITY

Relational systems have been designed to provide increased ease of use and availability of data. These characteristics can create unique challenges to system security. Relational systems allow end users to manipulate and share data in ways that were not possible with more traditional hierarchical, network, and flat file database applications. For example, the capabilities of Structured Query Language (SQL) allow users to enter real-time, ad hoc queries to access and modify data; such power and flexibility create exposures that may not be anticipated by EDP auditors who are unfamiliar with relational systems.

The inherent flexibility of relational systems must be balanced by security policies that limit users' access to only the data they need to perform their jobs. A policy of least privilege can be implemented, requiring that each user be granted the most restrictive set of privileges needed to perform a set of authorized tasks. The use of such a policy helps limit the damage that can result from accident and error as well as from unauthorized use.

Highly granular access controls can also be used to enforce separation of functions. Separation of functions involves dividing sensitive tasks into smaller subtasks and then assigning these subtasks to different individuals. This practice prevents one person from performing, and perhaps compromising, the entire function.

Unfortunately, most systems do not support a sufficiently granular assignment of privileges to enforce an effective level of separation of functions; for example, under most systems, the database administrator is assigned all privileges. This is problematic because it is particularly important to enforce such controls on database administrators and security personnel. It should also be noted that managing privileges on large, multiuser systems running complex databases can be tedious and can consume significant resources.

The security of relational systems is further complicated by the increased use of distributed processing. With distributed systems, several issues arise:

- Should the database be administered globally or by each site?
- How should users of networked database resources be identified and authenticated to the system?
- Can such distributed system use be audited centrally?

To be accepted, security controls must not introduce undue complication or inconvenience to users and database administrators; end users should be insulated as much as possible from the security mechanisms of the underlying operating systems, networks, and database management systems. Security controls should not inhibit the use of such sophisticated front ends to database applications Graphical User Interface and fourth generation languages. Security mechanisms must also support the full range of database functions and interfaces (in fact, to gain user acceptance, these controls should be seen to simplify security administration).

Exhibit 56-1. TCSEC security levels.

Class	Description
A1	Verified Design
B3	Security Domains
B2	Structured Protection
B1	Labeled Security Protection
C2	Controlled Access Protection
C1	Discretionary Security Protection
D	Minimal Protection

With these objectives in mind, the auditor must evaluate the ability of database products to meet security requirements. Fortunately, database security standards and product evaluation criteria have been developed to help in the process.

DATABASE SYSTEM SECURITY STANDARDS

Security standards provide a good starting point for gaining a relatively broad perspective on the security issues related to relational technologies. Relevant standards include the US Department of Defense's Trusted Computer System Evaluation Criteria (TCSEC, also referred to as the Orange Book) and the corresponding Trusted Database Interpretation (TDI) of the TCSEC, which interprets the TCSEC guidelines and applies them to database management systems.[1] A similar effort in Europe has produced the Information Technology Security Evaluation Criteria (ITSEC), which is gaining in popularity among security professionals.[2] Security standards are also being developed by other countries, and several professional organizations are working to define the requirements of the commercial sector.

Government-Sponsored Standards

As shown in Exhibit 1, the TCSEC identifies seven classes of trusteed products, ranging from the highest level of security (class A1) to the lowest level (class D). Each rating class specifies the required functional abilities of such features as user identification and authentication, auditing, and data labeling; it also defines the level of assurance required to ensure that the product's security mechanisms are properly implemented and cannot be circumvented. The criteria for each class of security controls are cumulative; for example, whereas class C products incorporate discretionary security controls, class B products include mandatory controls and other requirements in addition to discretionary controls.

Many users have accepted the C2 rating as the minimum level of security for database and other systems processing sensitive business data. At a C2 security level, users are individually accountable for their actions through the use of log-on procedures, audit trails of security-related events, and resource isolation.

The B1 rating is considered appropriate for systems that process classified and other more highly sensitive information. The B1 security level enforces the use of data labeling and mandatory access control over specified subjects and objects.

Many currently available relational database products provide a subset of class C2 features; some vendors are developing products to meet the complete range of C2 requirements. Multilevel secure database products that satisfy B1 and higher criteria are also now entering the market.

In the US, a new security initiative is under way at the National Institute of Standards and Technology and the National Computer Security Center to develop a more comprehensive set of criteria that reflect international security standards, advances in computer and security technologies, and the security requirements of the commercial sector.

The Europeans have taken an approach to security that differs from that of the Orange Book in several respects. Unlike the Orange Book, the European Information Technology Security Evaluation Criteria addresses assurance-related criteria separately from the criteria for evaluating system functional abilities. Whereas the Orange Book focuses on protecting the confidentiality of information, the European criteria also address the integrity and availability of information.

Professional Standards Organizations

New standards are also being developed by various professional organizations that, though not focused primarily on security issues, may affect the security of databases and other systems. For example, the American National Standards Institute has developed data integrity specifications for SQL. Relational database product standards can also be expected from such sources as the International Standards Organization, The Institute of Electrical and Electronics Engineers, Portable Operating System Interface for Computer Environments, Federal Information Processing Standards, Open Systems Interconnection, and SQL Access. These standards should be referred to during the evaluation of trusted database products to ensure that they meet the full set of operational standards appropriate for their processing environments.

DISCRETIONARY ACCESS AND AUDIT CONTROLS

Discretionary access control is the most general form of access control in relational database products today. Discretionary access control mediates access to information through the assignment of privileges — the subject, which can refer to either the user or the processes run by the user, must have the appropriate privilege to access an object (e.g., a data table or view). This type of access control is referred to as discretionary because appropriately authorized users can grant other users access privileges at their discretion. For example, the owner of a database table may grant another user permission to select data from that table.

In most relational database systems, discretionary controls are implemented by means of SQL, which is the standard query language for relational systems. Under SQL, users can be granted various privileges to access tables and other objects. The implementation of discretionary controls vary according to the vendor-specific extensions of SQL and the degree of granularity enforced.

In a relational database, views can support the enforcement of discretionary controls. Views are virtual tables consisting of a subset, union, or join of the columns of one or more tables. Data managers can provide users with access to relevant subsets of data, in the form of views, while restricting them from direct access to complete database tables. Data access privileges can also be stored in data dictionary views, providing an effective method of managing these privileges.

Although discretionary controls are sufficient for many applications, they do not always provide necessary security. For example, the management of privileges may be difficult, as illustrated by the following scenario. User A grants user B access to table, with the intention that no other users be granted such access; however, user B may promulgate access privileges to user C, thereby defeating user A's intention to limit access to the table. With discretionary controls, this problem can be avoided only through painstaking management of privileges. Newer relational database products that implement mandatory access controls can virtually eliminate the problem.

All relational database systems offer some audit capabilities, but the audit capabilities of most products are incomplete and the tools for analyzing audit data are insufficient. In addition, audit facilities are often unused because of concerns that these facilities may degrade overall system performance. As discussed in the next section, new database products are being developed that provide more comprehensive and efficient audit features.

To be effective, both discretionary access and audit controls require that a system properly identify users. Typically, users identify themselves to a database system by entering a user ID, and they authenticate themselves by entering a password. (The management system typically stores the password in encrypted format in the database.) Although these measures can provide an effective level of security, their use is burdensome for users, who must remember passwords for at least one operating system and database system. This problem may be compounded in distributed environments.

In summary, although the security capabilities of relational database systems have improved in recent years, many areas still require improvement. The next section describes security features of newly emerging database products that are designed to provide more effective controls that are also more easily managed.

DEVELOPMENTS IN DATABASE SECURITY

New methods of securing databases are being introduced that should simplify administrative tasks, facilitate implementation of least privilege and separation of functions, and offer improved overall database capabilities. These features shift more of the burden of enforcing security controls from the application to the database, thereby providing greater consistency of security enforcement across multiple applications that use the same data.

Privilege Management

The proper enforcement of system and object privileges is of primary importance in database management. An object privilege refers to the right to perform a particular action on a specified table, view, or other named database object (e.g., to update the DEPARTMENT table). A system privilege refers to the right to execute a particular system command or to globally perform a particular action on a class of objects (e.g., to select from any table).

A new trend is to provide a finer granularity of database privileges, in particular, system privileges. It is possible to more narrowly define roles among administrative staff by unbundling system privileges from a fixed set of three or four present definitions. For example, rather than the database administrator having all system privileges, appropriate privileges can be granted for such specific functions as system backup, user account management, security, auditing, and application administration. This capability makes it easier to enforce controls on the basis of the principle of least privilege.

For example, Oracle Corp.'s relational database product, ORACLE Relational Database Management System, Version 7.0, allows database privileges to be grouped into entities called roles. The database administrator can create a role named CLERK and then grant to that role the database privileges needed for clerks to perform their duties. This role can be granted to all clerks in the organization, making it unnecessary to grant individual privileges to each clerk. The CLERK role can also be granted to the CLERK/MANAGER role, conveniently giving the manager all staff privileges. The use of roles greatly simplifies the assignment and maintenance of privileges in a relational database.

Cooperative Systems Security

Various system controls are becoming available that enhance database security. Database systems are being designed to interface with operating system mechanisms for user identification and authentication so that users need only identify themselves once to the operating system, rather than to both operating system and the database system. Users must remember only one password; passwords are sorted only once, and audit trail records reflect a one-to-one mapping between operating system users and database users.

Vendors are also beginning to provide database audit capabilities that meet TCSEC class C2 criteria. Several products now offer auditing of statement executions or failures, auditing of objects, auditing of individual users or groups of users, and auditing of audit trail management. This ability to specify areas to be audited should result in more concise audit reporting and reduce the need for additional tools for audit trail analysis. However, extensive use of these more comprehensive audit capabilities may degrade system performance and increase the time required for audit trail review; consequently, audit options should be carefully selected and used. Audit features should permit the auditor to examine only those actions necessary to ensure system security.

The ability to enforce limits on the use of database system resources can also enhance security. For example, the database administrator can set limits on the number of concurrent sessions allowed per use of the database, idle time per session, Central Processing Unit use, and logical block reads. In some systems, this can be done by specifying a resource limit profile for either individual users or roles. The use of such profiles can help protect against denial of service and ensure the availability of system resources. For example, limits can be imposed to control the use of long-running, resource-intensive queries during peak hours.

Database Integrity Controls

Four principal types of data integrity controls-referential integrity, transaction integrity, entity integrity, and value constraints-are supported in varying degrees by relational database products. It should be noted that database integrity is of particular importance in multilevel secure environments, as is discussed later in this chapter.

Referential integrity controls involve the comparison of a foreign key value to a primary key value. In the case of relational databases, for example, a rule may be defined for a column of a table to permit modification of a row only if the foreign key value associated with the column matches the primary key value associated with a column of a related table. In Exhibit 2, for example, to ensure that all department numbers assigned to employees are valid, the foreign key value DEPTNO from the column in the EMPLOYEE table containing the department identification number of each employee is compared with the primary key value DEPTNO in the column of the DEPARTMENT table containing all valid department numbers. Some

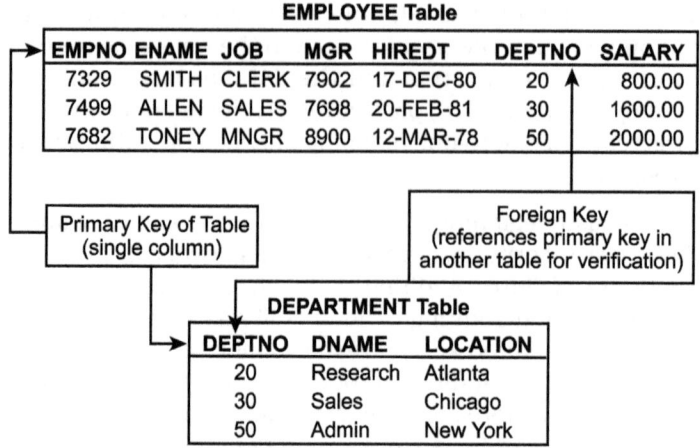

EMPLOYEE Table

EMPNO	ENAME	JOB	MGR	HIREDT	DEPTNO	SALARY
7329	SMITH	CLERK	7902	17-DEC-80	20	800.00
7499	ALLEN	SALES	7698	20-FEB-81	30	1600.00
7682	TONEY	MNGR	8900	12-MAR-78	50	2000.00

Primary Key of Table
(single column)

Foreign Key
(references primary key in
another table for verification)

DEPARTMENT Table

DEPTNO	DNAME	LOCATION
20	Research	Atlanta
30	Sales	Chicago
50	Admin	New York

Exhibit 56-2. Sample referential integrity controls.

relational database products allow users to code their own integrity constraints into database applications. With other products, SQL is used to declare integrity constraints to the database; the database stores these constraints in the data dictionary and automatically enforces them.

Transaction integrity controls are designed to ensure that a transaction can be rolled back if it is not executed successfully in its entirety. For example, if a financial posting involving a debit and credit transaction is not completely executed and stored, it must be rolled back to the stage before execution. To ensure transaction integrity, relational database products provide such security features as online redo log files, rollback segments, and distributed database recovery function.

Entity integrity controls identify each record in the database to ensure that the record is unique. For example, an automated sequence generator can be used to ensure unique primary key values in a relational database.

Value constraints can be used to check a data value to ensure that it falls within the limit of a predefined constraint; for example, salaries in the EMPLOYEE database table are checked to verify that they are within an appropriate numeric range. Value constraints can be defined using SQL when the table is created.

Stored Procedures

Enhanced relational database systems use stored procedures to access and modify data in a consistent and secure manner. A stored procedure logically groups a set of procedural language SQL statements that perform a specific task when the procedure is executed. A trigger is a type of procedure that is implicitly executed when such statements as INSERT or DELETE are entered against a table.

Stored procedures can be used to restrict the way in which data is accessed and updated. For example, a user may be allowed to update a specified table only by executing a stored procedure; the use of this procedure ensures that all updates are performed in a consistent way. In this example, the user is authorized only to execute the procedure; because the procedure itself owns the privilege of updating the table, the user does not have to be granted that privilege explicitly.

Triggers can be used to implement unique security requirements or complex business rules. For example, a trigger can be used to enforce referential integrity in a distributed database in which parent and child records reside on different network nodes and in which referential integrity between the parent and child records cannot be enforced using declarative SQL statements. If a change is made to the child's record in a table, a trigger associated with that table can execute a query against the remote table in which the parental record resides to perform the required integrity check. Triggers can also be used to enforce complex security rules, such as restrictions on data access and modification based on time of day.

Triggers can also support auditing activities. For example, a trigger can be written to record table values before and after an update to provide a detailed audit trail of change transactions.

MULTILEVEL SECURE DATABASES

A new generation of multilevel secure relational databases has been developed to provide a high degree of protection for proprietary and other sensitive data. Multilevel secure systems allow the simultaneous processing of data of various sensitivities by multiple users with various clearances. Most organizations have been hesitant to mix proprietary data with public data on the same system, preferring instead to segregate such data on separate computer systems. This approach is both costly and inefficient. Under multilevel secure systems, data residing on the same system is explicitly labeled or classified according to its degree of sensitivity to compromise; such classification schemes permit data isolation while simplifying management and reducing costs.

Multilevel secure database systems enforce mandatory access controls in addition to the discretionary controls commonly found in most current products. Mandatory controls restrict access to objects using two types of information: the security classification of the object, as represented by its sensitivity label; and the authority of the user to access and use the object. In a relational database, control is typically enforced on each row of a database table. If a user has not been authorized to the classification level

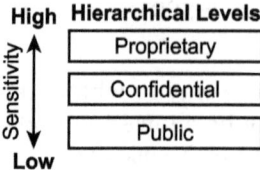

High	Hierarchical Levels	Nonhierarchical Categories within Each Level		
	Proprietary	Finance	Research	Marketing
	Confidential	Accounting	Development	Marketing
Low	Public	No Separate Categories		

(left axis label: Sensitivity, High at top, Low at bottom)

Exhibit 56-3. Sample labels.

associated with that row of data, access to that data will be denied regardless of any discretionary access rules that might otherwise permit access.

For example, a company might classify its data as being either proprietary, company confidential, or public. Each of these hierarchical classifications constitutes a security level within the database. Within each level, however, data can be further divided into descriptive, nonhierarchical categories. One category might identify proprietary data that belongs to a certain special project; another category might identify the department that controls the proprietary information. It is the combination of security level and category that forms the sensitivity label associated with the data object. Therefore, as shown in Exhibit 3, access to a relational database row labeled PROPRIETARY:FINANCE would be restricted to those users with sufficient clearance to access proprietary information belonging to the finance department.

Under a multilevel secure system, sensitivity labels are stored with the data object and can be changed only by users who have certain powerful mandatory access control privileges. Similarly, only users with such privileges are permitted to transfer access authority from one user to another; end users cannot transfer access privileges at their discretion. Mandatory access control privileges must be carefully administered and monitored to protect against their misuse.

Security Conflicts in Multilevel Database Applications

The use of multilevel secure data systems can create conflicts between data confidentiality and integrity. The enforcement of integrity rules can create covert channels for discovering confidential information and, in general lead to conflicts between other business rules and security policies.[3]

For example, enforcement of entity integrity requires that each database row be identified by its primary key, which cannot be a null value. A conflict between data confidentiality and integrity can arise if a user with a low-level access classification (e.g., unclassified) attempts to add a primary key that, in fact, already exists at a higher classification level (e.g., confidential). (A primary key at this high security level is not visible to an unclassified user.) If the database system permits the addition of this duplicate key, entity integrity is compromised; if the addition is denied, the secrecy of the existing key value for the confidential information is compromised. This problem can be avoided by using the security label as part of the primary key or by using an automated sequence generator to assign primary key within a specified value range for each security level.

It may also be possible to infer information about a database entity if referential integrity is enforced across multiple access classes. For example, if a user with a low-level access classification attempts to delete data at a higher classification level, a violation of referential integrity may occur. The user may be able to infer information about the targeted data item if the system returns an error on the basis of the access classification of the data item.

Transaction integrity conflicts can also arise in a multilevel database system. To maintain transaction integrity, all steps in a given transaction must be processed as an entire unit. Any expected transactions that pass across different security levels should be carefully reviewed to identify potential conflicts. These problems should be eliminated either by modification of the database design or through decomposition of multilevel transactions.

Weighing the Pros and Cons of Multilevel Security

Although multilevel secure database systems provide an enhanced level of security not previously available, this advantage must be weighed against the costs required to implement this technology and the security requirements of the organization. For some organizations, enhanced discretionary controls provide a more cost-effective alternative.

For organizations that process highly sensitive information, the implementation of a multilevel system is readily justified. Through the use of mandatory access controls, data access rules can be more explicitly defined and enforced, and controls can be more easily established around each category of system user. For organizations that rely solely on procedural or physical security measures, multilevel systems can provide an additional layer of controls. Reliance on redundant hardware and software systems and redundant data can be greatly reduced or eliminated, providing significant savings in system maintenance costs. For example, hardware systems that were formerly dedicated to processing confidential data can now be used of multiple application that access data of differing sensitivities.

These advantages, however, must be weighed against the additional complexity of multilevel application design and implementation. The database design must be analyzed to identify and eliminate conflicts in enforcing data integrity controls. The data must be thoroughly classified, and users must be assigned specific authorization. Multilevel applications must also be run on secure operating systems because mandatory controls cannot by reliably enforced by the relational database on nonsecure systems.

Some organizations may consider implementing multilevel databases only for selected applications that process proprietary information, while continuing to run other applications at a single security level on existing systems. If this configuration is selected, it should be verified that the multilevel product can support the interoperability of multilevel and single-level applications.

There are now several multilevel relational database products from which to choose. These products can be run either on standard multilevel operating systems or compartmented mode workstations, which are multilevel secure workstations that offer window capabilities.

IDENTIFYING SECURITY REQUIREMENTS

In reviewing the security of a database system, the auditor should not simply evaluate just the security features of the database product itself. It is also important to identify the security requirements of the overall system, of which the database is only one component. What is the minimum level of security required by the organization as a whole? Are there any specific applications that require enhanced data protection? Answers to such questions help determine whether discretionary or mandatory access controls are required.

The architecture of the relational database should also be evaluated to determine whither it provides a portable, transparent, and secure foundation for applications processing. A database management architecture that is independent of the operating system platform provides improved system portability as well as greater ease in evaluating and implementing system controls.

The prospective database system should be designed also to interface smoothly with other components of the overall system, including the operating system, network, user authentication devices, and other applications that affect security. Such a transparent user interface offers users a more seamless view of security controls by providing the appropriate controls at each level of the system (e.g., log-on security at the system access level, file security at the operating system level, and database security at the object level).

IMPLEMENTING DATABASE SECURITY

There are two basic approaches to implementing improved database security controls. As is done in most environments, existing database applications can be migrated to a more secure database management system; or, where possible, completely new applications can be built. In the case of migration, assuming that there are no major compatibility problems, implementation efforts focus on the transfer of data using export-import (i.e., migration) utilities and on the implementation of any new system control features.

In general, new database application should be designed to make effective use of the database system's security features. The design should be carefully planned and executed. Each database component should be reviewed to ensure that the appropriate security controls have been incorporated in the design for that component.

The following sections describe the process of designing and building new database application. It should be emphasized that the first step involves development of a sound security policy that defines how the organization manages, distributes, and protects sensitive information. A comprehensive security policy provides useful guidelines for designing the database and related controls and results in a cleaner, more simplified set of controls.

CASE Tools

Computer-aided systems engineering (CASE) tools can be used to design and build database applications. These tools can be used to model data flows and Entity Relationship and to build a unified repository of system data. Some CASE tools generate database application code from the repository data. CASE tools can also be useful in analyzing the design to ensure that the database conforms with the organization's policy objectives.

The Data Dictionary

The data dictionary can be used to store such information as the user names of database users, user privileges, the names of database objects, integrity constraints, and audit-related data. The data dictionary can serve as a reference guide during database development. It is also a useful tool for auditing database operations after implementation.

Because of the importance of the information stored in the data dictionary, access to it should be carefully controlled. In general, end users should be granted read-only privileges; write privileges should be restricted to database administrators.

APPLICATION DEVELOPMENT

The standard approach in building Oracle Relational Database Management System applications requires that the data be normalized, as needed, and tables created according to design specifications. referential integrity and value constraints should be included in table definitions Upon loading tables, the Oracle database system automatically checks that the data conforms to the rules. Triggers can be written after the tables have been developed or at a later date.

Views should be created to provide controlled access to portion of multiple tables rather than to the table themselves. Views can be used to grant users access only to that subset of data they require to perform their jobs. For example, a view of the EMPLOYEE table could be created and granted to managers so that only the records of employees in the manager's department can be accessed.

In the planning and design stages, the privileges to objects should be defined for all user. To facilitate this process, common database privileges can be grouped into roles. usually on the basis of shared job function. Using roles eliminates the need to create and maintain individual privileges for each user. In building applications, therefore, systems developers should create previously identified roles, grant privileges to these roles, and assign the roles to users who share related job duties.

As a final step, audit controls should be put into place, It is important to audit only those areas essential for ensuring system security. Audit options should be carefully selected to avoid performing superfluous audits that might degrade system performance and to ensure that audit reports are as concise as possible.

CONCLUSION

Security administration should be well supported by a relational database product. The mechanisms used to manage users and database privileges and the availability of roles and of other enhanced features should provide sufficient flexibility to implement the organization's security policies.

Because today's computing environment changes rapidly, it is also important for a product to be able to evolve to take advantage of emerging technologies. The security challenges posed by recent developments in client-server computing and distributed databases only dramatize the need for database systems that can adapt to the computing environment of the future.

Notes

1. Trusted Computer System Evaluation Criteria, DOD 5200-28-STD, United States Department of Defense, 1985; Trusted Database Interpretation of the Trusted Computer System Evaluation Criteria. NCSC-TC-021, Version 1, United States National Computer Security Center, 1991.
2. Information Technology Security Evaluation Criteria, Version 1.2, Commission of the European Communities. CD-71-91-502-EN-C, 1991.
3. R. Allen and B. Maimone, "Methods for Resolving the Security vs. Integrity Conflict," *Proceedings of the Fourth RADC Database Security Workshop* (Little Compton, RI. April 1991).

Chapter 57
Virus Activity in the Internet Environment
Terinia Reid

A COMPUTER VIRUS IS A PROGRAM DESIGNED TO REPLICATE AND SPREAD ON ITS OWN, USUALLY WITHOUT A PERSON'S KNOWLEDGE. Computer viruses spread by attaching themselves to another program — such as word processing or spreadsheet programs — or to the boot sector of a diskette. When an infected file is executed or the computer is started from an infected disk, the virus itself is executed. Often, it stays in memory waiting to infect the next program that is run or the next disk that is accessed.

There exists a perception that there are benign and malignant viruses. Considering that any type of virus is typically causing a computer to perform abnormally, whether causing damage or not, it would be difficult to class a virus as benign. However, the majority of viruses are harmless and do no real damage to a computer or files. A benign virus might do nothing more than display a message at a predetermined time or slow down the performance of a computer.

Destructive, or malignant, viruses can cause damage to a computer system by corrupting files or destroying data. These viruses do not corrupt the files they infect; that would prevent them from spreading. They infect and then wait for a trigger date to do damage. Just because a virus is classified as malignant does not mean the damage it causes is intentional. Sometimes, the damage is the result of poor programming or unintended bugs in the viral code.

TYPES OF VIRUSES

Boot Sector Infectors

All logical drives — hard disk and floppy — contain a boot sector, including disks that are not bootable. The boot sector contains specific information relating to the formatting of the disk and the data stored there. It also contains a small program called the boot program that loads operating system files. Boot sector viruses infect the boot program of the hard drive when an infected diskette is left in a floppy drive and the system is rebooted. When the computer reads and executes the boot sector program, the boot sector virus goes into memory and infects the hard drive. Later, when the user boots from the hard drive, the virus again gains control and can then infect each and every diskette used on the computer. Because every disk has a boot sector, boot viruses on a "data disk" that has no programs or operating system can infect computers.

Some symptoms of boot sector virus activity include:

- One cannot launch Windows.
- One's computer cannot perform a disk-based setup.
- One gets diskette errors.
- One gets hard drive errors.
- One gets non-system disk errors.

Macro Viruses (most common)

A macro virus is a piece of self-replicating code written in an application's macro language. Many applications have macro capabilities, such as the automatic playback of keystrokes available in early versions of Lotus 1-2-3. The distinguishing factor that makes it possible to create a macro virus is the existence of auto-execute macros in the language (e.g., Microsoft Word/Excel).

An auto-execute macro is one that is executed in response to some event and not in response to an explicit user command. Common auto-execute events are opening a file, closing a file, and starting an application. Once a macro is running, it can copy itself to other documents, delete files, and create general havoc in a computer system. These things occur without the user explicitly running that particular macro.

Another type of hazardous macro is one named for an existing Word command. If a macro in the global macro file or in an attached, active template has the name of an existing Word command, the macro command replaces the Word command. For example, if one creates a macro named FileSave in the "normal.dot" template, that macro is executed whenever the Save command on the File menu is chosen. There is no way to disable this feature.

Macro viruses spread by having one or more auto-execute macros in a document. By opening or closing the document or using a replaced command, one activates the virus macro. As soon as the macro is activated, it copies itself and any other macros it needs to the global macro file "normal.dot." After they are stored in normal.dot, they are available in all opened documents. An important point to make here is that Word documents (.DOC files) cannot contain macros; only Word templates (.DOT files) can contain macros. However, it is a relatively simple task to mask a template as a document by changing the file name extension from .DOT to .DOC.

An example of a Word Macro virus: the Nuclear macro virus with nine macros (AutoExec, AutoOpen, DropSuriv, FileExit, FilePrint, FilePrintDefault, FileSaveAs, InsertPayload, and Payload). It was the first macro virus known to cause damage, particularly to printouts and MS-DOS system files. Printing a document after infection may cause the following text to be appended to your printout: "STOP ALL FRENCH NUCLEAR TESTING IN THE PACIFIC!" Also, once infected, it will attempt on April 5th to delete your system files from your root directory, resulting in MS-DOS no longer starting.

File Infectors

These viruses attach themselves to or replace .COM and .EXE files, although in some cases they can infect files with the extensions .SYS, .DRV, .BIN, and OVL. This type of virus generally infects uninfected programs when they are executed with the virus in memory. In other cases, they infect programs when they are opened — using the DOS DIR command, for example — or the virus simply infects all of the files in the directory it was run from — a so-called direct infector. A sample:

File: VIRS0779.TXT
Name/Aliases: Smeg, Pathogen, Queeg
Platform: PC/MS-DOS
Type: Program
Disk Location: EXE application
COMapplication.
Features: Memory resident; TSR
Polymorphic
Damage: Overwrites sectors on the hard disk.
Size:
See Also: Junkie
Notes: Smeg and its variants are memory resident, polymorphic COM
  and EXE infectors. The Pathogen variant overwrites part of the disk
  drive between the hours of 17:00 and 18:00 on Monday evenings. It
  then prints the following message:

```
Your hard-disk is being corrupted, courtesy of PATHOGEN!

Programmed in the U.K. (Yes, NOT Bulgaria!) [C] The Black Baron
1993-4.

Featuring SMEG v0.1: Simulated Metamorphic Encryption
Generator!

Smoke me a kipper, I'll be back for breakfast...'

Unfortunately some of your data won't!!!!!
```

Virus Hoax

A virus hoax is an e-mail that is intended to scare people about a non-existent virus threat. Users often forward these alerts, thinking they are doing a service to their fellow workers; but this causes lost productivity, panic, and lost time. This increased traffic can soon become a massive problem in e-mail systems and cause unnecessary fear and panic. A sample of a virus hoax:

```
Dear All,

For your reference, take necessary precautions. If you
receive an e-mail with a file called California, do not
open the file. The file contains WOBBLER virus.

WARNING

This information was announced yesterday morning from
IBM; AOL states that this is a very dangerous virus, much
worse than "Melissa," and that there is NO remedy for it
at this time. Some very sick individual has succeeded in
using the reformat function from Norton Utilities,
causing it to completely erase all documents on the hard
drive. It has been designed to work with Netscape
Navigator and Microsoft Internet Explorer. It destroys
Macintosh and IBM-compatible computers. This is a new,
very malicious virus and not many people know about it.
```

HOW VIRUSES INFECT

Viruses, whether they are boot viruses, file viruses, or macro viruses, can employ none, one, or several of the following techniques to spread or conceal themselves.

Multi-partite Viruses

Multi-partite viruses often infect multiple targets instead of just one type of file or disk. For example, they will infect both files and boot records on hard disks, or both files and boot sectors on floppy disks.

Polymorphic Viruses

A polymorphic virus change segments of its own code so that it looks like a different virus from one infection to another. This technique is employed by virus creators to make it more difficult for anti-virus (AV) software to detect them, because detection software has a more difficult time comparing the changing virus to its inventory of known viruses.

Stealth Viruses

A stealth virus actively conceals itself from being discovered by AV software. There are two types of stealth viruses:

1. *Size stealth:* Once it infects a computer and becomes active in a computer's memory, a virus with size stealth capabilities monitors the opening and closing of all files. If it sees that a file it has infected earlier is about to be opened, it races to the file and un-infects it, so that the AV software does not know it has been infected. Once the file is closed, the virus then re-infects it. Another means these viruses have for hiding from AV software is by altering the disk directory data of a file to hide the additional bytes of an infecting virus. When possible, the virus can continue to infect any other files that are accessed on the hard drive.
2. *Full stealth:* Like a size stealth virus, a full stealth virus is memory resident and monitors all file activity. When it sees that an infected file is about to be opened, it redirects the call to an uninfected copy of the file that it made before infecting it. The virus stores the uninfected copy of the file at some other location on the hard drive for just this purpose.

These viruses actively conceal themselves while they are running in memory. If the anti-virus program does not scan in memory for these viruses, it will completely miss them when scanning files.

Retro viruses

Retro viruses are designed to actively attack anti-virus software. They are anti-anti-virus viruses. They will try to delete anti-virus data files, corrupt anti-virus programs, and more.

Triggered Event Viruses

Triggered event viruses activate based on some event. This event is known as a "trigger event"; hence, the characteristic name. An event can include a date, a certain keyboard action, or the opening of a particular file. The effect depends on the virus.

Memory Resident Viruses

Memory-resident viruses are copied to the computer's memory when its host program is executed. It no longer relies on the host program to remain active, as it stays active in memory, thereby infecting other files, until the computer is turned off.

Non-memory-Resident Viruses

A non-memory-resident viruses becomes memory resident when the host program is executed. It stays active in memory, infecting other files, until the host program is closed. It can only remain active while the host program is running.

Encrypting Viruses

An encrypting virus is transformed into something that does not look like a virus in order to avoid detection by anti-virus software. It does this with special code that allows the virus to convert, or encrypt, itself into program code that is non-infectious. But in order to infect, the virus must re-convert, or decrypt, itself into the original virus code, also making it visible to anti-virus software.

Combination Viruses

A combination virus can include one or more of the above characteristics, thus having a combination of characteristics. For example, a particular virus can be a polymorphic encryptor, which means that it combines both polymorphic and encryption characteristics.

OTHER DESTRUCTIVE PROGRAMS

As the name implies, a Trojan horse program comes with a hidden surprise intended by the programmer but totally unexpected by the user. The Trojan horse is not really a virus, but instead a means of virus delivery. The virus masquerades as a legitimate program so that the user will not realize it is a virus. For example, having downloaded from an online service what was thought to be a game program, but when one executes the program, only to find out it is a virus that infects one's computer.

A recent example: W95.Babylonia. According to Symantec, the virus was originally posted to an Internet newsgroup inside a Windows Help file named serialz.hlp. This file was claimed to be a list of serial numbers for "Warez" (pirated commercial software). But if the help file was opened, it exploited a little-known feature of Microsoft Windows that allows help files to contain executable programs. Merely opening the help file caused the Trojan horse program to be released within the computer system and begin wreaking mischief.

Worms are like viruses in that they do replicate themselves. However, instead of spreading from file to file, they spread from computer to computer, infecting an entire system.

Worms are insidious because they rely less (or not at all) on human behavior in order to spread themselves from one computer to another. The computer worm is a program designed to copy itself from one computer to another, leveraging some network medium: e-mail, TCP/IP, etc. The worm is more interested in infecting as many machines as possible on the network and less interested in spreading many copies of itself on a single computer (like a computer virus). The prototypical worm infects (or causes its code to run on) a target system only once; after the initial infection, the worm attempts to spread to other machines on the network.

The following is an example of the recent ExploreZip worm that uses an e-mail message to spread:

```
Hi (recipient name)

I received your email and I shall send you a reply ASAP.

Till then, take a look at the attached zipped docs.
```

After a user clicks on the attachment, the worm searches hard drives C through Z. It selects the Microsoft Word, Excel, and PowerPoint files, as well as source code files, and destroys the data on those files. When executed, the worm uses MAPI-enabled e-mail systems to automatically reply to received e-mail messages.

VIRUS PROTECTION

Viruses can be controlled at the desktop, the file server, the gateway, and on e-mail servers. Desktop and server anti-virus applications allow for virus scan and detection on an ongoing and periodic basis, as well as each time a file is downloaded or a computer is booted. More and more, computer users have anti-virus software running full-time in the background, scanning all files and diskettes the moment they are accessed. As macro viruses proliferate, scanning e-mail attachments at the desktop is critical. To protect networks, monitoring attachments at the e-mail gateway is just as important.

Recommendations:

1. Avoid installing any unknown software (e.g., games, screen-savers, etc.).
2. Be careful of software auto-installations from unknown/untrusted Web sites.
3. Write-protect diskettes (ensure floppy is clean first).
4. Install and auto-scan all hard drives, floppy disks, files, and programs with an anti-virus product at all times.
5. On a regular basis, update the signature files for the anti-virus program (as viruses are created and identified, the fixes are included in signature files).
6. Be aware of strange behavior on the computer system, such as the keyboard making strange noises, characters dropping from documents, etc.

HOW TO REMOVE A VIRUS

If the infection is file based (e.g., macro), running an anti-virus scanner with up-to-date signatures should clean the file and restore it to normal working order. If the infection is boot sector or hard-drive related, to keep downtime short and losses low, do the minimum required to restore the system to a normal state, starting with booting the system from a clean diskette. It is very unlikely that one will need to low-level reformat the hard disk.

If backups of the infected files are available and appropriate care was taken when making the backups, this is the safest solution, although it requires a lot of work if many files are involved.

More commonly, a disinfecting program is used. If the virus is a boot sector infector, one can continue using the computer with relative safety if one boots it from a clean system diskette; but it is wise to go through all diskettes, removing infection because, sooner or later, one may be careless and leave a diskette in the machine when it reboots. Boot sector infections on PCs can be cured by a two-step approach of replacing the MBR (on the hard disk), either by using a backup or by the FDISK/MBR command (from DOS 5 and up), and then using the SYS command to replace the DOS boot sector. Do not use FDISK/MBR if there is a Monkey or any other virus that encrypts the MBR (Master Boot Record). Confirm the above steps with a computer technician before completing to ensure the proper method is used.

ADDITIONAL VIRUS INFORMATION WEB SITES

- www.symantec.com — Norton Antivirus
- www.mcafee.com — McAfee VirusScan
- www.cai.com — Computer Associates
- www.ciac.org — Computer Incident Advisory Capability
- www.drsolomon.com — Dr. Solomon
- www.f-secure.com — formerly Data Fellows
- www.stiller.com/vintro.htm

The above list is not intended as an endorsement for any product or manufacturer.

About the Editor

SANJIV PURBA has a Bachelor of Science degree from the University of Toronto and has over 14 years of relevant Information Technology (IT) experience. He is a senior manager with Deloitte Consulting and leader of the Object-Oriented Practice in Canada.

Mr. Purba has extensive industry experience, with a focus on the financial and retail industry sectors. As a consultant, he has also gained relevant experience in other industries, such as telecommunications, travel and tourism, ticketing and reservation systems, and manufacturing. He has served in a large variety of roles in large organizations, including developer, senior developer, business analyst, systems analyst, team leader, project manager, consultant, senior architect, senior manager, and acting vice president.

Mr. Purba has written five IT-related textbooks published by John Wiley & Sons, New York. He has also written over 75 IT articles for *Computerworld Canada, Network World, Computing Canada, DBMS Magazine,* and the *Hi-tech Career Journal (HTC)*. Mr. Purba is a past editor of *ITOntario,* a publication of the Canadian Information Processing Society (CIPS). He has also written fantasy and science fiction graphic novels.

Mr. Purba is a regular speaker at industry symposiums on technical and project management topics. He has lectured at universities and colleges for the past 13 years, including Humber College, the University of Toronto, and Ryerson Polytechnic University. He recently hosted an IT forum for a television program in the Toronto area.

Prior to joining Deloitte Consulting, Mr. Purba ran his own computer consulting business, Purba Computer Solutions, Inc., during which time he consulted with Canadian Tire, Sun Life Assurance Company of Canada, and IBM in a variety of roles, including senior architect, facilitator, and project leader.

Mr. Purba also served as a senior architect and senior consultant with Flynn McNeil Raheb and Associates, a management consulting firm, for five years prior to owning his own business. During this time, he consulted with such organizations as IBM, ISM, The Workers Compensation Board, Alcatel, and The Ministry of Education.

Mr. Purba enjoys weightlifting, aerobics, Karate, Tae Kwon Do, Tae Bo, movies, and charity work.

Index

Index

A

Abstract
    entity types, concrete versus, 279
    Syntax Notation One, 363
Abstraction, level of, 168, 606
Access
    database, 504
    -user acquisition, 38
Accounting system, 198
    entity-relationship model of, 199
    information model diagram of, 203
    OMT diagram of, 206
Accounts payable, 267
Accounts receivable, 448
ACK/NAL code, see
    Acknowledgement/negative
    acknowledgement code
Acknowledgement/negative
    acknowledgement (ACK/NAK)
    code, 486
Active Server Pages (ASP), 500
ActiveX Data Objects (ADO), 501
Add entry screen, 534, 535
ADO, see ActiveX Data Objects
American National Standards Institute
    (ANSI), 19, 219, 359
Analysis diagrams, areas of
    effectiveness for, 64
ANSI, see American National Standards
    Institute
APIs, see Application programming
    interfaces
Applet, downloaded from, 502
Application(s)
    architecture example, 388
    development, 163, 561, 775
    directory, 528
    legacy, 438
    organization of, 537
    problems, 324

    programming interfaces (APIs),
      585, 728
    server, 386
    -specific
      bias, 318
      databases, 25
    transactional, 440
    Web-based, 109, 467, 621
    workarounds, 317
Appropriate use policy, 734–736
Arbitrary decomposition, 325
Architecture(s)
    multi-tiered, 386
    three-tiered, 387
ARI, see Attribute referential integrity
ASP, see Active Server Pages
Associative entity, 293, 294
Associative objects, 202, 209
ATM
    banking applications, 560
    transaction, 315
Atomic data, 571, 573
Attribute(s), 208, 399
    business rules, determining
      additional, 223
    data type, 212
    link, 209
    missing, 570
    names, 215
    non-foreign key, 433
Attribute referential integrity (ARI), 427,
    429
    constraint, enforcing, 433
    formal definition of, 430
    proposed notation for, 431
    specifying, 434
Audio compression, 715
Audit
    objectives, 452
    program, modifying of, 462
    records, 604

reports, checking of, 595
tests, 455, 458
tools, 746
Authentication, central, 443, 444
Automation, internal focus
    exacerbating lack of, 99
Autonumber, self-generated, 504
Avoidance techniques, 757

B

Back office systems, 626
Backup, 372, see also Loss and backup,
    how to handle
    accuracy of, 696
    incremental, 698
    system evaluation, 720–721
Batch
    cycles, 696
    processing, 675
B2B, see Business-to-business
BCNF, see Boyce-Codd Normal Form
Benchmarks, performance, 650–651
Bias, application-specific, 318
Billing organization jurisdiction, 238
Binary large objects (BLOBs), 702
Binary objects, 15
Bit-map indexing, 643
BLOBs, see Binary large objects
Boot sector infectors, 777–778
Borrow approach, 19
Boyce-Codd Normal Form (BCNF), 672
Bristol-Myers Products, 128
Browser, applet downloaded from, 502
B+ tree, 343
BT Tymnet, 490
Budget constraints, 683
Bulk load facilities, 585
Bureaucracy, eliminating layers of, 263
Business
    capture, difficult part of, 139
    classification, 114
    concurrence, distributing business
        rules for, 136
    data information, 28
    development life cycle, 113
    dilemma, lack of automation
        contributing to, 98
    education, 120
    information
        biased perspective of, 111
        derived, 229
        directory, 28, 32, 34
        externally controlled, 237

historical, 233
    planning for time-dependent, 232
    reason to include historical, 235
    redundant, 317
    time-dependent, 231, 234
leaders, internal focus of, 105
maintenance, 119
mismatches, 574
ownership, 118
publicity, 127
repository, 123
rule(s), 399
    acquisition sessions, 131
    administration, 118
    comprehensive, for nanny
        agency, 140–143
    consistency of, 116
    determining scope of, 129
    enforcing, 400
    first-version, 120
    historical perspective of, 112
    managing, 118
    nanny agency, 144
    organization of by subject, 134
    selling of, 119
    textual statement of, 145
    value added by, 112
source, obtaining consent from, 135
terms, evolving glossary of, 134
Business-to-business (B2B), 101, 103
    environment, 104
    interaction, 105
Business information data modeling,
    229–240
    derived business information,
        229–231
    externally controlled business
        information, 237–240
    historical business information,
        233–237
    time-dependent business
        information, 231–233
Business rules, capturing most elusive
    information asset, 111–128
    business rule classification, 114–115
    business rule development life
        cycle, 113–114
    business rule storage and
        automation, 121–127
        business rule publicity, 127
        business rule repository,
            123–125
        business rule repository and
            CASE tool, 126–127

CASE tools, 127
  word processors, 122
historical perspective of business
  rules, 112–113
managing business rules, 118–119
  business rule administration,
    118
  business rule maintenance, 119
  business rule ownership,
    118–119
  business rule and vendor
    packages, 119
selling business rules, 119–121
  business rule education, 120
  business rules in SDLC,
    120–121
  presentation of data models, 121
value added by business rules, 112
writing quality business rule, 115–117
  atomic, 115
  business, 116–117
  clarity, 117
  complete, 115–116
  consistency, 116
  independent, 116
Business rules, case study, 129–144
  classifying business rules into data
    modeling constructs, 137–139
  conducting business rule
    acquisition sessions, 131–134
  determining acquisition
    approaches, 131
  determining scope of business
    rules, 129–130
  developing project plan, 130
  distributing business rules for
    business concurrence, 136
  evolving glossary of business
    terms, 134
  identifying business rule sources, 131
  identifying business rule tools,
    interfaces, standards, and
    procedures, 131
  obtaining consent from business
    rule source, 135
  organizing business rules by
    subject, 134–135
  resolving conflicts, 136–137
Business rules, modeling, 145–155
  extending data and object models,
    146
  integrity constraints versus
    conditions, 147–148

modeling rules, 148–155
  derivatives, 154–155
  enablers and timers, 150–151
  inclusion rules, 152–153
  yield rules, 151–152, 153–154
rule types, 147

C

Calculators, 147
Capacity planning, 632, 636
Cardinality, 202, 243, 246, 291
  convention, 292
  effect of time on, 290
  James Martin, 247
  Oracle Method, 247
  violation, 293
  wrong, 597
Car rental company, 428
CASE, see Computer-assisted software
  engineering
Causal events, backwards trace from, 68
CDDL, see Conceptual database design
  language
CD-ROM, 7, 23
  disk, 491
  reader, 493, 494
Central data store, 442, 443
CEO, as ultimate business custodian, 139
CGI
  programs, 521
  scripts, 503, 525
Check-in/check-out capability, 95
Checkpoint processing, leveraging,
    661–669
  applying checkpoint restart to SQL
    based DBMS, 668–669
    generic checkpoints, 669
    generic restart, 669
  design considerations, 667–668
  general principles, 662–663
  IMS checkpoint/restart functions,
    663–666
    checkpoint call, 663–664
    checkpoint frequency, 663
    normal start paragraph, 665
    restart call, 665
    restart paragraph, 666
    sample program flow, 666
    save-areas, 664–665
Chen's relationships, 245
Childcare services, 132
Christmas club, 75
Class hierarchy, 177, 189, 190

Client
    data warehouse, 28, 36
    /server(s), 37
        computing, 357, 358
        databases, auditing of, 461
    servlet, creation of, 515
    single user node, 357
Clustering, 695–696
COBOL, 169, 387
Coding structures, inconsistent, 607
Communications
    back-flow, 485
    equipment, cost of, 471
    network, 357
Compact substyles, 250
Composite index, 350, 351
Composite semantic object, 379
Compound
    attributes, 184, 188
    semantic object, 379
Comprehensive analysis, keys to, see
    Data, processes, and events
Compression ratios, 711
COMPUSERVE, 354
Computer-assisted software
    engineering (CASE), 121
    -driven systems development, 566
    products, 41, 122
    technology, 447
        environments, 450
        repository, auditing of, 459
    tool(s), 11, 227, 254, 268, 428, 567, 775
        business rule repository and,
          126
        comprehensive organization
          model using, 269
        getting senior management to
          commit to, 274
Computer chassis, 369
Conceptual database design
    language (CDDL), 172
    using entity-relationship diagrams,
      174
    using relational diagrams, 176
    using SQL syntax, 175
Conceptual schema, 171, 219, 376, 337
Conditional words, 117
Conference room pilot (CRP), 8
Conflicting hierarchies, 325
Conflicts, resolving, 136
Consolidated data, 31
Consolidated reference, 444, 445
Constraining object, 150

Content
    management, 95, 100
    things affecting, 97
Contracts, 131, 138
Control information types, 42
Conversion
    approaches, 563
    efforts, 579
    programming of, 591, 594
    tools, 11
Copy management, 36
CORBA, 392
Core processes, 261
Corporate asset, data as, 26
Corporate database, 693
Corporate information factory, 438, 439,
    441
Corporate merger, 11
Corporation
    computer network, 353
    strategy planning, 356
Cost-based optimization, 655
CPU
    speeds, 642
    time, 603
Create-create, 53
Create-delete, 54
Create, read, update, and delete (CRUD)
    matrix, 10, 675
Create-update, 54
CRM, see Customer relationship
    management
CRP, see Conference room pilot
CRUD matrix, see Create, read, update,
    and delete
Customer
    applications, 131
    credit check, 113
    order size, average, 484
    relationship management (CRM), 102
    satisfaction, 263, 416
CVideoNow, 714

D

DAMA, see Data Administration
    Management Association
DASD, see Direct-access storage device
Data, 569–577
    access, boon to, 605
    administration, 127
        institutionalizing, 684
        as service provider, 165
    administrators, 87, 92

analysis
    of current, 615
    pre-relational, 616
architecture
    building of, 9
    framework, Zachman, 27
atomic, 571, 573
business rule mismatches, 574–576
chunk, melded, 81
classification scheme, 733–734
clean, 595
collection, 540
communications, 472, 490
consolidated, 31
control, 40
conversion, 559
    classifying, 580
    costs and benefits of, 590
    team (DCT), 589
correction, 593, 600
definition language (DDL), 122,
    124–126, 363
derived, 31
developed, 31
dictionary, 169, 217
dissemination, 639
dissimilarities of, 76
distillation, 544
element(s)
    attributes, multiple, 86
    definition, 85
    externally controlled, 240
    naming process, 83
    naming standards, 84
    poorly designed, 79
    redundant, 229
    standardization, 91
    structure, sample, 80
enhancement, 36
entry, real-time, 585
erroneous, 590
external, 442
facilitating end-user access to, 226
flow diagram (DFD), 62, 66
format, 278
guarding, 694–695
historical, 31
integration, at physical level, 167
integrity, 415
items
    accuracy of, 454
    names of corresponding, 606
kinds of change/mismatch, 570–571
land mines, 576

legacy, 617, 618
losing, 571–574
management, data component
    approach to, 397
manipulation
    language, 353, 363
    queries, 655
mapping, 390, 395, 592
migration
    tools, 610, 611
    /transformation process, 615
mirror image, 31
missing, 417, 608
model(s), 217, 375, 579
    administrative and directional,
       70
    benefits and applicability of, 226
    business rule database, 123
    characteristics of, 69
    conceptual, 384
    contents, quality of, 166
    enterprise, 161, 231
    extended, 146
    external, 69
    generic, 74
    high-quality, 277
    important constructs of, 215
    internal, 69
    knowledge base, 298
    logical, 159, 225
    physical, 159, 168
    prefabricated, 162
    Ron's Real Estate Business, 216
    separated levels of, 165
    supporting process model, 275
    verifying of, 9
modeler, 12, 240
modeling, 77, 242, 278
    characteristics, 213
    constructs, classifying
       business rules into, 137
    critical success factors in, 225
    critics of, 161
    major concepts of, 214
    steps within logical, 221
needs, defining, 489
non-atomic, 572
organization, 629
overlapping, 74
ownership, 28
placement, 658
preparation, 36
redundancy, 366, 405, 479
representative, 71

retrieval, 39
semantics and, 575
services management, 44
sharing, foundation of, 129
sourcing, 44
states, 31
structures, 269, 402
transaction, 460
transport, 44
Type Definition (DTD), 613
typing, poor, 613, 614
unstructured, 94, 98
warehouses, 440, 569, 601
Data, framework for classifying, 69–77
  administrative and directional data
    models, 70–77
    adding of ratings, 73–74
    generic data models, 74
    mutual exclusivity, 71
    other dissimilarities, 76–77
    overlapping data, 74–76
    rating of quadrants, 72–73
  internal and external data models,
    69–70
Data, processes, and events, 51–68
  analytical validation of analysis
    diagrams, 64–65
  applying of approach, 58–60
  documentation of events, 60
  ELH and process modeling, 52
  entity-life histories and data
    modeling, 51–52
  event networks, 61
  existence criteria and coupling, 53–57
    basis of event-driven
      approach, 56
    types of events, 56–57
    types of tightly coupled
      relationships, 53–56
  expanding coverage of diagrams,
    65–68
  items recorded about event, 61
  toward more powerful tool set, 57–58
  weaknesses in existing tools and
    techniques, 62–64
Data, what's wrong with, 415–425
  possible problems, 417–424
    different/changing business
      rules or logic, 418–419
    incorrect values, 422
    invalid values, 421
    missing data, 417
    missing/non-unique primary
      key, 419

    non-standardized and/or multi-
      element fields, 420
    redundant data with
      inconsistencies, 418
    referential integrity violations,
      422–423
    special cases, 423–424
  reason for caring, 415–417
Data Administration Management
  Association (DAMA), 687
Data Administration Users Group
  (DAUG), 687
Data administrative program, assessing
  of, 683–691
  assessment formation, 687–688
  data administration customer,
    686–687
  institutionalizing data
    administration, 684–685
  steps to conducting assessment,
    688–690
  using results from other surveys,
    690–691
Database(s)
  access, 504
    cost, 492
    layers, 168
    methods, 491
  administrator (DBA) 12, 171, 337, 609
  application-specific, 25
  auditing of client/server, 461
  availability, 693
  back-end, 503
  centralized, 469
  cluster management, 699
  conceptually linked, 481
  consolidations of, 482
  control environment, 450
  converting, 564, 566
  creation of working, 193
  custodial responsibility for, 448
  design, 305
    development of good initial
      physical, 352
    initial stage of, 383
    methodology, initial physical,
      339
    optimal, 214
    references, 253
    reviews, 409
    ultimate, 541
  development methodology
    high-level, 8
    selection of, 6

fine-tuning, 338, 351
flexible, 229
foreign, 366
implementation, of model, 218
integrity
    concerns, 448
    controls, 769
    maintaining, 413
    program, review of, 460
life cycle of, 338, 346
linkage, 485
management systems, 96
marketing, 416
master, 484
object-oriented, 385
operational procedures, 459
performance improvements, 335
pointers, 455
project names of, 22
prototype, 409
recovery, 453
relational, see Relational database
requirements, in e-business, 627
searching of, 515
security, 768
server, 11, 386
single functional, 479
structure, 406, 449
systems, legacy, 613
technology, complexity of, 449
Web, 711
Database, ensuring integrity of, 447–463
auditing case technology
    repository, 459–461
      defining repository
        characteristics, 460
      modification of audit program,
        461
      review of database integrity
        program, 460–461
auditing client/server databases,
    461–462
    defining client/server
      technology/platforms,
      461–462
    determination of number of
      databases in client/server
      environment, 462
    modification of audit program,
      462
    review of potential usage of
      data by clients, 462
audit objectives, 452–454
audit tests by objective, 455–459

custodial responsibility, 448
database control environment,
    450–451
database integrity concerns, 448–450
internal control review, 454–455
planning considerations, 451–452
recommended course of action,
    462–463
Database backup and recovery,
    managing, 693–703
accuracy of backups, 696–703
    administration tools, 699
    areas to protect, 699–701
    backing up in distributed
      LAN/WAN environment,
      698–699
    generic backup stream, 698
    incremental backups, 698
    Internet and intranet firewalls,
      702–703
    levels of protection, 701–702
    virus protection, 702
high availability vs. recoverability,
    693–694
methods of data protection, 694–696
    batch cycles, 696
    clustering, 695–696
    data guarding, 694–695
    duplexing, 695
    mirroring, 694
    partitioning, 695
    replication, 695
    tape backup, 694
Database compression technologies,
    705–716
audio compression, 715
case study, 705–706
DASD compression, 706–710
    IBM solutions, 708–710
    third-party solutions, 707–708
fractals, 714–715
JPEG, 712–713
MPEG, 713–714
UNIX database compression, 710–711
Web databases, 711–712
Database design, referential integrity
    for, 427–434
attribute referential integrity, 429–433
    E-R model, 431–432
    formal definition of attribute
      referential integrity, 430–431
    relational model, 432–433
common definition of referential
    integrity, 427–428

enforcing ARI constraint, 433–434
limits of common definition of
    referential integrity, 428–429
Database development methodology
    and organization, 5–13
    benefits, 6
    deliverables, 10–11
    high-level database development
        methodology, 8–10
    organization, 11–12
    pitfalls, 12
    selecting database development
        methodology, 6–8
    tools, 11
Database management system (DBMS),
    305, 375, 401, 434, 539, 549, see also
    EDMSs, integrating DBMSs and
    communications software
    installation, 370
    distributed, 365
    environment, homogeneous
        distributed, 359
    failure, 449
    index limitations posed by, 313
    nonstandard, 449
    products, 410
    self-organizing, 352
    software, 354, 369
    SQL based, 668–669
    technology, 470
    utility conversion routines of, 608
    vendors of, 193, 549
Data conversion, doing it right, 589–604
    common problems with data, 589–590
        cost and benefit of data
            conversion, 590
        cost of converting, 590
        cost of not converting, 590
    data quality, 595–599
        date inconsistencies, 598
        domain integrity, 596–597
        inconsistent redundancy,
            597–598
        intelligent keys, 598–599
        keeping data clean, 595
        miscellaneous inconsistencies,
            598
        missing information, 598
        orphaned records, 597
        other problems, 599
        referential integrity, 596
        types of data abnormalities,
            595–596
        uniqueness, 596

wrong cardinality, 597
wrong optionality, 597
designing of conversion, 601–603
    choice of language, 602
    control totals, 603
    extra space requirements, 602
    interoperability, 603
    processing time, 603
    routine error handling, 603
    special requirements for data
        warehousing, 601–602
    SQL as design medium, 602
error correction process, 599–600
    choices for correction, 599–600
    programming for data
        correction, 600
    resources for correction effort,
        599
recovery from error, 603–604
specifying of mapping, 600–601
    discovered requirements, 600
    existing documentation, 600–601
    model mismatches, 600
    possible mapping patterns, 601
    relational mathematics, 601
steps in data conversion process,
    590–595
    analyzing new physical data
        model, 592
    analyzing old logical data
        model, 592
    analyzing old physical data
        model, 591
    checking audit reports, 595
    conducting preliminary
        investigation of data quality,
        592
    correcting of data, 593–594
    determining data mapping, 592
    determining how to treat
        missing information, 592–593
    determining if conversion is
        required, 591
    documenting of requirements,
        593
    identifying problems, 593
    institutionalizing, 595
    planning conversion and
        determining conversion
        rules, 591
    programming of conversion, 594
    running of conversion, 594–595

Data conversion, practical example of, 579–587
  change in file access method, 582–583
  change in hardware, 580–581
  classifying data conversions, 580
  migrating from one application system to another, 583–587
  migrating from one operating system to another, 581–582
Data model, building of, 213–227
  benefits and applicability of data models, 226–227
  critical success factors in data modeling, 225–226
  data modeling characteristics, 213–214
  major concepts of data modeling, 214–219
    attributes, 216–219
    entities and relationships, 215
  role of three-schema architecture, 219–221
  steps within logical data modeling, 221–225
    adding detail to user views, 222
    adding keys to user views, 221–222
    building skeletal user views, 221
    determining additional attribute business rules, 223
    integrating user views, 223–225
    validating user views through normalization, 222–223
Data model, making readable, 241–259
  aesthetics, 242–256
    order, 242–243
    too many symbols, 243
    too many symbol types, 243–256
  goals of entity-relationship models, 241–242
  poor naming, 256–258
  presenting of model, 258–259
  what to do, 258
Data modeling, avoiding pitfalls in, 277–303
  attributes, 297–298
  completing data model knowledge base, 298
  critical considerations to improve data model quality, 277–278
    accuracy, 278
    completeness, 278
    semantics, 277
    technique, 277

data modeling, 278–295
  cardinality and optimality, 291–294
  entity role in data modeling, 287–290
  entity subtypes, 284–287
  entity type, 278–280
  recursive relationship, 294–295
  relationship, 280–284
  time-related situations, 290–291
  normalization, 295–296
  reference entity or minor entity, 296–297
Data quality, 435–445, 595
  FDS and corporate information factory, 438–442
  FDS implementation factors, 444–445
  FDS implementation strategies, 442–444
  FDS overview and benefits, 436–437
  foundation application framework, 437–438
  improvements, 437
DAUG, see Data Administration Users Group
DBA, see Database administrator
DBMS, see Database management system
DCT, see Data conversion team
DDBSs, see Distributed database systems
DDL, see Data definition language
Decision support system (DSS), 639
Delete-create, 55
Delete-delete, 56
Delete-update, 56
Deliverable walkthroughs, 23
Denormalization, 346
Denormalized entity identifiers, 307, 309
Department table, 345
Dependent entity, 252
Derivatives, 154, 155
Derived attributes, 297
Derived data, 31
Design languages, 171
  evaluation of for specifying conceptual database designs, 189
  example schemas using, 173
Developed data, 31
Development standards, 15
DFD, see Data flow diagram
Diagram notation, of information model, 201
Digital economy, 105
Direct-access storage device (DASD), 313, 705

Disk
  I/O, 642
  storage
    costs for, 593
    redundancy wasting, 597
Distributed database management
  systems, detailed design and
  application of, 365–374
  backup, recovery, and security
    protection, 372
  critical success factors, 372–373
  communications network design,
    367–368
    cost, 367
    open systems interconnection,
      368
    performance, 367–368
    reliability, 367
  DBMS communications software
    installation, 370–371
  design review, 368
  future issues, 373–374
  hardware design, 365–366
  hardware installation, 368–370
  installation of distributed database
    environment, 368
  installation review, 371
  network communications software
    installation, 370
  software design, 366–367
  support for distributed database, 371
  support review, 372
  tuning for better performance,
    371–372
  user training and resolving
    problems, 372
Distributed databases, design,
  implementation, and management
  of, 353–363
  consideration for standards, 362–363
  corporation strategy planning,
    356–357
  distributed database development
    phases, 355–356
    design phase, 355
    installation and implementation
      phase, 356
    planning phase, 355
    support and maintenance
      phase, 356
  distributed environment
    architecture, 359–362
    cooperation between sites, 361

interconnection of existing
  systems, 360
interconnection of newly
  purchases systems, 361–362
management motivation, 354–355
overall design of distributed
  database strategy, 357–359
  client/server computing,
    357–359
  heterogeneous distributed
    DBMS environment, 359
  homogeneous distributed
    DBMS environment, 359
  today's technology, 354
Distributed database systems (DDBSs),
  753
Distributed database systems, data
  communications requirements of,
  469–477
  data communications requirements,
    472
  distributed databases, 469–471
  network design considerations,
    475–476
  network expansion consideration,
    476–477
  performance considerations, 472–475
  pros and cons of distributed
    DBMSs, 471–472
  security considerations, 475
Distribution component, 37, 38
DNS, see Domain Name Server
Document
  management
    content versus, 95
    systems, 545
  virtual, 545
Documentation, existing, 600
Domain(s)
  integrity, 596
  Name Server (DNS), 632
  noisy name and address, 424
Dow Jones, 354, 490
DSS, see Decision support system
DTD, see Data Type Definition
Duplexing, 695

E

e-business, 93, 101, 102
  business-to-business, 103
  database requirements in, 627
e-commerce, 7, 102
Economic forecast, 71

EDM, see Enterprise data management
EDMS, see Electronic document
  management system
EDMSs, integrating DBMSs and, 539–547
  database management system,
    539–542
  DBMS and EDMS, 544–546
  electronic document, 542–544
  functional decomposition and data
    distillation, 544
Electrical power supply failure, 717
Electronic document management
  system (EDMS), 539
Electronic vaulting service, 719
ELH, see Entity-life history
Employee(s)
  entity constraint matrix, 327
  lacking motivation, 166
  table, 180, 345
Employment
  application, 133, 134
  contract, 133
  relationship, 132
Enablers, 150, 151
End-to-end testing, 633
End user
  computing, 561
  experience, factors influencing, 624
English rules, conceptual database
  design using, 173
Enterprise
  data
    scope, 26, 28
    standards, 16, 18, 21
    warehouse, 29, 30
  resource planning (ERP), 102
  warehouse, 28
    element states, 32
    manager, 42
  wide infrastructure, 104
Enterprise data management (EDM), 25–45
  benefits, 44
  business information directory, 32–33
  components, 28–29, 43
  control, 39–41
    control types, 41
    data control, 40
    process control, 40
    standards, 41
    user control, 40–41
  data copy management, 36
  data delivery, 36–38
  data states, 31
  enterprise data scope, 26–28

enterprise warehouse, 29–31
execution products, 43–44
manager processes, 41–43
metadata contents, 33–34
optimum source, 34–36
principles, 26
user acquisition, 38–39
Enterprise data modeling practices,
  161–169
  arguments against enterprisewide
    data models, 161–162
  organizational aspects, 164–166
    data administration as service
      provider, 165
    data types as entities, 166
    integration of data modeling
      activities into process of
      specification, 165
    quality of data model contents,
      166
    quality of upper model levels,
      166
    rate of change, 166
    separated levels of data model,
      165
  quality assurance and self-control,
    167–169
    database access layers, 168–169
    data dictionary product
      properties, 169
    data integration at physical
      level, 167–168
    data types, 169
    dialogs and data modeling, 168
    level of abstraction, 168
    quality objectives, 167
    reuse, 167
    transforming logical to
      physical data model, 168
  starting points for better data
    modeling, 162–164
Enterprise data standards, establishing,
  15–24
  architecture and physical
    environment category, 16–17
    benefits, 17
    objectives, 16–17
  categories of enterprise data
    standards, 18
  common pitfalls and traps, 22–23
  list of organization defining
    standards, 24
  measuring compliance and
    enforcing standards, 23

N-tier/layers category, 17–18
  benefits, 17–18
  objectives, 17
objectives and benefits, 15–16
procedures category, 17
  benefits, 17
  objectives, 17
process for defining enterprise data
  standards, 19–22
tips for getting started, 23
user interface category, 18
  benefits, 18
  objectives, 18
Entity(ies), 207
  associative, 293, 294
  billing account, 238
  boxes, text inside, 247
  constraint matrix, 326, 327, 328
  -CONTRACT, 138
  data types as, 166
  dependent, 252
  identifier(s), 160, 239, 307
    all-purpose, 311
    correction of denormalized, 310
    denormalized, 307, 309
    parochial, 311
    problems, 306, 318
    properties, 305
  intersecting, 259
  -life history (ELH), 51
    diagram, 52, 65
    ORDER entity, 56, 63
  minor, 296
  occurrence, identification of, 216
  reference, 296
  role, 287, 288, 289
  set(s), 173, 320, 589
  subtypes, 284
  summary-level, 230
  type, 278, 279
  weak, 184, 187
Entity identifiers, politics of, 305–318
  entity identifier problems, 306–312
    all-purpose entity identifiers, 311
    denormalized entity
      identifiers, 307–310
    nonuniversal or parochial
      entity identifiers, 311–312
    volatile entity identifiers,
      306–307
  solutions, 312–318
    application workarounds,
      317–318

redundant business
  information, 317
substitute keys, 316–317
surrogate key components,
  315–316
surrogate keys, 312–315
time stamps, 315
Entity-relationship (E-R), 195
  diagram (ERD), 51, 121, 180, 192, 436
    conceptual database design
      using, 174
    techniques, 327
  mapping, 539
  model, 196, 197, 209, 210, 431
E-R, see Entity-relationship
ERD, see Entity-relationship diagram
Ergonomics, 625
ERP, see Enterprise resource planning
Error
  correction process, 599
  handling, routine, 603
  recovery from, 603
ERWIN, 121
Erwin-entity relationship model, 138
Event(s), see also Data, processes, and
  events
  backwards trace from causal, 68
  documentation of, 60
  -driven approach, basis of, 56
  matrix for identifying, 59
  networks, 61, 63
  symbols, data flow diagram
    enhanced with, 66
  triggers, basic types of, 60
Existence criteria, 53
Extensive markup language (XML), 557,
  613
External administrative quadrant, 72
External data model, 69
External databases, providing access
  to, 489–494
  database access cost, 492
  defining data needs, 489
  economizing on multiple access
    requirements, 492–494
  information access methods, 490–491
  selecting external sources, 489–490
  update frequency, 491v492
External schema, 219
Extract component functions, 37

F

Fax modems, 493
FDS, see Foundation data store
Federal Reserve Bank of Boston, 491
Federal tax rate, 234
File
 access method, changes in, 582
 infectors, 779
 programming, relational versus, 562
 structures, determination of, 340
Fill-in-the-blank reference forms, 131
Financial instruments, data modeling
 for, 163
FireHunter, 630
Flat files, 15
Foreign databases, 366
Formula Translation, 367
Foundation data
 model, 437
 store (FDS), 435, 445
Fractals, 714
Front-end applications, to business rule
 tables, 123
Functional bridge, planning of, 482
Functional decomposition, 544
Fund assignment, 75

G

Garbage in, garbage out, 415
GDSS, see Group decision support
 systems
Generalization
 difference between specialization
 and, 198
 hierarchy, 212
 structure, 198
Generic data model, 74
Generic verbs, 116
GOSIP, see Government Open Systems
 Interconnection Profile
Government
 Open Systems Interconnection
 Profile (GOSIP), 362, 368
 -sponsored standards, 765
Group decision support systems
 (GDSS), 273
GSAM updates, 663

H

Hard disk crash, 717

Hardware
 changes in, 580
 design, 365
 diagnostic software, 369
 extra-fast, 603
Hashed file, 344
Hashed index, 348
Hash keys, 404
Health insurance payments, 236
Heap file organizations, alternative, 341
Hidden square, 255
Hierarchical files, 346, 347
Hierarchical storage management (HSM),
 699
Hierarchies, problem of conflicting, 328
Historical data, 31
Homogeneous valid values, 87
Horizontal concept, 264
Horizontal corporation, 262
Horizontal organization, integrating
 process and data models into,
 261–275
 creating horizontal organization,
 272–274
 horizontal corporation, 262–264
 integrating into horizontal
 organization, 268–272
 data structures, 269–272
 using Internet, 272
 IS methodologies, 265–268
 data-focused approach, 265–266
 process-focused approach,
 266–268
HSM, see Hierarchical storage
 management
HTML, see Hypertext markup language
HTTP, see HyperText Transfer Protocol
Hypertext markup language (HTML), 550
HyperText Transfer Protocol (HTTP), 506

I

IBM
 mainframe, 5
 solutions, 708
IDC, see Internet Database Connector
IDEF1X
 Data Modeling approaches, 268
 unique identifiers in, 253
Identifiers, unique, 251
IIS, see Internet Information Server
Imposter entities, 279
Incident, 200

Inclusion rules, 152, 153
Inconsistency, illustration of, 418
Incorrect values, example of, 422
Index(es)
  building of composite, 350
  hashed, 347
  for joins, 347
  names, 20
  tuning by adding, 405
  useless, 629
Indexed Sequential Access Method
    (ISAM), 343
Indexing, advancing art of, 639–651
  beginnings, 639
  client/server and networks, 640–641
  indexing, 642–644
  inverted indexing, 646–650
  performance benchmarks, 650–651
  performance dilemma, 641–642
  reign of 4GL, 639–640
  relational indexes versus inverted
    indexes, 644–645
  using inverted file indexes with
    applications, 645
Indicators
  higher-level, 90
  nonmeaningful, 90
Information
  failure, 264
  gathering, 49
  missing, 592, 598
  model, 199, 200, 208, 211
    diagram, of accounting system,
      203
    Shlaer and Mellor's, 195, 199
  providers, 489
  resource management, 297
  security, 753
  systems
    creation of, 261
    requirements, 213
    structure, simplified, 267
  technology (IT), 93, 730
Infoseek, 272
Input-user view, 65
Instance verifiers, 147
Insurance company, 573
Integrated database, migrating data to,
    605–612
  data migration tools and services,
    610–611
  recommended course of action, 611
  structural inconsistencies, 605–609
    different abstraction levels, 606

inconsistent coding
    structures, 607
  inconsistent data formats, 608
  naming issues, 605–606
  unneeded or missing data,
    608–609
  value inconsistencies, 609–610
Integration testing, 633
Integrity
  constraint, 147, 149, 150
  management, 553
Intelligent keys, 598
Internal administrative quadrant, 72
Internal business focus, unforeseen
    consequences of, 100
Internal control questionnaire, 456–457
Internal data models, 69
Internal schema, 219
International Standards Organization
    (ISO), 19, 359
Internet, 7, 101, 272
  business volumes conducted over,
    623
  database access through, 549
  Database Connector (IDC), 526
    operation, 527
    script, search, 530
  Information Server (IIS), 500, 526, 528
  service provider (ISP), 500
Internet, database management and,
    549–554
  browsing and filtering, 551
  data representation, 550
  integrity management, 553
  interoperability, 553
  metadata management, 553
  query management, 550–551
  security management, 552–553
  storage management, 552
  transaction management, 551–552
Invalid values, 421
Inverted file indexing, 643
IS
  management, corporate, 479
  methodologies, 265
ISAM, see Indexed Sequential Access
    Method
isa relationship, 250
ISO, see International Standards
    Organization
ISP, see Internet service provider
IT, see Information technology

J

James Martin cardinality and
  optionality, 247
Java
  code
    FortuneServer, 509
    RequestProcessor, 513
  programming language, 521
Java servlets and JDBC, developing
  client/server RDBMS applications
  using, 499–523
  back-end database, 503–506
  HTML front end, 506–507
  Java incentive, 500–502
  middleware, 507–521
    creating client servlet, 515
    how server works, 508–515
    searching of database, 515–521
  project, 502–503
  quick setup, 521
Joint Application design, 57
JPEG, 712
Jyra, 630

K

Key constraint, 177, 179
Knowledge workers, improved
  productivity of, 45

L

LAN, see Local area network
Language
  choice of, 602
  construct, causing confusion for
    reader, 117
Languages, evaluation of for specifying
  conceptual database designs,
  171–194
  design languages and conceptual
    schemas, 171–173
  example schemas using four design
    languages, 173–189
    class hierarchies, 189
    entity sets and attributes,
      173–177
    key constraint, 177–180
    many-to-many relationships,
      182–184
    one-to-many relationships,
      180–182
    weak entities, 184–189

evaluation of design languages,
  189–191
    necessity, 191
    sufficiency, 189–191
  recommendation, 193–194
  understandability and usability,
    192–193
    consistency, 192
    software support, 192–193
Legacy
  applications, 438
  database systems, 613
  feeder systems, 417
  programmers, departed, 614
  systems, 91, 415, 480, 639
Life cycle
  methodology, 10
  modeling technique, 211
LINE ITEM, 59
Link attributes, 209
List variability, 325, 329
Local area network (LAN), 368, 483, 492
  server farms, 98
  technology, 639
Logic, example of different, 419
Logical data
  model, 9, 159, 224
  structure, 402
Loose coupling, 360
Loss and backup, how to handle, 717–721
  backup method cost comparison, 721
  backup options, 718–720
    do nothing, 718
    employ system connected to
      multiple disks, 719
    funnel of data through in-house
      network for storage by
      mainframe and peripherals,
      720
    magnetic tapes and diskettes,
      718–719
    off-site, electronic vaulting
      service, 719
    purchase of mass storage
      equipment, 720
  backup system evaluation, 720–721
Lotus Notes, 7
Lycos, 272

M

Macro viruses, 778–779
Magnetic media, 491
Magnetic tapes, 718

Mainframe location, 615
Management motivation, 354
Manager processes, 43
Many-to-many relationships, 137, 182, 185, 205, 233
Mapping patterns, possible, 601
Market share, 76
Massively parallel processing (MPP), 654
Materials management, 583
Medicare benefits, 236
Metadata, 31, 32, 96, 442
    contents, 33
    tables, 329, 330
Microsoft, 538
    Access, 499
    -speak, 395
    transaction server (MTS), 394
Middleware, 487, 507
Minicomputers, 30
Minor entity, 296
Mirror image data, 31
Mirroring, 694
Model(s)
    comprehensive organization, 269
    data, 217, 375, 579
        conceptual, 384
        enterprise, 231
        extended, 146
        -focused, 270
        high-quality, 277
        knowledge base, 298
        logical, 159, 225
        physical, 159, 168
        prefabricated, 162
    database implementation of, 218
    entity-relationship, 196, 197, 199, 209, 376, 431
    foundation data, 437
    information, 199, 200, 208, 211
    mismatches, 600
    object, 146, 205
    presentation of, 258
    process, 271, 273, 274, 275
    quality, 298
    reference data, 164
    relational, 381, 432
    subdata, 392
    transaction, flexible, 551
    View Controller (MVC), 390
Modeling methodologies, comparison of three systems, 195–212
    comparison of modeling methods, 207–211
        attributes, 208–209

entities and objects, 207–208
        relationships, 209–211
    description of methodologies, 195–207
        entity-relationship modeling, 195–199
        Rumbaugh's object modeling technique, 204–207
        Shlaer and Mellor's Information Model, 199–203
MPEG, 713
MPP, see Massively parallel processing
MTS, see Microsoft transaction server
Multi-element fields, 420
Multiple databases, management of
    across heterogeneous hardware and software systems, 479–488
    evaluating alternatives, 482
    functional bridge solution, 482–488
        construction of bridge, 487–488
        making critical design decisions, 484–486
        planning functional bridge, 482–484
    managerial challenge, 480–482
    single functional database, 479–480
Multiplexers, 474
Mutual exclusivity, 71, 88
MVC, see Model View Controller

N

Name(s)
    dependence on, 85
    issues, 605
Nanny employment, 131
NAPs, see Network access points
NASA, 491
Natural languages, 145, 172, 194
Netscape, 538
Network(s)
    access points (NAPs), 632
    administrator, 12
    capacity, 472, 473
    communications software installation, 370
    corporation's computer, 353
    data manager, 371
    design, 475
    event, 61
    expansion, 476
    programming, 563
    structured event, 66
NIAM, 244

Non-database environment, 447
Non-foreign key attributes, 433
Nonprofit organization, 262
Normalization, 295
Normal start paragraph, 665
Not too many objects rule, 248
n-tier/layers category, 17, 20

O

Object(s), 207
  associative, 202, 209
  binary, 15
  constraining, 150
  Management Group (OMG), 553
  in many-to-many relationships, 205
  mapping, 389
  Modeling Technique (OMT), 195,
    204, 210, 211
    diagram, 206, 208
    notations, 209
    systems modeling techniques,
      212
    Yourdon's, 256
  -oriented (OO)
    analysis (OOA), 273, 667
    approaches, 146
    architectures, component-based,
      385
    lingo, 250
  proliferation, 325
  -property, single-valued, 382
  request broker (ORB), 553
  semantic, 376, 377, 378
  software, 204
  specification, 200
  technology, 7
ODA, see Office document architecture
ODBC, see Open Database Connectivity
ODS, see Operational data store
Office document architecture (ODA), 550
OLTP, see Online transaction processing
  applications
OMG, see Object Management Group
OMT, see Object Modeling Technique
One concept equals one data element,
  79–92
  analogy, 82–83
  benefits of flexibility, 80-82
  data element attributes, 86–90
    indicators, 90
    valid values, 86–90
  data element naming process, 83–86
    data element names, 83

    dependence on names, 85–86
    first step, 85
    modifiers, 83–85
  purpose of rule, 80
  supporting tools, 91–92
One-to-many relationship, 177, 180, 182
  existence of between current
    employee and employee
    assignment entities, 232
  with partial participation, 181
  with total participation, 183
One-to-one relationship, 282
Online query, 406
Online transaction processing
  applications (OLTP), 5
OO, see Object-oriented
OOA, see Object-oriented analysis
Open Database Connectivity (ODBC),
  501, 645
Open Systems Interconnection (OSI),
  367, 368
Operating system failure, 449
Operational data store (ODS), 438, 440
Operational systems applications, 34
Optionality, 246, 291
  James Martin, 247
  Oracle Method, 247
Optional-to-required theory, 321
Oracle
  cardinality and optionality, 247
  Method, 244, 246
  relationship names, 257
  unique identifiers, 252
ORB, see Object request broker
Order entry system, 55, 63
Organization(s)
  abundance of newly created, 101
  restructured, 263
Orphaned records, 597
Orthogonal subtypes, 250, 253
OSI, see Open Systems Interconnection
Out-of-process components, 394
Outside influence, 56

P

Paper documents, 15
Parallel databases, 653–659
  business benefits of parallel
    processing, 653
  how parallel performance is
    achieved, 655–659
    data placement and storage, 658

interprocess communication,
656–658
parallel database management,
658
principles of parallel execution,
655–656
query execution, 656
query optimization, 656
reorganization and
redistribution of data, 658–659
processor independence, 654–655
serial databases and parallel
processing performance,
653–654
Parallel execution, 655–656
Parallelogram, 67
Partitioning, 695
Password procedures, 455
Payback and systematization ratings, 73
Payroll, 267
Pentium machine, 581
Performance
benchmarks, 650
degradation, 316
Personal workstations, 30, 37
Person Health Risk Code, 90
Personnel department melded data
chunks, 84
Physical database design, 337–352
database fine-tuning, 351–352
initial physical database design
methodology, 339–351
building of composite indexes,
350–351
determination of file structures,
340–345
facilitation of frequent joins of
two tables, 345–347
identification and
implementation of secondary
search keys, 347–350
stages of database life cycle, 337–339
Physical data models, 159, 168
Physical environment category, 16
Pitfalls and remedies, chart of, 300–303
Platforms, compatibility of multiple, 453
Polymorphic operation, 205
Polymorphic viruses, 780
Portability, 467
Portable Operating System Interface for
Computer Environments (POSIX), 362
Position selectors, 147

POSIX, see Portable Operating System
Interface for Computer
Environments
Prefabricated data models, 162
Primary search keys, choosing, 344
Privacy risk, increased, 450
Procedures category, 17
Process(es), see also Data, processes,
and events
control, 40
-focused methodology, 266
model(s), 274
creation of overall, 273
data model supporting, 275
ELH and, 52
relationship between data and,
271
-oriented approaches, 145
time, 603
Processor independence, 654–655
Prodigy, 354
Productivity
information
monthly, 82
storage of, 80
report, revised, 82
Product number, 311
Professional standards organizations, 766
Project plan, development of, 130
Propagation delay, 472
Proprietary formats, 97
Publishing, to Web, 96

Q

QFH, 641
Quadrants, rating of, 72
Quality
assurance, 167
business rule, writing of, 115
Quantitative analysis, 541
Query(ies)
execution, 656
important, 340
management, 550
optimization, 470, 656
subtask, 657

R

RAD, see Rapid application
development
Radview software, 635
RAM, see Random access memory

Random access memory (RAM), 369
Rapid application development (RAD), 6, 599
RDA, see Remote data access
RDA/SQL standard, 373
RDBMs, see Relational database management systems
Recovery, 372
Recursive relationship, 294, 295
Redundant business information, 317
Redundant relationship, 281
Reference
    data models, 164
    entity, 296
Referential integrity, 307, 413, 596
    problems, 423
    violations, 422
Relational database, component design for, 385–397
    advantages/features of data-component approach, 389–391
    application architecture example, 388–389
    background of multi-tiered architectures, 386–388
    data component granularity considerations, 392
    data-component mining, 396–397
    disadvantages/limitations of data-component approach, 391
    implementation of component-based design using Microsoft's architecture, 392–396
    moving towards component-based architecture standard, 385–386
    why relational databases are here to stay, 385
Relational database, designing, 399–410
    benefits and applicability of relational database design methodology, 409–410
    critical success factors for relational database design methodology, 407–409
    major concepts of relational database design, 400–402
    steps in relational database design, 402–403
        translating logical data integrity, 402–403
        translating logical data structure, 402

tuning design by establishing storage-related access mechanisms, 403–407
    tuning by introducing controlled data redundancy, 405–406
    tuning by redefining relational database structure, 406–407
Relational database, understanding of and assessing security, 763–776
    application development, 775–776
    challenges in relational database security, 763–765
    database system security standards, 765–766
        government-sponsored standards, 765–766
        professional standards organizations, 766
    developments in database security, 768–771
        cooperative systems security, 768–769
        database integrity controls, 769–770
        privilege management, 768
        stored procedures, 770–771
    discretionary access and audit controls, 766–768
    identifying security requirements, 774
    implementing database security, 774–775
        CASE tools, 775
        data dictionary, 775
    multilevel secure databases, 771–774
        security conflicts in multilevel database applications, 772–773
        weighing pros and cons of multilevel security, 773–774
Relational database conversion, 559–568
    conversion approaches, 563–565
        converting databases, 564
        converting programs, 564–565
    programming in relational and nonrelational environments, 562–563
        relational versus file programming, 562–563
        relational versus hierarchical or network programming, 563
    pros and cons in converting to relational technology, 559–562
        cons, 560–561
        pros, 561–562

recommended course of action,
567–568
steps of relational conversion,
566–567
strategic issues, 565–566
Relational database management
systems (RDBMs), 557, 653
Relational database systems design,
denormalization decision in,
671–677
background, 671–672
functional dependency, 672–674
method for making
denormalization decision for
transitive functional
dependency, 674–677
examples, 676–677
usage of functional
dependency, 675–676
recommended course of action, 677
Relational diagrams, 172, 184
Relational mathematics, 601
Relational model, 432
Relational schema
design, 337
example of, 339
Relational technology, 469
Relationship(s)
attributes, 209
Chen's, 245
conditionality of, 202
identification, 280
isa, 250
misconstrued, 280
names, Oracle, 257
recursive, 294, 295
redundant, 281
semantics in, 283
spurious, 281, 282
Remote data access (RDA), 359
Remote procedure calls (RPCs), 17
RENTER relational table, 403
Replication, 695
RequestProcessor, 512
Requirements
document, 10
gathering process, 58
Restart call, 665
Retirement account contributions, 236
Role
entity, 287, 288, 289
name, 288
Ross Method, 146
RPCs, see Remote procedure calls

Rumbaugh's Object Modeling
Technique, 195

S

Scan efficiency, 404
Scheduled maintenance downtimes, 627
Schema refinement, 337, 346
Scratchpad, 705
Screen images, 23
SDK, see Sun Servlet Software
Development Kit
SDLC, see Systems development life
cycle
Search
key(s)
analysis, 345
hashing, 348, 349, 350
identification and
implementation of
secondary, 347
result screen, 532
screen, 529
Secure sockets layer (SSL), 739
Security, 471
log, 458
management, 550, 552
protection, 372
risk, increased, 450
threats, in distributed database, 754
Security controls, establishment of in
distributed database, 753–761
avoidance techniques, 757–759
external threats, 759
internal, accidental threats, 758
internal, intentional threats, 758
benefits and features of DDBSS,
753–754
conceptual security policy model,
755–757
classifying of data, 755–756
determining security needs, 756
selecting appropriate technique,
757
limitations of model, 761
security threats in distributed
database, 754–755
tolerance techniques, 759–761
techniques for protecting data
en route, 761
techniques for protecting data
in place, 759–761
Self-control, quality assurance and, 167

Semantic(s), 277
  data and, 575
  effect of time on, 290
  object, 376, 377, 378
    transforming of into relational
      model, 380
    types of, 379
    user orientation of, 383
  time dimensions affecting, 291
Semantic objects, relational database
  design using, 375–384
  building schema in semantic
    object, 377–380
  schemas, 375–377
    conceptual model, 376
    introducing semantic object,
      376–377
  transforming semantic object into
    relational model, 380–382
  user orientation of semantic object,
    383
Sequence verifiers, 147
Server(s)
  application, 386
  client, 37
  database, 386
  farms, LAN, 98
  Microsoft transaction, 394
  node, 358
  processing power of, 365
  software, Web, 499
  users, 714
  Web, 96, 386, 747
  working of, 508
Service provider, data administration as,
  165
SGML, see Standard generalized
  markup language
Shareholders, as ultimate business
  custodian, 139
Simple semantic object, 379
Simple sets, 319
Site autonomy, types of, 361
Software
  application, 367, 583
  DBMS, 354, 369
  design, 366
  front-end, 358
  hardware diagnostic, 369
  installation, network
    communications, 370
  objects, development of, 204
  packages, assessing, 226
  Radview, 635

  support, 191, 192
  tools, needed to build Web site, 626
  Web server, 499
Sorted file organizations, alternative, 342
Sourcing processes, optimum, 35
Specialization, difference between
  generalization and, 198
Specification object, 200
Spectrum Technology Group, Inc., 114
Split transactions, 486
SprintNet, 490
Spurious relationships, 281, 282
SQL, see Structured query language
SSADM, see Structured Systems
  Analysis and Design Method
SSL, see Secure sockets layer
Stage change
  in another entity, 57
  in same entity, 57
Standard generalized markup language
  (SGML), 550
Standardization policies, using sloppy, 92
Standards, list of organization defining, 24
State code table, 297
Statement cycle, 75
State-transition diagram (STD), 62, 64
Status-based subtype, 322
STD, see State-transition diagram
Storage management, 552
Stored procedures, 20
Strategy misalignment, 74
Structured data, 93
Structured event network, 66
Structured query language (SQL), 172,
  184, 194, 309, 499, 644, 764
  CREATE command, 191
  as design medium, 602
  editors, 193
  network service requests, 373
  statement, 531, 655
  syntax, conceptual database design
    using, 175
Structured Systems Analysis and Design
  Method (SSADM), 244, 256
Subdata model example, 392
Substitute keys, 316
Sub-table structures, embedded, 614
Subtype(s), 249
  modeling, 320, 330, see also
    Supertype and subtype
    modeling, practical guidelines
    for
      common uses of, 321
      effects, 321

implications, 323
problem with, 325
type-based, 322
multiple, 285
orthogonal, 250, 253
reduced ambiguity through, 324
schemas, 329
status-based, 322
type-based, 323
Sun Servlet Software Development Kit (SDK), 499
Super programmers, 669
Supertype(s), 249
goal-oriented approach to, 331
modeling, 320
multiple, 286
omission of, 286, 287
-subtype, 282, 284
Supertype and subtype modeling, practical guidelines for, 319–331
application problems, 324–326
arbitrary decomposition, 325
conflicting hierarchies, 325
list variability, 325–326
object proliferation, 325
entity sets, 320
practical solutions, 326–331
entity constraint matrix, 326–329
goals, 326
metadata tables, 329–331
simple sets, 319–320
supertype and subtype modeling, 320–324
subtype modeling effects, 321
subtype modeling implications, 323–324
subtype modeling uses, 321–323
Supply-chain collaboration, 103
Surrogate keys, 312, 314, 318
Surveys, opinion-only, 689
Symbol types, 243
System(s)
development life cycle (SDLC), 120
implementations, 579
management, 371

T

Table(s)
frequent joins of two, 345
names, 20
row, 589

TCP/IP interface, see Transmission Control Protocol/Internet Protocol interface
Technical competence, 624
Technology design information, 28
Telecommunications Act, 735
Telephone directory application, 526, 538
Ternary relationships, 212
Testing tools, 11
Test planning, 633
Text editors, 193
Threats
external, 759
internal
accidental, 758
intentional, 758
Three-schema architecture, 219, 220
Tight coupling, 54, 360
Timer, 150, 152
Time-related situations, 290
Time stamps, 315
T1 line, 483
Tolerance techniques, 759
Tool set, 57
Total Quality Management, 686
Transaction(s)
analysis, 9, 10, 539
applications, 440
carriers, 487
data, 460
handling, 470
management, 353, 551
models, flexible, 551
split, 486
Transmission Control Protocol/Internet Protocol (TCP/IP) interface, 657
Transparency, degrees of, 361
Tree indexes, 347, 349
TRIGGER commands, 191
Triggered event viruses, 781
Trigger events, 488

U

UML, see Universal Model Language
Union agreements, 584
Universal Model Language (UML), 172
UNIX, 580
database compression, 710
environments, 705
systems, 639
Unstructured data, 94, 98
Update controllers, 147
Update-create, 54

Update-delete, 55
Update-update, 54
User
  control, 40
  interface, 18, 21, 39
  training, 372
  views
    adding detail to, 222
    building skeletal, 221
    integrating, 223
    validating, 222

V

Valid values
  homogeneous, 87
  nonmutually exclusive, 89
Value(s)
  inconsistencies, 609
  valid, 87, 89
Variability problems, 328
Vendor packages, business rules and, 119
Verbs, generic, 116
Versioning capability, 95
Very large databases (VLDBs), 5, 653
Virtual document, 545
Virus
  hoax, 780
  protection, 702
Virus activity, in Internet environment,
    777–784
  how viruses infect, 780–782
    combination viruses, 782
    encrypting viruses, 782
    memory resident viruses, 781
    multi-parasite viruses, 780
    non-memory-resident viruses,
      782
    polymorphic viruses, 780
    retro viruses, 781
    stealth viruses, 781
    triggered event viruses, 781
  other destructive programs, 782–783
  types of viruses, 777–780
    boot sector infectors, 777–778
    file infectors, 779
    macro viruses, 778–779
    virus hoax, 780
  virus information Web sites, 784
  virus protection, 783
  virus removal, 784
Visual Basic, 387
VLDBs, see Very large databases
Volatile entity identifiers, 306

W

WAN, see Wide area network
Weak entities, 184, 187
Web, see also World Wide Web
  architectures, 7
  browser, 526
  databases, 711
  publishing to, 96
  server, 96, 386, 499
  site, appropriateness of, 624
  telephone directory application, 538
Web applications, building of database-
    enabled, with IDC, 525–538
  developing telephone directory
    application, 526–537
    add entry screen, 534–537
    application directory, 528
    database, 527–528
    organizing of application, 537
    requirements, 526–527
    search IDC script, 530–532
    search screen, 529–530
    search screen results, 532–534
  Internet database connector, 526
Web-based testing and capacity
    planning, 631–637
  added complexities, 631–632
  testing cycle, 632–636
    capacity planning, 636
    defining testing scope, 633
    test planning, 633–636
Web content management, 93–105
  automation of content and
    documents, 97–98
  content and business-to-business
    e-business, 103–104
  content versus document
    management, 95–96
  e-business and disaggregation,
    101–102
  e-business and e-commerce, 102–103
  internal focus exacerbating lack of
    automation, 99–100
  lack of automation in content and
    document management, 98–99
  structured data, 93
  unstructured data, 94
WebCrawler, 272
Web design and database performance,
    improving user experience through
    improved, 623–630
  database requirements in e-business,
    627-628

availability, 627
huge amounts of data processes in real time, 628
integration, 628
scalability, 627-628
security, 627
evaluating Web site performance, 630
FireHunter, 630
Jyra, 630
factors influencing end user experience, 624-625
content, 624
technical competence, 624
trust, 625
strategies to improve database performance, 628-629
architecture, 628
database design, 629
data organization, 629
sizing, 629
Web site design considerations, 625-627
business objective, 625
ergonomics, 625-626
investment in building of site, 626
investment in maintaining site, 626-627
size of site, 626
Wide area network (WAN), 37, 368, 483
WINTEL, 581
Without due cause, 137
Word processor, 121, 122
Work Order, unapproved, 298
Workstations, personal, 30, 37
World Wide Web (WWW), 497, 499, 525
server, 747
flaws, 749
management, 751
technologies, 728
World Wide Web, security management for, 727–752
appropriate use policy, 734–736
audit tools and capabilities, 746-749
data classification scheme, 733–734
internal/external applications, 736–737

Internet, intranet, and World Wide Web security architectures, 743–745
Internet/WWW security objectives, 731–732
Internet and WWW security policies and procedures, 732–733
path to Internet/browser technologies, 729–731
secure WWW client configuration, 745–746
users, 737–738
Web browser security strategies, 738–743
Secure Hypertext Transfer Protocol, 742–743
secure socket layer trust model, 739–742
WWW security flaws, 749–751
WWW security management, 751
WWW support infrastructure, 752
WWW, see World Wide Web

X

XML, see Extensive markup language
XML, bridging legacy data with, 613–618
data migration/transformation process, 615–617
analysis of current data, 615
clean up of current data, 615–616
transformation of data, 616–617
difficulties encountered with legacy data, 613–615

Y

Yahoo, 272
Yield
rules, 151, 152
value, 153, 154, 155
Yourdon's object-modeling technique, 256

Z

Zachman data architecture framework, 27

9 780367 455453